INDIAN BUILDINGS CONGRESS

PRACTICAL HANDBOOK ON ENERGY CONSERVATION IN BUILDINGS

INDIAN BUILDING CONGRESS

A NABHI PUBLICATION

Published by :
Ajay Kumar Garg
Managing Editor
NABHI PUBLICATIONS
P.O. Box. No. 37
New Delhi - 110 001

Composing & Processing by :
NABHI'S BOARD OF EDITORS

Visit us at : www.nabhipublications.com
For Complete Bibliography of our Publications and On-Line Ordering

PRICE : Rs. 700

1st Published, 2008

ISBN 81-7274-637-7

Printed at :
Salasar Imaging System
Delhi

Contents

Foreword

1. The Indian Buildings Congress is a national level and interdisciplinary NGO, which has made a dent on the emerging issues of Built Environment during the short period since its inception in 1992. The wide spectrum of membership of different disciplines has given it a unique place in the Construction Industry.

2. IBC has played a major role in the various facets of Built Environment through :
   (i) National level discussions, deliberations and dialogues.
   (ii) Dissemination of knowledge through publications.
   (iii) Promoting excellence in the field of Built Environment.
   (iv) Net working and collaboration with Govt./Local bodies/NGOs and Industry.
   (v) Professional Groups working on specific issues.

3. IBC has organized twenty nine National Seminars on Topical subjects, such as Information Technology, Energy Management, Water Management, Quality Management, Fire, Earthquakes, Urban Planning and Design etc. in the past. One of the important objectives of the IBC is to promote excellence in the field of Built Environment. In order to encourage the excellent work being done by Professionals, IBC Awards in six different categories are given at the time of Annual Convention. In addition awards have been instituted for outstanding technical papers presented during seminars. IBC constitutes Technical Committees, which bring out State of the Art Reports on various important subjects. Indian Buildings Congress bring out 'IBC Journal' and 'IBC News' containing vital information about Built Environment. A number of Handbooks on vital subjects like Fire Safety in Buildings, Seismic Retrofitting etc. are under preparation which will provide useful literature on the respective subject for engineers as well as working professionals. The present publication on energy conservation is also prepared with this aim.

4. Energy is a vital necessity for our existence, whether it is for lighting, heating or air conditioning, transportation, office equipments, operation of machineries, or for so many other innumerable aspects of modern living. The consumption of energy is increasing day by day and the stock of available fossil fuel, on which the bulk of energy production depends, is fast depleting. The situation will be rather alarming unless we take adequate steps towards energy conservation and use of renewable energy sources. There is still a general lack of awareness in matters pertaining to energy consumption and conservation.

5. The built environment is a major consumer of power and there is a need to address the issues pertaining to energy matters of this sector. Design of buildings adopting principles of solar passive architecture, selection of appropriate materials and processes for minimizing embodied energy, adoption of energy efficient systems and fittings, building automation, energy management, energy audit etc. have to become an inherent part of the design process, construction and maintenance of the built environment. All these aspects along with other related issues have been discussed in this publication.

6. The book extensively deals with a number of aspects, both technical as well as practical, of energy conservation and management in buildings. Starting with the correlation between climate and buildings, the book proceeds to discuss passive building design concepts, energy and buildings, parameters affecting energy consumption, calculation of cooling and heating load and thermal insulation and energy savings.

7. Certain newer aspects such as advanced windows, lighting techniques, integrated renewable energy technologies, energy audit and building automation have been discussed in the subsequent chapters of the book.

8. The book shall be of immense use for engineers/architects in preparing building designs and use of building materials, institutions, town planners, etc.

9. The Bureau of Energy Efficiency has recently finalized the Energy Conservation Building Code (ECBC 2007) for efficient use of energy and conservation in buildings. We are proud to say that this handbook is compatible with the provisions of ECBC 2007. I would like to express my sincere thanks to Prof. N.K. Bansal and Dr. Ing Jyotirmay Mathur, editors of this book, for their outstanding contribution in preparation of this publication.

10. Though every care has been taken to provide authentic information, yet some errors might have crept in inadvertently. The publisher, editors and authors are not legally or morally responsible for any loss or damage that may arise to any person from any error or omission in the book. We, however, always welcome suggestions and criticism from our esteemed readers for further improvement of this book which may please be sent in writing to Indian Buildings Congress.

(A. Chakrabarti)
President, Indian Buildings Congress
& Director General (W), CPWD
Sector VI, R.K. Puram
New Delhi-110022

Editors Prof. N.K. Bansal
Dr. Ing. Jyotirmay Mathur

Reviewers on behalf of IBC Shri P. Krishnan
Shri P.S. Chadha

Acknowledgement

Indian Buildings Congress acknowledges the contribution of Prof. N.K. Bansal and Dr. Ing. Jyotirmay Mathur for their contribution in drafting this handbook on behalf of Indian Buildings Congress. The contribution of S/Shri. P. Krishnan and P.S. Chadha in reviewing, getting feed back from several members of IBC on the contents, interacting with the editors and bringing this book in this shape is also acknowledged.

(A. Chakrabarti)

Introduction

The energy sector holds the key in accelerating the economic growth of India. Consumption of energy has been steadily increasing in tune with GDP growth. Indian energy sector, however, has constraints of resources, capital, technology and environment raising issues of energy security. Future economic growth of our country crucially depends on the long term availability of energy resources that are affordable, accessible and environmental friendly.

Looking at the pattern of energy consumption, one observes that although India ranks sixth in the total energy consumption, but per capita energy consumption remains very low (Figs. 1&2). Coal and oil are the main commercial fuels and the country remains a net importer of energy, more than 25% of primary energy needs are met through imports mainly in the form of crude oil. The rising oil import bill has been a cause of serious concern.

Regarding electrical power scenario in the country, thermal contributes nearly 70% while 28% is hydro and rest nuclear and wind (Fig 3). The absolute figures are given in Fig. 4. The gap between demand and supply persists throughout the year in most parts of the country. With this scenario of energy demand and supply, the solutions that are being discussed at the highest level are (1) abundantly available renewable energy sources like solar, wind, hydro and bio energy (2) improving the efficiency of energy uses by implementing energy conservation measures etc.

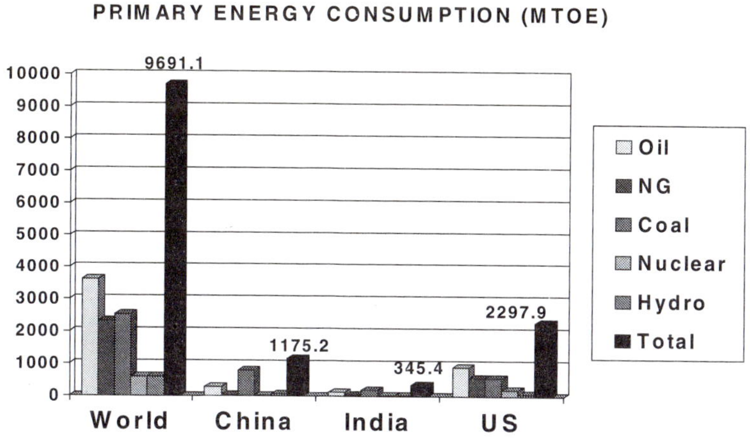

Fig. 1 : Primary commercial energy consumption for India and comparison with the World, China and US.

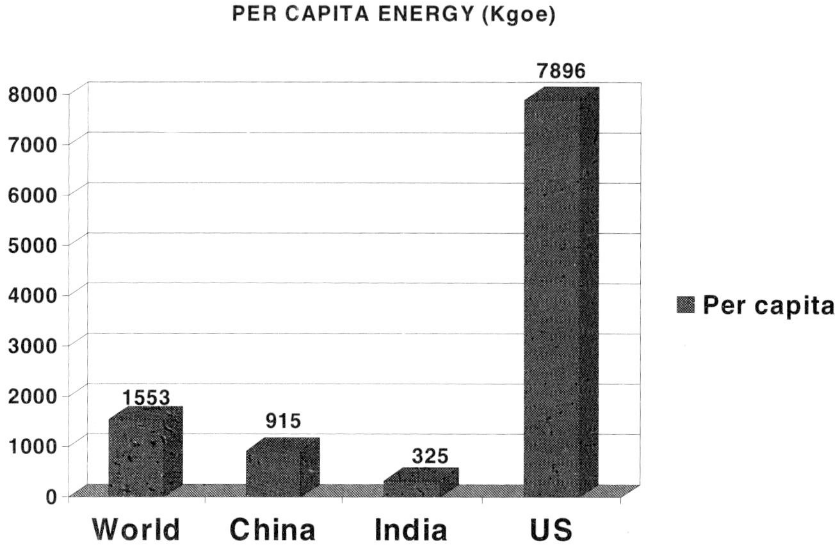

Fig. 2 : Per capita commercial energy comparison in India, China, US and the World

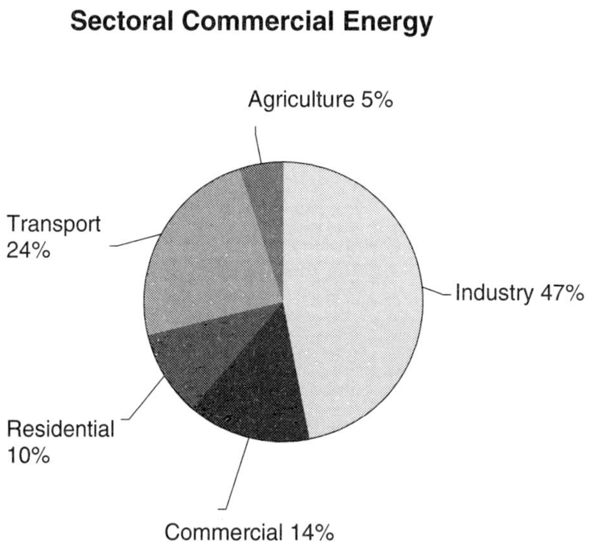

Fig. 3 : Sectoral Primary Commercial Energy Consumption in India

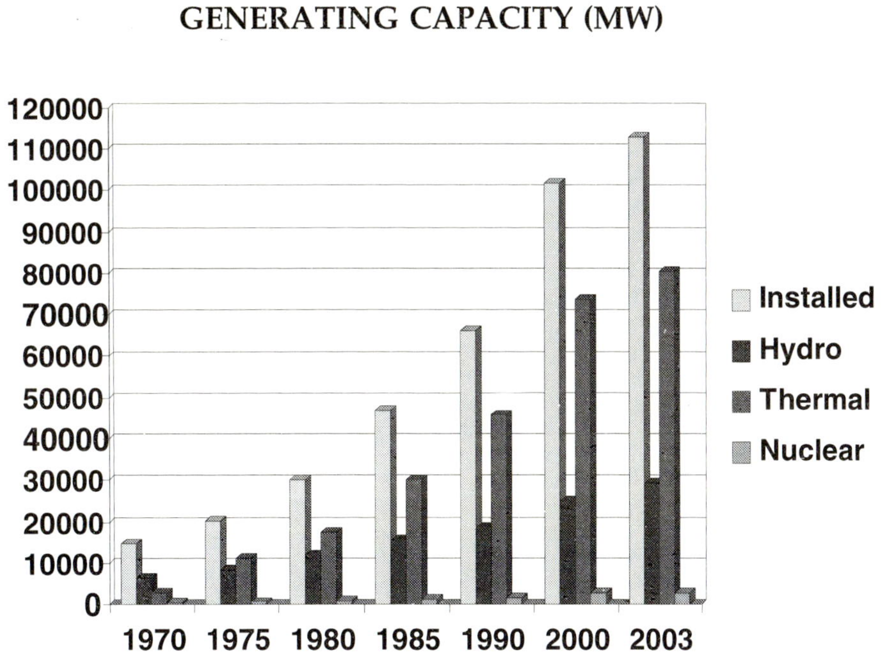

Fig. 4 : Resource-wise installed electrical power patterns in India

As on August 2004, the total installed electrical power capacity in India was 112,706 MW, with annual electricity generation of 558 billion units. There is an energy shortage of 8.8% on the average; at peak times the demand may exceed the supply by 15%. Over the next 10 years, the minimum capacity addition to meet the demand supply gap, is estimated to be 100,000 MW requiring a sum of approximately Rupees Eighty Thousand Crores (including T & D investments), which can not be met through public funds only. A series of measures are required to meet the situation, one of which is energy conservation.

Fig. 5 gives the sectoral electrical energy consumption in the country. Two major electricity consuming sectors are the domestic and agriculture respectively. In the domestic sector, electricity is used mainly in buildings for lighting, heating, ventilation and air–conditioning (HVAC), appliances etc.

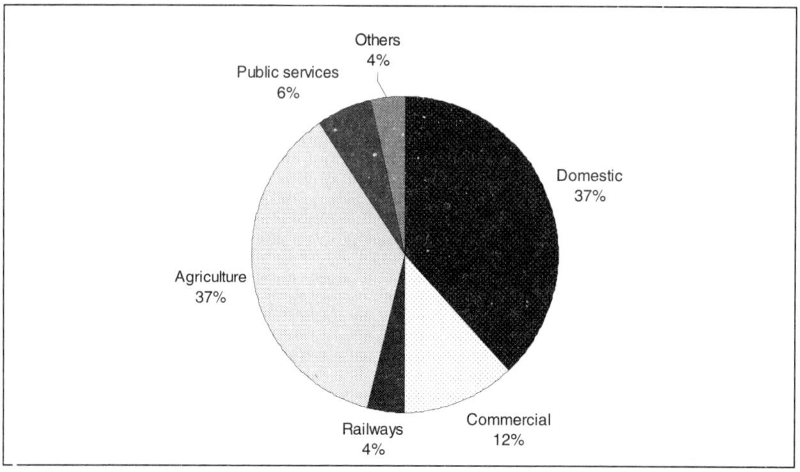

Fig. 5 : Electrical Consumption in different sectors in India

The buildings are mainly of two types namely, residential and commercial. The distribution of electricity consumption for various uses is given in Fig. 6.

Total Energy consumption in buildings = 180 billion Kwh.

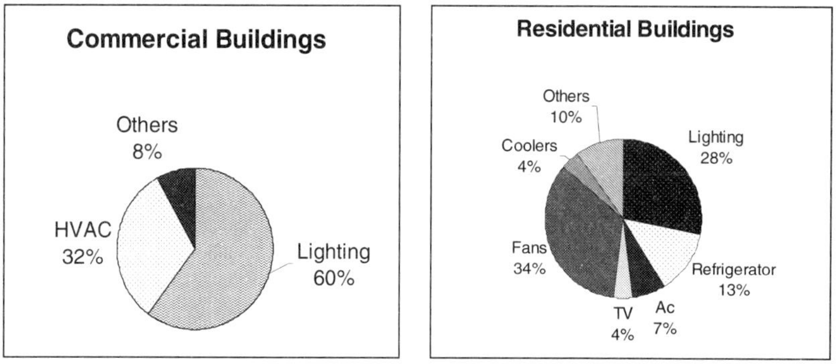

Fig. 6 : Distribution of electricity uses in residential and commercial buildings

With demand for room air conditioners on the increase, the air-conditioning energy use is likely to go very high. In commercial sector, the heating, ventilation and air-conditioning consumption has already been very high. Indian buildings are highly energy intensive in comparison to buildings in Europe and USA.

Energy Conservation Act (The Gazette of India 2001) introduced by the Government of India in the year 2001 requires the following in the context of energy consumption in buildings:

- take suitable steps to prescribe energy conservation codes for efficient use of energy and its conservation in buildings or building complexes;
- amend the energy conservation in building codes to suit the regional and local climatic conditions;
- direct every owner or occupier of the building or building complex, being a designated consumer to comply with the provisions of energy conservation in building codes for efficient use of energy and its conservation;
- direct, any designated consumer, if considered necessary, for efficient use of energy and its conservation in his building, to get energy audit conducted in respect of such building by an accredited energy auditor in such manner and intervals of time as may be specified by regulations;
- take all measures necessary to create awareness and disseminate information for efficient use of energy and its conservation;
- arrange and organize training of personnel and specialists in the techniques for efficient use of energy and its conservation;
- take steps to encourage preferential treatment for use of energy efficient equipment or appliances;

The Act also provides for financial assistance to institutions for promoting efficient use of energy and its conservation. All State Governments have been directed to constitute a fund to be called the State Energy Conservation Fund for the purposes of efficient use of energy and its conservation in the respective states.

Using appropriate architectural design, materials, building components along with the use of renewable energy, it is possible to reduce electrical energy consumption in buildings appreciably. Climate has greatly been responsible for indigenous human settlements. Indigenous buildings and great architectural traditions of the world have both demonstrated an understanding of climate responsive building design, which can be considered to be the first step to conserve energy in buildings. The first oil crisis of 1973 brought issues of oil dependence and energy cost to public awareness. Dependence for energy on Arab world has been the main reason for latest political conflicts between USA and Iraq and now with Iran. In most of the developed world, energy conservation in buildings was made part of national energy policies throughout the industrialized world. Solar energy was used for heating several homes. A decade later, around 1983, the passive and active solar heating was recognized as a science and part of construction industry activities to reduce fossil fuel use and heating costs without compromising on architectural styles and building practices. The integration of design, climate, and human comfort was first proposed by Olgyay and Olgyay (1950) as the bioclimatic approach to architecture regionalism. In the mid 1970s, the term "passive solar design" and "energy conscious design" were used to describe this attitude. One practical application of solar energy studied in that decade was day lighting. The energy management aspects that are being presented in this book are passive heating and cooling, lighting techniques, energy load calculations, thermal insulations, advanced windows, building integrated renewable energy buildings and building automation.

With the use of more and more thermal insulation in buildings, the glass industry came forward to produce high quality glass leading to highly energy efficient window systems, capable of matching an insulated wall with regard to thermal properties but at the same time providing adequate day lighting. The developed countries had developed building design and building materials to keep energy consumption low. In order to bring it down further, building automation techniques have been commercialized. Such building automation techniques are already being used in commercial and industrial buildings in India.

Building Energy Codes

Building energy codes establish minimum energy performance features in the residential and commercial buildings. Several countries have introduced building energy codes through regulation to ensure energy efficiency, environmental protection and fuel conservation measures.

Some countries like UK, New Zealand, have a national code that is adopted throughout the country as a single mandatory code for compliance. Other countries, such as USA and Canada, have a national model code that individual state or province may adopt as a whole or in part or not at all.

Most building energy codes throughout the world require a building to perform from an energy efficiency point of view. This requirement is inherent in the specific energy demand i.e. the annual energy required for heating, cooling, lighting of a building per unit floor area of the building. A building code usually differentiates between various sizes and usages of a building. For example, the UK code differentiates between dwellings and other buildings. A dwelling is a building designed for the residential use of a family. It includes attached or detached housing and individual units of multi-residential apartments but not the whole building as a single unit. It does not include accommodation for elderly persons, hostels, hotels/motels etc.

In the prescribed energy codes, a designer usually has to ensure compliance of prescribed methods and/or specifications. As an example, the designer may follow one of the three available methods specified in the approved document related to heat loss from a building. The three methods are used to demonstrate the method of limiting heat gain/loss through the building fabric, they are:

(a) **The elemental method:** The elemental method requires that certain building elements such as roof, floors, windows, doors etc. achieve the minimum thermal resistance (U-value).

(b) **The target U-value method:** This method requires that both a target U-value, and an average U-value, be calculated for a subject building. If the average U-value of the proposed dwelling does not exceed that target U-value, then compliance is shown. A target U-value is calculated using a formula that takes into account the floor area of the building in relation to the total area of exposed elements. The average U-value is calculated by summing the proposed U-values for each exposed surface and calculating the average U-value over the sum of the exposed surface areas.

(c) **The energy rating method:** The previous two methods only took into account the envelope components. The energy rating method is a holistic approach, which also takes into account ventilation rates, service water heating (SWH), internal heat gains, solar gains and the cost of fuel used.

The Indian Building Energy Code is based upon a combination of the above three methods and offers choice regarding compliance method. The code has good synergy with the American National Standard: 'Energy Standard for Buildings Except Low-Rise Residential Buildings' ANSI/ASHRAE/IESNA Standard 90.1-2004. Developers of the Indian code have taken good care to consider, Indian climatic conditions, available materials and prevailing practices in building industry. Nevertheless, development of the Building Energy Code in any country is an evolutionary process, which should take into account the contemporary building practices, availability of material and construction skills. The code needs to be updated and modified in a gradual process, which can be slowly implemented over wide range of buildings all over a region or a country.

This book, with sponsorship from the Indian Building Congress (IBC), describes above aspects of energy conservation and management in buildings. The first chapter deals with climate and human settlements correlating the elements of weather and climate with building architecture and materials. Examples have been drawn from a study of vernacular architecture in India (Bansal and Minke, 1995). The second chapter discusses solar passive concepts and elements for heating and/ or cooling of buildings followed by energy consumption in buildings. A lot of awareness is taking place regarding embodied energy. Chapter-3 discusses, embodied and operational energy demand related aspects of a building.

The Energy Conservation Building Code (ECBC) has been launched in India on May 27, 2007, with the purpose of providing minimum requirements for the energy-efficient design and construction of buildings. To start with, ECBC is proposed for adoption on a voluntary basis to take into consideration the transition required to make it mandatory. It is applicable to commercial buildings or building complexes that have a connected load of 500 kW or greater or a contract demand of 600 kVA or greater. The code is also applicable to all buildings with a conditioned floor area of 1,000 m^2 (10,000 ft^2) or greater. The code is also recommended for all other buildings. Provisions of the code apply to the areas of:

(a) Building envelopes, except for unconditioned storage spaces or warehouses,

(b) Mechanical systems and equipment, including heating, ventilating, and air conditioning,

(c) Service hot water heating,

(d) Interior and exterior lighting, and

(e) Electrical power and motors.

For ensuring compliance, plans and specifications shall show all pertinent data and features of the building, equipment, and systems in sufficient detail to permit the authority having jurisdiction to verify that the building complies with the requirements of this code. Details shall include, but are not limited to:

(a) Building Envelope: insulation materials and their R-values; fenestration U-factors, solar heat gain coefficients (SHGC), visible light transmittance (if the trade-off procedure is used), and air leakage; overhangs and side fins, building envelope sealing details;

(b) Heating, Ventilation, and Air Conditioning: system and equipment types, sizes, efficiencies and controls; economizers; variable speed drives; piping insulation; duct sealing, insulation and location; requirement for balance report;

(c) Service Hot Water and Pumping: solar water heating system;

(d) Lighting: lighting schedule showing type, number, and wattage of lamps and ballasts; automatic lighting shutoff, occupancy sensors and other lighting controls; lamp efficacy for exterior lamps;

(e) Electrical Power: electric schedule showing transformer losses, motor efficiencies, and power factor correction devices; electric check metering and monitoring system.

Different aspects of the ECBC have been discussed in this book, alongwith the respective topics. Chapter-1 describes effect of climate on energy demand in a building. Chapter-2 explains various passive heating and cooling approaches. This chapter also explains alternatives to conventional passive designs as per modern materials and constraints. Chapter-3 addresses a very important topic of striking a balance between operational energy demand and embodied energy in building. Since the topic of embodied energy is relatively new, a case study has also been included to develop a good insight of readers in this topic.

Chapter-4, first discusses various parameters that affect energy consumption in a building. Requirements of the code related to building envelope have been discussed at the end of Chapter-4 together with discussion on alternative paths for compliance. Discussion on the ECBC related requirements for HVAC system and hot water system have been presented towards the end of Chapter-5 after presenting method for calculating heating and cooling load. Although the insulation requirements for envelope have been discussed in Chapter-5, Chapter-6 would be useful in finding details about using insulation in buildings. Chapter-7 presents energy code related changes in the fenestration systems for buildings. Daylighting and artificial lighting related topics find place in the Chapter-8 alongwith requirements of the energy code. Various options of using building integrated renewable energy systems have been discussed in the Chapter-9. Requirements related to electrical power which included power factor, transformers, motors, have been presented after detailed discussion on energy audit, in the Chapter-10. Building automation has been discussed in Chapter-11. Automation and control related requirements for various services have been discussed along with their fields of application such as HVAC and lighting controls in their respective chapters.

1

Climate and Human Settlement

1.1 INTRODUCTION

Ancient architecture, all over the world, had many characteristics which led to thermal comfort in buildings. The buildings were shaped and different parts of the building (e.g. indoor spaces, doors, windows etc.) were located and oriented to take maximum advantage of the climate. The role of trees, vegetables and water around the building in determining the thermal comfort was well appreciated. The massive walls and clustered residences (to reduce the surface to volume ratio) for reducing the temperature swings were also commonly employed.

The Greek appreciated the importance of south (north in the southern hemisphere) aspect of houses as is evident from the statement of Socrates (400 B.C.: "Now in houses with south aspect, the sun's rays penetrate into porticos in winter, but in summer the path of sun is right over our heads and above the roof (so there is shade). If this is the best arrangement, we should build the south side loftier to get the winter sun and the north side lower to keep out the cold winds". Ancient Iranian architecture exploited the concepts of clustering (decreasing surface to volume ratio, to reduce the thermal load), of thick walls (whose large thermal storage capacity smoothed out the temperature fluctuation), of plantation of shade and living in the basement (during extreme heat and cold). Iranians also introduced the concept of wind towers, which along with cooling by earth and water evaporation made the buildings comfortable in summer. American Red Indians are also known to have used passive solar technique as early as A.D. 1100 in the construction of dwellings in Chaco Canyon and Mesa Verde.

Indigenous ancient Indian forts and domes are good examples of buildings responsive to the demands of sun and climate. As an example, the hot arid climate of Rajasthan is characterized by high daytime temperatures and uncomfortable low night temperatures. The solution best suited to such a wide temperature fluctuation is to delay the entry of heat into the building by such a period that it reaches the interior when it is least bothersome (or even welcome). The inhabitants of this area achieved this desired thermal performance by using materials of high thermal capacity, such as mud and stone which absorb the heat of the sun during the day and introduce it into the dwelling during night. By clustering their dwellings together, the Rajasthanis achieved maximum volume with minimum surface area exposed to the sun while increasing the mass of the building as a whole, thus increasing the thermal time lag. Indian and other ancient architectures are representative of the intuitive approach to building design for local climate conditions.

In hot dry climate conditions, the Islamic and Moorish architectural tradition, the courtyard shaded and graced with plants together with cooling water fountains became the architectural version of paradise on earth. Vernacular architecture in India illustrates a variety of concepts for climate responsive building design. All these features are affected by the local climate. It is, therefore, first essential to introduce the climate parameters and climate zone relevant for India.

1.2. CLIMATE PARAMETERS

1.2.1 Weather and Climate

Weather is an integration of all atmospheric variables at a given place for a brief period of time, whereas climate may be defined as average weather over a period of many years. Hence, both weather and climate are described by the same atmospheric variables, which are known as climatic parameters. Primarily, these parameters are:

- solar radiation
- air temperature
- air humidity
- precipitation
- wind

Another parameter is the atmospheric pressure, which determines the direction and speed of wind, as well as the temperature and moisture characteristics of the air masses. However, atmospheric pressure is not dealt with in this context, as it is of less relevance to the building design.

The basic information about climate parameters is available in the form of hourly and daily observations made at various stations all over India. The weather records of these stations are provided by calendar units (days, months, seasons and years). Climate, as the cumulative expression of the daily weather condition, is most frequently described by employing averages of climatic elements or variables, particularly temperature, precipitation, wind and sunshine. The use of monthly average displays the characteristics of seasonal changes. It is essential also to know the changes and extremes of temperature, the diurnal temperature ranges (difference between day and night temperatures), humidity, sky conditions, incoming and outgoing radiation, quantity and distribution of rainfall and the air movement (wind speed and direction).

The climatic data available at the meteorological stations is not in a form suitable to building designers. It is essential to make the information concise, classify the climates and present the data in the form easily understood by architects or non-professional builders. Before this presentation is attempted, it is useful to briefly describe the various climatic parameters which have an effect on building design. Factors, such as land and water, altitude and topography are also briefly dealt with, as these have an additional influence on building design.

1.2.2 Solar Radiation

The radiation of a large area is determined by the amount of solar radiation which falls upon that area during each season. Regions that are fully exposed to the sun for a larger part of the year are predominantly hot; those which receive sunshine only at low angles and for small portions of the year are predominantly cold. Considering the sun-earth relationship, one could expect the equatorial regions to be the hottest on the world map and the mean temperatures to drop steadily with increasing distance from the equator. It is, however, well known that the fall of temperature from equator to pole is not uniform and numerous deviations appear in the temperature maps.

Figure 1.1 gives the global radiation, which is the total amount of solar radiation (measured in kilowatt-hours per square meter) received on a horizontal surface, in various regions of India. It shows that the regions that receive more solar radiations are not necessarily the hottest. There are other factors which govern the temperature and which are discussed in this chapter. For a building designer, it is important to know the proportion of direct and diffuse radiation on a horizontal surface and on vertical walls oriented in different directions.

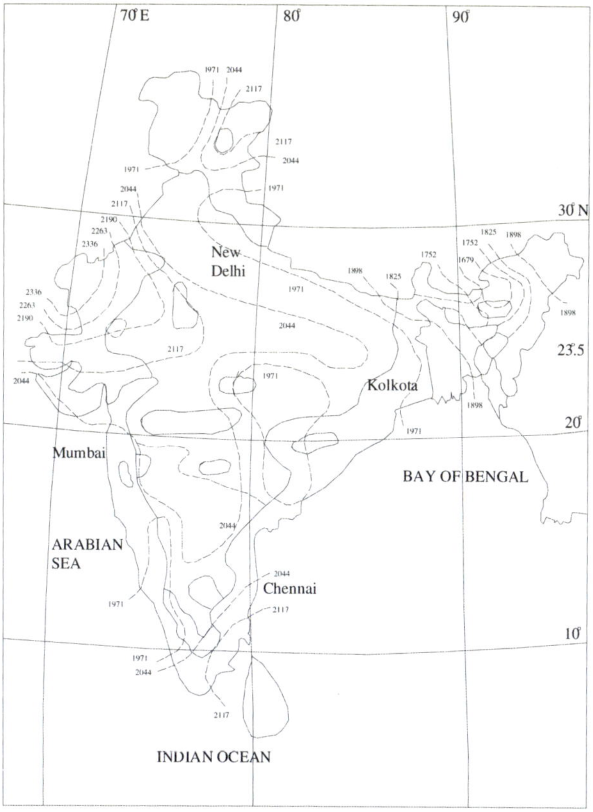

Figure-1.1: Annual global solar radiation kWh/m^2

Since the measured values are available only for a limited number of stations, it is possible to calculate solar radiations with reasonable accuracy. A comparison of measured and calculated values is given in Table-1.1.

Table 1.1 : Comparison of calculated and measured values of global solar radiation (kWh/m²) in New Delhi

Hour/ Month		6	7	8	9	10	11	12	13	14	15	16	17	18
JAN	Calculated	--	0.10	0.27	0.44	0.58	0.66	0.69	0.66	0.58	0.44	0.27	0.10	--
	Measured	--	0.01	0.10	0.27	0.43	0.56	0.62	0.62	0.55	0.43	0.27	0.10	--
FEB	Calculated	--	0.16	0.36	0.54	0.68	0.77	0.80	0.77	0.68	0.54	0.36	0.16	--
	Measured	--	0.02	0.16	0.36	0.54	0.67	0.73	0.73	0.66	0.53	0.36	0.17	--
MAR	Calculated	--	0.25	0.45	0.64	0.78	0.87	0.90	0.87	0.78	0.64	0.45	0.25	--
	Measured	--	0.07	0.26	0.48	0.66	0.78	0.85	0.84	0.77	0.64	0.46	0.25	--
APR	Calculated	0.12	0.32	0.53	0.71	0.85	0.94	0.97	0.94	0.85	0.71	0.53	0.32	0.12
	Measured	0.01	0.13	0.34	0.55	0.73	0.85	0.91	0.90	0.83	0.70	0.52	0.32	0.12
MAY	Calculated	0.18	0.39	0.59	0.76	0.90	0.98	1.01	0.98	0.90	0.76	0.59	0.39	0.18
	Measured	0.03	0.18	0.38	0.58	0.75	0.87	0.93	0.92	0.84	0.72	0.55	0.35	0.16
JUNE	Calculated	0.21	0.42	0.61	0.78	0.91	0.99	1.02	0.99	0.91	0.78	0.61	0.42	0.21
	Measured	0.02	0.16	0.34	0.51	0.66	0.76	0.81	0.81	0.75	0.64	0.48	0.32	0.16
JULY	Calculated	0.18	0.39	0.59	0.76	0.90	0.98	1 .01	098	0.90	0.76	0.59	0.39	0.18
	Measured	0.03	0.13	0.28	0.43	0.55	0.64	0.67	0.67	0.61	0.52	0.41	0.27	0.14
AUG	Calculated	0.12	0.32	0.53	0.71	0.85	0.94	0.97	0.94	0.85	0.71	0.53	0.32	0.12
	Measured	0.01	0.10	0.24	0.39	0.51	0.61	0.64	0.66	0.60	0.57	0.39	0.29	0.11
SEPT	Calculated	--	0.25	0.45	0.64	0.78	0.87	0.90	0.87	0.78	0.64	0.45	0.25	--
	Measured	--	0.08	0.25	0.43	0.59	0.70	0.76	0.76	0.69	0.57	0.42	0.24	--
OCT	Calculated	--	0.16	0.36	0.54	0.68	0.77	0.80	0.77	0.68	0.54	0.36	0.16	--
	Measured	--	0.04	0.20	0.41	0.58	0.70	0.76	0.76	0.69	0.57	0.39	0.19	--
NOV	Calculated	--	0.10	0.27	0.44	0.58	0.66	0.69	0.66	0.58	0.44	0.27	0.10	--
	Measured	--	0.01	0.13	0.32	0.50	0.62	0.69	0.68	0.61	0.49	0.32	0.13	--
DEC	Calculated	--	0.08	0.23	0.39	0.52	0.60	0.63	0.60	0.52	0.39	0.23	0.08	--
	Measured	--	0.00	0.09	0.26	0.43	0.54	0.61	0.61	0.54	0.42	0.26	0.09	--

1.2.3 Air Temperature

Air temperature, measured in degrees Celsius (°C), is the most important climatic parameter determining the requirement of heating or cooling at a given location. The temperature variations at a given place are, however, influenced by other climatic parameters, viz. wind speed and direction, besides the topography and altitude of the place.

Several devices, such as a liquid thermometer, platinum resistance sensor, thermocouple or bimetallic sensor, can be used to measure air temperature in the shade, for which they are usually mounted in a screened box, at a height of 1.50 to 2.00 m above the ground. A maximum and minimum thermometer can also be used to obtain the temperature values within a given period.

The observatories in India only publish the monthly mean, maximum and minimum temperatures, though for the building designer hourly variations of the air temperature and its average value are desirable. These can be estimated by using the ASHRAE algorithm.

1.2.4 Air Humidity

The humidity of air is measured as the amount of moisture present in it. The usual term used to express humidity is relative humidity (R.H.), which gives a direct indication of the evaporation potential. Relative humidity, which is a function of the temperature, is defined by the expression:

$$\text{R.H.} = \frac{\text{Absolute vapour pressure at temperature T}}{\text{Saturated vapour pressure at temperature T}}$$

which is practically equal to:

$$\frac{\text{Absolute humidity (A.H.)}}{\text{Saturated humidity (S.H.)}} \times 100\%$$

Where, A.H. is defined as the amount of moisture actually present in unit mass or unit volume of air, in terms of grams per kilogram (g/kg) or grams per cubic metre (g/m3), and S.H. is the maximum amount of moisture that a unit mass or unit volume of air can hold at that temperature.

Humidity is usually measured by noting the wet and dry bulb temperatures. The wet bulb temperature is measured in the same way as the dry bulb temperature, but the bulb (or sensor) in this case is covered with gauze or a wick, which is kept wet. The evaporation of moisture cools the thermometer and hence the wet bulb temperature will always be lower than the dry bulb temperature, except at a relative humidity of 100%, when the wet and dry bulb temperature will show identical readings. From the recorded observation of the Wet Bulb Temperature (WBT) and Dry Bulb Temperature (DBT) one can read the value of R.H. on the psychometric chart (Figure 1.2). For example, the DBT is 15 °C (59°F) and the WBT is 10 °C (40°F), the R.H. is about 53%, as shown in the figure 1.2.

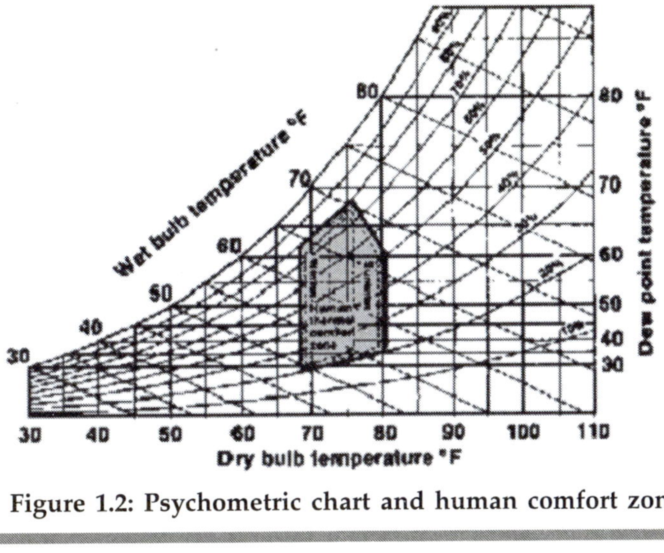

Figure 1.2: Psychometric chart and human comfort zone

Humidity measurements are also done by using a hydrograph, a device which draws a continuous graph on a paper mounted on a rotating cylinder. It works on the principle of the expansion and contraction of a human hair due to moisture differences. When continuous hydrograph readings are not available, the readings are taken when humidity is likely to be highest (just before sunrise, about 6.00 h) and when it is usually lowest (at 15.00 h). These are the values published by the meteorological department.

1.2.5 Precipitation

All forms of water, such as rain, snow, hail and dew, which descend on the earth's surface from the atmosphere, are called precipitation. Quantities of precipitation are generally measured by rain gauges, which show how many millimeters of water accumulate in them during the defined period (day or month). These values, recorded over several years, indicate the length and intensity of wet and dry seasons, which are important factors that have to be considered in building design.

1.2.6 Wind

Data on wind speed and direction is of importance to the building designer, when considering measures for cross ventilation in warm regions or exclusion of undesirable air infiltration in cool zones. Wind speed is measured in metre per second by an instrument called an anemometer, or by a pilot tube, as is used in aeroplane, while wind direction is measured by a wind vane. There are principally two types of anemometers:

(a) cup or propeller type, by which the number of rotations and hence the generated voltage is proportioned to the wind speed, and

(b) hot wire anemometer, which works on the principle of changing electrical resistance caused by temperature changes, so that the rate at which the hot wire cools depends on the wind speed.

Wind directions are usually grouped into eight categories, that is, north, north-east, east, south-east, south, south-west, west and north-west. The essential data required by a building designer is the prevailing wind direction, as this determines the orientation of the building and design of openings. It is also useful to know the typical daily and seasonal changes of wind speed and direction.

1.2.7 Land and Water

The temperature at a certain location is greatly affected by water masses, such as rivers and lakes that are close by. With the same amount of incident solar radiation, the soil gets heated up at least twice as easily as the same volume of water, while water additionally loses some energy by evaporation. Dry earth, therefore, gets heated to a higher temperature than water or wet earth, consequently air in contact with dry earth will be warmer than air in contact with water or wet ground. This explains why dry areas have higher temperatures than locations with high humidity.

For a particular latitude and altitude, the air temperatures in summer will be lower over large bodies of water and higher over large tracts of dry land. In winter, the reverse can be true, since the land cools down more quickly than water, when it is not exposed to sunshine. It is, therefore, evident that the annual variations in ambient temperature will be highest over dry land and lowest over large bodies of water. The diurnal variations will follow the same general pattern.

1.2.8 Altitude

In a free atmosphere, the temperature decreases with increasing altitude, at a rate of about 0.65°C per 100 m (standard atmosphere). This gradual temperature change could also be expected near the ground, if it were not for several factors which upset the general pattern. For instance, cold air tends to sink into depression in the terrain and warm air tends to rise up the hillsides, creating an inversion of the temperature. Ground surfaces exposed to a clear night sky lose a considerable quantity of heat by radiation, thus reducing the temperature of the air in contact with it. This also results in an inversion.

Nevertheless, the fall of air temperature with increasing altitude is fairly constant in most cases. Many of the world's highest elevations are within or close to the geographical tropics. For instance, the equator traverses the Andes of South America and the highlands of East Africa, and passes close to the snow covered mountains in New Guinea, while the Himalayas and the southern part of the Rocky Mountains lie close to the Tropic of Cancer. Since the climate changes with altitude, these elevations add to the variety of climates within the tropical belt and most of these are represented on the Indian subcontinent.

1.2.9 Topography

The climatic parameter that is most influenced by topography is the wind pattern. Valleys tend to channel wind along their own axis. Rising contours opposed to the wind produce up-currents over the crest on the leeward side and calms at the base of the slope on the leeward side. Wind speed begins to decrease on the windward side of the wind break and regains its full magnitude at a distance, depending on the type of barrier (opaque or perforated) as shown in Figures 1.3a and b.The figures show that the wind speed drops rapidly below 40% just behind the building and increases to 60% at a distance of twice height of the barrier, whereas in the case of row of trees, the drop is not as rapid, but regains 60% of the original speed only after a distance of 4.5 times the height of the barrier (h).

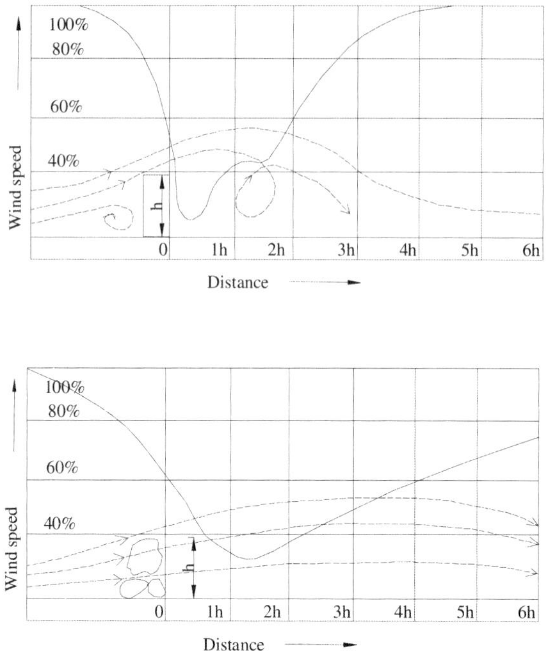

Figure 1.3: (a) Reduction of free wind speed (100%) by an opaque wind barrier (building), (b) Reduction of free wind speed (100%) by a perforated barrier (trees)

1.3 CLIMATIC ZONES IN INDIA

1.3.1 Characterization

A major prerequisite of good building design is to have sufficient knowledge of the climatic conditions of the given location. Since different locations within large areas have very similar climatic characteristics, these can be grouped together to form a more or less accurately defined climatic zone, within which the climatic design requirements for buildings are generally the same, with minor differences only due to the local environmental conditions. Thus, the division of a country into different climatic zones is an important instrument of climatic design.

The primary objective of house construction is not only to provide shelter against adverse weather conditions, but even more to provide a comfortable and healthy habitat. Therefore, only those climatic parameters that influence the thermal comfort of human beings merit consideration for the functional design of buildings. In the classification of a climate, only those parameters are taken into account that influence heat exchange between the body and the environment, and that are essentially important from the point of view of building design. India possesses a large variety of climates, ranging from extremely hot desert regions to high altitude locations with severely cold conditions, similar to Northern Europe. On the basis of monthly mean data recorded in 233 stations, located in all parts of India, Bansal and Minke (1995) divided the country into the following 6 climatic zones.

I. Hot and dry (HD)

II. Warm and humid (WH)

III. Moderate (MO)

IV. Cold and cloudy (CC)

V. Cold and sunny (CS)

VI. Composite (CO)

Air temperature and humidity are the most important parameters that determine weather & climate. The two other factors, namely solar radiation and precipitation are those that influence building design. Since the data available for all the meteorological stations does not include absolute values of radiation, it was only possible to express this factor in "number of clear days" (Table 1.2).

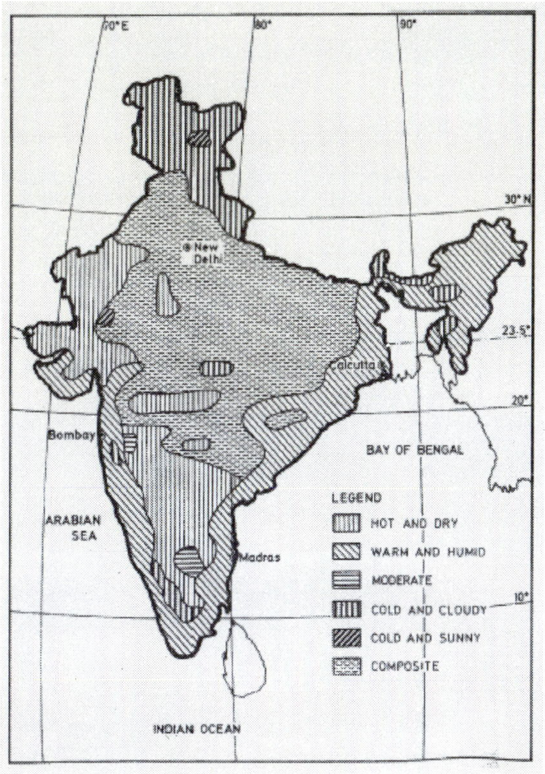

Figure 1.4: Climatic zones of India

The criteria for allocation of a station to one of the first five climatic zones are that the defined conditions prevail for more than 6 months. In case, where none of these categories can be identified for six months or longer, the climatic zone is called "composite". On this basis, the evaluation of the mean monthly climatic data from the 233 stations made it possible to delineate the six climatic zones on the map of India (Figure 1.4).

Figure-1.5 shows six locations which can be considered typical of each climatic zone: in Jodhpur 7 months can be classified as hot and dry, in Mumbai 10 months are typically warm and humid, and Bangalore has moderate conditions for 10 months of the year. Srinagar can be called cold and cloudy for 8 months, while Leh cold and sunny all through the year. Since New Delhi's climate does not correspond to any of the previous categories for more than half an year, it falls into the composite zone.

The 6 climatic zones are summarized in the form of a chart, which gives a general view of each zone at a glance and facilitates between them. The brief information on the main climatic features is sufficient to understand the principal requirements of climatic design, such as the need to decrease or increase solar heat gain, provide ventilation or wind protection, store heat and/ or absorb moisture, to name only a few design factors.

Table 1.2: Criteria for the classification of climate

Climate	Mean monthly temperature (°C)	Relative humidity (%)	Precipitation (mm)	No. of clear days
Hot and dry (HD)	>30	<55	<5	>20
Warm and humid (WH)	>30	>55	>5	<20
Moderate (MO)	25-30	<75	<5	<20
Cold and cloudy (CC)	<25	>55	>5	<20
Cold and sunny (CS)	<25	<55	<5	>20
Composite (CO)	This applies, when six months or more do not fall within any of the above categories.			

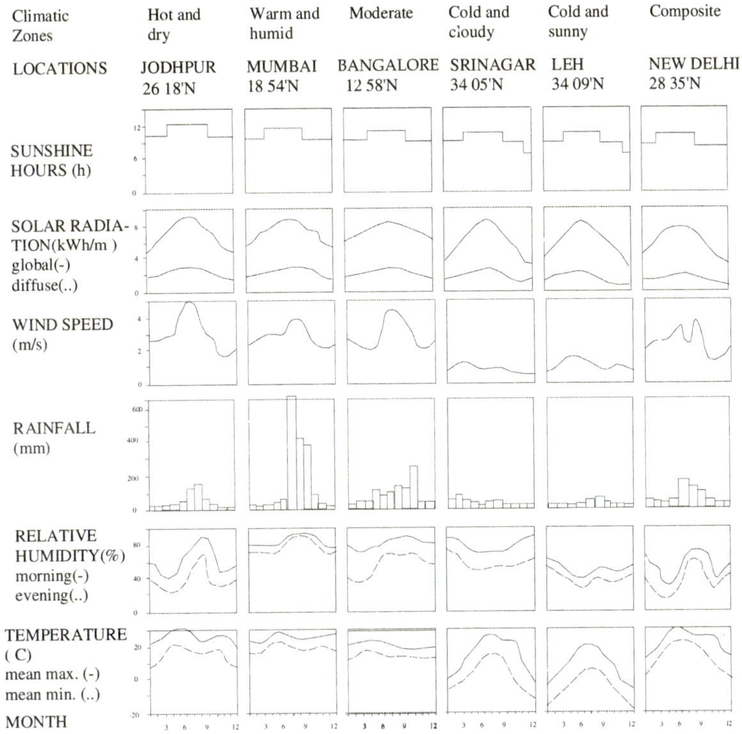

Figure 1.5 : Climatic data of representative locations

Table 1.3 Summary of Typical Climatic Features of the 6 Climatic Zones in India.

Climatic features	*Hot and dry*	*Warm and humid*	*Moderate*
Typical landscape and vegetation	Relative flat; sandy or rocky ground conditions; scarce vegetation, generally consisting of grass, cacti or thorny trees and bushes. Low water level.	Generally low altitude, relatively flat regions with abundant vegetation.	Generally hilly or high plateau region with fairly abundant vegetation.
Solar radiation	Intense (800-950 W/m^2)	Usually diffuse radiation (somtimes causes glare) due to cloud cover or vapour content of the air; intense radiation on clear days; dissipation of accumulated heat from	More or less uniformly moderate all through the year

Climatic features	*Hot and dry*	*Warm and humid*	*Moderate*
		the earth to the night sky usually prevented by clouds and humid air.	
Mean Temperature Summer midday Summer night Winter midday Winter night Diurnal variations	 40° - 45°C 20° - 30°C 5° - 25°C 0° - 10°C 15 – 45 deg.C	 30° - 35°C 25° - 30°C 25° - 30°C 20° - 25°C 5 - 8 deg.C	 30° - 34°C 17° - 24°C 27° - 33°C 16° - 18°C 8 - 13 deg.C
Relative humidity	Very low (25-40 %)	High (70-90 %)	Variable, between 30 and 80 %
Precipitation	Low, generally less than 500 mm per year	High, generally in excess of 1200 mm per year	Fairly well distributed over the year; total annual rainfall usually exceeding 1000mm, relatively dry winter.
Winds	Dust laden local winds (often developing into sandstorms) in the afternoons, and isolated whirlwinds in the evenings	Usually one or two prevailing directions, with velocity ranging from extremely low to very high (during rain storms)	Variable, generally high during summer; intensities and direction mainly dependent on topography
Sky conditions	Cloudless sky with high solar radiation, causing glare in dust laden air; occasional darkening of the sky due to sandstorms	Generally overcast (cloud cover ranging between 40 and 80%), causing unpleasant glare	Mainly clear; occasionally overcast with dense low clouds in summer
Miscellaneous	Radiant heat emanating from the ground and surrounding objects during afternoons and evenings can cause considerable thermal discomfort	High humidity levels and low diurnal temperature variations cause great discomfort, if there is no air movement	Climatic conditions generally within a favourable range, which requires no special building design to improve indoor comfort

Climatic features	*Cold and cloudy*	*Cold and sunny*	*Composite*
Typical landscape and vegetation	Highland regions with abundant vegetation in summer	Mountainous regions with little vegetation	Extremely variable landscapes, with seasonal changes in vegetation
Solar radiation	Low in winter with a higher percentage of diffuse radiation	Intense with low percentage of diffuse radiation	Intense in the summer and winter with a low percentage of diffuse radiation, but very low in

Climatic features	*Cold and cloudy*	*Cold and sunny*	*Composite*
			monsoon with predominantly diffuse radiation
Mean temperature Summer midday Summer night Winter midday Winter night Diurnal variations	 20° - 30° C 17° - 21° C 4° - 8° C -3° - 4° C 5 - 15 deg C	 17° - 24° C 4° - 14° C -7° - 8° C -14° - 0° C 20 - 25 deg C	 32°-43°C Monsoon 27°-32°C midday 27°-32°C 10°-25°C night 27°-32°C 4°-10°C 3-22 deg C
Relative humidity	Varies between 70-80%	Consistently low (10-50%)	In dry periods 20 to 55% and 1300 mm per year, during monsoon reaching 250 mm in the wettest month. Little or no rain in the dry season
Winds	Generally intense, especially during rainfall; mainly dependent on topography	Occasionally intense	Hot and dusty during summer; strong winds in monsoon from south-east; dry, cold winds in winter from north-west
Sky conditions	Overcast for most part of the year, except during the brief summer period	Fairly clear throughout the year with cloud cover less than 50%	Varying, overcast and dull in the monsoon, clear during summer and winter. Occasional dust haze during the summer period
Miscellaneous	Summers are usually pleasant, with higher rainfall	Exceptionally harsh cold desert climatic conditions	Seasonal changes in relative humidity cause rapid weakening of building materials.

1.4 CONSTRUCTION MATERIALS

Construction materials have several properties that influence interaction of the building with its surrounding climate. Comfort in the building is the result of this interaction and skillful use of material. From this point of view, walls and roof are the two most important components of any building. Several studies have been conducted to find the most suitable combination of materials and their laying. In a survey of rural households, it has been possible to detail the wall and roof construction. The data is given in Tables 1.4 and 1.5 respectively.

Table 1.4: Summary of Identified Wall Construction Materials in the Various Climatic Zones

Wall material	Horizontal section	Climatic zone
Compacted earth rendered with cow dung slurry		Hot and dry warm & Humid composite
Unburnt brick in mud mortar with a. lime plaster, b. cement plaster	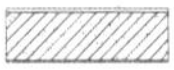	Cold and sunny composite
Burnt brick in mud mortar with a. lime plaste b. cement plaster		Cold and cloudy composite
Burnt brick in lime mortar		Warm and humid
Sandstone, upright slabs		Hot and dry
Stone masonry in mud mortar, unplaster		Cold and cloudy composite
Stone masonry in mud mortar with cow dung finish		Cold and cloudy
Stone masonry in mud mortar between wooden frame		Cold and cloudy
Stone masonry in lime mortar	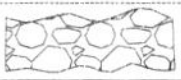	Moderate
Woven bamboo matting, without plaster		Warm and humid
Bamboo mat with mud plaster and cow dung finish on both sides.	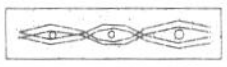	Cold and cloudy
Poles and twigs plaster with mud mortar	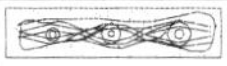	Composite
Frame of bamboo and bundled straw and loose straw cover.		Cold and cloudy

Table 1.5 Summary of Identified Roof Construction Materials in the Various Climatic Zones

Roof material	Detail (Not to scale)	Climatic zone
Straw thatch on pole timber on bamboo substructure		Hot and dry warm & humid, cold cloudy, composite
Straw thatch on bamboo frame clad with coconut leaf mat	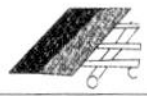	Cold and cloudy
Straw thatch on frame of timber and grass bundles		Cold and dry
Straw thatch on frame of bamboo and grass bundles (Toda roof)		Cold and cloudy
Natural stone state on timber substructure	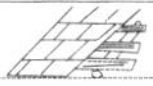	Cold and cloudy
Locally made 'Country' or 'Spanish ' tiles on timber substructure		Hot and dry, Warm & humid, composite
"Manglore" tiles on timber substructure		Warm and humid moderate composite
Poles and twigs covered with straw and mud layer (Ladakhi roof)		Cold and sunny
Wooden beams and board covered with straw and protective mud layer.		Hot and dry composite
Timber beams supporting stone slabs covered with lime concrete screed.		Moderate
Timber substructure carrying clay tiles covered with mud.		Composite
Timber beams, bricks and lime screed covered with clay tiles(Madras terrace)	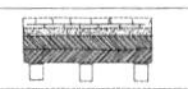	Warm and humid
Asbestos cement sheeting on timber substructure	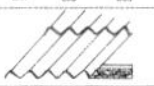	Cold and cloudy

1.5 ENERGY CONSERVING CONCEPTS IN RURAL BUILDINGS

Rural buildings in India exhibit the indigenous use of locally available materials and techniques in buildings that are adapted to local climatic conditions. A detailed study of traditional Indian buildings in rural areas has brought out many concepts and design patterns relevant for energy efficient building design.

1.5.1 Energy Efficient Features and Concepts

An examination of traditional buildings brings out many attractive features of design, which are valid even for contemporary architecture. Manali in Himachal Pradesh, has very cold climatic conditions with low precipitation. The common material used for building is mud with very thick walls. This construction helps to reduce the temperature variation indoors, in spite of the large diurnal fluctuations of ambient temperature. The living areas here are usually on the first floor. The ground floor is meant for the animals and the second floor is for the kitchen. The living space is thus sandwiched between two heat sources (Fig. 1.6). Another common feature of most houses in Manali is very small openings so the heat losses are reduced. The kitchen is used as the daytime living space in these regions, to benefit from warmth of the cooking stove.

Another striking example of climatic conscious building design is the vernacular architecture in the hot and dry regions of Rajasthan (Fig. 1.7). The building form in this region results in minimum surface area and heavy insulation in the form of thatch on the roof.

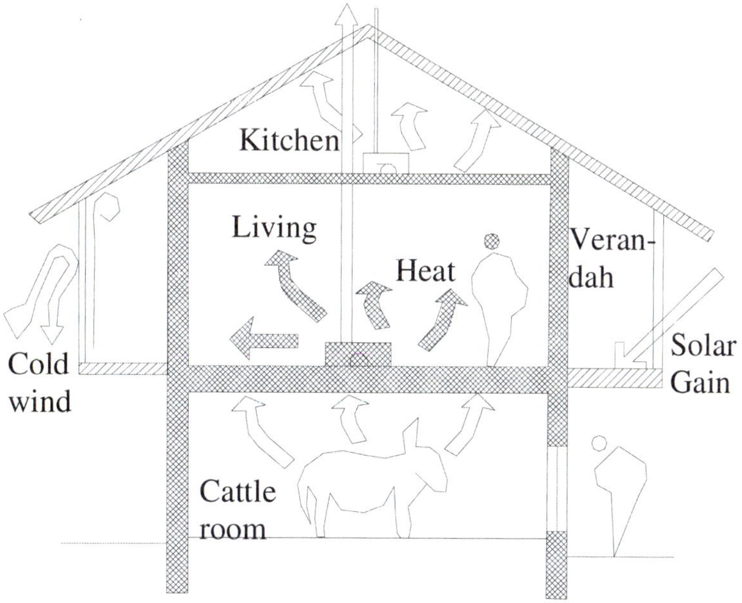

Figure 1.6 : Passive feature for cold climates

Passive and energy efficient architectural features identified for buildings in Manali are:

* Increase of solar heat gain
  - by facing the longer side towards south, to catch maximum sun in winter
  - by providing a sheltered verandah for use in sunny days
* Increase of internal heat gain
  - by utilizing heat from cattle accommodated below the living space
  - by utilizing the kitchen stove as a fireplace and placing the living room between two warm spaces (cattle room and kitchen)
* Decrease of heat loss
  - by low entrances to cattle room and living spaces
  - by reducing exposure to cold winter breeze, with canvas hung around the verandah, creating a buffer zone
  - by locating the house on the leeward side of a hill
* Balance of temperature fluctuations
  - by thick stone/mud walls.

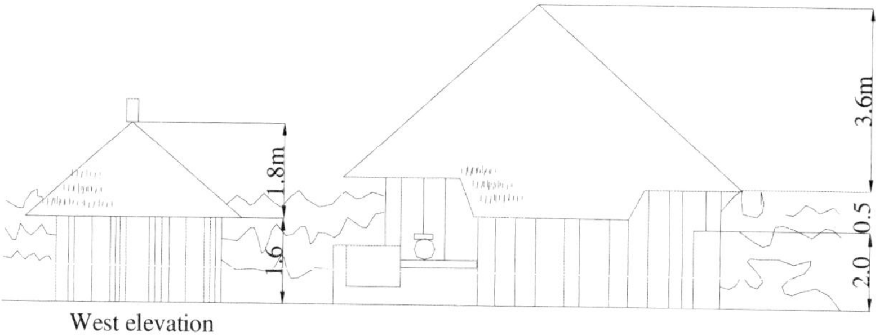

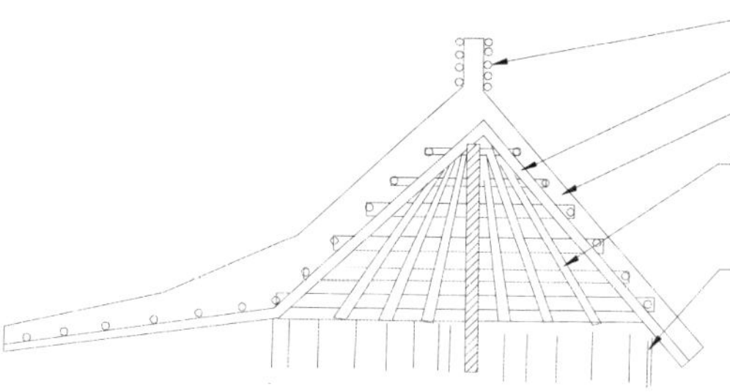

Figure 1.7: Passive features of hot and dry climate

Energy efficient features identified through architecture in Rajasthan, representative of hot & dry climatic conditions are as follows:

* Reduction of solar heat gain
    - by small surface-to-volume ratio, achieved by circular plan of house
    - by partial shading of walls, by overheating eaves and fence (on the east side)
    - by avoiding openings other than the door
* Reduction of heat transmission to the interior
    - by thermally insulating thatch roof
    - by wind-breaker/fence for protection against hot winds
* Increase of heat loss
* Reduction of solar heat gain
    - by roof overheating
* Reduction of internal heat gain
    - by locating the kitchen outside the house
* Increase of heat loss
    - by raising the structure on stilts
    - by ventilation through walls
    - by light roof

With such construction, the interception of solar radiation is reduced and then the transmission of heat through the roof is minimized. Here too, the openings are very small to avoid heat-gain through hot winds during the day. The people also build wind barriers to reduce wind speeds. During the night time, people sleep outdoors. Even in the urban context, Rajasthani architecture shows characteristics of climatic conscious building design. Mutual shading, overhangs, orientation, courtyards, large surface areas for increasing radiation losses during the night and many other aspects are useful for increasing energy efficiency in buildings in the cotemporary context.

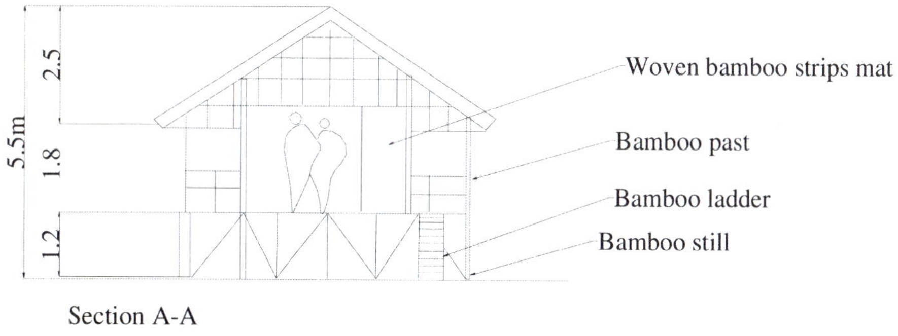

Figure 1.8 : Passive features for warm and humid climate

In warm and humid climates along the coast, people build light houses with large openings to facilitate natural ventilation. The roofs are sloped for easy drainage of rainwater (Fig. 1.8).

In the cold and cloudy conditions of North-Eastern India, people build their huts in the form of inverted catenaries so that the loads are transferred to the foundation and the rain water drains off immediately (Fig. 1.9). The following concepts can be listed for keeping the inside space of a building warm in cold and cloudy climatic conditions:

* Decrease of heat loss
    - by high thermal insulation of walls and roof
    - by providing only small doors and openings to reduce air infiltration
    - by providing a wind-shaded pit
    - by providing a small exposed surface area in the form of a vault-shaped structure.

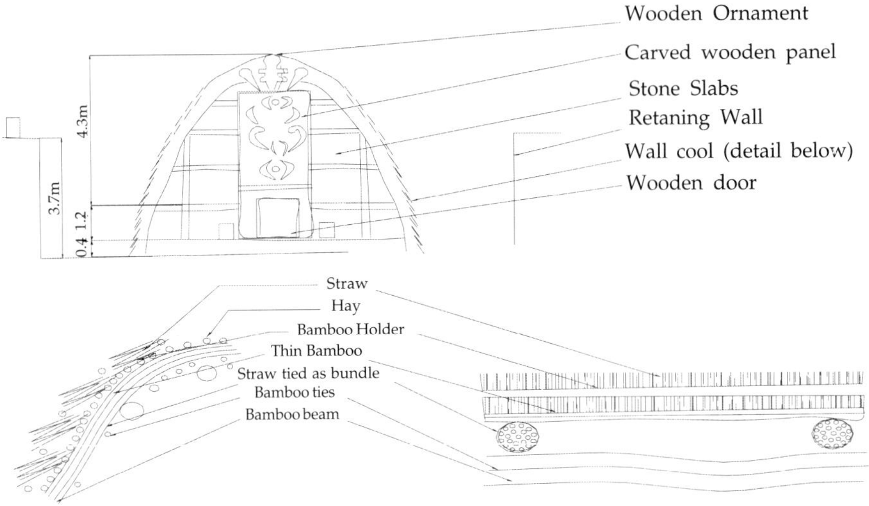

Figure 1.9: Passive features for cold and cloudy climate

1.5.2 Concepts for Heating in Cold Regions

In cold regions where the inside spaces need heating, the first step is to use concepts of building design which result in reduction of heat losses. The use of thermal insulation, advance windows, building forms with low surface-to-volume ratio, reduced air infiltration and shelter from cold winds are a few concepts that help to reduce heat losses in buildings.

After an architect has conceived a design to reduce heat losses to the maximum possible, the next step is to increase solar heat gain in the buildings. Orientation of the building, particularly of windows, can play a major role in reducing heating energy demand in buildings. Of course the windows in this case have to be constructed with insulated glass or even advance glazing systems. The use of different glazing systems and transparent insulation has been one of the major technological advances in recent years. Many countries, like France, Germany and Holland, have introduced advanced windows commercially with governmental support.

Passive heating techniques, like a thermal storage wall, Trombe wall, attached green houses, etc. have been used in many buildings all around the world with positive results. The performance of each of these passive concepts depends upon the climate and the type of building and the architects have to understand each of them in this context before applying them in a building design.

1.5.3 Concepts for Cooling in Hot Climatic Conditions

For achieving natural cooling for buildings in hot climates, there are basically three principles that have to be used intelligently by the architect.

1. Reduce solar radiation that reaches the building envelope,
2. Reduce heat transmission through the building envelope,
3. Increase heat losses from the building by convection, radiation and evaporation.

In order to reduce the amount of solar radiation that reaches the building, the natural way is to use the shade of neighboring buildings and vegetation, to provide overhangs and louvers and even use reflecting surfaces wherever possible (taking care to avoid causing glare). Sometimes a boundary of shrubs or trees around the house is very useful to effectively reduce the speed and even the temperature of incoming hot winds.

After the designer has done his best to reduce the interception of solar radiation, the next natural step is to reduce the heat transmission into the building. In this context the use of air cavities and thermal insulation is very well known. However, one has started thinking of using ventilated cavities which can remove the transmitted heat more effectively. Such cavities were built in a few old buildings at Jaisalmer, but their effect has not been quantified yet, particularly for the cooling.

Once the heat has been transmitted into the building, it has to be removed and discharged to the outside. The most natural way to remove heat is by ventilation. The arrangement of windows again plays a vital role in this regard. The use of courtyards is an effective way to discharge heat and to create natural ventilation and is a common practice in many countries. Additionally, wind towers and air vents have been used effectively in Persian architecture.

It is a well known fact that the temperature of the earth a few meters below the surface is constant and normally equal to the annual average temperature of the ambient air. It is due to this that cellars are cooler in summer and warmer in winter. Building underground has been one of the traditional ways of protection from scorching heat. Additionally, an underground tunnel can be used to cool the ambient air. The ambient air is drawn into this tunnel and the cold air is then discharged into the building. Efforts are going on to optimize this system, especially in Germany.

The thermal capacity of the building material can delay the entry of heat and reducing the temperature amplitude inside (difference between maximum and minimum temperature). The thermal storage effect increases with increasing compactness, density and specific heat of the materials. This is the reason why the temperature of the ocean fluctuates over only a small range during the year, whereas a thin metal sheet immediately assumes the temperature of the ambient air. All building elements, such as walls, roof and floor can be used for thermal storage. In order to dampen the effect of diurnal variations of the exterior environment and thus maintain the internal temperature at a relatively constant value, a heavy wall is used. This wall can store heat and has the ability to resist heat flow. The most effective way of maximizing these two properties in a building is to use a combination of material with a large thermal capacity (concrete, brick etc.) and a material with low thermal conductivity or high resistance to heat flow (such as expanded polystyrene). Insulation is an ideal way to reduce the effect of diurnal temperature fluctuations.

In hot and dry climatic conditions, evaporation of water is a very effective way of cooling the outdoors as well as indoor. This concept has been used very effectively in the past as well as in contemporary architecture.

In mixed climatic conditions, where cooling in summer and heating in winter is needed, the concepts for both heating and cooling are relevant. The building, however, has to be heavy to balance the temperature fluctuations. Overhangs and louvers should be provided intelligently to shade the building in summer and yet allow exposure to the winter sun. Detailed coverage on these topics is presented in subsequent chapters.

The next chapter on passive concepts describes various options for incorporating specific features in buildings located in such composite climatic conditions along with detailed discussion on other passive concepts.

2

Passive Building Design Concepts*

For almost all types of climatic conditions, there are few passive design concepts that help building designers to develop buildings that are comfortable with very little or even without use of any artificial device. These concepts have been classified in the following categories:

1. Passive heating systems
2. Passive cooling systems
3. Passive ventilation systems

2.1 PASSIVE HEATING SYSTEMS

The concept of passive heating essentially consists of increasing the heat gain and reducing the heat loss inside a building without conventional heating methods that utilize fossil fuels or electrical energy. Such concepts are typically useful for buildings located in cold climates where the buildings are to be kept warmer than their surroundings. Almost all the concepts of passive heating utilize combination of the following three elements or stages:

(i) Collection of naturally available energy/heat

(ii) Storage of collected energy

(iii) Use of stored energy in a controlled fashion for achieving thermal comfort

Passive heating systems can be classified in three categories depending upon the source of heat:

(a) Use of solar energy

(b) Use of ambient energy (other than solar energy)

(c) Use of internal sources of heat

2.1.1 Use of Solar Energy for Heating

Sun is the largest and most preferred naturally available source of energy for passive heating. Concepts that utilize solar energy for heating of buildings are termed as 'solar passive concepts'. Performance of the solar passive heating concepts is based upon maximizing solar exposure and capture of solar radiation. In addition, heat losses from any building are to be minimized for

* Base document for this Chapter is Bansal N.K. and Minke G (1995), Climatic Zones and Rural Housing in India, Research Centre, Juelich, Germany.

ensuring a high value of net solar heat gain. Capture of solar radiation alternatively termed as 'solar heat gain' in a building can be achieved either through entry of solar radiation in a building or through some indirect methods that capture the heat of solar radiation and transfer the heating effect to the building. All the solar passive heating concepts have been arranged in three groups:

(i) Direct solar heat gain

(ii) Indirect solar heat gain

(iii) Combined direct and indirect solar heat gain

2.1.1.1 *Direct Solar Heat Gain*

This is a straight forward concept in which the solar radiation is admitted through a window or wall of glass facing south direction to admit maximum solar radiation in winter and to heat walls, floors and objects (consequently the room air) lying in the room as shown in Figure 2.1(a). Double glazing is used to reduce heat loss and during night time, curtains or any other form of insulation is used to cover the window/curtain wall. A suitable overhang provided over the window/wall helps to keep out the summer sun and hence avoids undesired heating.

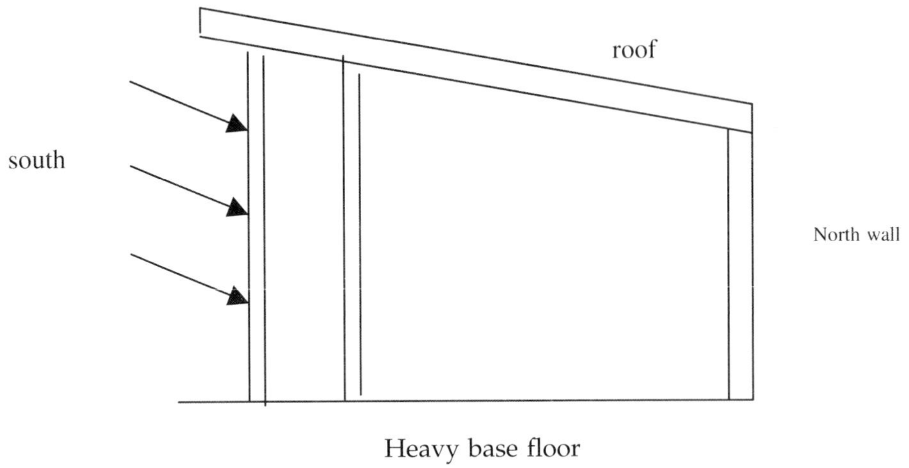

Figure 2.1(a): Direct Gain concept

Similarly, 'Solar Hemicycle' is another concept shown in Figure 2.1(b). The plan of building is shaped like a 'rising sun', with the north wall buried into the earth up to the window-sill level. The ring-shaped earth wall protects the ground floor from wind and weather.

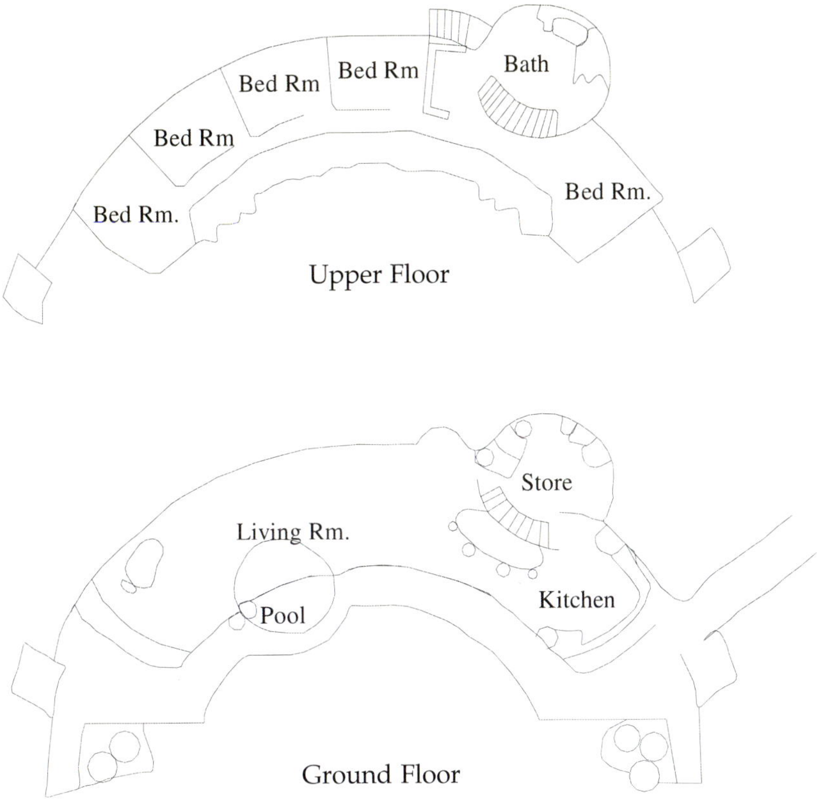

Figure 2.1(b) : Solar Hemicycle

A tunnel through the northern wall provides the way to the south oriented garden of the house. The gallery and roof overhang protect the house from hot summer sun. Thermal storage is provided in the floor, north wall and a circular shaped swimming pool.

The efficiency of direct heat gain through glazing depends upon the overall heat transfer coefficient i.e. the U-value and the Solar Heat Gain Coefficient 'g'. These terms have been explained with details in the Chapter-5.

To combine the above two parameters, "U-value' and 'g-value', a new term 'U-equivalent: U_{eq}' has been introduced. The amount of heat flow 'Q' can then be expressed by the formula:

$$Q = U_{eq} .A .DD \qquad \text{(eq. 2.1)}$$

where, A is the area of building element and 'DD' is the number of degree days. The term 'Degree Days' defines joint effect of duration and severity of the hot/cold climate and is very helpful in estimating the extent of heating/cooling requirement in any building. The number of degree-days on any particular day is equal to the degrees by which the average outdoor air temperature on that day falls below or above the desired indoor temperature. This number, multiplied by the number of total such days in a year gives the total number of degree-days for that season. Similarly, the number of degree days for any year can also be found.

The value of 'U_{eq}' in the formula 2.1 is given by:

$$U_{eq} = U_f - g_f . S_f \qquad \text{(eq. 2.2)}$$

where:

U_{eq} : equivalent heat transfer of transparent building element (window)

U_f : U-value of the window

g_f : Solar gain factor (g-value) of the window

S_f : Solar energy gain coefficient of the window

g_f can be found through:

$$g_f = \iota + u_f [\{(\alpha_i + \alpha_o)/h_0\} + \alpha_i/C] \qquad \text{(eq. 2.3a)}$$

where:

g_f is solar energy gain factor of double glazed window, ι is the total transmittance, α_I, α_o are the solar absorption coefficients of the inside and outside glazing, h_0 is the external heat transfer coefficient and C is conductance of air gap between glass panes.

and S_f can be found through:

$$S_f = (Q_{ws} - Q_{ms})/\ (A_f . g_f . DD) \qquad \text{(eq. 2.3b)}$$

where:

Q_{ws} is heating energy requirements of a building space without solar gain (Wh)

Q_{ms} is the heating energy requirement of a building space with incident solar radiation

The value of S_f depends upon the heating energy requirement through the term 'DD' in the denominator and hence depends upon the climatic conditions along with type, size and orientation of the window. Figure 2.2 shows solar energy gain coefficient through a typical double glazed window used in an office building of Germany as a typical example of cold climate.

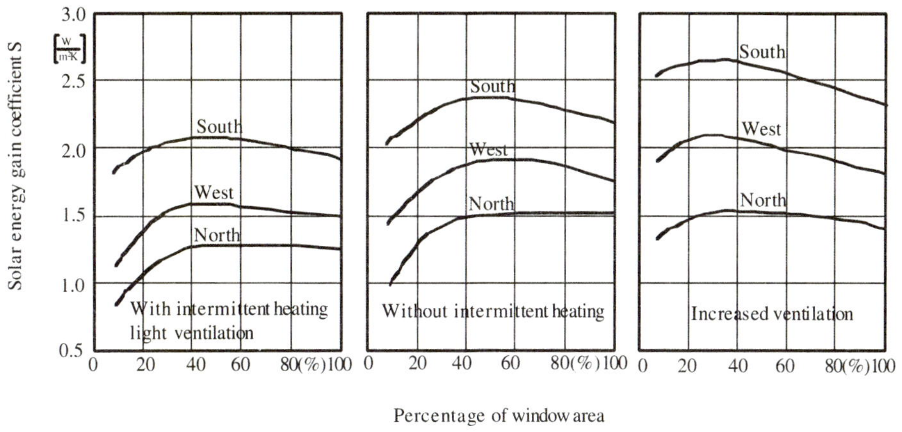

Figure 2.2: Solar Energy Gain Coefficient for Windows of different size and orientation

Performance of windows for direct heat gain can further be improved with use of movable insulation that is put-on during no-sunshine hours for reducing the heat loss through the window element.

The windows in direct heat gain systems should also allow the penetration of solar radiation deeper into the space to let it fall on surfaces that can absorb and store heat. Figure 2.3 (a), (b) display splaying the walls and window frames that help in increasing the solar gain.

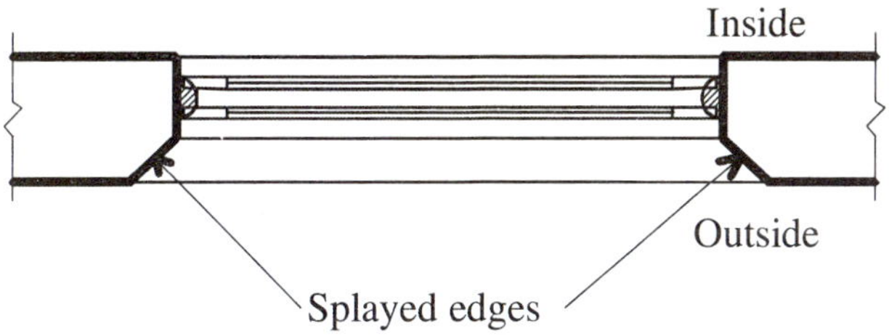

Figure 2.3(a) : Splaying of walls and window frames for increasing solar gain

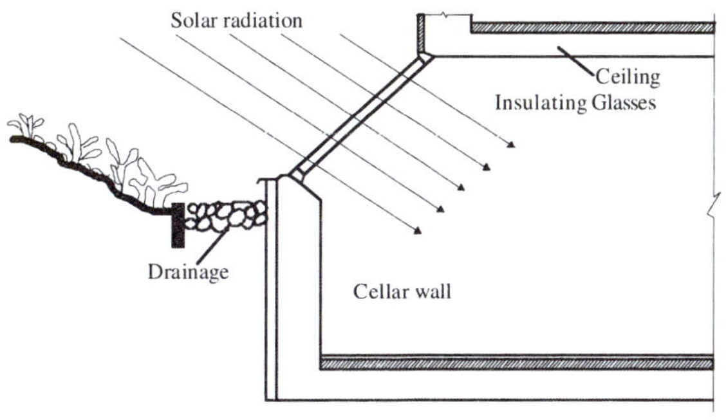

Figure 2.3(b) : Use of cellar windows for deep penetration of solar radiation

The admittance of direct sunlight through south facing windows is not feasible in many situations. In such cases, the clerestory and skylights help in admitting the desired amount of solar radiation as shown in Figure 2.4. The size of a solar window determines the average temperature in a space over the day. Hence it should be determined corresponding to the local parameters of each location such as heating degree days and availability of solar radiation.

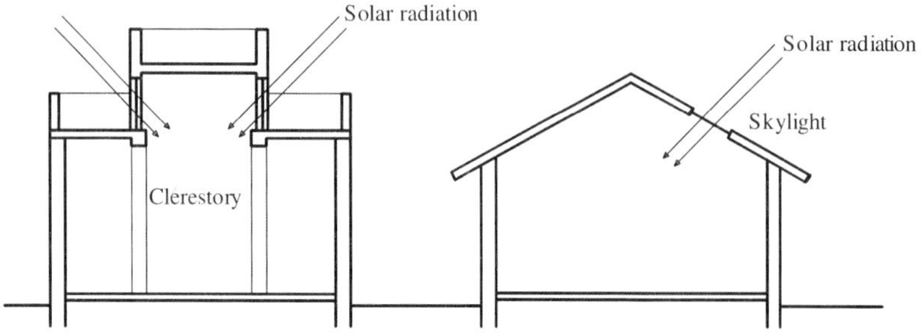

Figure 2.4: Clerestory and skylights for admitting solar radiation

(a) Using reflectors

The amount of solar radiation received at any window opening is fixed by the season and time. Although the intensity of directly incident solar radiation cannot be increased, irradiation received by the surrounding surfaces can be reflected into the opening, thereby increasing the effective collector area of the window.

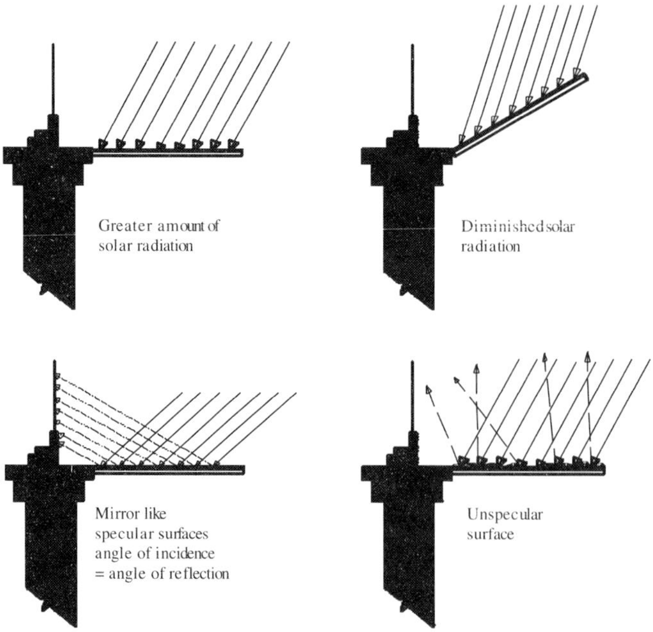

Figure 2.5: Methods for gaining more solar radiation through window by reflectors

Exterior insulating window shutters can also serve as sun reflectors during the day time and thereby increase the amount of heat gained through windows. For a reflector, three conditions must be met to maximize heat gain through a window:

(i) There must be a significant quantity of direct sunlight striking the reflecting surface of the shutter.

(ii) The reflecting surface must be as mirror-like as possible.

(iii) The radiation from the reflector must reach the window at a steep angle to ensure penetration through the glass.

These three conditions have been demonstrated in Figure 2.5.

Use of hinged shutters on top and bottom, for increasing the solar gain has also been demonstrated in Figure 2.6. Top hinged shutters can be employed on windows beneath a large overhang. An overhang above this type of shutters is essential for protection against snow and ice. Top hinged shutter reflector is very useful in the months of December and January, when the sun goes very low. With this arrangement, angle of shutter can be lowered to increase the heat gain without affecting the outside view.

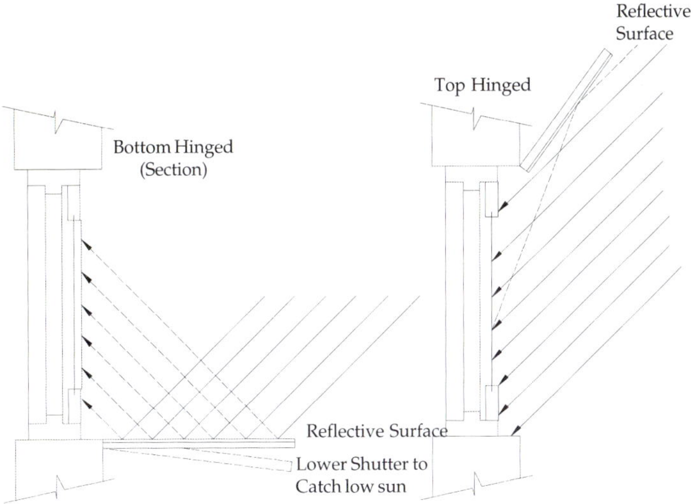

Figure 2.6: Two types of hinged shutter-reflectors for increasing solar heat gain

The length of reflector and its tilt has to be adjusted according to the window height and orientation. Figure 2.7(a) shows the horizontal reflector for a vertical glazing with a tilt of 95^0. Usually a tilt of more than 90^0 is recommended to overcome the water drainage problem. Use of reflectors with skylight is shown in Figure 2.7(b). At altitudes lower than 36^0N, normally skylights are not used due to abundance of sun.

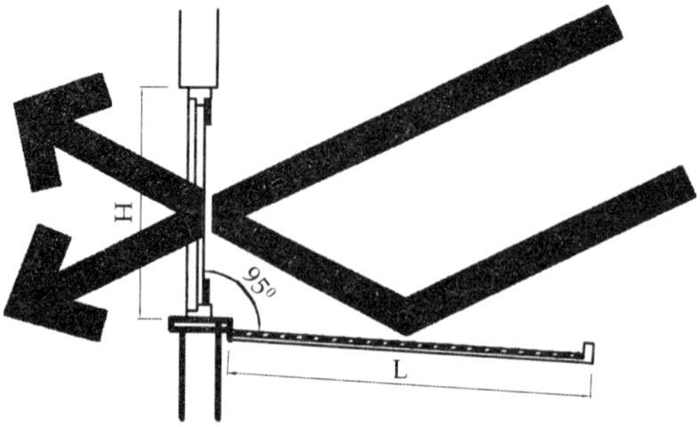

Figure 2.7(a): Vertical glazing with horizontal reflector

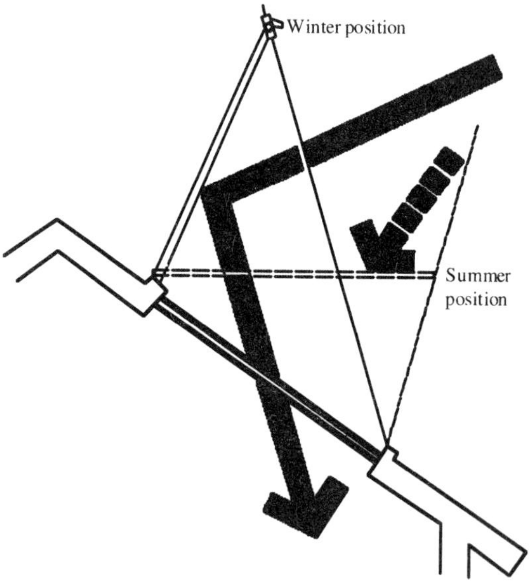

Figure 2.7(b): Skylight with hinged reflector

For composite climates, where heat gain is required in winters and protection from direct solar radiation is required in summer, staircase arrangement having horizontal reflectors and vertical glazing, as shown in Figure 2.8 can be adopted. In this technique of combining vertical glazing and horizontal reflector, solar radiation enters the living space when sun is at low altitude i.e. during winters. In summer months, when sun takes a higher altitude, solar radiation is reflected back by the reflectors to the sky as shown in the figure.

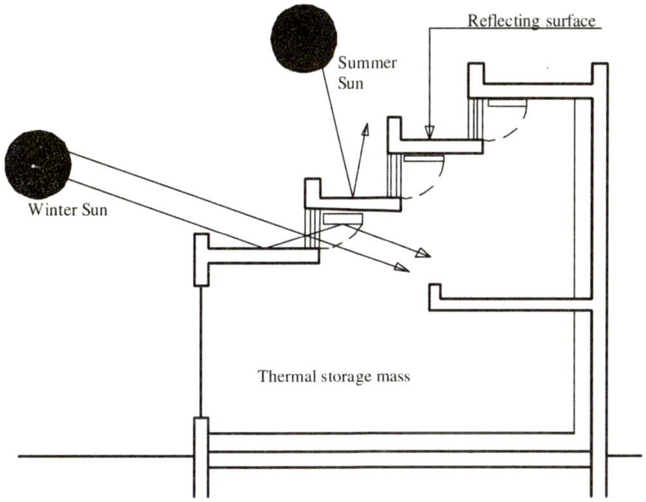

Figure 2.8: Staircase variation for heat gain in composite climate

(b) Increasing absorption of solar heat on exposed surfaces

Glazing on opaque exposed wall areas can be used to increase the solar gain factor g_w, defined by the equation:

$$g = q_g/I = U\alpha/h_o \qquad \text{(eq. 2.4)}$$

where

- g is solar gain factor
- q_g is net heat flux into the building space through the building component e.g. wall in W/m^2
- I is incident solar radiation on the corresponding building component in W/m^2
- U is overall heat transfer coefficient through the building component in W/m^2K
- h_o is total heat transfer coefficient from the external absorbing surface of the building component to the ambient in W/m^2K.
- α is the absorptivity of the wall surface

As evident from equation 2.4, increasing the absorptivity and decreasing 'h_o' can increase the solar gain factor through the opaque surfaces. Use of dark colors having high absorptivity is one widely known method to increase heat gain. Use of glazing over the wall reduces the outside heat transfer coefficient to about 25% of its value without glazing, thereby increasing the solar heat gain by five times.

2.1.1.2 Indirect Heat Gain

Unlike the direct heat gain, in the concept of indirect heat gain, solar energy is introduced into the room in an indirect fashion. Various options of indirect heat gain have been explained in this section.

(a) Normal glazed thermal storage wall

In this technique, heat from solar radiation is indirectly taken as a result of conduction through the wall and subsequent convection and long-wave radiation emitted by thermal wall. A thermal mass wall of concrete or masonry usually facing south, blackened and glazed is used for this purpose as shown in Figure 2.9. The advantage of this method is that it greatly reduces temperature fluctuations in the room air which is the disadvantage of direct solar heat gain methods. In addition, use of this method allows the heat to be delivered to the room at a later time (with time lag) from the availability of solar radiation.

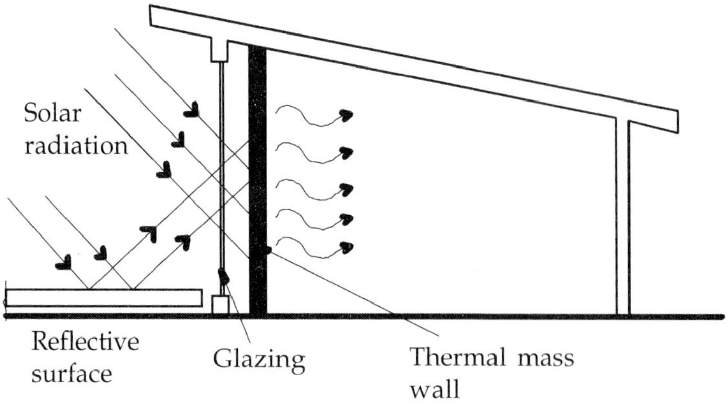

Figure 2.9: Use of normal glazed thermal storage wall for indirect heat gain

The arrangement shown in Figure 2.9 is also known as Trombe Wall without vents as there are no openings in the wall placed next to the glazing. For a simple glazed wall of thickness 'L' and thermal conductivity 'k', the average/instantaneous heat flux coming into the room to be maintained at temperature 'T_r' can be found by:

$$Q_t = U_L A\left[\frac{(\quad)I_t}{h_o} + (T_a - T_r)\right] \qquad \text{(eq. 2.5)}$$

where, Q_t, I_t are heat inflow and solar radiation intensity respectively. For finding out average heat flow into the living space behind Trombe Wall, value of average solar radiation throughout a day is to be kept in equation-2.5, for approximate calculations. The terms, $\alpha\tau$, are absorptivity of wall surface and transmissivity of glazing, h_0 is heat loss coefficient from the wall surface to the ambient through the glazing. U_L is total U-value from ambient to the room air, given by:

$$\frac{1}{U_L} = \frac{1}{h_o} + \frac{L}{k} + \frac{1}{h_{si}} \qquad \text{(eq. 2.6)}$$

The efficiency of a thermal storage wall system is largely determined by the wall's thickness, material and surface color. For each type of wall material there is an optimum thickness as indicated in Table 2.3. Different construction materials and thickness offer different amount of fluctuations in the indoor temperature.

Table 2.3: Effect of wall thickness on indoor air temperature fluctuations for 0.5 air changes per hour

Material	Thermal conductivity (W/mK)	Recommended thickness (cm)	Approx. indoor temp. fluctuations as a function of wall thickness
Adobe	0.53	20-30-40	10° 4° 4°
Brick	0.74	25-35	13° 6° 4°
Concrete	1.76	30-45	15° 8° 5°

It should be noted that if additional thermal mass is present in the building space such as heavy masonry walls and/or heavy flooring, temperature fluctuations will be less than those listed in Table 2.3.

The required elements of this technique of passive heating are a large south facing glazed collector area with thermal storage mass directly behind it. Such an arrangement is found to be effective upto a depth of 5-6 meters behind the thermal wall since this is considered to be maximum distance for an effective radiative heating. In buildings where the length of south wall is not much, staggered design as shown in Figure 2.10 can be used to increase the exposed wall area where indirect heat gain can be ensured. The predominant requirement for heat gain is a south facing glass, which functions as a heat trapping material.

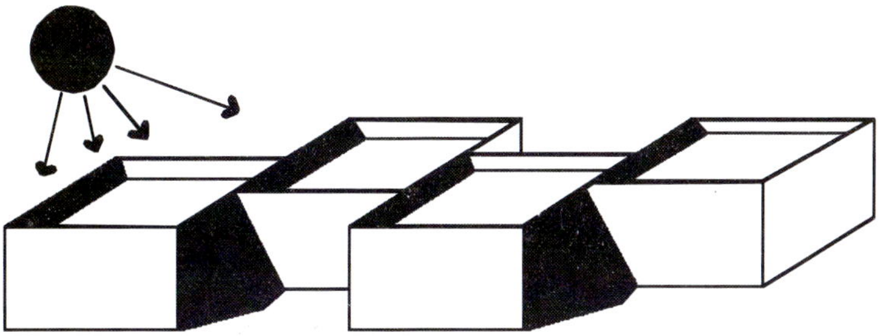

Figure 2.10: Staggered building design for increasing heat gain

(b) Trombe Wall

This concept can be considered as a modification of the thermal storage wall. It has openings in the thermal storage wall towards the top and the bottom to allow the self-sustaining distribution of heat in the building. On a clear winter day, it is possible to get temperature of air between the glazing and the absorber up to 70^{0}C. By properly sizing the thermal storage, it is possible to get a heat flow into the room even 2-3 hours after sunset till the wall surface gets cooled. The system is schematically shown in Figure 2.11.

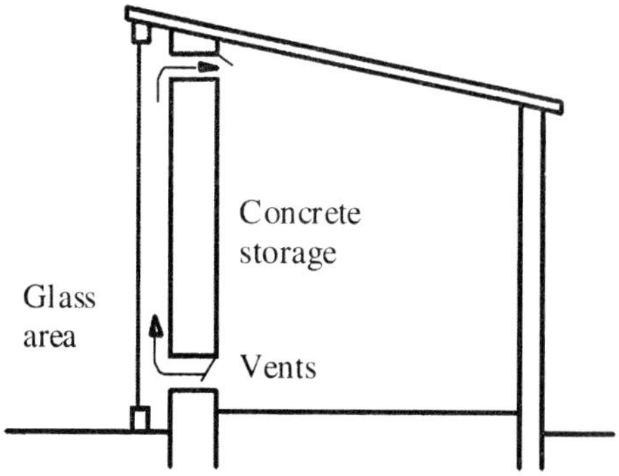

Figure 2.11: Use of Trombe Wall for Indirect Heat Gain in Building

In the system, the thermal storage lies just behind the glazed area. The openings of vents allow a convective heat transfer from the absorber surface to the room air. The openings of vents should follow the rule:

Total opening area = W*H/100 (eq. 2.7)

where,

W is the width of wall

H is the height between the openings

Normally the ratio of the opening area to the wall area should be between 1/100 to 3/100. The air space between the glazing and the absorbing surface should be 10-15cm. The constructional elements of a Trombe wall are shown in Figure 2.12. For reducing heat losses during the night, the glazing of the solar wall is usually covered with an insulation during night time.

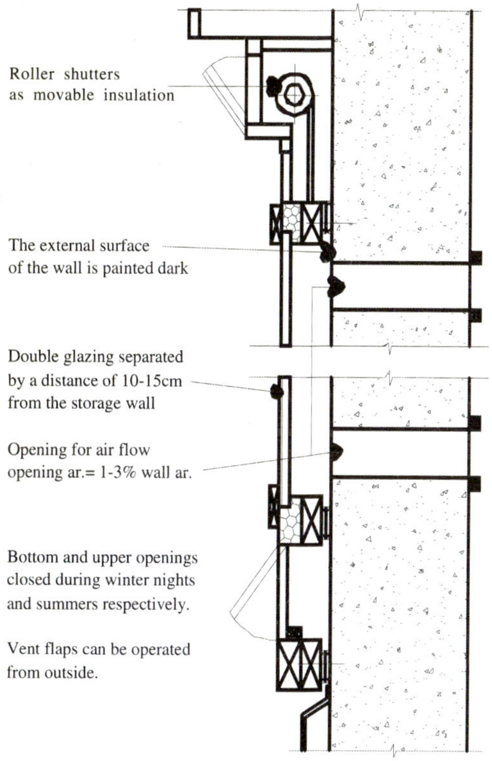

Figure 2.12: Constructional Elements of a Trombe Wall

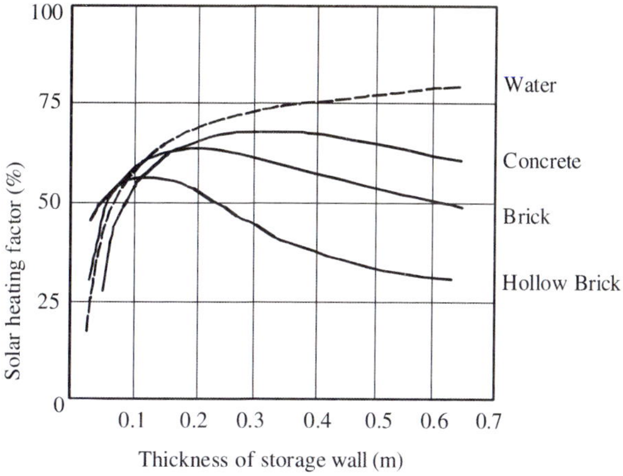

Figure 2.13: Dependence of solar heating fraction with wall thickness

Important parameters for determination of solar wall area are availability of radiation, average ambient temperature and depth of room. Thickness of the wall is another important design feature besides wall area. Figure 2.13 shows variation of solar heating fraction on the wall thickness using different construction materials. Comparing the four curves it can be seen that the efficiency of solar wall increases with an increase in the thermal conductivity of the material of the wall. Water as wall material offers highest efficiency due to its high thermal conductivity. For less conducting materials, increase in thickness though increases the thermal storage capacity, but at the same time it also increases the thermal resistance for heat flow from the backside of the wall. This combined effect results into net reduction in heat gain and therefore a dip in the curves for concrete, brick and hollow brick in Figure 2.13 is seen.

The heat collection capacity of thermal storage wall goes on decreasing after continuous heating due to increase of temperature of wall. This effect has been shown in Figure 2.14 and it can be seen that due to large thermal storage capacity efficiency of water wall gets least affected. The curves show that concrete is able to take only 50% of the heat after 3 hours and just 40% after 6 hours of exposure to radiation. Water containers are able to collect 70-80% of the incident heat even after 10 hours.

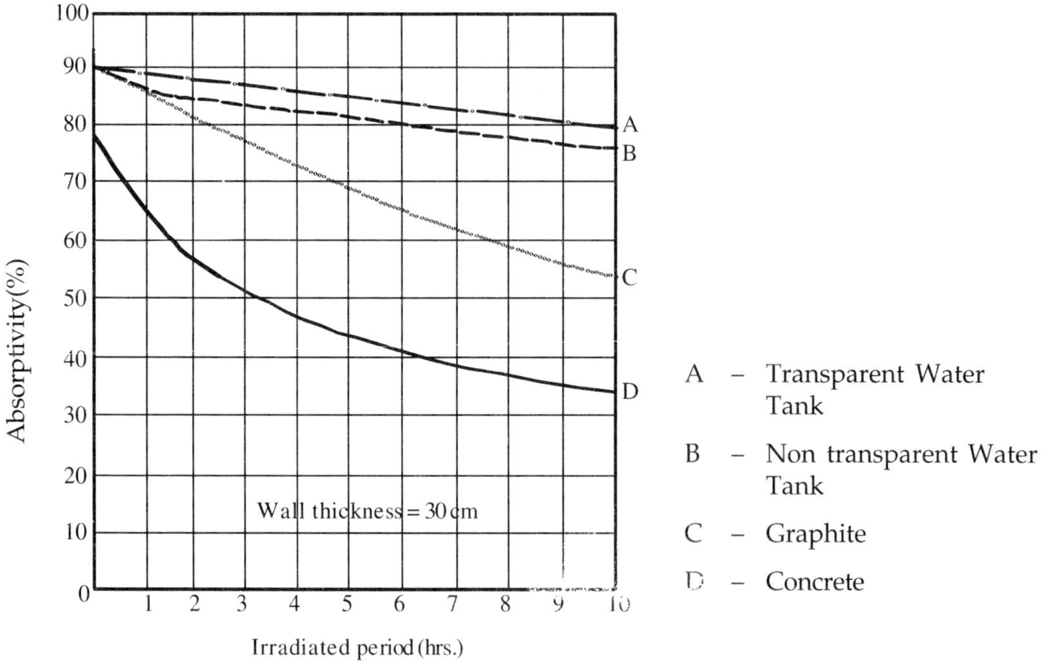

Figure 2.14: Effect of irradiated period on heat absorption in thermal storage wall (with average ambient temperature 12°C)

Simplified calculations of heat transfer through the water wall can be carried using the following equation:

$$Q = U_L A(T_{solair} - T_r) \qquad \text{(eq. 2.8)}$$

T_{solair} is the sol air temperature* for the water drum surface that receives radiation.

U_L for the above equation can be found through:

$$\frac{1}{U_L} = \frac{1}{h_o} + \frac{1}{h_1} + \frac{1}{h_2} + \frac{1}{h_{si}} \qquad \text{(eq. 2.9)}$$

where h_1 is convective heat transfer coefficient from metallic surface of water drum to water, h_2 is convective heat transfer coefficient from water inside drum to metallic surface of drum facing the inner side of room.

2.1.1.3 Combined Direct and Indirect Heat Gain

The disadvantage of direct heat gain for space heating, is that the space gets heated up rapidly. Similarly, after sunset, space gets cooled rapidly too. In contrast, a thermal storage wall for indirect heat gain absorbs solar radiation for several hours before it begins to heat-up the living space but it continues to provide heat even after the sunset. The most appropriate strategy for overcoming the disadvantages of individual direct and indirect heat gain methods would be through a combination of direct and indirect gain methods in a building. Major concepts of combined direct and indirect heating are explained below.

(a) Thermosiphon Air Panel (TAP)

A TAP is essentially a solar energy collector for air heating without a storage medium that is usually fitted in the south wall of a building for supplying warm air to the building space. It is typically suitable to the cold desert climatic conditions. Movement of air in TAP takes place due to density gradient that gets generated due to localized heating of air beneath/inside the panel. The schematic of TAP is shown in Figure 2.15. The absorber plate can have several design variations for increasing the collection and transfer of heat. Few such versions have been shown in Figure 2.16.

---

* For definition of solair temperature, see section 4.2.4.

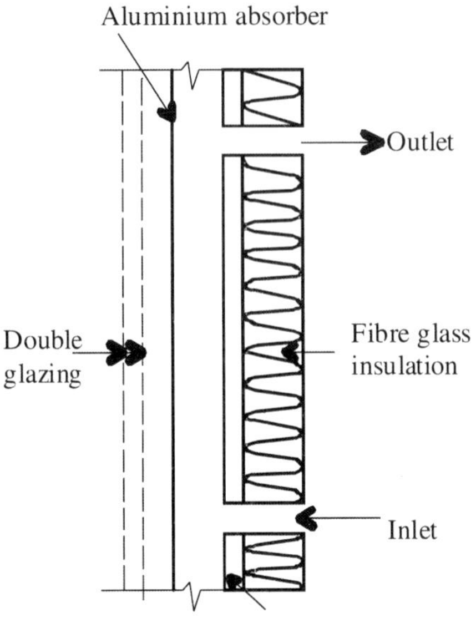

Figure 2.15: Schematic of a Thermosiphon Air Panel (TAP)

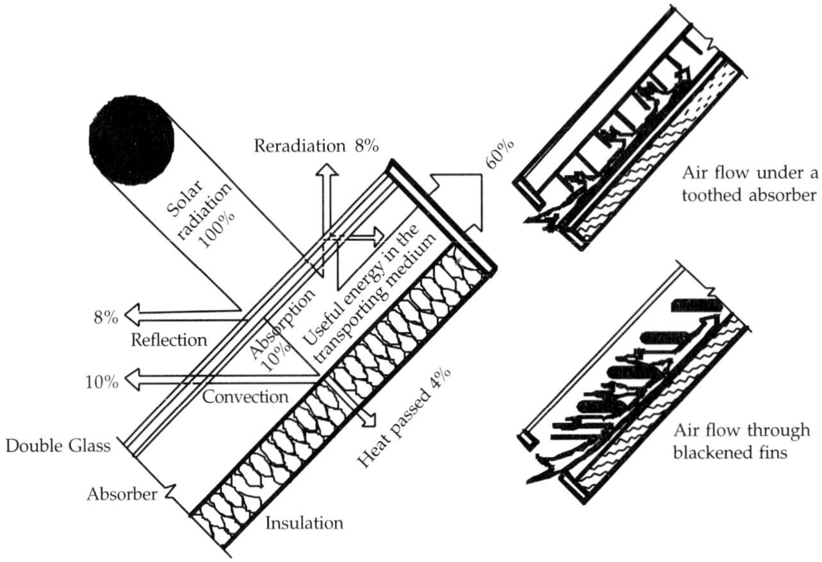

Figure 2.16: Energy balance of a TAP with variations in absorber plate design

A thermosiphon air panel is normally installed at a level below the space/storage that is to be heated, as shown in Figure 2.17. With such an arrangement, air after becoming warm, directly flows into the building space and replaces colder air. When solar radiation is not available, the collector is disconnected using a three way valve as shown in Figure 2.17(a), and the living space collects heat from the heat storage device. In summer, the collector is also disconnected to avoid overheating of room air.

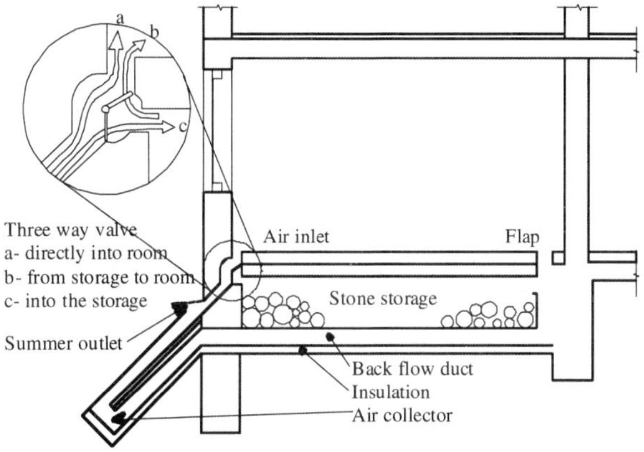

Figure 2.17(a): An air heating TAP with operating conditions

The TAP can also be installed on sloping roofs or on south facing façade walls. The warm air collected in attic space can be channeled into the desired rooms as shown in Figure 2.17(b). The inclined collector is about 20% more effective as compared to a vertical collector due to the fact that on vertical south facing wall, the amount of incident solar radiation is less than a corresponding southwards inclined surface. However, installation of vertical collector is much easier. The overall solar heat gain efficiency of a TAP is found to be of the order of 25-30%.

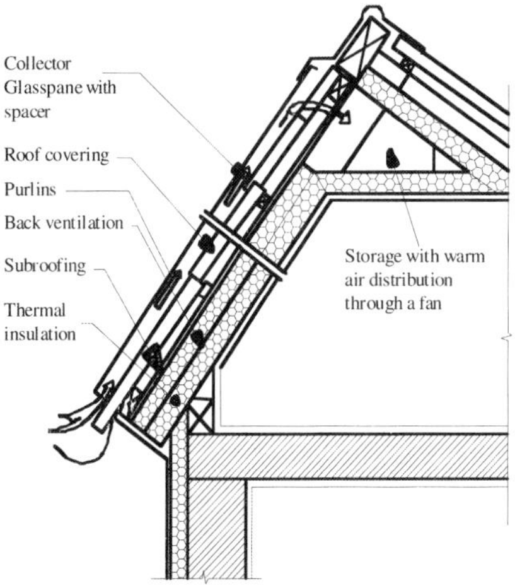

Figure 2.17(b): Use of TAP on inclined roof

The TAP can additionally be useful for summer ventilation by using a valve that vents out hot air from the top as shown in Figure 2.18. With such an arrangement, the TAP acts as a barrier for direct heat gain in summer. The movement of air removes the heat collected by collector continuously away. This concept has been explained properly in the section of passive cooling and ventilation.

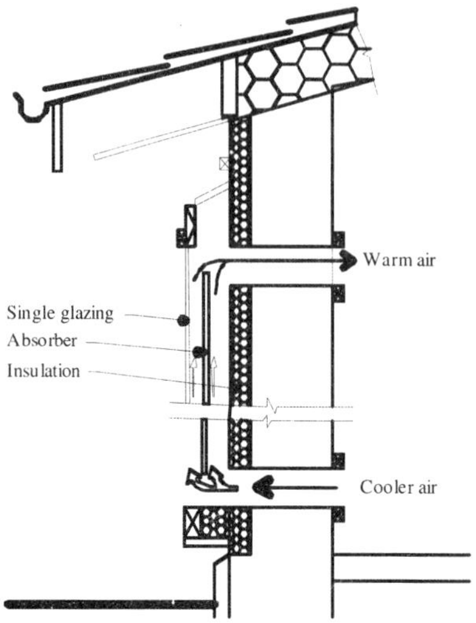

Figure 2.18: TAP installed on vertical wall

(b) Glass House

As the name suggests, glass houses are closed envelopes made of glass. These are also one form of combination of direct and indirect heat gain that offer scope of integrating appealing architectural elements in a building with passive heating opportunity.

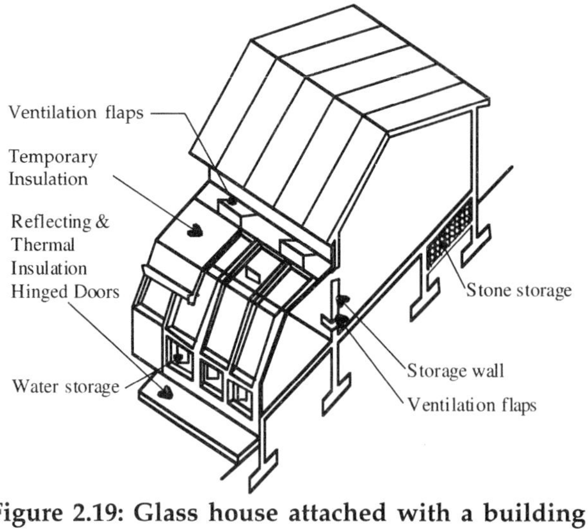

Figure 2.19: Glass house attached with a building

By constructing a glass house, a buffer zone is created between the living space and the outdoor conditions. During the sunny hours, the glass house, which can alternatively be called as greenhouse, accumulates heat that can be used to heat other parts of the building. Glasshouses quickly get heated due to the greenhouse effect, even with diffused incident radiation. In the absence of solar radiation, however, thermal losses from the greenhouse are large; therefore, it is necessary to install heat storage components or movable insulation with the glass houses. A typical glass house attached with a building has been shown in Figure 2.19. A glass house can be integrated to a building in different ways:

- As an attached greenhouse
- As a single, double or three sided integrated lobby
- As a double layered solarium or a climatic buffer zone
- As a climatic envelope, even in the external regions, such as a stair case or a glass covered courtyard.

The geometry of the glass house, its integration with the building, details of the thermal storage used govern the performance of the amount of heat gain through the glass house. Few versions of the concept have been shown in Figure 2.20.

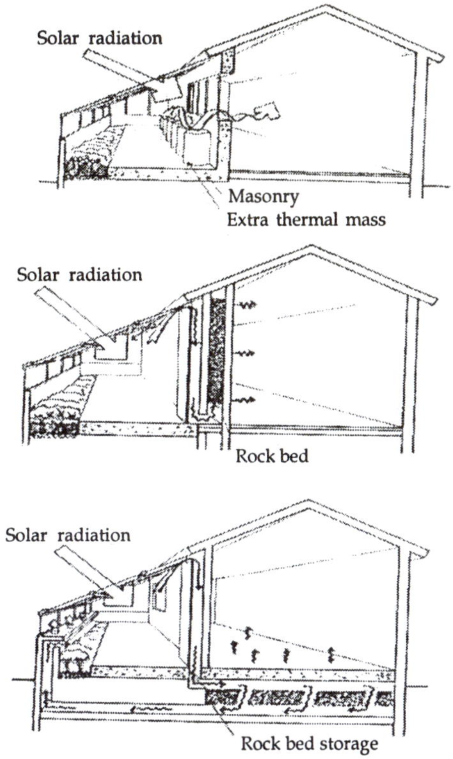

Figure 2.20: Different variations in the use of glass house for space heating

Simple version of the solar glass house attached with living space is called 'Solarium'. The system looks quite similar to the Trombe Wall concept but the difference between this type of system and Trombe wall without vents is that in case of solarium, there is a large distance between the absorbing surface and glazing. Due to this reason, there is almost no direct link between absorber and ambient in solarium. This space acts as a separate zone in itself. Simplified mathematical treatment of glass house using sun-space or solarium can be done through the similar approach used for Water wall, Transwall, except for the heat loss coefficient 'U_L' given by the following equation:

$$\frac{1}{U_L} = \frac{1}{h_o} + \frac{L}{k} + \frac{1}{h_{si}} + \frac{1}{h_{TS}} \qquad \text{(eq. 2.10)}$$

where, all other symbols carry the same meaning as before, additional term 'h_{TS}' is for the heat transfer coefficient between the absorbing wall and the sun-space.

2.1.2 Use of Ambient Heat for Space Heating

The ambient heat available around the buildings (in ground and water) can either be used for reducing transmission losses or it can be used to preheat the ambient air before it enters into the building thereby reducing the heat losses due to ventilation. Basics about these concepts have been explained in the following sub-sections.

2.1.2.1 Energy From Ground

Hourly, daily and seasonal fluctuations in the ambient temperature are found only in the atmosphere and upper layers of the ground. With increasing depth below the ground level, the temperature fluctuations decrease and remain close to the annual mean ambient temperature only. Figure 2.21 shows the annual variations in ground temperature at different depths and corresponding attenuation of fluctuations in temperature.

Due to this stability of temperature, if the external surface of any building remains in contact with ground instead of being exposed to ambient air, it would attract heat exchange with the ground itself. During winters, since the temperature below the ground would be higher than ambient, there would be less heat loss in underground spaces. As a result, underground spaces remain warmer during winters as compared to spaces above ground level.

Another possibility of utilizing the ground heat is the earth air tunnel system. In such system, air is passed through a tunnel before its entry to building. In the tunnel, due to temperature difference between cooler air and warmer tunnel surface, heating of air takes place. The performance of such a system depends upon the meteorological parameters such as solar radiation, air temperature, humidity, wind velocity etc, besides the ground characteristics such as thermal conductivity, heat storage capacity, depth of water table. Geometric parameters of the tunnel are also quite important such as depth below ground level, length and diameter of tunnel. Same arrangement can also be utilized for passive cooling during summer. More details about this concept have been given in the section of passive cooling.

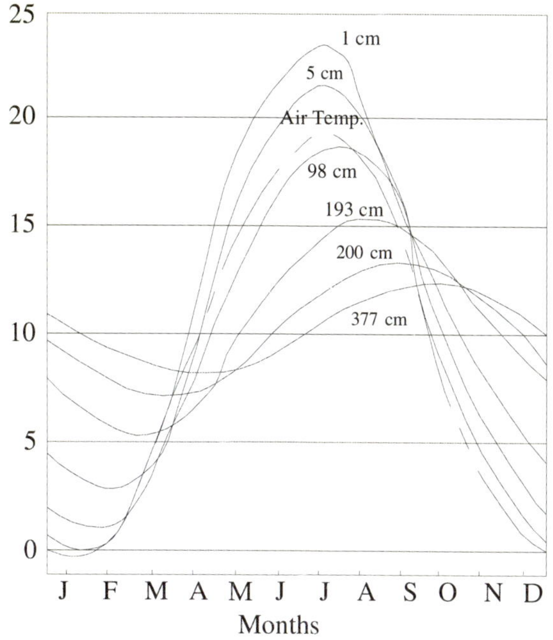

Figure 2.21: Annual variation in ground temperature at different depths

2.1.2.2 Energy From Water

Due to large heat capacity of water, there is relatively less fluctuation in its temperature as compared to the fluctuations in ambient air temperature. Similar to the concept of earth air tunnel, under water tubes can be laid to exchange heat from warmer water to heat ambient air. On passing through such tubes, ambient air becomes warmer before entering the building, thereby requiring less heating for reaching comfort temperature. The temperature of water and thus the amount of pre-heating of air depends upon the depth of the water body. With small size water bodies and shallow depths, such systems are not very effective. Practical problem with such systems is that buildings are to be located close to the water bodies. With such locations, other problems such as attack of excess moisture on building material etc. arise; hence, the concept has found very little application in practice.

2.1.3 Use of Internal Sources of Heat

There are several living as well as non-living sources of heat in a building that can be utilized for keeping the building warm. Living sources of heat are human beings or occupants, animals, micro-organisms; whereas non-living sources of heat are various equipments such as lighting, cooking appliances, washing machine etc. Methods for utilizing heat available from internal sources have been described in this section.

2.1.3.1 Heat Production by Human Beings

Due to metabolic reactions taking place continuously in human body, there is release of heat from human body that varies considerably according to the activity level. Dissipation of this heat to surroundings depends upon the clothing, ambient temperature, movement of air, surface temperature of surrounding building elements etc. A human being weighing 60-70 kg has a skin surface area of 1.7-1.9 m^2 and a mean skin temperature of about 33^0C, the heat production in relation to various activities is shown in Table 2.4.

Table 2.4: Total heat dissipation from human body during different activities

Activity	Heat dissipation	
	W	W/m^2
Sleeping	60	35
Lying	80	45
Sitting, normal office work	100	55
Type writing	150	85
Walking slowly (3 km/hr)	200	110
Walking quickly (6 km/hr)	250	140
Hard work (sawing, digging)	Over 300	Over 170

2.1.3.2 Heat Production by Animals

Similar to the heat released by human beings, animals also release heat that is much more in amount as compared to heat released from human beings. The heat produced by animals can be used to heat up living room for ensuring heat gain from the room floor. Care is to be taken for avoiding direct entry of warm air in the living space and to use indirect heating method. This would ensure no adverse affect on the quality of air due to impurities and ingredients exhaled by animals. Such examples can be seen in Kullu Valley, Himachal Pradesh (India). Several houses of this region utilize the heat production of cattle accommodated on the ground floor. Living rooms on the first floor are heated-up indirectly as shown in Figure 2.22.

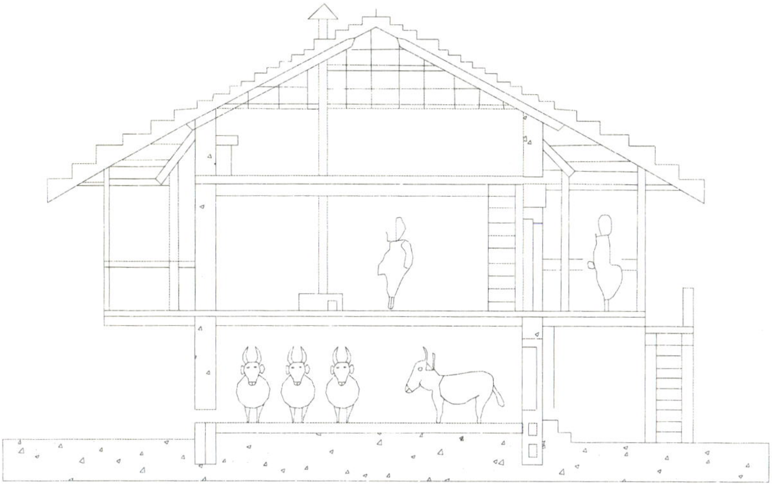

Figure 2.22: Utilisation of animal heat for space heating

Disadvantage of this option is that due to close vicinity of animal dwelling, there may be unpleasant smell in the living area due to animal excreta for which necessary arrangements such as proper orientation of openings for ventilation of air are necessary.

The heat produced by animals depends upon their weight and activity. It can be calculated by the following formulae:

For animals at rest (sitting/sleeping): $Q_o = 3.6\ M^{0.75}$ W/animal

For animals with normal activity: $Q = 7.2\ M^{0.75}$ W/animal

where 'M' is the mass of animal in kg.

2.1.3.3 Heat Production by Micro-Organisms

Garden debris, including pruning waste from trees and hedges, brushwood from forests and other timber waste, which is piled up to make a compost heap, gets decayed in due course of time (in 6-12 months). During the process of decay, energy is released in the form of low-temperature heat in the range of 50-70^{0}C. By putting a heat exchanger within the decaying compost-heap, it is possible to utilize this energy for indoor space heating. Figure 2.23(a) shows the working principle of a compost container of 30 m^3 capacity, corresponding to about 12 ton brushwood, with a heat exchanger. With this system, water can be heated from 40^{0}C to 60^{0}C with a flow rate of 50 liter per hour. The 12 ton of brushwood, once filled in the container, thus can substitute about 1000 liter of fuel oil as one ton of brushwood produces approximately 230 watts over a period of about 6 months.

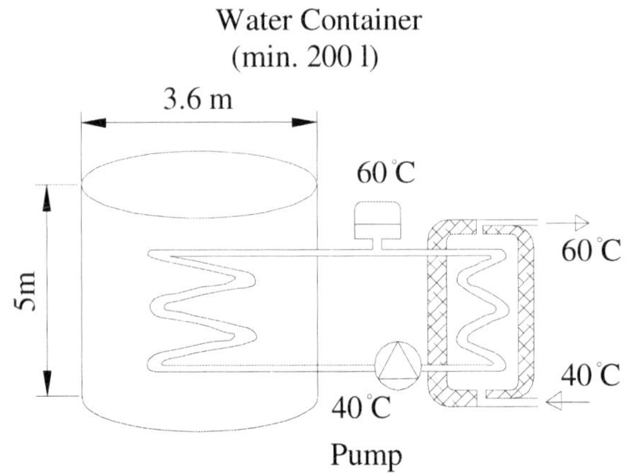

Figure 2.23(a) : Batch type compost container for water heating

Operation of the above system is like a batch reactor that would need emptying and refilling after the entire energy of wood is released. To overcome this difficulty, continuous operation type composters can be used as shown in Figure 2.23(b).

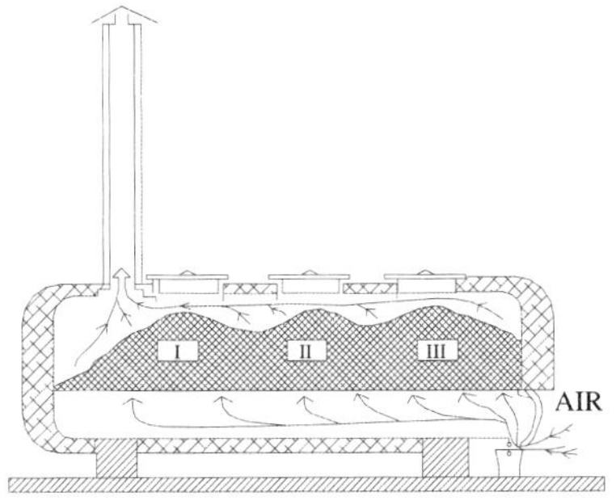

Figure 2.23(b) : Continuous operation composter

Continuous operation is achieved by dividing the tank into three sections such that the decomposed material from one section is removed after 3-4 weeks and refilled with fresh organic decomposable material. Care is to be taken while keeping the decomposed material in a well-ventilated space to render the micro-organisms inactive. Due to relatively high temperature in the container, almost all the disease-causing organisms get destroyed and any seeds if present are rendered incapable of germination, therefore, the compost produced is directly suitable for cultivation of plants.

Composters can also be integrated with lower parts of buildings for utilizing the released heat for keeping the living space warm. Location of the container for composting should be below the living space with proper insulation of outer walls so as to facilitate better utilisation of heat produced as shown in Figure 2.24.

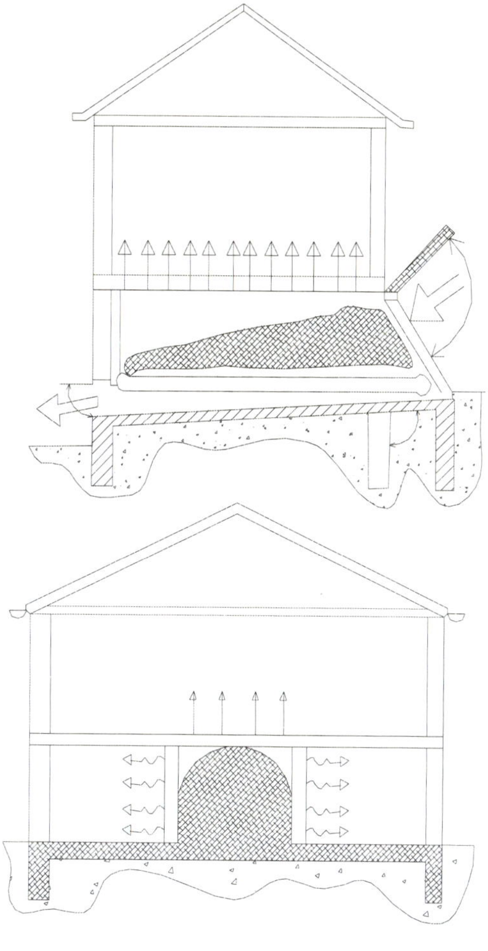

Figure 2.24: Compost container located beneath and within building

2.1.4 Waste Energy of Domestic Equipment

Domestic appliances such as refrigerators, release waste heat in the building, which can be used for heating the rooms. The amount of energy or heat released varies with the equipment rating and duration of its use. Refrigerator offers the most attractive scope of waste heat utilization among all domestic equipment, as it works almost continuously during the entire day. Additionally, due to its fixed location, it is easier to capture the waste heat as compared to the heat of vacuum cleaner rating of which is much higher than that of refrigerator but is not used in a fixed place. Table 2.5 gives power consumption of common domestic appliances.

Table 2.5: Power consumption of common domestic appliances

Equipment	*Watt (W)*
Radio	15
Television (B&W)	110
Refrigerator	120
Television (colour)	250
Coffee machine	400
Vacuum cleaner	800
Washing machine	2500
Dish washer	3000
Water heater	3500

2.1.5 Heat Storage

The need of energy or heat storage in a building arises due to mismatch between the availability and requirement of naturally available heat. Usually, when the heat is available i.e. in the noon, the ambient temperature is also higher and when this heat is required most i.e. during night, it is not available. Heat storage in a building, balances out this mismatch and thus reduces fluctuations in the room air temperature. Usually heat is contained in building elements like wall, roof having heavy mass and hence large heat capacity. Few concepts are quite similar to the idea used in Trombe wall, Transwall as explained earlier. Depending upon the art of collecting heat, heat storage systems can be classified into two categories namely:

- sensible heat storage systems
- latent heat storage systems

Sensible heat storage systems use the specific heat of the material, whereas latent heat storage use the heat of phase change of materials. As an example, Glauber Salt requires nearly eight times more energy to change its state from solid to liquid than that required by water at the same temperature. In the reverse process, i.e. change of state from liquid to solid, the same amount of heat energy will be released. Though the potential for heat storage in latent heat based systems is more, but the former only is used in buildings due to ease in application. Further, depending upon whether the heat storage mass is directly irradiated by the sun or not, classification of heat storage systems in three categories namely, primary, secondary and tertiary can be done.

(a) Primary Heat Storage Systems

Storage systems like glazed wall, Trombe wall, water wall as explained in indirect heat gain, fall in this category of primary storage systems as solar radiation directly falls on their surface. The efficiency of primary storage system depends upon their capability of absorbing the solar radiation and its reflected components besides the amount of re-radiated heat energy to the living space as already explained. For effective heating of space, in primary storage systems, solar radiation should fall within the room over a larger area of the storage medium. This amount of heating varies with variation in the proportion of the ratio between glazing area to storage area. Figure 2.25 shows, three different cases of glazing to surface area ratio 1:1.5, 1:3, 1:9.

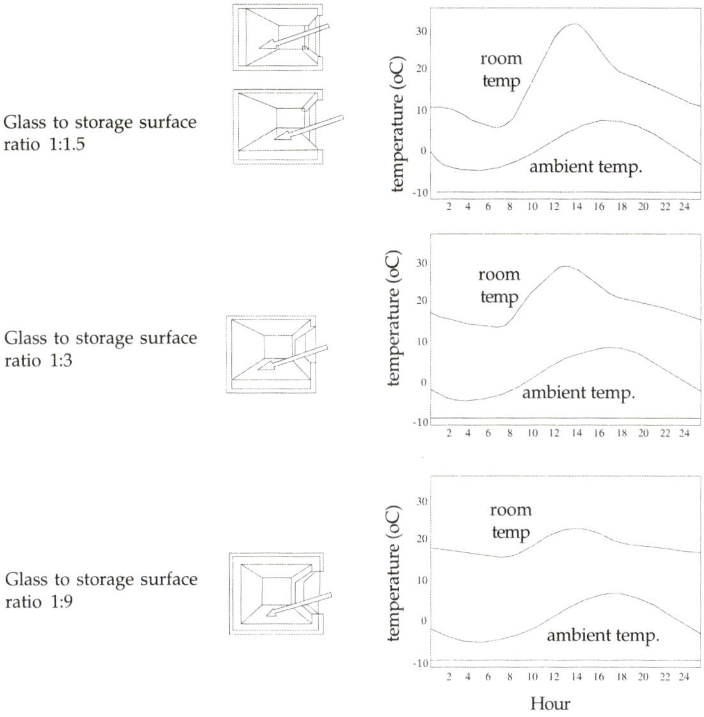

Fig. 2.25: Room temperature variation for different heat storage area

It can be seen that with more surface area per unit glazed area from where radiation enters, fluctuations in room temperature are much less as compared to the other two cases having less area available for heat storage. The room air fluctuations are 22°C, 14°C and 7°C respectively in the three cases. These results are for buildings having exposed to about 4 kWh/m^2 solar radiation per day. Further, in such an arrangement, it has been found that with increase in thickness of concrete wall beyond (10 cm thickness), not much change in room air profile takes place. This is due to the combined effect of increase in heat storage capacity and decrease in absorption of solar radiation.

(b) Secondary Heat storage systems

Similar to the concepts of indirect solar heat gain, in secondary heat storage systems, the space is not directly irradiated by the sun, but receives reflected, convected or re-radiated solar/heat energy. Usually convection is the dominant mode of heat transfer in such storage systems. The amount of heat stored and their performance depends upon air velocity, temperature difference between air and heat storing mass and surface area. Such storage systems are suitable for cold and sunny regions. Example of one such system is shown in Figure 2.26, where very less solar radiation is directly falling on the wall located on the right hand side. A major part of total radiation received by it is coming through reflections taking place on the horizontal surface which also acts as primary heat storage wall. Secondary storage systems are often used to improve the performance of primary systems that are not able to collect sufficient amount of heat. This requirement typically comes at places where surface area for direct exposure cannot be increased due to space limitation.

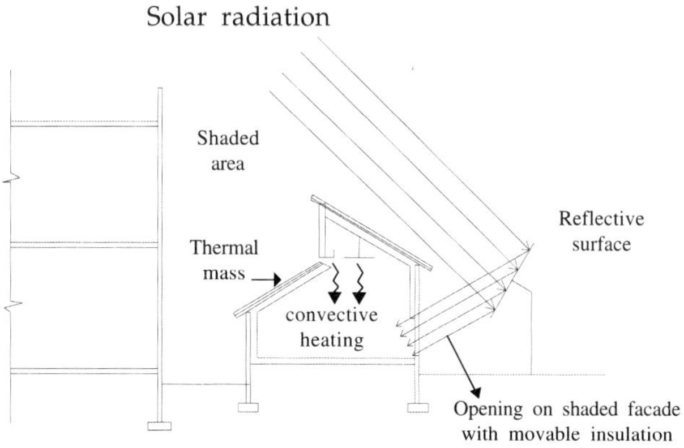

Figure 2.26: Use of Combined Primary and Secondary Heat Storage System

The surface area available for heat storage can further be increased by using translucent glass or plastic to achieve scattering or diffusion of radiation over a wide interior surface area. If water is used as storage media, then attempts should be made to get as much direct radiation on the surface of water as possible. Though water walls are used as primary heat storage devices, their performance can be improved by using it as secondary storage system as shown in Figure 2.27.

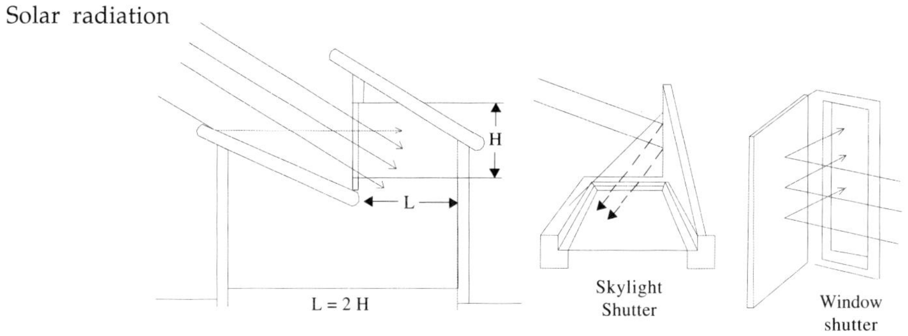

Figure 2.27: Use of reflective and convective methods for heat storage in water

(c) Tertiary Heat Storage Systems

These are isolated heat storage systems located outside the living space. They are usually coupled with thermal collector systems and heat transfer in such cases takes place through air movement. Such isolated storage systems are useful for storing high amount of heat and holding it for a larger period of the order of few days unlike few hours in primary and secondary storage systems. Use of such systems is typical case of large changing weather conditions.

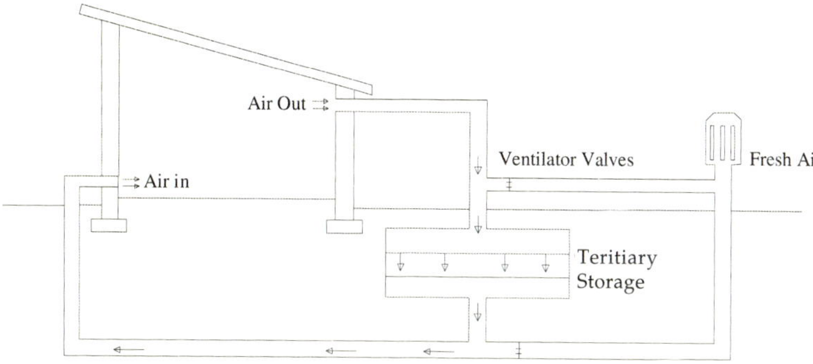

Figure 2.28: Tertiary Heat Storage System

Tertiary systems are usually made of stones, pebble beds of small stones with average diameter greater than 10 cm are used to make such systems. Figure 2.28 shows schematic and Figure 2.29 shows details of one example of such system commonly known as rock bed storage system. Use of stones, due to their large weight, enables the system to store large amount of heat. It is important to have a pebble bed and not to use less number of stone pieces of larger mass, to ensure presence of sufficient air pockets. These pockets become useful for utilization of stored heat, air can be blown through the bed to increase the heat recovery if found necessary.

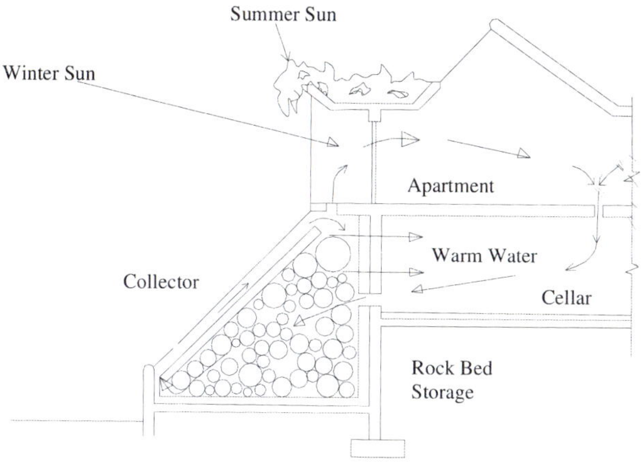

Figure 2.29: Underground Rock bed Storage System

Rock bed storage systems are usually located in cellars due to two reasons. Weight of stones does not cause any problem to structural requirements of building and additionally, this location also offers possibility of utilization of earth's heat. In humid climates, use of such systems may cause problems such as generation of algae and bacteria that are to be kept in mind before designing a system.

2.2 PASSIVE COOLING CONCEPTS

The first step to achieve natural cooling in a building is to reduce unnecessary thermal loads that might enter it. Usually, there are two types of thermal loads i.e.

(1) exterior loads due to the climate and

(2) internal loads due to people, appliances, cooking, bathing, lights etc.

Proper zoning of different components and local ventilation of the major heat sources can reduce the overall impact of internally generated heat loads. Depending on the weather, the heat gain in a building can occur in three major ways:

- Penetration of direct beam of sunlight.
- Conduction of heat through walls, roofs
- Infiltration of outside air.

An exercise of building design for warm climatic conditions would attempt to exclude any of the above major heat gains arising due to the prevailing ambient temperature and intensity of solar radiation. Following sections present coverage on the principles and practices for reducing thermal load.

2.2.1 Reduction of solar and convective heat import

In tropical regions like most places in India, interaction of solar radiation with the building envelope is the largest source of heat gain into the building space. The natural way for keeping a building cool is, therefore, through minimizing the incidence of solar radiation by choosing proper orientation of the building, selecting adequate layout with respect to neighbouring buildings and by using proper shading devices to help control the incident solar radiation. Good combination of shading strategies can save upto 20% of the energy required for cooling. Properly designed roof overhangs can provide adequate sun protection, especially for sun facing surfaces. Vertical shading surfaces such as trees, trellises, trellised vines, shutters, shading screens, awnings and exterior roll blinds are also effective. These options are recommended for east-facing and west-facing windows and walls.

If, ambient temperatures are higher than the room temperature, heat enters into the building by convection due to undesirable ventilation termed as infiltration. Best strategy therefore is to control infiltration of hot air from outside, that comes from frequently/partly opening doors and windows and also through cracks and joints in construction. Adequate wind shelter and sealing of windows reduces the air infiltration and this requires proper planning and landscaping.

2.2.1.1 Orientation of building

In countries like India, during the summers, maximum solar radiation is interrupted by the roof (horizontal surface) followed by the east and west walls and then the south and north walls. It is therefore desirable that the building is oriented with the longest walls facing north and south, so that only short face receives radiation from the east and west directions. Thus only the smallest walls are exposed to intense morning and evening sun. The east and west windows are the sources of most solar gain and should therefore, be eliminated or reduced in size. It is also advisable to place unconditioned space (garages, closets and other buffer spaces) on east and west sides. These spaces act as thermal barrier to inflow of heat.

Selection of proper orientation is also important to take advantage of prevailing breezes in warm and humid climate and for prevention of hot winds in hot and dry climate. It is, however, not as critical as an east-west orientation for sun control.

Table 2.6 gives the amount of incident solar radiation per sq. m. of floor space at 30^{0}N latitude for cubic, rectangular and square form buildings with one, two and four floors. It is seen that as far as the reduction of solar heat gain is concerned, the multi-floor structure has an advantage over a single floor building.

Table 2.6: Variation in incidence of solar radiation (MJ/h) with shape and orientation on buildings per sqm. of floor area at 28N

Type	Orientation[1]	Summer			Winter		
		12.00 Hours	15.00 Hours	Average	12.00 Hours	15.00 Hours	Average
Square 2 Storey	N	0.204	0.287	0.246	0.216	0.181	0.199
	NW	0.210	0.322	0.266	0.273	0.147	0.210
	W	0.204	0.276	0.240	0.233	0.184	0.209
Square 1 Storey	N	0.385	0.409	0.398	0.268	0.189	0.229
	NW	0.385	0.427	0.406	0.328	0.168	0.248
	W	0.385	0.379	0.382	0.296	0.189	0.243
Rectangular 1 Storey	N	0.358	0.358	0.358	0.308	0.176	0.243
	NW	0.358	0.420	0.389	0.319	0.139	0.279 [2]
	W	0.358	0.403	0.381	0.253	0.181	0.217
Square 4 Storey	N	0.119	0.266	0.193	0.223	0.212	0.217
	NW	0.119	0.322	0.220	0.293	0.160	0.227
	W	0.119	0.252	0.186	0.228	0.214	0.221

1. Building have simple gable roofs with ridge at right angles to orientation.
2. Average for types with rectangular base at intermediate oritentation include projections for 9.00 hours. (although not given in table)

2.2.1.2 Shading by neighboring buildings

The buildings in a cluster can be spaced such that they shade each other mutually as shown in Fig. 2.30. The amount and effectiveness of the shading, however, depends on the type of building clusters. Building clusters can be classified into three basic types, i.e. Pavilions, Streets and Courts as shown in Figure 2.32. "Pavilions" are isolated buildings, single or in clusters, surrounded by large open spaces. The "Streets" are long building blocks arranged in parallel rows, separated by actual streets in open spaces. "Courts" are defined as open spaces surrounded by buildings on all sides. Rather than defining the street by its width, it is possible to express it as a fraction H_w equal to the ratio of the building height to the street width (Fig. 2.30). This has the advantage that the percentage of overshadowing of one building by another, which is a function of the obstruction angle, remains constant for different building heights with the same H_w. Effective parameters determining the thermal performance of various building clusters are given in Table 2.7.

To compare the performance of these types of building clusters, it is necessary to assume a reference building volume and floor area. As a base case, we take a reference volume of 800,000 m^3. For different number of blocks in a building cluster (N) and heights of blocks (H), the variation of surface area for the building cluster is shown in Figure 2.30:

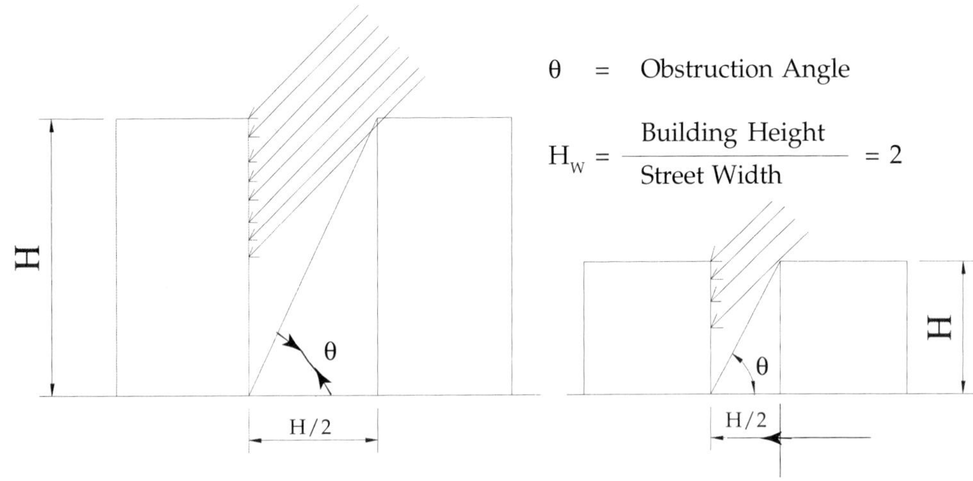

Figure 2.30: Shading effect due to adjacent buildings

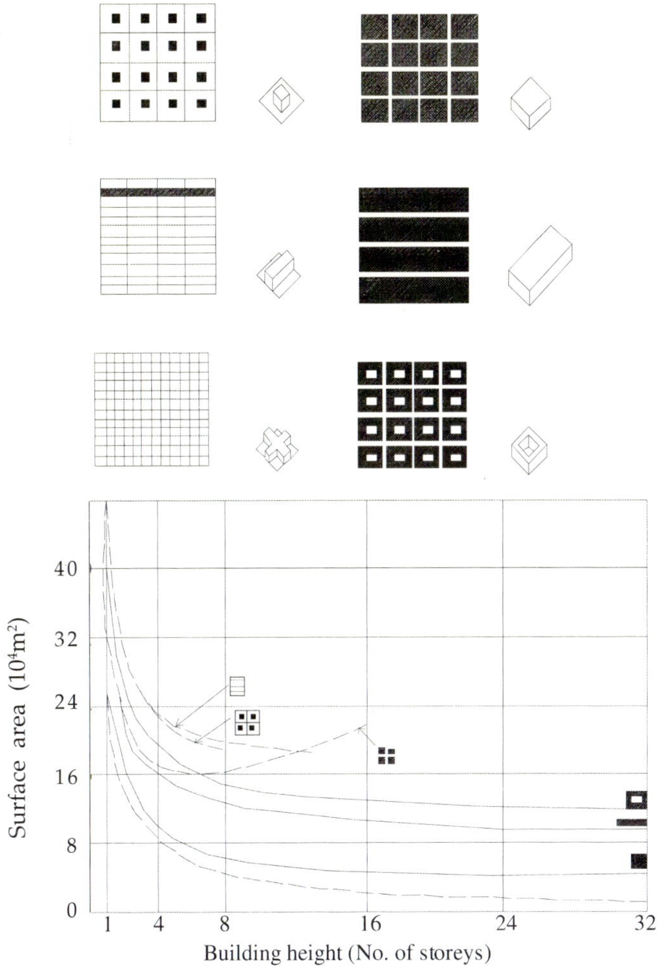

Figure 2.31: Different types of building clusters and their mutual shading effect

The roof area of a building cluster, which is independent of the plan form and depends on the building height only, is shown by the dotted line. The solid lines show the surface area of a single block only, while the broken lines show the areas for building clusters. It is seen that the least area is obtained for Pavilion and it is not much larger than the roof area. For all cluster forms, the surface area decreases sharply as the height of the building is increased from one to four floors, after which the increase in height does not change the area very much. Table 2.7 presents calculation of volume, exposed surface area and roof area for different types of building clusters.

Table 2.7:Different parameters for three types of building clusters

Type	*Variables*	*Volume*	*Surface area*	*Roof area*
Pavilion	L,H,N,W	L^2. H. N	NL (L+4H)	L^2.N
Street	L,W,H,N	L.W.H.N	N.W.L+2H(L+W)	N.LW
Court	L,W,H,N	4HN (L^2–W^2)	4HN(L+W)	(L^2 –W^2).N

N = Number of blocks in a building cluster

L = Length of a block

H = Height of a block

W = Width of a block

In case of courtyard, W has been considered width of courtyard and L as overall length of building with square shape.

2.2.1.3 *Shading by Vegetation*

Shading by trees and vegetation is a very effective method of cooling the ambient hot air and for protecting the building from solar radiation. The solar radiation absorbed by the leaves is mainly utilized for photosynthesis and evaporative heat losses. A part of the solar radiation is stored as heat by the fluids in the plants or trees as shown in figure Fig. 2.32.

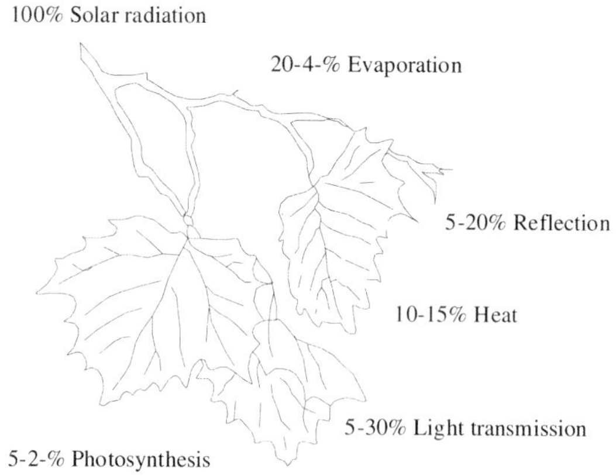

Figure 2.32: Energy balance on a leaf

The best place to plant shady trees is to be decided by observing, which windows admit the most sunshine during peak hours in the hottest months. Usually east and west oriented windows and walls receive about 50% more sunshine than the north and south oriented windows/walls during summer months. Trees should be planted at positions determined by lines from the center of the windows on the west or east walls toward the position of the sun at the designated hour and date. On the south side, only deciduous trees should be planted.

The precise distance for planting trees will depend on the space available in the yard and the size of the tree one would select. A species that grows to nearly 20 meters should be planted farther away than one that usually reaches 13 meters. The general rule, however, is that trees should be located fairly close to a residence so that after a five year growth period, the canopies will extend to a few meters beyond the roofline. A study shows that the ambient air under a tree adjacent to the wall is about 2°C to 2.5°C cooler than air in non-shaded areas. This cooler microclimate immediately adjacent to the house results in less heat gain through conduction by walls and windows.

Some commonly employed trees and shrubs are shown in Table 2.8. In coastal regions, salt in the soil or salt spray, seriously compounds salt problems. Many trees will not survive saline conditions. The categories of salt tolerance have been identified for various categories alongwith their suitability for different climatic zones.

Table 2.8 (a): Deciduous trees

Common Name	Uses	Ultimate height (m)	Colored foliage	Flowering season	Climate zone	Salt tolerance
Florida Elm	S	15			CC	low
Gumbo Limbo	A	9-15	blue purble flowers	spring	HD, MO	none
Mulberry	S, R	18-24			HD, MO	low
Laurel oak	R, S	18-24			CC	none
Red Mulberry	S	12-15	red brown	round	CO, MO	none
Sweet Gum	S	24	red brown	fall	WH	low
Sycamore	S	30	yellow	fall	WH	medium

Table 2.8(b) : Evergreen trees

Common Name	Uses	Ultimate height (m)	Colored foliage	Flowering season	Climate zone	Salt tolerance
Cocoplum	S	6	white flowers	spring	WH, CO	medium
Gallberry	H	3	black fruit	winter	CC,CS,WH	medium
Inkberry	C	2	white flowers	spring and summer	WH,HD,CO	high
Marlberry	S	6	white flowers, black fruit	all year	WH,MD,CO	high
Sea Lavender	C	2	white flowers, black fruit	all year	WH	high
Spanish Bayonet	B	6-7.5	white flowers	spring	CC,CO,WH	medium
Wild Coffee	H	2.4	white flowers	spring, summer	WH,HD	

Uses: B = barriers; C = coastal locations; H = hedges; S = Screens

Climatic zones: CC = cold and cloudy
CO = composite
CS = cold and sunny
HD = hot and dry
WH = warm and humid

2.2.1.4 Shading by overhangs, louvres and textured facades

Few building elements help in blocking direct entry of sunlight into building envelope which is the most important strategy in passive cooling. Such elements may be integral part of the building or they may even be externally added as described below. The devices that provide shading to an opening (door or window) can be classified into three types (Fig. 2.33):

(a) Movable opaque, e.g. roller blind, curtain, etc; can be highly effective in reducing solar gains but eliminates view and impedes air movement.

(b) Louvres. May be adjustable or fixed, affect view and air movement to some degree, can also provide security.

(c) Fixed overhangs. Easy to attain on single storey buildings with overhanging roof. Also gives rain protection to walls and openings. Little or no effect on view and air movement.

In practice, shading devices are very varied and sometimes consist of combinations of the above types.

(a) Movable blinds or curtains

Movable blinds or curtains effectively block the transmission of solar radiation through glazed windows, especially on the east and west walls. In hot and dry climates, when the ambient air is hotter than the room air, these devices also help to reduce the convective heat gain. In warm and humid climates, however, where airflow is desirable, they seriously impede ventilation. For air-conditioned buildings, the flow of outside air has to be blocked. In such cases, opaque (or translucent) blinds could be considered as means to reduce the cooling load.

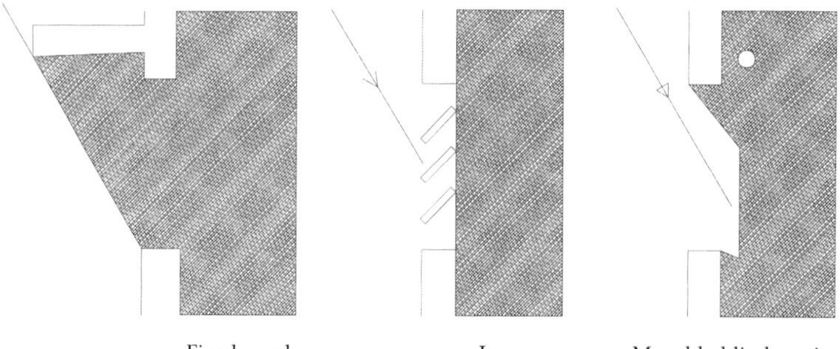

Figure 2.33: Classification of shading types

Furthermore, in composite climatic conditions, such devices block the undesirable solar radiation very effectively during summer. It is always desirable to choose light colored reflective blinds than dark colored ones, which absorb solar radiation and transmit it into the room in the form of long wave heat radiation (Fig. 2.34).

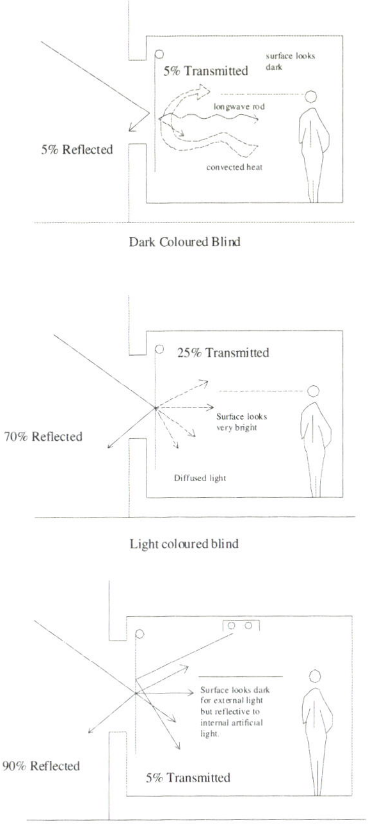

Figure 2.34: Performance of various blind materials

Fabrics are now available, which have aluminized finishes on one side and are preferable to ordinary fabrics. These are highly opaque but still look light colored from the inside of the building, when illuminated from inside as shown in Fig. 2.34. Alternatively, reflective plastic films could be considered. These could be permanently integrated with the glazing systems and in new buildings would be replaced by the use of reflective glass. However, all of these measures tend to redirect solar radiation in such a way that they increase glare to external spaces

(b) Overhangs and louvers (geometric shading)

Overhangs or louvers are utilized to block that part of the sky through which the sun passes. This leaves the low angle view and entry of air unimpeded. In the tropics, fixed overhangs are used as shading devices with careful consideration for orientation. The principles are illustrated in Fig. 2.35.

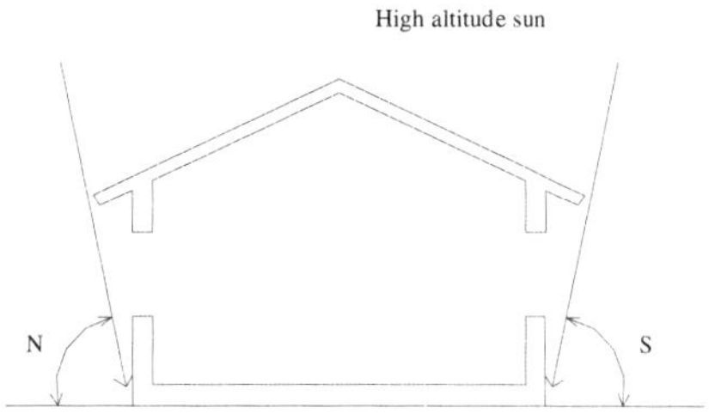

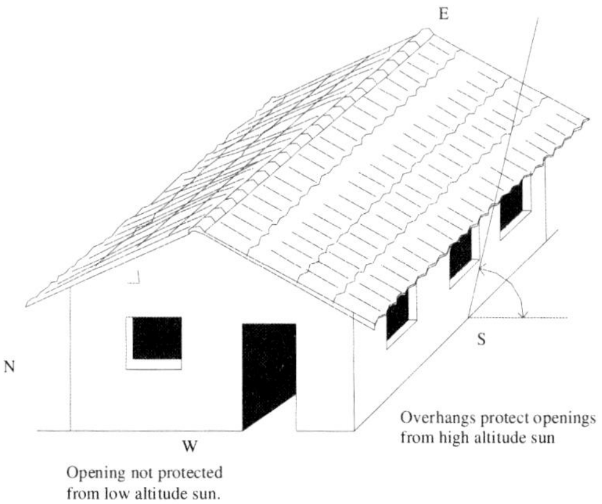

Figure 2.35: Shading of openings on long walls in E-W oriented building

Overhangs on south oriented windows provide very effective shading from the high altitude sun. Even an extended roof shades the entire north or south wall effectively from the noon sun. East and west openings on the other hand need much bigger sized overhangs, which sometimes may not be possible. Vegetation, shading by neighbouring buildings and/or placement of a portico or veranda on these sides protect the building from the morning and afternoon sun.

Geometry of overhangs and louvres

There are several possibilities for ensuring protection of direct entry of sunlight using horizontal, vertical, combination of horizontal and vertical, inclined shades. Few commonly used shading devices are shown in Fig. 2.36.

Requirement of shading largely depends upon the climatic conditions. According to climatic zones, there are three categories of shading requirement:

(a) complete year round shading

(b) complete year round shading but only during major sunshine hours

(c) shading during summer months alone.

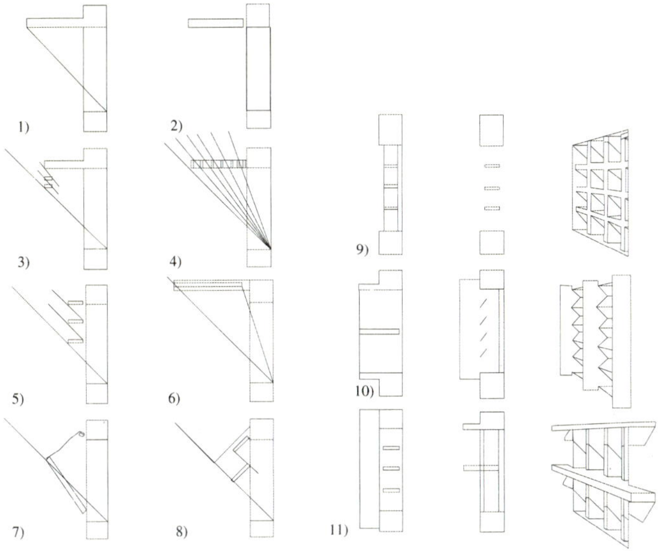

Figure 2.36: Commonly used shading elements

Table 2.9 summarizes preferences for shading devices in different climatic zones.

Table 2.9: Shading requirements in different climatic zones

Climatic Zone	*Requirement*
Hot and dry	Complete year round shading
Warm and humid	Complete year round shading but design should be made such that ventilation is not affected
Temperate	Complete year round shading but only during major sunshine hours
Cold and cloudy	No shading
Cold and sunny	Shading during summer months alone
Composite	Shading during summer months alone

Even though, the designer has his own freedom to design the shading devices in various shapes, some basic shapes in common usage are identified to present design tools to size them. Shadow obtained by use of different shading devices are shown in Figure 2.37.

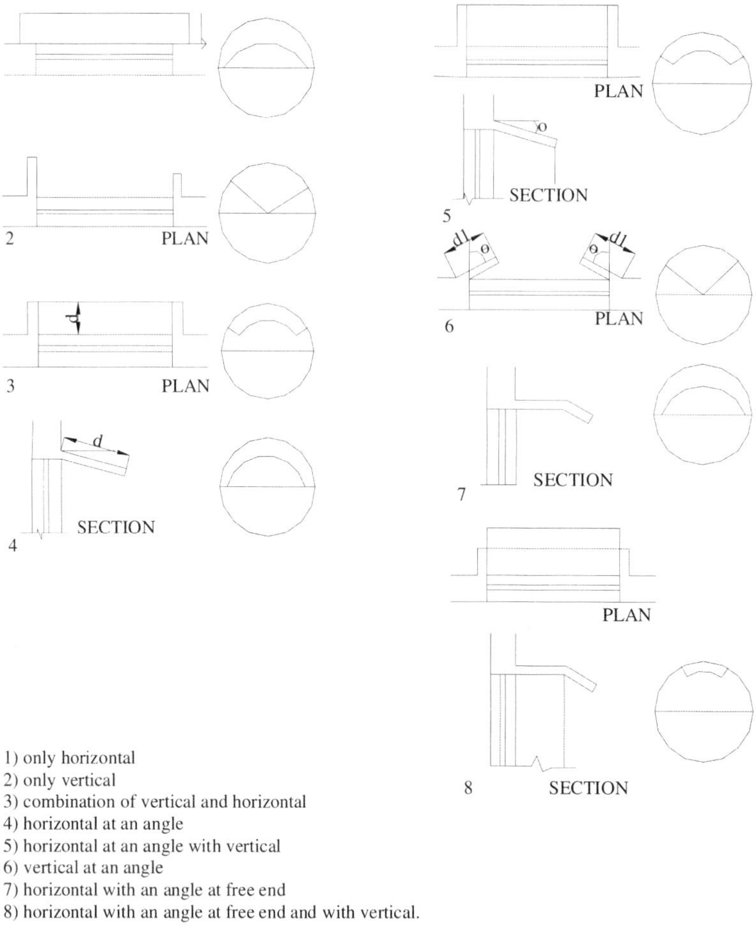

Figure 2.37: Various types of shading devices and their corresponding shadows

The size of the overhang in relation to height and width of window can be found after knowing solar altitude and solar azimuth angles on critical periods when shading is to be provided.

Overhang design for south facing clerestory windows

On a south facing clerestory, the roof that shades the clerestory is often angled upward. In this case one has to use the solar angles (Fig. 2.38). The best location for all south facing overhang extensions is the point, at which angle α crosses angle β. Angle β originates at the bottom of the window glass and angle α originates at the top of the window glass.

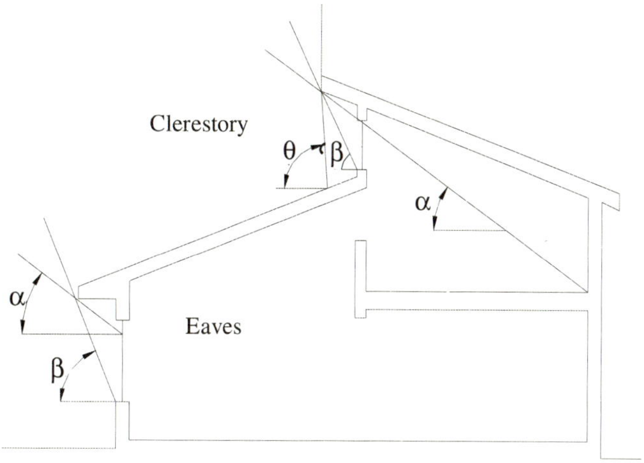

α = solar altitude at 12.00 noon on Dec. 21
θ = solar altitude at 12.00 noon on June 21
β = solar altitude in spring /fall (e.g. March 7th and October 5th for 28 N latitude)

Figure 2.38: Overhang calculation for south facing clerestory

The intersection of the lines is the optimum point for the end of the overhang. If the end point cannot be used because of the roof slope, then use the point at which angle β intersects the roof plane as the end point of the overhang.

Shading of roof and walls

During summer, since maximum solar radiation is incident on the roof, it is therefore, advisable to protect the roof from the sun up to maximum possible extent. Surface shading can be provided as an integral part of the building element or it can be provided using a separate cover. Highly textured walls have a portion of their surfaces in the shade (Fig. 2.39). The radiation absorbing area of such a textured surface is less than its radiation emitting area and therefore, it will be cooler than a smooth flat surface. The increased surface area will also result in an increased coefficient of convective heat transfer, which will permit the building to cool down faster at night, when the ambient temperature is lower than the building temperature.

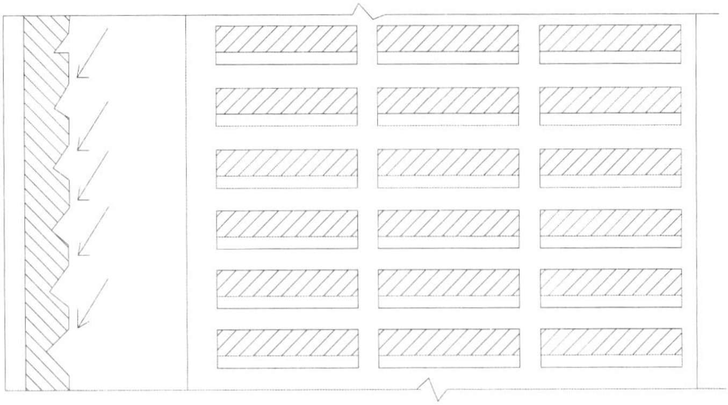

Figure 2.39: Shading by texture

Shading provided by external means should be such that it does not interfere with nighttime cooling. This is particularly important for roof surfaces, which are exposed to the cool night sky as shown in Figure 2.40. A cover over the roof provided by solid concrete or galvanized iron sheets provides protection from direct radiation, but it will not permit radiation escaping to the night sky. An alternative method is to provide a cover of deciduous plants or creepers. Because of the evaporation from the leaf surfaces, the temperature of such a cover will be lower than the daytime air temperature and at night, it may even be lower than the sky temperature.

Another shading device used in some traditional buildings is the covering of the entire roof surface area with small closely packed inverted earthen pots as shown in Figure 2.40. In addition to shading, this arrangement provides an increased surface area for radiative emission, and an insulating cover of still air over the roof, which impedes heat flow into the building, while still permitting upward heat flow at night. Although, the system of earthen pots is thermally efficient, the method suffers from practical difficulties, because the roof is rendered unusable and its maintenance is difficult.

A removable canvas cover can also serve as an effective roof shading device, as shown in Figure 2.40. This can be mounted close to the roof in the day time and at night, it can be rolled up to permit radiative cooling. The upper surface of the canvas should be painted white to minimize the amount of absorbed radiation by the canvas and the consequent conductive heat gain through it.

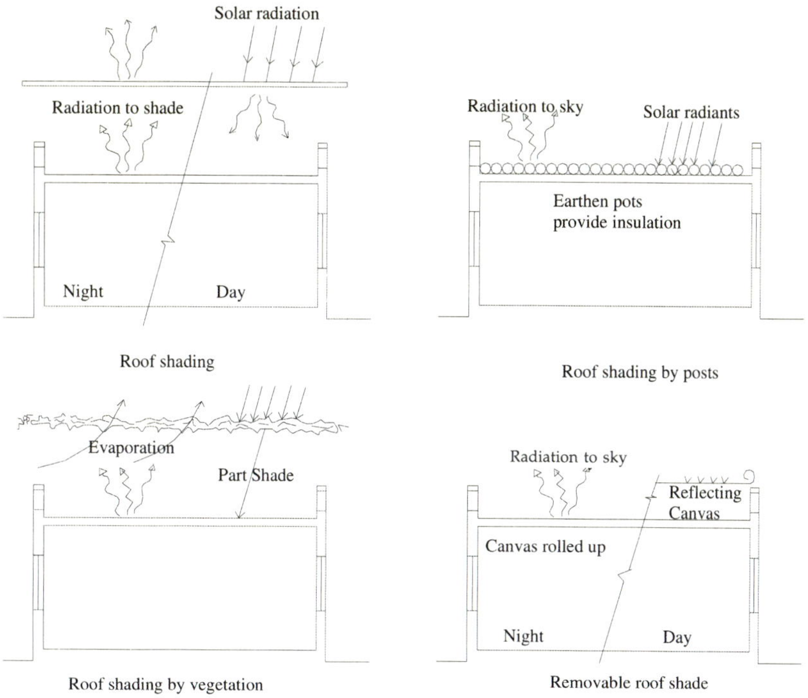

Figure 2.40: Different techniques for roof shading

2.2.1.5 *Reflecting surfaces*

If, the external surfaces of the building are painted with such colours that reflect solar radiation (in order to have minimum absorption), but the emission in the long wave region is high, then the heat flux transmitted into the building is reduced considerably. In the Table 2.10, the reflectivity of the surfaces for solar radiation and their emission in the long wave region are given for some common building materials.

The table shows that whitewash has a lower reflectivity than aluminum, but it will stay cooler, when exposed to solar radiation, because of its very high emissivity at low temperatures.

The effect of external surface colour is more evident in case of the light structures, which offer low resistance to heat flow, and because of low thermal capacity. Figure 2.41 shows the room air temperature in a 20cm thick brick walled room, which is painted black and white for the climatic conditions of New Delhi.

Table 2.10 : Reflectivity of surfaces to radiation

Material	Reflectivity (Solar radiation)	Emissivity (Low Temp.)
Aluminium foil bright	0.95	0.05
Aluminium foil oxidized	0.85	0.12
Polished aluminium	0.80	0.05
Aluminium paint	0.50	0.50
Galvanized steel bright	0.75	0.25
Whitewash new	0.88	0.90
White oil paint	0.80	0.90
Grey Colour, light	0.60	0.90
Grey colour, dark	0.30	0.90
Green colour, light	0.60	0.90
Aluminium foil bright	0.30	0.90
Red brick	0.40	0.90
Glass	0.08	0.90

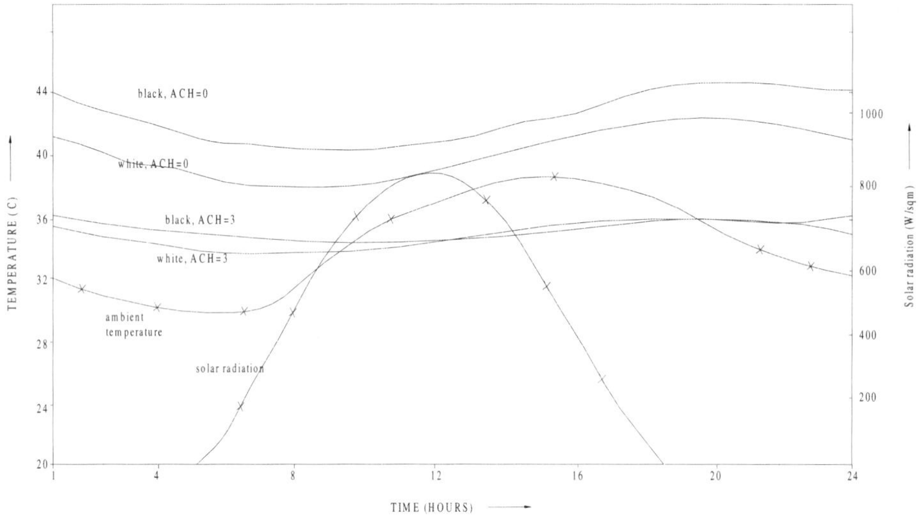

Figure 2.44: Room temperature for summer conditions inside a room (4mX4mX3m)

2.2.1.6 Shelter against hot winds

Hot winds in summer in hot and dry climatic conditions are a source of large convective heat gain and a source of extreme thermal discomfort. It is, therefore, advisable to protect a building against these hot winds.

Wind shelter for a building can be provided either by taking the advantage of the existing topography, such as an elevated land mass, or by creating wind barriers in the form of trees, shrubs, fences or walls. The reduction in the wind speed due to such barriers is illustrated in Figure 2.42. Usually, an opaque barrier creates a turbulent flow of wind and one has to avoid the accumulation of heat from the sun-irradiated surfaces between the barrier and the surface.

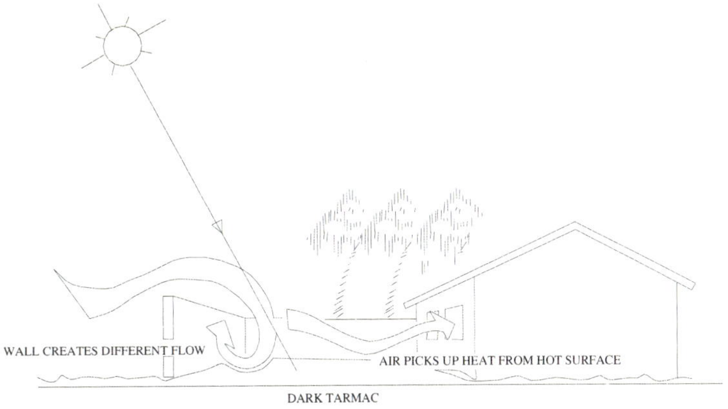

Figure 2.42: Heat accumulation due to opaque wind barrier

Similar to solar shading, relative placement of buildings also creates wind shades as shown in Figure 2.43. Depending upon whether the climate is hot and dry or warm and humid one can decide on the arrangement (a) or (b) respectively. Length of the wind shades for various building forms is given in Table 2.11.

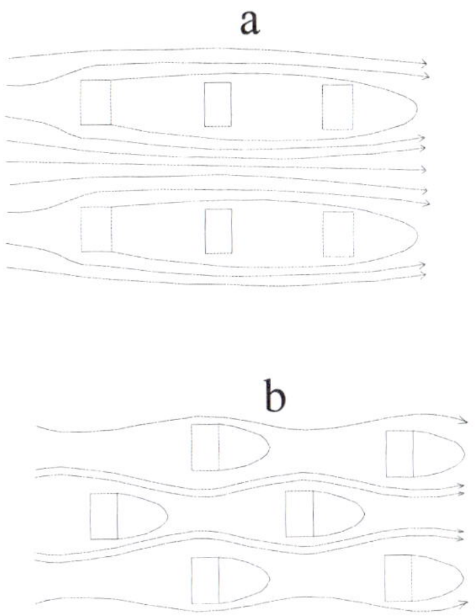

Figure 2.43: Effect of layout on wind shadowing

Table 2.11: Length of wind shadow for major building forms

Building form Width (W)	Height (H)	Roof Pitch	Wind shadow length (xH) Length of the building (l)					Wind Direction
			2A	4A	8A	16A	25A	
A	A	0°	2 1/2	3 1/4	5 1/4	8	8 1/4	
2A	A	0°	2	2 1/4	3 1/4	6	7	
3A	A	0°	2 1/4	3 1/4	4 1/2	5 1/4	5 1/2	
A	2A	0°	5 1/4	8 1/4	11 3/4	16 1/2	18	
A	3A	0°	6 3/4	11 1/2	16 1/2	18 2/4	20 2/4	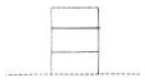
2A	2A	45°	2 3/4	5 1/4	9 1/4	13 1/4	15	
2A	1.6A	30°	3	4	6 3/4	10	13	
2A	1.5 A	15°	3	5 1/4	8 1/4	11 1/2	14 1/2	
2A	1.5A	15°	2 1/2	4 1/2	6 1/2	11	13 3/4	

2.2.2 Reduction of heat transmission into the building

As a result of the absorbed solar radiation and due to convective heat gain from the hotter ambient air, the external surface of a building gets heated. This heat gets transmitted through the building fabric to the internal envelope. Following sections describe various principles and methods to reduce such heat transfer.

2.2.2.1 Solar heat gain factor

One solar heat gain factor (g) or sometimes also called as Solar Heat Factor, is an indication of fraction of the heat of solar radiation transmitted into the building. It is defined as the ratio of the heat transmitted into the building to the incident solar energy on that surface. The solar heat gain factor is calculated as follows:

$$g = \frac{\text{Transmitted Solar Energy H}}{\text{Incident Solar Energy S}}$$

The factors that affect the value of 'g' are:

(a) absorptivity of the external surface

(b) the insulation value of the envelope

(c) the mass of the envelope.

The relative position of insulating and thermal mass layers in the construction has a significant effect on the 'g'. The value of 'g' over a period of 24 hours, in massive and insulated buildings, may also be influenced by the infrared emissivity of the external surface. SHF is usually expressed as a percentage. 'g' values for some typical constructions are given in Table 2.13 alongwith the U-values and the corresponding time lag values.

It is recommended that the Solar Heat Gain Factor (g) should be less than 4% and the time lag should be less than 4 hours in warm and humid climates. The time lag should be more than 6 hours for hot and dry climatic conditions. These recommendations for 'g' and time lag are made only for non-air-conditioned buildings. In air-conditioned buildings, where temperatures are consistently below the ambient temperature, much higher levels of insulation, especially in roofs, will be economical.

Table 2.12: Solar heat gain factor, U-value and time lag for walls and roofs

Construction	*U-value for hot season (W/m^2 °K)*	*Solar heat gain factor (%)*	*Time lag (hours)*
Roofs			
1. Aluminium sheet	8.7	10.2	0.5
2. GI sheet	8.5	20.0	0.5
3. Aluminium sheet, roof cavity, asbestos cement sheet ceiling	1.9	4.4	1.0
4. As(4) with 50mm fiber glass in the cavity	1..3	3.0	1.0
5. As(6) with 50mm fiber glass	1.3	5.2	1
6. 150mm concrete slab	3.3	9.1	4
7. As(8) with 50mm internal wood wool slab	1.13	3.1	4.5
8. As(9) bus with external insulation	1.13	3.1	13
9. As(8) with internal and external insulation	0.75	2.1	13.5
10. As(8) whitewashed externally	3.3	4.1	4
11. As(9) whitewashed externally	1.13	1.4	4.5
12. As(10) whitewashed externally	1.13	1.4	13
13. As(11) whitewashed externally	0.75	0.9	13.5
14. 300mm concrete slab	2.46	6.7	9.2
Walls			
1. 250mm hollow concrete blocks	1.7	4.7	11
2. As(17) whitewashed externally	1.7	2.1	11
3. 230mm brick wall	2.7	9.5	8
4. 280mm brick wall	1.7	6.0	10.5
5. As(23) whitewashed externally	1.7	2.1	10.5

2.2.2.2 Thermal insulation

Use of insulation is a well-known and well-practiced concept used for energy conservation in buildings. In hot climatic conditions, it should be ensured that the thermal mass is weakly coupled with external heat source (i.e. solar radiation), but strongly coupled with the interior in order to be able to absorb internal gains easily. For cold climatic conditions, approach gets reversed. The principle is illustrated in Figure 2.44.

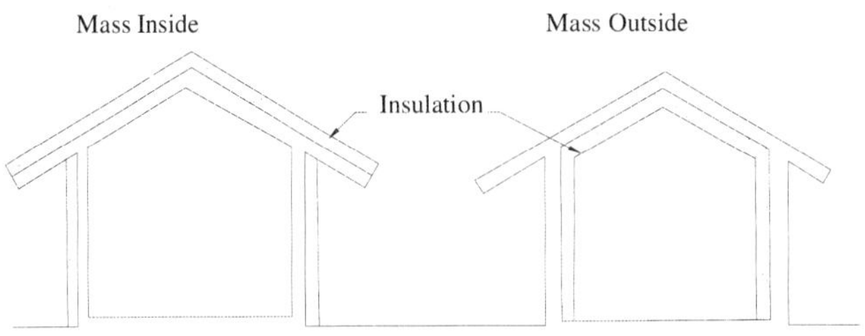

Figure 2.44: Coupling of thermal mass for hot and cold climate

Depending on the type and thickness of insulation, it is easy to calculate the U-value of the building component. If, one knows the absorptivity of the outside surface then the solar heat gain factor can be read from Figure 2.45 using the following steps:

- Find the absorptivity of the surface at the right-hand side of the graph
- Calculate the U value and locate U value on the second scale at the top of the graph.
- Find where the two lines intersect. If the solar heat value exceeds the required standard, then either the insulation should be increased or the absorptivity lowered.

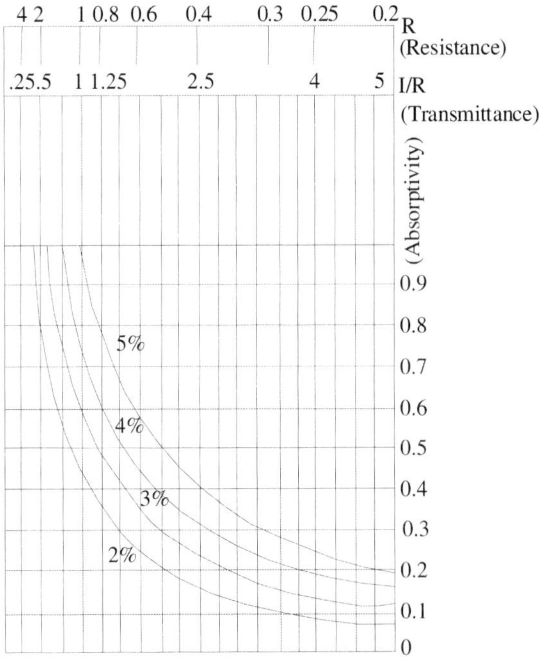

SHF Calculator (Evans, 1980)

Figure 2.45: SHF calculator chart for combinations of U-value and absorptivity

2.2.2.3 *Air cavities*

Air cavities within walls or an attic space in the roof-ceiling combination reduces the solar heat gain factor (SHF). Performance gets further improved, if the void is ventilated. Heat is transmitted through the air cavity by convection and radiation. The cavity represents a resistance, which is nearly proportional to the thickness of the air cavity upto 20mm as shown in Figure 2.46. It is seen that for thickness greater than 20 mm, the resistance to heat flow does not increase much and becomes nearly constant. Some typical values of the thermal resistance for air cavities are given in Table 2.13.

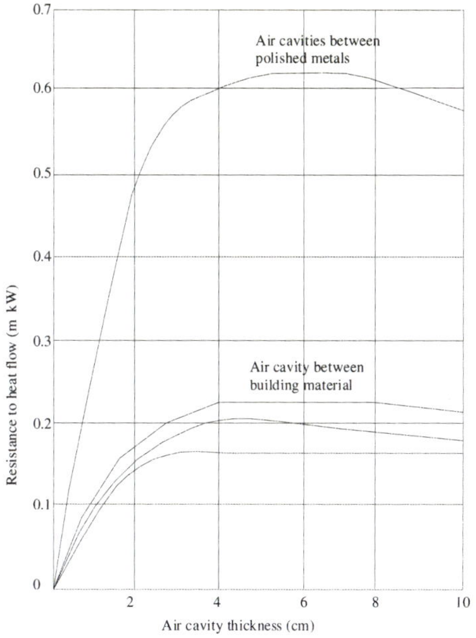

Figure 2.46: Thermal resistance of various thickness of air cavity

Table 2.13 : Thermal resistance to heat flow for air cavities

Air cavity placement	Thickness of air layer (mm)	Thermal resistance m k/W
Vertical	10-20 20-500	0.14 0.17
Horizontal Heat flow from bottom to top Heat flow from top to bottom	10-500	0.17 0.21

If it is possible to ventilate the air gap between the roof and the ceiling, then we could expect a further reduction of heat transfer. If, the ventilation is effective, then the temperature of air in the void will remain close to the ambient temperature, thus reducing the convective heat transfer to nearly zero. Ventilated air, however, does not reduce the radiative heat transfer from the roof to the ceiling. The radiative component of the heat transfer may be reduced by using low emissivity or high reflective coating (e.g. aluminium foil) on either surface facing the cavity as shown in Figure 2.47.

(a) Ventilated air cavity
(b) Radiation insulation in cavity

Figure 2.47: Ventilated cavity and radiation insulation in cavity to reduce heat transmission

2.2.3 Increasing heat loss

2.2.3.1 Increase of heat loss from the building by radiation

The emission of longwave radiation from building surfaces continuously takes place during day and night. During the daytime, however, the radiating surface is exposed to solar radiation. The absorbed solar radiation at the surface (depending on the solar absorptivity of the surface) produces heat, which in most cases outweighs the cooling effect produced by the emission of longwave radiation. With the materials presently available, radiant cooling can be obtained only during the night hours. Radiative cooling often operates simultaneously with convection and evaporation. In humid climates, the evaporation is limited and hence the radiative cooling plays a more important role in total heat losses from surfaces exposed to the sky. In such a climate, the nocturnal sky is usually the coldest available heat sink. Typically the effective nocturnal sky temperature is about 10°C below the ambient temperature near the ground.

Three types of problems are involved in the design of systems for using nocturnal long-wave radiation based passive cooling system:

(a) The first problem involves the estimation of the meteorological potential for radiant heat loss. This includes the estimation of the effective sky temperature or emissivity, and the convective heat exchange for calculating the net radiant and total heat losses from ordinary surfaces.

The radiative heat loss, can be calculated by using the formula

$Q_R = \sigma T_{sky}^4$ W/m² (eq. 2.11)

where $T_{sky} = å_s^{1/4} T_a$ (K) (eq. 2.12)

where ó is the Stefan Boltzmann constant, T_{sky} is the sky temperature in Kelvin, T_a is the ambient temperature in Kelvin and $å_s$ is the emissivity of the sky given in Table 2.14.

Table 2.14: Emissivity of clear sky at varying dew point temperatures

Temperature (dew point C)	e_s	$e_s^{1/4}$
0	0.74	0.93
5	0.77	0.94
10	0.80	0.95
15	0.83	0.95
20	0.86	0.96
25	0.89	0.97
30	0.92	0.98
35	0.95	0.99

(b) The second type of problem involves the development and application of techniques for augmenting the net radiative heat loss from the radiating surface above its natural level, and reducing the convective heat gain from the ambient air by such means as infrared (IR) transparent wind screens and use of IR selective surfaces. While considering these problems, attention should be paid to the possibilities of deviations from the theoretical ideal performance due to such factors as dew formation and dust settling, as well as the durability of wind-screen materials and structural details.

(c) The third type of problem is related to using the cooling effect produced by nocturnal radiation, that is, the transfer of this cooling effect to the building and the way in which it is used to improve indoor comfort conditions. In practice it means the choice and design of the type of cooling system, whether direct cooling of the thermal storing mass (e.g. a roof itself), or the use of a heat transfer medium and specialized longwave radiator.

The equation for radiative heat loss suggests that an increase of the surface area will result into an enhanced radiative loss, provided that while doing so, there is no increase in the intercepted solar radiation during the daytime.

2.2.3.2 Increased radiation by movable elements

A movable insulation like a canvas permits protection of the roof from the daytime solar radiation and also the convective heat gain and during the night time it can be removed to expose the roof to the sky. Movable insulation can also be in the form of horizontal movable panels (as in a roofpond system) or hinged panes which are positioned vertically during the night so as to expose the roof mass below. These hinged panels should be covered on both sides with a reflective layer (e.g. aluminium foil) so that the thermal radiation emitted obliquely will be reflected towards the sky. Horizontally movable panels require an area at the roof level for their storage while the roof is exposed. The area allocated to this function may take about one quarter of the roof area and this area cannot be cooled by radiation. In small buildings, the garage or a porch area can be allocated for the storage of the panels when the roof is exposed. In large buildings, an area has to be set aside for this function. Hinged panels, on the other hand, can expose effectively the whole roof area when in a vertical position. Although physically they cover an area corresponding to their thickness (about 5 to 10% of their height), it is possible to minimize this blocking effect by covering the two sides of the panes with a reflective layer.

A modified radiative cooling system in which, a metallic deck placed a few centimeters above an insulated nearby flat roof, can also be used. It should be painted white to provide good reflectivity for the solar radiation and good emissivity for the thermal radiation. The expected temperature depression of such a radiator would be from 4 to 5K under stagnation conditions for humid regions and about 6 to 7 K in desert regions.

Assuming the conditions for an exposed radiator in use, the utilized radiant cooling would be about 34 W/m^2. With an air flow rate of 30 m^3/h per m^2 of the floor area (3000 m^3/h for a building of 100 m^2 and net volume of 250 m^3), the temperature depression of the air would be about 3.8K below the ambient night temperature. If, this cooled air is used to cool the building by ventilation, the air change rate would be 3000/250 = 12 air changes per hour, quite adequate for ventilation cooling. It would be of interest to compare this radiant/convective cooling with pure convective cooling by ambient night air. Typical differences between the indoor air and the outdoor air at night, in buildings, which are ventilated at night, are about 3-4°K. As the temperature depression of the air cooled by nocturnal radiation is also about 3-4°K, it means that the radiant cooling can double the net convective cooling achieved by nocturnal ventilation.

In regions, where night winds with a known direction are available in summer, it is possible to induce the air flow under the radiator and through the building by the wind force, augmented by the thermosyphonic effect. This can be achieved by providing an air inlet, for the flow under the radiator, facing the prevailing night air. The wind then can force the flow under the radiator and into the building (e.g. through a small covered courtyard). Warmer indoor air can be exhausted through a chimney, assisted by outlet details which produce a venturi suction effect, so that the same wind force produces pressure at the inlet to the nocturnal radiator and suction at the outlet for the discharge of the indoor air. In regions lacking persistent night winds, the air flow can, of course, be induced by a fan.

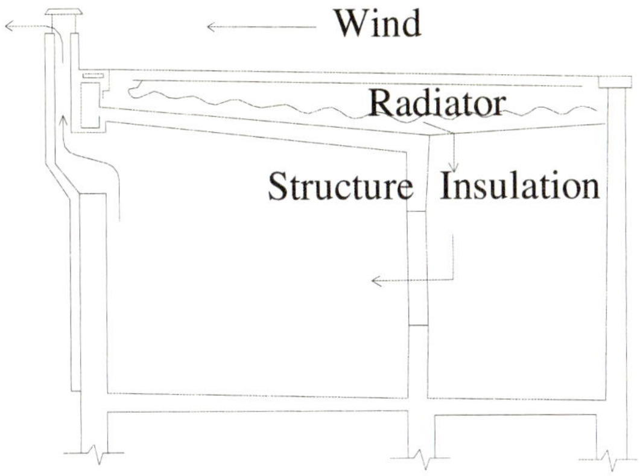

Warm indoor air can be discharged when air is forced under the radiator into the building, and then out again through a chimney. The air flow may be induced either by wind force or a fan

Figure 2.48: Modified roof radiative cooling combined with chimney effect

2.2.3.3 Increase of heat loss from the building by convection

Ventilating the building by cooler ambient air is one of the most effective ways of cooling non-conditioned buildings. Traditional architecture of the hot regions is dominated by the provision of air movement, particularly in the humid regions. In inland areas, where wind speeds are low, one has to adopt extreme measures such as stilts.

Convective cooling can take place by either creating an air movement, such as the use of fans etc., or by natural or forced ventilation in which the ventilated air is replaced by the ambient air. Thus the ventilation creates a heat loss from the interior (of a building) by replacing outgoing air with cooler incoming air, whereas the air movement reduces the effective temperature by increasing convective cooling and evaporative cooling of the body. In air-conditioned buildings, ventilation has to be kept to a minimum level that is governed by the requirements of fresh air as shown in Table 2.14.

Convective heat loss due to ventilation is in proportion to

- the air exchange rate
- the temperature difference between inside and outside
- the heat capacity of the air

Though the heat capacity of the air varies slightly with humidity, but with reasonable accuracy, the ventilation losses can be calculated by the formula

$Q_v = 0.33\ NV\ (t_i - t_a)$ (eq. 2.13)

where N is the number of air exchanges per hour, V is the volume of the building (m^3), t_i is the inside air temperature in the building and t_a is the ambient air temperature.

Table 2.15: Fresh air requirements

Activity	*Specially for room*	*Fresh air reqd. ac. Air change*
For CO_2 removal - person working - person relaxing	 All rooms All rooms	 12 m^3/h 4 m^3/h
For removal of gases of combustion (person smoking)	All rooms	20 m^3/h
Removal of odour	Bathroom	6 ac/h
Removal of gases of combustion (latent heat moisture)	Kitchen	8 ac/h
Removal of carbon monoxide	Garages	12 ac/h

2.3 VENTILATION FOR PASSIVE COOLING OF BUILDINGS

Airflow in a building is either due to the pressure differences, caused by temperature differences (stack effect) or due to pressure differences of the wind. Windows play a dominant role in inducing indoor ventilation due to wind forces. The various parameters that affect the ventilation are:

- climate
- wind direction
- area of fenestration/location
- size of inlet and outlet openings
- volume of the room
- shading devices
- wire meshes/fly screens
- internal partitions

2.3.1 Stack effect

Stack ventilation, the principle of which is shown in Figure 2.49, depends upon the buoyancy of the warmer air causing the air to rise and leave the building from a higher outlet. This way, the heavier cooler air is replaced via a lower inlet.

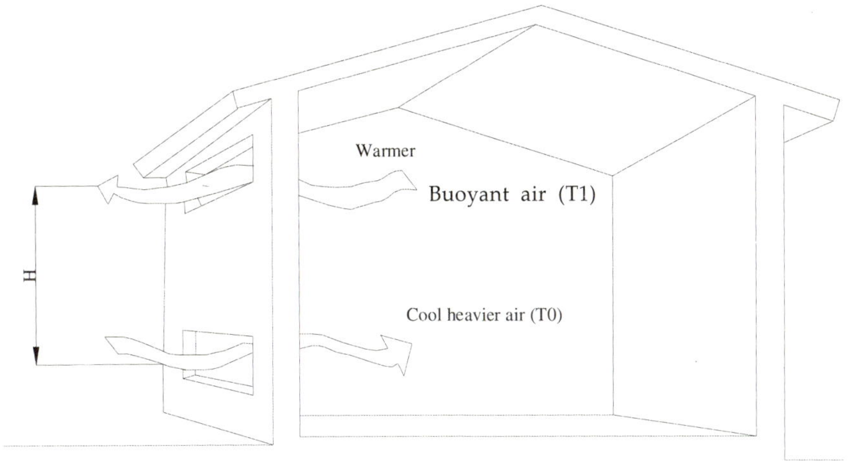

Figure 2.49: Stack effect ventilation

The rate of flow induced by thermal force is given by the formula

$$V=0.117A[h(t_i-t_a)]^{1/2} \quad \text{(eq. 2.14)}$$

where: V is Ventilation rate (m^3/s), A is Free area of the inlet opening (m^2), h is Vertical distance between inlet and outlet (m), t_i Average temperature of indoor air (^0C), t_a Average temperature of ambient air (^0C).

To attain the required velocity per m^2 of the opening, the height and temperature difference graph is given in Fig. 2.50. By a conventional design, it is difficult to achieve the required ventilation rates or air velocity. For example, Figure-2.50 shows that to achieve a velocity of 0.5 m/s over a height of 1.8 m, one needs to have a temperature difference of 10^0C. This temperature difference will not be acceptable in an occupied space. So, additional features to create a draught and which do not interfere with the occupied space, like a solar chimney (discussed later), have to be provided to achieve the desired air motion.

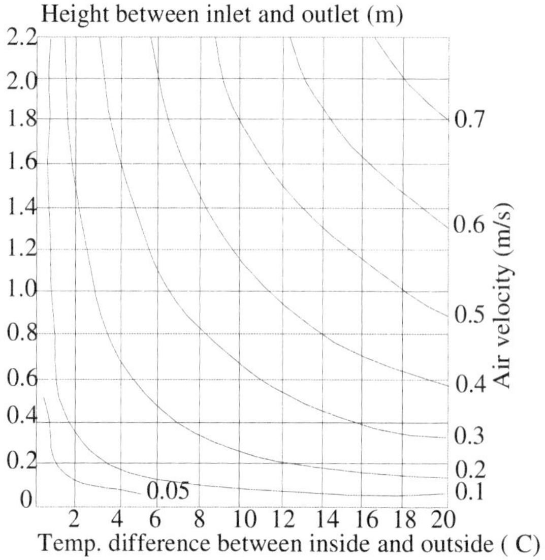

Figure 2.50:Stack effect ventilation rate diagram

2.3.2 Ventilation due to wind forces

When wind strikes a building, a region of higher pressure is created across the building in the direction of the incident wind (windward wall). The sides, leeward wall and roof, are all subjected to reduced pressure. Therefore, a pressure gradient is created in the direction of the incident wind. This pressure gradient causes the air to flow through the building from openings in the region of higher pressure to openings located in lower pressure. In the simple case of an isolated enclosure, in which openings are provided in each of two opposite walls, the rate of airflow can be calculated by the equation:

$Q = KAV$

where

Q rate of air flow in m^3/h

A area of smaller opening in m^2

V outdoor wind speed in m/h

K coefficient of effectiveness

The coefficient of effectiveness, K depends upon the direction of the wind relative to the opening, and on the ratio between the areas of the two openings. It is maximum, when the wind blows directly on to the opening and it increases with the relative size of the larger opening. Figure-2.51 gives the values of K for various ratios of the two openings, for winds perpendicular to the opening and at 45° to it. Changes in wind directions up to 30° on either side of the normal to the window wall have little effect on the value of K. For wind directions outside these limits, the value of K may be considered to change linearly with the wind direction.

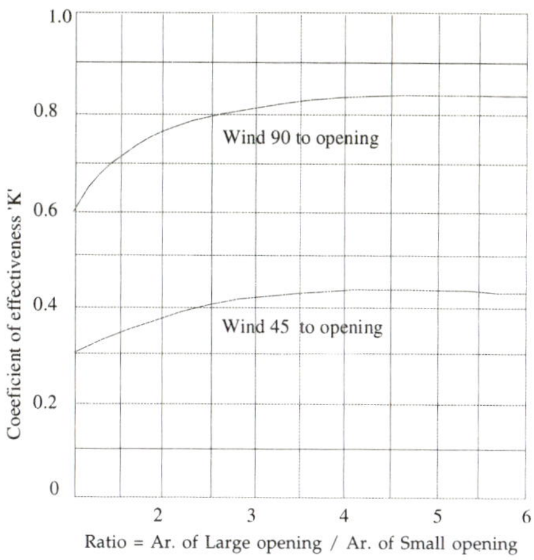

Figure 2.51: Values of coefficient of effectiveness K for flow through buildings

2.3.3 Ventilation due to combined effect of wind and thermal forces

Actual flow in a building results from the combined effect of thermal and wind forces. The two forces may either reinforce or oppose each other, depending on the direction of the wind and on whether the internal or the external temperature is higher. When acting simultaneously, the rate of airflow through the building may be computed by the equation

$$v^2 = v_w^2 + v_t^2 \qquad \text{(eq. 2.15)}$$

where:

v = resultant volume of air flow (m^3/s)

v_w = volume of air due to wind force (m^3/s)

v_t = volume of air flow due to thermal forces (m^3/s)

2.3.4 Room with windows on one wall only

The available wind velocity in a room with a single window on the windward side is about 10% of the outdoor velocity at point up to a distance one-sixth of the room width from the window. Beyond this, the velocity decreases rapidly and hardly any air movement is produced in the leeward half portion of the room. The effect of one window and the opening size on an average internal wind speed is shown in Fig. 2.52 along with the curve for the cross ventilation.

Figure 2.52: Average internal wind speed for different areas of the openings

In case of unequal inlet and outlet sizes, the area of the inlet window is first expressed as a percentage of the total area of fenestration. Following which, the corresponding value of the performance efficiency is determined from Figure-2.53(a). The average indoor velocity v_i is then calculated by multiplying the value of E with that of v_s. The local air movement velocity at different points shows a deviation from that of the average taken over the whole room area. For a given value of the ratio of the inlet window to the total fenestration, the Root Mean Square Deviation (RMSD) of local velocity from the average value may be obtained from Figure 2.53(b).

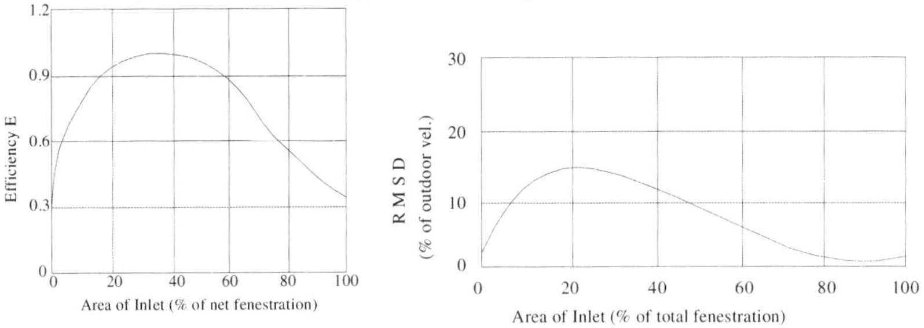

(a) (b)

Fig. 2.53: Effect of size of inlet on the performance efficiency and root mean square deviation

2.3.5 Effect of Orientation on Ventilation

The orientation of a window with respect to the most probable wind direction has considerable effect on the internal wind speed. For oblique incidence, the value of indoor wind speed gets reduced as compared to normal incidence. The value of indoor wind speed is also influenced by change in the location of openings with respect to the outdoor wind. Figure-2.54 gives the indoor speed for various outdoor wind speeds as a function of the fenestration area and for inlet and outlet opening ratios of 1 and 0.5 respectively. Table 2.16 shows effect of relative window location with respect to each other and also with respect to incident wind direction.

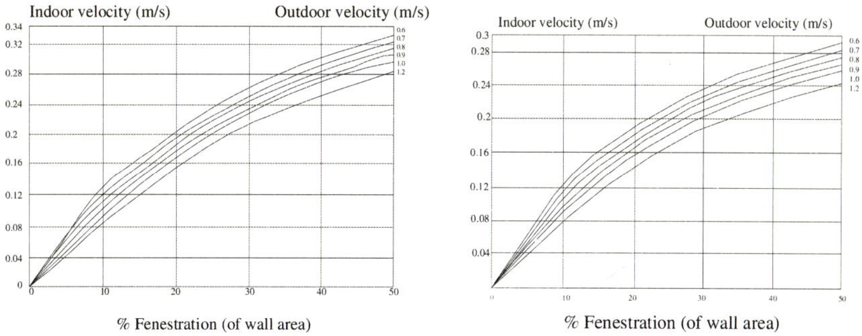

Fig. 2.54: Indoor air speed as a function of fenestration area

Table 2.16: Effect of window location on indoor air motion

Orientation → / Window Location ↓	Change in %	
	0° wind 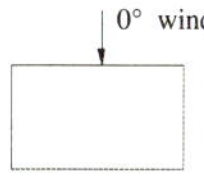	45° wind 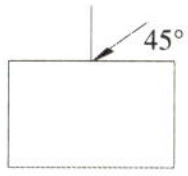
	0	0
	-10	+40
	-10	-15
	-15	0
	-15	0
	0	0
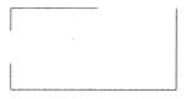	-10	+40
	-10	-15
	0	-60
	-20	-10
	-20	-60

2.3.6 Outdoor wind management

Local topography and surface texture can greatly affect the wind conditions for any building. Obstruction such as vegetation can greatly reduce wind speed, whereas the land relief can enhance or diminish the wind speed as shown in Figure 2.55. Wind speed usually increases with altitude, and as a result, high floors of buildings generally have good access to breeze, except for a location having high building densities as shown in Figure 2.55(b).

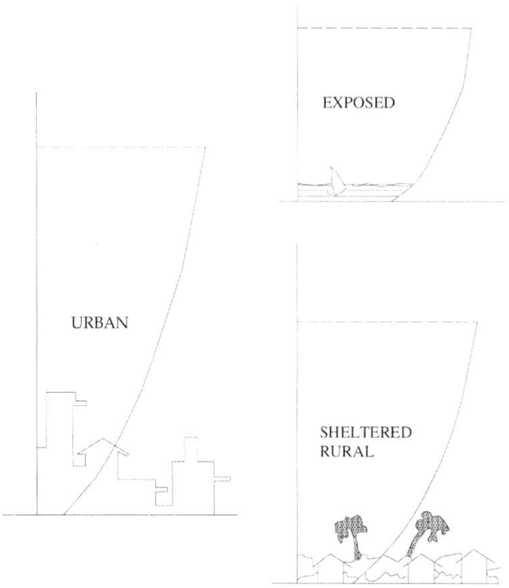

Figure 2.55(a): Effect of terrain on wind velocity gradients

Next to be considered is the immediate surrounding. By careful consideration of various buildings, an unimpeded airflow can be provided in all the buildings. In a grid-iron layout, a spacing of six times the building height is necessary to ensure adequate air movement for the second row. In a checkerboard pattern, the flow field is more uniform, stagnant air zones are eliminated.

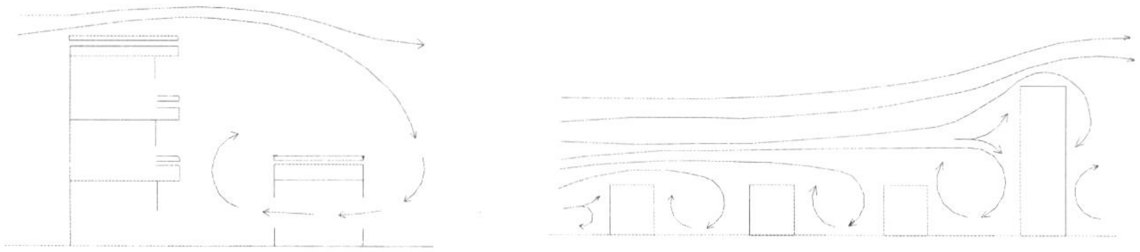

Fig. 2.55(b): Effect of tall buildings

The air stream separates on the face of a tall block, part of it moving up and over the roof, part of it down, to form a large vortex leading to a very high-pressure build up. An increased velocity is found at ground level at the sides of the tall block. When a very tall building faces the wind with a shorter block behind, a reverse flow can be experienced because of a strong negative pressure zone.

Wind shadow created by different building orientations and roof profiles have been shown in Figure 2.56.

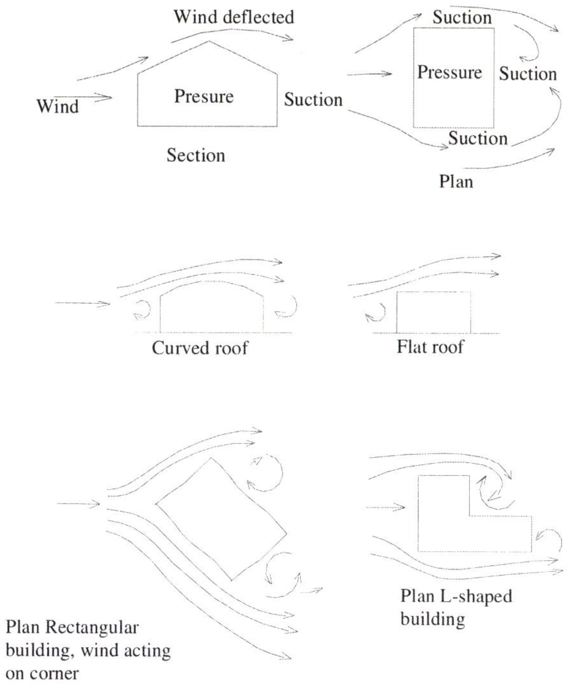

Figure 2.56: Wind shadow created by orientations and profiles

Actual problem arises in the tropical warm and humid areas, where ventilation is a must and when the orientation resulting from the wind movement does not match with the one that minimizes solar heat gain. In that case, one should orient buildings according to the motion of Sun and deflect or tamper the wind by suitable deflectors, in order to catch as much wind as possible.

2.3.7 Effect of louvers, verandah and fly screen

Various construction elements such as louvers, a verandah before the windows, subdivision of the internal space and the presence of fly screens effect the air movement inside.

Effect of louvers

Louvers, which are provided for protection against rain and for prevention of direct entry of sun through the windows, have a bearing on the indoor air flow pattern. The influence of some simple types of louvers on room air motion is summarized in Table 2.17.

Table 2.17: Influence of louvers on indoor air motion

Type of Louver	% change in indoor air velocity	
	0^0	45^0
Horizontal (sunshade)	-20	-20
L-type (horizontal and vertical)	+5	+10
Box type:		
Contraction ratio 1:1	0	-25
Contraction ratio 1:2	0	0
Multiple horizontal	-10	-13
Multiple vertical	-15	-25

Results of studies on airflow pattern with use of different types of shades and openings are shown in Figure 2.57.

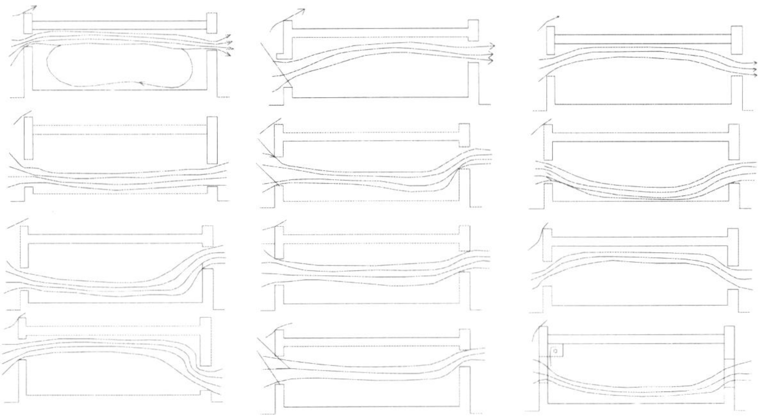

(a) (b) (c)

Figure 2.57:
(a) Airflow relating to the position of inlet in wall
(b) The effect of external sunshades
(c) The effect of different types of window openings

Effect of verandah before the windows

The presence of a verandah on the windward or leeward side of a room influences the room air motion. Table 2.18 shows the effect on average indoor wind velocity of some of the common types of verandah. To get the value of average indoor wind velocity for the given type, location and orientation of a verandah in front of a window, the correction factor may be taken from Table 2.18 and applied to the value of wind velocity for a case without verandah. The value remains almost unaffected, in case the verandah height is lower than that of the room.

Table 2.18: Effect of verandah on indoor air motion

Type of verandah	Location	Change in v (as % of v)	
		0^0	45^0
Open on three sides	Windward Leeward	+15 +15	+10 +10
Open on two sides	Windward Leeward	0 0	0 0
Open side parallel to the room wall	Windward Leeward	-10 0	-10 0
Open side perpendicular to the room wall	Windward Leeward	-50 0	–30 +15

Effect of fly screens

Fly screens or mosquito nets are an absolute necessity not only in malaria infested areas, but also if any kind of lamp is used indoors at night. Without it, thousands of insects would gather around the lamp. Such screens and nets can substantially reduce the airflow. Cotton net can give a reduction of 70% in air velocity. A smooth nylon net is better, with a reduction factor of only approximately 35%. The reduction is greater with higher wind velocities and is also increased with the angle of incidence, as shown in Table 2.19.

Table 2.19: Reduction of wind velocities with the incident angle

Outside velocity	*Normal incidence*		*67.5⁰ Incidence*	
m/s	*Inside velocity m/s*	*Reduction (%)*	*Inside velocity (m/s)*	*Reduction (%)*
0.75	0.49	35	0.40	47
1.23	0.87	29	0.75	40
2.50	1.33	30	1.00	60
3.30	1.79	47	1.33	50
3.80	2.64	46	2.23	43
Average		37.4		50.0

2.3.8 Trees as wind deflectors

It may not always be possible to locate the openings in the windward direction due to reasons like the site restriction, solar radiation, privacy etc. To some extent, the limitations can be overcome by designing suitable wind deflectors, as shown in Fig. 2.58. Interior partitions are provided in a building for the purpose of privacy, which may not allow openings in the partition. In warm and humid climatic zones, where ventilation becomes very essential, cross-ventilation becomes the major solution. Sometimes it is not possible in dense urban areas. This can be overcome by providing ridge ventilation or ventilating ducts or shafts for deeper rooms.

Figure 2.58(b): Wind deflectors

2.3.9 Wind tower

The principle of the wind tower is explained in Figure 2.59. The hot ambient air enters the tower through the openings in the tower and is cooled, when it comes in contact with the cool tower and thus becomes heavier and sinks down. When an inlet is provided to the rooms with an outlet on the other side, there is a draft of cool air. After a whole day of heat exchange, the wind tower becomes warm in the evening.

Figure 2.59 : Daytime and nighttime operation of a wind tower

During night, the reverse happens: due to warm surface of wind tower and drop in temperature of ambient air, due to buoyancy effect, warm air rises upwards. As a result of rise and escape of warm air from the tower, cooler ambient air is sucked into the room through the window. As a bye-product of this process, wind tower looses the heat that was collected during the daytime and it becomes ready for use in cold condition upto the morning. This system can work very effectively in hot and dry types of climate, where daily variations in temperatures are high with high temperature during daytime and low temperature during night time. As a result of clear sky conditions during the night, radiative losses are high. The openings of the wind tower are provided in the direction of the wind and outlets on the leeward side take advantage of the pressure difference created by wind speed and direction. Normally, the outlets have thrice the area of the inlet for better efficiency. As a thumb rule, over a height of 3 to 4 meter, a temperature difference of 4 to 5°C in air temperature can be obtained.

A combination of sensible cooling in the ground and evaporative cooling with the flow of air induced by the wind tower can be achieved by a configuration, shown in Fig. 2.60. The heat loss from air (on account of sensible cooling) results in a decreased air temperature, but no change in the water vapor content of the air.

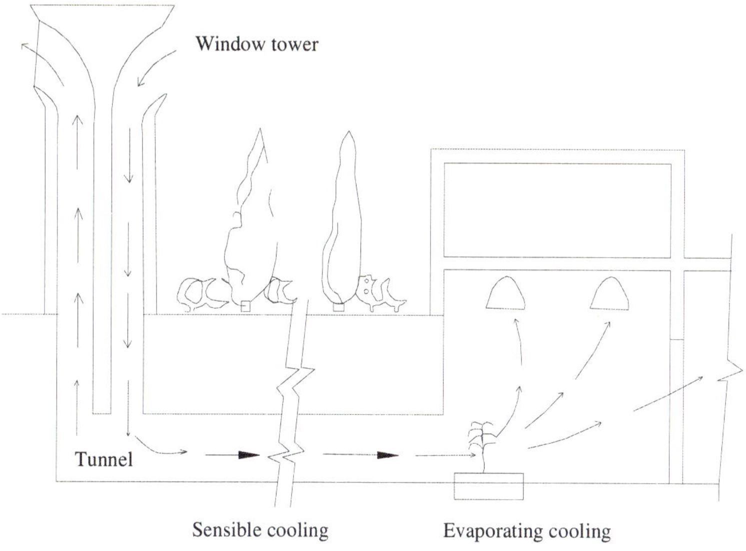

Figure 2.60 : Wind tower with evaporative cooling

Air in the upper part of a wind tower is cooled in conventional way. In addition, if water is introduced into this system, evaporative cooling also occurs. Such cooling involves a change in the water-vapor content and the temperature of the air. When unsaturated air comes in contact with water, some water is evaporated, thus lowering the temperature of the air and increasing its water vapor content. A wind-tower system that cools air evaporatively as well as sensibly is particularly effective in dry climates.

In few locations, where water table is high, water in the ground seeps through to the inside of the basement wall of the tower, so that air passing over the wall is evaporatively cooled. The wind tower can even be placed far away from the building and can be connected to it by a tunnel. The trees, shrubs and grass in the ground over the tunnel can be watered so that water seeps through the soil and keeps the inside surfaces of the tunnel walls damp. Thus air from the tower is evaporatively cooled, as it passes through the tunnel.

Pool and fountain in the basement of the building further cool the air. Whenever underground streams are present, the wind can be made to flow over them and the fountain dispensed with. Wind towers are normally employed with curved roofs, which offer a larger area for heat transfer to the ambient air. Since the wind velocity over a curved roof is higher than that over a flat roof, the corresponding heat transfer coefficient (surface-outside air) is also higher. Further hot air from the room gathers below the roof and thus the heat transfer from the roof to inside air gets further reduced.

When the wind direction is unpredictable, it is better to provide openings on all four sides and also have the additional effect due to wind pressure (Fig. 2.61a). The rate of heat transfer mainly depends upon the surface area with which, the air comes in contact. Here, the surface area is increased by having vertical conduits, which give less resistance to airflow. Further, the effectiveness is further increased by having sprinklers to promote the evaporative cooling as shown in Fig. 2.61(b).

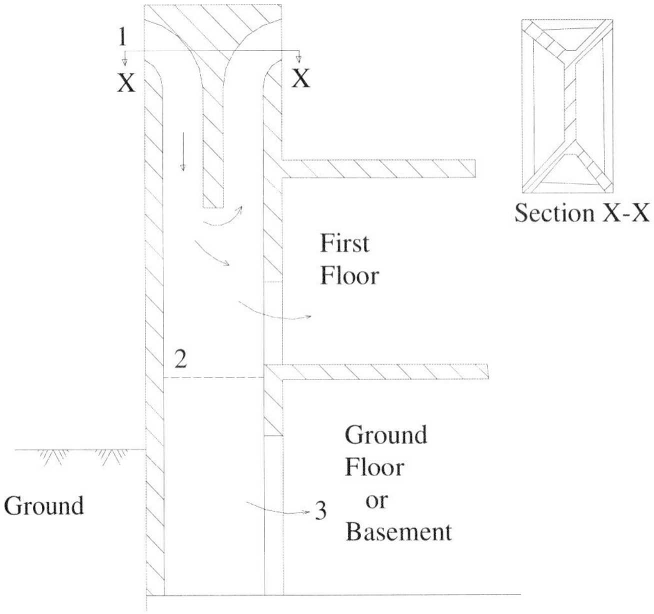

Fig. 2.61(a): Wind tower design with openings on all four sides

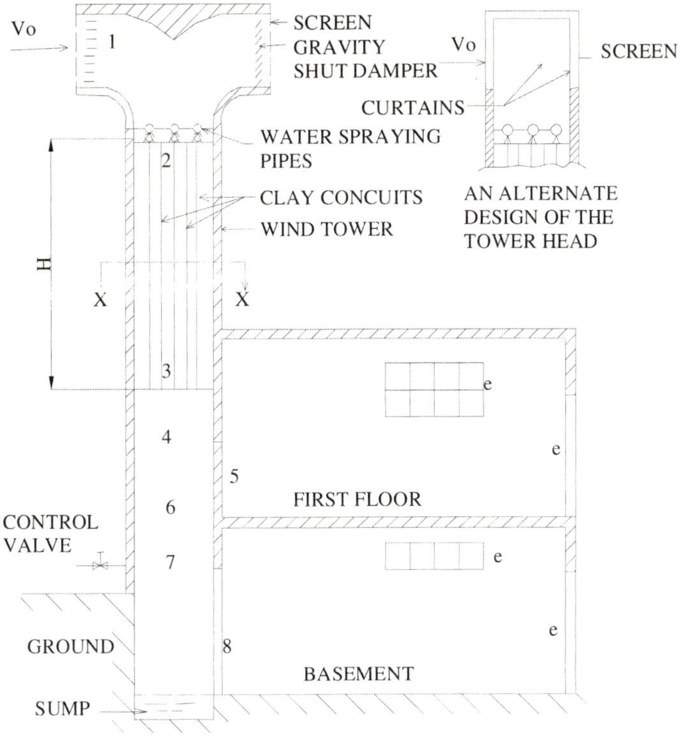

Fig. 2.61(b): Wind tower with evaporatively cooled system

Limitations of wind tower

- Concepts of wind tower may work well in the case of individual units and not in multi-storied apartments. For multi-storied buildings, multiple wind towers are needed.
- In a dense urban area the wind tower has to be very high to be able to catch enough air.
- The surface of the wind tower accumulates dust in due course and the heat transfer from the surface of wind tower to the air becomes slower. Protection from driving rain is difficult.

2.3.10 Solar Chimney

A solar chimney utilises the stack effect, as already described, but here the air is deliberately heated by solar radiation in order to create an exhausting effect (Fig. 2.62).

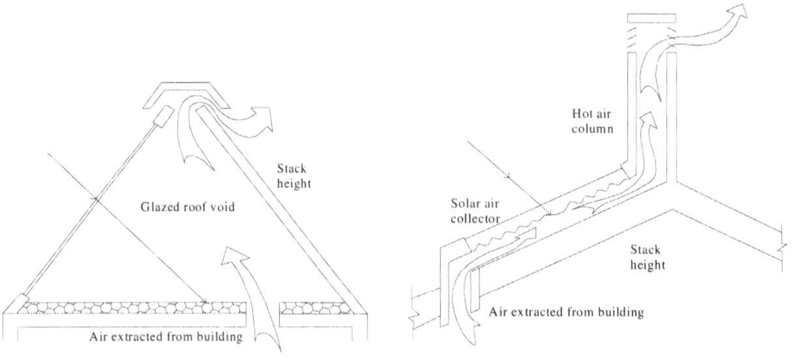

Fig. 2.62: Solar chimneys

One should distinguish between the stack effect ventilation due to heating of the building itself and that due to a solar chimney. In the former case, one tries to keep the increment in the building temperature as small as possible (ventilation is being used for cooling) and hence the stack effect is weak. In the case of a solar chimney, there is no limit to the temperature increment within the chimney, since it is almost isolated from the living space connected to it. The chimney can therefore be designed to maximise the solar gains for maximising the ventilation effects. The parameters affecting the ventilation rates are:

- height between inlet and outlet
- cross-sectional area of the inlet and the outlet
- geometrical construction of the solar absorbing plate
- inclination angle

The use of solar chimneys is advisable for regions, where very low wind speeds exist.

This system is a combined system for both the winter heating and summer cooling quite similar to Trombe Wall discussed earlier. Figure 2.63 shows implementation of the concept in a building.

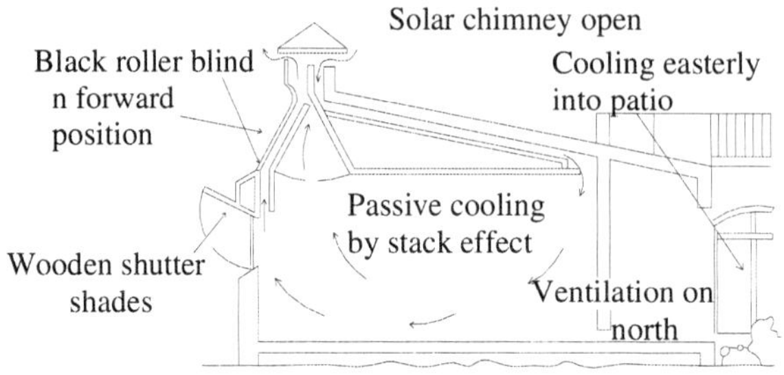

Fig. 2.63: Building with a solar chimney

On a summer day, when the interior is overheated, the black roller blind is drawn over the internal reflector panels behind the tilted windows. The stack effect is increased by opening the ventilators in the solar chimney and north façade windows to promote the draft.

2.3.11 Courtyard effect

The principle of the courtyard effect is shown in Figs. 2.64(a) and 2.64(b).

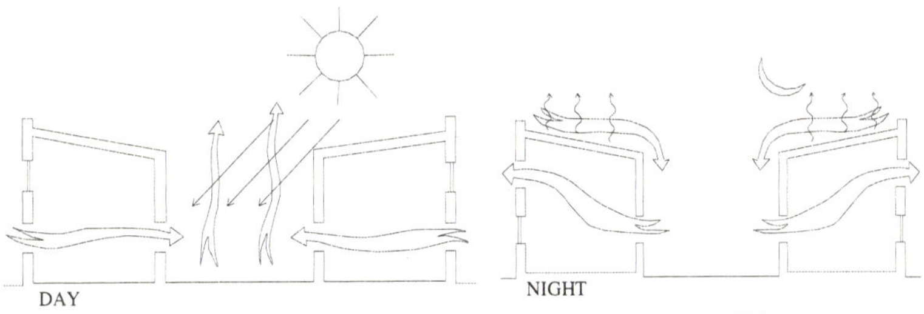

(a) **(b)**

Fig. 2.64: Courtyard effect in day and night

Due to the incident solar radiation in the courtyard, the air in the courtyard becomes warmer and rises up. To replace it, cool air from the ground level flows through the louvered openings of the room, thus producing the airflow.

During the night, the process is reversed. As the warm roof surface gets cooled by convection and radiation, a stage is reached, when its surface temperature equals the dry bulb temperature of the ambient air. Further cooling by radiation continues, as the night sky temperature is lower than the ambient temperature. If the net heat exchange reduces the roof surface temperature to the wet bulb temperature of the surrounding air, condensation of the atmospheric moisture takes place on the roof and the heat gained due to condensation limits further cooling. If the roof surfaces are sloped towards an internal courtyard, the cooled air sinks into the court and enters the living spaces through the low level openings and leaves through higher level openings. To make it work efficiently, a parapet wall is to be raised around the roof to prevent air mixing.

This concept can very well be applied in a warm and humid climate. It also should be made certain that the courtyard gets adequate radiation to produce a draft through the interior. Temperature depressions of 4-7^{0}C below ambient are obtainable during clear night sky conditions. The problem, however, remains to ventilate the roof adequately with this cool air.

An airflow inside the room can be maintained by a dual courtyard concept, where one courtyard is kept cool by shady trees/vegetation and another courtyard to sun as shown in Fig. 2.65.

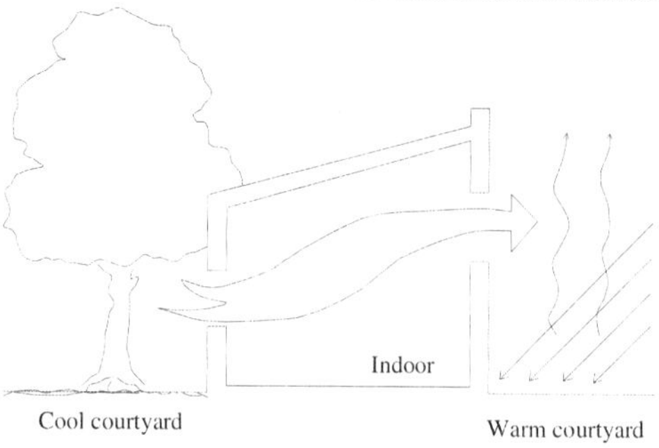

Fig. 2.65: Courtyard effect (night)

The efficiency can be increased by providing an evaporative cooling system in the cool courtyard, as shown in Fig. 2.66.

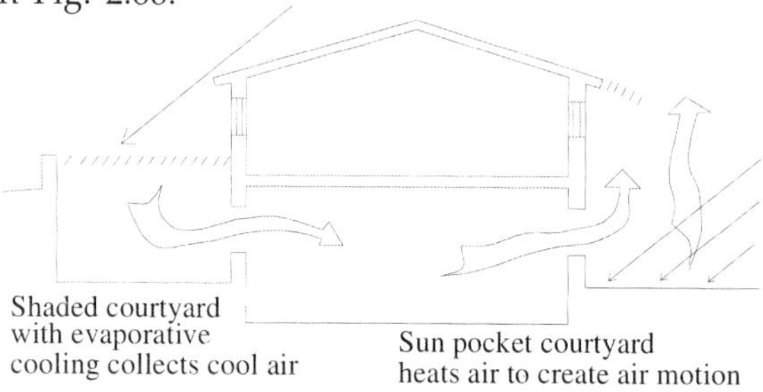

Fig. 2.66: Courtyard effect with evaporative cooling

When the courtyard is small and does not get enough radiation during the daytime, it acts as shown in Fig. 2.67.

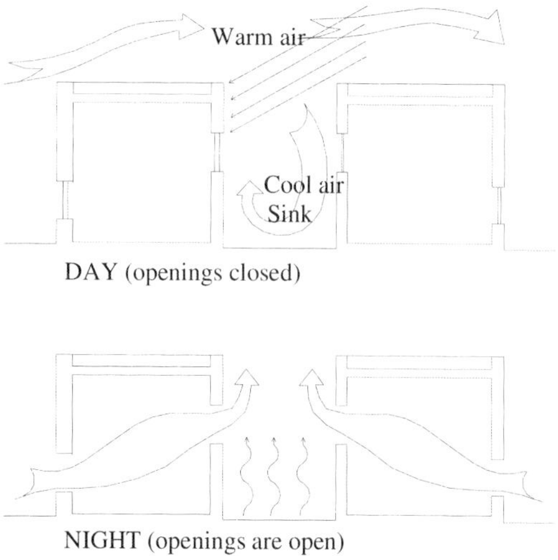

Fig. 2.67: Ventilation mechanism in small courtyards

This system can work very effectively in hot and dry climates, where daytime ventilation is undesirable, as it brings heat inside and night time air temperature is lower and allows us to ventilate the building. Also, the night sky is clear for the radiative cooling of the courtyard surfaces.

Limitations

- When the courtyard is allowed to receive intense solar radiation much heat is conducted and radiated into the rooms as against the induced draft of air, which may be problematic.
- The intense solar radiation in the courtyard also produces immense glare indoors.

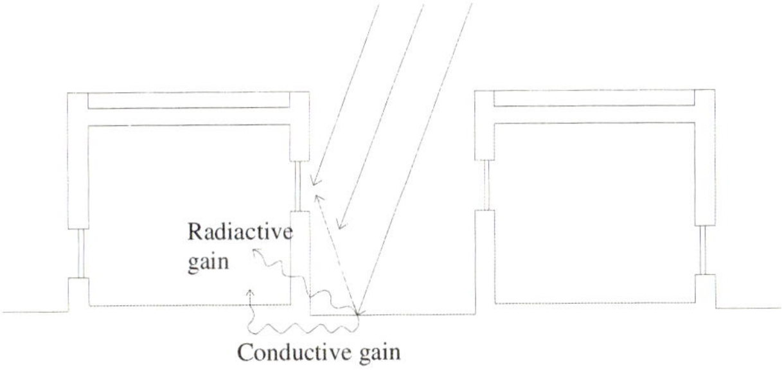

Fig. 2.68: Improperly designed courtyards can bring in undue reflected and transmitted solar heat

The best way is to keep the courtyard shaded and only partially open to sky.

2.3.12 Air vent

A typical vent is a hole cut in the apex of a domed or cylindrical roof (Fig. 2.69). Openings in the protective cap over the vent direct wind across it. When air flows over a curved surface, its velocity increases resulting in lowering of the pressure at the apex of the curved roof, thereby, inducing the hot air under the roof to flow out through the vent. In this way, air is kept circulating through the room under the roof. Air vents are usually placed over living rooms, often with a pool of water directly under the vent to cool the air, which is moving up to the vent, by evaporation.

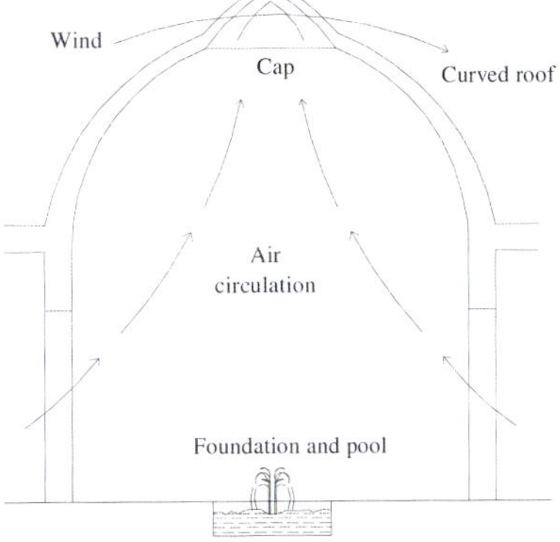

Fig. 2.69: Air vent

Air vents are employed in areas, where dusty winds make wind towers impractical. It works well both in hot and dry zones and warm and humid zones unlike a wind tower, which works only in hot and dry zones. It is most suited for single units, just above frequently used livable space.

Limitations

- The special form of domes restricts its usage to the top floor only
- Acoustic concentration often occurs in this type of ceiling.

2.4 PASSIVE CONCEPTS AND ECBC

Although there is no direct provision in the Energy Conservation Building Code for giving credit or conditions for use of passive concepts, however, through use of passive concepts, relaxation in requirements for other building components can be enjoyed by the building designer/owner. For example use of good shading devices relaxes the requirements for properties of glazing. It may be noted that maximum credit of passive systems can only be taken by showing reduction of overall energy consumption in a building through energy simulation of whole building.

SUMMARY

Numerous design options are available for making the buildings comfortable by using passive design concepts. Care should be taken while selecting most appropriate passive concept that matches with the climatic conditions and building usage. Use of such passive concepts in any building can be very helpful in eliminating or reducing the energy consumption through use of active devices for heating or cooling of buildings. Ventilation devices can also be eliminated by use of passive ventilation techniques as described in this chapter. In modern buildings, though, there are several constraints that do not allow designers to use many of the passive concepts described in this chapter, non-availability of land being most crucial of these constraints. However, wherever possible, these concepts should be accommodated to the best possible extent in building design for reducing dependence of active systems that require energy consumption in building.

3

Energy in Buildings

Historically, focus has been on understanding energy use during the operational period of the building (use phase). With this approach, an important factor had been neglected; the embodied energy of construction materials.

The initial embodied energy in buildings represents the non-renewable energy consumed in the acquisition of raw materials, their processing, manufacturing, transportation to site and construction.

The recurring embodied energy in buildings represents the non-renewable energy consumed to maintain, repair, restore, refurbish or replace materials, components or systems during the life of the building.

Material and product selection can influence heating and cooling energy, e.g. through insulation, mass and window design and specifications. Design changes to reduce operational energy can result in increased material usage, and hence the embodied energy. Implicit in the measure of embodied energy are the associated environmental implications of resource depletion, greenhouse gases and environmental degradation.

As a rule of thumb, embodied energy is a reasonable indicator of the overall environmental impact of building materials. Therefore, there is a need to adopt an integrated approach to study the impact of both Operational and Embodied Energy of the building/components.

Typically, embodied energy is measured as a quantity of non-renewable energy per unit of building material, component or system. For example, it may be expressed as mega joules (MJ) or giga joules (GJ) per unit of weight (kg or ton) or area (square meter). The embodied energy per unit mass of materials used in building varies enormously, from about two giga joules per ton for concrete to hundreds of giga joules per ton for aluminium (refer Chart 01). But using these values alone to determine preferred materials is inappropriate because of the differing lifetimes of materials, differing quantities required to perform the same task and different design requirements.

Embodied energy is the energy consumed by all of the processes associated with the construction of a building, from the acquisition of natural resources to product delivery. This includes the mining and manufacturing of materials and equipment, the transport of the materials and the administrative functions. Embodied energy is a significant component of the lifecycle impact of a building.

'While there is a growing awareness of the need to reduce operating energy consumption in buildings, reflected through numerous rating tools and planning requirements, embodied energy has typically been considered as too difficult or too abstract to consider. However, the future will impact significantly on various mainstream groups including valuers, architects, banks and lenders, investors and real estate agents.

Every building is a complex combination of many processed materials, each of which contributes to the building's total embodied energy. Renovation and maintenance also add to the embodied energy over a building's life.

It was thought until recently that the embodied energy content of a building was small compared to the energy used in operating the building over its life. Most efforts were therefore put into reducing operating energy by improving the energy efficiency of the building envelope. Research has shown that this is not always the case. Embodied energy can be the equivalent of many years of operational energy.

Choices of materials and construction methods can significantly change the amount of energy embodied in the structure of a building.

True low energy building design will consider this important aspect and take a broader life cycle approach to energy assessment. Merely looking at the energy used to operate the building is not really acceptable.

Operational energy consumption is dependent on the occupants. Embodied energy is not occupant dependant- the energy is built into the materials.

Embodied energy content is incurred once (apart from maintenance and renovation) whereas operational energy accumulates over time and can be influenced throughout the life of the building.

Embodied building content varies greatly with different construction types.

Whereas the energy used in operating of a building can be readily measured, the embodied energy contained in the structure is difficult to assess. This energy in use is often hidden and can be fully quantified through a complete Life Cycle assessment (LCA).

It also depends on where 'boundaries' are drawn in the assessment process. For example, whether to include:

(a) The energy used to transport the materials and workers to the building site.

(b) Just the materials for the construction of the building shell or all materials used to complete the building such as bathroom and kitchen fittings, driveways, outdoors paving, etc.

(c) The upstream energy input in making the materials (such as factory/office lighting, the energy used in making and maintaining the machines that make the materials, etc.).

Gross Energy Requirement (GER) is a measure of the true embodied energy of a material, which would ideally include all of the above and more. In practice this is usually impractical to measure.

Process Energy Requirement (PER) is a measure of the energy directly related to the manufacture of the material, this is simpler to quantify. Consequently, most figures quoted for embodied energy are based on the PER. This would include the energy used in transporting the raw materials to the factory but not energy used to transport the final product to the building site.

In general, PER accounts for 5 to 80 % of GER. Even within this narrower definition, arriving at a single figure for a material is impractical as it depends on:

Efficiency of the individual manufacturing process.

The fuel used in manufacturing of the materials.

The distances materials are transported.

The amount of recycled product used, etc.

Each of these factors varies according to product, process, manufacturing and application. They also vary depending on how the embodied energy has been assessed.

Materials with the lowest embodied energy intensities, such as concrete, bricks and timber, are usually consumed in large quantities. Materials with high energy content such as stainless steel are often used in much smaller amounts. As a result, the greatest amount of embodied energy in a building can be either from low embodied energy materials such as concrete or high-embodied energy materials such as steel.

For most people it is more useful to think in terms of building components and assemblies rather than individual materials. For examples, a brick veneer wall will contain bricks, mortar, tiles, timber, plasterboard and insulation.

Comparing the energy content per square meter of construction is easier for designers than looking at the energy content of all the individual materials used.

There are two forms of embodied energy in buildings:

- Initial embodied energy; and
- Recurring embodied energy

The initial embodied energy in buildings represents the non-renewable energy consumed in the acquisition of raw materials, their processing, manufacturing, transportation to site and construction. This initial embodied energy has two components:

- Direct energy is the energy used to transport building products to the sites, and then to construct the building.
- Indirect energy is the energy used to acquire, process and manufacture the building materials, including any transportation related to these activities.

The recurring embodied energy in buildings represents the non-renewable energy consumed to maintain, repair, restore, refurbish or replace materials, components or systems during the life of the building.

As buildings become more energy-efficient, the ratio of embodied energy to lifetime consumption increases. Clearly, for buildings claiming to be "zero-energy" or "autonomous", the energy used in construction and final disposal takes on a new significance.

Typically, embodied energy is measured as a quantity of non-renewable energy per unit of building material, component or system. For example, it may be expressed as Mega Joules (MJ) or Giga Joules (GJ) per unit of weight (kg or ton) or area (square meter).

Implicit in the measure of embodied energy are the associated environmental implications of resource depletion, greenhouse gases, environmental degradation and reduction of biodiversity. As a rule of thumb, embodied energy is a reasonable indicator of the overall environmental impact of building materials, assemblies or systems. However, it must be carefully weighed against performance and durability since these may have a mitigating or compensatory effect on the initial environmental impacts associated with embodied energy.

The amount of embodied energy in buildings varies considerably. Initial embodied energy consumption depends on the nature of the building, the materials used and the source of these materials (this is why data for a building material in another country). The recurring embodied energy is related to the durability of the building materials, components and systems installed in the building, how well these are maintained and the life of the building (the longer the building survives, the greater the expected recurring energy consumption.

Research carried out by the Cole and Keman(1) using a model based on Canadian construction of a generic 4620 m^2 (50,000 ft^2) three storey office building with underground parking, considered three different construction systems (wood, steel and concrete) and yielded the following results for average total initial embodied energy. (Note: Data were averaged for the three construction systems as the overall differences between the building types were not significant).

The building envelope, structure and services contribute fairly equally and account for about three-quarters of total initial embodied energy. The finishes, which represent only 13% of the embodied energy initially, typically account for the highest increase in recurring embodied energy.

The quantification of embodied energy for any particular material is an inexact science, requiring a "long view" look at the entire manufacturing and utilization process and filled with a large number of potentially significant variables.

Consequently, the complexity of embodied energy calculations is frustrating even for scientists and it is easy for the individual homeowner, builder, designer or government specifier to become discouraged at the difficulty of obtaining accurate figures. Fortunately, precise figures are not absolutely necessary for informed decisions on which building materials to use in order to lower the embodied energy in a structure. Builders need to only recognize the potential differences in relative embodied energy to make wise material and system choices.

3.1 INTRODUCTION

Very often, one discusses the energy consumption in buildings only during its operation i.e. for its lighting, heating and cooling and ventilation etc. This seems logical because in un-insulated buildings the operational energy demand (for air-conditioned buildings) far exceeds the energy needed to construct a building, including the energy in manufacturing of the materials and procuring them. The conversion of resources in a building takes many dimensions and is done over a broad time frame. It begins when a building is conceived and does not end until the building has been retired and its materials and site have been returned to the resource bank. In their use of resources, these building strategies are different from development purposes for industry and transportation. Of the three major sectors of energy economy (industry, transportation and building), buildings require the largest investments in all countries.

The Indian construction industry is a very fast growing sector accounting for 25% of gross domestic product (GDP). With an employment potential of over 30 million people, this sector assumes vital importance in the growth of Indian economy. With increasing construction activity, the use of building materials has also increased. The consumption of key building materials like cement, steel, brick and timber has increased by nearly forty percent or more in the last five years (Fig. 3.1), where as the use of plastics has shown tremendous increase of ten times more in the ten twelve years and the consumption is likely to increase much more rapidly.

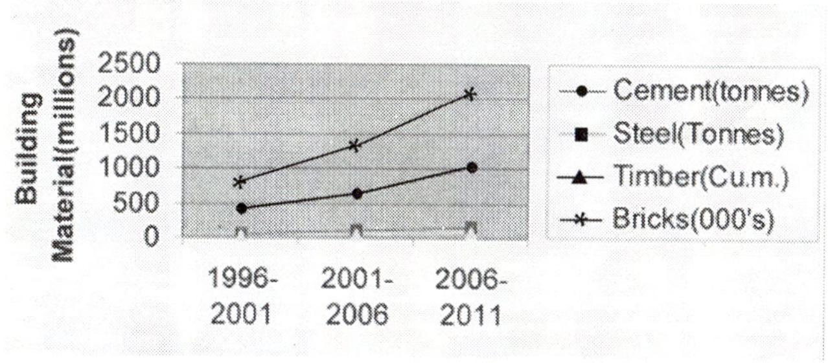

Figure 3.1: Consumption of building materials in India

Since all these materials are energy intensive, their increasing use also results in increasing energy consumption (Fig. 3.2) and the environmental emissions given in Fig. 3.3.

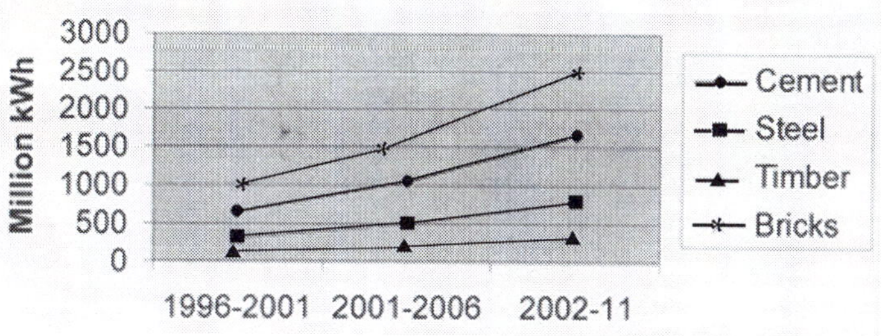

Figure 3.2: Embodied Energy in building materials

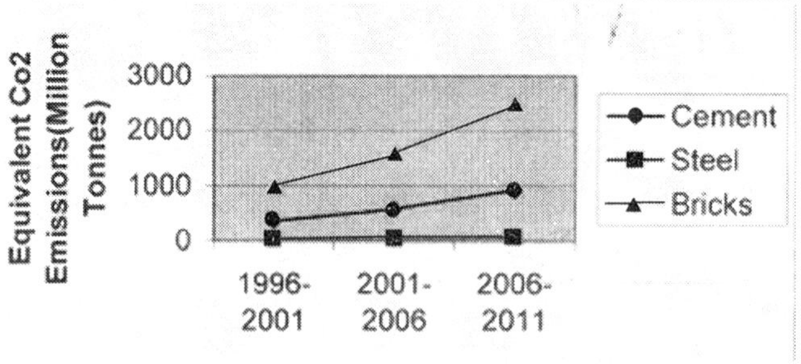

Figure 3.3: Equivalent greenhouse emission due to use of building materials in India

Plastic is another construction material, which is gradually replacing traditional materials like steel, wood and cement concrete. The past and future demand projections of plastic consumption alongwith the embodied energy and equivalent CO_2 emissions are given in Table 3.1. It is to be noted that out of this demand of plastics, nearly 20% is consumed for various building applications.

Table 3.1 : Past and projected plastic consumption in India with the embodied energy and Carbon-dioxide emissions

Year	Consumption (million tonnes)	Embodied Energy (million kWh)	CO_2 Emissions (million tonnes)
1985	0.45	9.21	9.0
1990	0.75	15.3	1.5
1995	1.71	35.0	3.42
1996	1.88	38.5	3.76
Estimates 2002	4.5	92.1	9.0
2007	8.0	163.8	16.0

Another factor that needs to be considered in the Indian context is the growing number of households in the higher income group. It is estimated that middle to high increase group households will be around 40 to 50% of the total households in the year 2007. This is evident from the increasing electricity consumption in the country, which will be more than 35% of total electricity consumption in the country. The reason is more and more of air conditioning used by the people. The two important facts about the sustainability in buildings, therefore, are (1) the materials that are used in the construction of buildings and the associated: embodied energy and the greenhouse gas emissions and (2) the operational energy that is used for heating and cooling of buildings and also the associated carbon-di-oxide emissions.

3.2 BUILDING MATERIALS AND ENVIRONMENTAL CONCERNS

Building materials used for construction and maintenance of a building consume energy at different stages. The most important of these stages from the point of view of energy are:

- Use and operations
- Manufacturing
- Raw material acquisition, transportation and preparation
- Disposal and reuse.

In the estimation of embodied energy, one usually considers the manufacturing at the production stage. For many materials, however, the use phase of the product is very significant because of the relatively long lifetime over which the building materials are in use. Following the stage of raw material extraction and preparation phase, the disposal stage can be very important because of the volume of materials that buildings embody.

In the following section, we empirically define various steps in assessing the environmental impact of the building materials.

3.2.1 The first three steps: the Use Phase

Two of the most significant sources of environmental impact from building materials are energy use in the building and possible impacts on occupants' health. Considerations of impacts in the use phase depend not only on the material in question, but also on the application for the material.

Step 1-Energy use: will the material in question (in the relevant application) have a measurable impact on building energy use? If not, proceed to step 2.

If, yes (as for materials such as glazing, insulation, mechanical systems), avoids options that do not minimize energy use. Also take care to design the application to minimize energy use. For materials that can be used in an energy-efficient manner only with the addition of other components, the impact of including those additional components must be factored in. Examples include glazing systems that require exterior shading systems for efficiency, and light-gauge steel framing that requires form sheathing to prevent thermal bridging.

Step 2-Occupants' health : Will the products in this application affect the health of building occupants? If not, proceed to Step 3.

If, yes (interior furnishings, interior finishes, mechanical systems), avoid materials that are likely to adversely affect occupants' health and design systems to minimize any possible adverse effects when sources of indoor pollution cannot be avoided.

Step 3 -Durability and maintenance: Are products in this application likely to need replacement, special treatment, or repair multiple times during the life of the structure? If not, proceed to step 4.

If, yes (roofing, coating, sealants), avoid products with short expected life spans (Unless they are made from low-impact, renewable materials and are easily recycled, or products that require frequent, high impact maintenance procedures. Also, design the structure for flexibility so that materials that become obsolete before they wear out (such as wiring) can be replaced with minimal disruption and cost.

Next Step: Manufacturing

The remaining steps pertain less to the application (how a material or product is used) and more to the material itself. They require knowledge of the raw materials that go into each product.

Step 4 -Hazardous by-products: Are significant toxic or hazardous intermediaries or by-products created during manufacture, and if so, how significant is the risk of their release to the environment or risk of hazard to worker's health? If these are not significant, proceed to step 5.

Where toxic by-products are either generated in large quantities or in small but uncontrolled quantities (smelting of zinc, production of petrochemicals), the building material in question should be avoided if possible, or sourced from a company with strong environmental standards.

Step 5 -Energy use: How energy intensive is the manufacturing process? If not very intensive, proceed to step 6.

If, the manufacture of a building material is very energy-intensive compared to the alternatives (aluminium, plastics), its use should be minimized. It is not the energy use itself that is of concern, however, but the pollution from its generation and use: industries using clean-burning or renewable energy sources have lower burdens than those relying on coal or petroleum.

Step 6-Waste from manufacturing: How much solid waste is generated in the manufacturing process? If not much relative to the quantity of product manufactured, proceed to step 7.

If, significant amounts of solid waste are generated that are not readily usable for other purposes (tailings from mining of copper and other metals), seek alternative materials, or material from companies with progressive recycling programs.

Further Steps: Raw Materials

Step 7 -Resources limitations: Are any of the component materials from rare or endangered resources? If not, proceed to step 8.

If, yes (endangered or threatened tree species), avoid these products, unless they can be sourced from recycled material.

Step 8 -Impacts of resource extraction: Are there significant ecological impacts from the process of mining or harvesting the raw materials? If not, proceed to step 9.

If, yes (damage to rainforests from bauxite mining for aluminium, or from certain timber harvesting practices), seek suppliers of material from recycled stock, or those with credible third-party verification of environmentally sound harvesting methods.

Step 9 -Transportation: Are the primary raw materials located a great distance from your site? If not, proceed to step 10.

If, yes (Italian marble, tropical timber, New Zealand wool), seek appropriate alternative material from more local sources.

Final Steps: Disposal or Reuse?

Step 10 -Demolition waste; can the material be easily separated out for reuse or recycling after its useful life in the structure is over? If so, proceed to step 11.

While most materials that are used in large quantities in building construction (steel, concrete) can be atleast partially recycled, others are less recyclable and may become a disposal problem in the future. Examples include products that combine different materials (such as fibreglass composites) or that undergo a fundamental chemical change during manufacture (thermo set plastics such as polyurethane foams). Consider the future recyclability of products chosen.

Step 11-Hazardous materials from demolition: Will the material become a toxic hazardous waste problem after the end of its useful life? If not, proceed to step 12.

If, yes (preservative-treated wood), seek alternative products or construction systems that require less of the material in question.

Step 12 -Review the results: Go over any concerns that have been raised about the products under consideration, and look for other life-cycle impacts that might be specific to a particular material.

For example, with drywall and spray-in open-cell polyurethane foam insulation, waste generated at the job site is a potential problem that should be considered. A flow chart of these various steps for assessment is given in Fig. 3.4.

Selecting materials with the best environmental life cycle and performance is not the only factor in designing green buildings in most cases; it is not even the most important. Nevertheless, it is an area where specifications provided by designers can sometimes make a big difference in the overall environmental impact of a building for relatively little cost. It is also an area where building designers can influence manufacturing industries to improve their processes.

1. Energy Use	Little impact on energy use in building	
2. Occupants' Health	Potential (minor) off-gassing of formaldehyde from binder	Specify OSB with MDI Binder
3. Durability	Good durability if properly installed	
4. Hazardous By-Products	Potential air pollutants from manufacturing especially from dryers	Determine that plant is meeting or exceeding air emission standards
5. Energy Intensity	Fairly efficient manufacturing process	
6. Process Waste	Potentially air pollutants from manufacturing especialy from dryers	
7. Resource Limitation	Minimal resource impacts produced from small-diameter, low-quality trees	
8. Resource Extraction	Potentially significant impacts from logging if clearcutting on slopes with unstable soils	Determine the wood is from well managed forests
9. Transportation	OSB plants distributed fairly widely, so transportation is reasonable	
10. Recyclability	Limited possibilities for recycling OB from existing buildings	
11. Hazardous Demolition	Material not hazardous	
12. Review Results	No other significant problems	

Figure 3.4 : Flow chart for assessing environmental impact of building materials

3.3 ENERGY IN BUILDING CONSTRUCTION

There is an enormous variation in what is required to build buildings, what is required to produce the materials for buildings, what the relationship is between capital energy – that is, the energy to build the buildings and the operational energy, the energy to permit them to serve their intended purposes throughout their useful lifetimes. In order to understand these variations and to go to the next step, which is to improve the efficiency of energy use throughout the entire building sector, the nature of the building process and the way in which energy is embodied in fabrication and erection of components of the building must be given quantitative value.

The building industry is a complex amalgam of material producers, manufacturers, designers and assemblers. It includes the mining and lumbering sectors as well as the steel mills, sawmills, aluminium smelters, and cement factories. It includes glass factories, curtain-wall manufacturers, and millwork plants. It includes the electrical and plumbing jobbers, contractors, architects and engineers, building tradesmen, and subcontractors. Its product is an assembly of thousands of parts produced by a wide range of industries and brought to the job-site or to the assembly plant, shaped to fit compatibly with all of its neighbouring products, and finally assembled into a building, no two of which are identical. The number of different skills and procedures that are called into play is enormous. As a result, it is a difficult process to understand; and after one understands it, it can be seen that it is a formidable one to change.

In most industrially developed countries bricks are produced by sophisticated technology using fully mechanised and automated systems right from the winning of clay to the burning of bricks in oil-fired tunnel kilns. Manufacturers of the bricks in a fully mechanised plant requires much more energy than in the manual methods, where fuel is consumed only in the burning process. The production of several other building materials like cement, lime, plastic etc., consumes higher rate of energy in more sophisticated technological processes than in small-scale semi-mechanised or manual methods of production. With a view to collecting information on energy consumption in the production techniques used in India, a questionnaire was sent out to building materials manufacturers. At the same time data were also collected from literature to supplement the information obtained through the questionnaire survey.

The energy consumption computed through the two sources, i.e. questionnaire and literature, was compared. It was found that there was only a slight variation in the energy figures computed from literature and those obtained directly from manufacturers. The mean energy costs of some of the important materials are given in Table 3.2. Human energy consumed in the processes has been excluded from the scope of this study.

Table 3.2: Energy costs of various building materials in India

Materials	*Basis*	*Energy (k/cal) x 10^3*
Cement	Kg	1.93
Burnt clay bricks	1000	1020.6
Surkhi	Kg	0.330
Quick lime	Kg	1.51
Mild steel	Kg	6.3
PVC	Kg	27.75
Sheet glass	Sq.m	63.8
L.D.Polyethylene	Kg	5.2
Burnt clay roofing tiles	1000 Nos.	1060
Sand-lime bricks	1000 Nos.	665.0
Wood particle board	Kg	0.74
Linoleum	Sq.m	39.8
Sanitary ware	kg	7.80
Stoneware pipes	kg	5.07
Aluminium	Kg	34.3
Clay flyash bricks	1000 Nos.	553.0
Bloated clay aggregate	Kg	1.27
Gypsum (calcined)	kg	0.3613
Crushed aggregate	Kg	0.0516

The energy computations in some of newly developed processes and techniques such as semi-mechanised brick making, use of fly-ash in brick making, use of rice husk in brick making and use-of-coal washery rejects in brick making have been given in Table 3.2. In addition some other energy saving processes in building materials have been briefly mentioned in Table 3.3.

Table 3.3: Energy savings in brick making

S.No.	*Process Description*	*Coal saving (%)*
1.	Heat draught kiln in brick firing	15-20
2.	Use of flyash in making bricks	10-30
3.	Use of coal washery rejects in making bricks	25-75
4.	Use of rice husk in firing bricks	20-25

Table 3.4: Energy saving processes in building materials

S. No.	*Process*	*Use of industrial wastes*	*Approximate (%) savings in energy*
1.	Portland-Pozzolana and Portland blast furnace slag cement	Flyash, Mining wastes, blast furnace slag	15-20
2.	Lima-Pozzolana mixtures	Lime kiln rejects industrial ashes	30-40
3.	Lime Rice-husk-ash- Pozzolana	Rice-husk-ash or Rice husk	30-40
4.	Lime-sludge, Rice-husk Pozzolana	Rice-husk-ash or Rice husk	40-50
5.	Sand-flyash bricks	Flyash, Mining wastes	30-50
6.	Masonry cement	Mining, mineral wastes, lime sludges	10-20
7.	Cement-concrete tiles	Mining, mineral wastes	10-15

On the basis of energy consumption for various materials, the energy consumption of several types of building components was also calculated and data are presented in Tables 3.5 to 3.9. However, the energy consumed in transport to the site has not been included in these figures as for obvious reasons; transport energy costs vary considerably from place to place.

The data gives an idea about the type of construction to be preferred with a view to savings in energy. Table 3.5 shows various mortar mixes, 1:6 cement-sand mortar seems to be the cheapest, while 1:2 lime surkhi to be the costliest. Even though lime and surkhi are produced mainly in inefficient country kilns in India, the energy input in the manufacture of these materials is much less than in cement. But the quantity of lime required in mortars is always more than that of cement and therefore energy consumption in lime mortar is higher than in 1:6 cement-sand mortar. Surkhi also needs energy for preparation viz. firing and grinding. Hence, it could be recommended that from the energy saving point of view that cement-sand mortar is to be preferred. With the use of improved manufacturing processes for lime and surkhi, the energy costs of lime-pozzolana mortar could be substantially reduced, so that its use could be encouraged.

Table 3.5: Comparative energy economics* of mortar mixes (basis-one cu.m. of wet mortar)

Materials	Cement: 1 Qty.	Sand: 6 Energy (kcal)	Cement 1 Qty.	Lime: 6 Energy (kcal)	Lime : 1 Qty.	Surkhi: 2 Energy (kcal)	Lime 1 Qty.	Surkhi 1	Sand: 1 Energy (kcal)
Cement (tonne)	0.250	4.82×10^5	0.250	4.82×10^5	-	-	-	-	-
Lime (Tonne)	-	-	0.113	1.70×10^5	0.301	4.55×10^5	0.301		4.55×10^5
Sand (cu.m.)	1.07	-	1.07	-	-	-	0.475		-
Surkhi (tonne)	-	-	-	-	1.140	3.74×10^5	0.570		1.87×10^5
Total Energy	-	4.82×10^5	-	6.52×10^5	-	8.29×10^5	-		6.42×10^5
Comparison	-	100	-	135	-	172	-		133

Tables 3.6-3.9 compare energy costs of construction techniques for walling, roofing, partitioning and flooring. It is seen that with the use of brick and cement, the energy cost goes up. RBC roofing compares favourably with RC slab as in this case, bricks are partly replaced by concrete. A close look at Table 3.4 would show that use of new-energy conserving processes in building materials manufacture would also promote exploitation of local waste materials and the saving of cement.

Table 3.6: Comparative energy economics* of walls

(basis-one sq. m. of wall)

Materials	*23 cm thick brick wall plastered on both sides*		*30 cm thick random rubble stone masonry wall plastered on both sides*	
	Quantity (kcal)	*Energy*	*Quantity*	*Energy (kcal)*
Brick Stone (m^3)	112	114×10^5	-	-
Mortar (cement: sand) 1:6 (m^3) (for masonry work	0.057	0.275×10^5	0.11	0.53×10^5
Mortar (cement: sand) 1:6 (m^3) (for plaster work)	0.316	1.52×10^5	0.448	2.16×10^5
Mortar (cement: sand) 1:6 (m^3) Total Energy	-	2.935×10^5	-	2.69×10^5
Comparison		100		92

* not including energy consumed in transportation

Table 3.7: Comparative energy economics for roofing (basis-one sq. m. of partition wall)

Materials	*Reinforced cement concrete slab*		*(3.5 M Span) Reinforced brick Slab*		*Reinforced brick conc.Slab*		*Cored units slab*		*Channel units slab*	
	Qty.	*Energy (kcal)*	*Qty.*	*Energy (kcal)*	*Qty.*	*Energy (kcal)*	*Qty.*	*Energy (kcal)*	*Qty.*	*Energy (kcal)*
Cement (bags)	0.81	78×10^3	0.57	55×10^3	0.53	51.1×10^3	0.61	58×10^3	0.46	5.3×10^3
Sand (m^3)	0.06		0.05		0.04		0.04		0.03	
Coarse Agg. (m^3)	0.10	10.32×10^3		7.23×10^3	0.06	6.2×10^3	0.08	8.25×10^3	0.06	6.18×10^3
Bricks (Nos)			66	67.3×10^3	26	27.4×10^3				
Steel (kg.)	5.736	36.10×10^3	4..50	28.4×10^3	5.04	31.8×10^3	5.47	34.5×10^3	5.35	33.7×10^3
Total energy		124.42×10^3	150.7×10^3	150.7×10^3		116.5×10^3		100.7×10^3		85.18×10^3
Comparison		100		121		94		81		68

Table 3.8: Comparative energy economics* of flooring (basis-10 sq. m. of floor area)

Materials	*40 cm thick RCC 1:2:4 flooring with a neat coat of cement*		*Alternatives 40 mm thick marble chips flooring with a underlayer of 31 mm thick PCC 1:2:4 and top layer of 9 mm thick with marble chips*	
	Quantity	*Energy (kcal)*	*Quantity*	*Energy (kcal)*
Cement (bags)	30	290x10^3	3.20	30.80 x10^3
Sand (m^3)	0.178		0.14	
Coarse Aggregate (m^3)	0.356	36.7 x10^3	0.28	28.8 x10^3
Marble chips (m^3)			140	7.23 x10^3
Marble powder (m^3)			0.012	1.55 x10^3
Total energy		326.7x 10^3		345.58 x10^3
Comparison		100		106

Table 3.9 : Comparative energy economics of partition walls basis-one sq. m. of partition wall

Materials	11.5 cm thick brick wall in cem. Mortar: 1:6 and plastered on both sides with cem. Mortar : 1:6		10 cm thick hollow concrete block wall in composite mortar 1:2:9 and plastered on both faces with 1:16 mortar		10 cm thick foam concrete block wall in composite mortar 1:2:9 and plastered on both faces with 1:2:9 mortar		Timber frame with plywood panels		10 cm thick precast stone masonry block wall in the cem. Mortar 1:6 and plastered on both sides with cem. Mortar 1:6	
	Qty.	Energy (kcal)	Qty.	Energy (kcal)	Qty.	Energy (kcal)	Qty.	Energy (kcal)	Qty.	Energy (kcal)
Cement (bags)	0.47	45.4x 10^3	0.42	40.5x10^3	0.40	38.6x10^3			0.385	37.20x10^3
Sand (m^3)	0.07		0.06		0.036				0.34	
Coarse Agg. (m^3)			0.07	7.23x10^3					0.05	5.15x10^3
Hydrated lime (m^3)			0.005	8.25x10^3	0.005	8.25x10^3				
Stone (m^3)									0.022	
Timber (dm^2)							4.20	0.086x10^3		
Bricks (Nos.)	56	57x10^3					1.05	4.94x10^3		
Sheet covering (m^2) plywood							1.05	4.85x10^3		
Total energy		102.4x10^3		55.98x10^3		46.95x10^3		4.94x10^3		42.35x10^3
Comparison		100		55		46		4.8		41

In one of the studies at the University of Essen, Germany, the distribution of cumulative energy demand over the buildings lifetime shows that the construction materials constitute about 87% of the total energy demand, construction and transport 11% and dismantling recycling about 2% (Fig. 3.5)

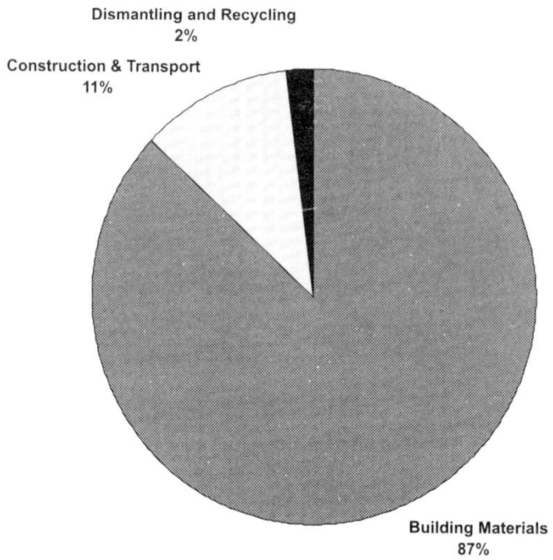

Fig. 3.5 : Share of different phases of life cycle in a embodied energy

Most of the embodied energy is consumed in the walls, floors, foundation and a basement (Fig. 3.6)

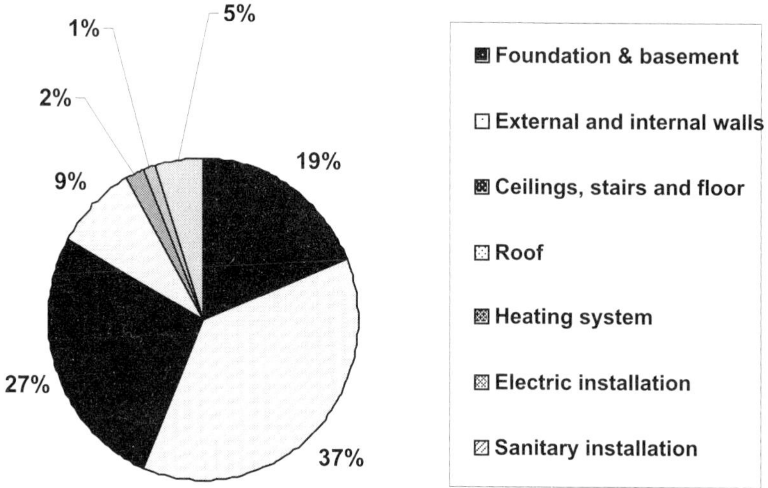

Fig. 3.6 : Share of different Components in total embodied energy

The energy consumed in various building components and activities may however differ from building to building and place to place.

The embodied energy calculations require a detailed inventory of all the materials used in the construction starting from their procurement to their placement. Based on detailed energy analysis, the energy consumed in producing a unit of material is calculated. These are given in Table 3.10 for various construction materials. For some materials, the associated emissions released in the production process are also given. Using the material, the quantities of works and the required materials are calculated for various building components such as:

- Foundation
- Floor
- Walls
- Roof
- Doors and windows

The various items, their quantities and the total embodied energy for each of these items are given in Table 3.11. It is seen that the earth berm contributes about 10% of the total embodied energy. The embodied energy for the case, when the walls and roof are insulated, is equivalent to 31.25 terra Joules (8.68 million kWh). The operational energy however shows reverse trend, being the maximum for normal construction (323 MWh (231 kWh/m^2a). The calculations correspond to city of Ahmedabad in the hot and dry zone.

3.4 BUILDING ENERGY USE

The most significant energy consumption in building use is that for heating and cooling of buildings. This energy consumption depends upon the climatic conditions as well as for the type of building. In most developing countries, the energy consumption is excessively high. The total specific energy consumption may range from 280 kWh/m2a to about 400 kWh/m2a. Before the year 1973, the year of energy crisis all over the world, the energy consumption in developed countries was also very high i.e. of the order of 300 kWh/m2a. A large amount of efforts have been made to reduce this energy consumption to 70 kWh/m2a or even less (Fig. 3.5), through a series of actions, which include building codes and mandatory implementation.

Table 3.10: Embodied energy and emissions for building materials

EMBODIED ENERGY AND EMIISIONS FOR BUILDING MATERIALS

Name	Specific CEA	CO_2(g/kg)	CO	No_x	SO_2	CH_4	NMVOC	Dust
Primary Aluminum	204 MJ/Kg	11687	26.683	24.769	15.139	19.907	2.538	1.754
Secondary Aluminum	15.7 MJ/Kg	860	0.834	1.496	625	2.063	0.127	0.096
Reinforce Steel	16.3 MJ/Kg	1500	1.15	2.9	8.15	6.6	0.21	0.5
Cotton	17.6 MJ/Kg							
Concrete	0.7 MJ/Kg	123	0.0037	0.318	0.084	0.104	0.011	0.011
Prefab. concrete	2.3 MJ/kg	242	0.147	0.457	0.744	0.677	0.036	0.055
Burnt lime	4.6 MJ/kg	1059	0.296	0.453	0.303	1	0.022	0.19
Roof tile	4.2 MJ/kg							
Roof tile cement	6.8 MJ/kg							
Insulating plate	9.5 MJ/kg	3836	2.074	15.064	18.304	15.074	11.67	2.461
Paint Cement	0.9 MJ/kg							
Foam concrete	3.6 MJ/kg							
Gypsum	1.5 MJ/kg	87	0.075	0.171	0.044	0.179	0.013	0.009
Gypsum plane	3.5 MJ/kg	155	0.141	0.24	0.051	0.373	0.017	0.013
Glass wall	16.5 MJ/kg	1011	0.705	12.77	1.135	2.599	0.09	0.112
Cavity brick	2.5 MJ/kg							
Wood	12 MJ/kg	80						
Furniture wood	16 MJ/kg	372						
Wood board hard	23 MJ/kg	1180	1.104	2.412	0.861	1.168	0.343	0.132
Drainage pipe	125 MJ/kg	5200	2.9	12.9	11.9	16	11	1.7
Insulate pipe	95.6 MJ/kg	3005						
Cable	77 MJ/kg	2200						
Calcium hydrate	3.5 MJ/kg	804	0.225	0.344	0.231	0.762	0.017	0.144
Sand stone	1 MJ/kg	128	0.061	0.176	0.087	0.128	0.015	0.026
Cast iron	39.4 MJ/kg	446						
Pipe	66 MJ/kg	2.1	1.7	7.6	5.3	5.9	3.8	0.9
Gravel	0.044 MJ/kg	3	0.004	0.024	0.003	0.003	0.003	0.002
Hard burned brick	3.1 MJ/kg	175	0.171	0.42	0.53	0.421	0.019	0.04
Primary copper	44.2 MJ/kg	2749	3.549	9.656	4.723	5.984	1.07	0.71
Secondary copper	30.7 MJ/kg	1413	1.162	2.845	1.017	8.303	0.245	0.205
Mud brick	2.4 MJ/kg							
Light concrete	5 MJ/kg	567	0.299	1.045	1.604	0.996	0.068	0.106
Wall light concrete	1.7 MJ/kg	252	0.112	0.812	0.196	0.201	0.046	0.036
Wall Brick Tile	2.5 MJ/kg	292	0.114	0.42	0.107	0.237	0.014	0.04
Brass	105 MJ/kg							
Polypropylene	73.7 MJ/kg							
Polypropylene	72.5 MJ/kg							
Poly styrene	69.3 MJ/kg	2856	1.788	8.545	8.68	10.385	10	1.17
Pores concrete	4 MJ/kg							
PP Foil moisture barrier	73 MJ/kg							
PV foam plate	95 MJ/kg	4900	3.3	5.8	3	10.3	2.55	0.36
Insulating Paint	3.2 MJ/kg	527	0.16	1.2	0.4	0.5	0.033	0.045
Inner Paint	0.7 MJ/kg	91	0.046	0.14	0.035	0.1	0.013	0.02
Outer Paint	1.4 MJ/kg	250	0.07	0.6	0.17	0.23	0.017	0.022
Gun metal	83.1 MJ/kg	64						
Sand	0.044 MJ/kg	3	0.004	0.024	0.003	0.003	0.003	0.002
Scarf wool	16.4 MJ/kg							
Foam glass	23.5 MJ/kg							
RCC	2.4 MJ/kg	258	0.153	0.586	0.788	0.719	0.032	0.056
Stone wool	20.90 MJ/kg							
Cellulose fibre	3.2 MJ/kg							
Cement high oven	1.7 MJ/kg	233	0.071	0.534	0.157	0.0238	0.019	0.019
Portland cement	4.3 MJ/kg	893	0.184	1.874	0.59	0.754	0.017	0.043

Table 3.11: Embodied energy calculations

EMBODIED ENERGY CALCULATIONS

FOR A BUILDING IN GUJARAT HAVING EARTH BERMS IN SOUTH, EAST AND WEST DIRECTIONS

	Description of Materials	Qty.	Unit	Energy	Per Unit	Total (MJ)
1	Earthwork in filling for berms	3448.10 6.75x 10^6	M^3 Kg	0	MJ/Kg	0
2.	Filling of sand @ 2" under flooring	36.12	M^3	0	MJ/M^3	0
3.	Lean concrete (p.c.c.) with graded aggregate 40 mm nominal size (1:3:6) & fine sand	23.39 42102	M^3 Kg	1.9	MJ/Kg	0.08X 10^6
4.	Dump proof course 40 mm thick cement concrete(1:2:4) coarse sand	141.40 1.3	M Run. M^3	3180	MJ/M^3	4134
5.	Brickwork					
	1st class in foundations and upto plinth with cement mortar (1:4)	113.78	M^3	4482	MJ/M^3	0.5 X 10^6
	1st class in superstructure with cement sand mortar(1:4) including exposed brickwork in first floor	568.95	M^3	4482	MJ/M^3	2.55 X 10^6
6.	Reinforced cement concrete(RCC)(1:2:4)	519.48	M^3	3180	MJ/M^3	1.65 X 10^6
	Roof slabs	202.17	M^3			
	Staircases	3.17	M^3			
	Water storages	31.28	M^3			
	Beams	82.77	M^3			
	Columns	33.59	M^3			
	Chajjas and lintels	9.75	M^3			
	Plinth beam	4.94	M^3			
7.	Steel reinforcement					
	Tor steel reinforcement for RCC	4.7 x 10^5	Kg	43	MJ/Kg	20.21X 10^6
	Mild steel including staircases	75.6	Kg	43	MJ/Kg	3250.8
8.	Wood works for					
	Windows	215.24	M^2	216	MJ/M^2	46491.84
	Doors	50.06	M^2	482	MJ/M^2	24128.92
9.	Flooring					
	Laying p.c.c 1:3:6 over 50 mm sand	77.1 .13 X 10^6	M^3	1.9	MJ/Kg	0.26X10^6
	40mm thick cement concrete flooring 1:2:4,stone agg 20mm nominal size finished with neat cement slurry	1542	M^2	1465	MJ/M^2	2.25X10^6
	Stone flooring –if done	(inc.)				
	Cement plaster skirting upto 150mm	(inc.)				
10	Roofing					
	100mm thick mud phuska of damped brick earth grouted with 1:3 cement mortar	0	M^3	0	MJ/M^3	0
	Gola 1:2:4 in cement conc.	141.2	M	26.84	MJ/M	3789.8
	16mm cement plaster	552.11	M^2	30	MJ/M^2	16563
	Roof Tiling	0	M^2	0	MJ/M^2	0
11	Finishing					
	12mm cement plaster of 1:6 mix	2932.30	M^2	30	MJ/M^2	87969
	6mm cement plaster of 1:3 mix in ceilings	1192.86	M^2	85	MJ/M^2	0.101X10^6
	White washing with lime	2932.30	M^2	1	MJ/M^2	2932.30
	Finishing on outer walls with water proof cement paint	(n.a.)				
	Painting with enamel paint	2932.30	M^2			
		=538	Kg	94	MJ/Kg	50572
12	Glazing (float 4mm single)	1.36	M^3	37550	MJ/M^3	50824
	Grand Total					**27.89X10^6**

3.4.1 Indian scenario

For various Indian climatic zones mentioned in Section 1.3 of this book, the numbers of degree-days for each of these representative locations (with set point temperature of 20°C) are given in Table 3.12.

Energy gains/losses take place through windows, walls, roof and floor and in addition ventilation losses contribute to the energy consumption for heating/cooling especially in an air-conditioned building.

Table 3.12: Degree days for representative locations of different climatic zones in India (set point temperature = 20°C)

	Leh	Shillong	Delhi	Jodhpur	Madras	Bangalore
January	880	326	178	93	140*	0*
February	714	232	90	0	163*	87*
March	620	124	81*	161*	245*	174*
April	432	33	258*	310*	312*	219*
May	313	12	419*	447*	394*	214*
June	183	0	430*	429*	372*	129*
July	81	0	430*	429*	372*	129*
August	81	0	347*	316*	332*	100*
September	207	0	279*	282*	290*	100*
October	415	84	183*	236*	251*	100*
November	582	201	0	78*	174*	51*
December	766	298	133	421	143*	0

* Cooling Degree days

In addition to building design and construction details, the energy consumption in a building is influenced by weather parameters such as ambient temperature, sky conditions, rainfall, solar radiation etc. However, out of these parameters ambient temperature and solar radiation are most important. The evaluation of solar radiation on building facades has been the subject of considerable scientific and practical work. However, it is possible now to predict the amount of solar radiation incident on various facades with reasonable accuracy. Only thermal simulation programs can accurately evaluate the effect of energy consumption in buildings.

3.4.2 Energy saving potential in buildings

Energy saving in buildings can be achieved through efficient lighting, careful design of building envelope and using solar energy for water heating.

In an air-conditioned building, the cooling loads are excessively high. This also leads to higher energy consumption. In cold climates, though exact estimates are not available, but based on simulation, the specific energy consumptions are given in Table 3.13, for typical building construction in India.

Table 3.13: Specific energy consumption in Indian buildings in different locations representative of six climatic zones

Location	*Specific energy consumption (Thermal) kWh/m²a*
Leh (CS)	674
Simla (CC)	120
Delhi (CO)	440
Jodhpur (HD)	485
Mumbai (WH)	489
Bangalore (MO)	178

A building with 28 m^2 floor area has been simulated by using a sophisticated dynamic simulation model DOE 2.1 E. The total peak load comes out to be 3.763 kW for cooling. The analysis corresponds to Delhi type of mixed climatic conditions where no occupancy, no equipment and no lighting has been considered. From the Figure it is clear that there is a vast potential of energy saving by using suitable wall and roof elements. In office buildings, however, the equipment (about 300 VA per person) also contributes significantly by increasing the cooling load and the annual energy consumption.

The relative importance of windows in this case is much less. Roofs and walls, which can resist heat and the energy efficient equipment, can substantially lower the peak load and annual energy consumption at least for cooling. From the point of view of building design however, we have concentrated on a building which is not occupied and simulated it for different climatic zones and for different variations of roof, wall construction, windows and also computed the effect of raising the set point temperature of the a/c equipment for 24^{0}C to 26^{0}C for cooling and from 20^{0}C to 16^{0}C for heating purposes.

The peak load for cooling and heating at different locations, which represent various climatic zones are given in Table 3.13(a) and the corresponding specific energy consumption rationalised in terms of kWh per sq. m of floor area are given in Table 3.14. Some of the observations that are important from the point of view of energy efficiency through building design are:

I. Double glazed windows are much more effective in cold climatic conditions where heating is required.

II. A cavity in roof and walls can reduce the peak load between 20% to 29%. In extreme climates, a cavity is less effective.

III. Provision of insulation in walls and roof (about 5 cm of glass wool) can reduce the load between 50% to 67%. For cooling requirements, the effect of insulation is more.

Tolerating higher or cooler temperature in summer and winter respectively (26°C instead of 24°C and 16°C instead of 20°C) can save energy consumption between 15 to 22%.

Table 3.13(a) : Specific cooling and heating loads in different climatic conditions

Case No.	*Cases*	*Annual cooling/heating loads (kW/m^2a)*					
		Delhi (CO)	*Jodhpur (HD)*	*Bombay (WH)*	*Bangalore (MO)*	*Simla* (CC)*	*Leh* (CS)*
1.	Base case (brick wall, RCC Roof, south window (20% floor area) ach=1, set (pt. =24)	3.763	3.831	2.998	2.086	2.229 (set pt.=18)	5.329 (set pt.=18)
2.	1 + double glazed windows	3.629	3.640	2.938	2.054	2.058	5.027
3.	1+ cavity roof	3.278	3.393	2.568	1.781	1.993	4.963
4.	3 + cavity walls	2.703	2.875	2.100	1.470	1.689	4.265
5.	1 + roof insulation	2.504	2.751	1.866	1.392	1.703	4.329
6.	1 + cavity walls + roof insulation	1.957	2.237	1.397	1.160	2.413	5.518
7.	Case 1 but window is in north	3.778	3.834	3.010	2.061	2.413	5.518
8.	Case 1 but ach = 3	3.949	4.196	3.069	2.241	2.353	5.638
9.	1 + insulation on walls and roof	1.242	1.579	0.861	0.889	0.970	2.544
10.	1 but set pt = 26 (16 for heating)	3.319	3.370	2.564	1.649	1.817	4.979

* Heating

Table 3.14: Specific energy consumption and percentage savings by energy conserving measures in different climatic conditions (Figures in Parentheses show the percentage reduction)

Case No.	*Cases*	*Annual cooling/heating Energy Demand (kWh/m^2a)*					
		Delhi (CO)	*Jodhpur (HD)*	*Bombay (WH)*	*Bangalore (MO)*	*Simla* (CC)*	*Leh* (CS)*
1	Base case	440.82 (-)	485.46(-)	489.39 (-)	178.46 (-)	119.86 (-)	674.29 (-)
2	1 + double glazed windows	431.43 (2.1)	469.43 (3.3)	480.64 (1.8)	183.07 (-2.6)	104.96 (12.4)	617.75 (8.4)
3	1+ cavity roof	392.68 (10.9)	442.18 (8.9)	435.43 (11.0)	150.43 (15.7)	109.71 (8.5)	635.43 (5.8)
4	3 + cavity walls	326.39 (26.0)	376.61 (22.4)	363.71 (25.7)	124.96 (30.0)	96.79 (19.2)	566.79 (15.9)
5	1 + roof insulation	310.46 (29.6)	370.00 (23.8)	339.75 (30.6)	104.32 (41.5)	98.61 (17.7)	579.64 (14.0)
6	1 + cavity walls + roof insulation	244.82 (44.5)	304.96 (37.2)	268.07 (45.2)	79.64 (55.4)	86.61 (27.7)	515.32 (23.6)
7	Case 1 but window is in north	432.36 (1.9)	473.54 (2.5)	478.89 (2.1)	172.11 (3.6)	137.39 (-14.6)	686.89 (-1.9)
8	Case 1 but ach = 3	452.7 (-2.7)	516.21 (-6.3)	499.71 (-2.1)	179.04 (-0.3)	131.14 (-9.4)	720.11 (-6.8)
9	1 + insulation on walls and roof	145.71 (67)	204.57 (57.9)	153.04 (68.7)	51.39 (71.2)	60.96 (49.1)	398.54 (40.9)
10	1 but set pt = 26 (16 for heating)	343.61 (22.1)	377.71 (22.2)	360.82 (26.3)	90.43 (49.3)	73.68 (38.5)	574.29 (14.8)

* Heating

Subsequent chapters of this book discuss with details, the energy required for keeping a building comfortable and methods to reduce the energy demand.

3.5 CASE STUDY OF EMBODIED AND OPERATIONAL ENERGY IN A HOTEL

Two patterns of Hotel's guest rooms have been identified each having a total area of 4000 square meters (800 square meters x 5 floors). Following are the main details of the hotel building that have been used for the analysis of embodied and operational energy:

(i) **External wall**: 200mm thick Autoclaved Aerated Concrete Block 15mm thick cement plaster with white paint

(ii) **Internal walls**: 115mm thick Autoclaved Aerated Concrete blocks with 15mm thick plaster finish and off-white emulsion paint

(iii) **Windows**: 6mm thick clear float glass in wooden frame 30mm thick. Overall Dimension of Windows in Rooms:

(iv) **Room Dimensions**: 3.75m x 4.85m

(v) **Corridor Dimensions**: 2.00m wide

(vi) **Roof Construction**: 150mm thick R.C.C roof with 50mm Polyurethane insulation, 100mm thick cement screed and 50mm thick brick tile top finish.

(vii) **HVAC**: Chilled water system. No Heating.

(viii) Occupancy levels: Occupancy levels @60% were considered throughout the year.

(ix) Time Scheduling: Mid Night to Mid night.

(x) **Set points**: 72.5F DBT for occupied rooms, 80.0F DBT for unoccupied rooms.

Figure 3.7 and Figure 3.8 describe the two hotel guest room patterns identified for the analysis of the embodied and operational energy.

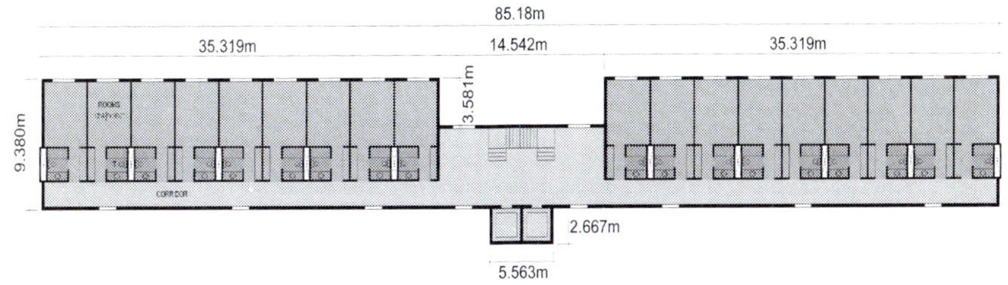

Figure 3.7: Pattern one: Linear Pattern.(Hotel Guest Block with singly loaded corridor)

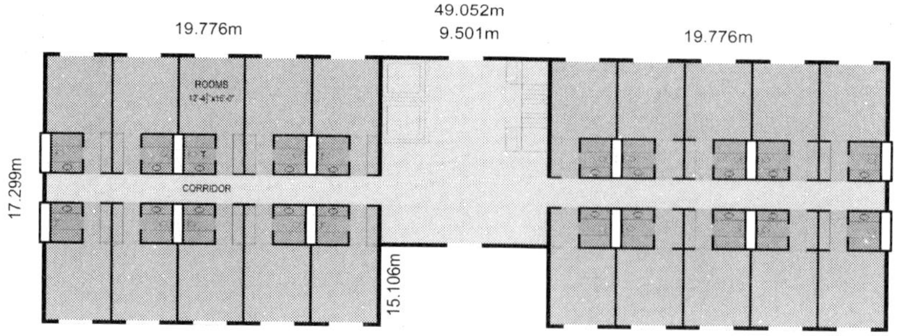

Figure 3.8 : Pattern Two: Doubly Loaded Corridor

EMBODIED ENERGY ANALYSIS:

The building was divided into seven main components (By Material choice) and the Embodied Energy of the building components was calculated separately for the Envelope and the Interior spaces by multiplying the amount of material with the specific energy content of that material.

Embodied energy (Pattern 1&2) :

Table 3.15 : Envelope components (Pattern 01)

Material components	*Specific energy contents (MJ/unit)**	*Qty.*	*Energy contents MJ*
Window single glass (m²)	216	468	101088
External plaster (m²)	40	3439	137580
External paint (m²)	6.5	3439	22356
Roof insulation (m²)	117	800	93600
Roof tiles (m²)	34	800	27200
Cement screed (m³)	1800	80	144000
RCC roof slab (m³)	3180	120	381600
Reinforcement in slab (kg)	43	7200	309600
Concrete block wall 200mm (m²)	1800	688	1238400
Total EE (Envelope)			2455424 MJ

Table 3.16 : Envelope components (Pattern 02)

Material components	*Specific energy contents (MJ/unit)**	*Qty.*	*Energy contents MJ*
Window single glass (m^2)	216	396	85536
External plaster (m^2)	40	2434	97360
External paint (m^2)	6.5	2434	15821
Roof insulation (m^2)	117	800	93600
Roof tiles (m^2)	34	800	27200
Cement screed (m^3)	1800	80	144000
RCC roof slab (m^3)	3180	120	381600
Reinforcement slab (kg)	43	7200	309600
Concrete block wall 200mm (m^2)	1800	487	876600
Total EE (Envelope)			2031317 MJ

Table 3.17 : Internal components (Pattern 01)

Material components	*Specific energy contents (MJ/unit)**	*Qty.*	*Energy contents MJ*
Flooring room & toilet (m^2)	40	2730	109200
Flooring corridor (m^2)	40	1270	50800
Plaster Rooms and toilet (m^2)	40	13300	532000
Plaster Corridor (m^2)	40	4665	186600
Timber door (m^2)	482	351.5	169423
Timber cupboard (m^2)	3332	475	1582700
Paint Rooms (m^2)	6.5	11875	77187
Paint Corridor (m^2)	6.5	4665	30322
Tile dado in toilet (m^2)	565	1448	818543
RCC slab (m^3)	3180	480	1526400
RCC column beam (m^3)	3180	135.5	429300
Reinforcement in column/beam (kg)	43	13550	582650
Reinforcement slab (kg)	43	28800	1238400
Block work for walls (m^3)	1800	484.5	872100
Total EE (Internal components)			8205625 MJ

Grand Total EE (Internal component+component) **10661049 MJ**

Table 3.18: Internal components (Pattern 02)

Material components	*Specific energy contents (MJ/unit)**	*Qty.*	*Energy contents MJ*
Flooring room & toilet (m^2)	40	3005	120200
Flooring corridor (m^2)	40	995	39800
Plaster Rooms and toilet (m^2)	40	14000	560000
Plaster Corridor (m^2)	40	3370	134800
Timber door (m^2)	482	370	178340
Timber cupboard (m^2)	3332	500	1666000
Paint Rooms (m^2)	6.5	12500	81250
Paint Corridor (m^2)	6.5	3370	21905
Tile dado in toilet (m^2)	565	1525	861625
RCC slab (m^3)	3180	480	1526400
RCC column beam (m^3)	3180	115	365700
Reinforcement in column/beam (kg)	43	11425	491275
Reinforcement slab (kg)	43	28800	1238400
Block work for walls (m^3)	1800	510	918000
Total EE (Internal components)			8203695 MJ

Grand Total EE (Int comp+ Env comp) 10235012 MJ

As is observed from the computation of the embodied energy, reinforcement and concrete are the two largest contributors of the total embodied energy related to the envelope. Among the internal components, besides the reinforcement and concrete, timber cupboards also feature among the significant contributors.

Pattern Two has the total initial Embodied Energy of 10235012 MJ ($EE_{Envelope}$ + $EE_{Internal\ Components}$).

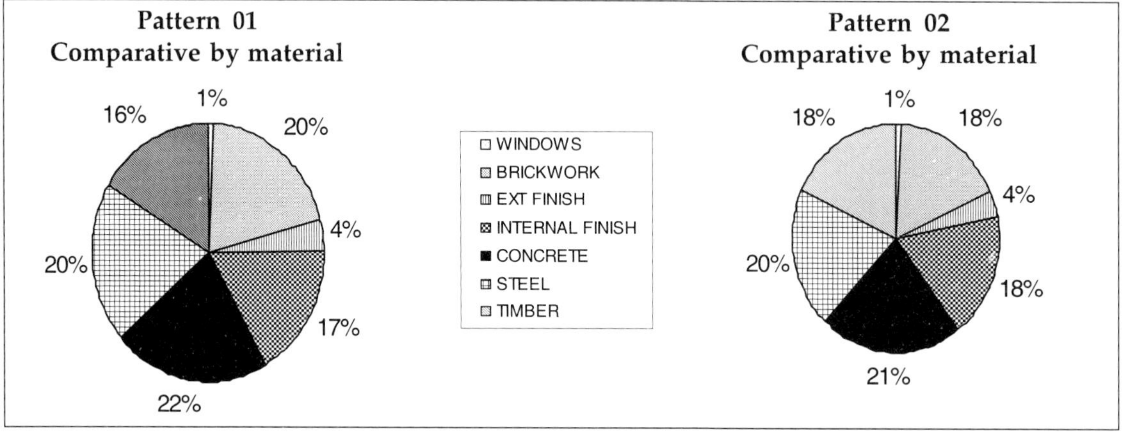

Figure 3.8(a) : Comparison of embodied energy by material type

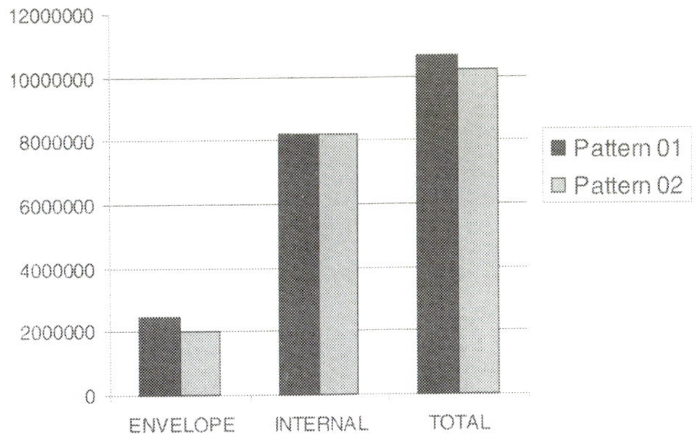

Figure 3.9: Comparative embodied energy in Pattern 01 & 02

OPERATIONAL ENERGY ANALYSIS

Energy requirement during the operational life of the hotel was estimated by using an energy simulation tool 'eQUEST'. The two design patterns were simulated for various orientations and two climatic zones – a) Composite Climate – New Delhi India, b) Warm & Humid Climate – Calcutta, India.

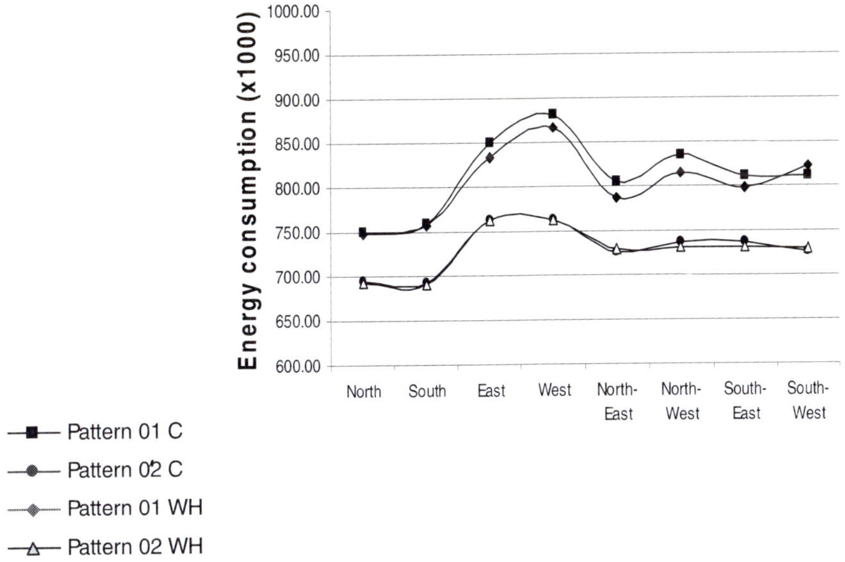

Figure 3.10: Comparative Annual Energy Consumption (KWh x 1000)

Table 3.19: Comparative: Annual Energy Consumption Table (The values are in Kwh and equivalent MJ)

Orientation	*Pattern 01 (Composite Climate)*	*Pattern 02 (Composite Climate)*	*Pattern 01 (Warm & Humid)*	*Pattern 02 (Warm & Humid)*
North	749650 KWh (2698740 MJ)	695140 KWh (2502504 MJ)	748850 KWh (2695860 MJ)	691910 KWh (2490876 MJ)
South	758710 KWh (2731356 MJ)	692660 KWh (2493576 MJ)	758320 KWh (2729952 MJ)	691180 KWh (2488248 MJ)
East	850330 KWh (3061188 MJ)	762830 KWh (2746188 MJ)	833010 KWh (2998836 MJ)	762830 KWh (2746188 MJ)
West	882250 KWh (3176100 MJ)	762820 KWh (2746152 MJ)	866220 KWh (3118392 MJ)	762740 KWh (2745864 MJ)
North-East	806040 KWh (2901744 MJ)	725710 KWh (2612556 MJ)	786440 KWh (2831184 MJ)	729140 KWh (2624904 MJ)
North-West	834800 KWh (3005280 MJ)	737150 KWh (2653740 MJ)	813940 KWh (2930184 MJ)	732090 KWh (2635524 MJ)
South-East	812010 KWh (2923236 MJ)	737170 KWh (2653812 MJ)	797710 KWh (2871756 MJ)	732100 KWh (2635560 MJ)
South-West	811400 KWh (2921040 MJ)	725700 KWh (2612520 MJ)	821440 KWh (2957184 MJ)	729130 KWh (2624868 MJ)

For a typical North orientation in a Composite Climate, the results of the analysis of energy consumption for Pattern 01 & 02 are discussed below.

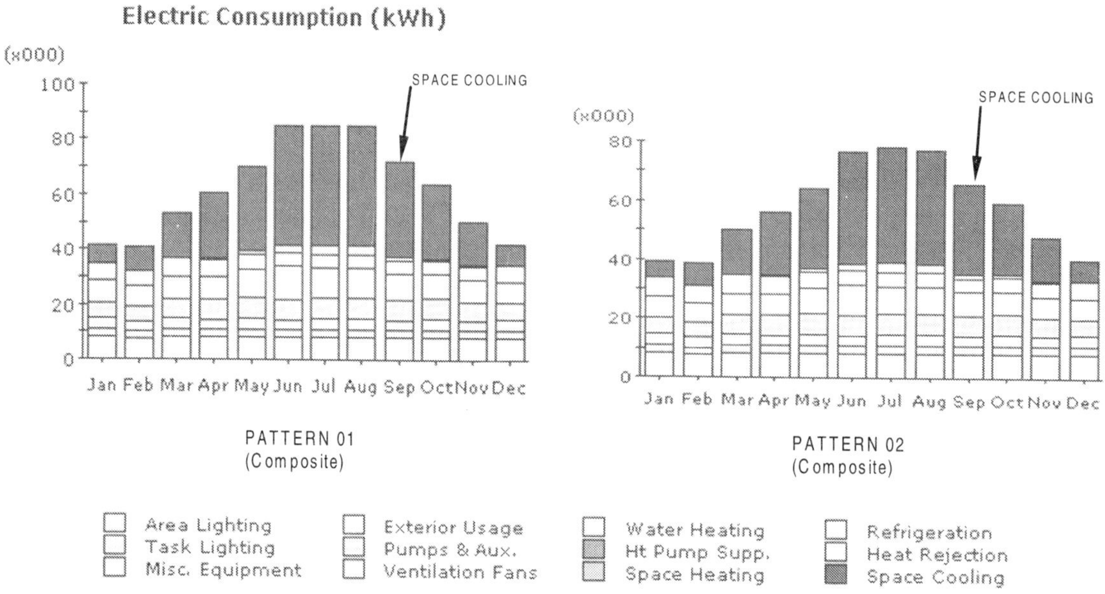

Figure 3.11: Annual Electricity Consumption

Pattern 01 (Composite Climate): The electricity consumption in the building varies over a wide range from 41250 KWh for the month of January to 85310 KWh for the month of July.

Out of the total annual consumption of 749650 KWh, 40.2% is due to the electricity requirement for cooling.

Pattern 02 (Composite Climate): The electricity consumption in the building varies over a wide range from 39350 KWh for the month of January to 78130 KWh for the month of July.

Out of the total annual consumption of 695140 KWh, 38.88% is due to the electricity requirement for cooling.

The annual electricity consumption in KWh can be expressed in MJ by converting KWh into equivalent Joules unit. Further, considering the potential efficiency for India i.e. .35 this electrical energy can be converted into the primary energy.

LIFE CYCLE ASSESSMENT

With the help of the two steps in which the total embodied energy demand and the annual operational energy demand have been calculated, the life cycle assessment can be done.

The third stage, i.e. demolition stage has not been covered due to the fact that information related to recoverable material and energy requirements for demolition are quite unclear. Reliable literature about the condition of material regarding fitness for reuse or recycling, after spending such long life span has great deal of uncertainty. It has therefore, been assumed that the share of that energy demand is negligible as compared to the other two stages.

The order of magnitude for cumulated energy demand during construction and the annual operational energy demand is comparable. Hence, it can be concluded that for normal building life i.e. 50 years*, the share of embodied energy becomes negligible as compared to the operational energy. Exact ratio of these two values would however, be a function of building life.

The above analysis can be extended for comparison of alternative building forms, alternative construction materials, use of special insulation or incorporation of passive architectural concept in the building for the purpose of energy conservation.

It is hypothesized that the total life of the building is determined when the cumulative maintenance cost equals the initial cost of the building, which excludes the land cost.

Life Cycle Assessment for Pattern 01 (Composite, North Orientation)

(1) Total embodied energy (incl. maintenance, repairs and replenishments) : 10661049 MJ

(2) Total operational energy through life of bldg.(50 years) :
(749650 KWh x 50 yrs x 3.6) = 134937000 MJ

(3) Total Cumulative Energy (1+2) : 145598049 MJ

Life Cycle Assessment for Pattern 02 (Composite, North Orientation)

(1) Total embodied energy (incl. maintenance, repairs and replenishments) : 10235012 MJ

(2) Total operational energy through life of bldg.(50 years) (695140 KWh x 50 yrs x 3.6) = 124678800 MJ

(3) Total Cumulative Energy (1+2) : 134913812 MJ

The results of the Life Cycle Assessment of the Patterns suggest that the embodied energy is approximately 4 times the annual operational energy. The decision about building design should be considering the fact that pattern-2 is much more efficient as compared to pattern-1. In a typical trade-off case, where the operational energy is lower than the base case design, but due to use of large amount of insulation or material with higher embodied energy, decision should be made on the basis of lower total cumulative energy and not just lower operational energy or lower embodied energy.

4

Parameters Affecting Energy Consumption in Buildings

This chapter describes various thermo-physical parameters that govern the energy consumption in a building for cooling or heating. To enhance the understanding of these parameters, basic scientific concepts have been presented in this chapter followed by discussion on role of each parameter.

4.1 FUNDAMENTALS OF HEAT TRANSFER

Study of heat transfer plays a very important role in understanding the thermal behavior of any building in response to weather and the climatic conditions. This understanding equips a reader to predict more scientifically, the change in internal environment of any building envelope due to change in weather conditions. With this objective, fundamental concepts of three modes of heat transfer namely conduction, convection and radiation and their relevance in buildings have been explained below.

Heat

Heat is energy in transit due to a temperature difference. The thermal energy is transferred from one region to another by three modes of heat transfer: conduction, convection and radiation. Almost every building exchanges heat with its surroundings through all of the three modes. In S.I. units, heat energy is expressed in units 'Joules' (J) or 'kilo Joules' (kJ). Other alternative units in use and their inter-conversion has been given in Table 4.1. The time rate at which heat is transferred is called 'Heat Flux (Φ)'. Units used to express heat flow are corresponding to energy flow per unit time i.e. 'Joules per second' or 'Watts (W)'. 'Heat flux density (q)' is the heat flux per unit area expressed in units 'watts per square meter (w/m^2)'.

Table 4.1: Conversion factors of different units used for heat energy

1 Calorie (M.K.S. units)	=	4.187 Joules (S.I. units)
1 kWh (kilo watt hour)	=	3.6 MJ
1 Btu (British Thermal Unit)	=	1.055 kJ
1 kgoe (kilogram oil equivalent)	=	42 MJ

Specific heat (c) is the amount of heat energy necessary to cause unit temperature increase in a unit mass of any substance. It is usually measured in 'Kilo Joules per kilogram per degree centigrade (KJ/kg °C)' or 'Kilo Calories per kilogram per degree centigrade (kcal/ kg °C)'. The higher the specific heat of any substance is, the more heat it will absorb for a given increase in temperature. Of all the commonly used substances, water has the highest specific heat 4.187 KJ/ kg °C. Unlike solids and liquids, gases have two different values of specific heats, specified as specific heat at constant pressure (c_p) and specific heat at constant volume (c_v) respectively. For our purpose, the one with constant pressure is more important due to the nature of thermodynamic processes usually occurring in nature and in buildings. Specific heat of air at atmospheric pressure and temperature can be taken as 1.0057 KJ/kg °C corresponding to a mass density of 1.1774 kg/m^3. However, it is advised to see exact values for accurate calculation of heat transfer from data tables for heat transfer.

Latent heat of a substance is the amount of heat energy absorbed by unit mass of that substance for change of state from solid to liquid or from liquid to vapour (gaseous) without change in its temperature. If the substance is changing state from vapour to liquid or liquid to solid, heat shall be released instead of getting absorbed. For water, the latent heat for evaporation i.e. for changing liquid into vapour is 2261 kJ/kg at atmospheric pressure. Latent heat for fusion of solid water (i.e. ice) at atmosphere is 335 kJ/kg.

Thermal capacity or heat capacity of a body is the product of its mass and the specific heat of its material. It can be understood as the amount of heat required to cause unit temperature increase of a body expressed in units kJ/^{0}C. More is the value of the thermal capacity, more becomes the tendency of any body to store heat within itself rather than passing it through or increasing its temperature. Therefore, it finds a very important place in buildings for storage of thermal energy.

4.1.1 Thermal conduction

Conduction in simple bodies

This is the mechanism of heat transfer whereby energy is transferred between parts of a continuum (say a body or medium) by transfer of kinetic energy between particles or groups of particles at the atomic level. Thermal energy transfer through conduction occurs in the direction from higher to lower temperature. In solid bodies including building components, thermal conduction takes place when one part of the component is subjected to higher temperature and other part to lower temperature condition.

Most of the cases of thermal conduction are usually analysed and treated in their simplified form as one dimensional heat flow cases, i.e. heat flow in directions other than the main direction are neglected. Similarly, if the change in atmospheric conditions (inside and/or outside) are assumed to be very slow, neglecting these changes, the process of heat transfer can be assumed to be 'Steady-State Heat Transfer' in its simplified form. For one dimensional, steady state heat transfer through conduction, heat flow is expressed by Fourier's law as given in equation 4.1 below:

$$Q = -kA\frac{dT}{dX} \qquad \text{(eq. 4.1)}$$

where:

Q is heat flow rate (W)

k is thermal conductivity (W/m^{0}C), a property of material, explained below

dT/dX is temperature gradient (^{0}C/meter) in the direction of heat flow

The term 'Thermal Conductivity (k)' in the above equation is a property of material through which heat transfer takes place. Heat flow rate is directly proportional to this property expressing friendliness of material to heat flow through conduction, area through which heat transfer takes place, temperature difference between both sides of the component (for example wall of building). It is inversely proportional to the distance through which heat has to flow e.g. thickness of wall.

The value of thermal conductivity varies over a wide range from about 0.02 W/m ^{0}C for insulating materials to about 400 W/m ^{0}C for good conductors like copper. The lower the conductivity, the better insulator a material is.

Another related term, Thermal Resistivity is the reciprocal of thermal conductivity (1/k) measured in "m ^{0}C/W". It expresses the resistance offered by material for heat flow. Good insulators are supposed to have high resistivity values. A material having thickness 'L' would offer thermal resistance of 'L/k'. It can be noted that for higher thermal resistance, more thickness or less value of thermal conductivity is desirable.

Thermal conductivity of water at atmospheric conditions is 0.58 W/m ^{0}C whereas air has only 0.026 W/m ^{0}C as its conductivity. This clearly indicates that air is a poor conductor of heat. This property of air makes it useful for insulation of buildings. One interesting use of poor conductivity of air and good conductivity of water in buildings is through use of porous materials. Due to poor conductivity of air, porous materials since have air filled in their pores, are bad conductors of heat.

If this air in pores is replaced by water, the same material will have higher conductivity. Hence, the nature of building component with respect to heat transfer can be altered by simply adding moisture to it. Their conductivity gets increased with increase in moisture content and decreases when the moisture content decreases and air takes place of moisture. Similarly, if density of any material is altered and it is made more compact, relatively less air resides in the pores and hence conductivity of that material increases. Figure 4.1 shows variation of thermal conductivity with density of a dried construction material, Figure 4.2 shows increase in thermal conductivity of construction materials with change in share of moisture content in its total volume.

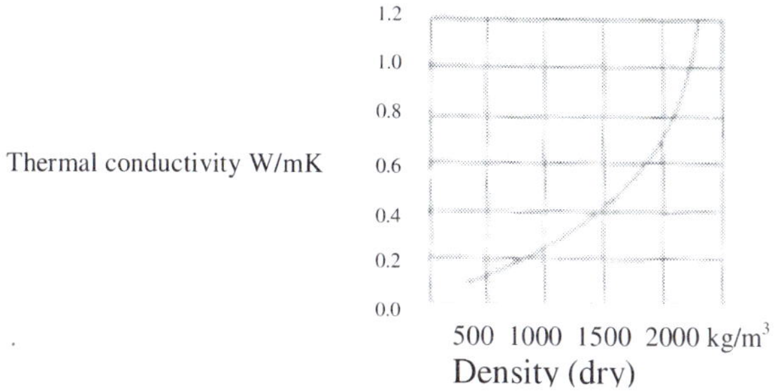

Figure 4.1: Variation in thermal conductivity of air dried construction material with density changes

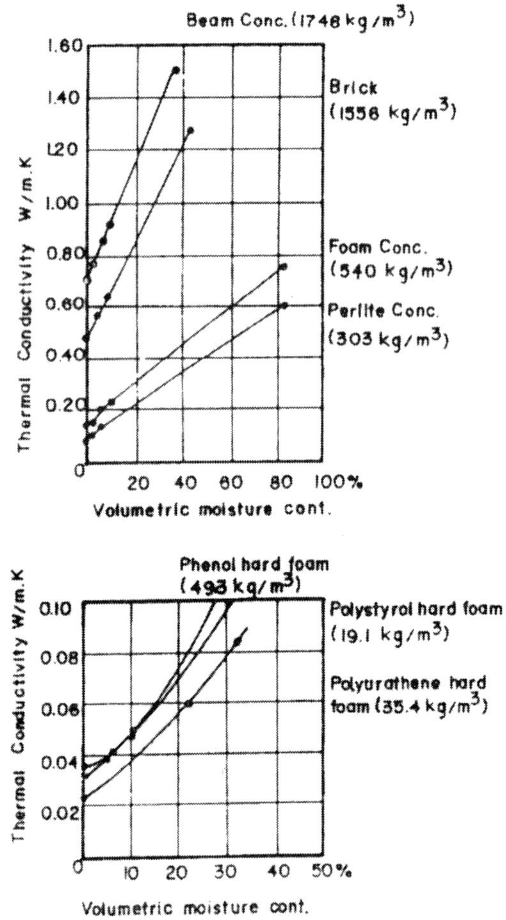

Figure 4.2: Variation in thermal conductivity of different construction materials with volumetric moisture content

Whilst thermal conductivity (or thermal resistivity are properties of a material, the corresponding properties of a body for a given thickness are described as 'Thermal Conductance (C)' and its reciprocal 'Thermal Resistance (R)' respectively such that C=1/R.

Conductance is the heat flow rate through a unit area of a body (i.e. the heat flux density 'q') when the temperature difference between the two surfaces is in unit degree centigrade. The unit of its measurement is $W/m^2\ ^0C$ and resistance is measured in $m^2\ ^0C/W$.

Thermal Resistance of a body is the product of its thickness and the resistivity of its material:

$R = b \times (1/k) = b/k$ (eq. 4.2)

where, b is the thickness in meters.

Thermal conduction in multi-layered bodies

If the body consists of several layers of different materials, its total resistance (R_b) will be the sum of the resistance of individual layers. The conductance of such a multi-layer body (C_b) can be found by finding its total resistance and taking its reciprocal as given below:

$R_b = R_1 + R_2 + R_3 + \ldots\ldots = b_1/k_1 + b_2/k_2 + b_3/k_3 + \ldots\ldots = \Sigma\, b/k$ (eq. 4.3)

$C = 1/R = 1/(\Sigma\, b/k)$ (eq. 4.4)

It is to be noted that conductance of different materials cannot be added directly, only the resistance can be added. Details of this concept have been mentioned under the heading 'electrical analogy of heat transfer' later in this chapter.

Role of Surface conductance

In addition to the resistance of a body to flow of heat, a resistance is also offered by its surface where a thin layer of air film separates the body from the surrounding air. The measure of this phenomenon is the 'surface or film resistance' expressed in units of resistance and reciprocal of it being film-conductance (f) with units $W/m^2\ {}^0C$.

In the preceding discussion, heat flow from one surface of the body to another surface was considered therefore the temperature difference was taken between the two surfaces for calculation of heat transfer. If the layer of air on both sides of wall is considered as per the concept of surface conductance, heat transfer from air on one side to air on other side takes place. Hence the overall 'air-to-air resistance (R)' will be the sum of the body's resistance and the surface resistance on both sides of wall:

$R = 1/f_o + R_b + 1/f_i$ (eq. 4.5)

where:

$1/f_o$ is film resistance on outer side of wall

$1/f_i$ is film resistance on inner side of wall

R_b is the resistance of wall or body

All resistance values in the above expression are in units $m^2\ {}^0C/W$.

The value of surface or film conductance (f) is a function of surface qualities such as smoothness and of the velocity of air surrounding the surface.

4.1.2 Thermal Convection

This form of heat transfer involves energy transfer by fluid movement and molecular conduction. The fluid movement required to cause convection if produced by external sources (for example a blower or pump), the heat transfer is termed as 'forced convection'. If the fluid flow or motion gets generated due to the difference in density and due to action of gravity, heat transfer is called 'natural convection' or 'free convection'.

The rate at which heat gets transferred through convection is given by the following equation:

$$Q = h_c A (T_s - T_f) \qquad \text{(eq. 4.6)}$$

where:

Q is rate of heat transfer (W)

A is area over which heat transfer is taking place (m^2)

T_s is temperature of body (^0C)

T_f is temperature of fluid (^0C)

h_c is convective heat transfer coefficient (W/m^2K)

From the above equation it is evident that if fluid is cooler than the body, heat loss or cooling of body shall take place. If the fluid (for example ambient air in hot climate) is warmer than the body or wall, due to negative value of the term (T_s-T_f), heat gain takes place. The term 'convective heat transfer (h_c)' depends upon the following factors:

- Surface and air temperature
- Air flow velocity
- Roughness of the surface
- Orientation of surface

Its value varies over a wide range from '0' to about 100 W/m^2 ^0C depending upon the case.

Calculation of Convective Heat Transfer Coefficient

The method of calculation of exact value of 'h_c' is slightly complicated and involves use of concepts of fluid mechanics along with heat transfer. In most engineering applications related to buildings however, empirical relationships can be used to find the heat transfer coefficient. Table 4.2 shows important empirical relationships that can be used to find convective heat transfer coefficient in selected cases related to building components.

Table 4.2: Simplified relations for natural convection with air at atmospheric pressure and moderate temperatures

Geometry	*Mean heat transfer coefficient h_c ($W/m^2\,^0C$)*
Vertical wall or surface (flat or cylindrical)	$h_c = 1.42\ (\Delta T/L)^{1/4}$ (laminar flow) $h_c = 1.31\ \Delta T^{1/3}$ (turbulent flow)
Horizontal cylindrical surface	$h_c = 1.32\ (\Delta T/D)^{1/4}$ (laminar) $h_c = 1.24\ \Delta T^{1/3}$ (turbulent)
Horizontal surface: (a) upper surface hotter (b) lower surface hotter	 $h_c = 1.32\ (\Delta T/L)^{1/4}$ (laminar) $h_c = 1.52\ DT^{1/3}$ (turbulent) $h_c = 0.59\ (\Delta T/L)^{1/4}$ (laminar)

In the above table, 'L' or 'D' is characteristic length. 'L' is equivalent to the length for a plane surface and 'D' is the diameter of cylindrical surface. ΔT is the temperature difference between the body and the surrounding fluid.

4.1.3 Thermal Radiation

The phenomenon of thermal radiation is described as the transport of energy through electromagnetic waves. Unlike conduction and convection, radiative heat transfer is not bound with material, it can even occur through vacuum. Every body whose temperature is above absolute zero (i.e.–273.14^{0}C) radiates energy in the form of electromagnetic radiation. The spectral distribution of the energy radiated from any body depends upon the temperature of its surface. The higher the temperature of the body, the lower is the wavelength of the radiation that makes major portion of the total emitted radiation.

Due to this dependence only, on heating, as the temperature of any body increases its colour changes to orange and then on further heating changes to red. While doing so, wavelength of majority of radiation emitted at is equal to the wavelength of orange colour in visual spectrum and hence the body mainly emits orange radiation or orange light. Similar emission of red colour light takes place on further increase in temperature. Temperature of the sun being around 6000 K, the spectral distribution of its emitted radiation becomes such that maximum of its radiation fall in the visible region i.e. majority of radiation having wavelength between 0.35 to 0.75 µm. The range of various zones in the electromagnetic spectrum is shown in Figure 4.3. Distribution of different wavelengths in solar radiation has also been shown in Figure 4.4.

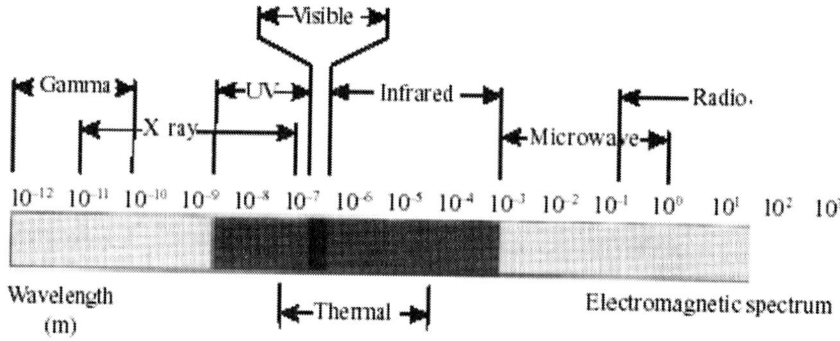

Figure 4.3: Electromagnetic spectrum

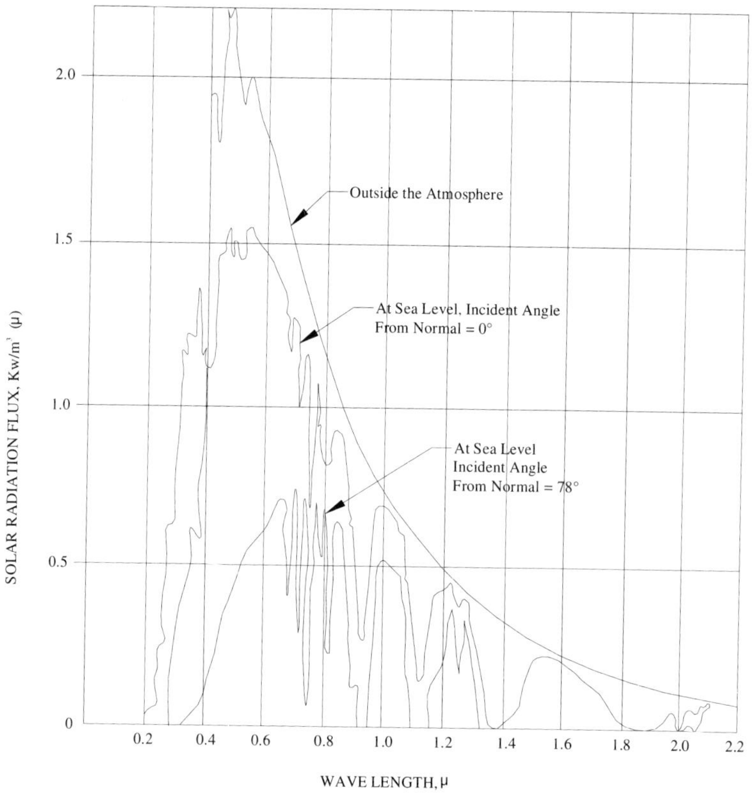

Figure 4.4: Distribution of different wavelengths in solar radiation

Since the temperature of most building components and their surroundings is much less as compared to that of sun, the spectral distribution of their emitted radiation has more share of longer wavelength. It means, radiation emitted from such bodies is thermal radiation. Typical wavelengths of radiation from building components is in the range of 3 to 800 μm that makes the basis of radiative heat exchange in buildings with their surroundings.

Important terms in radiation

Few important terms that are very useful for estimating the radiative heat transfer have been explained below:

Black body: a body which radiates radiation as per Stefan-Boltzman's law expressed by the following expression:

$$Q_{emitted} = \sigma A T^4 \qquad \text{(eq. 4.7)}$$

where:

σ is Stefan-Boltzman constant (value $5.669 * 10^{-8}$ $W/m^2 K^4$)

A is surface area emitting radiation

T is temperature of surface in Kelvin

Another characteristic of a perfect black body is that it absorbs all the radiation that falls on it and acts as perfect emitter too.

Emissivity (ε): it is the ratio of radiation emitted by any non-black body to the radiation emitted by black body of similar shape and temperature.

$$\varepsilon = q_{gray}/q_{black} \qquad \text{(eq. 4.8)}$$

thus for gray bodies, the emitted radiation can be found by:

$$Q_{gray} = \varepsilon\sigma A T^4 \qquad \text{(eq. 4.9)}$$

It is important to note that emissivity of any surface is not uniform for radiation of all wavelengths. This dependence of emissivity on wavelength is of great importance in buildings that has been discussed later in this chapter while discussing heat gain through windows. Emissivity values of different materials used in buildings have been given in Table 4.3.

Table 4.3: Emissivity of different building materials

Material	*Heat Radiation Emissivity* 'ε' *(at 20°C)*
Solid red brick	0.93
Roof brick (dark brown)	0.94
Lime/sand stone	0.96
Concrete (plain surface)	0.96
Plaster (white)	0.97
Anodised aluminium	0.90
Polished aluminium	0.02 to 0.04
Window glass	0.90

Grey Body: Grey bodies are those bodies that have same value of emissivity for all wavelengths of radiation.

Absorptivity (α): It is the ratio of amount of radiation absorbed by any surface of unit area to the total radiation that is incident on it. Value of this property plays an important role in governing the amount of radiation absorbed by any surface and hence affects its temperature. Like emissivity, absorptivity is also wavelength dependent. Values of absorptivities of various types of surfaces for solar radiation i.e. low wavelength radiation and the low temperature radiation or terrestrial radiation i.e. long wavelength radiation are given in Table 4.4.

Table 4.4 : Comparison of absorptivities of various surfaces to solar and terrestrial Radiation

Surface	*Absorptivity*	
	For solar radiation	*For terrestrial radiation (at 20 °C)*
Polished aluminium	0.15	0.04
Polished copper	0.18	0.03
Cast iron	0.94	0.21
Polished stainless steel	0.37	0.60
White marble	0.46	0.95
Asphalt	0.90	0.90
Red brick	0.75	0.93
Gravel	0.29	0.85
White paint	0.12	0.90-0.95

Shape factor: This factor expresses the fraction of radiation emitted by one surface as captured by other surface kept in its surroundings. Its value depends upon the relative orientation and size of the two surfaces. To understand this factor let us consider a rectangular small surface (say surface-1) fully covered by another surface (say surface-2). The entire amount of radiation emitted by surface-1 shall be captured by surface-2 i.e. hemispherical surface covering surface-1. Hence the shape factor of surface-1 with respect to surface–2 written as F_{12} is unity. The vice-versa of this is not true. Only a part of the radiation emitted by surface-2 shall be captured by surface-1 and hence the shape factor of surface-2 with respect to surface-1 written as F_{21} shall be less than unity.

Universally applicable form of equation for radiative heat transfer

If, there are two gray bodies, kept close to each other at temperature T_1 and T_2, each one shall emit radiation according to its own temperature and emissivity. Entire or only some part of the radiation emitted by one shall be captured by the other according to their shape factors with respect to each other as explained above. Net heat exchange between the two shall be equal to the difference between radiation of first received by second and radiation of second received by first one. This can be expressed by a generic equation:

$$Q = F_\varepsilon F_G \sigma (T_1^4 - T_2^4) \qquad \text{(eq. 4.10)}$$

Where F_ε represents factor due to emissivity and F_G represents factor due to geometry.

Table 4.4 gives values of shape factors of various types of surfaces with different relative orientations.

Table 4.4: Shape factors of different combination of surfaces

Configuration	*Formula for configuration factor*
Radiation from	*Elementary area dA_1 falling on Finite area A_2*
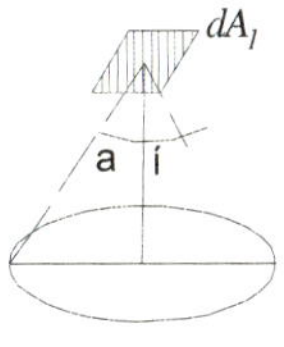	$F_{1\text{-}2} = sin^2 a \quad cos i$
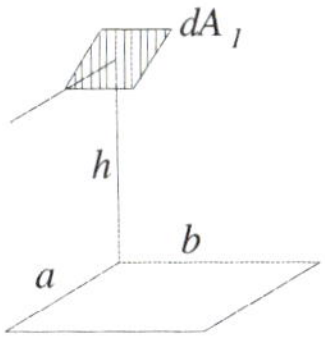	$F_{1\text{-}2} = \frac{1}{2p}\left[\frac{a}{\sqrt{a^2+h^2}} tan^{-1} \frac{b}{\sqrt{a^2+h^2}} tan^{-1} + \frac{b}{\sqrt{a^2+h^2}} tan^{-1} \frac{a}{\sqrt{a^2+h^2}}\right]$
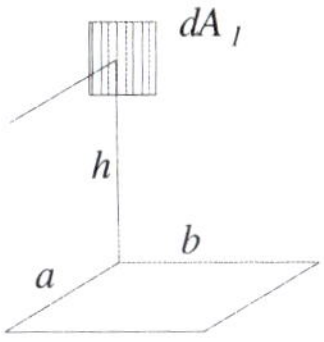	$F_{1\text{-}2} = \frac{1}{2p}\left[tan^{-1} \frac{b}{h} \quad \frac{b}{\sqrt{a^2+h^2}} tan^{-1} \frac{b}{\sqrt{a^2+h^2}}\right]$
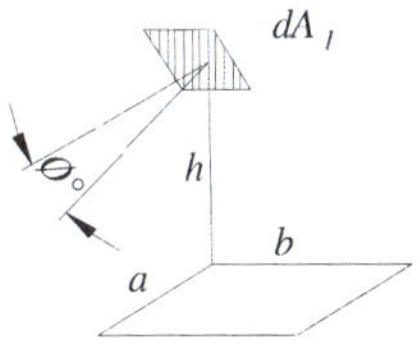	$F_{1\text{-}2} = F_{p,1\text{-}2} cos d + F_{n,1\text{-}2} sin d$

4.1.4 Electrical analogy to analyse cases of heat transfer

Flow of heat can be considered analogous to electricity. In both the cases, flow quantity is directly proportional to the driving potential and inversely proportional to the flow resistance. In electricity, the voltage potential and electrical resistance of the material governs flow of current in a conductor. Likewise, in case of heat transfer, temperature difference acts like the driving force for heat that together with the thermal resistance (i.e. inverse of thermal conductance) decide the amount of heat flow.

From Ohm's law for electricity;

Current (i) = voltage potential (dV)/electrical resistance (R_{el})

and from Fourier's law of heat transfer:

Heat flow rate (Q) = thermal potential (dT)/thermal resistance (R_{th})

Thermal resistance, R_{th} is reciprocal of thermal conductance and has units 'degree per watt'.

In case of conduction, the equation for heat transfer is written as:

$Q = kA\,\Delta T/dx$

Re-writing the above equation:

$Q = \Delta T/(dx/kA)$ it can be compared with the electric current flow equation:

$i = V/R$

Therefore, the entire term (dx/kA) can be considered as thermal resistance for conduction.

Similarly, in case of convection:

$Q = h_c\,A\,\Delta T = \Delta T/(1/\,h_c\,A)$

Therefore, '$1/(h_c\,A)$' would be thermal resistance.

In case of radiative heat exchange between two bodies, net heat transfer equation is:

$Q_{12} = A_1\,F_{12}\,\sigma\,(T_1^4 - T_2^4) = (T_1 - T_2)/\,[1/\,A_1\,F_{12}\,\sigma\,(T_1^2+T_2^2)(T_1+T_2)]$

Using the above mentioned formulae for thermal resistance, complex cases of heat transfer can be solved as shown below:

Case-1: Resistance in series

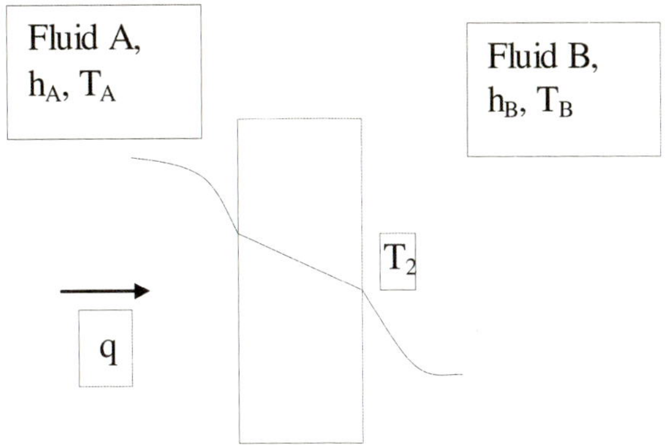

Equivalent electric circuit:

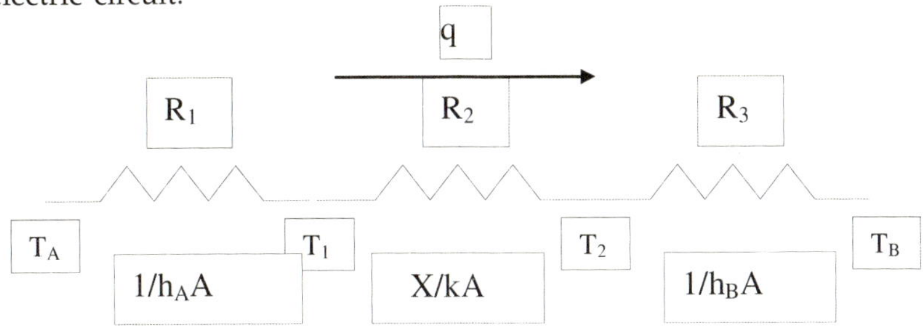

Hence net heat transfer can be found using:

$$q = \Delta T/R_{th} = (T_A - T_B)/ \{(1/h_A A) + (\Delta X/kA) + (1/h_B A)\}$$

Case-2: Resistance in combined series and parallel arrangement.

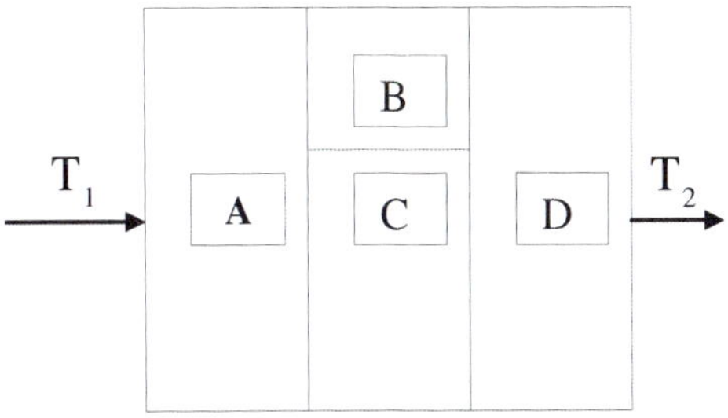

In the figure shown above, first net resistance between the two extreme points is to be found:

$$R_{net} = R_A + (R_B R_C/(R_B+R_C) + R_D$$

Net heat transfer can thus be found using:

$$Q_{net} = (T_1 - T_2)/R_{net}$$

This approach using electrical analogy is very useful in analysis of components such as composite walls having several doors and windows.

4.2 APPLICATION OF HEAT TRANSFER FUNDAMENTALS IN BUILDINGS

After understanding the basic concepts of heat transfer, commonly used applications of heat transfer in buildings have been briefly described here in this chapter, only their working principle has been covered.

4.2.1 Thermal Insulation and R-Value

Although there is a separate chapter on thermal insulation in this book, but to highlight the relative importance of insulation along-with other important parameters, this topic has been touched briefly here in this chapter too.

Insulation for any wall or building component is provided by applying layer of a material that is poor conductor of heat. For analyzing the effect of insulation, the approach described under heading 'thermal conduction in multi-layered bodies' can be adopted to find total thermal resistance to conduction. As the insulating materials have low thermal conductivity and hence high thermal resistivity, the total thermal resistance on applying layer of insulating material only increases and hence blocks the flow of heat. Mathematically:

$$R_{total} = R_{wall} + R_{insulation} = (b_{wall}/k_{wall}) + (b_{insulation}/k_{insulation}) \qquad \text{(eq. 4.11)}$$

Where 'R' stands for thermal resistance, 'b' for thickness and 'k' for thermal conductivity. The term R-value for any building component thus refers to combined thermal resistance offered by different layers any building component such as wall, roof, fenestration. This concept is further explained in the section describing U-value.

Conductive heat transfer 'Q' can thus be found by :

$$Q = A_{wall}\,(T_{outside} - T_{inside})/R_{total} \qquad \text{(eq. 4.12)}$$

Where 'A' is area through which heat transfer is taking place, 'T' is temperature.

Depending upon the composition, conductivity and operating temperature range, insulating material can be chosen to suit any application and required thickness can be found using equation 4.11 with 4.12 knowing permissible heat flow and terms other than '$b_{insulation}$'.

4.2.1 Air cavity as insulation

If an air space is left between two layers making a wall or roof of any building, the air trapped between the layers being poor conductor of heat acts as barrier to heat transfer. The thickness of air cavity is a very important parameter that governs its effectiveness by controlling the heat transfer coefficient. It has been found that with gaps broader than 50 mm., movement of trapped air due to temperature gradient starts that in turn increases the coefficient of heat transfer due to convection coming into picture. Therefore, cavities broader than 50 mm. are normally not preferred. This concept also finds very important place in development of insulating windows using double glazing i.e. air or other poor conducting gases trapped between two layers of glazing.

4.2.2 Reducing radiative heat gain on building surfaces

In radiation heat transfer, as explained earlier, besides depending upon the temperature of surfaces, heat transfer also depends upon the emittance and absorptance. Radiation received by a surface can partly be absorbed, partly be reflected and partly be transmitted, the fractions depend upon the coefficients known as absorptance (α), reflectance (r), and transmittance (ι). As no other effect can take place out of the radiation falling on any surface, the sum total of these coefficients for any surface is always unity:

$$\alpha + r + \iota = 1$$

For opaque surfaces value of transmittance is zero. Light coloured, smooth and shiny surfaces tend to have high reflectance. Therefore, for a perfect opaque reflector, r=1 and therefore the value of α has to be zero.

For a perfect absorber, i.e. the black body, as the absorptance is having a value of unity, reflectance 'r' has to have a value of zero. The coefficient 'emittance' (ε) expresses its value similar to the absorptance (α) for radiation of any particular wavelength. For the same surface, value of emittance and hence also of absorptance may have different values for radiation of different wavelengths. As the wavelength of solar radiation is much lower than that of the radiation emitted by terrestrial bodies, behavior of various surfaces in buildings is also different for these radiations. For example white paint has very less absorptance (0.1-0.3) for solar radiation but it has emittance of the order of 0.8-0.9 for radiation due to terrestrial bodies. On the contrary, a surface of bright metal foil has a typical absorptance for solar radiation in the range 0.1-0.3 whereas the emittance for radiation corresponding to terrestrial temperatures is of the order of 0.05-0.2.

Practical use of this is that if both of the above mentioned surfaces are exposed to sun, both will absorb the same amount of heat as their absorptances are same but the white painted surface will re-emit much of the absorbed energy, whereas the bright metal surface will not as its emittance (terrestrial) is much less. Therefore, the later will attain a much higher temperature as compared to the former.

4.2.3 'U'-value and 'R'-value: important parameters for buildings

In real life situations in almost all the building components, heat transfer takes place through all the three modes. For example, the wall shown in Figure 4.5 receives heat through convection from the ambient air, through conduction the heat gets transmitted upto the inner surface where again through convective heat transfer due to inside/room air, heat goes into the building. Using the concept of thermal resistance, the overall heat transfer can be found using:

$$Q = \frac{T_{outside} - T_{inside}}{\frac{1}{h_o A} + \frac{b}{kA} + \frac{1}{h_i A}} \qquad \text{(eq. 4.13)}$$

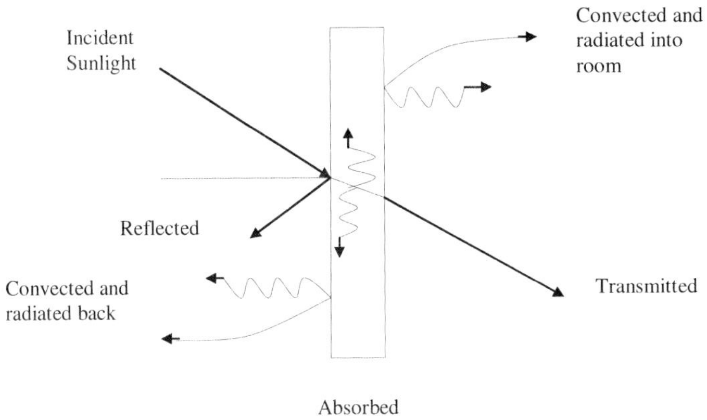

Figure 4.5: Combined heat transfer from ambient air to room air through wall

Equation 4.13 can be written to take the simplified form as :

$$Q = U\,A\,(T_{outside} - T_{room}) \qquad \text{(eq. 4.14)}$$

Where

$$U = \frac{1}{\frac{1}{h_o} + \frac{b}{k} + \frac{1}{h_i}} \qquad \text{(eq. 4.15)}$$

The term 'U' represents overall thermal conductance or overall heat transfer coefficient from outside to inside covering all modes of heat transfer. Units for U-value in SI units are W/m^2K. Corresponding unit in the BTU system is $BTU/(ft^2.h.^0F)$. In case, radiative heat gain on outer surface and radiative heat loss from inner surface to room are also to be added to make the case actual, the overall thermal resistance can be found using electrical analogy as explained earlier. Reciprocal of the overall thermal resistance shall become the 'overall heat transfer coefficient' termed as the 'U-value' of building component. From equation 5.14, the 'U-value' can be defined as "the rate of heat flow over unit area of any building component through unit overall temperature difference between both sides of the component".

Besides depending upon properties and physical details of components through the details of components through the parameter 'b/k', the value of 'U' depends upon climatic conditions such as wind velocity, orientation (as they together decide the value of 'h_o' and 'h_i') and also on temperature of surroundings and sky conditions for radiative heat exchange. However, variation in 'U-value' due to change in climatic conditions is not found to alter its value by more than 15% from the average. Hence average 'U-value ' of any building parameter is a good parameter for gauging the amount of heat that can flow through it.

The term R-value for any building section is the inverse of its U-value. Normally, in building codes, R-value is specified without considering resistance offered by air film close to the wall or roof since it depends upon climatic conditions, air velocity in particular. Considering resistance of air film further enhances the R-value in real life situation.

As standard practice, the alphabet 'R' followed by a number specifies resistance offered by certain section. For example R-4 refers to any section combined thermal resistance of which is 4 m^2K/W. Same R-value can be achieved through various combinations of materials and thickness. It may be noted that since R-value is based on steady-state heat transfer, sequence of layers does not affect the R-value. However, actual heat transfer in buildings is a transient phenomenon, the effect of relative positioning of different layers is explained later in this chapter. Chapter-6 also deals with this topic in further details.

4.2.4 Sol-Air Temperature

Sol-air temperature is the temperature of the outdoor air that, in the absence of all radiation changes, gives same rate of heat transfer through the surface as would occur with the combination of incident solar radiation, radiative heat transfer with the outdoor surroundings including sky, and convective heat exchange with the outdoor air.

Heat flux through a sunlit surface can be written as:

$$Q/A = \alpha I + h_o (T_a - T_x) - \varepsilon \Delta R \qquad \text{(eq. 4.16)}$$

Where:

α is absorptance of surface for solar radiation

I is solar radiation incident on surface (W/m^2)

h_o is coefficient of heat transfer by longwave radiation and convection at outer surface (W/m^2K)

$T_{a,}$ T_x are temperature of ambient and surface (^0C)

ε is hemispherical emittance of surface

ΔR is difference between longwave radiation on surface from surroundings including sky and radiation emitted by black body at outdoor temperature (W/m^2)

using eq. 4.16, the rate of heat transfer can be expressed in terms of the sol-air temperature 'T_{solair}' by the following equation:

$$Q/A = h_o (T_{solair} - T_x) \quad \text{(eq. 4.17)}$$

Where

$$T_{solair} = T_a + (\alpha I / h_o) - (\varepsilon \Delta R / h_o) \quad \text{(eq. 4.17a)}$$

For horizontal surfaces that receive longwave radiation from the sky only, an appropriate value of ΔR can be taken as $110W/m^2$, so that if ε is 1.0, and h_o is $17W/m^2$, the long wave radiation correction is about -6.5^0C.

Vertical surfaces receive solar radiation from the ground, surrounding buildings as well as from the sky and therefore, accurate estimation of the term ΔR is difficult. When the solar radiation is high, surfaces usually have a higher temperature than the outdoor air, their longwave radiation compensates to some extent, for the low emittance of sky. Therefore, it is common practice to assume ΔR = 0, for vertical surfaces.

4.2.5 Solar Heat Gain Factor for opaque surfaces

Similar to the concept of defining sol-air temperature, it might be useful to consider effect of reflective surfaces and thermal insulation in a simplified manner. For the reduction of solar heat gain, a dark, highly absorptive surface with good insulation may be just as effective as a more reflective but poorly insulated element. Good insulation with highly reflective surface is of course, better than both. From equation 4.16 the temperature equivalent to the effect of radiation i.e. radiative gain (or sol-air excess temperature) can be written as:

$$T_{solair} - T_0 = I * \alpha / h_0 \quad \text{(eq. 4.18)}$$

Thus the rate of extra heat flow caused by radiation per unit area can be written as:

$$Q_{extra} = (I * \alpha / h_0) * U * A \quad \text{(eq. 4.19)}$$

Rearranging the above equation a non-dimensional number can be defined:

$$Q_{extra} / I * A = U \alpha / h_0 = \text{Solar Heat Gain Factor (g)} \quad \text{(eq. 4.20)}$$

The solar heat gain factor thus can be defined as a fraction of the incident solar radiation that enters the building spaces as heat.

4.2.6 Heat Transfer through glazed windows

There are two means of indicating the amount of solar radiation that passes through a window. These are solar heat gain coefficient (SHGC) and shading coefficient (SC). In both cases, the solar heat gain is the combination of directly transmitted radiation and the inward-flowing portion of absorbed radiation. However, SHGC and SC have a different basis for comparison or reference. SHGC is same as 'g-factor' defined in Chapter-2.

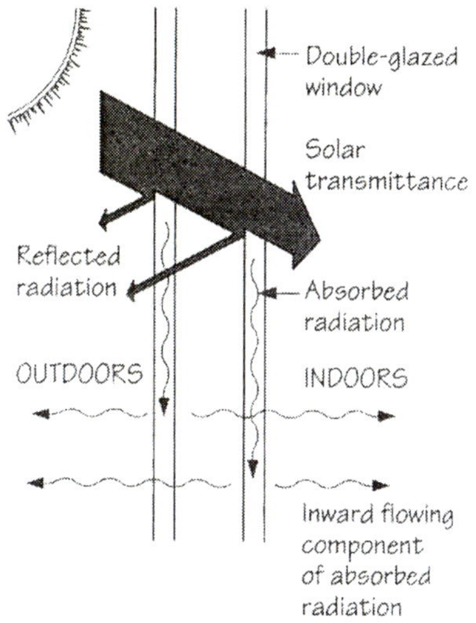

Fig 4.6 : Simplified view of the components of solar heat gain. Heat gain includes the transmitted solar energy and the inward flowing component of absorbed radiation

The window industry is now moving away from use of the shading coefficient to the solar heat gain coefficient (SHGC), which is defined as that fraction of incident solar radiation that actually enters a building through the window as heat gain. The SHGC generally refers to total window system performance and is a more accurate indication of solar gain under a wider range of conditions. The solar heat gain coefficient is expressed as a dimensionless number from 0 to 1.0. A high coefficient signifies high heat gain, while a low coefficient means low heat gain.

4.2.7 Shading Coefficient

Until recently, the shading coefficient (SC) was the primary term used to characterize the solar control properties of glass in windows. Although it is being replaced by the solar heat gain coefficient, but it can still be found referenced in books or product literature. The SC was originally developed as a single number that could be used to compare glazing solar control under a wide range of conditions. Its simplicity, however, is offset by a lack of accuracy in a number of circumstances.

The shading coefficient (SC) is only defined for the glazing portion of the window and does not include frame effects. It represents the ratio of solar heat gain through the system relative to that through 1/8-inch (3 mm) clear glass at normal incidence. The SC has also been used to characterize performance over a wide range of sun positions; however, there is some potential loss in accuracy when applied to sun positions at high angles to the glass. The shading coefficient is expressed as a dimensionless number from 0 to 1.0. A high, shading coefficient means high solar gain, while a low shading coefficient means low solar gain.

The total window SC value is strongly influenced by the type of glass selected. The shading coefficient can also include the effects of any integral part of the window system that reduces the flow of solar heat, such as multiple glazing layers, reflective coatings, or blinds between layers of glass. The SHGC is influenced by all the same factors as the SC, but since it can be applied to the entire window assembly, the SHGC is also affected by shading from the frame as well as the ratio of glazing and frame. For any glazing, the SHGC is always lower than the SC. If you find an older information source with SC values only, you can make an approximate conversion to SHGC for the glazing by multiplying the SC value by 0.87.

Visible transmittance is the amount of light in the visible portion of the spectrum that passes through a glazing material. This property indirectly affects heating and cooling loads in a building, and it is an important factor in evaluating energy-efficient windows. Transmittance is influenced by the glazing type, the number of layers, and any coatings that might be applied to the glazings. Visible transmittance of glazings ranges from above 90 percent for water-white clear glass to less than 10 percent for highly reflective coatings on tinted glass.

Visible transmittance is an important factor in providing daylight, views, and privacy, as well as in controlling glare and fading of interior furnishings. These are often contradictory effects: a high light transmittance is desired for view out at night, but this may create glare at times. These opposing needs are often met by providing glazing that has high visible transmittance and then adding window attachments such as shades or blinds to modulate the transmittance to meet changing needs.

In the past, products that reduced solar gain (with tints and coatings) also reduced visible transmittance. However, new spectrally selective tinted glasses and selective coatings have made it possible to reduce solar heat gain with little reduction in visible transmittance. Because the concept of separating solar gain control and light control is so important, we now characterize this differential effect by referring to the light-to-solar-gain ratio (LSG), which is simply the ratio of visible transmittance to solar heat gain coefficient values for typical glazings which are listed in Table 4.5.

Table 4.5: Solar heat gain and visible transmittance characteristics of windows

	Window					
General Glazing Description	*Single-glazed clear*	*Double-glazed clear*	*Double-glazed Bronze*	*Double-glazed spectrally selective*	*Double-glazed spectrally selective*	*Triple-glazed low-E*
			Center-of-glass			
SHGC	0.86	0.76	0.62	0.41	0.32	0.49
SC	1.00	0.89	0.72	0.47	0.38	0.57
VT	0.90	0.81	0.61	0.72	0.44	0.68
LSG	1.04	1.07	0.98	1.75	1.38	1.39
			Total Window			
SHGC	0.79	0.58	0.48	0.31	0.26	0.37
VT	0.69	0.57	0.43	0.51	0.31	0.48
LSG	0.87	0.98	0.89	1.65	1.19	1.29

SHGC: Solar Heat Gain Coefficient; SC: Shading Coefficient; VT: Visible Transmittance

LSG: Light-to-solar-gain ratio (VT/SHGC)

4.3 TRANSIENT HEAT TRANSFER AND ITS USE IN BUILDINGS

The approach for calculation of heat transfer, explained so far in this chapter is valid only for steady state heat transfer cases i.e. for average conditions or for the case when the outdoor and indoor temperatures are constant. If the fluctuations of temperatures on either side do not exceed ±3°C, the case can be treated as steady state case with relatively accurate results. Such a variation can prevail in actual practice only during the moderate climatic conditions when the interior is heated or cooled and kept at a desired temperature through use of cooling/heating equipment.

The U-value and SHGC values of building components (roof, walls, windows) obtained from steady state assumptions are useful to determine the cooling/heating load that may be useful for determination of the size of cooling/heating equipment. Prediction of thermal behavior of the building cannot be done without taking into account the variations in temperatures with time for which transient analysis becomes necessary. With transient analysis of heat transfer, it may be found that the size of cooling/heating equipment calculated on the basis of steady state approach is oversized. The designers have to be careful about the effects and differences between such approaches.

4.3.1 Periodic Heat flow

Diurnal variations of weather conditions produce an approximately repetitive 24-hour cycle of increasing and decreasing temperatures. As the cycle is repetitive, it can be described as periodic heat flow. Figure 4.7 shows the diurnal variations of external and internal temperatures in a periodically changing thermal regime. In the morning, as the outdoor temperature starts increasing, heat starts entering the outer surface of the wall. Each particle of the wall material absorbs certain amount of heat depending upon its mass and specific heat jointly known as heat capacity.

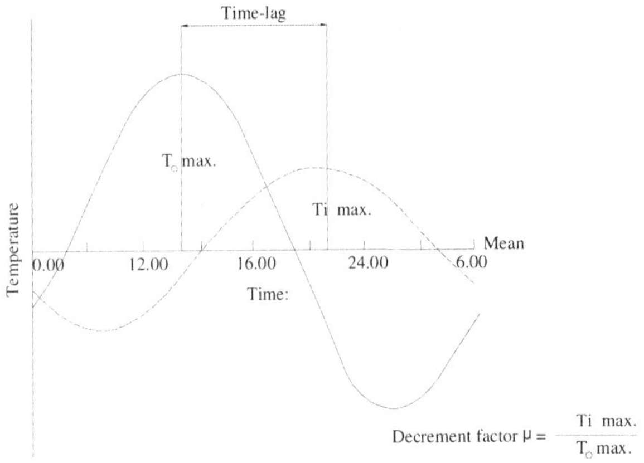

Figure 4.7: Time-lag and decrement factor

For every degree of temperature rise in surroundings, there will be some corresponding heat storage in particles of outer layer. After the temperature of the first layer increases due to storage of heat, it is transmitted to the next layer, thus the process of heat transfer induces a delay. In such a process, the out-door temperature reaches its peak and starts decreasing before the inner surface reaches its peak. By the time, peak arrives in the inner layers out-door temperature starts decreasing and as a result heat starts flowing back in the outward direction. Due to such effect, the peak at the inner surface remains lower as compared to the peak at outer atmosphere or in outer layers as shown in Figure 4.7.

Two quantities characterize the above mentioned phenomenon, namely 'time-lag (φ)' or phase shift and 'decrement factor (μ)' or amplitude attenuation. Decrement factor is the ratio of the maximum outer surface temperature and the maximum inner surface temperature amplitudes taken with reference from daily mean.

Value of these two parameters depends upon the rate at which heat transfer from outer to inner surface takes place. The rate of heat transfer in turn depends upon the thermal conductivity, density and specific heat of the material. Jointly, these three terms make one single important property known as 'Thermal Diffusivity' given by equation:

$$K = k/(\rho * c) \qquad \text{(eq. 4.21)}$$

where;

K is thermal diffusivity in m^2/s

k is thermal conductivity in W/m ^{0}C

ρ is density of material kg/m^3

c is specific heat of material in J/kg ^{0}C

In actual practice, the time lag and the decrement factor values can either be calculated for individual case taking the properties and dimensional details of construction or can directly be read from compiled information. Figure 4.8 shows graphic indication of these values for massive walls. As a thumb rule of massive masonry made of earth and concrete, for each thickness of 0.3 meters, a time lag of 10 hours can be taken.

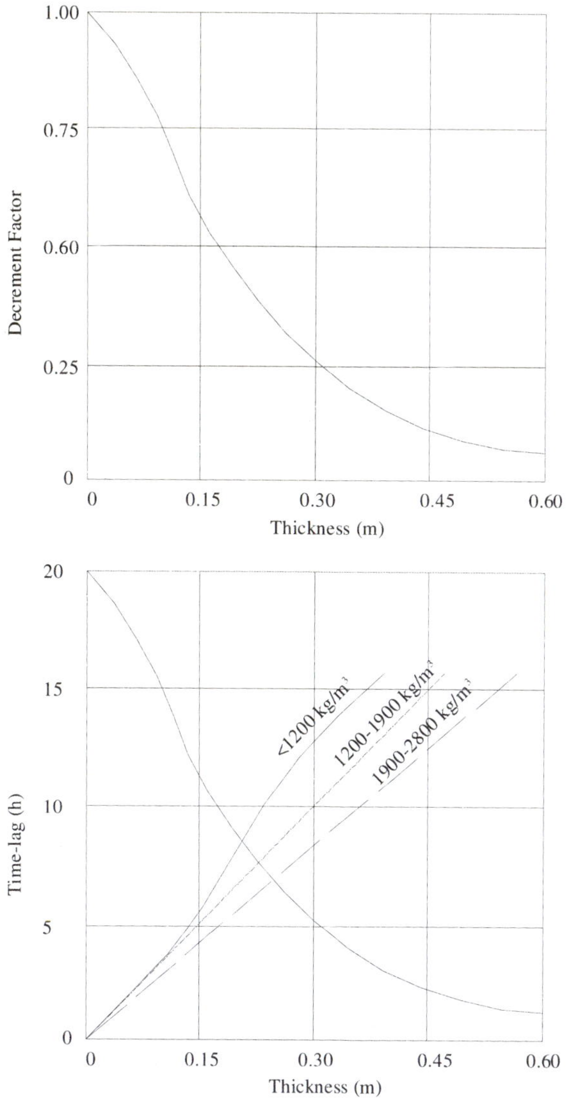

Figure 4.8: Time lag and decrement factor for massive walls

Table 4.6 shows, time-lag and decrement factors for different types of construction materials that are commonly found in buildings. In this table, cases of different materials, their different positions and varying thickness have been taken. A clear effect of each one of these can be seen on the time lag and decrement factor.

4.3.2 Heat Flow Calculation with Periodic Fluctuations

Due to periodic fluctuations, it has been explained that at every instance, the amount of heat flow would be different. To find momentary heat transfer in buildings with reasonable accuracy, the indoor temperature can be assumed to be constant. Doing this is justified as the amount of temperature fluctuation inside is much less than outside. With such assumption, momentary heat transfer would depend upon the time-lag, the decrement factor and the outdoor conditions (both momentary and average). Following equation can be used for this purpose:

$$Q = U\,A\,[(T_m - T_i) + \mu(T_\phi - T_m)] \qquad \text{(eq. 4.22)}$$

where:

q is momentary heat transfer rate in W

A is area in m^2

U is U-value in $W/m^2\,^0C$

T_m is daily mean outdoor temperature

T_i is indoor temperature (assumed to be constant)

T_ϕ is outdoor sol-air temperature φ hours earlier than the time of investigation

μ is decrement factor

φ is time lag in hours

Knowledge of decrement factor and time lag for different thickness of combination of materials in various construction elements is very important for designers. By taking into account these parameters, buildings can be designed to perform better. For example, an office or school building can be designed in such a way that the heat arrives into the building when either natural cooling starts taking place (cool breeze in the evening) or when building is not in use at all i.e. after school or office hours.

Table 4.6: Time lag and amplitude decrement factor for different wall constructions

Wall construction (Outside to Inside)			Physical Properties			Amplitude Decrement Factor	Time Lag
Thickness (cm)			k (W/mK)	ρ (kg/m^2)	c (J/kgK)	μ (-)	Ö (h)
	10.5 5.0	Brick Insulation	0.84 0.04	1700 25.0	800.0 1380.0	0.876	2.66
	5.0 10.5	Insulation Brick	0.04 0.84	25.0 1700.0	1380.0 800.0	0.07	6.64
	22.0 5.0	Brick Insulation	0.84 0.04	1700 25.0	800.0 1380.0	0.37	6.82
	5.0 22.0	Insulation Brick	0.04 0.84	25.0 1700.0	1380.0 800.0	0.03	9.33
	1.6 5.0	Wood Insulation	0.13 0.04	600.0 25.0	2000.0 1380.0	0.99	0.68
	5.0 1.6	Insulation Wood	0.04 0.13	25.0 600.0	1380.0 2000.0	0.47	4.32
	20.0 5.0	Concrete Insulation	1.4 0.04	2100.0 25.0	800.0 1380.0	0.56	5.23
	5.0 20.0	Insulation Concrete	0.04 1.4	25.0 2100.0	1380.0 800.0	0.03	8.12
	30.0 5.0	Concrete Insulation	1.4 0.04	2100.0 25.0	800.0 1380.0	0.27	7.95
	5.0 30.0	Insulation Concrete	0.04 1.4	25.0 2100.0	1380.0 800.0	0.016	10.47
	10.0 5.0	Concrete Insulation	1.4 0.04	2100.0 25.0	800.0 1380.0	0.94	1.94
	5.0 10.0	Insulation Concrete	0.04 1.4	25.0 2100.0	1380.0 800.0	0.06	6.41

Wall construction (Outside to Inside)			Physical Properties			Amplitude Decrement Factor	Time Lag
Thickness (cm)			k (W/mK)	ρ (kg/m^2)	c (J/kgK)	μ (-)	Ö (h)
	14 4 9.5	Concrete Insulation Gyp. Board	2.1 0.04 0.21	2500 100 900	1000 1500 1000	0.1024	10.265
	14 10 9.5	Concrete Insulation Gyp. Board	2.1 0.04 0.21	2500 100 900	1000 1500 1000	0.416	12.20
	11.5 12 24	Brick Insulation Brick	0.96 0.04 0.56	2000 100 1200	1000 1500 1000	0.0076	16.83
	1.6 14 1.9	Ph. Wood Insulation Wood Board	0.13 0.04 0.13	600 100 600	2000 1000 2000	0.102	9.92
	17.5	Wood	0.13	600	2000	0.0807	12.252
	11.5 2.55 11.5	Brick Cavity Brick	0.45 0.147 0.45	1000 0.34 1000	1000 1000 1000	0.1818	8.8936
	7.5 2.5 15	Concrete Insulation Concrete	2.1 0.04 0.22	2500 100 500	1000 500 1000	0.1837	8.332
	20 10 2	Loam Brick Timber	0.9 0.56 0.13	1000 12000 0600	1000 1000 2000	0.2078	9.248
	10.5	Solid Brick (Unplastered)	0.84	1700	800	0.88	2.32
	22.0	Solid Brick (Unplastered)	0.84	1700	800	0.38	6.48
	33.5	Solid Brick (Unplastered)	0.84	1700	8000	0.153	9.84

Wall construction (Outside to Inside)		Physical Properties			Amplitude Decrement Factor	Time Lag
Thickness (cm)		k (W/mK)	ρ (kg/m²)	c (J/kgK)	μ (-)	Ö (h)
10.5 1.6	Solid Brick Dense Plaster	0.84 0.5	1700 1300	800 1000	0.82	2.96
22.0 1.6	Solid Brick Dense Plaster	0.84 0.5	1700 1300	800 1000	0.34	6.98
33.5 1.6	Solid Brick Dense Plaster	0.84 0.5	1700 1300	800 1000	0.14	10.32
10.5 1.6	Solid Brick Light Plaster	0.84 0.16	1700 600	800 1000	0.85	2.72
22.0 1.6	Solid Brick Light Plaster	0.84 0.16	1700 600	800 1000	0.36	6.81
33.5 1.6	Solid Brick Light Plaster	0.84 0.16	1700 600	800 1000	0.144	10.16
10.5 2.0 10.5 1.6	Brick Cavity Brick Dense Plaster	0.84 0.147 0.84 0.5	1700 0.34 1700 1300	800 3600 800 1000	0.23	7.78
10.5 2.0 10.5 1.6	Brick Cavity Brick Light Plaster	0.84 0.147 0.84 0.16	1700 0.34 1700 1300	800 3600 800 1000	0.25	7.65
15.0 5.0 1.6	Concrete Wood Wool Dense Plaster	1.4 0.1 0.5	2100 500 1300	800 1000 1000	0.435	7.34
20.0 5.0 1.6	Concrete Wood Wool Dense Plaster	1.4 0.1 0.5	2100 500 1300	800 1000 1000	0.31	8.88

Wall construction (Outside to Inside)			Physical Properties			Amplitude Decrement Factor	Time Lag
Thickness (cm)			k (W/mK)	ρ (kg/m²)	c (J/kgK)	μ (-)	Ö (h)
	7.5 2.5 15.0	Concrete Expended Polystyrene Light Wt. Concrete	1.4 0.04 0.38	2100 25.0 1200	800 1380 1000	0.07	9.65
	1.5 7.5 15.0 1.5	Asphalt Sweed... Dense Concrete Dense Plaster	0.5 0.4 11.4 0.5	1700 1200 2100 1300	1000 840 800 1000	1.166	7.92
	1.9 15.0 1.5	Asphalt Aerated Conc. Dense Plaster	0.5 0.16 0.5	1700 500 1300	1000 840 1000	0.288	7.26

4.4 ECBC REQUIREMENTS AND COMPLIANCE

Under the requirements of Energy Conservation Building Code (ECBC), the building envelope shall comply with the mandatory provisions and either the prescriptive criteria or the trade-off option. This means, a designer has three major options:

Option-1 :

Under the prescriptive criteria, the envelope has to meet standards prescribed separately for each building component such as walls, roofs, windows, skylights etc.

Option-2 :

This option is given considering the fact that in any building, it may not be possible to meet the prescribed criteria for one component, whereas, for any other component it may be possible to provide much better specification than the prescribed value. A typical example would be providing better insulation than prescribed value in roof can be balanced with not-meeting the prescribed value for walls or windows. Care has to be taken in this trade-off option regarding the calculation of Energy Performance Factor which has been explained later in appendix to this chapter.

Option-3 :

Third option for ensuring compliance is through the Whole Building Performance Method alternatively known as Energy Budget Method. In this method, performance of the designed building is to be compared with standard building of similar shape, usage and HVAC equipment. There are several simulation tools, such as Visual DOE, Energy Plus, eQUEST, Ecotect, that are capable of providing such comparison between designed building and standard building. Details of the standard building with which comparison is to be done, are provided in appendix to this chapter.

Under the requirements of ECBC, the following areas of the enclosed building envelope shall be sealed, caulked, gasketed, or weather-stripped to minimize air leakage:

(a) Joints around fenestration and door frames,

(b) Openings between walls and foundations and between walls and roof and wall panels,

(c) Openings at penetrations of utility services through, roofs, walls, and floors

(d) Site-built fenestration and doors,

(e) Building assemblies used as ducts or plenums, and

(f) All other openings in the building envelope.

4.4.1 Requirements for Roofs

Roofs shall comply with either the maximum assembly U-factor or the minimum insulation R-value in Table 4.7. R-value is for the insulation alone and does not include building materials or air films. The roof insulation shall not be located on a suspended ceiling with removable ceiling panels. It may be noted that the usual practice of specifying the heat transfer coefficient is U-value and R-value. However, in few references and in ECBC, the term U-factor has been used in its place.

Table 4.7: Roof insulation U-factor and R-value requirements

Climate Zone	24-Hour use buildings Hospitals, Hotels, Call Centers etc.		Daytime use buildings Other Building Types	
	Maximum U-factor of the overall assembly (W/m^2-°C)	Minimum R-value of insulation alone (m^2-°C/W)	Maximum U-factor of the overall assembly (W/m^2-°C)	Minimum R-value of insulation alone (m^2-°C/W)
Composite	U-0.261	R-3.5	U-0.409	R-2.1
Hot and Dry	U-0.261	R-3.5	U-0.409	R-2.1
Warm and Humid	U-0.261	R-3.5	U-0.409	R-2.1
Moderate	U-0.409	R-2.1	U-0.409	R-2.1
Cold	U-0.261	R-3.5	U-0.409	R-2.1

Roofs with slopes less than 20 degrees shall have an initial solar reflectance of no less than 0.70 and an initial emittance no less than 0.75. Solar reflectance shall be determined in accordance with ASTM E903-96 and emittance shall be determined in accordance with ASTM E408-71 (RA 1996).

For calculating the overall U-factor of a typical roof construction, the U-factors from the typical wall construction type and effective U-factor for insulation shall be combined according to the following equation:

$$U_{Total\ Roof} = \frac{1}{\frac{1}{U_{Typical\ Roof}} + \frac{1}{U_{Tyipcal\ Insulation}}}$$

where:

$U_{totalRoof}$: overall U-factor for roof assembly

$U_{Typical\ Roof}$: U-factor for roof from Table 4.8

$U_{Typical\ Insulation}$: U-factor of the effective insulation from Table 4.9.

Table 4.8: Defaults of typical roof constructions

Type	U-factor (W/m²-°K)	U-factor (Btu/h-ft²-°F)
RCC slab with mud phuska and clay tiles	2.797	0.493
RCC slab with foam concrete or perlite	0.069	0.012
Inverted clay/pots with mud phuska	2.244	0.396

Table 4.9: Defaults for effective U-value for exterior insulation layers

Thickness	R-value	U-factor (W/m²-°K)	U-factor (Btu/h-ft²-°F)
15 mm (0.5")	0.70 (4)	1.420	0.250
20 mm (0.75")	1.06 (6)	0.946	0.167
25 mm (1.0")	1.41 (8)	0.710	0.125
40 mm (1.5")	2.11 (12)	0.568	0.100
50 mm (2.0")	2.82 (16)	0.406	0.071
65 mm (2.5")	3.52 (20)	0.284	0.050
75 mm (3.0")	3.70 (21)	0.270	0.048

The method of calculating overall U-value/R-value has already been described with detail previously in this Chapter. It is advised that U-value or R-value should be found as per design rather than taking default value for calculations.

4.4.2 Requirements for Opaque Walls

Opaque walls shall comply with either the maximum assembly U-factor or the minimum insulation R-value in Table 4.10. R-value is for the insulation alone and does not include building materials or air films.

Table 4.10: Opaque Wall Assembly U-factor and Insulation R-value Requirements

Climate Zone	Hospitals, Hotels, Call Centers (24-Hour)		Other Building Types (Daytime)	
	Maximum U-factor of the overall assembly (W/m^2-°C)	Minimum R-value of insulation alone (m^2-°C/W)	Maximum U-factor of the overall assembly (W/m^2-°C)	Minimum R-value of insulation alone (m^2-°C/W)
Composite	U-0.44	R-2.10	U-0.44	R-2.10
Hot and Dry	U-0.44	R-2.10	U-0.44	R-2.10
Warm and Humid	U-0.44	R-2.10	U-0.44	R-2.10
Moderate	U-0.431	R-1.80	U-0.397	R-2.00
Cold	U-0.369	R-2.20	U-0.352	R-2.35

For calculating the overall U-factor of a typical wall construction, the U-factors from the typical wall construction type and effective U-factor for insulation shall be combined according to the following equation:

$$U_{Total\ Roof} = \frac{1}{\dfrac{1}{U_{Typical\ Roof}} + \dfrac{1}{U_{Tyipcal\ Insulation}}}$$

where:

$U_{total\ Wall}$: overall U-factor for wall assembly

$U_{Typical\ Wall}$: U-factor for wall from Table 4.11

$U_{Typical\ Insulation}$: U-factor of the effective insulation from Table 4.12, 4.13.

Table 4.11: Default values of U-factor for typical wall constructions

Type	Description	U-factor (W/m²-°K)	U-factor (Btu/h-ft²-°F)
Mass single wall	Single wall with no insulation, plaster on both sides	1.99	0.351
Mass double wall	Double brick wall with air gap	1.23	0.216
Curtain wall	Curtain wall	2.11	0.371

Table 4.12: Defaults for U-factor for exterior insulation

Thickness	R-value	U-factor (W/m²-°K)	U-factor (Btu/h-ft²-°F)
15 mm (0.5")	0.70 (4)	1.262	0.222
20 mm (0.75")	1.06 (6)	0.874	0.154
25 mm (1.0")	1.41 (8)	0.668	0.118
40 mm (1.5")	2.11 (12)	0.454	0.080
50 mm (2.0")	2.82 (16)	0.344	0.061
65 mm (2.5")	3.52 (20)	0.277	0.049
75 mm (3.0")	3.70 (21)	0.264	0.047

Table 4.13: Defaults for U-factor for interior insulation

Thickness	R-value	U-factor (W/m²-°K)	U-factor (Btu/h-ft²-°F)
15 mm (0.5")	0.70 (4)	4.732	0.833
20 mm (0.75")	1.06 (6)	3.549	0.625
25 mm (1.0")	1.41 (8)	2.988	0.526
40 mm (1.5")	2.11 (12)	2.103	0.370
50 mm (2.0")	2.82 (16)	1.670	0.294
65 mm (2.5")	3.52 (20)	1.385	0.244
75 mm (3.0")	3.70 (21)	1.183	0.208

APPENDIX 4.1

ENVELOPE TRADE OFF METHOD FOR COMPLIANCE OF ECBC

The building envelope complies with the code if the building envelope performance factor (EPF) of the proposed design is less than the standard design, where the standard design exactly complies with the criteria following prescriptive approach.

The envelope performance factor shall be calculated using the following equations.

$$EPF_{Total} = EPF_{Roof} + EPF_{Wall} + EPF_{Fenest}$$

where

$$EPF_{Roof} = c_{Roof} \sum_{s=1}^{n} U_s A_s$$

$$EPF_{Wall} = c_{Wall,Mass} \sum_{s=1}^{n} U_s A_s + c_{Wall,Other} \sum_{s=1}^{n} U_s A_s$$

$$\begin{aligned} EPF_{Fenest} = {} & c_{1Fenest,North} \sum_{w=1}^{n} SHGC_w M_w A_w + c_{2Fenest,North} \sum_{w=1}^{n} U_w A_w + \\ & c_{1Fenest,NonNorth} \sum_{w=1}^{n} SHGC_w M_w A_w + c_{2Fenest,NonNorth} \sum_{w=1}^{n} U_w A_w + \\ & c_{1Fenest,Skylight} \sum_{s=1}^{n} SHGC_s A_s + c_{2Fenest,Skylight} \sum_{s=1}^{n} U_s A_s \end{aligned}$$

where:

EPF_{Roof} : Envelope performance factor for roofs. Other subscripts include walls and fenestration

As, A_W : The area of a specific envelope component referenced by the subscript "s" or for windows the subscript 'w'.

$SHGC_W$: The solar heat gain coefficient for windows (w). $SHGC_S$ refers to skylights.

M_W : A multiplier for the window SHGC that depends on the projection factor of an overhang r sidefin

U_S : The U-factor for the envelope component referenced by the subscript "s".

c_{Roof} : A coefficient for the "Roof" class of construction. Values of "c" are taken from Tables A4.1.1 to A4.1.5 given below.

Table A4.1.1: Envelope Performance Factor Coefficients – Composite Climate

	Daytime Occupancy		24-Hour Occupancy	
	U-factor	SHGC	U-factor	SHGC
Mass Walls	6.01	-	13.85	-
Curtain Walls, Other	15.72	-	20.48	-
Roofs	11.93	-	24.67	-
North Windows	-1.75	40.65	-4.56	58.15
Non-North Windows	-1.25	54.51	0.68	86.57
Skylights	-96.35	311.71	-294.66	918.77

Table A4.1.2: Envelope Performance Factor Coefficients – Hot & dry Climate

	Daytime Occupancy		24-Hour Occupancy	
	U-factor	SHGC	U-factor	SHGC
Mass Walls	5.48	-	15.01	-
Curtain Walls, Other	6.38	-	22.06	-
Roofs	11.14	-	25.98	-
North Windows	-2.40	36.57	-1.49	56.09
Non-North Windows	-1.86	46.79	1.187	81.79
Skylights	-96.27	309.33	-295.81	923.01

Table A4.1.3: Envelope Performance Factor Coefficients – Hot and Humid Climate

	Daytime Occupancy		24-Hour Occupancy	
	U-factor	SHGC	U-factor	SHGC
Mass Walls	6.42	-	9.60	-
Curtain Walls, Other	14.77	-	19.71	-
Roofs	9.86	-	14.11	-
North Windows	-1.58	34.95	-7.29	64.19
Non-North Windows	-1.00	43.09	-6.48	76.83
Skylights	-96.11	305.45	-295.45	893.55

Table A4.1.4: Envelope Performance Factor Coefficients – Moderate Climate

	Daytime Occupancy		24-Hour Occupancy	
	U-factor	SHGC	U-factor	SHGC
Mass Walls	2.017	-	3.11	-
Curtain Walls, Other	2.72	-	4.11	-
Roofs	5.46	-	5.86	-
North Windows	-3.10	29.66	-11.95	62.14
Non-North Windows	-2.98	34.86	-11.62	68.45
Skylights	-96.21	298.82	-294.12	876.70

Table A4.1.5: Envelope Performance Factor Coefficients – Cold Climate

	Daytime Occupancy		24-Hour Occupancy	
	U-factor	SHGC	U-factor	SHGC
Mass Walls	5.19	-	5.19	-
Curtain Walls, Other	6.76	-	6.76	-
Roofs	5.69	-	5.67	-
North Windows	1.55	9.13	1.55	9.13
Non-North Windows	-1.13	16.32	-1.13	16.32
Skylights	-93.44	283.18	-93.44	283.18

Details related to windows and HVAC system have been discussed later in this book along with their respective chapters.

APPENDIX 4.2

DETAILS OF STANDARD BUILDING FOR COMPLIANCE METHOD OF ENERGY BUDGET BUILDING

A building complies with the whole building performance method when the estimated annual energy use of the proposed design is less than the standard design, even though it may not comply with the specific requirements of the prescriptive requirements.

Annual Energy Use

Annual energy use for the purposes of the whole building performance method shall be calculated in kilowatt-hours (kWh) of electricity use per year. Energy sources other than electricity which are used in the building shall be converted to kWh of electric energy at the rate of 0.75 kWh per Mega Joule.

The whole building performance method may be used for building permit applications that include less than the whole building; however, any design parameters that are not part of the building permit application shall be identical for both the proposed design and the standard design. Future improvements to the building shall comply with both the mandatory and prescriptive requirements.

Documents required for showing compliance

Compliance shall be documented and submitted to the authority having jurisdiction. The information submitted shall include the following:

(a) The annual energy use for the proposed design and the standard design.

(b) A list of the energy-related building features in the proposed design that are different from the standard design.

(c) The input and output report(s) from the simulation program including a breakdown of energy usage by at least the following components: lights, internal equipment loads, service water heating equipment, space heating equipment, space cooling and heat rejection equipment, fans, and other HVAC equipment (such as pumps). The output reports shall also show the amount of time any loads are not met by the HVAC system for both the proposed design and standard design.

(d) An explanation of any error messages noted in the simulation program output.

Requirements for simulation method

The simulation program shall be a computer-based program for the analysis of energy consumption in buildings and be approved by the authority having jurisdiction. The simulation program and shall model the following:

(a) Energy flows on an hourly basis for all 8,760 hours in the year,

(b) Hourly variations in occupancy, lighting power, miscellaneous equipment power, thermostat setpoints, and HVAC system operation, defined separately for each day of the week and holidays,

(c) Thermal mass effects,

(d) Ten or more thermal zones,

(e) Part-load and temperature dependent performance of heating and cooling equipment,

(f) Air-side and water-side economizers with integrated control, and

(g) All of the standard design characteristics specified in this chapter.

Climatic data

The simulation program shall use hourly values of climatic data, such as temperature and humidity from representative climatic data, for the city in which the proposed design is to be located. For cities or urban regions with several climatic data entries, and for locations where weather data are not available, the designer shall select available weather data that best represent the climate at the construction site.

Compliance calculations

The proposed design and standard design shall be calculated using the following:

(a) Same simulation program,

(b) Same weather data, and

(c) Same building operation assumptions (thermostat setpoints, schedules, internal gains, occupant loads, etc.).

Comparing Energy Consumption of the Proposed Design and the Standard Design

The simulation model for calculating the proposed design and the standard design shall be developed in accordance with the requirements in Table 10.3.1 of the code.

The HVAC system type and related performance parameters for the standard design shall be determined from Table A4.2.1.

Table A4.2.1: HVAC systems map for ECBC compliance

	Residential		Non-residential	
	More than 3 stories	Less than 3 floors or less than 7,500 m^2	4 or 5 floors or less than 7,500 m^2 or 5 floors or less and 7,500–15,000 m^2	More than 5 floors or more than 15,000m^2
Code	PTAC	PSZ	RHFS	RHFS
System type	Packaged terminal air conditioner	Packaged rooftop air conditioner	Central cooling plant with constant volume AHU for each zone	Central cooling plant with constant volume AHU for each zone
Fan control	Constant Volume	Constant volume	Constant volume air handler for each zone	Constant volume air handler for each zone
Cooling type	Direct expansion	Direct expansion	Air cooled reciprocating chiller	Water cooled centrifugal chiller
Heating type	Electric resistance	Electric resistance	Electric resistance	Electric resistance

Components and parameters not listed in Table A4.2.1 or otherwise specifically addressed in this subsection shall be identical to those in the proposed design. Exception to these specifications for standard building would be applicable where there are specific requirements as per overall guidelines of the code, the component efficiency in the standard design shall be adjusted to the lowest efficiency level allowed by the requirement for that component type.

(a) All HVAC and service water heating equipment in the standard design shall be modeled at the minimum efficiency levels, both part load and full load, in accordance with general guidelines.

(b) Where efficiency ratings, such as EER and COP, include fan energy, the descriptor shall be broken down into its components so that supply fan energy can be modeled separately.

(c) Minimum outdoor air ventilation rates shall be the same for both the standard design and the proposed design.

(d) The equipment capacities for the standard design shall be sized proportionally to the capacities in the proposed design based on sizing runs; i.e., the ratio between the capacities used in the annual simulations and the capacities determined by the sizing runs shall be the same for both the proposed design and standard design. Unmet load hours for the proposed design shall not differ from unmet load hours for the standard design by more than 50 hours.

APPENDIX 4.3

EXAMPLES OF HEAT TRANSFER

Example 4.1

The wall of a cold storage consists of three layers – an outer layer of ordinary bricks, 25 cm thick, a middle layer of cork, 10 cm thick, and an inner layer of cement, 6 cm thick. The thermal conductivities of the materials are – brick: 0.7, cork: 0.043, and cement: 0.72 W/m°C. The temperature of the outer surface of the wall is 30°C, and that of the inner is –15°C. Calculate (a) the steady state rate of heat gain per unit area of the wall, (b) the temperatures at the interfaces of the composite wall, and (c) the percentages of the total heat transfer resistance offered by the individual layers. What additional thickness of cork should be provided to make the rate of heat transfer 30% less than the present value?

Solution:

Let the three layers be layer 1: brick; layer 2: cork; and layer 3: cement. If we consider unit area of the wall ($1 m^2$), then from Eq. (5.9), we get

Thermal resistance of the brick layer,

$$R_1 = \frac{l_1}{k_1 A} = \frac{0.25\,\text{m}}{(0.7\,\text{W/m}\,^\circ\text{C})(1\,\text{m}^2)} = 0.357^\circ\text{C/W}$$

Thermal resistance of the cork layer,

$$R_2 = \frac{l_2}{k_2 A} = \frac{0.10\,\text{m}}{(0.043\,\text{W/m}\,^\circ\text{C})(1\,\text{m}^2)} = 2.326^\circ\text{C/W}$$

Thermal resistance of the cement layer,

$$R_3 = \frac{l_3}{k_3 A} = \frac{0.06\,\text{m}}{(0.72\,\text{W/m}\,^\circ\text{C})(1\,\text{m}^2)} = 0.083^\circ\text{C/W}$$

Total thermal resistance = $R_1 + R_2 + R_3$ = 0.357 + 2.326 + 0.083 = 2.766°C/W

Temperature driving force = 30 - (-15) = 45°C

(a) Rate of heat gain by the wall, Q = 45°C/(2.766°c/w) = 16.27 W

(b) The temperature drop across the brick layer

$$T_1 - T^1 = Q\frac{l_1}{k_1 A} = (16.27)(0.357) = 5.8^\circ\text{C}$$

Now T_1 = 30°C; therefore, T′ = 30°C – 5.8°C = 24.2°C (interface temperature between brick and cork).

Similarly, $T' - T'' = Q \dfrac{l_2}{k_2 A} = (16.27)(2.326) = 37.8°C$

Therefore,

T″ = 24.2 – 37.8 = -13.6°C (Interface temperature between cork and cement).

(c) Per cent thermal resistance offered by the

brick layer $= \dfrac{0.357}{2.766} \times 100 = 12.9\%$

cork layer $= \dfrac{2.326}{2.766} \times 100 = 84.1\%$

cement layer $= \dfrac{0.083}{2.766} \times 100 = 3.0\%$

Second Part

Desired rate of heat flow (30% less than the present value) = (16.27)(0.7) = 11.39 W

Required thermal resistance $= \dfrac{\text{Driving force}}{\text{Rate of heat flow}} = \dfrac{45}{11.39} = 3.95°C/W$

Additional thermal resistance to be provided = 3.95 – 2.766 = 1.184°C/W

Additional thickness of cork to be provided = (1.184)(0.043)(1) = 51 cm

Example 4.2

The walls of a house in a very cold region consist of three layers – an outer brickwork of 15 cm thickness and an inner wooden panel of 1.2 cm thickness. The intermediate layer is made of an insulating material 7 cm thick. The thermal conductivities of the brick and the wood used are 0.70 W/m°C and 0.18 W/m°C, respectively. The inside and outside temperatures of the composite wall are 21°C and –15°C, respectively. If the layer of insulation offers twice the thermal resistance of the brick wall, calculate (a) the rate of heat loss per unit area of the wall and (b) the thermal conductivity of the insulating material

Solution:

Consider 1 m^2 of the wall area.

(a) If l = thickness of a layer, A = area, and k = thermal conductivity, then

thermal resistance $= \dfrac{l}{kA}$ in the given case, A = 1.0 m^2

Thermal resistance of the layer of brick (l = 0.15 m; k = 0.70 W/m °C)

$$= \frac{0.15}{(0.70)(1.0)} = 0.2143\ ^\circ C/W$$

Thermal resistance of the layer of wood (l = 0.012 m; k = 0.18 W/m °C)

$$= \frac{0.012}{(0.18)(1.0)} = 0.0667\ ^\circ C/W$$

Thermal resistance of the insulating layer (2)(0.2143) = 0.4286 °C/W
Total thermal resistance = 0.2143 + 0.4286 + 0.0667 = 0.7096 °C/W

Temperature driving force = 21 – (-15) = 36°C

$$\text{Rate of heat loss} = \frac{36^\circ C}{0.7096\ ^\circ C/W} = 50.7\ W$$

(b) For the insulating layer, l = 0.07 m; A = 1.0 m²; thermal resistance = l/kA = 0.4286 °C/W

Therefore,

$$\text{Thermal conductivity, } k = \frac{0.07}{(1.0)(0.4286)} = 0.1633\ W/m\ ^\circ C$$

Example 4.3

Estimate the heat transfer from a 40-W incandescent bulb at 127°C to 27°C quiescent air. Approximate the bulb as a 50-mm-dia. sphere. What percent of the power is lost by free convection? Use the following relationship for Nusset's number:

$$Nu = \frac{\bar{h}D}{k} = (0.60)(Gr_L\ Pr)^{1/4}$$

Solution:

From appendices, the required parameters, evaluated at $T_f = (T_s + T_\infty)/2 = 77^\circ C$, are:
$\nu = (22.38 \times 10^{-5})(0.0929) = 2.079 \times 10^{-5}\ m^2/s$ $Pr = 0.697$
$k = (0.01735)(1.729) = 0.0300\ W/m\text{-}K$, $\beta = 1/T = 1/350 = 2.857 \times 10^{-3}\ K^{-1}$

Evaluating the Grashof number, where the characteristic length L is the diameter of the sphere, gives

$$Gr_L = \frac{g\beta(T_s - T_\infty)D^3}{\nu^2}$$

$$= \frac{(9.80 m/s^2)(2.857 \times 10^{-3}\ K^{-1})(100 K)(0.050 m)^3}{(2.079 \times 10-5)^2\ m^4/s^2} = 8.1 \times 10^5$$

Equation given in problem governs the heat transfer, hence,

$$\frac{\bar{h}D}{k} = (0.60)(Gr_L Pr)^{1/4}$$

$$\bar{h} = \frac{0.0300 W/m\text{-}K}{0.050 m}(0.60)[(81 \times 10^5)(0.697)]^{1/4} = 9.87 W/m^2\text{-}K$$

The heat transfer is

$$q = \bar{h}A(T_s - T_\infty) = \left(9.87 \frac{W}{m^2\text{-}K}\right)\pi(0.050\,m)^2(100\,K) = 7.75\,W$$

$$\frac{7.75}{40}(100\%) = 19.37\%$$

Example 4.4

What heat load is generated in a restaurant by a 1.0-m by 0.8-m cooking grill which is maintained at 134°C? The room temperature is 20°C.

Solution:

The appropriate parameters from appendices, evaluated at the mean film temperature, are:

$$T_f = \frac{T_s + T_\infty}{2} = 77°C$$

$\nu = (22.38 \times 10^{-5})(9.29 \times 10^{-2}) = 2.08 \times 10^{-5}\ m^2/s$

$k = (0.01735)(1.729) = 0.0300\ W/m\text{-}K$

$Pr = 0.697$

For air, $\beta = 1/T = 1/350 = 2.857 \times 10^{-3}\ K^{-1}$, and the Grashof number is

$$Gr_L = \frac{g\beta(T_s - T_\infty)L^3}{\nu^2}$$

where L = 0.9 m, the average of the lengths of the two edges.

$$Gr_L = \frac{(9.80\,m/s^2)(2.857 \times 10^{-3}\,K^{-1})(114 K)(0.9 m)^3}{(2.08 \times 10^{-5})^2\,m^4/s^2}$$

Using empirical relation for this case of a heated plate facing up,

$$\frac{\bar{h}L}{k} = (0.14)(Gr_L Pr)^{1/3}$$

$$\bar{h} = \frac{0.0300 W/m\text{-}K}{0.9 m}(0.14)[(538 \times 10^9)(0.697)]^{1/3} = 7.25 W/m^2\text{-}K$$

This gives a heat transfer of

$$q = \bar{h}A(T_s - T_\infty) = \left(7.25 \frac{W}{m^2\text{-}K}\right)[(1.0 \times 0.8)\,m^2](114 K) = 661.2 W$$

Example 4.5

It is desired to cut down the radiation loss between two parallel surfaces by inserting a sheet of aluminium foil midway between them. The temperatures of the two surfaces are maintained at 40 and 5°C, and the emissivity of both surfaces is 0.85. The emissivity of aluminium foil is 0.05. Calculate the percentage reduction in heat loss rate by radiation using the aluminium foil, assuming that the surface temperature are the same in both cases and that all surfaces are grey. Neglect end effects.

Solution:

Without the aluminium foil, for two long parallel surfaces, for 1 m^2 of surface, combined thermal resistance due to emissivity and geometric factor can be found using:

$R_T = (1/\varepsilon_1) + (A_1/A_2)\{(1/\varepsilon_2) - 1\}$

As A_1 and A_2 are equal in this case, it becomes:

$$R_T = (1/\varepsilon_1) + (1/\varepsilon_2) - 1 = (2/0.85) - 1$$

i.e. $R_T = 1.353$

Therefore, heat transfer can be found using:

$$\dot{Q}_{1-2} = \frac{\sigma(T_1^4 - T_2^4)}{R_T} = \frac{5.67 \times (3.13^4 - 2.78^4)}{1.353}$$

where $T_1 = 40 + 273 = 313$ K and $T_2 = 5 + 273 = 278$ K

i.e. $\dot{Q}_{1-2} = 151.92 \text{ W/m}^2$

With the aluminium foil, let the temperature of the foil be 'T' K. Now using the same approach used above, heat transfer from surface-1 to foil,

$$\dot{Q}_{1-F} = \frac{\sigma(T_1^4 - T^4)}{R_{T1-F}}$$

and from the foil to surface 2

$$\dot{Q}_{F-2} = \frac{\sigma(T^4 - T_2^4)}{R_{TF-2}}$$

Since both sides of the foil act in a similar way, and since $\varepsilon 1 = \varepsilon 2$, then $R_{T1-F} = R_{TF-2}$. Therefore,

$$(T_1^4 - T^4) = (T^4 - T_2^4) \quad \text{or} \quad T^4 = \frac{T_1^4 + T_2^4}{2}$$

$T^4 = 77.85 \times 10^8$

Also $R_{T1-F} = R_{TF-2} = (1/0.85) + (1/0.05) - 1 = 20.176$

Then from the equation for heat transfer:

$$\dot{Q}_{1-F} = \frac{\sigma(T_1^4 - T^4)}{R_T} = \frac{5.67 \times (3.13^4 - 77.85)}{20.176}$$

i.e.

Therefore, $\dot{Q}_{1-F} = 5.09 \text{ W/m}^2$

Percentage reduction in heat loss

$$= \left(\frac{151.92 - 5.09}{151.92}\right) \times 100 = 96.7\%$$

5

Cooling and Heating Load Calculation*

This chapter explains method for estimating the cooling/heating load in any building. This estimation is one of the most important steps from the point of view of both, thermal comfort and energy consumption. Under-estimation of load would result into uncomfortable indoor conditions and over-estimation would cause excessive energy consumption. Later part of this chapter presents various options for reduction of cooling/heating load in buildings.

5.1 PRINCIPLES OF LOAD CALCULATION

Basic meaning of thermal load is heat to be supplied or extracted from the interior of any building in order to maintain desired thermal conditions. Calculation of thermal load does not include any detail of cooling or heating equipment, it encompasses only the sources and sinks of heat inside the building. Thermal load in any building does not have any fixed value, it changes with variation in any of the many variables such as solar radiation outside, occupancy level, equipment being used inside. For HVAC engineers, peak load or maximum load is of primary importance as it determines the capacity of heating or cooling equipment to be used. The set of conditions that governs rating of equipment is called 'Design Conditions'. Thermal load calculation involves detailed accounting of all the thermal energy terms in any building. In this chapter, detailed methodology for conducting such calculation has been presented.

First thing that governs thermal load is the indoor conditions that one wants to maintain inside the building. It is important to understand that design conditions corresponding to the peak load or worst conditions is not always the best choice. If such extreme conditions occur for less than 1% duration of the year, there is not much sense in deciding the equipment rating corresponding to this condition and under-load the equipment in remaining 99% duration. Doing this has double loss, one, it requires more investment due to higher equipment rating, second, during under-loading efficiency often decreases resulting into more energy consumption by the equipment. However, for critical places such as operation theatre, desired conditions even in this 1% duration have to be met.

5.1.1 Numerical approach for cooling load calculation

In the attempt of calculating the cooling load in any building, all the factors contributing to heat gain are to be addressed separately. A systematic approach to this has been explained in this article.

* Base document for this Chapter is ASHRAE Handbook 'Fundamentals' (2005).

Heat Transmission through building components

(a) Conduction of heat from ambient

One of the most important terms in the heat balance of buildings is the heat flow across the envelope. Assuming the heat flow to be one-dimensional, heat flow through each building component can be found as the product of its area, U-value and the temperature difference through which heat transfer takes place. The calculation of 'U' or its inverse 'R' value has already been described in Chapter-4. Total conductive heat flow between interior and exterior is calculated using the following equation with the sum running over all the parts of building envelope:

$$Q_{cond} = \sum_{k} U_k A_k (T_i - T_o)$$

Where: U_k is U-value of building component 'k' (as described in previous chapter)

A_k is area through which conductive heat transfer takes place.

T_i, T_o are inside temperature and outside temperature respectively.

For most buildings envelope contains large number of parts. As a simplification, few major groups can be considered like glass, walls, roof. However, more is the detailed calculation e.g. considering east, wall, north, south walls separately, more accurate would be the result. With the grouping approach heat transfer can be found through:

$$\dot{Q}_{cond} = \left[U_{wall}A_{wall} + U_{roof}A_{roof} + U_{glass}A_{glass}\right](T_i - T_o)$$

(b) Solar heat gain

In case of surfaces on which solar radiation is incident, in place of the formula given above, heat inflow can be calculated using the term solar gain factor given by:

$$Q = UA(T_i - T_o) - gAI$$

Where: g is solar heat gain factor,

I is intensity of solar radiation,

solar heat gain factor can be calculated as :

$$g = \frac{U\alpha_s}{h_o}$$

α_s is absorptivity of external surface on which solar radiation is incident

h_o is outside convective heat transfer coefficient

In case of transparent surfaces, through which solar radiation can pass causing direct heat gain in the space, heat inflow can be calculated using the same equation except calculation of solar heat gain coefficient given by:

$$g = \tau + \frac{U\alpha}{h_o}$$

Above equation is valid only for unshaded single glazed window. For shaded windows, windows with multiple glazing, with selective coatings, with low-E coating, heat gain can be calculated using values of SHGC compiled and given in ASHRAE or other standard references.

Heat gain by air exchange

Intake of fresh air in building is essential from health point of view. If the amount of fresh air is less, building results into a sick building, on the contrary, if there is excess fresh air, energy consumption increases. The rate of air exchange is defined through a term 'air change per hour'. In brief, air change rate is defined as the number of times, air equal to volume of a room or building is exchanged with the surroundings. Air change in a building may take place in uncontrolled and undesired way called 'infiltration of air'. On the other hand it may be accomplished in controlled way called 'ventilation'. Either of these contribute towards heat gain or loss in buildings that can be found through the following equation:

$$\dot{Q} = c_p \dot{V} (T_i - T_o)$$

where:

ρ: density of air

c_p: specific heat of air

V: air exchange rate (m^3/s)

From above equations, it is convenient to combine terms that are proportional to (T_i-T_o) in the following form:

$$\dot{Q} = \left[c_p \dot{V} + \sum U_k A_k \right] (T_i - T_o) = K_{total} (T_i - T_o)$$

The bracketed term in the above equation has been replaced by single term 'K_{total}' that represents 'total heat transmission coefficient' of the building as a sum of conductive and air change effects.

Internal heat gain

Besides contribution of the climate and exterior conditions, there are several sources within the conditioned space that also contribute towards thermal load. Method to incorporate their contribution in total load has been described in this section.

People

Due to metabolic heat release from the bodies of human beings and all living creatures, there is heat gain in buildings. The rate of such heat release mainly depends upon the level of activity in addition to few other factors such as sex, type of clothing. Table 5.6 shows representative rates of heat gain corresponding to different states of activity.

It may be noted from Table 5.1 that the heat gain can further be split in two components sensible and latent heat gain. For accurate calculation, these two components are to be dealt in a separate way, as the net sensible heat gain from people is also affected by the thermal storage characteristics of the conditioned space. Such analysis is carried out with use of 'Room Transfer Functions' (RTF) coverage of which is beyond the scope of this book.

Table 5.1: Rate of heat gain from occupants of conditioned space

Degree of activity	Total heat, W		Sensible heat	Latent heat	% sensible heat that is radiant	
	Adult male	Adult female			Low V	High V
Seated at theatre	115	95	65	30	60	27
Seated very light work	130	115	70	45		
Moderately active office work	140	130	75	55		
Standing light work	160	130	75	55	58	38
Walking standing	160	145	75	70		
Light bench work	235	220	80	140	49	35
Moderate dancing	265	250	90	160		
Walking 5 km/hr, light machine work	295	295	110	185		
Heavy work	440	425	170	255	54	19
Athletics	585	525	210	315		

Notes : Tabulated values are based on 24^{0}C dry bulb temp of room, low and high V are low air velocity and high air velocity of air surrounding the occupant.

Source : Reprinted with permission from ASHRAE Handbook Fundamentals, Volume, 2005.

Lighting

In cases of space cooling, use of artificial lighting in conditioned space is often necessary as use of sunlight brings in solar heat gain that results into increase in total load on air conditioner. All the artificial lighting devices consume electricity that ultimately gets converted into heat. Such heat gain has two components, one, convective heat transfer from the fitting through moving conditioned air, second, radiative heat gain that comes through radiation emitted by the light. These radiation after illuminating the space, get absorbed by various surfaces present in the space and their energy is re-released by these surfaces such as walls, floors, furniture. There is a significant delay between the time of switching lights on and the re-radiation of heat absorbed by surfaces. It is recommended that in commercial buildings having higher illumination levels, such as showrooms, such time lag should be taken into consideration for calculation of peak load.

Instantaneous heat gain from light emitting elements or lamps can be found using:

$$\dot{Q}_{el} = W F_{ul} F_{sa}$$

where:

Q_{el} : heat gain in W

W : total lighting wattage

F_{ul} : lighting use factor

F_{sa} : lighting special allowance factor

The total wattage is obtained from ratings of installed lamps. The utilisation factor F_{ul} is the ratio of wattage in use to the total installed wattage. This factor is close to unity for commercial places such as departmental stores but may be very low for residential buildings where all the lights are not used simultaneously. Special allowance factor is for fluorescent fixtures or fixtures that are either ventilated or installed in such a way that only a part of their heat goes into the conditioned space. Value of this factor is as low as 0.4 for ventilated fixtures in which heat releases is taken away by ventilation air and does not enter the conditioned space. For non-ventilated fluorescent lamps its value can be as high as 2.2, for general appliances its value can be taken as 1.20.

Electric appliances

Instantaneous heat gain from equipment and appliances uses in conditioned space can be found through:

$$\dot{Q}_{em} = \left(\frac{P}{E_m} \right) F_{um} F_{Lm}$$

where:

Q_{em} is heat gain due to equipment operation in W

P: appliance/motor power rating in W

E_m: appliance/motor efficiency, as decimal fraction (<1.0)

F_{um}: appliance/motor use factor, as decimal fraction (< 1.0)

F_{Lm}: appliance/motor load factor, as decimal fraction (< 1.0)

The use factor is to be applied when the appliance is not to be operated continuously and the load factor is applied to cover, consumption of less power with use as under loaded appliance. In the above equation it is assumed that both the motor and the driven equipment are placed in the conditioned space. If the motor is placed outside the conditioned space and the end-effect is in the conditioned space, the above formula gets modified as given below:

$$\dot{Q}_{em} = P\left(\frac{1 - E_m}{E_m}\right) F_{um} F_{Lm}$$

Limitation of the above discussed approach is that it covers only instantaneous heat gain and does not cover the dynamic effects that deviate the actual heat gain from the instantaneous heat gain.

5.1.2 CLTD/CLF method for cooling load calculation

Due to the storage of energy in the path of transmission as explained in chapter-IV, transient effects of heat transfer come into picture. These effects attenuate the amplitude of temperature variation inside the space and bring in some time lag. To account for transient effects without having to resort to a full-fledged dynamic analysis, a special shorthand method has been developed that uses the *Cooling Load Temperature Difference (CLTD)* and *Cooling Load Factor (CLF)*. This method has been described in this section that is convenient to use and avoids many steps of calculations. As has been explained earlier, heat transfer under static conditions across an envelope element of area A and conductance U would be:

$$Q_{C,\ cond} = U\ A\ (T_0 - T_i)$$

Static conditions in the above equation mean that indoor temperature T_i and outdoor temperature T_o are both constant. In actual practice, when the temperatures vary, this equation does not hold good. But if the temperatures follow a periodic pattern, day after day, $Q_{c,cond}$ will also follow a periodic pattern. To simplify the task of calculating heat flow using periodic pattern, the values of CLTD are compiled in ASHRAE. These values are specific for different types of construction and outdoor weather conditions. These values can directly be taken and used in the above equation for quick determination of the load. Thus the conductive cooling load is:

$$Q_{c,cond} = U\ A\ (CLTD_t)$$

where the subscript 't' indicates hour 't' of the day.

Figure 5.1 a & b show CLTD for two different types of sunlit walls with different orientations for 40^0 N on July 21. Figure 5.2 shows CLTD for three roof types.

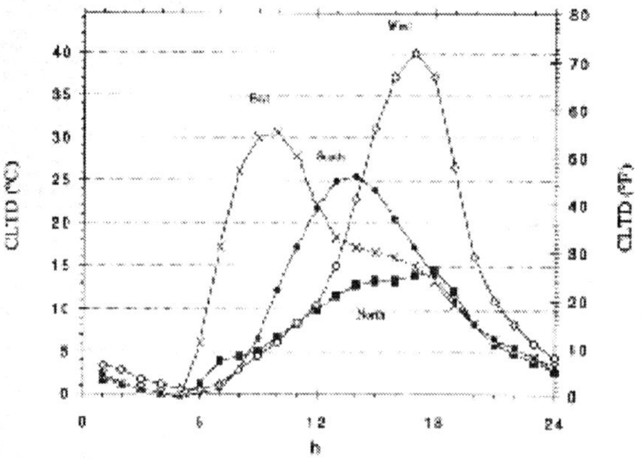

Figure 5.1a: CLTD for sunlit wall, group-A type (8-inches thick concrete with insulation)

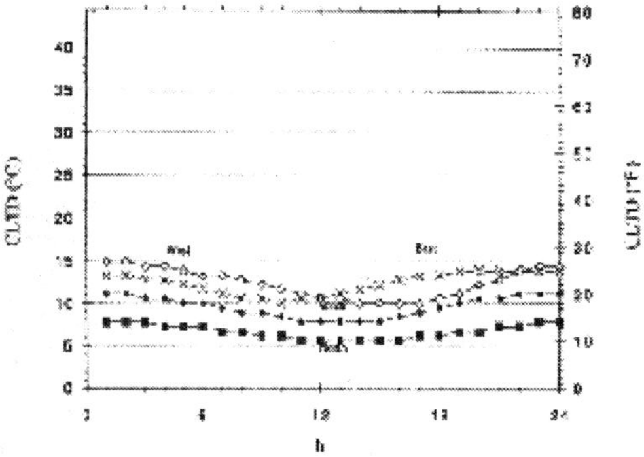

Figure 5.1b: CLTD for sunlit wall, group-G type (light wall, frame wall or curtain wall)

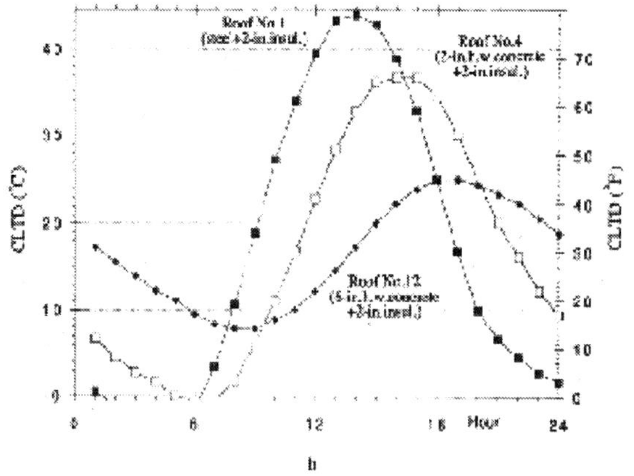

Figure 5.2: CLTD for three roof types

Above figures are for inside temperature 25.5⁰C and outside mean temperature as 29.4⁰C. Corrected CLTD should be calculated in the following manner for any deviation in above conditions:

$$CLTD_{corr} = (CLTD + LM)K + (25.5^0C + T_i) + (T_{o,av} - 29.4^0C)$$

where:

LM is the correction factor for latitude and month (from ASHRAE)

K is colour adjustment factor

T_i, $T_{o,av}$ are actual values of inside temperature and average outside temperature

If there is a constant radiative gain in a zone, the corresponding cooling load is simply equal to that heat gain. If the radiative heat gain follows a periodic pattern, the cooling load also follows a periodic pattern. The Cooling Load Factor (CLF) is defined such that it yields the cooling load at hour 't' when multiplied by the daily maximum Q_{max} of heat gain:

$$Q_{c,rad,t} = \dot{Q}_{\max} (CLF_t)$$

The CLF accounts for the fact that radiative gains (solar, lights etc.) are first absorbed by the mass of building, becoming a cooling load only as they are being transferred to the air. Only convective gains can be counted as cooling load without delay. Some heat gains, e.g. from occupants, are partly convective and partly radiative as explained in preceding section, are also taken care of by CLF.

The CLTDs and CLFs have been calculated by means of transfer functions compiled by ASHRAE. Selected tables have been given in appendices of this book. The value of CLTD is sensitive to latitude, type of construction (R-value of wall/mass per sq meter) and orientation of wall. Therefore, careful reading of CLTD tables is suggested. For using the CLTD/CLF method, it is further advised to use a computerised worksheet given as Table 5.2 below. It is to be filled for every hour/critical hours for finding the maximum cooling load value.

Table 5.2: Worksheet for CLTD/CLF method of load calculation

Job ID	Date		Initials	
Site	Latitude		Longitude	
Design conditions	Indoor temp.	Rel. humid.	Outdoor temp.	Rel. humid.
Room	Identification		Dimensions	

Latent loads					Instantaneous
	$\dot{V}$	W_o	W_i	$\Delta W = W_o - W_i$	$\dot{Q}_{lat} = \rho \times h_{fg} \times \dot{V} \times \Delta W$
Air exchange					
	N = number			$\dot{Q}_{lat/unit}$	$\dot{Q}_{lat} = N \times \dot{Q}_{lat/unit}$
Appliances					
People					
TOTAL LATENT					

Sensible loads					hour t			hour t		
Component and orientation	Construction type		U	A	$CLTD_t$			$\dot{Q}_t = U \times A \times CLTD_t$		
Walls										
Roof										
Glazing conduction										
Glazing solar		A	SC	$SHGF_{max}$	CLF_t			$\dot{Q}_t = A \times SC \times SHGF_{max} \times CLF_t$		
Air exchange		V	$\dot{V}$	T_i	T_o			$\dot{Q} = \rho \times c_p \times \dot{V} \times (T_o - T_i)$ (instantaneous)		
Internal partitions			U	A	ΔT across partition			$\dot{Q} = U \times A \times \Delta T$ (instantaneous)		
Ceiling										
Floor										
Sides										
Ducts										
Internal gains		number	gain /unit	$\dot{Q}$	CLF_t			$\dot{Q}_t = \dot{Q} \times CLF_t$		
Appliances										
Fans										
Lights										
Motors										
People										
TOTAL SENSIBLE										

Similar to the conductive heat transfer through walls and roof, heat gain through windows can also be simplified using CLTD method. Total heat gain through glass is sum of conductive heat gain and solar heat gain as given below:

Heat gain through glass = {Conduction due to $(T_i - T_o)$} + heat gain due to solar radiation transmitted or absorbed by glass.

Using the CLTD for glazed surfaces from appendices, the conductive part can be calculated as:

$$Q_{c,cond,glaz,t} = UA\,(CLTD_{glaz,t})$$

Solar heat gain through glazing is treated through the solar heat gain factor (SHGF). It is defined as instantaneous heat gain (W/m^2) due to solar radiation through reference glazing as described earlier in this book. There are two components in this solar load, the radiation absorbed and re-radiated by the glazing and the radiation transmitted through it. The later is assumed to be totally absorbed by the interior of the building. The radiation absorbed in glass increases its temperature thereby changing the conductive heat flow. The SHGF combines the latter contribution with the radiation transmitted. For finding the cooling load at time 't' following formula can be used:

where:

A is the area of glazing

SC is shading coefficient (to be used for non reference glazing)

$$Q_{c,solar,t} = A * SC * SHGF_{\max}\,(CLF_t)$$

$SHGF_{max}$ is maximum solar heat gain factor (W/m^2), from appendix/ASHRAE

CLF_t cooling load factor for time 't', from appendix/ASHRAE

$SHGF_{max}$ is the value of SHGF when the radiation attains its maximum for a particular month, orientation and latitude. CLF takes into account the variation of the solar radiation during the day as well as dynamics of its absorption and re-radiation.

Similar to above approach, CLFs for other sources of heat can be computed. Such as, for occupancy load:

$$Q_{occ,t} = Q_{occ}\,(CLF_{occ,t})$$

Load due to lighting:

$$Q_{light,t} = Q_{light}\,(CLF_{light,t})$$

and load due to appliances:

$$Q_{app,t} = Q_{app}\,(CLF_{app,t})$$

For each of the above three equations, for each load profile, there is a different set of CLFs that also depends upon the thermal inertia of interiors. In these cases also thermal load gets attenuated and delayed as shown in Figure 5.3.

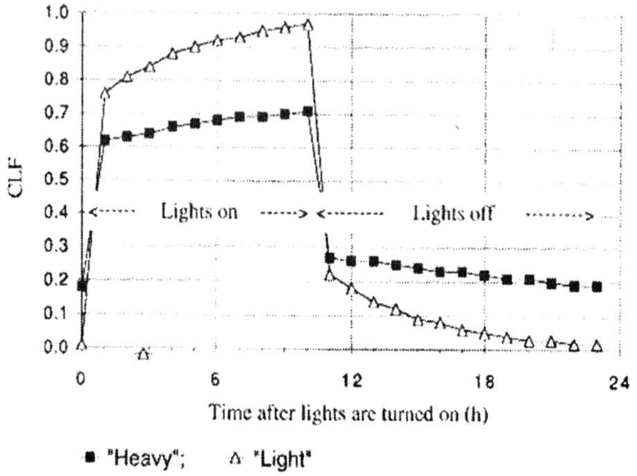

Figure 5.3: CLFs for lights that are on for 10 hrs/day with two construction types

Similarly, Figure-5.4 shows CLFs for Type-A and Type-D zones (as specified by ASHRAE, depending upon thermal inertia), due to occupant loading of space for 12 hour occupancy.

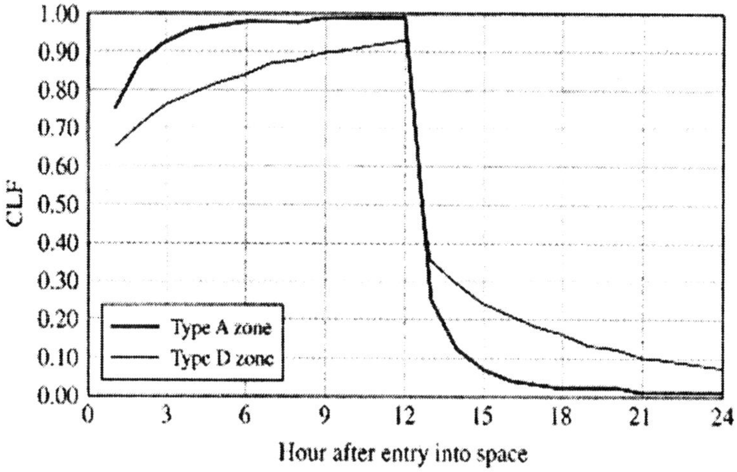

Figure 5.4: Occupant cooling load factors for space occupied for 12 hours

Ventilation and infiltration air as immediately contributes to the load does not usually require a CLTD/CLF based approach. It must be carefully noted that the cooling/heating load itself does not determine rating of equipment to be used, however, it forms the most important parameter for its rating. Important tables for load calculations that are useful for understanding the solutions of examples, are given in this chapter itself. Remaining important information is also provided in appendices.

Example on Cooling load calculation

Problem:

A single-family detached house (as shown in figure) is located at 30°N latitude has following constructional details:

Roof construction : Roof-attic-ceiling combination, vented to remove moisture with 150 mm of fibrous batt insulation and vapour retarder [U = 0.28 W/(m^{2}K)].

Wall construction : Frame with 100mm face brick, 90mm fibrous batt insulation, 19mm polystyrene sheathing, and 13mm gypsum wall board [U=0.34W/(m^{2}K)]. Ceiling height is 2.4m throughout. Floor construction. 100mm concrete slab on grade.

Fenestration : Clear double glass, 3mm thick, in and out. Assume closed, medium-colour venetian blinds. The window glass has a 600mm overhang at the top.

Doors: Solid core flush with all-glass storm doors [U=1.82 W/(m^{2}K)].

Outdoor design

Conditions : Temperature of 36°C dry bulb with a 13° daily range and a humidity ratio of 0.0136 kg vapor/kg dry air (23.7°C wet bulb) *U-factors*: for all external surfaces are based on a 3.4 m/s (12 km/h) wind velocity.

Indoor design

Conditions : Temperature of 24°C dry bulb and 50% RH.

Occupancy : Four persons, based on two for the master bedroom and one for each additional bedroom. Assign to the living room.

Appliances and lights : Assume 470 W for the kitchen, and assign 50% to the living room. Assume 470 W for the utility room, and assign 25% to the kitchen and 25% to the storage room.

The conditioning equipment is located in the garage, and the construction of the house is considered medium. Find the sensible, latent, and total cooling load; size the cooling unit; and compute the air quantity for each room.

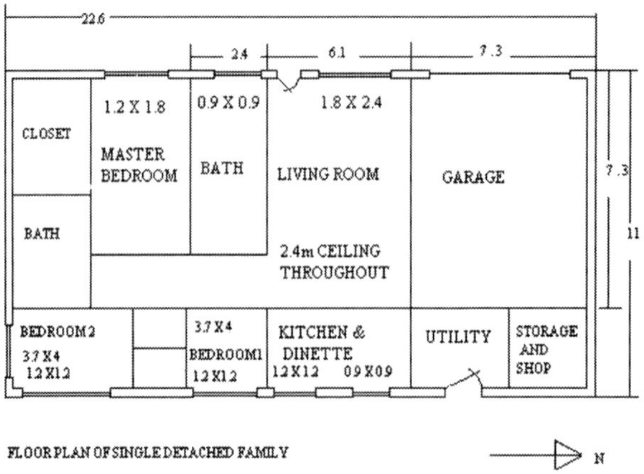

Figure 5.5: Floor plan of single family detached house

Source : Reprinted with permission from ASHRAE Handbook Fundamentals, Volume, 2005.

Solution

The cooling load must be made on a room-by-room basis to determine the proper distribution of air. The calculations follow the procedure outlined in the section on Load Components.

Walls, roof, windows, and doors: The calculations for the living room and the kitchen, where q = UA(CLTD) for the walls, roof, and door and q = A(CLF) for the windows, are outlined in Table-5.3. The glass shaded by the overhang is treated as north-facing glass, with the shaded area computed using Table 5.4.

Table 5.3: Transmission Cooling Load

Item	Net area m^2	CLF W/m^2	U-factor $W/(m^2K)$	CLTD (K)	Cooling load (kW)
Living room					
West wall	8.4		0.34	14	0.040
Partition (garage)	17.5		0.4	7	0.049
Roof	44.5		0.28	27	0.336
West door	1.9		1.82	14	0.048
West glass	3.168	141			0.446
Shaded glass	1.152	63			0.072
Kitchen					
East wall	12.4		0.34	14	0.059
Roof	22.6		0.28	27	0.171
East glass	1.24	141			0.174
Shaded glass	1.0	63			0.063

Source : Reprinted with permission from ASHRAE Handbook Fundamentals, Volume, 2005.

Table 5.4: Shade line factors

Direction window faces	Latitude, degree north						
	24	32	36	40	44	48	52
East	0.8	0.8	0.8	0.8	0.8	0.8	0.8
SE	1.8	1.6	1.4	1.3	1.1	1.0	0.9
South	9.2	5.0	3.4	2.6	2.1	1.8	1.5
SW	1.8	1.6	1.4	1.3	1.1	1.0	0.9
West	0.8	0.8	0.8	0.8	0.8	0.8	0.8

Note: Shadow length below the overhang equals the shade line factor times the overhang width.

Source : Reprinted with permission from ASHRAE Handbook Fundamentals, Volume, 2005.

Internal and infiltration sensible cooling loads: Compute as follows,
For the living room: Infiltration, using table :
Volume inflow rate V = ACH (room volume) * 1000/3600
V = 0.5 * 106.9 * 1000/3600 = 14.85 l/s
$q = 1.2\ V\ (T_o - T_i)$
q = 1.2 * 14.85 (63-24) = 214 W

Occupants, assuming 67 W per person:
q = 67 * (no. of persons)
q = 67 * 4 = 268 W

Appliances, assuming that 50% of the kitchen appliance load is picked up in the living room:
q = 0.5 * (kitchen appliance load)
q = 0.5 * 470 = 235 W

For the kitchen:
Volumetric rate of infiltration,
V = 0.5 * 54.2 * 1000/3600 = 7.5 l/s
q = 1.2 * 1.75 (36-24) = 108 W
since there are no occupants, corresponding heat gain is zero.

Appliances

assuming 25% of the utility appliance load is picked up in kitchen,
q = (470/2) + (470/4) = 352.5 W

For the total sensible cooling load for these two rooms and the cooling load for the remaining rooms, Table 5.5 can be seen. At this point, the sensible cooling load for the house is 5.75 kW. Depending on the design of the air distribution system, heat losses from the supply and return ducts may add to the cooling load. There may be more accuracy estimated after designing the system; however, to size the cooling unit, duct losses should be included initially. If all ducts are in the attic space, a duct loss of 10% of the space sensible cooling load is reasonable. For a counter-flow system, with ducts below the slab, a 5% loss is more reasonable.

Table 5.5 : Summary of sensible cooling load estimate

Room	Roof, walls, doors	Glass	people	appliances	infiltration	Total kW (q_{rm})	Room l/s (V_{rm})
Living room	0.47	0.518	0.27	0.24	0.21	1.708	142
Kitchen	0.23	0.237		0.35	0.11	0.927	77
Utility and storage	0.41			0.35	0.13	0.89	74
Bedroom no. 1	0.17	0.16			0.08	0.41	34
Bedroom no. 2	0.19	0.25			0.08	0.52	34
Master bedroom and bath	0.50	0.24			0.24	0.98	82
Bath	0.16	0.08			0.08	0.32	27
Total	2.13	1.48	0.27	0.94	0.93	5.755	479
Duct loss (10%)				0.5755			
Outdoor ventilation air				0.47			
			Total	**6.80 kW**			

Source : Reprinted with permission from ASHRAE Handbook Fundamentals, Volume, 2005.

An infiltration rate of 0.5 ACH may not be adequate for good indoor air quality, so some outdoor air should be introduced. This additional cooling load may be estimated in the same way as the infiltration load.

Assuming that the entire duct system is in the attic, that is, the total sensible cooling load with a 10% duct loss is 1.1 x 5.75 = 6.33 kW. Also, assume that additional outdoor air is needed to assure good indoor air quality, so the total infiltration and outdoor ventilation air is 0.75 ACH. This increases the infiltration rate by 50%, or about 0.47 kW. The total sensible cooling load is then increased to 6.80 kW (Table 5.5).

The total cooling load (sensible plus latent) may be estimated by applying the latent factor (LF) from Table 5.1. For a design humidity ratio of 0.0136 kg vapour per kg dry air, LF = 1.15 for a house of medium construction.

Hence, the total cooling load equals 1.15 x 6.80 = 7.82 kW.

The load raises the temperature of the cooling air 9 to 12 K as it leaves the rooms. The total design flow from the air conditioner can be estimated by the following equation:

$$V_{total} = 1000q/(1.2\Delta t)$$

where:

V_{total} is total air flow, l/s

q = total sensible load, W

1.2 = density times specific heat of cooling air

Δt is temperature difference of air entering and leaving room, K

For a temperature difference of 10 K, the total airflow is estimated from above equation as:

$$V_{total} = (1000 * 5.75)/(1.2 * 10) = 479 \text{ l/s}$$

The exact design flow can be determined only after the cooling unit has been selected. Then, the supply of air quantities can be composed. Air should be supplied to each room on the basis of the room sensible cooling load:

$V_{rm} = V_{total} (q_{rm}/q)$

where:

V_{rm} is air flow in each room, l/s

Q_{rm} is room sensible cooling load, W

Thus:

$V_{rm} = (479/5.75)q_{rm}$

If the living space in above example were a multifamily unit (assume that the north, south, and east walls are not exposed surfaces), the calculation procedure would be the same, except that different tables would have been used for the CLTDs and GLFs. Assumptions regarding infiltration, ventilation, and appliance loads are different for smaller multifamily units.

5.2 REDUCTION OF THERMAL LOAD AND ENERGY CONSUMPTION

After the gulf crisis in 1973, with increase in energy prices worldwide, efforts towards conservation of energy got started. Buildings of the new era, are now equipped with energy conservation measures. For understanding the scope of energy conservation in buildings, the total energy consumption in modern buildings can be covered under three major heads:

(i) Energy consumption for maintaining thermal comfort

(ii) Energy consumption for illumination

(iii) Energy consumption for operation of equipment e.g. lifts, geysers, computers, television etc.

Out of the three major heads mentioned above, energy consumption for maintaining thermal comfort accounts for the largest share in air-conditioned buildings. Therefore, it also offers largest scope of energy conservation in buildings. In this chapter, measures for controlling the energy consumption towards maintaining thermal comfort are discussed.

As already described, energy requirement for thermal comfort arises due to various reasons like heat transmission through building elements, solar heat gain, occupants and their activities, equipment used etc. Measures for conservation of energy in any building for maintaining thermal comfort can be divided in three categories:

(i) reduction of thermal load due to heat transmission through building elements

(ii) reduction of thermal load due to mass transfer between building and surroundings

(iii) reduction of thermal load through heat recovery

In cold climates efforts are made to prevent outflow of heat whereas in hot climates, inflow of heat is to be prevented. In cold places, more exposure to sun during day is suggested but in hot locations, less exposure is recommended. Since the underlying principles with most of the energy conservation concepts is same, a combined coverage of energy conservation possibilities for hot and cold climates has been done under following sections.

5.2.1 Heat Transmission Related Measures

For reduction in the thermal load arising due to inflow/outflow of heat through the building components mainly, walls, roofs and windows, several measures and options are available. Out of those, three main options are:

(i) use of insulation

(ii) use of air cavities

(iii) use of advanced windows

5.2.1.1 Insulation

Insulation for any wall or building component is provided by applying layer of a material that is poor conductor of heat. Doing this increases the thermal resistance of that building component thereby reducing the heat transfer, taking place through it. For analysis of effect of insulation, the approach described under heading 'thermal conduction in multi-layered bodies' in section 5.1 of this chapter, can be adopted to find total thermal resistance to conduction. As the insulating materials have low thermal conductivity and hence high thermal resistivity, the total thermal resistance on applying layer of insulating material only increases and hence blocks the flow of heat. The amount of heat flow through the insulated building element depends upon the thermal conductivity and thickness of insulating material used besides conductivity and thickness of the main component on which insulation is being applied. Mathematically:

$$R_{total} = R_{wall} + R_{insulation} = (b_{wall}/k_{wall}) + (b_{insulation}/k_{insulation})$$

Conductive heat transfer can thus be found by :

$$Q = A_{wall}\,(T_{outside} - T_{inside})/R_{total}$$

Depending upon the composition, conductivity and operating temperature range, insulating material can be chosen to suit any application and required thickness can be found using above two equations. knowing permissible heat flow and terms other than '$b_{insulation}$'. Table 5.6 shows properties of important insulating materials.

Different options for application of insulating material are usually available such as on outer surface, on inner surface, sandwiched between two layers. From the heat transfer point of view, choice can be made considering the transient analysis as explained earlier in this chapter, as the time lag with respect to the variation taking place outside shall be different for all of these cases. Maximum time lag appears when insulation is applied on outer surface of building if surroundings of that are hotter than inside. Depending upon the usage pattern of building decision about location and thickness of insulation can be chosen to have appropriate effect inside. However, practical considerations such as durability, ease of application etc. are also to be considered.

Table 5.6: Properties of different building materials used for insulation

	Density (kg/m^3)	Conductivity (W/mK)	Specific heat	
			(J/kgK)	(Wh/kgK)
Fibreboard	300	0.06	1000	(0.28)
Mineral fibre (rock mat or quilt)	25	0.040	960	(0.27)
Semi-rigid felted	130	0.036		
Loose, felted slab or mat	180	0.042	1000	(0.28)
Foamed plastics				
phenolic foam board	30	0.038	1400	(0.39)
expended polystyrene board	15	0.037	1400	(0.39)
expended polysterene board	25	0.034	1210	(0.34)
extruded polystyrene board smooth skin	36	0.029	1210	(0.34)
extruded polystyrene board cut skin	28	0.036	1400	(0.39)
Polyurethane foam board (aged)	30	0.026	1570	(0.44)
Urea formaldehyde foam	10	0.04	1400	(0.39)
Sprayed urethane foam	32	0.02		
Brown cellulose fibres	37-51	0.045	1350	(0.38)
Thatch				
reed	270	0.09	1000	(0.28)
straw	240	0.07	1000	(0.28)
Vermiculite granules	100	0.065		
Insulating render (sand cement and polystyrene beads)		0.66		
Cellular glass	175	0.17	1000	(0.28)
Foam glass	150	0.053-0.07		
Cotton	80	0.056	1420	(0.39)
Hairfell	270	0.07		
Silk	100	0.052		
Sheepswool	135	0.049	1260	(0.35)
Straw fiber	140	0.047		
Feathers	80	0.037		
Paste board	700	0.07		
Corrugated board	35	0.041		
Chalk dust	200	0.058-0074	960	(0.266)

5.2.1.2 Air Cavities

In principle, use of air cavities is similar to use of insulating material. If an air space is left between two layers making a wall or roof of any building, the air trapped between the layers being poor conductor of heat acts as barrier to heat transfer. The mathematical treatment of air cavity would also be similar to that of insulation as explained above if natural convection in air is neglected. The thickness of air cavity is a very important design parameter that governs its effectiveness by controlling the heat transfer coefficient as in case of insulation. Considerable difference arises for air cavities having more than 50mm thickness. It has been found that with gaps broader than 50mm, movement of trapped air due to temperature gradient starts that in turn increases the coefficient of heat transfer. This increase in heat transfer takes place due to convective heat transfer taking place in addition to conductive heat transfer. Therefore, cavities broader than 50mm are normally not preferred. However, if more thickness of air cavity is required for getting heavy insulation, by putting partitions in the main broad cavity multiple cavities can be used as an alternative. Figure 5.6 shows U-value obtained in air cavities of different thickness, location and orientation with use of coatings having different emissivity.

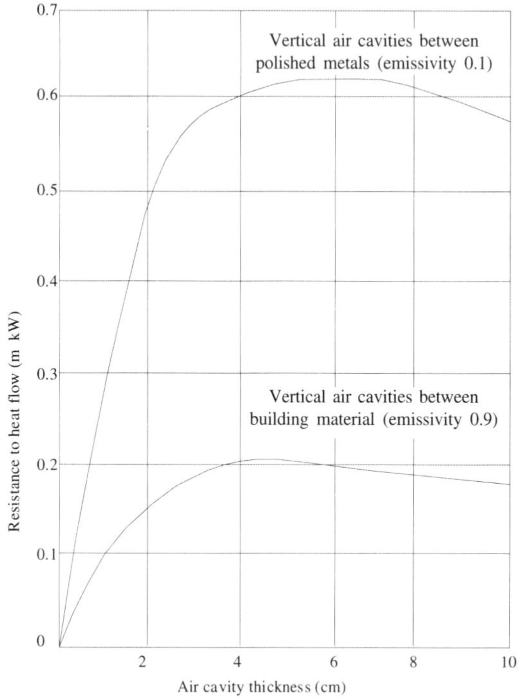

Figure 5.6: Variation in U-Value of air cavities

In addition to application on walls and roofs, the concept of air cavities also finds very important place in development of insulating windows using double and triple glazing details of which have been covered below.

5.2.1.3 Use of Advanced Windows

Windows are one of the most interesting elements of any building as they provide sunlight, and heat into the building. Size and type of window is a very critical issue while designing any building as windows many a times become the single largest source of heat gain/loss in buildings. Construction of an ordinary window comprises of one layer of glass as a shield that allows sunlight to come into the building space. The most common form of single glazed window typically has an overall U-value ranging from 6-10 W/m^2 ^{0}C depending upon the wind velocity and orientation of window. As compared to the U-value of concrete wall in the range of 1-1.5 W/ m^2 ^{0}C this value is quite high and as a result heat transmission through windows needs proper attention.

For reducing the heat transmission through the windows, three main technological improvements have taken place:

(a) Use of multiple layers of glazing

By use of more than one layer of glass in window, typically two or three layers named double glazed and triple glazed windows respectively, a drastic reduction in U-value can be achieved. Air between the layers of glass, acts like an air cavity as described above. Figure 5.7 shows various parts of a typical double glazed window.

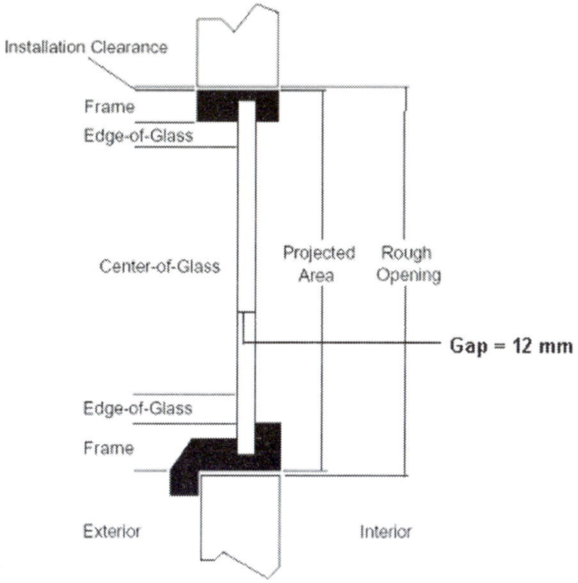

Figure 5.7: Construction of a double glazed window

There are several critical technological issues related to double/triple windows such as spacing between glazing, use of metal spacers between glazing, moisture proof sealing-coverage of these topics is beyond the scope of this book.

Few inert gases mainly Argon and Krypton, can also be used in place of air filled between the layers of glass. These gases have lower thermal conductivity as compared to air and additionally, being heavier than air, convection currents are not set so easily as compared to air offering low U-value. Figure 5.8 shows variation in different types of windows that have much different U-values due to variation in number of glazing, spacing and frame material.

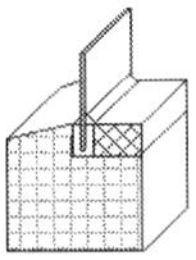

Single Glazing (3mm)
Frame Material: Wood, Vinyl & Aluminum.
Glass E_{mis} = 0.840
Visible Transmittance = 0.90
Spectrally Selective Coating - No

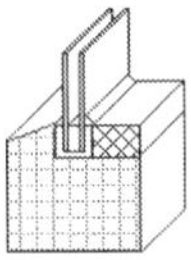

Glazing Material: 3mm clear glass.
Gap Between Glazing Layers = 12.7 mm.
Gas: Air
Frame Material: Wood, Vinyl & Aluminum.
Glass E_{mis} = 0.840
Visible Transmittance = 0.82
Spectrally Selective Coating - No

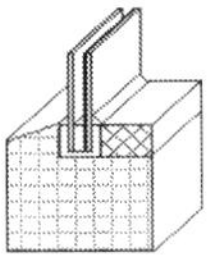

Glazing Material: 3mm clear glass.
Gap Between Glazing Layers = 12.7 mm.
Gas: Air
Frame Material: Wood, Vinyl & Aluminum.
Glass E_{mis} = 0.840
Visible Transmittance = 0.77
Spectrally Selective Coating – Outer side of inner Glazing

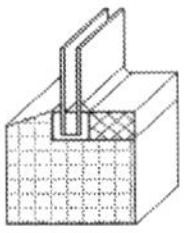

Glazing Material: 3mm clear glass.
Gap Between Glazing Layers = 12.7 mm.
Gas: Argon
Frame Material: Wood, Vinyl & Aluminum.
Glass E_{mis} = 0.840
Visible Transmittance = 0.82
Spectrally Selective Coating - Nil

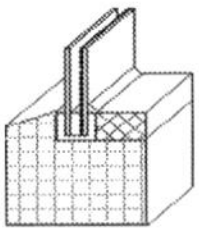

Glazing Material: 3mm clear glass.
Gap Between Glazing Layers = 12.7 mm.
Gas: Argon
Frame Material: Wood, Vinyl & Aluminum.
Glass E_{mis} = 0.840
Visible Transmittance = 0.77
Spectrally Selective Coating – Outer side of inner Glazing

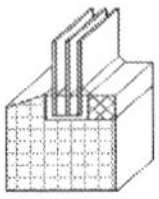

Glazing Material: 3mm clear glass
Gap Between Glazing Layers = 12.7 mm.
Gas Air
Frame Material: Wood, Vinyl & Aluminum.
Glass E= 0.840
Visible Transmittance = 0.75
Spectrally Selective Coating No.

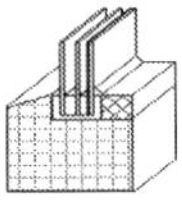

Glazing Material: 3mm clear glass.
Gap Between Glazing Layers = 12.7 mm.
Gas: Air, Argon
Frame Material: Wood, Vinyl & Aluminum.
Glass E_{mis} = 0.840
Visible Transmittance = 0.70
Spectrally Selective Coating - Outer side of inner Glazing

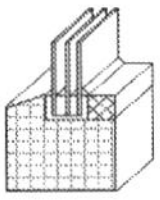

Glazing Material: 3mm clear glass
Gap Between Glazing Layers = 12.7 mm.
Gas Argon
Frame Material: Wood, Vinyl & Aluminum.
Glass E= 0.840
Visible Transmittance = 0.75
Spectrally Selective Coating No.

Figure 5.8: Different types of multiple glazed windows

(b) Use of special coatings

Heat transfer through a window comprises effects of all the three modes of heat transfer conduction, convection and radiation. Radiative heat transfer through the glazing can be reduced by using special coating called 'Low-E coatings' that have low emissivity specially for long wavelength radiation i.e. heat. At the same time, it is important to have high transmissivity in these coatings to keep the advantage of illumination almost unaltered. Application of these coatings reduces the emission of long wave radiation (i.e. heat) from the glazing thereby reducing the U-value. These coatings can either be coated on the surface of glass or are also available in the form of film that can be suspended between the layers of glass.

Due to the fact that these coatings get deteriorated when exposed to open atmosphere, they are normally not applied on exposed side of glass. It should be therefore applied to the first available protected surface of glass in the direction of heat flow. For cold climates where main objective is to prevent heat flow from inside to outside, coating is applied to the outer surface of the inner glass. On the contrary, in hot climates, these are applied on the inner surface of the outer glass. Figure 5.8 besides U-value of other multiple glazed windows, also shows U-value for windows with low-e coatings. High-transmission low-E, Selective-transmission low E, and Low-transmission low-E. High transmission products are best suited to buildings located in heating-dominated climates and particularly to south-facing windows in passive solar designs. Selective-transmission products are suited for buildings that have both winter heating and summer cooling requirements. The low-emittance characteristics of this glass reduce winter heat loss. In the summertime, the selective properties allow natural daylighting, but block a large fraction of the solar infrared energy, thus reducing cooling loads. A similar effect can be achieved by combining a high-transmittance, high SHGC, low-E coating with a spectrally selective tinted glass. Placing a low-E coating on dark tinted glass, and/or increasing the solar reflectance of the coating itself, creates a product with the insulating capability of low –E coatings, along with glare control and a high-level solar heat rejection. This is especially suited to- controlling solar gain and glare in cooling-dominated climates.

Spectrally selective coatings on plastic can also be applied to existing glass as a retrofit measure, thus reducing the SHGC of an existing clear glass considerably while maintaining a high visible light transmittance. Other conventional tinted and reflective films will also reduce the SHGC but at the cost of lower visible transmittance. Reflective films can also lower the U-factor, since the surface facing the room has a lower emittance than uncoated glass. These are special type of coatings that can be applied on surface of glass or even on any opaque surface. These coatings have different spectral properties for short and long wavelength radiation. Usual coatings employed are silver coatings on glass. Copper and nickel coatings have higher heat emissivity and therefore offer relatively higher U-value as compared to silver. Selective coatings, unlike low-e coatings can be used on both, exposed and unexposed surfaces.

The technology to produce low-E and selective coatings has been evolving quickly, and the market price has been dropping at a corresponding rate. Once the initial hurdle of making a substantial investment in the necessary production machinery has been met, there is a market incentive for manufacturers to provide coatings on as much of the glass produced as possible.

Thus, windows with low-E coatings have become a standard residential window product. Approximately 40 percent of window products now sold in the United States have low-E coatings, and the figure will continue to rise. The improvement in insulating value due to the low-E coating is roughly equivalent to adding another pane of glass to a multipane unit.

(c) Moisture prevention between glazing

Moisture is often a problem on the interior side of the cold single glazed glass. The visual problem due to condensation is not severe, since it usually evaporates during the day time as the window glass warms up and if necessary, it can be wiped off. However, moisture between the layers of glazing can be a serious problem. Simplest method for removing this problem is proper sealing of windows to prevent entry of moisture between glazing. Further prevention can be done by use of desiccant filled metal spacer between the two layers. Another option for absorption of moisture between the glass layers is fitting desiccant filled balloon.

5.2.2 Mass Transfer Related Measures

After discussing methods for reducing the heat transmission through building components, next important scope of energy conservation is by controlling air-infiltration that causes unwanted air-changes between building envelope and its surroundings through cracks, clearances and openings. Knowing the measures for air infiltration proper measures can be taken to minimize it for conserving energy.

Air infiltration depends upon the following facts:

(a) The meteorological variables-wind forces which include average velocity, prevailing direction, seasonal and daily variation in velocity and direction.

(b) The shape of house and the nature of its surroundings, local obstacles such as nearby buildings, hills, trees etc. These determine the distribution of wind generated pressure or pressure difference between interior and exterior of the building.

(c) The position and air flow characteristics of all opening and flow path.

(d) The temperature difference between the inside and outside. Temperature difference causes density difference between the outside and inside air, creating a difference in pressures and leading to infiltration.

A typical plot of air infiltration measures in air changes per hour as a function of time is shown in Figure 5.9 which also shows the corresponding values of air velocity and temperature difference between the inside and the outside.

Concepts and Elements of Natural Climatic Control

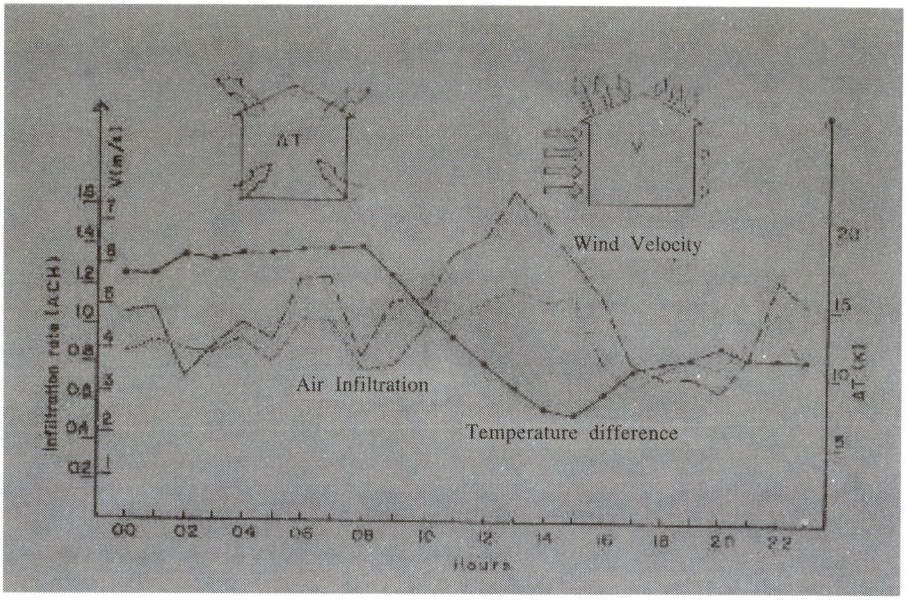

Figure 5.9: Wind and temperature induced infiltration

Heat gain/losses due to air infiltration are proportional to the number of air exchanges and hence to the volume of the building. This volume of air change is given by formula:

$V = a.l.\ \Delta p^n$

where,

a: joint discharge coefficient

l: joint length

Δp: pressure difference

n: exponent of pressure difference

The pressure difference is primarily dependent upon the flow of air with respect to the building and secondarily on the temperature difference. Due to suction on leeward side, if the pressure is assumed to be half of the static pressure, then the pressure difference across the building component is 0.75 times of the static pressure. Table 5.7 shows values of discharge coefficients and exponent 'n' that may be useful for estimation of infiltration.

Table 5.7: Joint discharge coefficient 'a' and exponent 'n'

b	Building component thickness									
	1 mm		*10 mm*		*50 mm*		*82 mm*		*100 mm*	
mm	*a*	*n*	*a*	*n*	*a*	*n*	*a*	*n*	*a*	*n*
0.4	-	-	2.14	0.66	0.48	0.89	0.31	0.93	0.24	0.95
0.6	-	-	4.67	0.60	1.75	0.77	1.14	0.82	0.88	0.87
0.8	-	-	7.57	0.56	3.98	0.67	2.72	0.73	2.31	0.75
1.0	-	-	11.21	0.53	7.0	0.60	5.15	0.65	4.19	0.70
2.0	-	-	25.0	0.51	21.8	0.53	20.8	0.52	19.8	0.53
3.0	-	-	38.0	0.51	35.8	0.51	33.5	0.52	32.6	0.52
5.0	-	-	66	0.50	60.3	0.51	60.6	0.51	58	0.52
7.0	95	0.50	93	0.50	87	0.51	88.5	0.50	86	0.51

5.2.2.1 Modifying External Features of Building to Prevent Infiltration

The infiltration of ambient air, as a first step, be reduced by the shape and orientation of the building that collectively can be termed as attempts to modify external features of building for energy conservation. Details of few major concept are discussed below.

(a) **Long inclined roof:** The infiltration of ambient air can be reduced by using a long, windowless, inclined roof surface as shown in Figure 5.10. This type of surface provides a good aerodynamic effect and deflects the air flow smoothly over the house in a streamline fashion. This diversion avoids the 'air dam effect' in which a straight vertical wall acts like a dam for flowing air thereby creating conditions for enhanced air pressure near the wall that in turn increases infiltration.

(b) **Earth berming:** Due to preference of house owners towards symmetry of buildings from aesthetic point of view in some cases, the option mentioned above may not be adaptable. In such a case, an earth berm may be made in the windward direction having a slope matching with that of roof, as shown in Figure 5.11. In this case surface of berm and inclined roof surface starting in continuity with it together make the total surface needed for desired movement of air. This type of berming or earth sheltering, eliminates infiltration of air, both from the roof as well as the vertical wall. Creation of earth berm though might add to the initial cost but in addition to prevention of infiltration, but it also reduces heat transmission through the wall adjacent to berm. Therefore, use of earth berm offers double advantage and hence can be thought as one option for energy conservation if availability of space permits.

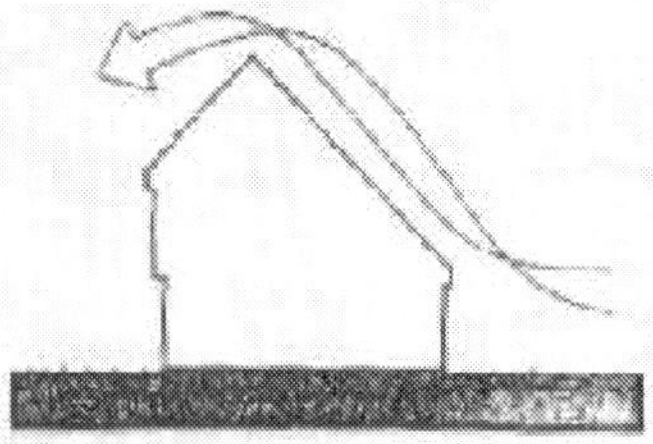

Figure 5.10: Air flow over long inclined roof

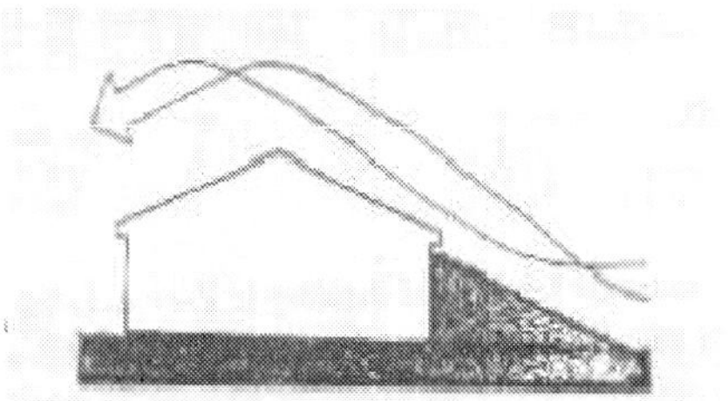

Figure 5.11: Air flow over earth berming

(c) Compact form and orientation: Use of compact form of building envelope is one of the basic rules for minimising wind exposure. Besides compact form, if the building is given proper orientation, air infiltration can be controlled. Figure 5.12 shows three options for the same built-up area having different response to wind and hence having different infiltration of outside air.

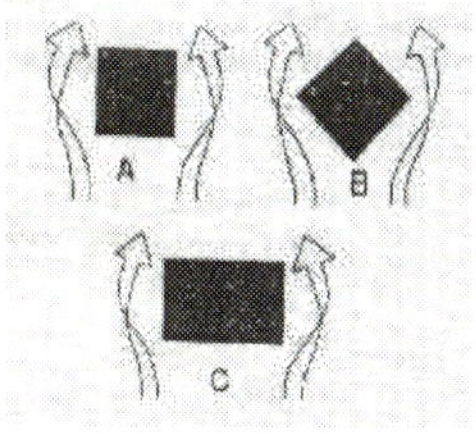

Figure 5.12: Form and orientation of building affecting wind exposure

(d) Protected entrances: Entrance provided in buildings for their use also causes air infiltration that though cannot be avoided but definitely can be minimised. The main entrance of a building should be made a small-enclosed space that provides a double entry or air lock between the main building and exteriors as shown in Figure 5.13. Doing this will prevent a large quantity of warmed/ cooled air from leaving the building each time the door is opened since only the air within the enclosed space can escape out. The infiltration of cold/hot air that normally occurs around exterior doors will be virtually eliminated because the entry creates a still-air space between the interior and exterior doors. The entrance should be oriented away from the prevailing winter/summer winds or provided with a windbreak to reduce the wind's velocity against entrance. The entry space should be used for storage of unheated/uncooled items, as a place to remove shoes, winter clothing etc.

Figure 5.13: Protected entrance for minimising infiltration

(e) Wind shelter: Hot winds in summer and cold winds in winters are a large source of heat gain/loss in a building due to increased air infiltration. Strong winds also increase convection heat transfer due to high wind velocity and larger temperature difference. Infiltration can be reduced by providing a wind shelter by proper site planning and landscaping. An analysis of the building site should be made to determine if there are existing wind protected areas. In siting a house, the builder should avoid open areas, hilltops and valley floors that are directly exposed to prevailing winter/summer winds as shown in Figure 5.22.

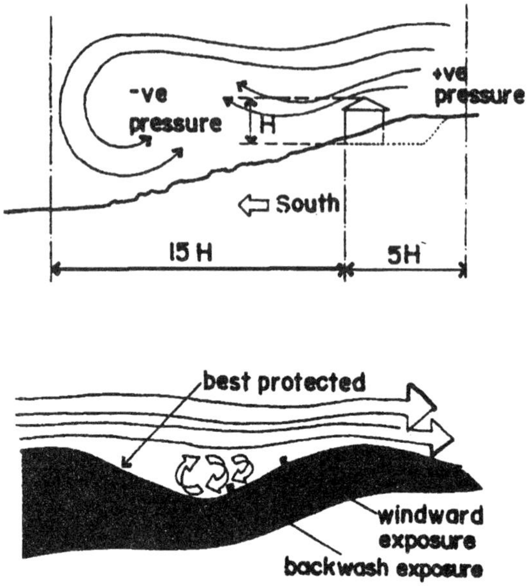

Figure 5.14: Avoiding direct exposure of building to wind on hilltops, valleys

In cold climates, as the cold air flows downhill just like water, special care should be taken while locating a building. A valley may seem to be shielded from cross winds, it may actually be in midst of a steady downstream night time cold current. Figure 5.14 shows flow of wind with respect to a valley and best location of a building in cold climate. In hot climates, the treatment becomes opposite to cold climates as hot air has a natural tendency of rising upwards.

(f) **Fencing & wall as barriers to wind flow:** Existing hedge rows, hillocks and tree stands may be available for any building to act as wind shields. In the absence of, or to augment, existing land forms and tree masses, barriers can be created for wind control. Trees and shrubs are the most common of these, but berms, fences and walls can also provide the desired protection from wind. It should be noted carefully that solid or wind-impenetrable barriers are not a good choice as they cause creation of turbulent areas on the leeward direction as shown in Figure 5.16.

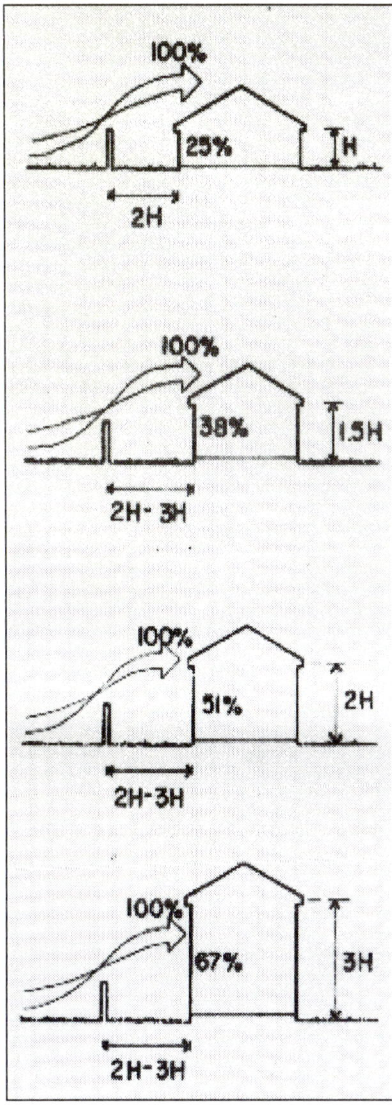

Distance from fence	Average wind speed at façade
1H	26%
3H	28%
4H	36%
5H	42%
6H	46%
8H	54%
10H	62%

Distance from fence	Average wind speed at façade
1H	42%
4H	43%
5H	47%
6H	51%
8H	58%
10H	66%

Distance from fence	Average wind speed at façade
1H	55%
4H	54%
5H	57%
6H	59%
8H	64%
10H	70%

Distance from fence	Average wind speed at façade
1H	69%
4H	68%
5H	69%
6H	70%
8H	73%
10H	77%

Figure 5.15: Impact of man-made barriers in wind exposure of buildings

The most desirable windbreaks, from the heat gain/loss point of view, are those that range in porosity from 25% to 60%. High porosity (about 50%) usually means more protection over a distance 5 to 20 times the height of barrier in the downwind direction where the wind velocity is reduced to about 30% of free stream velocity. Lower porosity (about 25%) usually indicates more protection up to a distance 4 times the height of barrier, where wind velocity reduces to 10% but from 4 to 20 height distance, wind velocity becomes 60% of the free stream velocity.

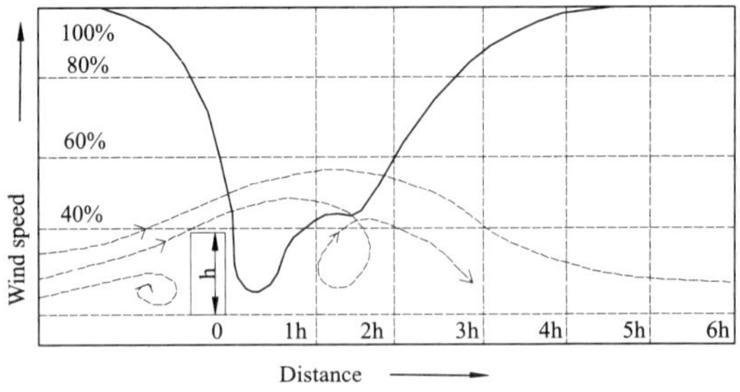

solid barrier (wall)

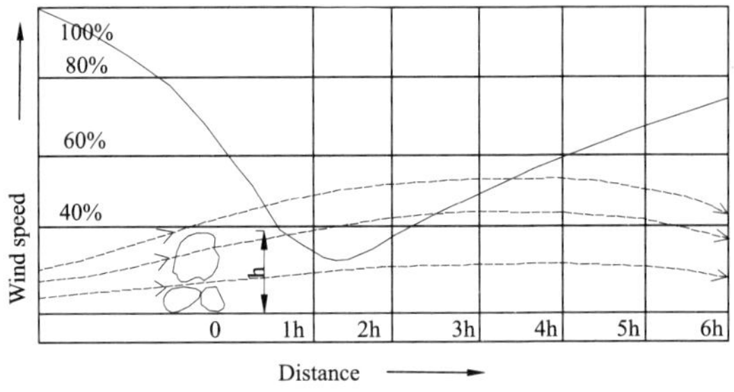

perforated barrier

Figure 5.16: Wind pattern change due to solid and non-solid wind shields

5.2.2.2 Improved Materials and Designs of joints

Heat gain/loss due to air infiltration through cracks can be minimised by using jointless building components. For necessary joints within the building, the following methods are possible for reducing air leakage:

(a) **Sealing Compounds:** On the outside and inside of the joints, usually sealing materials like silicon, thiokol, polyurethene or acrylic are used. In using these materials, one should take care of good foundation and use of appropriate materials. Large expansion/ contraction like shrinkage of wood should not be allowed to take place. Sealing components if exposed to atmospheric conditions, have a life of 8-15 years and need to be changed after that for maintaining their effectiveness in preventing air infiltration.

(b) **Profile Seals :** Such types of seals may be characterized as clamping profiles, compression profiles and impregnated foam profile. Clamping profiles are very sensitive to tolerances and are only practically useful in prefabricated building components with predetermined joint geometry. Compression profiles are usually made of synthetic rubber and are pressed into the joint. Because of the elasticity of the material, a surface pressure always exists and provides the required sealing. The tolerance of these systems is relatively large. Impregnated foam sealing bands are mostly manufactured from chloroparaffin or from bitumen soaked porous polyurethene foam. These profiles are compressed to about $1/5^{th}$ of their final volume and they expand gradually. These profiles are, however, not completely air tight, water vapour diffuses through these sealings but the renovation is relatively easy.

(c) **Joint Bands :** Joint bands are mostly made from polysulphides silicon rubber, tarpolyurethane or polyurethane. They are pasted on the flank of the joint to cover it. The visual quality of the building is strongly influenced in use of this technique.

(d) **Foils :** Over the planar areas, foils are air tight. These are pasted on the boundaries or on slots. These could also be fixed and made air tight by using compressed bands as shown in Figure 5.17.

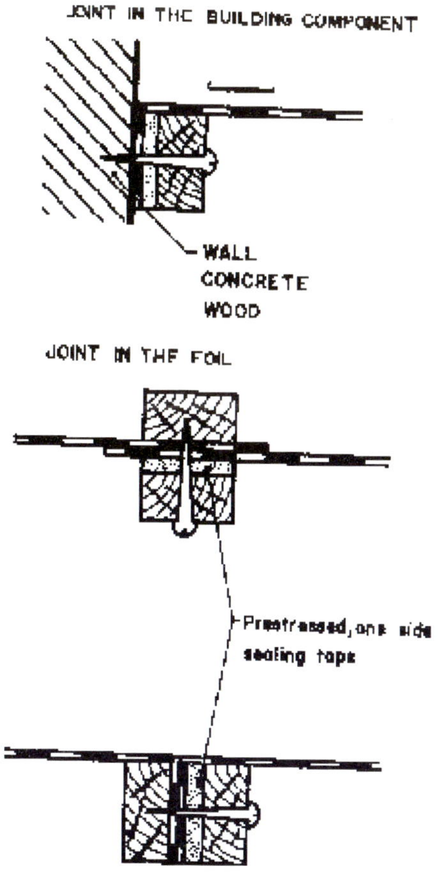

Figure 5.17: Schematic representation of details of reducing air infiltration

5.5.3 Heat Recovery in Buildings for Energy Conservation

A reduction in heating energy demand of building is possible by recovering part of the waste heat. It is possible to recover heat from various mechanisms. The heat energy from building is lost by the following mechanisms:

(a) Ventilation losses

Heat losses due to ventilation can be recovered partly through mechanical component and partly through constructed building element. The most important mechanical techniques are summarized in Figure 5.18.

Overview of the heat recovery methods				
Methods of heat recovery	Only heat exchange		Heat and mass transfer	Heat transfer for an increase in the energy
	1	2	3	4
Systems	Recuperators	Regenerators		Heat Pump
Examples	1.1 Plate Heat Exchanger 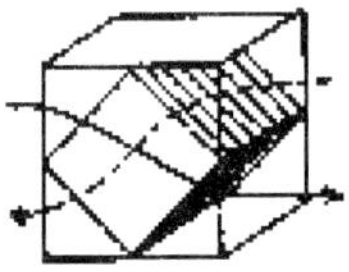	Closed Loop Connected tube h.E. (a) water circulation system (forced flow) 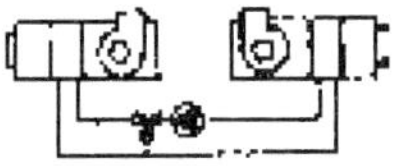	Rotating solid storage systems (a) Slowly Moving 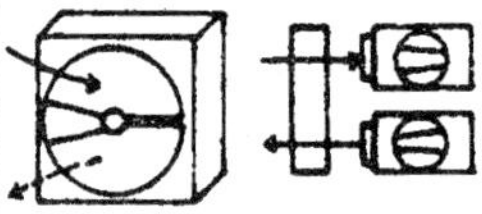	4.1 Compressors 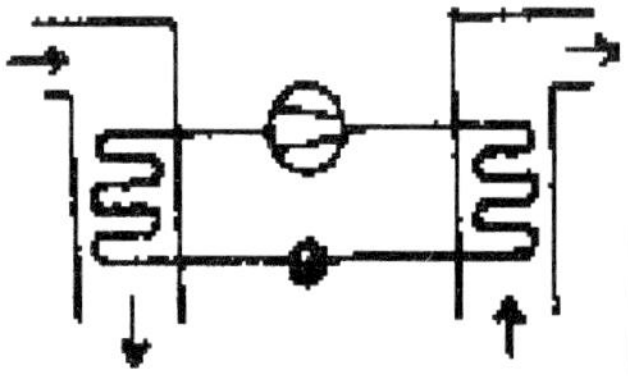
	1.2 Smooth Tube Heat Exchanger e.g. in industry (furnace)	(b) Heat pipe (with gravitatior flow) 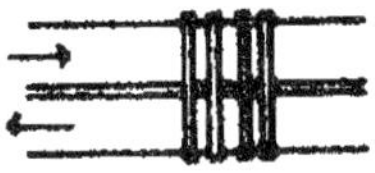	(b) Fast moving as capillary ventilator (alternator) 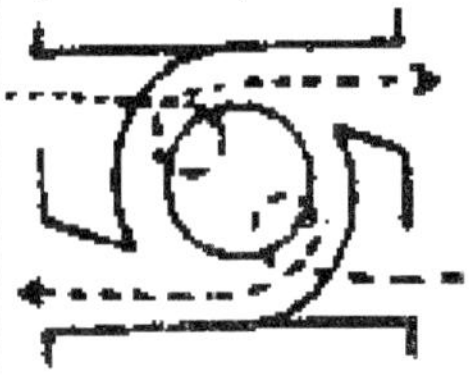	4.2 Absorption systems Absorption Media e.g. / Working with Water-ammonia, Lithium-bromide water / Earth gas LPG Thermal oil
		(c) Heat pipe (with capillary force)	(c) By direct contact (air washer principle)	Working wise like a cooling machine
Remarks	Separation wall	Flowing heat transfer media	Rotating solid heat transport material storage (a) and (b)	Working wise like a cooling machine.

	Heat recovery systems	Schematic	Efficiency (%)
Recuperators	Plate heat exchanger		20-80
Regenerators	Circulating fluid systems	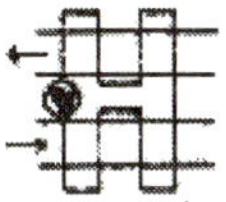	10-80
	Heat pipe	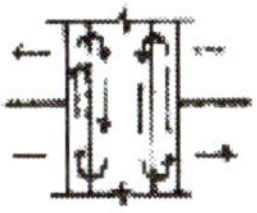	60-90
	Rotating heat exchanger		70-90
	Capillary ventilator		40-50

Figure 5.18: Overview of heat recovery methods

Recuperators are essentially heat exchangers, their use in building can be done to have heat transfer from warm outgoing ventilation air to the cool incoming ambient air. The two fluids are separated by a heat conducting wall made of metals or glass. In this type of equipment there is no direct mixing of the fluids. In the other category, regenerators, a fraction of warm outgoing air is mixed with cool incoming air. The outgoing and incoming masses in addition to partial mixing, are stored closely for a short period to facilitate heat transfer. Few examples of waste heat recuperates and regenerators are shown in Figure 5.19.

(b) Transmission heat losses

In cold climates, considerable amount of heat is lost by outward transmission of heat through building components. This escaping heat can be recovered and utilized for reuse in the building either for space heating itself or for heating of incoming cool ventilation air. In one type of systems, the incoming air is passed through the porous building material of the external building elements

Recuperators

Plate heat exchanger (in counter current flow) for heat transfer between two air streams.

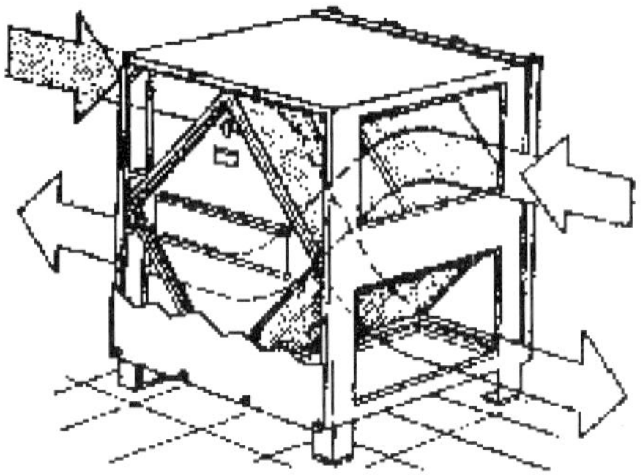

Regenerators

Closed loop heat exchanger for local air streams.

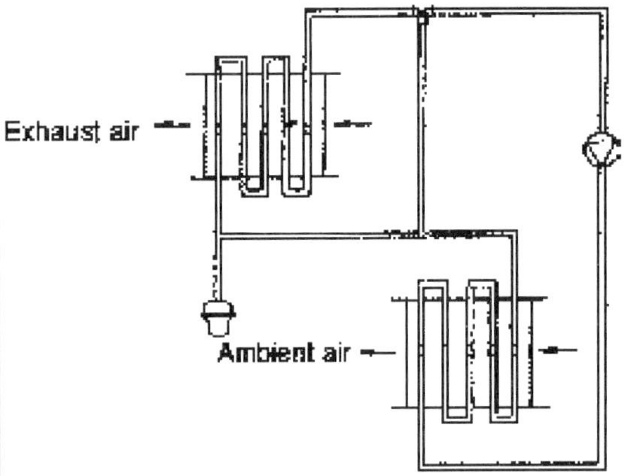

Heat pipe makes the heat transfer possible between two air streams by using a refrigerating material without auxiliary energy.

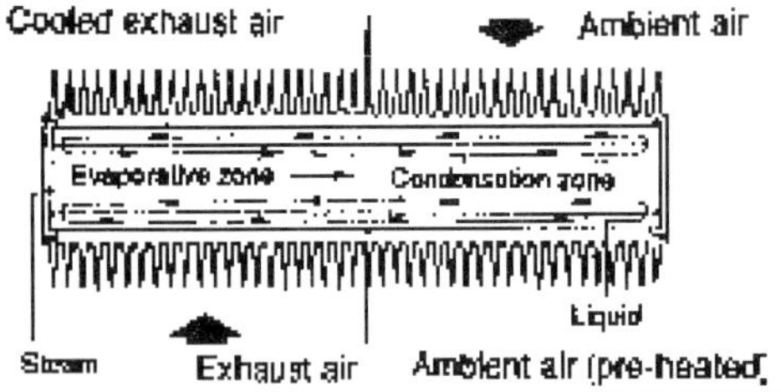

Capillary ventilator for single room ventilation units; the individual components are:

a. hollow cylinder of storage material
b. wall
c. chamber for entering exhaust air
d. exhaust air duct
e. chamber for entering ambient air
f. ambient air duct.

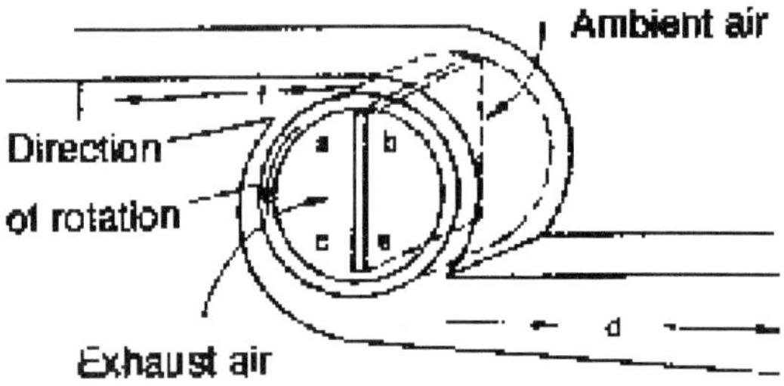

Regenerative heat exchanger with rotating storage mass for centrally ventilating systems;

a. rotors of storage material
b. housing with connecting to air ducts
c. circulation zone for ambient and exhaust air streams
d. rotoroperation.

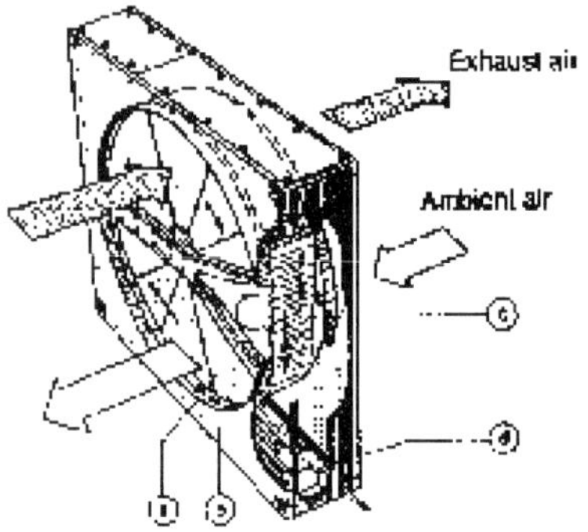

as shown in Figure 5.20. The porous material suitable for such application should also be an insulating material for better system efficiency. The direction of flow of ventilation air in such cases should be normal to the plane of the building element to have better utilisation of waste heat.

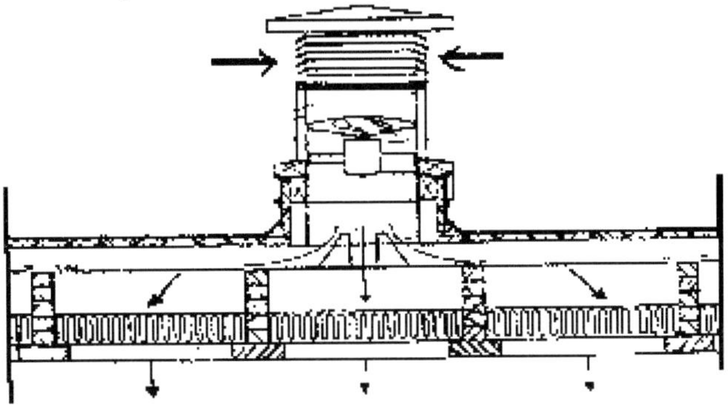

Figure 5.20: Working principle of dynamic insulation

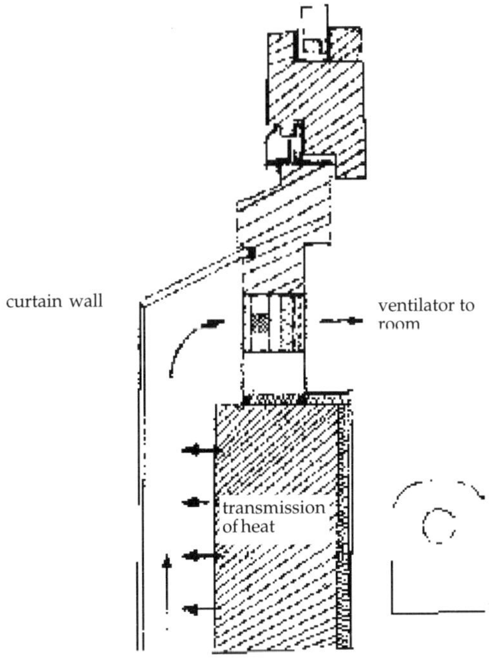

Figure 5.21: Schematic representation of façade with air flow for preheating ventilation air

In other type of systems, air is flown along the plane of the building element using a translucent or transparent cover over the building element. The transparent cover helps increasing the solar heat gain as has already been explained earlier. An example of such systems has been shown in Figure 5.21.

Use of the above mentioned systems may require a small blower or fan for ensuring sufficient flow of air over the façade. Application of such system in one building is shown in Figure 5.22.

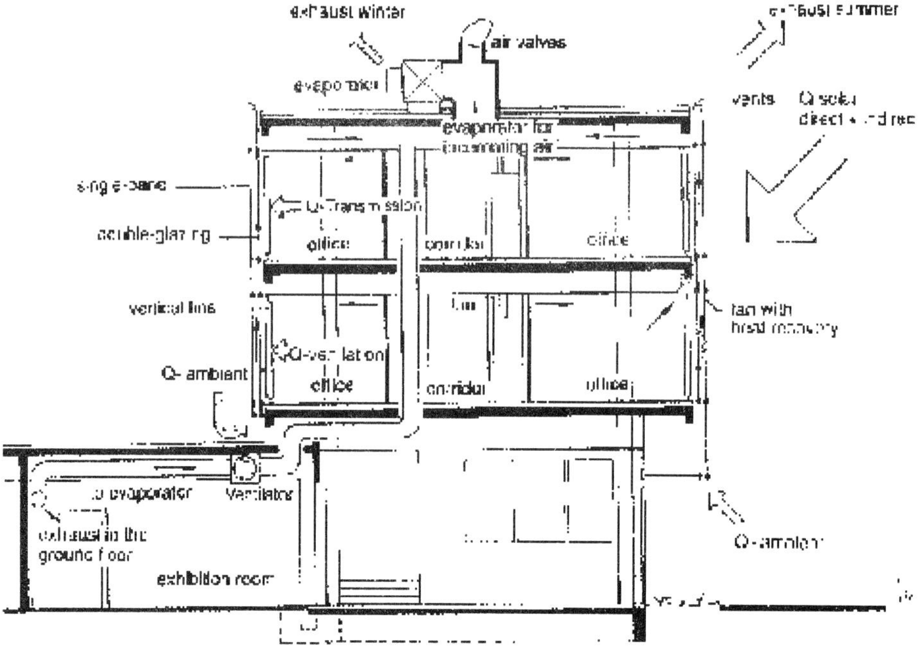

Figure 5.22: Use of façade system in an east elevation office building

(c) Warm water heat losses

Warm water is lost from buildings and especially from a multifamily house in appreciable quantities as a result of:

- body hygiene (washing, bathing etc.)
- cleaning (dish washers, washing machines etc.)

This energy flows down the house drains and it is possible to recover a part of these heat losses by using appropriate heat recovery systems. One disadvantage of this system is, however, the fluctuation in the quantity of heat over various time periods. One method could involve the flow of water in non-insulated tubes through the building and thus, by keeping the space temperature at a lower level, contributing to the space heating. The heat of the waste water can also be used to preheat water for domestic use. In any case, it is essential to incorporate a waste water storage to compensate for erratic supplies of the recovered heat. The use of a recuperative heat exchanger is usually of limited use and expensive in these cases. The use of a heat pump is, however, recommendable. In both cases, the pollution in the drained water poses a big problem. Mature systems for using warm water waste heat are still not developed to a commercial stage.

5.2.4 Other Concepts for Energy Conservation

Besides the above mentioned methods for conservation of energy, kept under the categories of reducing heat transmission, reducing mass transfer and waste heat recovery, few other concepts are also there that have been covered under this section.

5.2.4.1 Movable Insulation

Since in many cases, increase in window area is associated with increase in heat gain and better illumination during the day time and more heat losses during the night hours, it is difficult to take decision about the window area. In cold climates, it is desired to reduce the heat loss during night keeping high heat gain during the day. On the contrary, in hot climates, it is desired to reduce the heat gain during the day but heat dissipation during the night hours is required to keep a building comfortable. These combinations of different behavior in a single window can be achieved using the concept of movable insulation. Schematic representation and practical details of movable insulation in building is shown in Figure 5.23(a).

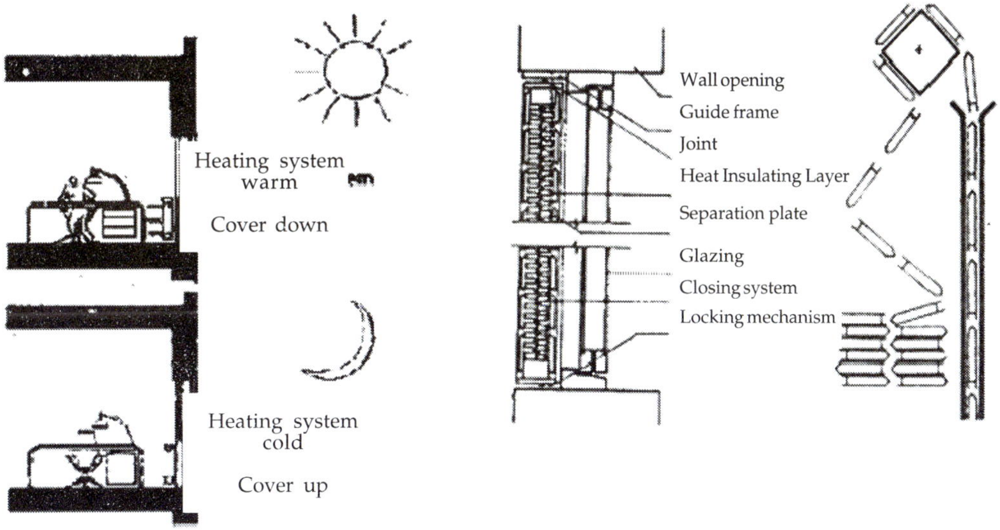

Figure 5.23(a): Schematic details and practical details of movable insulation system

In cold climates, it allows the solar radiation to enter during the day and when put during the night, heat loss can be prevented. Few form of such type of insulators are venetian blinds, shutters, sliding door, curtains. Figure 5.23(b) shows various versions of movable insulation systems with their corresponding 'U-value' with insulation and the 24-hour efficiency values with respect to the double glazed window.

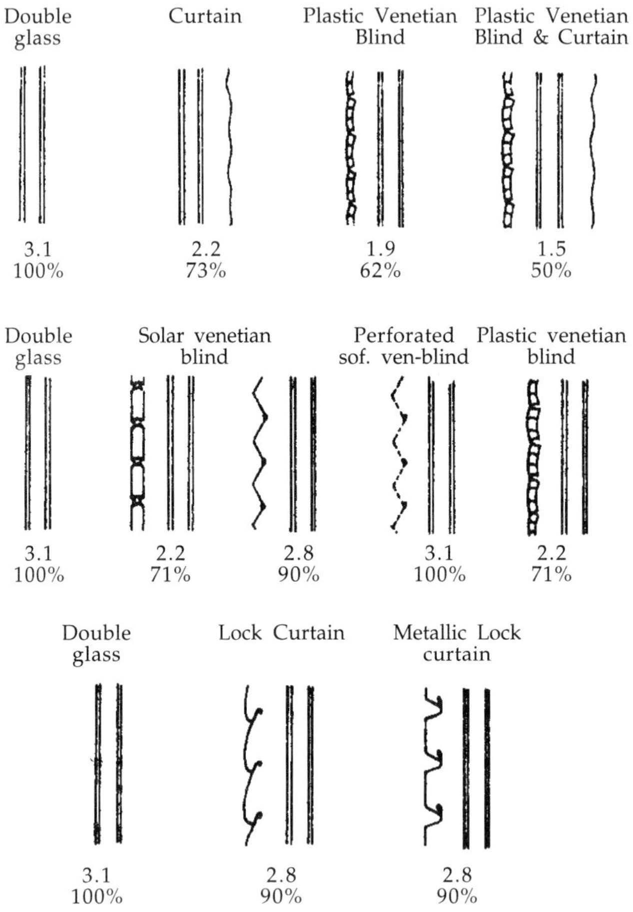

Figure 5.23(b): U-values of different types of movable insulation systems

5.2.4.2 Building Forms and Surroundings

Shape and surroundings of any building plays a very important role in governing the energy consumption in any building. Such factors may cause heat gain when cooling is required and heat loss when heat gain is required. These concepts are however, similar to the concepts described in chapter-2 while discussing shading, wind shelters, and other related topics.

5.3 HEAT LOAD ESTIMATION FORM

For systematic calculation of the heat load, practicing HVAC engineers use standard heat load estimation forms. A typical format of such a form is given below. In this form, heat gain is separated into the room sensible heat, room latent heat, room total heat and grand total heat, to facilitate the calculations for the air quantity required. The required air quantity is a key factor in equipment selection.

Following are the main causes for heat gain in buildings:

A. Effective Gain through glazed area:

A.1 Solar radiation enters the conditioned space through glass. Materials and air in the conditioned space absorb the heat brought by the radiation. Such heat gain not only occurs through the sun-exposed sides, but the sides, that do not face sun, also transmit heat inside. Though, this amount is less than the sides having direct solar exposure. ASHRAE gives the value of this heat gain in heat units per hour per unit area for different orientation, time of the year, time of the day and for various latitudes.

As the heat gain depends upon the orientation of each side of the building, the gain has to be worked out individually for each side (i.e. north, north-east, east, etc.). The values given in design tables are generally for exposed ordinary glass. The heat gain is less for colored/ tinted glass, double panel glass, shaded glass (with venetian blinds, shading, etc.) and for the glass which is not directly exposed. Multiplying factors for different types of glass, inside/outside venetian blinds, outside shading/ awning etc. are to be used (available from the tables) on value for ordinary glass. The heat gain is:

Heat gain = A x R x MF

Where, A: Area of glass in m^2 or ft^2

R: Solar gain in $kcal/h/m^2$ or $BTU/h/ft^2$

MF: Multiplying factor's for the type of glass, shading etc.

A2. Solar Transmission Gain through the Walls and Roof: As a result of the absorption of direct radiation of the sun, the temperature of walls/roof rises above the ambient temperature. This results in larger temperature difference with respect to the air conditioned space. The design tables provide the following information.

(a) Equivalent temperature difference for a standard outside temperature (say 35°C or 95°F) and inside temperature (say 26.7°C or 80°F).

(b) Correction factors for different outside and inside temperatures to be added/subtracted from standard values (a).

(c) Correction factors for different types of shading, to be added/subtracted to (a).

(d) Transmission coefficients for the most commonly used construction materials in heat units/h/unit area/degree temperature difference.

The heat gain = A x U x EqTD

Where A: area of the wall or roof in m^2 or ft^2
U: transmission coefficient in kcal/h/m^2/°C r BTU/h/ft^2/°F.
EqTD: corrected equivalent temperature difference in °C or °F

A3. Transmission Gain through Glass and Partitions: In addition to the solar gain through the glass, as described above, there is a heat gain by transmission through the glass because of the temperature difference between the surroundings and the conditioned space. Also heat gain occurs through the partition walls/partitions between the non-conditioned and the conditioned space.

The heat gain = A x U x TD
Where A: area of the wall or roof in m^2 or ft^2
U: transmission coefficient for glass/partitions (from tables) in kcal/h/m^2/°C r BTU/h/ft^2/°F.
TD: Temperature difference between the surroundings and the conditioned space (°C or °F)

A4. Heat Gain-(1) through Infiltration and (2) (by passed) Fresh Air.

(a) Design tables give the infiltration air quantity for various types of doors/windows, for observable cracks and for infiltration due to the openings of the doors. This load is generally ignored as this can be merged with the load due to fresh air intake for ventilation.

(b) The room load due to the by passed fresh air (through the cooling coil) is:
Q_u x ñ x C x BF x TD
i.e. Heat gain in kcal/h = m^3/min.x60xñxCxBFxTD(°F) [where, ñ= 1.2 kg/m^3; C=0.24]

or in BTU/h = cfmx60ñxCxBFxTD(°F) [where, ñ= 0.075 lb/cft; C=0.24]
= 1.08 cfm x BF x TD (°F)

Table: Heat Load Estimation Form – Cooling and De-humidifying

(I) Time (Peak Load)

Condition	*D B*	*W B*	*% RH*	*Moisture Content*	
(a) Outside (b) Room (c) Difference				$ù_o$ $ù_2$ $ù_0 - ù_1$	DB and WB: °C or °F Moisture content; $ù_0 - ù_1$ Kg/kg dry air (or) Gr./lb dry air

(II) Outside air-through apparatus-ventilation

(a) No. of people x Q_p/person or floor area x Q_1/per unit area		Q_p = m^3/min. (or) fcm/person Q_1 = m^3/m^2 (or) cfm/ft^2 per unit area
(b) Ventilation air quantity Q_y	(a+b)	Q_U = m^3/min. (or) cfm

(III) Infiltration

(a) No. of doors x Q_d/door		Q_d = m³/min./door (or) fcm/door
(b) Q_L x crack length		Q = m³/min./m length of crack (or) cfm/ft² per feet of crack
(c) Exhaust Fan Q_e	(a+b)	Q_e = m³/min. (or) cfm
Total infiltration air quantity Q_i	(a+b+c)	

Heat Load

A.1 Sun Gain – Glass

Item	Area of Quantity		Sun Gain or Temp. Def.		Factor	Heat Gain per Hour	
Glass	A_1	x	R_1	x	f_1	=	A_1 to A_5: Area: m²(or) ft²
Glass	A_2	x	R_2	x	f_2	=	R_1toR_5: Solar gain wrt orientation, in kcal/h/m² (or) BTU/h/ft²
Glass	A_3	x	R_3	x	f_3	=	$f_1$toRf_5: Multiplier for coloured/shaded glass
Glass	A_4	x	R_4	x	f_4	=	
Sky light	A_5	x	R_5	x	f_5	=	

A.2 Solar and Transmission Gain- Walls and Roof

Item	Area of Quantity		Sun Gain or Temp. Def.		Factor	Heat Gain per Hour	
Wall	A_1	x	U	x	TD_1	=	A_1 to A_6: Area: m²(or) ft²
Wall	A_2	x	U	x	TD_2	=	U: Transmission coefficient in kcal/h/m² (or) BTU/h/ft²
Wall	A_3	x	U	x	TD_3	=	TD_1toTD_6: Equivalent temp. difference °C or °F
Wall	A_4	x	U	x	TD_4	=	
Roof directly exposed to sun	A_5	x	U	x	TD_5	=	
Shaded roof	A_6	x	U	x	TD_6	=	

A.3 Transmission Gain Except Walls and Roof

All glass	A_G	x	U_G	x	TD	=	A_G to A_F: Respective Areas: m²(or) ft²
Partition	A_P	x	U_P	x	TD	=	U_P to U_F Respective Transmission coefficient in kcal/h/m²/°C or BTU/h/ft²/°F
Ceiling	A_C	x	U_C	x	TD	=	TD: Temperature difference between the outside and conditional space
Floor	A_F	x	U_F	x	TD	=	

A.4 Infiltration and Ventilation Air

Infiltration	Q	x	60	x	TD	ñ	x	=	Q_i and Q_v : Infiltration and ventilation: m³/min. or cfm.
Ventilation Air	QxBF	x	60	x	TD	ñ	x	=	TD: Between outside and inside °C/ °F BF: Coil by-pass factor ñ x C: Air density x Sp. heat

A.5 Internal Heat

People	N	x	Sñ	=	N: No. of people Sñ: sensible heat per person
Horsepower	BHP	x	*f*	=	
Lights	Watts	x	*f* ù	=	
Appliances	Watts	x	*f* ù	=	
Others	Watts	x	*f* ù	=	
A.(T)	Room sensible heat sub-total				(A.1+A.2+A.3+A.4+A.5) = Credit for thermal storage =

A.6 Supply duct heat gain, leak and safety factor- 5% =

A.7 Effective room sensible heat = A.(T) + A.6

B.1 Room latent heat

Infiltration	Q_i x 60 x (w_o – w_i)	x	p x h	=	Q_v and Q_i : As in A-4
Ventilation	Q_v x BF x (w_o – w_i)	x	p x h	=	w_o – w_I: as in I
People N	x w_p	x	h	=	H: L.H. of condensation of moisture- kcal/kg (or) BTU/gr.
Steam	W_s	x	hs	=	w_p: Moisture released per hour per person: kg/person, Gr./person/h
Appliance	w_a	x	h	=	w_s – Weight of steam; kg or lb./h
Room latent heat sub-total					w_a : Moisture from appliance/h kg/h or Gr./h
Supply duct leak and safety factor- 5%					hs: LH of steam; kcal/kg or BTU/lb

B.2 Effective room latent heat =

C: Effective room total heat A.7 + B.2 =

D: Total heat gain

Outside Air (Ventilation) Heat Sensible	Q_v x (1-BF) 60 x TD x ñ x C	=	Q_v : quantity of fresh air intake (m^3/min. or cfm)
Latent	Q_v x (1-BF) 60 x ($w_o - w_i$) x ñ x C	=	ñ : density of air (kg/m^3or lb/cft) C: specific heat of air (0.24)

D.1 Grand total heat sub-total C + D =

E. Return duct heat gain, leakage: 2%

Ch. Water pump hp x *f* =

Ch. W.pipe heat gain =

F. Grand total : Heat gain D.1 + E =

Note: The by-pass factor depends on the number of rows deep of the coil, fin pitch and coil face (air) velocity. Since the cooling coil and air quantity can be selected/established only after knowing the full load, an approximate value for BF is to be assumed. After working out the heat load and selecting the equipment, the heat gain under this head has to be recalculated for the BF of the coil and cfm selected. The total load is then accordingly corrected.

So far the load originating from the surroundings of the air conditioned space has been dealt with.

A5. Internal Heat Gain : The general sources of internal heat are listed below. Some or all of these items may be present in the conditioned space. Diversity factor should be considered for higher loads.

(a) People: Heat is generated within the human body by the process of metabolism. The metabolic rate for women is about 85% and for children it is 75%. The metabolic rate varies with the type of activity of the individual. Design tables provide the sensible and latent heat generated per person. Multiply the sensible heat per person by the number of persons to get the sensible heat gain due to occupancy.

(b) Lights: Load due to the following is calculated below:

Fluorescent light = total watts x 1.25 x 0.86 kcal/h

or total watts x 1.25 x 3.4 BTU/h

Incandescent light= total watts x 0.86 kcal/h

or total watts x 3.4 BTU/h

Note: The fan horsepower and lights contribute to the sensible heat only.

(c) Fan horsepower in the draw-through systems: For calculating this value, multiply the brake horsepower of the fan by 641 to get the value in kcal/h or, 2545 for BTU/h.

(d) Appliances: Some appliances give off both sensible and latent heats; the latent heat being given off directly or as a result of their function such as cooking, drying etc. Refer to the data provided by manufacturers of the appliances or the design tables, for arriving at the sensible heat contributed by the appliances. In bigger installations such as in hotels, exhaust hoods with positive exhaust are provided which remove considerable amount of sensible heat and moisture. Also, all the appliances may not be functional at the same time. So the diversity factors have to be judiciously arrived at for such applications.

A.6 Safety Factor : An additional 5% on RSH is taken as a safety factor and this also covers items such as heat gain by the supply duct, leak, etc.

A.7 Effective Room Sensible Heat (ERSH) Gain: It is obtained by adding up the items (A.1) to (A.6).

B. Effective Room Latent Heat Gain (ERLH)

B.1. Room Latent Heat

(a) *Infiltration:* This is generally ignored as explained earlier in the section A.4.

(b) *Outside air (by passed air) :* The latent heat portion (i.e. latent heat removal for condensation of the excess moisture from the by passed fresh air) forms a part of the room latent heat gain. The heat gain depends on the amount of moisture to be condensed and drained off. And this is equal to the difference between the surrounding and inside moisture contents and can be found out from the psychrometric chart.

The heat gain is thus
$= Q_v \times 60\ \tilde{n} \times h \times BF \times (\grave{u}_o - \grave{u}_i)$
where Q_v : Fresh air quantity is m³/min. or cfm.
ñ : Density of air
BF: latent heat of condensation of water vapour in kcal/kg or BTU/lb of moisture.
$(\grave{u}_o - \grave{u}_i)$: difference of moisture content at outside and inside conditions respectively in grams of water vapour/kg dry air or grains of water vapour/lb dry air.

Thus the heat gain is:
In kcal/h $= m^3/min. \times 60 \times 1.2 \times 588.3/1000 \times BF(\grave{u}_o - \grave{u}_i)$
$= m^3/min. \times 60 \times 1.2 \times 0.5883 \times BF(\grave{u}_o - \grave{u}_i)$
$= 42.36 \times m^3/min \times BF\ (\grave{u}_o - \grave{u}_i)$
$= 0.706\ cmh \times BF(\grave{u}_o - \grave{u}_i)$
($\grave{u}_o$ and $\grave{u}_i$ in gr. Moisture/lb dry air)
(lb = 7000 Gr.)
(Density of air: 1.2 kg/m³ or 0.075 lbs/ft³
Latent heat of water vapour: 588.3 kcal/kg or 0.588 kcal/f or 1059 BTU/lb.

(c) *People (occupancy) :* The moisture released by the occupants has to be condensed. For the moisture

Heat gain = ç x ù x h

ç: No. of persons

ù: Moisture released/person in g/person or in gr.person

h: Latent heat of condensation of moisture in kcal/g or BTU/gr.

i.e. kcal h = ç x ù x 588.3/1000

= ç x ù x 0.5883

or BTU/h = ç x ù/7000 x1059

= ç x ù x 0.15

(d) *Steam :* In comfort application steam as such, or steam appliances are seldom used in the conditioned space. In industrial or special applications, where steam is used, the corresponding heat gain has to be taken into account.

(e) *Appliance :* If moisture-generating appliances are used in the conditioned space, find the moisture generation from the appliance rating.

Heat gain: ù x h

Where ù: moisture generated per hour in or gr.

h: latent heat of moisture in kcal/g or BTU.gr.

in kcal/h: ù x 0.5883 (ù= g. moisture generated per hour)

BTU/h: ù x 0.15 (ù= gr moisture generated per hour)

(f) *Vapour transmission :* As the water vapour content in the air increases, its water vapour pressure increases. Thus the surrounding air will have higher water vapour pressure than in the air conditioned space. This difference in pressure results in a flow of the water vapour into the conditioned space from the surroundings. The flow can be through cracks around the doors/windows, cracks in the walls and doors openings, thereby necessitating the condensation of the excess moisture. However this is ignored in comfort applications. But in applications where low RH is specified, this load will have to be taken into account.

(g) *Supply duct leakage :* This loss is generally ignored.

B.2. Adding up the values of B.1(a) to (g) and adding up 5% as safety factor, effective room latent heat (ERLH) is obtained.

C. Effective Room Total Heat Gain (ERTH)

It is the sum of ERSH (item A.7) and ERLH (item B.2)

D. Outside Air Heat

The sensible and latent heat removal from the fresh air taken in for ventilation purposes (i.e. bringing the fresh air from outside conditions to the conditions in the conditioned space) causes a load on the air conditioning apparatus. The heat gain due to the by passes outside air has already been accounted for under the ERTH gain. So the heat removal from balance (1-BF) fresh air intake is to be accounted for under this caption. As explained under the section (A.4) and (B.1.b), the heat gain on account of the fresh air intake is:

Sensible heat: Q_v x 60 x C x (1-BF) x ñ x TD

In kcal/h: 17.28 x m^3/min. (1-BF) x TD (°C)

In BTU/h: 1.08 x (1-BF) x TD(°F)

Latent heat:

kcal/h = 42.36 x m^3/min x (1-BF) ($ù_o$ – $ù_i$)

or = 0.706 cmh x (1-BF) ($ù_o$ – $ù_i$) ($ù_o$ and $ù_i$ in gr. Moisture/lb dry air)

in BTU/h = 0.68 x cfm (1-BF)($ù_o$ – $ù_i$) ($ù_o$ and $ù_i$ in gr. Moisture/lb dry air)

E. Return Duct Heat Gain

(a) Return-air-heat gain, are generally ignored, as return-air-passage/ducts are insulated, if running through non-conditioned area and the aspect of leakage is taken care of, by proper sealing of the return-air passage/duct against leaks.

(b) The heat gain due to the fan horsepower is to be taken under the grand total heat if the system is of the blow-through type. (This gain in the draw-through system, as already explained, forms part of the room load).
The gain due to the fan horsepower (blow-through system only)
in kcal/h: 641xBHP of fan
BTU/h: 2545 x BHP of fan

(c) In chilled water system, the heat gain due to the chilled water pump horsepower and the gain through the chilled water pumping (even if insulated) gets added to the load on the refrigeration plant.

F. Grand Total Heat (GTH)

Adding up the items (D) and (E) to the effective room total heat (item C) gives the total heat, the refrigeration plant has to handle.

Diversity in cooling loads

The methods of working the heat load form explained so far is on the assumption that the system is subjected to all possible loads and the surrounding conditions are also at the design peak all the time. However in large buildings, such as offices, banks, hotels, restaurants, etc. this is not the case. For example, some office rooms and apartments may not be occupied all the time; in hotels a number of guest rooms may not be occupied during the day time, but service areas such as dining halls, restaurants, conference halls, lobby/reception can be fully occupied during the day time, particularly dining halls in lunch time. For such jobs, a diversity factor can be applied on people and light loads to arrive at a realistic heat load. Proper judgement should be exercised in selecting the diversity factor.

Table below gives typical values of the diversity factors for big buildings. Please note that this Table is presented only as a guideline. Every job has to be examined thoroughly and then only the diversity factor should be applied.

Suggested Diversity Factors:

Type of application	*Diversity factor*	
	People	*Light*
Big offices	0.75 to 0.9	0.70 to 0.85
Apartment, Hotel	0.40 to 0.60	0.30 to 0.50
Department Store	0.80 to 0.90	0.90 to 1.00

Source : Basic Refrigeration and Air-Conditioning 3rd Edition, P.N. Ananthanarayanan.

Having arrived at the heat load, the next step is the selection of various equipments of the system. The first item to be selected is the air quantity that has to be handled by the air-handling equipment.

Determination of Air Quantity (m³/min. or cfm)

The air quantity selected should offset the room sensible and latent heat load. It should also handle the total sensible and latent heat loads, i.e. including the outdoor (fresh) air loads, etc.

The air can be determined from the formula

Q_{dt} = ERSH / $(t_{rm}-t_{adp})$ (1-BF)60 x ñ x C

Q_{dt} = Dehumidified air quantity (m^3/min. or cfm)

ERSH = Effective Room Sensible Heat (kcal/h or BTU/h)

t_{rm} = Room design temperature (°C or °F)

t_{adp} = Apparatus due point temperature (°C or °F)

C= Specific heat of air (0.24)

BF= By-pass factor of the coil

ñ = Density of air (1.2 kg/m^3 or 0.075 lbs/ft^3)

Air Quantity in m^3/min. = ERSH / 17.28$(t_{rm}-t_{adp})$ (1-BF)

(or) CFM = ERSH / 1.08$(t_{rm}-t_{adp})$ (1-BF)

Out of the two, i.e. the rating based upon cooling/heating load and the CFM requirement, whichever, gives higher equipment rating, that rating is to be selected.

SUMMARY

Heating and cooling load calculation has so many parameters that it is quite easy to over or under estimate the actual load. Under estimation results into uncomfortable conditions in the conditioned space whereas, over-estimation results into excess energy consumption for conditioning the space. To simplify their job, many field engineers use thumb rules for load estimation and equipment sizing. However, these thumb rules are not able to take into account, the effect of change in each parameter on cooling/heating load. With better understanding of load estimation, as described in this chapter, such crude estimation can be made more accurate and considerable energy can be saved. In some cases, crude estimation has been cross checked with detailed load estimation, and as much as 30-40% difference in equipment sizing has been found.

5.4 ECBC REQUIREMENTS FOR HVAC SYSTEMS

Although the building energy code does not put any check to ensure system sizing according to the actual lad for preventing over-sizing of equipment, it does restricts installation of inefficient equipment. Oversizing has been checked through demanding high Integrated Part Load Value (IPLV) of the coefficient of performance (COP). For a properly sized equipment only, IPLV requirements and COP requirements can be conveniently met.

All heating, ventilation and air conditioning equipment and systems shall comply with the mandatory provisions and the prescriptive criteria.

5.4.1 Mandatory Provisions for HVAC system

5.4.1.1 Natural Ventilation

Natural ventilation shall comply with the design guidelines provided for natural ventilation in the National Building Code of India 2005 Part 8, 5.4.3 and 5.7.1.1

5.4.1.2 Equipment efficiencies

Cooling equipment shall meet or exceed the minimum efficiency requirements presented in Tables 5.8 through 5.12. Heating and cooling equipment not listed here shall comply with ASHRAE 90.1-2004 § 6.4.1.

Table 5.8: Requirements for Unitary Air Conditioning Equipment

Equipment Class	Minimum COP	Minimum IPLV	Test Standard
Unitary Air Cooled Air Conditioner ≥19 and <40 kW (≥5.4 and <11 tons)	3.08		ARI 210/240
Unitary Air Cooled Air Conditioner ≥40 to <70 kW (≥11 to <20 tons)	3.08		ARI 340/360
Unitary Air Cooled Air Conditioner ≥70 kW (≥20 tons)	2.93	2.99	ARI 340/360
Unitary Water Cooled Air Conditioner <19 kW (<5.4 tons)	4.10		ARI 210/240
Unitary Water Cooled Air Conditioner ≥19 and <40 kW (≥5.4 and <11 tons)	4.10		ARI 210/240
Unitary Water Cooled Air Conditioner ≥<40 kW (≥11 tons)	3.22	3.02	ARI 210/240

*COP = Energy Efficiency Ratio (EER) ÷ 3.6

Table 5.9: Requirements for Chillers

Equipment Class	Minimum COP	Minimum IPLV	Test Standard
Air Cooled Chiller <530 kW (<150 tons)	2.90	3.16	ARI 550/590-1998
Air Cooled Chiller ≥530 kW (≥150 tons)	3.05	3.32	ARI 550/590-1998
Centrifugal Water Cooled Chiller < 530 kW (<150 tons)	5.80	6.09	ARI 550/590-1998
Centrifugal Water Cooled Chiller ≥530 and <1050 kW (≥150 and <300 tons)	5.80	6.17	ARI 550/590-1998
Centrifugal Water Cooled Chiller ≥ 1050 kW (≥ 300 tons)	6.30	6.61	ARI 550/590-1998
Reciprocating Compressor, Water Cooled Chiller all sizes	4.20	5.05	ARI 550/590-1998
Rotary Screw and Scroll Compressor, Water Cooled Chiller <530 kW (<150 tons)	4.70	5.49	ARI 550/590-1998
Rotary Screw and Scroll Compressor, Water Cooled Chiller ≥530 and <1050 kW (≥150 and <300 tons)	5.40	6.17	ARI 550/590-1998
Rotary Screw and Scroll Compressor, Water Cooled Chiller ≥ 1050 kW (≥ 300 tons)	5.75	6.43	ARI 550/590-1998

Table 5.10: Requirements for heat pumps heating mode

Equipment Type	Size Category (Input)	Subcategory or Rating Condition	Performance Required[a]	Test Procedure[b]
Air Cooled (Heating Mode)	<19 kW (Cooling Capacity)	Split System	6.8 HSPF (before 1/23/2006) 7.4 HSPF (as of 1/23/2006)	ARI 210/240
		Single Package	6.6 HSPF (before 1/23/2006) 7.4 HSPF (as of 1/23/2006)	
Air Cooled (Heating Mode)	≥19 kW and <40 kW (Cooling Capacity)	8°C db/6°C wb Outdoor air	3.2 COP	ARI 340/360
		-8°C db/-9°C wb Outdoor Air	2.2 COP	
	≥40 kW (Cooling Capacity)	8°C db/6°C wb Outdoor air	3.1 COP	
		-8°C db/-9°C wb Outdoor Air	2.0 COP	

[a] IPLVs and Part load rating conditions are only applicable to equipment with capacity modulation.

[b] Section 12 of ASHRAE 90.1-2004 contains a complete specification of the referenced test procedure, including the referenced year version of the test procedure.

Table 5.11: Requirements for furnaces

Equipment Type	Size Category (Input)	Subcategory or Rating Condition	Performance Required[a]	Test Procedure[b]
Warm Air Furnace, Gas-Fired	<66 kW		78% AFUE or 80% E_t[d]	DOE 10 CFR Part 430 or ANSI Z21.47
	≥66 kW	Maximum Capacity[e]	80% E_c[c]	ANSA Z21.47
Warm Air Furnace, Oil-Fired	<66 kW		78% AFUE or 80% E_t[d]	DOE 10 CFR Part 430 or ANSI Z21.47
	≥66 kW	Maximum Capacity[e]	81% E_t[f]	UL 727
Warm- Air Duct Furnaces, Gas-Fired	All Capacities	Maximum Capacity[e]	80% E_c[g]	ANSI Z83.9
Warm Air Unit Heaters, Gas-Fired	All Capacities	Maximum Capacity[e]	80% E_c[g]	ANSI Z83.8
Warm Air Unit Heaters, Oil-Fired	All Capacities	Maximum Capacity[e]	80% E_c[g]	UL 731

[a] E_t = thermal efficiency. See test procedure for detailed discussion.

[b] Section 12 of ASHRAE 90.1-2004 contains a complete specification of the referenced test procedure, including the referenced year version of the test procedure.

[c] E_c = combustion efficiency. Units must also include an interrupted or intermittent ignition device (IID), have jacket losses not exceeding 0.75% of the input rating, and have either power venting or a flue damper. A vent damper is an acceptable alternative to a flue damper for those furnaces where combustion air is drawn from the conditioned space.

[d] Combination units not covered by NAECA (3-phase power or cooling capacity greater than or equal to 65,000 Btu/h may comply with either rating.

[e] Minimum and maximum ratings as provided for and allowed by the unit's controls.

[f] E_t = thermal efficiency. Units must also include and interrupted or intermittent ignition device (IDD), have jacket losses not exceeding 0.75% of the input rating, and have either power venting or a flue damper. A vent damper is an acceptable alternativ3 to a flue damper for those furnaces where combustion air is drawn form the conditioned space.

[g] E_c = combustion efficiency (100% less flue losses). See test procedure for detailed discussion.

Table 5.12: Requirements for boilers

Equipment Type	Size Category (Input)	Subcategory or Rating Condition	Performance Required[b]	Test Procedure[c]
Boilers, Gas-Fired	<88 kW	Hot Water	80% AFUE	DOE 10 CFR Part 430
		Steam	75% AFUE	
	≥88 kW and ≤733 kW	Maximum Capacity[d]	75% E_t[b]	H.I. Htg Boiler Std.
	>733 kW[a]	Hot Water	80% E_c	
	>733 kW[a]	Steam	80% E_c	
Boilers, Oil-Fired	<88 kW		80% AFUE	DOE 10 CFR Part 430
	≥88 kW and ≤733 kW	Maximum Capacity[d]	78% E_t[b]	H.I. Htg Boiler Std.
	>733 kW[a]	Hot Water	83% E_c	
	>733 kW[a]	Steam	83% E_c	
Oil-Fired (Residual)	≥88 kW and ≤733 kW	Maximum Capacity[d]	78% E_t[b]	H.I. Htg Boiler Std.
	>733 kW[a]	Hot Water	83% E_c	
	>733 kW[a]	Steam	83% E_c	

[a] These requirements apply to boilers with rated input of 2,345 kW or less that are not packaged boilers, and to all packaged boilers. Minimum efficiency requirements for boilers cover all capacities of packaged boilers.

[b] E_t = thermal efficiency. See reference document for detailed information.

[c] Section 12 of ASHRAE 90.1-2004 contains a complete specification of the referenced test procedure, including the referenced year version of the test procedure.

[d] Minimum and maximum ratings as provided for and allowed by the unit's controls.

5.4.1.3 Controls

All mechanical cooling and heating systems shall be controlled by a timeclock that:

(a) Can start and stop the system under different schedules for three different day-types per week.

(b) Is capable of retaining programming and time setting during a loss of power for a period of atleast 10 hours, and

(c) Includes an accessible manual override that allows temporary operation of the system for upto 2 hours.

Exceptions to above are permitted to:

(a) Cooling systems < 28 kW (8 tons)

(b) Heating systems < 7 kW (2 tons)

All heating and cooling equipment shall be temperature controlled. Where a unit provides both heating and cooling, controls shall be capable of providing a temperature dead band of 3°C (5°F) within which the supply of heating and cooling energy to the zone is shut off or reduced to a minimum. Where separate heating and cooling equipment serve the same temperature zone, thermostats shall be interlocked to prevent simultaneous heating and cooling.

All cooling towers and closed circuit fluid coolers shall have either two speed motors, pony motors, or variable speed drives controlling the fans.

5.4.1.4 Piping and duct work

Piping for heating systems with a design operating temperature of 60°C (140°F) or greater shall have at least R-0.70 (R-4) insulation. Piping for heating systems with a design operating temperature less than 60°C (140°F) but greater than 40°C (104°F), piping for cooling systems with a design operating temperature less than 15°C (59°F), and refrigerant suction piping on split systems shall have at least R-0.35 (R-2) insulation. Insulation exposed to weather shall be protected by aluminum sheet metal, painted canvas, or plastic cover. Cellular foam insulation shall be protected as above, or be painted with water retardant paint. The ductwork shall be insulated in accordance with Table 5.13.

Table 5.13: Requirements for Ductwork Insulation

	Required Insulation[a]	
Duct Location	**Supply Ducts**	**Return Ducts**
Exterior	R-1.4 (R-8)	R- 0.6 (R-3.5)
Ventilated Attic	R-1.4 (R-8)	R- 0.6 (R-3.5)
Unventilated Attic without Roof Insulation	R-1.4 (R-8)	R- 0.6 (R-3.5)
Unventilated Attic with Roof Insulation	R- 0.6 (R-3.5)	No Requirement
Unconditioned Space[b]	R- 0.6 (R-3.5)	No Requirement
Indirectly Conditioned Space[c]	No Requirement	No Requirement
Buried	R- 0.6 (R-3.5)	No Requirement

[a] Insulation R-value is measured on a horizontal plane in accordance with ASTM C518 at a mean temperature of 24°C (75°F) at the installed thickness

[b] Includes crawlspaces, both ventilated and non-ventilated

[c] Includes return air plenums with or without exposed roofs above.

5.4.1.5 System Balancing

Construction documents shall require that all HVAC systems be balanced in accordance with generally accepted engineering standards. Construction documents shall require that a written balance report be provided to the owner or the designated representative of the building owner for HVAC systems serving zones with a total conditioned area exceeding 500 m^2 (5,000 ft^2).

Air System Balancing

Air systems shall be balanced in a manner to first minimize throttling losses. Then, for fans with fan system power greater than 0.75 kW (1.0 hp), fan speed shall be adjusted to meet design flow conditions.

Hydronic System Balancing

Hydronic systems shall be proportionately balanced in a manner to first minimize throttling losses; then the pump impeller shall be trimmed or pump speed shall be adjusted to meet design flow conditions. Exceptions to be considered for:

(a) Impellers need not be trimmed nor pump speed adjusted for pumps with pump motors of 7.5 kW (10 hp) or less,

(b) Impellers need not be trimmed when throttling results in no greater than 5% of the nameplate horsepower draw, or 2.2 kW (3 hp), whichever is greater.

5.4.1.6 Condensers

Location of condensers

Care shall be exercised in locating the condensers in such a manner that heat sink is free of interference from heat discharge by devices located in adjoining spaces and also does not interfere with such other systems installed nearby.

Treated water for condensers

All high-rise buildings using centralized cooling water system shall use soft water for the condenser and chilled water system.

5.4.2 Prescriptive Requirements for HVAC systems

Compliance shall be demonstrated with the requirements in 5.4.2.1 through 5.4.2.1 for each

HVAC system that meets the following criteria:

(a) Serves a single zone,

(b) Cooling (if any) is provided by a unitary packaged or split-system air conditioner or heat pump,

(c) Heating (if any) is provided by a unitary packaged or split-system heat pump, fuelfired furnace, electric resistance heater, or baseboards connected to a boiler, and

(d) Outside air quantity is less than 1,400 l/s (3000 cfm) and less than 70% of supply air at design conditions.

Other HVAC systems shall comply with ASHRAE 90.1-2004, § 6.5.

5.4.2.1 Economizers

Air side economizers

Each individual cooling fan system that has a design supply capacity over 1,200 l/s (2,500 cfm) and a total mechanical cooling capacity over 22 kW (6.3 tons) shall include either:

(a) An air economizer capable of modulating outside-air and return-air dampers to supply 100 percent of the design supply air quantity as outside-air; or

(b) A water economizer capable of providing 100% of the expected system cooling load at outside air temperatures of 10°C (50°F) dry-bulb/7.2°C (45°F) wet-bulb and below.

Exception for above requirements to § 5.3.1.1:

(a) Projects in the Hot-Dry and Warm-Humid climate zones are exempt.

(b) Individual ceiling mounted fan systems < 3,200 l/s (6,500 cfm) are exempt.

5.3.1.2 Where required by 5.3.1.1 economizers shall be capable of providing partial cooling even when additional mechanical cooling is required to meet the cooling load.

5.3.1.3 Air-side economizers shall be tested in the field following the requirements in Appendix 15 to ensure proper operation.

Exception to 5.3.1.3: Air economizers installed by the HVAC system equipment manufacturer and certified to the building department as being factory calibrated and tested per the procedures in Appendix 15.

Variable Flow Hydronic System

5.3.2.1 Chilled or hot-water systems shall be designed for variable fluid flow and shall be capable of reducing pump flow rates to no more than the larger of:

(a) 50% of the design flow rate, or

(b) the minimum flow required by the equipment manufacturer for proper operation of the chillers or boilers.

5.3.2.2 Water cooled air-conditioning or heat pump units with a circulation pump motor greater than or equal to 3.7 kW (5 hp) shall have two-way automatic isolation valves on each water cooled air-conditioning or heat pump unit that are interlocked with the compressor to shut off condenser water flow when the compressor is not operating.

5.3.2.3 Chilled water or condenser water systems that must comply with either 5.3.2.1 or 5.3.2.2 and that have pump motors greater than or equal to 3.7 kW (5 hp) shall be controlled by variable speed drives.

5.4.3 ECBC Requirements for Service Hot water and Pumping

All service water heating equipment and systems shall comply with the mandatory provisions that Residential facilities, hotels and hospitals with a centralized system shall have solar water heating for at least 1/5 of the design capacity. Exception is given to systems that use heat recovery for at least 1/5 of the design capacity. Service water heating equipment shall meet or exceed the minimum efficiency requirements presented in Table 5.14.

Table 5.14 : Minimum Efficiencies for Service Water Heating Equipment

Equipment Type	Size Category (Input)	Subcategory or Rating Condition	Performance Required[a]	Test Procedure[b]
Electric Water Heaters	≤12 kW	Resistance ≥76 L	0.93-0.00132V EF	DOE 10 CFR Part 430
	>12 kW	Resistance ≥76 L	20 + 35 √V SL, Btu/h	ANSI Z21.10.3
	≤24 Amps and ≤250 Volts	Heat Pump	0.93-0.00132V EF	DOE 10 CFR Part 430
Gas Storage Water Heaters	≤23 kW	≥76 L	0.62-0.0019V EF	DOE 10 CFR Part 430
	>23 kW	<310 W/L	80% E_t (Q/800 + 110 √V) SL, Btu/h	ANSI Z21.10.3
Gas Instantaneous Water Heaters	>15 kW and <59 kW	≥310 W/L and <8 L	0.62-0.0019V EF	DOE 10 CFR Part 430
	≥59 kW[c]	≥310 W/L and <38 L	80% E_t	ANSI Z21.10.3
	≥59 kW	≥310 W/L and ≥38 L	80% E_t (Q/800 + 110 √V) SL, Btu/h	
Oil Storage Water Heaters	≤31 kW	≥76 L	0.59-0.0019V EF	DOE 10 CFR Part 430
	>31 kW	<310 W/L	78% E_t (Q/800 + 110 √V) SL, Btu/h	ANSI Z21.10.3
Oil Instantaneous Water Heaters	≤62 kW	≥310 W/L and <8 L	0.59-0.0019V EF	DOE 10 CFR Part 430
	>62 kW	≥310 W/L and <38 L	80% E_t	ANSI Z21.10.3
	>62 kW	≥310 W/L and ≥38 L	78% E_t (Q/800 + 110 √V) SL, Btu/h	
Hot Water Supply Boilers, Gas and Oil	≥62 kW and <3664 kW	≥310 W/L and <38 L	80% E_t	ANSI Z21.10.3
Hot Water Supply Boilers, Gas		≥310 W/L and ≥38 L	80% E_t (Q/800 + 110 √V) SL, Btu/h	
Hot Water Supply Boilers, Oil		≥310 W/L and ≥38 L	78% E_t (Q/800 + 110 √V) SL, Btu/h	
Pool Heaters Oil and Gas	All		78% E_t	ASHRAE 146
Heat Pump Pool Heaters	All		4.0 COP	ASHRAE 146
Unfired Storage Tanks	All		R-2.2	(none)

[a] Energy factor (EF) and thermal efficiency (E_t) are minimum requirements, while standby loss (SL) is maximum Btu/h based on a 38.9°C temperature difference between stored water and ambient requirements. In the EF equation, *V* is the rated volume in liters. In the SL equation, V is the rated volume in liters and *Q* is the nameplate input rate in W.

[b] Section 12 of ASHRAE 90.1-2004 contains a complete specification, including the year version, of the referenced test procedure.

[c] Instantaneous water heaters with input rates below 58.62 W must comply with these requirements if the water heater is designed to heat water to temperatures 82.2°C or higher.

Supplementary Water Heating System

Supplementary heating system shall be designed to maximize the energy efficiency of the system and shall incorporate the following design features in cascade:

(a) Maximum heat recovery from hot discharge system like condensers of air conditioning units,

(b) Use of gas fired heaters wherever gas is available, and

(c) Electric heater as last resort.

Piping Insulation

Piping insulation shall comply with § 5.2.4.1. The entire hot water system including the storage tanks, pipelines shall be insulated conforming to the relevant IS standards on materials and applications.

Heat Traps

Vertical pipe risers serving storage water heaters and storage tanks not having integral heat traps and serving a non-recirculating system shall have heat traps on both the inlet and outlet piping as close as practical to the storage tank.

Swimming Pools

Heated pools shall be provided with a vapor retardant pool cover on or at the water surface. Pools heated to more than 32°C (90°F) shall have a pool cover with a minimum insulation value of R-2.1 (R-12).

Exception to § 6.2.6: Pools deriving over 60% of their energy from site-recovered energy or solar energy source.

Compliance Documentation

The application for approval shall furnish detailed calculation showing the design to ensure that at least 20% of the heating requirement shall be met from solar heat/heat recovery and not more than 80% of the heat shall be met from electrical heating. Wherever gas is available, not more than 20% of the heat shall be met from electrical heating.

6

Thermal Insulation and Energy Savings*

Thermal insulations are materials or combination of materials that help retard the flow of heat energy by conductive, convective and/or radiative modes of heat transfer. Thermal insulation materials can be of several types: fibrous, particulate, film, block or composites of these materials. By retarding the heat flow, thermal insulations can serve one or more of the following functions:

1. Conserve energy by reducing heat loss or gain of structures and ducts.
2. Control surface temperature of structures for comfort.
3. Prevent vapor condensation on surfaces having temperature below the dew point temperature of the surrounding atmosphere.
4. Reduce temperature fluctuations within an enclosure when required heating or cooling is not available.
5. Reduce temperature variations within a conditioned space for increasing personal comfort.

Additionally, thermal insulation can also serve the following purposes:

1. Add structural strength to wall, ceiling or floor section
2. Provide support to surface finish
3. Impede water vapor transmission and air infiltration
4. Reduce noise and vibration

Limiting value of use of any thermal insulation material is its own survival temperature. Nevertheless, selection of thermal insulation material may involve secondary criteria in addition to the primary criteria of low thermal conductivity. The first section of this chapter therefore, covers all such properties of insulating materials that are vital for making a choice.

On the basis of their origin, all the thermal insulation materials can be classified in three categories:

First category is of inorganic, fibrous or cellular materials such as glass wool, rock wool, or slag wool and calcium silicate, bonded perlite, vermiculite or ceramic products. Use of asbestos has been identified as carcinogen and extreme care is to be taken for using it as insulating material.

---

* Base document for this Chapter is ASHRAE Handbook 'Fundamentals', 2005

Second category of insulating materials is organic fibrous materials such as cellulose, cotton, animal hair, wood, pulp, cane or synthetic fibers, and organic cellular materials such as cork, foamed rubber, polystyrene, polyurethane and other polymers.

Third category is metallic or metallic organic reflective membranes. These surfaces must face an air, gas filled or evacuated space to be effective.

6.1 PROPERTIES OF INSULATING MATERIALS

6.1.1 Physical properties

Following are major forms of insulation materials:

(a) *Loose-fill insulation:* these materials consist of fibres, powders, granules, or nodules that are usually poured or blown into walls or other spaces.

(b) *Insulating cement:* it is a loose material that is mixed with water or a suitable binder to obtain plasticity and adhesion. It is toweled or blown wet on a surface and dried in place. It is particularly useful for filling irregular places.

(c) *Flexible and semi-rigid insulation:* These consist of organic and inorganic materials, with and without binders and have a wide range of compressibility and flexibility. These insulations are generally available as blanket, batt, or felt insulation and in either sheets or rolls. Covering the facings may be fastened to one or both sides and serve as reinforcing, air or vapor retarder or both, reflective surfaces, or surface finishes. These coverings include combinations of laminated foil, glass, cloth or plastics and paper, wire mesh, or metal lath.

(d) *Rigid materials:* such materials are available in rectangular blocks, boards or sheets, which are performed during manufacture of standard lengths, widths and thicknesses.

(e) *Reflective materials:* these are available in the form of sheets and rolls of single layer or multilayer construction and in pre-formed shapes with integral air spaces.

(f) *Foam-in-place insulations:* they are available as liquid components or expandable pellets that can be poured, frothed or sprayed in place to form rigid or semi-rigid foam insulation. Fibrous materials mixed with liquid binders can also be sprayed in place, and in some products, the binder is also a foam.

(g) *Accessory material:* these materials include mechanical and adhesive fasteners, exterior and interior finishes, vapor and air retarder coatings, jackets and weather coatings, sealants, lagging adhesives, membranes and flashing compounds.

ASTM Standard C 168 defines more details related to thermal insulating materials.

6.1.2 Thermal Properties

Thermal resistance of insulation is a measure of the effectiveness of thermal insulation to retard the heat flow. A material with high thermal resistivity (low thermal conductivity) is an effective insulator. Heat transmission in most thermal insulations is accomplished by a combination of gas and solid conduction, convection and radiation. Major factors that control heat transfer are length of heat flow path, temperature difference for heat flow and environmental conditions such as wind velocity.

Thermal conductivity of any material may not be same at all the conditions. Specially for the reflective insulation materials, 'apparent thermal conductivity' can be defined to represent its insulation equivalent to any conventional mass type insulation material. Reflective insulations impede radiative heat transfer because the surfaces have high reflectance and low emittance values. To be effective, the reflective face of both the single and multi-layer reflective materials must face an air or evacuated space. Multiple layers of reflective materials along with smooth and parallel air spaces increase overall thermal resistance. Care must be taken to inhibit any air leakage or movement within the air space.

Mass type insulation can be combined with reflective surfaces and air spaces to obtain a higher thermal resistance. However, each design must be evaluated because maximum thermal performance of these systems depends upon factors such as condition of the insulation, shape, air leakage/movement, condition of reflective surface and aging characteristics. Design values of effective or apparent thermal conductivity, thermal conductance and thermal resistance of common insulations are given in Table 6.1. Other thermal properties that can be important are specific heat, heat capacity, thermal diffusivity, coefficient of thermal expansion and maximum permissible temperature. Heat capacity is the product of mass and specific heat, it shows the amount of heat any material can store within itself without becoming hot or cold. Thermal diffusivity of insulation becomes important for applications where temperature varies with time, since the rate of temperature change within an insulation is proportional to its thermal diffusivity for a given thickness.

The R-value

If the conductance of an insulating material is given by, $C = k_{ins}/L_{ins}$, where, k_{ins} and L_{ins} are thermal conductivity and thickness of insulating material, the R-value of the insulation is defined as $R=1/C = L_{ins}/k_{ins}$. This means that, for obtaining a higher R-value of insulation, either more thickness of insulating material or a material of low conductance should be used.

For example, a 6" thick blanket of fiberglass whose thermal conductivity k= 0.027BTU/hr/°F, the R-value can be found by using the above formula. The value comes out to be R = 0.5/0.027 = 18.5.

As per the practice of nomenclature, for such R-value calculated in BTU units, the above combination of material and thickness is said to have an insulating effectiveness of R-19. Names like R11, R-12 represent ratio of thickness and thermal conductivity in BTU system of units.

In appendix to this chapter, typical thermal properties of common building and insulating materials are given.

6.1.3 Mechanical Properties

Some insulation materials have sufficient structural strength to act as load bearing members. They are used occasionally to support load bearing roofs and floors, form self-supporting partitions or stiffen structural panels. For such applications following properties are important: compressive strength, tensile strength, shear strength, impact resistance, flexural rigidity, resistance to vibration. These mechanical properties vary with basic composition such as density, composition, cell size, fiber diameter and orientation, type and amount of binder and temperature.

6.1.4 Health and Safety

Most thermal insulations have good resistance to potential risks to health such as fire, vermin, rot, objectionable odors and vapors. The potential risks from insulation materials can be put in two categories: —

(a) risks related to storage, handling and installation

(b) risks that can occur after installation e.g. aging

Potential health effects range from temporary irritation to serious changes in body functions. Insulation materials containing asbestos are of special concern. Potential traumatic injury can occur from direct contact with materials that are sharp, rough, have protrusions or abrasive surfaces, permit overheating or transmit electrical energy. Combustion of insulating materials may also release heat, hazardous gases, fibers and particulates. Correct handling, installation and precautionary measures can reduce or eliminate these problems. Manufacturer's recommendations and government codes must be concerned before using insulating materials.

6.1.5 Acoustics

Some thermal insulation materials can also serve purpose of acoustic control. Acoustic efficiency depends upon physical structure of the material. Materials with open, porous surfaces have sound absorption capability. Those with high density and resilient character can be used for absorption of vibrations. Insulation for sound conditioning includes flexible and semi-rigid, formed-in-place fibrous materials and rigid fibrous insulation.

Sound absorption insulation materials are installed on interior surfaces. Rigid materials are fabricated into tile or blocks, edge treated to facilitate mechanical or adhesive application, and pre-finished during manufacturing stage itself. Some insulation materials have natural porous surface others have artificial perforations to facilitate entry of sound waves. Such materials are available in variety of thickness and density to suit different applications. When density is increased by compacting the material, sound absorption generally decreases.

Thermal insulation materials improve their sound insulation when installed with discontinuous construction. A wall of staggered stud construction that uses resilient clips or channels on one side of the stud or resilient boards of special manufacture to prevent acoustic coupling mechanically between the surfaces, reduces sound transmission. Sound absorption by thermal insulation blanket in a cavity wall reduces sound transmission.

In floor construction, resilient channels for separate floor and ceiling joists form a discontinuous construction. Sound absorbing thermal insulation placed within the construction further reduces sound transmission. Thermal insulation boards can be placed under mechanical equipment to isolate vibration.

6.2 FACTORS AFFECTING THERMAL PERFORMANCE OF INSULATION MATERIALS

6.2.1 Physical parameters

Thermal conductivity of materials 'k' is a property of insulating materials but for most materials, conduction is not the only mode of heat transfer. Consequently, the term 'apparent thermal conductivity' describes the heat flow properties of most materials. The apparent thermal conductivity of insulation materials varies with their form, structure, environmental conditions and application conditions. Typical variations include density, cell size, diameter and arrangement of fibers/particles, degree and extent of bonding element, transparency to thermal radiation and type and pressure of gas within the insulation. Environmental and space conditions include, temperature gradient, moisture content, air infiltration, orientation and direction of heat flow. Variation of apparent thermal conductivity of materials is shown in Figure-6.1(a). Variation of apparent thermal conductivity with fiber diameter and density is shown in Figure 6.1(b).

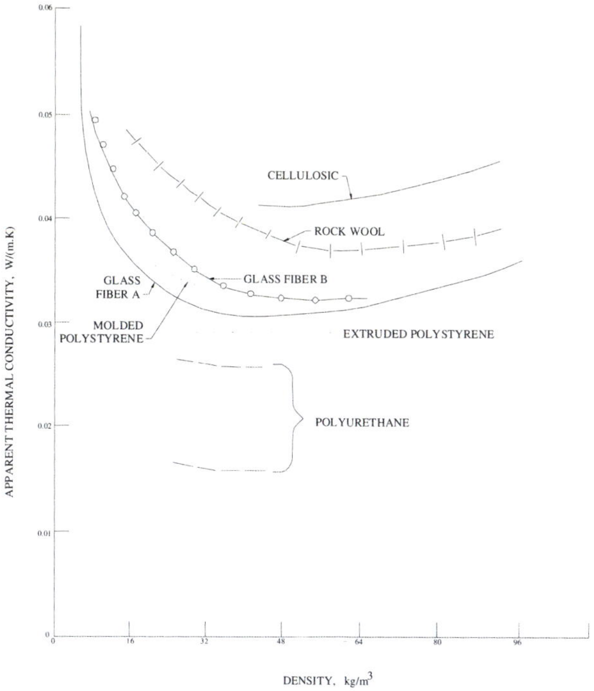

Figure 6.1(a): Apparent thermal conductivity variation of thermal insulating materials

Source : Reprinted with permission from ASHRAE Handbook Fundamentals, Volume, 2005.

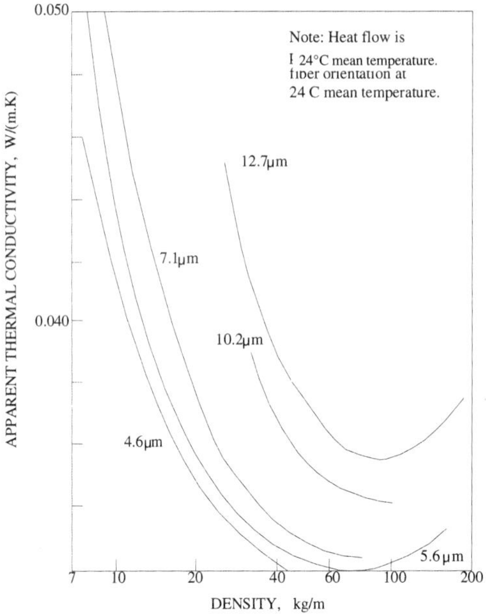

Figure 6.1(b): Apparent thermal conductivity variation of thermal insulating materials
Source : Reprinted with permission from ASHRAE Handbook Fundamentals, Volume, 2005.

Other factors that affect thermal performance include compaction and settling of insulation, air permeability, type and amount of binder used, additives that may influence the bond or contact between fibers/particles, and if used, the type and form of radiation inhibitor.

A change in density caused by the degree of compaction of insulating powders affects the effective thermal conductivity. Insulation materials with lightweight aggregates can be produced with a wide range of densities, with corresponding thermal conductivities.

6.2.2 Environmental parameters

At low temperatures below 200-300^{0}C, a large portion of heat transfer across most insulation materials takes place, mainly due to conduction through the air or other gas in the material. With change in density and temperature, conductivity of this medium, air or gas, changes and as a result the apparent conductivity also changes.

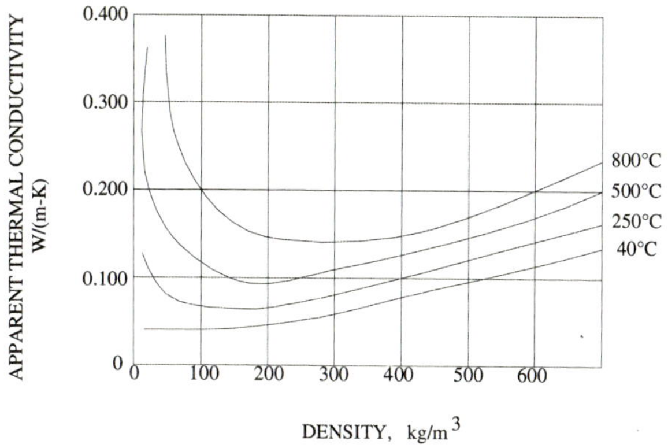

Figure 6.2 (a): Variation of apparent thermal conductivity with mean temperature and density of fibrous insulation

Source : Reprinted with permission from ASHRAE Handbook Fundamentals, Volume, 2005.

Figure 6.2(b) shows typical variation of thermal conductivity of several insulating materials with temperature.

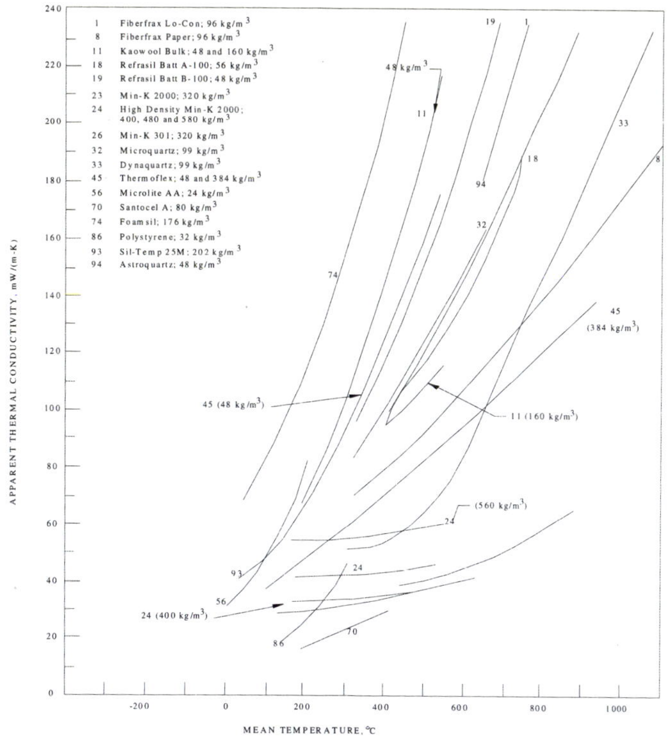

Figure 6.2(b) Apparent thermal conductivity versus mean temperature of materials

Source : Reprinted with permission from ASHRAE Handbook Fundamentals, Volume, 2005.

With increase in temperature, additional effects such as excessive linear shrinkage, softening, de-composition also come into consideration. Additionally, with increase in temperature, convection and air-infiltration through the fibers may increase the heat transfer across them. Low density, loose-fill, large open-cell and fibrous insulation materials are more susceptible to increased heat transfer by air infiltration and convection at elevated temperatures. Similarly, gaps between both board and batt type insulation can lower insulation effectiveness. About 4% void area between batt insulation can produce a 50% loss in effective thermal resistance for a ceiling application with thermal resistance of 3.4 m^2.K/W. If moisture condenses in within the insulation, it further reduces the thermal resistances in addition to damaging the insulation as a whole. Reduction in thermal resistance depends upon distribution of condensed moisture within insulation.

6.2.3 Surface conductance

In order to calculate the overall coefficient of heat transmission through any building component, information about apparent thermal conductivity, thickness of homogenous components, surface conductance of both sides of construction and conductance of air spaces in the construction, is required.

Surface-conductance is the heat transfer to and from the surface by combined effects of radiation, convection and conduction. Heat transfer by conduction and convection is controlled by surface roughness, air movement and temperature difference between the air and surface. Heat transfer by radiation is governed by emittance and reflectivity of surface, temperature difference between surfaces and solid angle between them.

In several construction types, thermal resistance of the internal parts of the wall is very high as compared to surface resistance (reciprocal of surface conductance). In such cases, this factor may be neglected while calculating heat flow. However, for surfaces such as window with single plane of glass this factor plays an important role.

The convective part of surface conductance is notably affected by nature of air movement as shown in Figure 6.3.

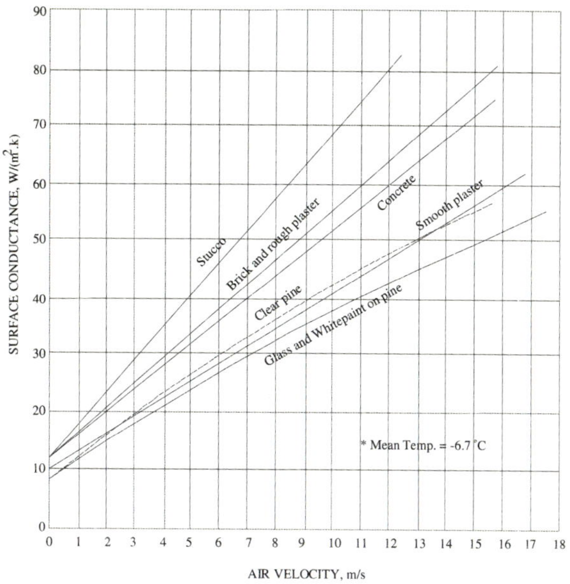

Figure 6.3: Surface conductance for different surfaces as affected by air movement

Source : Reprinted with permission from ASHRAE Handbook Fundamentals, Volume, 2005.

Table-6.1 shows surface conductance for ordinary building materials.

Table-6.1: Surface Conductance and Resistance for Air

Position of Surface	Direction of Heat Flow	Surface Emittance, ε					
		Non-reflective ε= 0.90		Reflective ε= 0.20		ε=0.05	
STILL AIR		**hi**	**R**	**hi**	**R**	**hi**	**R**
Horizontal	Upward	9.26	0.11	5.17	0.19	4.32	0.23
Sloping-45°	Upward	9.09	0.11	5.00	0.20	4.15	0.24
Vertical	Horizontal	8.29	0.12	4.20	0.24	3.35	0.30
Sloping-45°	Downward	7.50	0.12	3.41	0.29	2.56	0.39
Horizontal	Downward	6.13	0.16	2.10	0.48	1.25	0.80
MOVING AIR (Any Position)		**Ho**	**R**				
Wind (for winter) 6.7m/s (24 km/h)	Any	34.0	0.030	-	-	-	-
Wind (for summer) 3.4m/s. (12 km/h)	Any	22.7	0.044	-	-	-	-

Source : Reprinted with permission from ASHRAE Handbook Fundamentals, Volume, 2005.

Notes:

1. Surface conductance, hi and ho measured in $W/(m^2/K)$, resistance R in m^2K/W.
2. No surface has both an air space resistance value and a surface resistance value
3. Conductances are for surface of the stated emittance facing virtual blackbody surroundings at the same temperature as the ambient air. Values are based on a surface air temperature difference of 5.5^0 C and for surface temperature of 21^0C.

6.3 AIR CAVITIES FOR INSULATION

As already discussed briefly in Chapter-5, use of air cavity for insulation of buildings is a very common practice. Heat transfer across any air space is affected by the following factors:

(a) Nature of boundary surface between material and intervening air cavity
(b) Orientation of air cavity
(c) Distance between boundary surfaces
(d) Direction of heat flow

Air cavity conductance coefficient represents the total conductance from one surface bounding the air space to the other surface. Total conductance is the sum of radiation, convection and conduction components. In all cases, the air cavities are considered to be air tight. The radiation component is affected only slightly by the thickness of air space, orientation and direction of heat flow. Heat transfer by conduction and convection is markedly affected by these parameters. Table 6.2 shows thermal resistance of sealed air spaces of different types.

Table 6.2: Thermal Resistances of Plane Air Spaces, $K.m^2/W$

Position of Air Space	Direction of Heat Flow	Air Space	Temp.	13mm Air Spaces[c]					20mm Air Spaces[c]				
		Mean Temp.[d], °C	Diff.[d], °C	Effective Emmitance $å_{eff}^{d,e}$					Effective Emmitance $å_{eff}^{d,e}$				
				0.03	**0.05**	**0.2**	**0.5**	**0.82**	**0.03**	**0.05**	**0.2**	**0.5**	**0.82**
Horizontal	Up ↑	32.2	5.6	0.37	0.36	0.27	0.17	0.13	0.41	0.39	0.28	0.18	0.13
		10.0	16.7	0.29	0.28	0.23	0.17	0.13	0.30	0.29	0.24	0.17	0.14
		10.0	5.6	0.37	0.36	0.28	0.20	0.15	0.40	0.39	0.30	0.20	0.15
		-17.8	11.1	0.30	0.30	0.26	0.20	0.16	0.32	0.32	0.27	0.20	0.16
		-17.8	5.6	0.37	0.36	0.30	0.22	0.18	0.39	0.38	0.31	0.23	0.18
		-45.6	11.1	0.30	0.29	0.26	0.22	0.18	0.31	0.31	0.27	0.22	0.19
		-45.6	5.6	0.36	0.35	0.31	0.25	0.20	0.38	0.37	0.32	0.26	0.21
45° Slope	Up ↗	32.2	5.6	0.43	0.41	0.29	0.22	0.18	0.31	0.31	0.27	0.22	0.19
		10.0	11.1	0.36	0.35	0.31	0.25	0.20	0.38	0.37	0.32	0.26	0.21
		10.0	5.6	0.45	0.43	0.32	0.21	0.16	0.51	0.48	0.35	0.23	0.17
		-17.8	5.6	0.39	0.38	0.31	0.23	0.18	0.37	0.36	0.30	0.23	0.18
		-17.8	16.7	0.46	0.45	0.36	0.25	0.19	0.48	0.46	0.37	0.26	0.20
		-45.6	5.6	0.37	0.36	0.31	0.25	0.21	0.36	0.35	0.31	0.25	0.20
		-45.6	11.1	0.46	0.45	0.38	0.29	0.23	0.45	0.43	0.37	0.29	0.23

Source : Reprinted with permission from ASHRAE Handbook Fundamentals, Volume, 2005.

Position of Air Space	Direction of Heat Flow	Air Space	Temp.	13mm Air Spaces[c]					20mm Air Spaces[c]				
		Mean Temp.[d], °C	Diff.[d], °C	Effective Emmitance $å_{eff}^{d,e}$					Effective Emmitance $å_{eff}^{d,e}$				
Vertical	Horizontal	32.2	5.6	0.43	0.41	0.29	0.19	0.14	0.62	0.57	0.37	0.21	0.15
		10.0	5.6	0.45	0.43	0.32	0.22	0.16	0.51	0.49	0.35	0.23	0.17
		10.0	16.7	0.47	0.45	0.33	0.22	0.16	0.65	0.61	0.41	0.25	0.18
		-17.8	5.6	0.50	0.48	0.38	0.26	0.20	0.55	0.53	0.41	0.28	0.21
		-17.8	11.1	0.52	0.50	0.39	0.27	0.20	0.66	0.63	0.46	0.30	0.22
		-45.6	5.6	0.51	0.50	0.41	0.31	0.24	0.51	0.50	0.42	0.31	0.24
		-45.6	5.6	0.56	0.55	0.45	0.33	0.26	0.65	0.63	0.51	0.36	0.27
45° Slope	Down	32.2	16.7	0.44	0.41	0.29	0.19	0.14	0.62	0.58	0.37	0.21	0.15
		10.0	5.6	0.46	0.44	0.33	0.22	0.16	0.60	0.57	0.39	0.24	0.17
		10.0	11.1	0.47	0.45	0.33	0.22	0.16	0.67	0.63	0.42	0.26	0.18
		-17.8	5.6	0.51	0.49	0.39	0.27	0.20	0.66	0.63	0.46	0.30	0.22
		-17.8	5.6	0.52	0.50	0.39	0.27	0.20	0.73	0.69	0.49	0.32	0.23
		-45.6	16.7	0.56	0.54	0.44	0.33	0.25	0.67	0.64	0.51	0.36	0.28
		-45.6	5.6	0.57	0.56	0.45	0.33	0.26	0.77	0.74	0.57	0.39	0.29
Horizontal	Down	32.2	11.1	0.44	0.41	0.29	0.19	0.14	0.62	0.58	0.37	0.21	0.15
		10.0	5.6	0.47	0.45	0.33	0.22	0.16	0.66	0.62	0.42	0.25	0.18
		10.0	5.6	0.47	0.45	0.33	0.22	0.16	0.68	0.63	0.42	0.26	0.18
		-17.8	16.7	0.52	0.50	0.39	0.27	0.20	0.74	0.70	0.50	0.32	0.23
		-17.8	5.6	0.52	0.50	0.39	0.27	0.20	0.75	0.71	0.51	0.32	0.23
		-45.6	11.1	0.57	0.55	0.45	0.33	0.26	0.81	0.78	0.59	0.40	0.30
		-45.6	5.6	0.58	0.56	0.46	0.33	0.26	0.83	0.79	0.60	0.40	0.30
				40mm Air Spaces[c]					90mm Air Spaces[c]				
Horizontal	Up	32.2	5.6	0.45	0.42	0.30	0.19	0.14	0.50	0.47	0.32	0.20	0.14
		10.0	16.7	0.33	0.32	0.26	0.18	0.14	0.27	0.35	0.28	0.19	0.15
		10.0	5.6	0.44	0.32	0.32	0.21	0.16	0.49	0.47	0.34	0.23	0.16
		-17.8	11.1	0.35	0.34	0.29	0.22	0.17	0.40	0.38	0.32	0.23	0.18
		-17.8	5.6	0.43	0.41	0.33	0.24	0.19	0.48	0.46	0.36	0.26	0.20
		-45.6	11.1	0.34	0.34	0.30	0.24	0.20	0.39	0.38	0.33	0.26	0.21
		-45.6	5.6	0.42	0.41	0.35	0.27	0.22	0.47	0.45	0.38	0.29	0.23
45° Slope	Up	32.2	5.6	0.51	0.48	0.33	0.20	0.14	0.56	0.52	0.35	0.21	0.14
		10.0	11.1	0.38	0.36	0.28	0.20	0.15	0.40	0.38	0.29	0.20	0.15
		10.0	5.6	0.51	0.48	0.35	0.23	0.17	0.55	0.52	0.37	0.24	0.17
		-17.8	5.6	0.40	0.39	0.32	0.24	0.18	0.43	0.41	0.33	0.24	0.19
		-17.8	16.7	0.49	0.37	0.37	0.26	0.20	0.52	0.51	0.39	0.27	0.20
		-45.6	5.6	0.39	0.38	0.33	0.26	0.21	0.41	0.40	0.35	0.27	0.22
		-45.6	11.1	0.48	0.46	0.39	0.30	0.24	0.51	0.49	0.41	0.31	0.24
Vertical	Horizontal	32.2	5.6	0.70	0.64	0.40	0.22	0.15	0.65	0.60	0.38	0.22	0.15
		10.0	5.6	0.45	0.43	0.32	0.22	0.16	0.47	0.45	0.33	0.22	0.16
		10.0	16.7	0.67	0.62	0.42	0.26	0.18	0.64	0.60	0.41	0.25	0.18
		-17.8	5.6	0.49	0.47	0.37	0.26	0.20	0.51	0.49	0.38	0.27	0.20
		-17.8	11.1	0.62	0.59	0.44	0.29	0.22	0.61	0.59	0.44	0.29	0.22
		-45.6	5.6	0.46	0.45	0.38	0.29	0.23	0.50	0.48	0.40	0.30	0.24
		-45.6	5.6	0.58	0.56	0.46	0.34	0.26	0.60	0.58	0.47	0.34	0.26

Source : Reprinted with permission from ASHRAE Handbook Fundamentals, Volume, 2005.

Position of Air Space	Direction of Heat Flow	Air Space	Temp.	40mm Air Spaces[c]					90mm Air Spaces[c]				
		Mean Temp.[d], °C	Diff.[d], °C	Effective Emmitance å$_{eff}^{d,e}$					Effective Emmitance å$_{eff}^{d,e}$				
45° Slope	Down	32.2	16.7	0.89	0.80	0.45	0.24	0.16	0.85	0.76	0.44	0.24	0.16
		10.0	5.6	0.63	0.59	0.41	0.25	0.18	0.62	0.58	0.40	0.25	0.18
		10.0	11.1	0.90	0.82	0.50	0.28	0.19	0.83	0.77	0.48	0.28	0.19
		-17.8	5.6	0.68	0.64	0.47	0.31	0.22	0.67	0.64	0.47	0.31	0.22
		-17.8	5.6	0.87	0.81	0.56	0.34	0.24	0.81	0.76	0.53	0.33	0.24
		-45.6	16.7	0.64	0.62	0.49	0.35	0.27	0.66	0.64	0.51	0.36	0.28
		-45.6	5.6	0.82	0.79	0.60	0.40	0.30	0.79	0.76	0.58	0.40	0.30
Horizontal	Down	32.2	11.1	1.07	0.94	0.49	0.25	0.17	1.77	1.44	0.60	0.28	0.18
		10.0	5.6	1.10	0.99	0.56	0.30	0.20	1.69	1.44	0.68	0.33	0.21
		10.0	5.6	1.16	1.04	0.58	0.30	0.20	1.96	1.63	0.72	0.34	0.22
		-17.8	16.7	1.24	1.13	0.69	0.39	0.26	1.92	1.68	0.86	0.43	0.29
		-17.8	5.6	1.29	1.17	0.70	0.39	0.27	2.11	1.82	0.89	0.44	0.29
		-45.6	11.1	1.36	1.27	0.84	0.50	0.35	2.05	1.85	1.06	0.57	0.38
		-45.6	5.6	1.42	1.32	0.86	0.51	0.35	2.28	2.03	1.12	0.59	0.39

Source : Reprinted with permission from ASHRAE Handbook Fundamentals, Volume, 2005.

One important classification of air cavities is the width making it narrow or wide cavity. If the product of temperature difference in Kelvin(K), and the cube of air space thickness in millimeters (mm) is less than 27000 for horizontal air space with downward heat flow, it is called narrow air cavity or narrow air space. For installations having upwards heat flow, this product if lower than 9000, makes an air space eligible for being called narrow. In narrow air cavities, convective heat transfer is suppressed and can be neglected. To obtain high thermal resistance with reflective insulation, a series of multiple air cavities bounded by reflective surfaces can be adopted. Except for thick horizontal air cavities, there is very little improvement in thermal insulation by adding second highly reflective surface in the same air cavity. If the air cavity has only one reflective surface, placing the reflective side on the warm side prevents condensation. Emittance of surface in the air cavity should be kept low to minimize the radiative heat flow through the air cavity.

6.4 BUILDING INSULATION PRACTICES

Selection of insulation in buildings is based upon thermal properties of materials, space availability, compatibility of materials with adjacent materials and interior and exterior climatic conditions. Insulation practices differ from the type of basic construction. Major practices for important construction types are as follows:

6.4.1 Insulation for wood frame construction

Since the construction with wooden framework provide limited resistance to heat flow, it is very much suited for both, cavity insulation and surface applied insulation. Most common materials for cavity insulation are glass-fiber, mineral fiber, cellulose and spray-applied foams. For surface applications, a variety of sheathing insulations are found in market, such as rigid foam panels. Pre-finished insulating paneling may be used as an inside finish on the exterior walls or on either side of internal partition. It can also underlay other finishes. Wooden or metallic roof decks may be insulated on the top side or below the deck. Structural monolithic insulating decks must be at least 75mm thick to provide an acceptable reduction in the overall heat transfer coefficient. Additional insulation can be placed on the top or below the deck.

Attic construction with conventional rafters and ceiling joists or roof trusses can be insulated between the framing members with batt, blanket or loose-fill insulation. In warm climatic conditions, radiant barriers and reflective insulations can provide additional reduction to cooling load.

Frames of construction can be insulated by blowing-in insulation in the form of loose-fill material. The material must be packed to match the density prescribed by the manufacturer for desired thermal performance.

In addition to being properly insulated, the exterior envelope of buildings should be constructed to minimize flow of air into or through the building. As explained in previous section, airflow may degrade the performance of insulation and may cause accumulation of moisture.

6.4.2 Steel Frame Insulation

Structures having steel framing and exterior metal cladding are to be insulated between the frame and cladding with faced blanket or spray insulation as shown in Figure 6.4. In the climatic conditions, where heating is required, the facing may serve as a combination of vapor retarder and exterior finish and must be protected against physical damage. Other types of insulation materials can be applied by adding framing or furring to the inside of frame or exterior side. Securing insulation as shown in Figure-6.4, reduces the thermal resistance offered by insulation since the screw or bolt penetrating the insulation acts as a thermal bridge.

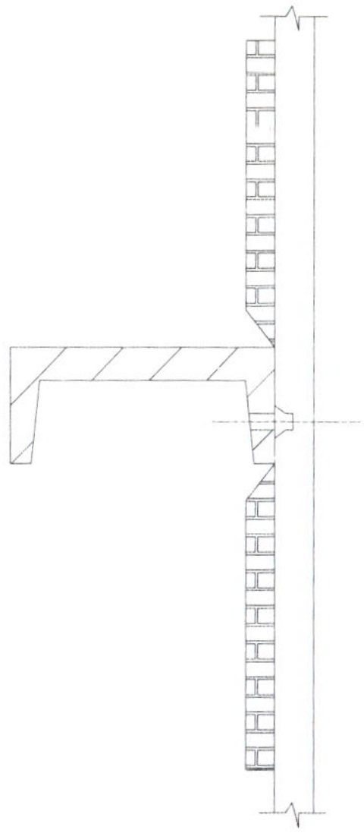

Figure 6.4: Steel frame building wall with flexible blanket insulation

To withstand the elements, single-thickness facings are usually inserted in sub-framing with the windows to form a veneer over separate backup walls. Thermal insulation is integral with or added to the exterior of the back-up wall and covers the edge of the floor slab or spandrel beam. This method is especially useful for cold climates since the floor is kept warm at their exterior edges. Insulation of the exterior of framing reduces thermal movement of building structure as shown in figure 6.5a.

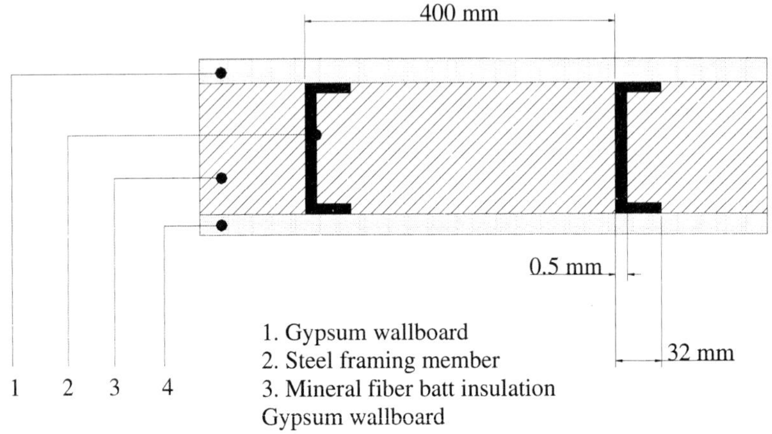

Figure 6.5a: Insulated sheet frame wall

Source : Reprinted with permission from ASHRAE Handbook Fundamentals, Volume, 2005.

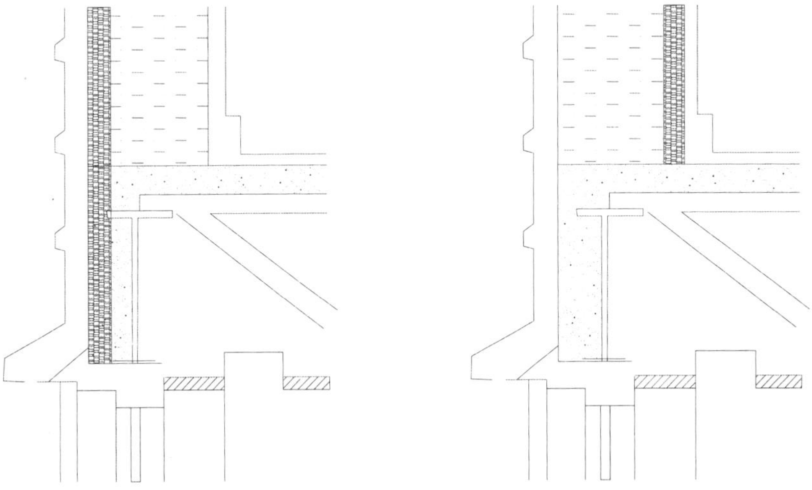

Figure 6.5b: Placement of insulation for structural frame

Source : Reprinted with permission from ASHRAE Handbook Fundamentals, Volume, 2005.

Sandwich construction or adhesive bonded panels consists of three ply: exterior skin, core material and interior skin. These type of panels are manufactured with concrete faces and a core of insulating material. They are available in large sizes and can be attached directly to the exterior of the building frame.

Mechanically fastened panels are usually of hollow box type with exterior facing nesting over the interior facing. The cavity is filled with flexible or semi-rigid insulation as shown in Figure 6.6. The edges should vent to the exterior of the building to allow the panel to additionally serve as rain shield. The panels are installed in a sub framing system.

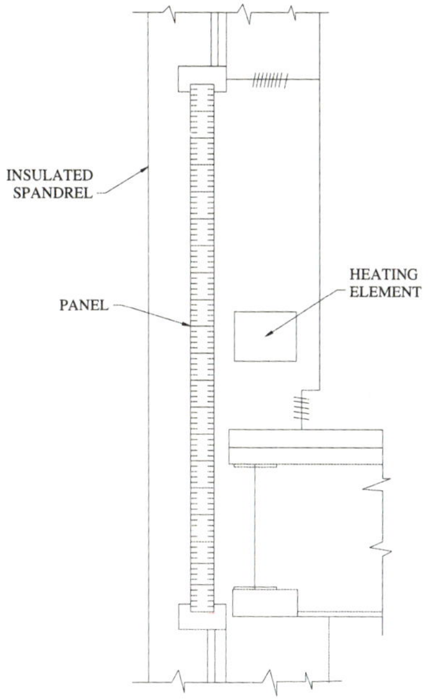

Figure 6.6: Insulated pan type panel

Source : Reprinted with permission from ASHRAE Handbook Fundamentals, Volume, 2005.

All the curtain wall panels with insulation in the cavity or as core material, should be sufficiently tight at the edges to prevent entrance of water and moisture. However, if there is a possibility of entry of moisture from inside or outside through wall, the wall should be capable of drying out. Therefore, panel edges should not be hermetically sealed. For cold climates, sub framing members or wall mullions should be of non-continuous construction. The exterior to interior path should have a thermal break or insulated mullion cover to reduce the moisture condensation as shown in Figures 6.7 and 6.8.

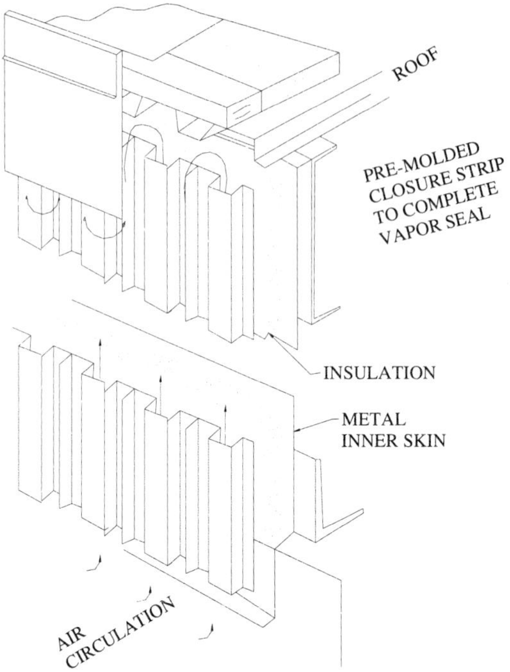

Figure 6.7: Ventilated and insulated field-fabricated curtain wall

Source : Reprinted with permission from ASHRAE Handbook Fundamentals, Volume, 2005.

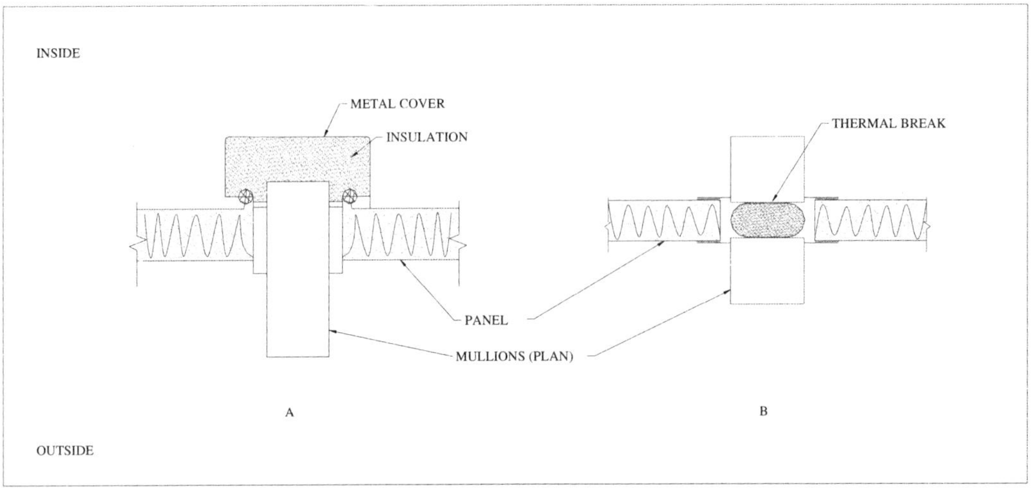

Figure 6.8 : Use of thermal break and insulation mullion

Source : Reprinted with permission from ASHRAE Handbook Fundamentals, Volume, 2005.

6.4.3 Masonry Construction

Since concrete masonry walls and masonry cavity walls have hollow vertical cavities, insulating materials are usually placed within the wall itself. Loose fill insulation, such as water repellent perlite and vermiculite, foam inserts and in-situ-foamed insulation, are commonly used. This insulation method is more effective as compared to low-density masonry units. Rigid insulation can be placed between the veneered construction or with furring on the inner side of the wall as shown in Figure 6.9. The thermal mass and inertia of such heavy construction causes a time-lag in heat migration, that may lower the peak gains or losses. Insulation placed on outer side of the wall increases the time lag as compared to placement inside. In addition, placement of insulation on outer side protects the structure from thermal expansion or contraction due to temperature fluctuations.

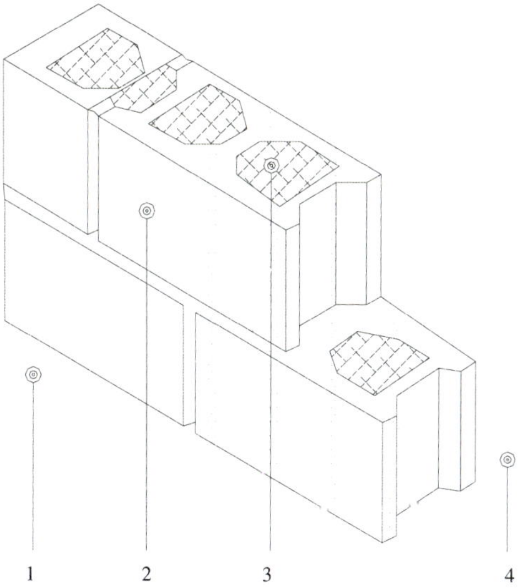

1. Outside surface
2. Concrete block
3. Expanded perlite insulation
4. Inside surface

Figure 6.9: Insulated concrete block wall

Source : Reprinted with permission from ASHRAE Handbook Fundamentals, Volume, 2005.

Pre-cast or poured-in-place concrete walls are insulated the same way as solid masonry construction. The design and fabrication method of panels governs the type of most appropriate insulation material. Figure 6.10 shows insulation on pre-cast concrete panel, the break in insulation shown in this figure is an undesired situation since it may create a thermal short circuit.

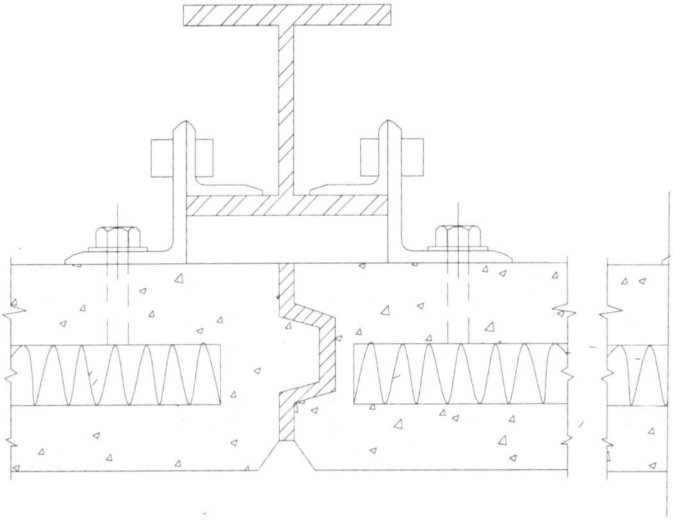

Figure 6.10: Plan of insulated pre-cast concrete panel

Source : Reprinted with permission from ASHRAE Handbook Fundamentals, Volume, 2005.

6.4.4 Foundation and Floor System Insulation

Insulation of perimeter should be applied vertically on the inside or outside of foundation walls as shown in Figure 6.11. Rigid mineral fiber or cellular plastic insulation are used as perimeter outside insulation. Perimeter insulation needs protection from physical damage and protection from ultraviolet radiation if it extends above the grade level. Insulation can also be installed under the slab, horizontally, from the foundation wall inwards for a distance of about 600mm or more, with vertically placed insulation.

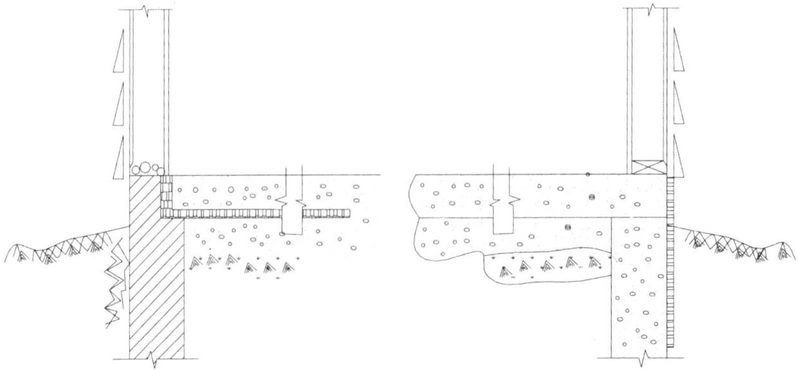

Figure 6.11: Perimeter insulation

Source : Reprinted with permission from ASHRAE Handbook Fundamentals, Volume, 2005.

Below grade, back-filled walls enclosing usable and heated space can be insulated and finished in the same way as solid masonry or concrete walls. Unoccupied or unheated spaces below heated areas e.g. crawl spaces, may have insulated walls to maintain temperatures and minimize need for underground insulation, in cold areas.

Floor construction with joists can be insulated between the joists as shown in Figure 6.12. Such insulation may require supplemental support. Material with an integral vapor retarder, installed with an vapor retarder up, can be secured with the flange provided for this purpose. Laced wires, barbed-end wires spanning the joist space, wire mesh, screening, or ceiling finish support loose fill insulation. Another floor insulation method is with use of double sided, perforated aluminium foil draped and stapled over floor joists. For a sag depth of about 100mm, R-values of 1.0 to 2.0m^2.K/W can be obtained. Carpeted floors over good installations with a sag of 100mm can have R-value of 2.5m^2.K/W.

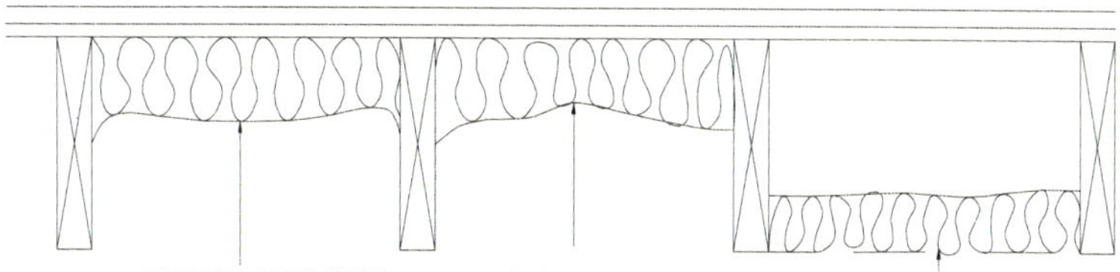

Figure 6.12: Insulation method for framed doors

Source : Reprinted with permission from ASHRAE Handbook Fundamentals, Volume, 2005.

6.4.5 Roof Deck Insulation

Insulation is required with almost all the common types of roof-deck construction systems to maintain the indoor temperature within comfortable limits. For flat and low-slope roofs, insulation should be placed on the top of the deck, on the outside of the structure. As described earlier, placing the insulation outside, reduces thermal movement of deck and the potential of underdeck condensation in cold climatic conditions. Traditionally, insulation is placed under the roof membrane so that it serves the purpose of base for the built up roof. For a stable base, a good bond must be established between the insulation and the roof deck, between the insulation and the built-up-roof.

Single-ply membrane roofs are commonly installed with ballasted, loose-laid, mechanically/ adhesively fastened systems. Adhesion to the insulation is usually not desirable. Insulation can also be placed above the membrane in a protected membrane roof system. In this type of system, a roof membrane is installed on the deck, where it functions as a water proofing membrane and vapor retarder. Insulation can be placed above or below membranes to work as the base, as membrane protector and as an insulator.

Roofs systems designed to sustain heavy movement of persons, should have a secondary structure, supported on a curb system, above the waterproof membrane of the roof system. Insulation of pitched roofs covered with shingles, tile or other mechanically fastened water-shedding materials, should be placed above the ceiling directly on the roof of attic floor. If the undersurface of pitched roof is exposed to the interior, insulation can be applied over the roof framing or decking. In such case, insulation is covered with nailing base for the roofing application. Pre-finished roof planks having the required thermal resistance can also be placed over the rafters.

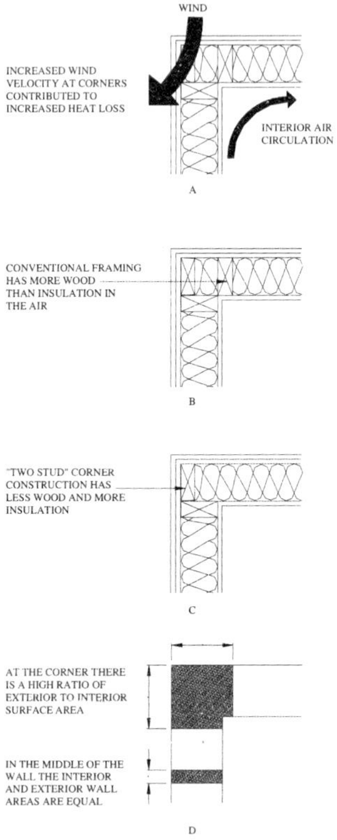

Figure 6.13: Heat loss at building corners

Source : Reprinted with permission from ASHRAE Handbook Fundamentals, Volume, 2005.

6.5 INSULATION OF DUCTS

In buildings, insulation ducts carrying cold/warm air is a very important field. The requirement of insulating any duct is governed by the following factors:

(a) Duct location, indoor or outdoor
(b) The effect of heat loss or gain on equipment size and operating cost
(c) The need to prevent condensation at low temperature ducts
(d) The need to control temperature change in long duct lengths
(e) The need to control noise with interior duct lining

Ducts that are exposed to outdoor conditions, and ducts that pass through unconditioned space, should be properly insulated. Analysis of temperature change, heat loss/gain and other factors influencing the economics of thermal insulation are usually not carried out for residential buildings. For commercial and industrial buildings, such analysis is essential from the point of view of performance as well as economics.

The overall heat transfer coefficient, the U-factor for un-insulated duct, is affected by air velocity, emittance of surface, and the shape of duct. An approximate value of 5.5 to 6.0W/m^{2}K may be used for this purpose. For insulated ducts, U-factors in the range of 0.74 to 1.4 can be attained with rigid insulation of 50mm and 25mm respectively using material having thermal conductivity of 0.039W/mK at 25^{0}C.

Material selection for ducts, insulation and liners

Ducts fitted inside buildings can be of insulated sheet metal or fibrous glass, both of which provide combined air barrier, thermal insulation and sound insulation. Ducts embedded in or fitted just below the floor slabs may be of compressed fiber, ceramic tile or any other rigid material. Ducts installations include semi-rigid boards and flexible blanket composed of organic or inorganic materials in fibrous, cellular or bonded particle forms. Insulations for exterior surfaces may have attached vapor barriers. When applied to the interior of duct as liner, insulation serves dual purpose, thermal insulation and sound absorption. Duct liner insulations have sound-permeable coatings or other treatment on the side facing the air-stream to withstand air velocities without deterioration.

Fibrous glass ducts are available as preformed round ducts or in form of board for fabrication of rectangular ductwork. Maximum recommended air velocity inside such ducts is 10m/s to prevent erosion of fibers. For heating ducts, maximum recommended temperature is 120^{0}C.

Various duct installations and fibrous glass duct materials must meet the fire hazard requirements to restrict spread of smoke, heat and fire through duct and to minimize ignition sources.

Exterior duct insulation can be attached with adhesive, with supplemental pre-attached pins and clips, with wiring or bands. Liners can be attached with adhesive and supplemental pins/clips. Manufacturers usually provide information on the construction of fiber glass duct systems. Preformed round ducts for straight runs can be combined with fittings fabricated from straight ducts. Rectangular ducts and fittings are fabricated by grooving, folding, and taping with metal accessories such as turning vanes, splitters, and dampers incorporated into the system. If rectangular ducts exceed the pre-determined dimensions for particular static pressure, the ductwork must be reinforced.

The effect of duct insulation in commercial buildings is more pronounced as compared to residential buildings. However, insulation can significantly reduce operating costs that depend upon the unit cost of heating and cooling energy, extent of duct exposed to outside conditions. In addition, duct insulation maintains the supply air temperature unaltered thereby, maintaining the conditioned space within acceptable temperature range. Vapor retarders are required on exterior insulation of ducts that are used for alternate cooling and heating.

Insulation can reduce operating cost and size of the cooling system significantly. The advantage of adequate insulation can be clearly seen in the areas with high dry-bulb temperature and dew-point temperature. Ducts with summer air-conditioning are insulated with the same material as heating ducts. Ducts in an unconditioned space should be insulated and have vapor retarders to prevent condensation. Joints and laps must be properly sealed. Flexible closed-cell insulation does not always need a supplemental vapor retarder, but care must be taken to form vapor tight seams at joints.

APPENDIX

Table 6.3: Typical thermal properties of common building and insulating materials

Description	*Density kg/m³*	*Conductivity [b](k), W/(m.K)*	*Conductance (C), W/(m².K)*	*Resistance (R)*		
				Per-Inch Thickness (1/k), K.m/W	*For Thickness Listed (1/C), W/(m².K)*	*Specific Heat, kJ, (kg.K)*
BUILDING BOARD						
Asbestos-cement board..	1900	0.58	-	1.73	-	1.00
Asbestos-cement board........3.2mm	1900	-	187.4	-	0.005	-
Asbestos-cement board........6.4mm	1900	-	93.7	-	0.011	-
Gypsum or plaster board.....9.5mm	800	-	17.6	-	0.056	1.09
Gypsum or plaster board....12.7mm	800	-	12.6	-	0.079	-
Gypsum or plaster board.....15.9mm	800	-	10.1	-	0.099	-
Plywood (Douglas Fir)[d]	540	0.12	-	8.66	-	1.21
Plywood (Douglas Fir)........6.4mm	540	-	18.2	-	0.055	-
Plywood (Douglas Fir).........9.5mm	540	-	12.1	-	0.083	-
Plywood (Douglas Fir)......12.7mm	540	-	9.1	-	0.11	-
Plywood or wood panels....15.9mm	540	-	7.3	-	0.14	-
Plywood (Douglas Fir)......19.0mm	540	-	6.1	-	0.16	1.21
Vegetables fiber board						
Sheathing, regular density....12.7mm	290	-	4.3	-	0.23	1.30
....................................19.8mm	290	-	2.8	-	0.36	-
Sheathing, intermediate						
density...12.7mm	350	-	5.2	-	0.19	1.30
Nail-base sheathing [c]..........12.7mm	400	-	5.3	-	0.19	1.30

Source : Reprinted with permission from ASHRAE Handbook Fundamentals, Volume, 2005.

Description	*Density kg/m³*	*Conductivity ᵇ(k), W/(m.K)*	*Conductance (C), W/(m².K)*	*Resistance (R)*		
				Per-Inch Thickness (1/k), K.m/W	*For Thickness Listed (1/C), W/(m².K)*	*Specific Heat, kJ, (kg.K)*
Shingle backer....................9.5mm	290	-	6.0	-	0.17	1.30
Shingle backer....................7.9mm	290	-	7.3	-	0.14	-
Sound deadening board	240	-	4.2	-	0.24	1.26
..................................12.7mm	290	0.058	-	17	-	0.59
Tile and lay-in panels, plain or acoustic..12.7mm	290	-	4.5	-	0.22	-
Tile and lay-in panels, plain or acoustic..19.0mm	290	-	3.0	-	0.33	-
Laminated paperboard	480	0.072	-	13.9	-	1.38
Homogenous board from repulped paper	480	0.072	-	13.9	-	1.17
Hard board[c]						
Medium density	800	0.105	-	9.50	-	1.30
High density, service-tempered grade and service grade.......	880	0.82	-	8.46	-	1.34
High density, standard-tempered grade	1010	0.144	-	6.93	-	1.34
Particle board[c]						
Low density..........	590	0.102	-	9.77	-	1.30
Medium density.........	800	0.135	-	7.35	-	1.30
High density.............	1000	0.170	-	5.90	-	1.30
Underlayment 15.9mm	640	-	6.9	-	0.14	1.21
Waferboard.................	590	0.01	-	11.0	-	-
Wood subfloor....................19.0mm	-	-	6.0	-	0.17	1.38
BUILDING MEMBRANE						
Vapor-permeable felt..................	-	-	94.9	-	0.011	-
Vapor seal, 2 layers of mopped 0.73 kg/m²felt	-	-	47.4	-	0.21	-
Vapor seal, plastic film.......	-	-	-	-	Negl.	-
FINISH FLOORING MATERIALS						
Carpet and fibrous pad..........	-	-	2.73	-	0.37	1.42

Source : Reprinted with permission from ASHRAE Handbook Fundamentals, Volume, 2005.

Description	*Density kg/m³*	*Conductivity ᵇ(k), W/(m.K)*	*Conductance (C), W/(m².K)*	*Resistance (R)*		
				Per-Inch Thickness (1/k), K.m/W	*For Thickness Listed (1/C), W/(m².K)*	*Specific Heat, kJ, (kg.K)*
Carpet and rubber pad..........	-	-	4.60	-	0.22	1.38
Cork tile...........3.2mm	-	-	20.4	-	0.049	2.01
Terrazzo...........25mm	-	-	71.0	-	0.014	0.80
Tile- asphalt, linoleum, vinyl,						
rubber..........	-	-	113.6	-	0.009	1.26
Vinyl asbestos.............						1.01
Ceramic..................						0.80
Wood, hard wood finish.........19mm	-	-	8.35	-	0.12	-
INSULATING MATERIALS						
Blanket and Batt[f,g] Mineral fiber, fibrous form processed from rock, slag, or glass						
Approx. 75-100mm...............	6.4-32	-	0.52	-	1.94	-
Approx. 90mm...............	6.4-32	-	0.44	-	2.29	-
Approx. 90mm...............	12-26	-	0.38	-	2.63	-
Approx. 140-165mm...............	6.4-32	-	0.30	-	3.32	-
Approx. 140mm...............	10-16	-	0.27	-	3.67	-
Approx. 150-190mm...............	6.4-32	-	0.26	-	3.91	-
Approx. 210-250mm...............	6.4-32	-	0.19	-	5.34	-
Approx. 250-330mm...............	6.4-32	-	0.15	-	6.77	-
Board and Slabs						
Cellular glass.......................	136	0.050	-	19.8	-	0.75
Glass fiber, organic bonded......	64-140	0.036	-	27.7	-	0.96
Expanded perlite, organic bonded....	16	0.052	-	19.3	-	1.26
Expended rubber (rigid)...........	72	0.032	-	31.6	-	1.68
Expended polystyrene, extruded (smooth skin surface) (CFC-12 exp.)...	29-56					
Expended polystyrene, extruded (Smooth skin surface) (HCFC-142 exp.)[h]...	29-56	0.029	-	34.7	-	1.21

Source : Reprinted with permission from ASHRAE Handbook Fundamentals, Volume, 2005.

Description	*Density kg/m³*	*Conductivity* [b]*(k), W/(m.K)*	*Conductance (C), W/(m².K)*	*Resistance (R)*		*Specific Heat, kJ, (kg.K)*
				Per-Inch Thickness (1/k), K.m/W	*For Thickness Listed (1/C), W/(m².K)*	
Expended polystyrene, molded beads...........	16	0.037	-	26.7	-	-
	20	0.036	-	27.7	-	-
	24	0.035	-	28.9	-	-
	28	0.035	-	28.9	-	-
	32	0.033	-	30.2	-	-
Cellular polyurethane / polyisocyanurate[i] (CFC-11 exp.) (unfaced)..................	24	0.023-0.026	-	43.3-38.5	-	1.59
Cellular polyisocyanurate[i] (CFC-11 exp.) (gas permeable facers)..................	24-40	0.023-0.026	-	43.3-38.5	-	0.92
Cellular polyisocyanurate[i] (CFC-11 exp.) (gas permeable facers)..................	32	0.020	-	48.8	-	0.92
Cellular phenolic (closed cell) (CFC-11, CFC-113 exp.)[k]	32	0.017	-	56.8	-	-
Cellular phenolic (open cell)........	29-35	0.033	-	30.5	-	-
Mineral fiber with resin binder......	240	0.042	-	23.9	-	0.71
Mineral fiberboard, wet felted Core or roof insulation............	260-270	0.049	-	20.4	-	-
Acoustical tile..............	290	0.050	-	19.8	-	0.80
Acoustical tile...............	340	0.053	-	18.7	-	-
Mineral fiberboard, wet molded Acoustical tile[1]	370	0.060	-	16.5	-	0.59
Wood or cane fiberboard Acoustical tile[1] 12.7mm	-	-	4.5	-	0.22	1.30
Acoustical tile[1] 19.0mm	-	-	3.0	-	0.33	-
Interior finish (plank, tile)	240	0.050	-	19.8	-	1.34
Cement fiber slabs (shredded wood with Portland cement blinder).........	400-430	0.072-0.076	-	13.9-13.1	-	-

Source : Reprinted with permission from ASHRAE Handbook Fundamentals, Volume, 2005.

Description	*Density kg/m³*	*Conductivity [b](k), W/(m.K)*	*Conductance (C), W/(m².K)*	*Resistance (R)*		
				Per-Inch Thickness (1/k), K.m/W	*For Thickness Listed (1/C), W/(m².K)*	*Specific Heat, kJ, (kg.K)*
Cement fiber slabs (shredded wood with Magnesia oxysulfide blinder)... Loose fill	350	0.082	-	12.1	-	1.30
Cellulosic insulation (milled paper or wood pulp).........	37-51	0.039-0.046	-	25.6-21.7	-	1.38
Perlite, expended..................	32-66	0.039-0.045	-	25.6-22.9	-	1.09
	66-120	0.045-0.052	-	22.9-19.4	-	-
	120-180	0.052-0.060	-	19.4-16.6	-	-
Mineral fiber (rock, slag, or glass)[g]						
Approx. 95-130mm...............	9.6-32	-	-	-	1.94	0.71
Approx. 170-220mm...............	9.6-32	-	-	-	3.35	-
Approx. 190-250mm...............	9.6-32		-	-	3.87	-
Approx. 260-350mm...............	9.6-32	-	-	-	5.28	-
Mineral fiber (rock, slag, or glass)[g]						
Approx. 90mm (closed side wall application)...............	32-56	-	-	-	2.1-2.5	-
Vermiculite, exfoliated................	110-130	0.068	-	14.8	-	1.34
	64-96	0.063	-	15.7	-	-
Spray Applied						
Polyurethane foam..............	24-40	0.023-0.026	-	43.3-38.5	-	-
Ureaformaldehyde foam..........	11-26	0.032-0.040	-	31.5-24.7	-	-
Cellulosic fiber..........	56-96	0.042-0.049		23.9-20.4		
Glass fiber.............	56-72	0.038-0.039		26.7-25.6		

Source : Reprinted with permission from ASHRAE Handbook Fundamentals, Volume, 2005.

Description	*Density kg/m³*	*Conductivity* ᵇ*(k), W/(m.K)*	*Conductance (C), W/(m².K)*	*Resistance (R)*		
				Per-Inch Thickness (1/k), K.m/W	*For Thickness Listed (1/C), W/(m².K)*	*Specific Heat, kJ, (kg.K)*
Reflective insulation						
Reflective material (Σ<0.5) in center of 20mm cavity forms two 10mm vertical air space[m]..................			1.76		0.57	
METALS						
ROOFING						
Asbestos – cement shingles............	1900		27.0		0.037	1.00
Asphalt roll roofing..................	1100		36.9		0.026	1.51
Asphalt shingles.....................	1100		12.9		0.077	1.26
Built-up roofing..........10mm	1100		17.0		0.058	1.46
Slate.......................13mm			114		0.009	1.26
Wood shingles, plain and plastic film faced............			6.0		0.166	1.30
PLASTERING MATERIALS						
Cement plaster, sand aggregate...	1860	0.72		1.39	-	0.84
Sand aggregate...............10mm			75.5		0.013	0.84
Sand aggregate...............10mm			37.8		0.026	0.84
Gypsum plaster:						
Lightweight aggregate.......13mm	720		17.7		0.056	
Lightweight aggregate.......16mm	720		15.2		0.066	
Lightweight aggregate on metal lath...19mm			12.1		0.083	
Perlite aggregate	720	0.22	-	4.64		1.34
Sand aggregate...................13mm	1680	0.81		1.25		0.84
Sand aggregate................16mm	1680		63.0		0.016	
Sand aggregate on metal lath....13mm	1680		51.7		0.019	
Sand aggregate on metal lath..19mm			43.7		0.023	
Vermiculite aggregate..................	720	0.24		4.09		

Source : Reprinted with permission from ASHRAE Handbook Fundamentals, Volume, 2005.

Description	Density kg/m³	Conductivity [b](k), W/(m.K)	Conductance (C), W/(m².K)	Resistance (R)		
				Per-Inch Thickness (1/k), K.m/W	For Thickness Listed (1/C), W/(m².K)	Specific Heat, kJ, (kg.K)
MASONRY MATERIALS (Masonry Units)						
Brick, fired clay....................	2400	1.21-1.47		0.83-0.68		
	2240	1.07-1.30		0.94-0.77		
	2080	0.92-1.12		1.08-0.89		
	1920	0.81-0.98		1.24-1.02		0.79
	1760	0.71-0.85		1.42-1.18		
	1600	0.61-0.74		1.65-1.36		
	1440	-0.52-0.62		1.93-1.61		
	1280	0.43-0.53		2.31-1.87		
	1120	0.36-0.45		2.77-2.23		
Clay tile, hallow						
1 cell deep..........................75mm			7.10		0.14	0.88
1 cell deep..........................100mm			5.11		0.20	
2 cell deep..........................150mm			3.75		0.27	
2 cell deep..........................200mm			3.07		0.33	
2 cell deep..........................250mm			2.56		0.39	
3 cell deep..........................300mm			2.27		0.44	
Concrete blocks[n,o]						
Limestone aggregate						
200mm, 16.3kg, 2210 kg/m³ concrete, 2 cores........						
Same with perlite filled cores............		2.73		0.37		
300mm, 25kg, 2210 kg/m³ concrete, 2 cores........						
Same with perlite filled cores.........			1.53		0.65	
Normal mass aggregate (sand and gravel)200mm, 15-16kg, 2020-2180 kg/m³ concrete, 2 or 3 cores........			5.1-5.8		0.20-0.17	0.92
Same with perlite filled cores.........			2.84		0.35	

Source : Reprinted with permission from ASHRAE Handbook Fundamentals, Volume, 2005.

Description	*Density kg/m³*	*Conductivity ᵇ(k), W/(m.K)*	*Conductance (C), W/(m².K)*	*Resistance (R)*		*Specific Heat, kJ, (kg.K)*
				Per-Inch Thickness (1/k), K.m/W	*For Thickness Listed (1/C), W/(m².K)*	
Same with vermiculite filled cores...			3.0-4.1		0.34-0.24	
300mm, 22.7kg, 2000 kg/m³ concrete, 2 cores........			4.60		0.217	0.92
Medium mass aggregate (combinations of normal and low mass aggregate) 200mm, 12-13kg, 1550-1790 kg/m³ concrete, 2 or 3 cores........			3.3-4.4		0.30-0.22	
Same with perlite filled cores.........			1.5-2.5		0.65-0.41	
Same with vermiculite filled cores......			1.70		0.58	
Same with molded EPS (beads) filled cores			1.82		0.56	
Same with molded EPS inserts in cores...........			2.10		0.47	
Low mass aggregate (expended shale, clay, slate oe slag, pumic) 150mm, 7.3-7.7kg, 1360-1390 kg/m³ concrete, 2 or 3 cores........			3.0-3.5		0.34-0.29	
Same with perlite filled cores.........			1.36		0.74	
Same with vermiculite filled cores...			1.87		0.53	
200mm, 8.6-10.0kg, 1150-1380 kg/m³ concrete, ...			1.8-3.1		0.56-0.33	0.88
Same with perlite filled cores............			0.9-1.3		1.20-0.77	
Same with vermiculite filled cores...			1.1-1.5		0.93-0.69	
Same with molded EPS (beads) filled cores			1.19		0.85	
Same with UF foam foam filled cores...........			1.25		0.79	
Same with molded EPS inserts in cores...........			1.65		0.62	

Source : Reprinted with permission from ASHRAE Handbook Fundamentals, Volume, 2005.

Description	*Density kg/m³*	*Conductivity [b](k), W/(m.K)*	*Conductance (C), W/(m².K)*	*Resistance (R)*		
				Per-Inch Thickness (1/k), K.m/W	*For Thickness Listed (1/C), W/(m².K)*	*Specific Heat, kJ, (kg.K)*
300mm, 14.5-16.3kg, 1280-1440 kg/m³ concrete, 2 or 3 cores........			2.2-2.5		0.46-0.40	
Same with perlite filled cores.........			0.6-0.9		1.6-1.1	
Same with vermiculite filled cores...			0.97		1.0	
Stone, lime and sand Quartzitic and sandstone...........	2880	10.4		0.10		
	2560	6.2		0.16		
	2240	3.5		0.29		
	1920	1.9		0.53		0.79
Calcitic, dolomitic, limestone, marble, and granite.......	2880	4.3		0.23		
	2560	3.2		0.32		
	2240	2.3		0.43		
	1920	1.6		0.63		0.79
	1600	1.1		0.90		
Gypsum partition tile						
75 by 300 by 760 mm, solid.........			4.50		0.222	0.79
75 by 300 by 760 mm, 4 cells.........			4.20		0.238	
100 by 300 by 760 mm, 3 cells.........			3.40		0.294	
Concretes[c]						
Sand and gravel or stone aggregate concretes (concretes with more than 50% quartz or quartzite sand have conductivities in the higher end of the range)..............	2400	1.4-2.9		0.69-0.35		
	2240	1.3-2.6		0.77-0.39		0.8-1.0
	2080	1.0-1.9		0.99-0.53		
Limestone concrete.............	2240	1.60		0.62		
	1920	1.14		0.88		
	1600	0.79		1.26		

Source : Reprinted with permission from ASHRAE Handbook Fundamentals, Volume, 2005.

Description	*Density kg/m³*	*Conductivity ᵇ(k), W/(m.K)*	*Conductance (C), W/(m².K)*	*Resistance (R)*		
				Per-Inch Thickness (1/k), K.m/W	*For Thickness Listed (1/C), W/(m².K)*	*Specific Heat, kJ, (kg.K)*
Gypsum-fiber concrete (87.5% gypsum, 12.5% wood chips)	816	0.24		4.18		0.88
Cement/lime, mortar and stucco......	1920	1.40		0.71		
	1600	0.97		1.04		
	1280	0.65		1.54		
Lightweight aggregate concretes Expended shale, clay, or slate; expended slages; cinders; pumice (with density upto 1600 kg/m³) and scoria (sanded concrete have conductivities in the higher end of the range).............	1920	0.9-1.3		1.08-0.76		
	1600	0.68-0.89		1.48-1.12		0.84
	1280	0.48-0.59		2.10-1.69		0.84
	960	0.30-0.36		3.30-2.77		
	640	0.18		5.40		
Perlite, vermiculite and polystyrene beads.........	800	0.26-0.27		3.81-3.68		
	640	0.20-0.22		4.92-4.65		0.63-0.96
	480	0.16		6.31		
	320	0.12		8.67		
Foam concretes...........	1920	0.75		1.32		
	1600	0.60		1.66		
	1280	0.44		2.29		
	1120	0.36		2.77		
Foam concretes and cellular concretes	960	0.30		3.33		
	640	0.20		4.92		
	320	0.12		8.67		

Source : Reprinted with permission from ASHRAE Handbook Fundamentals, Volume, 2005.

Description	Density kg/m^3	Conductivity ^{b}(k), W/(m.K)	Conductance (C), W/(m^2.K)	Resistance (R) Per-Inch Thickness (1/k), K.m/W	Resistance (R) For Thickness Listed (1/C), W/(m^2.K)	Specific Heat, kJ, (kg.K)
SIDING MATERIALS (on flat surface)						
Shingles:						
Asbestos cement…………	1900		27.0		0.037	
Wood, 400mm, 190-mm exposure……..	-		6.53		0.15	1.30
Wood, double, 400mm, 300-mm exposure……….	-		4.77		0.21	1.17
Wood, plus insul, backer board, 8mm …	-		4.03		0.25	1.30
Siding:						
Asbestos – cement, 6.4mm, lapped…			27.0		0.037	1.01
Asphalt roll siding…………..			36.9		0.026	1.47
Asphalt insulating siding (12.7 mm bed)…			3.92		0.26	1.47
Hardboard siding, 11mm……..			8.46		0.12	1.17
Wood, drop, 20 by 200mm……..			7.21		0.14	1.17
Wood, bevel, 13 by 200mm lapped….			6.98		0.14	1.17
Wood, bevel, 19 by 250mm lapped….			5.40		0.18	1.17
Wood, plywood, 9.5mm lapped………			9.60		0.10	1.22
Aluminum, steel, or vinyl[p,q], over sheathing						
Hollow-backed…………..			9.31		0.11	1.22[q]
Insulating-board backed……….						
9.5mm nominal…………..			3.12		0.32	1.34
9.5mm nominal, foil backed …………			1.93		0.52	
Architectural (soda-lime float) glass …			56.8		0.018	0.84
WOODS (12% moisture content)[e,r]						
Hardwoods						1.63[s]
Oak……………	659-749	0.16-0.18		6.2-5.5		
Birch…………	682-726	0.167-0.176		6.0-5.7		
Maple…………	637-704	0.157-0.171		6.4-5.8		

Source : Reprinted with permission from ASHRAE Handbook Fundamentals, Volume, 2005.

Description	Density kg/m^3	Conductivity [b](k), W/(m.K)	Conductance (C), W/(m^2.K)	Resistance (R)		
				Per-Inch Thickness (1/k), K.m/W	For Thickness Listed (1/C), W/ (m^2.K)	Specific Heat, kJ, (kg.K)
Ash…………	614-670	0.153-0.164		6.5-6.1		
Softwoods						1.63[s]
Southern pine……………	570-659	0.144-0.161		6.9-6.2		
Douglas Fir-Larch………..	536-581	0.137-0.145		7.3-6.9		
Southern Cypress……….	502-514	0.130-0.132		7.7-7.6		
Hem-Fir, Spruce-Pine-Fir…………..	392-502	0.107-0.130		9.3-7.7		
West Coast Woods, Cedars…………..	347-502	0.098-0.130		10.3-7.7		
California Redwood……………..	392-448	0.107-0.118		9.4-8.5		

Source *:* Reprinted with permission from ASHRAE Handbook Fundamentals, Volume, 2005.

Table 6.4 : Assembly U-Factors for Roofs with Deck above

Rated R-Value of Insulation Alone	*Overall U-Factor for Entire Assembly*	*Rated R-Value of Insulation Alone*	*Overall U-Factor for Entire Assembly*
R-0	U-1.282	R-19	U-0.051
R-1	U-0.562	R-20	U-0.048
R-2	U-0.360	R-21	U-0.046
R-3	U-0.265	R-22	U-0.044
R-4	U-0.209	R-23	U-0.042
R-5	U-0.173	R-24	U-0.040
R-6	U-0.147	R-25	U-0.039
R-7	U-0.129	R-26	U-0.037
R-8	U-0.114	R-27	U-0.036
R-9	U-0.102	R-28	U-0.035
R-10	U-0.093	R-29	U-0.034
R-11	U-0.085	R-30	U-0.032
R-12	U-0.078	R-35	U-0.028
R-13	U-0.073	R-40	U-0.025
R-14	U-0.068	R-45	U-0.022
R-15	U-0.063	R-50	U-0.020
R-16	U-0.060	R-55	U-0.018
R-17	U-0.056	R-60	U-0.016
R-18	U-0.053		

*R&U Values are in BTU system

Source *:* Reprinted with permission from ASHRAE Handbook Fundamentals, Volume, 2005.

Table 6.5: U-values of different types of roof assemblies

Insulation System	Rated R-Value of Insulation	Total Rated R-Value of Insulation	Overall U-Factor for Entire Base Roof Assembly	Overall U-Factor for Assembly of Base Roof Plus Continuous Insulation (Uninterrupted by framing) Rated R-Value of Continuous Insulation					
				R-5.6	R-11.2	R-16.8	R-22.4	R-28.0	R-33.6
Standing Seam Roofs with Thermal Blocks									
Single Layer	None	0	1.280	0.162	0.087	0.059	0.045	0.036	0.030
	R-6	6	0.167	0.086	0.058	0.044	0.035	0.029	0.025
	R-10	10	0.097	0.063	0.046	0.037	0.031	0.026	0.023
	R-11	11	0.092	0.061	0.045	0.036	0.030	0.026	0.022
	R-13	13	0.083	0.057	0.043	0.035	0.029	0.025	0.022
	R-16	16	0.072	0.051	0.040	0.033	0.028	0.024	0.021
	R-19	19	0.065	0.048	0.038	0.031	0.026	0.023	0.020
(Multiple R-values are listed in order from inside to outside)									
Double Layer	R-10+R-10	20	0.063	0.047	0.037	0.031	0.026	0.023	0.020
	R-10+R-11	21	0.061	0.045	0.036	0.030	0.026	0.023	0.020
	R-11+R-11	22	0.060	0.045	0.036	0.030	0.026	0.022	0.020
	R-10+R-13	23	0.058	0.044	0.035	0.029	0.025	0.022	0.020
	R-11+R-13	24	0.057	0.043	0.035	0.029	0.025	0.022	0.020
	R-13+R-13	26	0.055	0.042	0.034	0.029	0.025	0.022	0.019
	R-10+R-19	29	0.052	0.040	0.033	0.028	0.024	0.021	0.019
	R-11+R-19	30	0.051	0.040	0.032	0.027	0.024	0.021	0.019
	R-13+R-19	32	0.049	0.038	0.032	0.027	0.023	0.021	0.019
	R-16+R-19	35	0.047	0.037	0.031	0.026	0.023	0.020	0.018
	R-19+R-19	38	0.046	0.037	0.030	0.026	0.023	0.020	0.018
Screw Down Roofs									
	R-10	10	0.153	0.082	0.056	0.043	0.035	0.029	0.025
	R-11	11	0.139	0.078	0.054	0.042	0.034	0.028	0.025
	R-13	13	0.130	0.075	0.053	0.041	0.033	0.028	0.024
Filled Cavity With Thermal Blocks									
	R-19+R-10	29	0.041	0.033	0.028	0.024	0.021	0.020	0.017

Table 6.6: Assembly U-Factors for Attic Roofs with Wood Joists

Rated R-Value of Insulation Alone	*Overall U-Factor for Entire Assembly*
Wood framed attic, standard framing	
None	0.613
R-11	0.091
R-13	0.081
R-19	0.053
R-30	0.034
R-38	0.027
R-49	0.021
R-60	0.017
R-71	0.015
R-82	0.013
R-93	0.011
R-104	0.010
R-115	0.009
R-126	0.008
Wood framed attic, advanced framing	
None	0.613
R-11	0.088
R-13	0.078
R-19	0.051
R-30	0.032
R-38	0.026
R-49	0.020
R-60	0.016
R-71	0.014
R-82	0.012
R-93	0.011
R-104	0.010
R-115	0.009
R-126	0.008
Wood joists, single-rafter roof	
None	0.417
R-11	0.088
R-13	0.078
R-15	0.071
R-19	0.055
R-21	0.052
R-25	0.043
R-30	0.036
R-38	0.028

Table 6.7: Assembly U-Factors for attic Roofs with Steel Joists (4.0 ft. on center)

Rated R-Value of Insulation Alone	*Overall U-Factor for Entire Assembly*
R-0	U-1.282
R-4	U-0.215
R-5	U-0.179
R-8	U-0.120
R-10	U-0.100
R-11	U-0.093
R-12	U-0.086
R-13	U-0.080
R-15	U-0.072
R-16	U-0.068
R-19	U-0.058
R-20	U-0.056
R-21	U-0.054
R-24	U-0.049
R-25	U-0.048
R-30	U-0.041
R-35	U-0.037
R-38	U-0.035
R-40	U-0.033
R-45	U-0.031
R-50	U-0.028
R-55	U-0.027

Table 6.8: U-value variation with framing type

Framing Type and Depth	*Rated R-Value of Insulation Alone*	*Assembly U-Factors for 8 in. Normal Weight 145 lb/ft³ Solid Concrete Walls*	*Assembly U-Factors for 8 in. Medium Weight 115 lb/ft³ Concrete Ball Walls: Solid Grouted*	*Assembly U-Factors for 8 in. Medium Weight 115 lb/ft³ Concrete Ball Walls: Partially Grouted (cores un-insulated expected where specified)*
No framing	*R-0*	*U-0.740*	*U-0.580*	*U-480*
	Up grouted Cores Filled with Loose- Fill Insulation	*N.A.*	*N.A.*	*U-3.350*
Continuous metal framing at 24 in. on center horizontally				
3.5 in.	R-11.0	U-0.168	U-0.158	U-0.149
3.5 in.	R-13.0	U-0.161	U-0.152	U-0.144
3.5 in.	R-15.0	U-0.155	U-0.147	U-0.140
4.5 in.	R- 17.1	U-0.133	U-0.126	U-0.121
4.5 in.	R- 22.5	U-0.124	U-0.119	U-0.114
4.5 in.	R- 25.2	U-0.122	U-0.116	U-0.112
5.0 in.	R- 19.0	U-0.122	U-0.117	U-0.112
5.0 in.	R- 25.0	U-0.115	U-0.110	U-0.106
5.0 in.	R- 28.0	U-0.112	U-0.107	U-0.103
5.5 in.	R- 19.0	U-0.118	U-0.113	U-0.109
5.5 in.	R- 20.9	U-0.114	U-0.109	U-0.105
5.5 in.	R- 21.0	U-0.113	U-0.109	U-0.105
5.5 in.	R- 27.5	U-0.106	U-0.102	U-0.099
5.5 in.	R- 30.8	U-0.104	U-0.100	U-0.096
6.0 in.	R- 22.8	U-0.106	U-0.102	U-0.098
6.0 in.	R- 30.0	U-0.099	U-0.095	U-0.092
6.0 in.	R- 33.6	U-0.096	U-0.0.93	U-0.090
6.5 in.	R- 24.7	U-0.099	U-0.096	U-0.092
7.0 in.	R- 26.6	U-0.093	U-0.090	U-0.087
7.5 in.	R- 28.5	U-0.088	U-0.085	U-0.083
8.0 in.	R- 30.4	U-0.083	U-0.081	U-0.079
1 in. metal clips at 24 in. on center horizontally and 16 in. vertically				
1.0 in.	R- 3.8	U-0.210	U-0.195	U-0.182
1.0 in.	R- 5.0	U-0.184	U-0.172	U-0.162
1.0 in.	R- 5.6	U-0.174	U-0.163	U-0.154
1.5 in.	R- 5.7	U-0.160	U-0.151	U-0.143
1.5 in.	R- 7.5	U-0.138	U-0.131	U-0.125
1.5 in.	R- 8.4	U-0.129	U-0.123	U-0.118
2.0 in.	R- 7.6	U-0.129	U-0.123	U-0.118

Framing Type and Depth	*Rated R-Value of Insulation Alone*	*Assembly U-Factors for 8 in. Normal Weight 145 lb/ft³ Solid Concrete Walls*	*Assembly U-Factors for 8 in. Medium Weight 115 lb/ft³ Concrete Ball Walls: Solid Grouted*	*Assembly U-Factors for 8 in. Medium Weight 115 lb/ft³ Concrete Ball Walls: Partially Grouted (cores un-insulated expected where specified)*
No framing	*R-0*	U-*0.740*	U-*0.580*	U-*480*
	Up grouted Cores Filled with Loose- Fill Insulation	*N.A.*	*N.A.*	U-*3.350*
2.0 in.	R- 10.0	U-0.110	U-0.106	U-0.102
2.0 in.	R- 11.2	U-0.103	U-0.099	U-0.096
2.5 in.	R- 9.5	U-0.109	U-0.104	U-0.101
2.5 in.	R- 12.5	U-0.092	U-0.089	U-0.086
2.5 in.	R- 14.0	U-0.086	U-0.083	U-0.080
3.0 in.	R- 11.4	U-0.094	U-0.090	U-0.088
3.0 in.	R- 15.0	U-0.078	U-0.076	U-0.074
3.0 in.	R- 16.8	U-0.073	U-0.071	U-0.069
3.5 in.	R- 13.3	U-0.082	U-0.080	U-0.077
3.5 in.	R- 17.5	U-0.069	U-0.067	U-0.065
3.5 in.	R- 19.6	U-0.064	U-0.062	U-0.061
	1 in. metal clips at 24 in. on center horizontally and 16 in. vertically			
4.0 in.	R- 15.2	U-0.073	U-0.071	U-0.070
4.0 in.	R- 20.0	U-0.061	U-0.060	U-0.058
4.0 in.	R- 22.4	U-0.057	U-0.056	U-0.054
5.0 in.	R- 28.0	U-0.046	U-0.046	U-0.045
6.0 in.	R- 33.6	U-0.039	U-0.039	U-0.038
7.0 in.	R- 39.2	U-0.034	U-0.034	U-0.033
8.0 in.	R- 44.8	U-0.030	U-0.030	U-0.029
9.0 in.	R- 50.4	U-0.027	U-0.027	U-0.026
10.0 in.	R- 56.0	U-0.024	U-0.024	U-0.024
11.0 in.	R- 61.6	U-0.022	022U-0.	U-0.022
	Continuous insulation un-interrupted by framing			
No Framing	R-1	U-0.425	U-0.367	U-0.324
No Framing	R-2	U-0.298	U-0.269	U-0.245
No Framing	R-3	U-0.230	U-0.212	U-0.197
No Framing	R-4	U-0.187	U-0.175	U-0.164
No Framing	R-5	U-0.157	U-0.149	U-0.141
No Framing	R-6	U-0.136	U-0.129	U-0.124
No Framing	R-7	U-0.120	U-0.115	U-0.110
No Framing	R-8	U-0.107	U-0.103	U-0.099

Framing Type and Depth	*Rated R-Value of Insulation Alone*	*Assembly U-Factors for 8 in. Normal Weight 145 lb/ft³ Solid Concrete Walls*	*Assembly U-Factors for 8 in. Medium Weight 115 lb/ft³ Concrete Ball Walls: Solid Grouted*	*Assembly U-Factors for 8 in. Medium Weight 115 lb/ft³ Concrete Ball Walls: Partially Grouted (cores un-insulated expected where specified)*
No framing	*R-0*	U-*0.740*	U-*0.580*	U-*480*
	Up grouted Cores Filled with Loose- Fill Insulation	*N.A.*	*N.A.*	U-*3.350*
No Framing	R-9	U-0.097	U-0.093	U-0.090
No Framing	R-10	U-0.088	U-0.085	U-0.083
No Framing	R-11	U-0.081	U-0.079	U-0.076
No Framing	R-12	U-0.075	U-0.073	U-0.071
No Framing	R-13	U-0.070	U-0.068	U-0.066
No Framing	R-14	U-0.065	U-0.064	U-0.062
No Framing	R-15	U-0.061	U-0.060	U-0.059
No Framing	R-16	U-0.058	U-0.056	U-0.055
No Framing	R-17	U-0.054	U-0.053	U-0.052
No Framing	R-18	U-0.052	U-0.051	U-0.050
No Framing	R-19	U-0.049	U-0.048	U-0.047
No Framing	R-20	U-0.047	U-0.046	U-0.045
No Framing	R-21	U-0.045	U-0.044	U-0.043
No Framing	R-22	U-0.043	U-0.042	U-0.042
No Framing	R-23	U-0.041	U-0.040	U-0.040
No Framing	R-24	U-0.039	U-0.039	U-0.038
No Framing	R-25	U-0.038	U-0.038	U-0.037
No Framing	R-30	U-0.032	U-0.032	031U-0.
No Framing	R-35	U-0.028	U-0.027	U-0.027
No Framing	R-40	U-0.024	U-0.024	U-0.024
No Framing	R-45	U-0.022	U-0.021	U-0.021
No Framing	R-50	U-0.019	U-0.019	U-0.019
No Framing	R-55	U-0.018	U-0.018	U-0.018
No Framing	R-60	U-0.016	U-0.016	U-0.016

Table 6.9: Assembly U-Factor, C-Factor, R_u and R_c and Heat Capacity

Density in lb/ft³	*Pro-perties*	*Thickness in inches*									
		3	4	5	6	7	8	9	10	11	12
20	U-factor	0.22	0.17	0.14	0.12	0.10	0.09	0.08	0.07	0.07	0.06
	C-factor	0.27	0.20	0.16	0.13	0.11	0.10	0.09	0.08	0.07	0.07
	R_u	4.60	5.85	7.10	8.35	9.60	10.85	12.10	13.35	14.60	15.85
	R_c	3.75	5.00	6.25	7.50	8.75	10.00	11.25	12.50	13.75	15.00
	HC	1.0	1.3	1.7	2.0	2.3	2.7	3.0	3.3	3.7	4.0
30	U-factor	0.28	0.22	0.19	0.16	0.14	0.12	0.11	0.10	0.09	0.09
	C-factor	0.37	0.28	0.22	0.18	0.16	0.14	0.12	0.11	0.10	0.09
	R_u	3.58	4.49	5.40	6.30	7.21	8.12	9.03	9.94	10.85	11.76
	R_c	2.73	3.64	4.55	5.45	6.36	7.27	8.18	9.09	10.00	10.91
	HC	1.5	2.0	2.5	3.0	3.5	4.0	4.5	5.0	5.5	6.0
40	U-factor	0.33	0.27	0.23	0.19	0.17	0.15	0.14	0.13	0.11	0.11
	C-factor	0.47	0.35	0.28	0.23	0.20	0.18	0.16	0.14	0.13	0.12
	R_u	2.99	2.71	4.42	5.14	5.85	6.56	7.28	7.99	8.71	9.42
	R_c	2.14	2.86	3.57	4.29	5.00	5.71	6.43	7.14	7.86	8.57
	HC	2.0	2.7	3.3	4.0	4.7	5.3	6.0	6.7	7.3	8.0
50	U-factor	0.38	0.31	0.26	0.23	0.20	0.18	0.16	0.15	0.14	0.13
	C-factor	0.57	0.43	0.34	0.28	0.24	0.21	0.19	0.17	0.15	0.14
	R_u	2.61	3.20	3.79	4.38	4.97	5.56	6.14	6.73	7.32	7.91
	R_c	1.76	2.35	2.94	3.53	4.12	4.71	5.29	5.88	6.47	7.06
	HC	2.5	3.3	4.2	5.0	5.8	6.7	7.5	8.3	9.2	10.0
85	U-factor	0.65	0.56	0.50	0.44	0.40	0.37	0.34	0.31	0.29	0.27
	C-factor	1.43	1.08	0.86	0.71	0.61	0.54	0.48	0.43	0.39	0.36
	R_u	1.55	1.78	2.01	2.25	2.48	2.71	2.94	3.18	3.41	3.64
	R_c	0.70	0.93	1.16	1.40	1.63	1.86	2.09	2.33	2.56	2.79
	HC	4.3	5.7	7.1	8.5	9.9	11.3	12.8	14.2	15.6	17.0
95	U-factor	0.72	0.64	0.57	0.52	0.48	0.44	0.41	0.38	0.36	0.33
	C-factor	1.85	1.41	1.12	0.93	0.80	0.70	0.62	0.56	0.51	0.47
	R_u	1.39	1.56	1.74	1.92	2.10	2.28	2.46	2.64	2.81	2.99
	R_c	0.54	0.71	0.89	1.07	1.25	1.43	1.61	1.79	1.96	2.14
	HC	4.8	6.3	7.9	9.5	11.1	12.7	14.3	15.8	17.4	19.0

Density in lb/ft³	*Properties*	*Thickness in inches*									
		3	4	5	6	7	8	9	10	11	12
105	U-factor	0.79	0.71	0.65	0.59	0.54	0.51	0.47	0.44	0.42	0.39
	C-factor	2.38	1.79	1.43	1.18	1.01	0.88	0.79	0.71	0.65	0.59
	R_u	1.27	1.41	1.56	1.70	1.84	1.98	2.12	2.26	2.40	2.54
	R_c	0.42	0.56	0.70	0.85	0.99	0.13	1.27	1.41	1.55	1.69
	HC	5.3	7.0	8.8	10.5	12.3	14.0	15.8	17.5	19.3	21.0
115	U-factor	0.84	0.77	0.70	0.65	0.61	0.57	0.53	0.50	0.48	0.45
	C-factor	2.94	2.22	1.75	1.47	1.25	1.10	0.98	0.88	0.80	0.74
	R_u	0.19	1.30	1.42	1.53	1.65	1.76	1.87	1.99	2.10	2.21
	R_c	0.34	0.45	0.57	0.68	0.80	0.91	1.02	1.14	1.25	1.36
	HC	5.8	7.7	9.6	11.5	13.4	15.3	17.3	19.2	21.1	23.0
125	U-factor	0.88	0.82	0.76	0.71	0.67	0.63	0.60	0.56	0.53	0.51
	C-factor	3.57	2.70	2.17	1.79	1.54	1.35	1.20	1.03	0.98	0.90
	R_u	1.13	1.22	1.31	1.41	1.50	1.59	1.68	1.78	1.87	1.96
	R_c	0.28	0.37	0.46	0.56	0.65	0.74	0.83	0.93	1.02	1.11
	HC	56.3	8.3	10.4	12.5	14.6	6.7	18.8	20.8	22.8	25.0
135	U-factor	0.93	0.87	0.82	0.77	0.73	0.69	0.66	0.63	0.60	0.57
	C-factor	4.55	3.33	2.70	2.22	1.92	1.67	1.49	1.33	1.22	1.11
	R_u	1.07	1.15	1.22	1.30	1.37	1.45	1.52	1.60	1.67	1.75
	R_c	0.22	0.30	0.37	0.45	0.52	0.60	0.67	0.75	0.82	0.90
	HC	6.8	9.0	11.3	13.5	15.8	18.0	20.3	22.5	24.8	27.0
144	U-factor	0.96	0.91	0.86	0.81	0.78	0.74	0.71	0.68	0.65	0.63
	C-factor	5.26	4.00	3.23	2.63	2.27	2.00	1.79	1.59	1.45	1.33
	R_u	1.04	1.10	1.16	1.23	1.29	1.35	1.41	1.48	1.54	1.60
	R_c	0.19	0.25	0.31	0.38	0.44	0.50	0.56	0.63	0.69	0.75
	HC	7.2	2.6	12.0	14.4	16.8	19.2	21.6	24.0	26.4	28.8

Product Size: in.	*Density in lb/ft³*	*Properties*	*Concrete Block Grouting and Cell Treatment*				
			Solid Grouted	*Partly Grouted, Cells Empty*	*Partly Grouted, Cells Insulated*	*Unreinforced Cells Empty*	*Unreinforced Cells Insulated*
6 in block	85	U-factor	0.57	0.46	0.34	0.40	0.20
		C-factor	1.11	0.75	0.47	0.60	0.23
		R_u	1.75	2.18	2.97	2.52	5.13
		R_c	0.90	1.33	2.12	1.67	4.28
		HC	10.9	6.7	7.0	4.2	4.6
	95	U-factor	0.61	0.49	0.36	0.42	0.22
		C-factor	1.25	0.83	0.53	0.65	0.27
		R_u	1.65	2.06	2.75	2.38	4.61
		R_c	0.80	1.21	1.90	1.53	3.76
		HC	11.4	7.2	7.5	4.7	5.1
	105	U-factor	0.64	0.51	0.39	0.44	0.24
		C-factor	1.38	0.91	0.58	0.71	0.30
		R_u	1.57	1.95	2.56	2.26	4.17
		R_c	0.72	1.10	1.71	1.41	3.32
		HC	11.9	7.7	7.9	5.1	5.6
	115	U-factor	0.66	0.54	0.41	0.46	0.26
		C-factor	1.52	0.98	0.64	0.76	0.34
		R_u	1.51	1.87	2.41	2.16	3.79
		R_c	0.66	1.02	1.56	1.31	2.94
		HC	12.3	8.1	8.4	5.6	6.0
	125	U-factor	0.70	0.56	0.45	0.49	0.30
		C-factor	1.70	1.08	0.73	0.84	0.40
		R_u	1.44	1.78	2.23	2.04	3.38
		R_c	0.59	0.93	1.38	1.19	2.53
		HC	12.8	8.6	8.8	6.0	6.5
	135	U-factor	0.73	0.60	0.49	0.53	0.35
		C-factor	1.94	1.23	0.85	0.95	0.49
		R_u	1.36	1.67	2.02	1.90	2.89
		R_c	0.51	0.82	1.17	1.05	2.04
		HC	13.2	9.0	9.3	6.5	6.9

Product Size: in.	*Density in lb/ft³*	*Properties*	*Concrete Block Grouting and Cell Treatment*				
			Solid Grouted	*Partly Grouted, Cells Empty*	*Partly Grouted, Cells Insulated*	*Unrein-forced Cells Empty*	*Unrein-forced Cells Insulated*
8 in block	85	U-factor	0.49	0.41	0.28	0.37	0.15
		C-factor	0.85	0.63	0.37	0.53	0.17
		R_u	2.03	2.43	3.55	2.72	6.62
		R_c	1.18	1.58	2.70	1.87	5.77
		HC	15.0	9.0	9.4	5.4	6.0
	95	U-factor	0.53	0.44	0.31	0.39	0.17
		C-factor	0.95	0.70	0.41	0.58	0.20
		R_u	1.90	2.29	3.27	2.57	5.92
		R_c	1.05	1.44	2.42	1.72	5.07
		HC	15.5	9.6	10.0	6.0	6.6
	105	U-factor	0.55	0.46	0.33	0.41	0.19
		C-factor	1.05	0.76	0.46	0.63	0.22
		R_u	1.81	2.17	3.04	2.44	5.32
		R_c	0.96	1.32	2.19	1.59	4.47
		HC	16.1	10.2	10.6	6.6	7.2
	115	U-factor	0.58	0.48	0.35	0.43	0.21
		C-factor	1.14	0.82	0.50	0.68	0.25
		R_u	1.72	2.07	2.81	2.33	4.78
		R_c	0.87	1.22	1.99	1.48	3.93
		HC	16.7	10.8	11.2	7.2	7.8
	125	U-factor	0.61	0.51	0.38	0.45	0.24
		C-factor	1.27	0.90	0.57	0.74	0.30
		R_u	1.64	1.96	2.62	2.20	4.20
		R_c	0.79	1.11	1.77	1.35	3.35
		HC	17.3	11.4	11.8	7.8	8.4
	135	U-factor	0.65	0.55	0.42	0.49	0.28
		C-factor	1.44	1.02	0.67	0.83	0.37
		R_u	1.54	1.83	2.35	2.05	3.55
		R_c	0.69	0.98	1.50	1.20	2.70
		HC	17.9	12.0	12.4	8.4	9.0

Product Size: in.	*Density in lb/ft³*	*Properties*	*Concrete Block Grouting and Cell Treatment*				
			Solid Grouted	*Partly Grouted, Cells Empty*	*Partly Grouted, Cells Insulated*	*Unrein-forced Cells Empty*	*Unrein-forced Cells Insulated*
10 in block	85	U-factor	0.44	0.38	0.25	0.35	0.13
		C-factor	0.70	0.57	0.31	0.50	0.14
		R_u	2.29	2.61	4.05	2.84	7.87
		R_c	1.44	1.76	3.20	1.99	7.02
		HC	19.0	11.2	11.7	6.5	7.3
	95	U-factor	0.47	0.41	0.27	0.37	0.14
		C-factor	0.77	0.62	0.35	0.55	0.16
		R_u	2.15	2.46	3.73	2.67	6.94
		R_c	1.30	1.61	2.88	1.82	6.09
		HC	19.7	11.9	12.4	7.3	8.1
	105	U-factor	0.49	0.43	0.29	0.39	0.16
		C-factor	0.85	0.68	0.39	0.59	0.19
		R_u	2.03	2.33	3.45	2.54	6.17
		R_c	1.18	1.48	2.60	1.69	5.32
		HC	20.4	12.6	13.1	8.0	8.8
	115	U-factor	0.52	0.45	0.31	0.41	0.18
		C-factor	0.92	0.73	0.42	0.64	0.21
		R_u	1.94	2.22	3.21	2.42	5.52
		R_c	1.09	1.37	2.36	1.57	4.67
		HC	21.1	13.4	13.9	8.7	9.5
	125	U-factor	0.54	0.48	0.34	0.44	0.21
		C-factor	1.01	0.80	0.48	0.70	0.25
		R_u	1.84	2.10	2.95	2.28	4.81
		R_c	0.99	1.25	2.10	1.43	3.96
		HC	21.8	14.1	14.6	9.4	10.2
	135	U-factor	0.58	0.51	0.38	0.47	0.25
		C-factor	1.14	0.90	0.56	0.79	0.32
		R_u	1.72	1.96	2.64	2.12	4.00
		R_c	0.87	1.11	1.79	1.27	3.15
		HC	22.6	14.8	15.3	10.2	11.0

Product Size: in.	*Density in lb/ft³*	*Properties*	*Concrete Block Grouting and Cell Treatment*				
			Solid Grouted	*Partly Grouted, Cells Empty*	*Partly Grouted, Cells Insulated*	*Unrein-forced Cells Empty*	*Unrein-forced Cells Insulated*
12 in block	85	U-factor	0.40	0.36	0.22	0.34	0.11
		C-factor	0.59	0.52	0.27	0.48	0.12
		R_u	2.53	2.77	4.59	2.93	9.43
		R_c	1.68	1.92	3.74	2.08	8.58
		HC	23.1	13.3	14.0	7.5	8.5
	95	U-factor	0.42	0.38	0.24	0.36	0.12
		C-factor	0.66	0.57	0.30	0.52	0.13
		R_u	2.30	2.60	4.22	2.76	8.33
		R_c	1.53	1.75	3.37	1.91	7.48
		HC	23.9	14.2	14.8	8.3	9.3
	105	U-factor	0.44	0.41	0.26	0.38	0.14
		C-factor	0.71	0.62	0.33	0.57	0.15
		R_u	2.25	2.47	3.90	2.62	7.35
		R_c	1.40	1.62	3.05	1.77	6.50
		HC	24.7	15.0	15.6	9.1	10.2
	115	U-factor	0.47	0.42	0.28	0.40	0.15
		C-factor	0.77	0.66	0.36	0.61	0.18
		R_u	2.15	2.36	3.63	2.49	6.54
		R_c	1.30	1.51	2.78	1.64	5.69
		HC	25.6	15.8	16.4	10.0	11.0
	125	U-factor	0.49	0.45	0.30	0.42	0.18
		C-factor	0.84	0.72	0.40	0.66	0.21
		R_u	2.04	2.23	3.34	2.36	5.68
		R_c	1.19	1.38	2.49	1.51	4.83
		HC	26.4	16.6	17.3	10.8	11.8
	135	U-factor	0.52	0.48	0.34	0.46	0.21
		C-factor	0.94	0.81	0.47	0.74	0.26
		R_u	0.91	2.08	2.98	2.19	4.67
		R_c	1.06	1.23	2.13	1.34	3.82
		HC	27.2	17.5	18.1	11.6	12.6

Table 6.10 : Effective R-Value for Insulation/Framing Layers Added to Above-Grade Mass Walls and Below-Grade Walls

Depth in	Framing Type	Rate R-Value of Insulation												
		0	1	2	3	4	5	6	7	8	9	10	11	12
		Effective R-Value if continuous insulation uninterrupted by framing (includes gypsum board)												
	None	0.5	1.5	2.5	3.5	4.5	5.5	6.5	7.5	8.5	9.5	10.5	11.5	12.5
		Effective R-Value if insulation is installed in cavity between framing (includes gypsum board)												
0.5	Wood	1.3	1.3	1.9	2.4	2.7	na	na	na	na	na	na	na	na
	Metal	0.9	0.9	1.1	1.1	1.2	na	na	na	na	na	na	na	na
0.75	Wood	1.4	1.4	2.1	2.7	3.1	3.5	3.8	na	na	na	na	na	na
	Metal	1.0	1.0	1.3	1.4	1.5	1.5	1.6	na	na	na	na	na	na
1.0	Wood	1.3	1.5	2.2	2.9	3.4	3.9	4.3	4.6	4.9	na	na	na	na
	Metal	1.0	1.1	1.4	1.6	1.7	1.8	1.8	1.9	1.9	na	na	na	na
1.5	Wood	1.3	1.5	2.4	3.1	3.8	4.4	4.9	5.4	5.8	6.2	6.5	6.8	7.1
	Metal	1.1	1.2	1.6	1.9	2.1	2.2	2.3	2.4	2.5	2.5	2.6	2.6	2.7
2.0	Wood	1.4	1.5	2.5	3.3	4.0	4.7	5.3	5.9	6.4	6.9	7.3	7.7	8.1
	Metal	1.1	1.2	1.7	2.1	2.3	2.5	2.7	2.8	2.9	3.0	3.1	3.2	3.2
2.5	Wood	1.4	1.5	2.5	3.4	4.2	4.9	5.6	6.3	6.8	7.4	7.9	8.4	8.8
	Metal	1.2	1.3	1.8	2.3	2.6	2.8	3.0	3.2	3.3	3.5	3.6	3.6	3.7
3.0	Wood	1.4	1.5	2.5	3.5	4.3	5.1	5.8	6.5	7.2	7.8	8.3	8.9	9.4
	Metal	1.2	1.3	1.9	2.4	2.8	3.1	3.3	3.5	3.7	3.8	4.0	4.1	4.2
3.5	Wood	1.4	1.5	2.6	3.5	4.4	5.2	6.0	6.7	7.4	8.1	8.7	9.3	9.8
	Metal	1.2	1.3	2.0	2.5	2.9	3.2	3.5	3.8	4.0	4.2	4.3	4.5	4.6
4.0	Wood	1.4	1.6	2.6	3.6	4.5	5.3	6.1	6.9	7.6	8.3	9.0	9.6	10.2
	Metal	1.2	1.3	2.0	2.6	3.0	3.4	3.7	4.0	4.2	4.5	4.6	4.8	5.0
4.5	Wood	1.4	1.6	2.6	3.6	4.5	5.4	6.2	7.1	7.8	8.5	9.2	9.9	10.5
	Metal	1.2	1.3	2.1	2.6	3.1	3.5	3.9	4.2	4.5	4.7	4.9	5.1	5.3
5.0	Wood	1.4	1.6	2.6	3.6	4.6	5.5	6.3	7.2	8.0	8.7	9.4	10.1	10.8
	Metal	1.2	1.4	2.1	2.7	3.2	3.7	4.1	4.4	4.7	5.0	5.2	5.4	5.6
5.5	Wood	1.4	1.6	2.6	3.6	4.6	5.5	6.4	7.3	8.1	8.9	9.6	10.3	11.0
	Metal	1.3	1.4	2.1	2.8	3.3	3.8	4.2	4.6	4.9	5.2	5.4	5.7	5.9

Depth in	Framing Type	Rate R-Value of Insulation												
		13	14	15	16	17	18	19	20	21	22	23	24	25
		Effective R-Value if continuous insulation uninterrupted by framing (includes gypsum board)												
	None	13.5	14.5	15.5	16.5	17.5	18.5	19.5	20.5	21.5	22.5	23.5	24.5	25.5
		Effective R-Value if insulation is installed in cavity between framing (includes gypsum board)												
0.5	Wood	na	na	na	na	na	na	na	na	na	na	na	na	na
	Metal	na	na	na	na	na	na	na	na	na	na	na	na	na
0.75	Wood	na	na	na	na	na	na	na	na	na	na	na	na	na
	Metal	na	na	na	na	na	na	na	na	na	na	na	na	na
1.0	Wood	na	na	na	na	na	na	na	na	na	na	na	na	na
	Metal	na	na	na	na	na	na	na	na	na	na	na	na	na
1.5	Wood	na	na	na	na	na	na	na	na	na	na	na	na	na
	Metal	na	na	na	na	na	na	na	na	na	na	na	na	na
2.0	Wood	8.4	8.7	9.0	9.3	na	na	na	na	na	na	na	na	na
	Metal	3.3	3.3	3.4	3.4	na	na	na	na	na	na	na	na	na
2.5	Wood	9.2	9.6	10.0	10.3	10.6	10.9	11.2	11.5	na	na	na	na	na
	Metal	3.8	3.9	3.9	4.0	4.0	4.1	4.1	4.1	na	na	na	na	na
3.0	Wood	9.9	10.3	10.7	11.1	11.5	11.9	12.2	12.5	12.9	na	na	na	na
	Metal	4.3	4.4	4.4	4.5	4.6	4.6	4.7	4.7	4.8	na	na	na	na
3.5	Wood	10.4	10.9	11.3	11.8	12.2	12.6	13.0	13.4	13.8	14.1	14.5	14.8	15.1
	Metal	4.7	4.8	4.9	5.0	5.1	5.1	5.2	5.2	5.3	5.4	5.4	5.4	5.5
4.0	Wood	10.8	11.3	11.9	12.4	12.8	13.3	13.7	14.2	14.6	14.9	15.3	15.7	16.0
	Metal	5.1	5.2	5.3	5.4	5.5	5.6	5.7	5.8	5.8	5.9	5.9	6.0	6.0
4.5	Wood	11.2	11.7	12.3	12.8	13.3	13.8	14.3	14.8	15.2	15.7	16.1	16.5	16.9
	Metal	5.4	5.6	5.7	5.8	5.9	6.0	6.1	6.2	6.3	6.4	6.4	6.5	6.6
5.0	Wood	11.5	12.1	12.7	13.2	13.8	14.3	14.8	15.3	15.8	16.3	16.7	17.2	17.6
	Metal	5.8	5.9	6.1	6.2	6.3	6.5	6.6	6.7	6.8	6.8	6.9	7.0	7.1
5.5	Wood	11.7	12.4	13.0	13.6	14.2	14.7	15.3	15.8	16.3	16.8	17.3	17.8	18.2
	Metal	6.1	6.3	6.4	6.6	6.7	6.8	7.0	7.1	7.2	7.3	7.4	7.5	7.6

Table 6.11 : Assembly U-Factors for Metal Building Walls

Insulation System	Rated R-Value of Insulation	Total Rated R-Value of Insulation	Overall U-Factor for Entire Base Wall Assembly	Overall U-Factor for Assembly of Base Wall Plus Continuous Insulation (un-interrupted by framing) Rated R-Value of Continuous Insulation					
Single Layer of Mineral Fiber	None	0	1.180	0.161	0.086	0.059	0.045	0.036	0.030
	R-6	6	0.184	0.091	0.060	0.045	0.036	0.030	0.026
	R-10	10	0.134	0.077	0.054	0.051	0.033	0.028	0.024
	R-11	11	0.123	0.073	0.052	0.051	0.033	0.028	0.024
	R-13	13	0.113	0.069	0.050	0.039	0.032	0.027	0.024
Double Layer of Mineral Fiber (Second layer inside of girts) (Multiple layers are listed in order from inside to outside)	R-6+R-13	19	0.070	N/A	N/A	N/A	N/A	N/A	N/A
	R-10+R-13	23	0.061	N/A	N/A	N/A	N/A	N/A	N/A
	R-13+R-13	26	0.057	N/A	N/A	N/A	N/A	N/A	N/A
	R-19+R-13	32	0.048	N/A	N/A	N/A	N/A	N/A	N/A

Table 6.12: Assembly U-Factors for Steel-Frame Walls

Framing Type & Spacing Width (actual depth)	Cavity Insulation R-Value: Rated/ (effective installed)	Overall U-Factor for Entire Base Wall Assembly	Overall U-Factor for Assembly of Base Wall Plus Continuous Insulation (un-interrupted by framing) Rated R-Value of Continuous Insulation																			
			R-1.00	R-2.00	R-3.00	R-4.00	R-5.00	R-6.00	R-7.00	R-8.00	R-9.00	R-10.00	R-11.00	R-12.00	R-13.00	R-14.00	R-15.00	R-20.00	R-25.00	R-30.00	R-35.00	R-40.00
Steel Framing at 16 in. OC																						
3.5 in depth	None (0.0)	0.352	0.260	0.207	0.171	0.146	0.128	0.113	0.102	0.092	0.084	0.078	0.072	0.067	0.063	0.059	0.056	0.044	0.036	0.030	0.026	0.023
	R-11 (5.5)	0.132	0.117	0.105	0.095	0.087	0.080	0.074	0.069	0.064	0.060	0.057	0.054	0.051	0.049	0.046	0.044	0.036	0.031	0.027	0.024	0.021
	R-13 (6.0)	0.124	0.111	0.100	0.091	0.083	0.077	0.071	0.066	0.062	0.059	0.055	0.052	0.050	0.048	0.045	0.043	0.036	0.030	0.026	0.023	0.021
	R-15 (6.4)	0.118	0.106	0.096	0.087	0.080	0.074	0.069	0.065	0.061	0.057	0.054	0.051	0.049	0.047	0.045	0.043	0.035	0.030	0.026	0.023	0.021
6.0 in depth	R-19 (7.1)	0.109	0.099	0.090	0.082	0.076	0.071	0.066	0.062	0.058	0.055	0.052	0.050	0.047	0.045	0.043	0.041	0.034	0.029	0.026	0.023	0.020
	R-21 (7.4)	0.106	0.096	0.087	0.080	0.074	0.069	0.065	0.061	0.057	0.054	0.051	0.049	0.047	0.045	0.043	0.041	0.034	0.029	0.025	0.022	0.020
Steel Framing at 24 in. OC																						
3.5 in depth	None (0.0)	0.338	0.253	0.202	0.168	0.144	0.126	0.112	0.100	0.091	0.084	0.077	0.072	0.067	0.063	0.059	0.056	0.044	0.036	0.030	0.026	0.023
	R-11 (6.6)	0.116	0.104	0.094	0.086	0.079	0.073	0.068	0.064	0.060	0.057	0.054	0.051	0.048	0.046	0.044	0.042	0.035	0.030	0.026	0.023	0.021
	R-13 (7.2)	0.108	0.098	0.089	0.082	0.075	0.070	0.066	0.062	0.058	0.055	0.052	0.049	0.047	0.045	0.043	0.041	0.034	0.029	0.025	0.023	0.020
	R-15 (7.8)	0.102	0.092	0.084	0.078	0.072	0.067	0.063	0.059	0.056	0.053	0.050	0.048	0.046	0.044	0.042	0.040	0.034	0.029	0.025	0.022	0.020
6.0 in depth	R-19 (8.6)	0.094	0.086	0.079	0.073	0.068	0.064	0.060	0.057	0.054	0.051	0.048	0.046	0.044	0.042	0.041	0.039	0.033	0.028	0.025	0.022	0.020
	R-21 (9.0)	0.090	0.083	0.077	0.071	0.066	0.062	0.059	0.055	0.052	0.050	0.048	0.045	0.043	0.042	0.040	0.038	0.032	0.028	0.024	0.022	0.020

Table 6.13 : Assembly U-Factors for Wood-Frame Walls

Framing Type & Spacing Width (actual depth)	Cavity Insulation R-Value: Rated/(effective installed)	Overall U-Factor for Entire Base Wall Assembly	Overall U-Factor for Assembly of Base Wall Plus Continuous Insulation (un-interrupted by framing) Rated R-Value of Continuous Insulation																			
			R-1.00	R-2.00	R-3.00	R-4.00	R-5.00	R-6.00	R-7.00	R-8.00	R-9.00	R-10.00	R-11.00	R-12.00	R-13.00	R-14.00	R-15.00	R-20.00	R-25.00	R-30.00	R-35.00	R-40.00
Wood Studs at 16 in. OC																						
3.5 in depth	None (0.0)	0.292	0.223	0.181	0.152	0.132	0.116	0.104	0.094	0.086	0.079	0.073	0.068	0.064	0.060	0.056	0.053	0.042	0.035	0.030	0.026	0.023
	R-11 (11)	0.096	0.087	0.079	0.073	0.068	0.063	0.059	0.056	0.053	0.050	0.048	0.046	0.044	0.042	0.040	0.038	0.032	0.028	0.024	0.022	0.020
	R-13 (13)	0.089	0.080	0.074	0.068	0.063	0.059	0.056	0.053	0.050	0.047	0.045	0.043	0.041	0.040	0.038	0.037	0.031	0.027	0.024	0.021	0.019
	R-15 (15)	0.083	0.075	0.069	0.064	0.060	0.056	0.053	0.050	0.047	0.045	0.043	0.041	0.039	0.038	0.036	0.035	0.030	0.026	0.023	0.020	0.019
5.5 in depth	R-19 (18)	0.067	0.062	0.058	0.054	0.051	0.048	0.046	0.044	0.042	0.040	0.038	0.037	0.036	0.034	0.033	0.032	0.027	0.024	0.021	0.019	0.018
	R-21 (21)	0.063	0.058	0.054	0.051	0.048	0.045	0.043	0.041	0.039	0.038	0.036	0.035	0.034	0.032	0.031	0.030	0.026	0.023	0.021	0.019	0.017
(+R-10 headers) in depth	R-19 (18)	0.063	0.059	0.055	0.052	0.049	0.047	0.045	0.043	0.041	0.039	0.038	0.036	0.035	0.034	0.033	0.031	0.027	0.024	0.021	0.019	0.017
	R-21 (21)	0.059	0.055	0.051	0.049	0.046	0.044	0 042	0.040	0.038	0.037	0.035	0.034	0.033	0.032	0.031	0.030	0.026	0.023	0.020	0.018	0.017
Wood Studs at 24 in OC																						
3.5 in depth	None (0.0)	0.298	0.227	0.183	0.154	0.133	0.117	0 105	0.095	0.086	0.079	0.074	0.068	0.064	0.060	0.057	0.054	0.042	0.035	0.030	0.026	0.023
	R-11 (11)	0.094	0.085	0.078	0.072	0.067	0.062	0 059	0.055	0.052	0.050	0.047	0.045	0.043	0.041	0.040	0.038	0.032	0.027	0.024	0.022	0.019
	R-13 (13)	0.086	0.078	0.072	0.067	0.062	0.058	0 055	0.052	0.049	0.047	0.045	0.043	0.041	0.039	0.038	0.036	0.031	0.026	0.023	0.021	0.019
	R-15 (15)	0.080	0.073	0.067	0.062	0.058	0.055	0 052	0.049	0.046	0.044	0.042	0.040	0.039	0.037	0.036	0.035	0.029	0.026	0.023	0.020	0.018
6.0 in depth	R-19 (18)	0.065	0.060	0.056	0.053	0.050	0.047	0 045	0.043	0.041	0.039	0.038	0.036	0.035	0.034	0.033	0.032	0.027	0.024	0.021	0.019	0.018
	R-21 (21)	0.060	0.056	0.052	0.049	0.046	0.044	0.042	0.040	0.038	0.037	0.036	0.034	0.035	0.032	0.031	0.030	0.026	0.023	0.020	0.018	0.017
(+R-10 headers) in depth	R-19 (18)	0.062	0.058	0.054	0.051	0.048	0.046	0.044	0.042	0.040	0.039	0.037	0.036	0.034	0.033	0.032	0.031	0.027	0.024	0.021	0.019	0.017
	R-21 (21)	0.057	0.053	0.050	0.047	0.045	0.043	0.041	0.039	0.037	0.036	0.035	0.033	0.032	0.031	0.030	0.029	0.025	0.023	0.020	0.018	0.017

Table 6.14: Assembly C-Factors for Below-Grade Walls

Framing Type and Depth	*Rated R-Value of Insulation Alone*	*Special C-Factors (wall only, without soil and air films)*
No Framing	R-0	C-1.140
Exterior Insulation, Continuous and uninterrupted by framing		
No Framing	R-5.0	C-0.170
No Framing	R-7.5	C-0.119
No Framing	R-10.0	C-0.092
No Framing	R-12.5	C-0.075
No Framing	R-15.0	C-0.063
No Framing	R-17.5	C-0.054
No Framing	R-20.0	C-0.048
No Framing	R-25.0	C-0.039
No Framing	R-30.0	C-0.032
No Framing	R-35.0	C-0.028
No Framing	R-40.0	C-0.025
No Framing	R-45.0	C-0.022
No Framing	R-50.0	C-0.020
Continuous Metal framing at 24 in. on center horizontally		
3.5 in.	R-11.0	C-0.182
3.5 in.	R-13.0	C-0.174
3.5 in.	R-15.0	C-0.168
5.5 in.	R-19.0	C-0.125
5.5 in.	R-21.0	C-0.120
1 in. metal clip at 24 in. on center horizontally and 16 in. vertically		
1.0 in.	R-3.8	C-0.233
1.0 in.	R-5.0	C-0.201
1.0 in.	R-5.6	C-0.189
1.5in.	R-5.7	C-0.173
1.5in.	R-7.5	C-0.147
1.5in.	R-8.4	C-0.138
2.0 in.	R-7.6	C-0.138
2.0 in.	R-10.0	C-0.116
20 in.	R-11.2	C-0.108
2.5 in.	R-9.5	C-0.114
2.5 in.	R-12.5	C-0.096
2.5 in.	R-14.0	C-0.089
3.0 in.	R-11.4	C-0.98
3.0 in.	R-15.0	C-0.82
3.0 in.	R-16.8	C-0.076
3.5 in.	R-13.3	C-0.085
3.5 in.	R-17.5	C-0.071
3.5 in.	R-19.6	C-0.066
4.0 in.	R-15.2	C-0.076
4.0 in.	R-20.0	C-0.063
4.0 in.	R-22.4	C-0.058

Table 6.15 : Assembly U-Factors for Mass Floors

Framing Type & Spacing Width (actual depth)	Cavity Insulation R-Value: Rated/(effective installed)	Overall U-Factor for Entire Base Wall Assembly	Overall U-Factor for Assembly of Base Wall Plus Continuous Insulation (un-interrupted by framing) Rated R-Value of Continuous Insulation																			
			R-1.00	R-2.00	R-3.00	R-4.00	R-5.00	R-6.00	R-7.00	R-8.00	R-9.00	R-10.00	R-11.00	R-12.00	R-13.00	R-14.00	R-15.00	R-20.00	R-25.00	R-30.00	R-35.00	R-40.00
Concrete Floor with Rigid Foam																						
	None (0.0)	0.322	0.243	0.196	0.164	0.141	0.123	0.110	0.099	0.090	0.083	0.076	0.071	0.066	0.062	0.058	0.055	0.043	0.036	0.030	0.026	0.023
Concrete Floor with Pinned Boards																						
	R-4.2 (4.2)	0.137	0.121	0.108	0.097	0.089	0.081	0.075	0.070	0.065	0.061	0.058	0.055	0.052	0.049	0.047	0.045	0.037	0.031	0.027	0.024	0.021
	R-6.3 (6.3)	0.107	0.096	0.088	0.081	0.075	0.070	0.065	0.061	0.058	0.054	0.052	0.049	0.047	0.045	0.043	0.041	0.034	0.029	0.025	0.023	0.020
	R-8.3 (8.3)	0.087	0.080	0.074	0.069	0.065	0.061	0.057	0.054	0.051	0.049	0.047	0.045	0.043	0.041	0.039	0.038	0.032	0.027	0.024	0.022	0.019
	R-10.4 (10.4)	0.074	0.069	0.064	0.060	0.057	0.054	0.051	0.049	0.046	0.044	0.042	0.041	0.039	0.038	0.036	0.035	0.030	0.026	0.023	0.021	0.019
	R-12.5 (12.5)	0.064	0.060	0.057	0.054	0.051	0.048	0.046	0.044	0.042	0.041	0.039	0.038	0.036	0.035	0.034	0.033	0.028	0.025	0.022	0.020	0.018
	R-14.6 (14.6)	0.056	0.053	0.051	0.048	0.046	0.044	0.042	0.040	0.039	0.037	0.036	0.035	0.034	0.033	0.032	0.031	0.027	0.023	0.021	0.019	0.017
	R-16.7 (16.7)	0.051	0.048	0.046	0.044	0.042	0.040	0.039	0.037	0.036	0.035	0.034	0.032	0.031	0.030	0.030	0.029	0.025	0.022	0.020	0.018	0.017
Concrete Floor with Spray-on Insulation																						
	(1 in.) R-4 (4.0)	0.141	0.123	0.110	0.099	0.090	0.083	0.076	0.071	0.066	0.062	0.058	0.055	0.052	0.050	0.047	0.045	0.037	0.031	0.027	0.024	0.021
	(2 in.) R-8 (8.0)	0.090	0.083	0.076	0.071	0.066	0.062	0.058	0.055	0.052	0.050	0.047	0.045	0.043	0.041	0.040	0.038	0.032	0.028	0.024	0.022	0.020
	(3 in.) R-12 (12.0)	0.066	0.062	0.058	0.055	0.052	0.050	0.047	0.045	0.043	0.041	0.040	0.038	0.037	0.036	0.034	0.033	0.028	0.025	0.022	0.020	0.018
	(4 in.) R-16 (16.0)	0.052	0.050	0.047	0.045	0.043	0.041	0.040	0.038	0.037	0.036	0.034	0.033	0.032	0.031	0.030	0.029	0.026	0.032	0.020	0.018	0.017
	(5 in.) R-20 (20.0)	0.043	0.041	0.040	0.038	0.037	0.036	0.034	0.033	0.032	0.031	0.030	0.029	0.028	0.028	0.027	0.026	0.023	0.021	0.019	0.017	0.016
	(6 in.) R-24 (24.0)	0.037	0.036	0.034	0.033	0.032	0.031	0.030	0.029	0.028	0.028	0.027	0.026	0.026	0.025	0.024	0.024	0.021	0.019	0.018	0.016	0.015

Table 6.16: Assembly U-Factors for Steel-Joist Floors

Framing Type & Spacing Width (actual depth)	Cavity Insulation R-Value: Rated/ (effective installed)	Overall U-Factor for Entire Base Wall Assembly	Overall U-Factor for Assembly of Base Wall Plus Continuous Insulation (un-interrupted by framing) Rated R-Value of Continuous Insulation																			
			R-1.00	R-2.00	R-3.00	R-4.00	R-5.00	R-6.00	R-7.00	R-8.00	R-9.00	R-10.00	R-11.00	R-12.00	R-13.00	R-14.00	R-15.00	R-20.00	R-25.00	R-30.00	R-35.00	R-40.00
Steel-Joist Floors with Rigid Foam																						
	None (0.0)	0.350	0.259	0.206	0.171	0.146	0.127	0.113	0.101	0.092	0.084	0.078	0.072	0.067	0.063	0.059	0.056	0.044	0.036	0.030	0.026	0.023
Steel-Joist Floors with Pinned Boards																						
	(1 in.) R-4.2 (4.2)	0.148	0.129	0.114	0.103	0.093	0.085	0.078	0.073	0.068	0.064	0.060	0.056	0.053	0.051	0.048	0.046	0.037	0.032	0.027	0.024	0.021
	(2 in.) R-8 (7.52)	0.096	0.088	0.081	0.075	0.070	0.065	0.061	0.058	0.054	0.052	0.049	0.047	0.045	0.043	0.041	0.039	0.033	0.028	0.025	0.022	0.020
	(3 in.) R-12 (10.80)	0.073	0.068	0.064	0.060	0.057	0.054	0.051	0.048	0.046	0.044	0.042	0.041	0.039	0.038	0.036	0.035	0.030	0.026	0.023	0.021	0.019
	(4 in.) R-16 (13.92)	0.060	0.056	0.053	0.051	0.048	0.046	0.044	0.042	0.040	0.039	0.037	0.036	0.035	0.034	0.032	0.031	0.027	0.024	0.021	0.019	0.018
	(5 in.) R-20 (17.00)	0.050	0.048	0.046	0.044	0.042	0.040	0.039	0.037	0.036	0.035	0.033	0.032	0.031	0.030	0.030	0.029	0.025	0.022	0.020	0.018	0.017
	(6 in.) R-24 (19.68)	0.044	0.042	0.041	0.039	0.038	0.036	0.035	0.034	0.033	0.032	0.031	0.030	0.029	0.028	0.027	0.027	0.024	0.021	0.019	0.017	0.016
Steel-Joist Floors with Butt Insulation																						
	None (0,0)	0.350	0.259	0.206	0.171	0.146	0.127	0.113	0.101	0.092	0.084	0.078	0.072	0.067	0.063	0.059	0.056	0.044	0.036	0.030	0.026	0.023
	R-11 (10.01)	0.078	0.072	0.067	0.063	0.059	0.056	0.053	0.050	0.048	0.046	0.044	0.042	0.040	0.039	0.037	0.036	0.030	0.026	0.023	0.021	0.019
	R-13 (11.70)	0.069	0.064	0.060	0.057	0.054	0.051	0.049	0.046	0.044	0.042	0.041	0.039	0.038	0.036	0.035	0.034	0.029	0.025	0.022	0.020	0.018
	R-15 (13.20)	0.062	0.059	0.055	0.052	0.050	0.047	0.045	0.043	0.042	0.040	0.038	0.037	0.036	0.034	0.033	0.032	0.028	0.024	0.022	0.020	0.018
	R-19 (16.34)	0.052	0.050	0.047	0.045	0.043	0.041	0.040	0.038	0.037	0.035	0.034	0.033	0.032	0.031	0.030	0.029	0.026	0.023	0.020	0.018	0.017
	R-21 (17.64)	0.049	0.047	0.044	0.043	0.041	0.039	0.038	0.036	0.035	0.034	0.033	0.032	0.031	0.030	0.029	0.028	0.025	0.022	0.020	0.018	0.017
	R-25 (20.25)	0.043	0.041	0.040	0.038	0.037	0.036	0.034	0.033	0.032	0.031	0.030	0.029	0.028	0.028	0.027	0.026	0.023	0.021	0.019	0.017	0.016
	R-30C (23.70)	0.038	0.036	0.035	0.034	0.033	0.032	0.031	0.030	0.029	0.028	0.027	0.027	0.026	0.025	0.025	0.024	0.021	0.019	0.018	0.016	0.015
	R-30 (23.70)	0.038	0.036	0.035	0.034	0.033	0.032	0.031	0.030	0.029	0.028	0.027	0.027	0.026	0.025	0.025	0.024	0.021	0.019	0.018	0.016	0.015
	R-38C (28.12)	0.032	0.031	0.030	0.029	0.029	0.028	0.027	0.026	0.026	0.025	0.024	0.024	0.023	0.023	0.022	0.022	0.020	0.018	0.016	0.015	0.014
	R-38 (28.12)	0.032	0.031	0.030	0.029	0.029	0.028	0.027	0.026	0.026	0.025	0.024	0.024	0.023	0.023	0.022	0.022	0.020	0.018	0.016	0.015	0.014

Table 6.17 : Assembly U-Factors for Wood-Joist Floors

Framing Type & Spacing Width (actual depth)	Cavity Insulation R-Value: Rated/ (effective installed)	Overall U-Factor for Entire Base Wall Assembly	Overall U-Factor for Assembly of Base Wall Plus Continuous Insulation (un-interrupted by framing) Rated R-Value of Continuous Insulation																			
			R-1.00	R-2.00	R-3.00	R-4.00	R-5.00	R-6.00	R-7.00	R-8.00	R-9.00	R-10.00	R-11.00	R-12.00	R-13.00	R-14.00	R-15.00	R-20.00	R-25.00	R-30.00	R-35.00	R-40.00
Wood Joists																				
(5.5 in.)	None (0.0)	0.282	0.220	0.180	0.153	0.132	0.117	0.105	0.095	0.087	0.080	0.074	0.069	0.064	0.060	0.057	0.054	0.042	0.035	0.030	0.026	0.023
	R-11 (11.0)	0.074	0.069	0.064	0.060	0.057	0.054	0.051	0.048	0.046	0.044	0.042	0.040	0.039	0.037	0.036	0.035	0.030	0.026	0.023	0.020	0.019
	R-13 (13.0)	0.066	0.062	0.058	0.055	0.052	0.049	0.047	0.045	0.043	0.041	0.039	0.038	0.036	0.035	0.034	0.033	0.028	0.025	0.022	0.020	0.018
	R-15 (15.0)	0.060	0.057	0.053	0.050	0.048	0.046	0.044	0.042	0.040	0.038	0.037	0.036	0.034	0.033	0.032	0.031	0.027	0.024	0.021	0.019	0.017
	R-19 (18.0)	0.051	0.048	0.046	0.044	0.042	0.040	0.038	0.037	0.036	0.034	0.033	0.032	0.031	0.030	0.029	0.028	0.025	0.022	0.020	0.018	0.017
	R-21 (21.0)	0.046	0.043	0.042	0.040	0.038	0.037	0.035	0.034	0.033	0.032	0.031	0.030	0.029	0.028	0.027	0.027	0.023	0.021	0.019	0.017	0.016
(7.25 in)	R-25 (25.0)	0.039	0.037	0.036	0.035	0.033	0.032	0.031	0.030	0.029	0.028	0.028	0.027	0.026	0.025	0.025	0.024	0.022	0.019	0.018	0.016	0.015
	R-30C (30.0)	0.034	0.033	0.032	0.031	0.030	0.029	0.028	0.027	0.026	0.026	0.025	0.024	0.024	0.023	0.023	0.022	0.020	0.018	0.016	0.015	0.014
(9.25 in)	R-30 (30.0)	0.033	0.032	0.031	0.030	0.029	0.028	0.027	0.027	0.026	0.025	0.024	0.024	0.023	0.023	0.022	0.022	0.020	0.018	0.016	0.015	0.014
(11.25 in)	R-38C (38.0)	0.027	0.026	0.025	0.025	0.024	0.024	0.023	0.022	0.022	0.021	0.021	0.020	0.020	0.020	0.019	0.019	0.017	0.016	0.015	0.014	0.013
(13.25 in)	R-38 (38.0)	0.026	0.026	0.025	0.024	0.024	0.023	0.023	0.022	0.022	0.021	0.021	0.020	0.020	0.019	0.019	0.019	0.017	0.016	0.015	0.014	0.013

Table 6.18 : Assembly F-Factors for Slab-on-Grade Floors

Insulation Description	Rated R-Value of Insulation												
	R-0	R-5	R-7.5	R-10	R-15	R-20	R-25	R-30	R-35	R-40	R-45	R-50	R-55
Uncoated Slabs													
None	0.73												
12 in. Horizontal		0.72	0.71	0.71	0.71								
24 in. Horizontal		0.70	0.70	0.70	0.69								
36 in. Horizontal		0.68	0.67	0.66	0.66								
48 in. Horizontal		0.67	0.65	0.64	0.63								
12 in. Vertical		0.61	0.60	0.58	0.57	0.567	0.565	0.564					
24 in. Vertical		0.58	0.56	0.54	0.52	0.510	0.505	0.502					
36 in. Vertical		0.56	0.53	0.51	0.48	0.472	0.464	0.460					
48 in. Vertical		0.54	0.51	0.48	0.45	0.434	0.424	0.419					
Heated Slabs													
None	1.35												
12 in. Horizontal		1.31	1.31	1.30	1.30								
24 in. Horizontal		1.28	1.27	1.26	1.25								
36 in. Horizontal		1.24	1.21	1.20	1.18								
48 in. Horizontal		1.20	1.17	1.13	1.11								
12 in. Vertical		1.06	1.02	1.00	0.98	0.968	0.964	0.961					
24 in. Vertical		0.99	0.95	0.90	0.86	0.843	0.832	0.827					
36 in. Vertical		0.95	0.89	0.84	0.79	0.762	0.747	0.740					
48 in. Vertical		0.91	0.85	0.78	0.72	0.688	0.671	0.659					
Fully Insulated Slabs		0.74	0.64	0.55	0.44	0.373	0.326	0.296	0.273	0.255	0.239	0.227	0.217

Table 6.19: Values for Cavity Air Spaces

Component	*Air space Thickness (in.)*	*R-Value* *Effective Emissivity*				
		0.03	0.05	0.20	0.50	0.82
Roof	0.50	2.13	2.04	1.54	1.04	0.77
	0.75	2.33	2.22	1.64	1.09	0.80
	1.50	2.53	2.41	1.75	1.13	0.82
	3.50	2.83	2.66	1.88	1.19	0.85
Wall	0.50	2.54	2.43	1.75	1.13	0.82
	0.75	3.58	3.32	2.18	1.30	0.90
	1.50	3.92	3.62	2.30	1.34	0.93
	3.50	3.67	3.40	2.21	1.31	0.91
Floor	0.50	2.55	1.28	1.00	0.69	0.53
	0.75	1.44	1.38	1.06	0.73	0.54
	1.50	2.49	2.38	1.76	1.15	0.85
	3.50	3.08	2.90	2.01	1.26	0.90

Table 6.20: Effective R-Values for Fibre Glass

Insulation R-Value at Standard Thickness									
Rated R-Value		38	30	22	21	19	15	13	11
Standard Thickness		12	9.5	6.5	5.5	6	3.5	3.5	3.5
Nominal Lumber Size (in.)	Actual Depth of Cavity (in.)	Effective Insulation R-Values when Installed in a Confined Cavity							
2x12	11.5	37	-	-	-	-	-	-	-
2x10	9.25	32	30	-	-	-	-	-	-
2x8	7.25	27	26	22	21	19	-	-	-
2x6	5.5	-	21	20	21	18	-	-	
2x4	3.5	-	-	14	-	13	15	13	11
	2.5	-	-	-	-	-	-	9.8	-
	1.5	-	-	-	-	-	-	6.3	6

Table 6.21 : R-Values for Building Materials

Material	*Nominal Size (in.)*	*Actual Size (in)*	*R-Value*
Carpet and Rubber pad	-	-	1.23
Concrete at R-0.0625/in.	-	2	0.13
	-	4	0.25
	-	6	0.38
	-	8	0.5
	-	10	0.63
	-	12	0.75
Flooring, wood sub-floor	-	.075	0.94
Gypsum board	-	0.5	0.45
	-	0.625	0.56
Metal deck	-	-	0
Roofing build up	-	0.375	0.33
Sheathing, vegetable fiber board, 0.78 in.	-	0.78	2.06
Soil at R-0.104/in.	-	12	1.25
Steel, mild	-	1	0.0031807
Stucco	-	0.75	0.08
Wood, 2x4 at R-1.25/in.	4	3.5	4.38
Wood, 2x6 at R-1.25/in.	6	5.5	6.88
Wood, 2x8 at R-1.25/in.	8	7.25	9.06
Wood, 2x410 at R-1.25/in.	10	9.25	11.56
Wood, 2x12 at R-1.25/in.	12	11.25	14.06
Wood, 2x14 at R-1.25/in.	14	13.25	16.56

Table 6.22: Thermal Conductivity of Concrete block Material

Concrete Block Density in lb/ft²	*Thermal Conductivity in Btu.in/h.ft².°F*
80	3.7
85	4.2
90	4.7
95	5.1
100	5.5
105	6.1
110	6.7
115	7.2
120	7.8
125	8.9
130	10.0
135	11.8
140	13.5

7

Advanced Windows and Energy Savings*

7.1 INTRODUCTION

Windows in a building play a dominant role in determining the consumption of electricity for lighting as well as for the HVAC, because the penetration of daylight through windows reduces demand of artificial lighting. On the other hand, as compared to other parts of building envelope, windows offer much less resistance to the entry or loss of heat. Fortunately, with technical breakthroughs, window technology has improved by leaps and bounds, providing significant improvements in solar control, and rate of heat gain/losses through a window system. With new innovative window design technologies, it is now possible to have windows performing at par with walls and may be even better.

7.2 TRENDS AND DEVELOPMENTS

The most important change in the trend related to windows came with the advent of insulating glazing, two panes of glass sealed together with an air gap in between. Other developments e.g. triple glazed system, selective glass, low-E glass, have also emerged over the period. Research efforts are being made in the direction of improving cost-performance relationship in energy efficient windows.

Technological development with integration of more elements of control into the window assembly has resulted in extremely energy efficient glazing system. Selected developments have been briefly described below for presenting overview of the current trends. These concepts are covered with greater depth in the chapters of their specific reference.

- **Glazing unit structure**
  Multiple layers of glass or plastic / alternate material films improve thermal resistance and reduce the heat loss attributed to convection between window layers. Additional layers also provide more surfaces for application of low-E or solar control coatings.
- **Low-emittance coatings**
  Low-emittance or low-E coatings are highly transparent and almost invisible. Their low emittance is associated with a high reflectance to long-wavelength infrared radiation. Putting a layer of low-E coating between two glass layers reduces long-wavelength radiative heat transfer by a factor of 5 to 10, thereby reducing total heat transfer through the window assembly. Low-emittance coatings may be applied directly to glass surfaces, or to thin sheets of plastic (films) which are suspended in the air cavity between the interior and exterior glazing layers.

* Base document for this Chapter is Bansal N.K., Mathur J. (2006), Energy Efficient Windows, Anamaya Publishers, India

- **Low-conductance gas fills**

  With the use of a low-emittance coating, heat transfer across a gap is dominated by conduction and natural convection. While air is a relatively good insulator, there are other gases (such as argon, krypton, and carbon-dioxide) with lower thermal conductivities. Using one of these nontoxic gases in an insulating glass unit can further reduce heat transfer between the glazing layers.

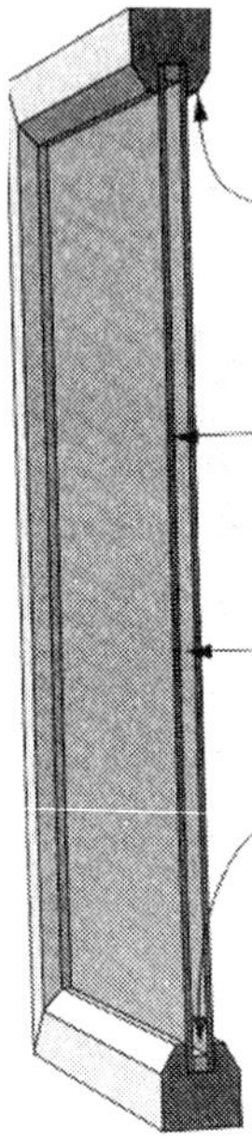

Figure 7.1 : Technological advances have significantly improved window energy performance in recent years

- **Warm edge spacers**

  Heat transfer through the metal spacers that are used to separate glazing layers can increase heat gain/loss and cause condensation at the edge of the window. "Warm edge" spacers use new materials and better design to reduce this effect.

- **Thermally improved sash and frame**

  Traditional sash and frame designs often contribute to heat gain/loss and can represent a large fraction of the total gain/loss through the window assembly, especially when high-performance glass is used. New materials and improved designs can reduce this loss.

- **Solar control glazing and coatings**

  New types of tinted glass and new coatings can be specified to reduce cooling loads that reduce the impact of the sun's heat without sacrificing view. Spectrally selective glazing and coatings absorb/reflect the infrared portion of sunlight while transmitting visible daylight, thus reducing solar heat gain coefficients and the resulting cooling loads. These solar control coatings can also be combined with low-emittance characteristics for further enhancement of window quality.

- **Improved weather-stripping**

  Weather strips play a crucial role in controlling the air leakage through the window assembly. Better weather-strips are now available that reduce air leakage and last over a longer time period.

7.2.1 Glazing Materials, Coatings and Frames

7.2.1.1 Properties of glazing materials

As the solar radiation passes through a glazing material, part of it is transmitted, other part is reflected and the balance is absorbed within the material itself as shown in Figure 7.2. These are the three components of solar impact that determine major energy performance properties of a glazing material; such as the solar heat gain coefficient and shading coefficient. The proportion of transmittance, reflectance, and absorptance for different wavelengths of solar radiation can now be controlled for altering performance of glazing material to suit different climatic conditions within the country.

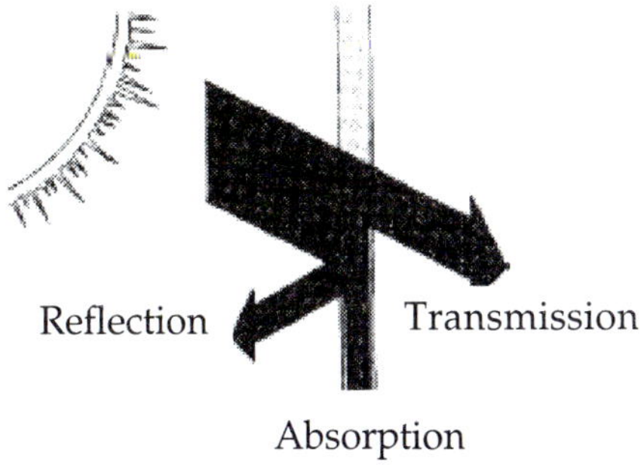

Figure 7.2: The passage of solar radiation through a glazing material

Depending upon the transparency and the material used, the properties and interaction of the glazing system varies for different wavelengths of the solar spectrum. For example, the tint in a particular glazing material allows radiations corresponding to that color to pass through. Similar phenomena takes place for the non-visible portion of the solar spectrum, as most of the transparent glazing material permit a portion of the UV radiations while the plastics resist to the UV band.

A strategic utilization of these properties of the materials can bring in significant change in reduction in overall building energy requirements.

There are four basic properties of glazing that affect the result of solar radiation incidence. These parameters, namely, transmittance, reflectance, absorptance and emittance are described below before discussing advances in glazing materials.

Transmittance

Transmittance is defined as the percentage of radiation that can pass through glazing. It depends upon the wavelength under consideration, e.g. "visible light transmittance," "UV transmittance," or "total solar energy transmittance". Each describes a different characteristic of the glazing. The concept of 'visible transmittance', has already been introduced in chapter-2 in the context of whole window assembly, but here in this chapter, it is related to only the glazed portion and there should not be any confusion between the two.

Transmission of visible light through glazing determines the effectiveness of a type of glass in providing daylight and a clear view through the window. For example, tinted glass has a lower visible light transmittance than a clear glass. The human eye is sensitive to radiation corresponding to wavelengths between 0.4 to 0.7 micrometers, but its peak sensitivity is for 0.55 micrometers wavelength. The sensitivity is low at the red and blue ends of the spectrum. This sensitivity is termed as the 'photopic sensitivity' of the eye.

More than half of the Sun's energy cannot be sensed with human eye and it reaches us as either ultraviolet (UV) or, predominantly, as infrared radiation. The term "total solar energy transmittance" describes how the glazing responds to the entire solar spectrum for its passing through. This term is very useful in characterizing the glazing on the basis of the amount of solar energy transmitted by the glazing.

Colors of materials are very sensitive to UV radiations, thus a reduction in UV is always considered beneficial for maintaining the colors of furniture, drapes and carpets. With the recent advances in glazing technology, manufacturers can control behavior of glazing materials for different parts of the solar spectrum. The basic properties of the substrate material (glass or plastic) can be altered, by adding special coatings to the surfaces of the substrates for achieving desired combination of properties. For example, a window optimized for daylighting and for reducing heat gains should transmit an adequate amount of light in the visible portion of the spectrum, while excluding unnecessary heat gain from the near-infrared part of the electromagnetic spectrum. These strategies related to combining different properties for enhancing properties of glazing, are described later in this very chapter. Ideal spectral transmittance for glazings in different climatic conditions.

Reflectance

Reflectance can be defined as the fraction or percent of a particular frequency or wavelength of electromagnetic radiation that is reflected from the surface of a substance without being absorbed or transmitted. The natural reflectance of glass for sunlight is dependent on the quality of the glass surface, the presence of coatings, and the angle of incidence of the light. The standard clear glass reflects about 50 percent or more of the light striking at an incident angle greater than 70 degrees. The incident angle is formed with respect to a line perpendicular to the glass surface. It has been found that oblique incidence is usually associated with more reflectance as compared to normal incidence as shown in Figure 7.3 and 7.4.

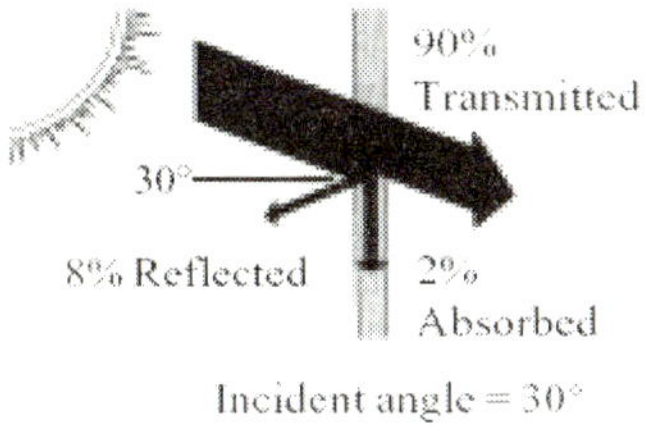

Fig 7.3 : Break-up of incident solar radiation at 30°

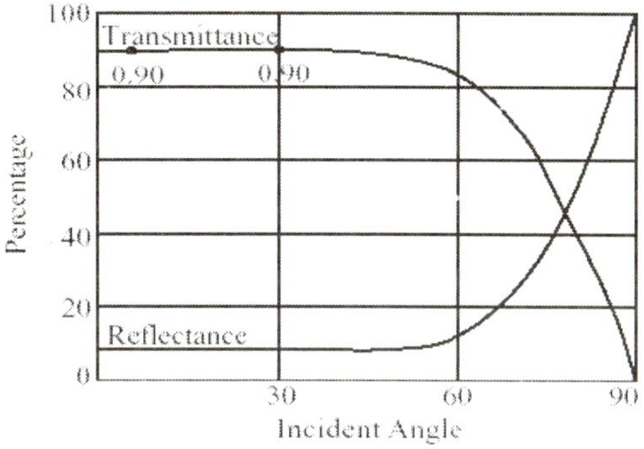

Fig 7.4 : Variation of transmitted and reflected light by 3mm clear glass with incident angle

The reflectance of various glass types becomes especially apparent during low light conditions. The surface on the brighter side acts like a mirror because the amount of light passing through the window from the darker side is less than the amount of light being reflected from the lighter side. A similar effect can be noticed from the outside during the day and from the inside during the night.

Coatings on the glazing can further change the properties of the overall window assembly. The reflectivity of glass can be increased by applying various metallic coatings to the surface. Thick coatings can be fully reflective and they make the glass virtually opaque. A thinner coating is partially reflective and partially transmitting. Recently use of "One-way glass" has become very popular for making glass-facades since these partial metallic coatings act like a full mirror when viewed from the side with brighter light conditions but appear transparent when viewed from the side with dimmer light.

Commonly used coatings reflect all portions of the solar spectrum. However, coatings have been developed that can be applied to glass and plastic to reflect only selected wavelengths of radiant energy.

Absorptance

Energy that is not transmitted through the glass or reflected off of its surfaces is absorbed. Once glass has absorbed any radiant energy, the energy is transformed into heat, raising the temperature of the glass.

Typical 3 mm clear glass absorbs only about 4 percent of incident sunlight. The absorptance of glass is increased by adding chemicals that absorb solar energy. If the visible light is absorbed, the glass appears dark. If the glazing material absorbs the non-visible spectrum, then there is virtually no change in the appearance of the glazing. The absorbed energy is converted into heat, warming the glass. Thus, when these "heat-absorbing" glasses are in the sun, they feel much hotter to the touch than clear glass. They are generally gray, bronze, or blue-green and are used primarily to lower the solar heat gain coefficient and to control glare. Since they block some of the sun's energy, they reduce the cooling load placed on the building and its air-conditioning equipment.

All glass and most plastics, however, are generally very absorptive of far-infrared energy. This property led to the use of clear glass for greenhouses, where it allowed the transmission of intense solar energy but blocked the retransmission of the low-temperature heat energy generated inside the green-house and radiated back to the glass.

Emittance

When heat or light energy is absorbed by glass, a large portion is convected away by moving air or even through still air through the natural convection phenomenon. Remaining heat in the glass is reradiated by the glass surface as the hot surface becomes source of emission. Such ability of any material to radiate energy by virtue of temperature is called its emissivity. Emission of radiant heat is one of the important routes in overall heat transfer through a window. Thus, reducing the window's emission of heat can significantly improve its insulating properties.

Standard glass has an emittance of 0.84 over the long wavelength portion of the spectrum. It means that it emits 84 per cent of the long-wave radiation striking the surface of the glass and only 16 per cent is reflected. By comparison, low-E glass coatings have an emittance as low as 0.04. This glazing would emit only 4 percent of the energy possible at its temperature, and thus reflect 96 percent of the incident long-wave infrared radiation. Utility of this property for energy conservation is covered in subsequent chapters of this book.

7.2.1.2 Advances in Glazing Materials

Glass

Traditionally, windows are made of clear glass. Almost all the glazing materials are based on the float glass technology in which the glass is "floated" over a bed of molten tin. This technique provides extremely flat surfaces, uniform thickness, and almost no visual distortions. Normally, the glass produced with this technique has a slight greenish tinge, due to iron impurities, but this is generally not noticeable except while looking from the direction of its edge. Higher-quality glass with reduced iron content has no greenness and also provides a higher solar energy transmittance.

Obscure glasses, used at places of privacy such as bathrooms, though transmit most of the light but break up the view in order to provide privacy. This effect is generally achieved either with the help of decorative embossed patterns or with a frosted surface that scatters the rays of visible light.

Colors can be added to glass by adding chemicals to form stained glasses. These glasses are used to get certain shade/color in the glass. The mechanical properties of glass can also be altered along with its basic composition and surface properties. For example, heat treatment for strengthening and tempering make glass more resistant to breakage. Heat-strengthened glasses are about twice as strong as standard glass. Tempering is the process of reheating followed by quick chilling. Tempered glass produced in this manner, on meeting an impact, breaks into small fragments, rather than observing long and possibly dangerous shards. Laminated glass is a sandwich of two outer layers of glass with a plastic inner layer that holds the glass pieces together in the event of breakage. Fully tempered and laminated glass finds a variety of uses in buildings as well as in automobiles.

Advanced technologies that have significantly improved the thermal performance of glass are discussed later in this chapter, in the section related to improved glazing products.

Plastics

During past few years, use of plastic has emerged even in the field of glazing materials. Plastic is primarily used in windows with special requirements and skylights.

Various plastic materials that can be used as glazing material are as given below:

- ***Clear acrylic:*** It is a widely available and relatively inexpensive material that is available with various tints and colors. It has very good visible light transmittance and longevity. Since the material is softer than glass, it is vulnerable to scratching.
- ***Frosted acrylic***: It is quite similar to clear acrylic, except for the property that it diffuses light rays and obscures the view. It comes in varying degrees of light transmittance. Most bubble skylights and openings at places of privacy use frosted acrylic as glazing material.
- ***Clear polycarbonate:*** Is like acrylic sheet, but it is harder and tougher, offering greater resistance to scratching and breakage. It is more expensive than acrylic.
- ***Fiber-reinforced plastic:*** Commonly known as FRP, it is a tough, translucent, flexible sheet material having good light-diffusing properties. Short lengths of fiberglass are embedded in a polymer matrix to form flat or ribbed sheets of FRP. These panels are stiff, insulating and translucent after being created by bonding double layers to a metal frame and adding fiberglass insulation. This material is also available in the form of corrugated sheets for use as a translucent roofing material. FRP has a drawback of surface erosion that often shortens its useful life.
- ***Extruded multicell sheet:*** These sheets are made with acrylic or polycarbonate plastic material in the form of a transparent or tinted plastic material extruded into a double- or triple-wall sheet with divider webs for stiffness, insulating value, and light diffusion.
- ***Polyester:*** It is a thin transparent film used to carry specialized coatings and/ or to divide the air space between two layers of glass into multiple air spaces. Such films have to be protected from abuse and weathering by the two exterior glass layers. It can also be made in tinted or coated forms that are glued to the inner surfaces of existing windows during retrofitting.

Comparison of glass and plastic as glazing material

Both the materials have their own advantages and disadvantages. The first and foremost advantage of glass over plastic is that it is extremely durable. Glass has low coefficient of thermal expansion therefore it can withstand higher or lower temperatures.

Further glass is impermeable to gases and moisture and thus can be used with hermetically sealed, gas-filled insulating units. Plastics are not normally fabricated in sealed units.

Rigid plastics are not normally coated with additional films since the process is to be carried out at very low temperature. On the other hand, glass can be coated easily by a variety of high and low- temperature processes.

Advantage of plastic over glass is that it is not as brittle as glass and they do not shatter when broken. Though, tempered glass are available that reduce injury potential in case of breakage. Plastics are tougher and can resist vandals. Conventional glass can be laminated with plastics to produce a wide range of burglar- and bullet-resistant glazings.

Additional advantage of plastic is their light weight for an equal thickness of glass. This advantage reduces structural requirements for frames.

From the health point of view, plastics can be formulated to screen out almost entire amount of Ultraviolet Radiation (UV) in the solar spectrum. Glass is usually not UV absorbing, unless special coatings and laminates are used. For safety against fire, both the materials have certain disadvantages. Although, glass is nonflammable but it may break in a condition of fire. Plastics are typically flammable, they may also melt in the heat released with fire, and may give off toxic fumes when they burn.

7.2.2 Improvements in performance of glazing

For improving the energy performance of glazing products, there are three fundamental approaches:

(a) Changing the chemical composition or physical characteristics of the glazing material itself.

(b) Apply a coating to the surface of glazing material for changing performance. Reflective coatings and films are developed to reduce heat gain and glare. Low-emittance and spectrally selective coatings have also been developed to improve performance in heating and cooling seasons.

(c) Assembling layers of glazing and controlling the properties of the spaces between the layers. These approaches include the use of two or more panes of glass or films; use of low-conductance gas fills between the layers, and thermally improved edge spacers.

The above three approaches are now well developed and well tested for energy conservation in buildings, as explained in the following sub-sections of this chapter.

7.2.2.1 Tinted Glass

Glass as well as plastic for use in windows are available in a large number of shades or tints. Due to it the glazing absorbs certain portion of the visible light and heating effect of the solar radiation. Additionally, the tint changes the color of window and can be helpful in increasing visual privacy with reasonable reduction in glare. Chemical composition of tinted glazing is specially formulated to maximize absorption of radiation over some or the entire solar spectrum. Entire absorbed solar energy is initially transformed into heat within the glazing itself, thus raising its own temperature. Such absorption of heat in glass is not a very preferred option for climate control, because up to 50 percent of the heat absorbed in a single layer of tinted glass may then be transferred *via* radiation and convection to the inside, in certain climatic conditions.

There are two categories of tinted glazing: the traditional tints that diminish light as well as heat gain, and spectrally selective tints that reduce heat gain but do not block visible light transmission to the interior as shown in Figure-7.5. In buildings, where day-lighting is not undesirable, use of the spectrally selective tint or coating along with other means of controlling solar gain is therefore, the obvious choice. Normal tinted glazing can provide a measure of visual privacy during the day when they reduce visibility from the outdoors. However, at night this effect gets reversed and it is more difficult to see outdoors from the inside with good visibility from outdoor to inside.

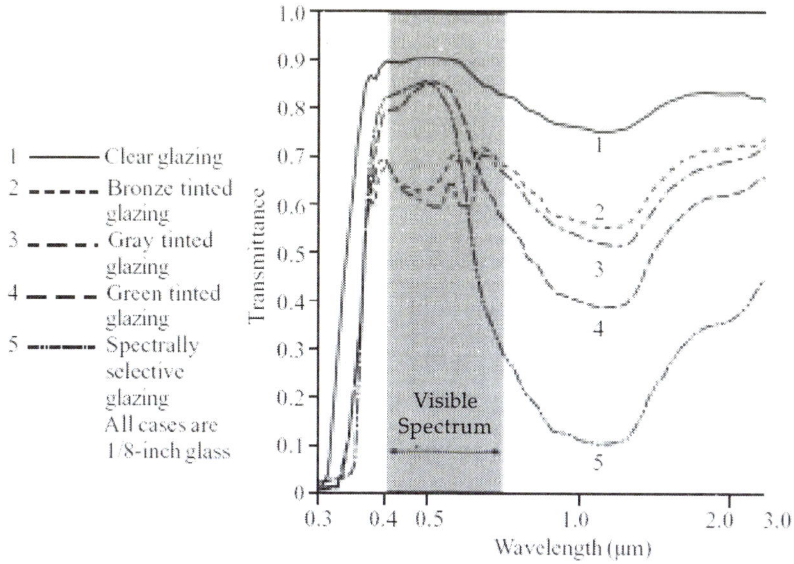

Fig 7.5 : Spectral transmittance curves for common tinted and spectrally selective glazing

Reduction in the Visible Light Transmittance (VT) due to traditional tinting is substantially more than the solar heat gain coefficient. A ratio between these two factors, termed as the Light-to-Solar Gain ratio (LSG ratio), represents the relative efficiency of different glass types in transmitting daylight while blocking solar gain as shown in Table 7.1. The LSG ratio is defined as a ratio between Visible Transmittance (VT) and Solar Heat Gain Coefficient (SHGC). For instance, for a clear glass having a Visible Light Transmittance (VT) of 0.90 and a Solar Heat Gain Coefficient (SHGC) of 0.86, LSG can be calculated as VT/SHGC = 1.05 whereas, in case of a Bronze-tinted glass having a visible transmittance of 0.68 and a solar heat gain coefficient of 0.71, which results in an LSG ratio of 0.96. This illustrates that while the bronze tint lowers the SHGC, it lowers the VT even more. A spectrally selective blue tint typically has a higher VT of 0.77 and a lower SHGC of 0.58, resulting in an LSG of 1.33-significantly better than the bronze tint. Table-7.1 shows similar relationships while comparing tinted double glazings, as well as units with a combination of tinted glass and low-E coatings. Glazings with low-E and spectrally selective coatings (discussed later in this chapter) can reduce the SHGC significantly but retain a relatively high VT, producing LSG ratio that are higher than those for simple tinted glass.

In residential buildings, solar gains are more typically controlled using blinds, drapes, or other decorative window treatments due to higher cost of glass with selective or low-e coating. However, tinted glazing can also be used in combination with the traditional ways for sun control to improve solar gain control or offer some privacy. In retrofit situations, when old windows are not being replaced by new ones, tinted plastic film may be applied to the surface of the glazing.

The tinted glazing requires no maintenance or operation from the inhabitants. On the other hand, it cannot respond to changing climatic conditions. It cuts out heat and light equally well in the summer and in the winter, when different combinations of cutting-out are needed.

Table 7.1: Light-to-Solar-Gain ratio (LSG) of various types of glass

Center-of-glass			
Glass Description	*Visible Transmittance VT*	*Solar Heat Gain Coefficient SHGC*	*Light-to-Solar-Gain Ratio LSG*
Single glass			
Clear	0.90	0.86	1.05
Bronze	0.68	0.71	0.96
Spectrally selective blue	0.77	0.58	1.33
Double glass [Inner layer is clear]			
Clear	0.82	0.75	1.20
Bronze	0.62	0.60	1.03
Spectrally selective blue	0.70	0.46	1.52
Double glass [Inner layer is clear with low-E coating]			
Clear	0.78	0.63	1.24
Bronze	0.58	0.49	1.18
Spectrally selective blue	0.66	0.35	1.84

7.2.2.2 Reflective Coatings and Films

Since the lowering of SHGC with use of single pane-tinted glass is associated with lowering of daylight transmission (VT), there are practical limits on lowering of SHGC using tints. In case, larger reduction in SHGC is required, a reflective coating can be used that increases the surface reflectivity of the glass. These coatings usually consist of thin metallic layers. Reflective coatings are normally available in few metallic colors such as silver, gold and bronze. They can be applied on a clear or even on tinted glazing. The reduction in solar heat gain coefficient of the glazing with use of such reflective coatings depends upon the thickness and reflectivity of the coating, and also on its location with respect to the glass.

Similar to use of tinted films in retrofit situations, reflective coatings may also be applied to the glass surface of an existing window by means of an adhesive-bonded, metallic-coated plastic film. The applied films are effective for reducing solar gains but are not as durable as pre-laminated or coated glass.

As with tinted glazing, the visible light transmittances of reflective glazing is reduced by a substantial amount as compared to reduction in the solar heat gain coefficient. Reflective glazing is usually used in commercial buildings having large windows, in hot climates, or on windows where substantial solar heat gains and/or glare are present. In residential applications, they are usually reserved for special cases. For example, a picture window opening in west direction over a large body of water experiences substantial solar gains and reflected glare during summer afternoons. Such windows require a reflective glazing.

While using reflective glazing, special thought should always be given for the effect of the reflective glazing on the outside. Acting like a mirror, the reflective glass intensifies the sun's effects, and could momentarily blind pedestrians or drivers, burn plants, or overheat a patio. It is also important to keep in mind that reflective glass acts like a mirror on the side that faces brighter light. Thus, a reflective window that acts like a mirror to the outside during the day will look like a mirror on the inside during the night.

7.2.2.3 Low-Emittance and Spectrally Selective Coatings

These coatings are especially useful with multi-pane glazing. The principal mechanism of heat transfer in multi-layer glazing is thermal radiation from a warm pane of glass to a cooler pane. Coating a glass surface with a low-emittance material and facing that coating into the gap between the glass layers prevents significant amount of this radiant heat transfer reducing the total heat flow. The improvement in insulating value due to the low-E coating is roughly equivalent to adding another pane of glass to a multipane unit.

The solar spectral reflectance of low-E coatings can be manipulated to include specific portion of the visible and infrared spectrum as explained in the previous section. The term "spectrally selective glazing", refers to system that allows only specific portions of the energy spectrum to be "selected" for certain behavior e.g. only desirable wavelengths of the spectrum are transmitted and others are reflected. A glazing material can then be designed to optimize energy flows to suit the purpose of solar heating, day-lighting and cooling. With conventional clear glazing, a significant amount of solar radiation passes through the window, and then heat from objects within the house is reradiated back through the window as shown in Figure 7.6. For example, a glazing design for maximizing solar gains in the winter would ideally allow entire solar spectrum to pass through, and would block the re-radiation of heat from the inside of the house. The first low-E coatings were designed to have a high solar heat gain coefficient and a high visible transmittance to transmit the maximum amount of sunlight into the interior while reducing the U-factor significantly.

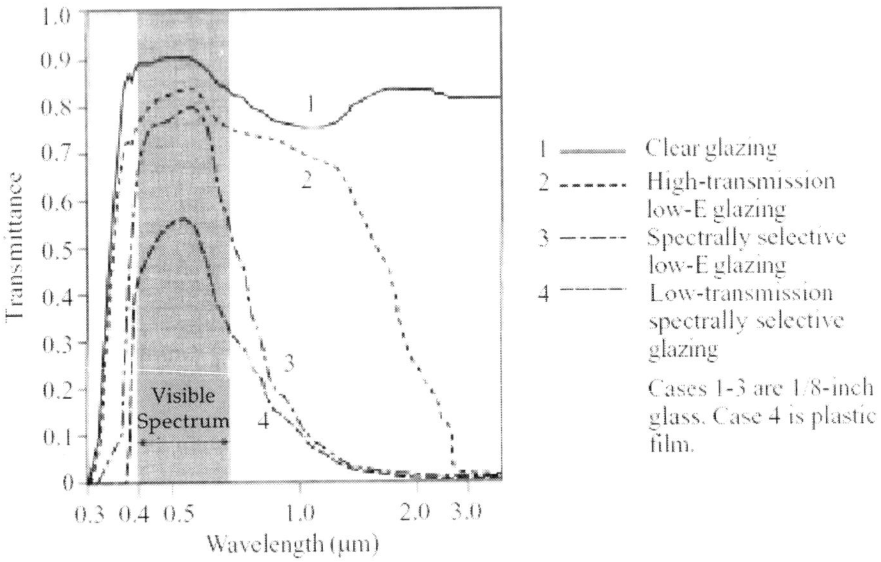

Figure 7.6: Curves representing spectral transmittance for glazing with low-emittance and spectrally selective coatings

On the other hand, a glazing designed to minimize summer heat gains but to allow daylighting effect would allow most portion of the visible light to pass through, while blocking all other portions of the solar spectrum, including ultraviolet, near-infrared, as well as long-wave heat radiated from outside objects such as paving and adjacent buildings.These second-generation low-E coatings are designed to reflect the near-infrared portion of solar radiation, thus reducing the total solar heat gain coefficient while maintaining high levels of light transmission. Variations on this design (modified coatings and/or glazing) can further reduce summer solar heat gain and control glare.

Low-E coatings can be classified in three categories:

(a) High-transmission low-E

High transmission products are most suitable for buildings located in cold and sunny or heating-dominated climates and particularly for south-facing windows in passive solar designs.

(b) Selective-transmission low E

Selective-transmission products are suitable for buildings in composite type of climate that have both the requirements: winter heating and summer cooling. The low-emittance characteristics of this glass reduce winter heat loss from the building. During summers, the selective properties allow natural daylighting to enter, but block a large fraction of the infrared radiation, thereby reducing cooling loads. A similar effect can be achieved by combining a high-transmittance, high SHGC, low-E coating with a spectrally selective tinted glass.

(c) Low-transmission low-E

Placing a low-E coating on dark tinted glass, and/or increasing the solar reflectance of the coating itself, a product can be created that has insulating capability of low –E coatings, combined with glare control and a high-level solar heat rejection. This is especially suited to- controlling solar gain and glare in hot climatic conditions or alternatively known as cooling-dominated climates.

Placement of Coatings

With the increase in number of panes, options for placing the coatings increase. In order to obtain best results, it is extremely important to place the coatings on surfaces that are best suited for their specific purpose. The placement of a low-E coating within the air gap of a double-glazed window does not change the U-factor but it does influence the value of Solar Heat Gain Coefficient (SHGC). That is why, in cold climates, placing a low-E coating on the #3 surface (outside surface of the inner pane in double glazed window) is recommended to minimize the heat loss from inside to outside. This is done at the expense of a slight reduction in the ability to control summer heat gain. On the other hand, in hot climates, a coating on the #2 surface (inside surface of the outer pane) is generally best to reduce heat gain from outside to inside. Multiple low-E coatings are also placed on surfaces within a triple-glazed window assembly, or on the inner plastic glazing layers of multipane assemblies referred to as super windows, described later in this chapter.

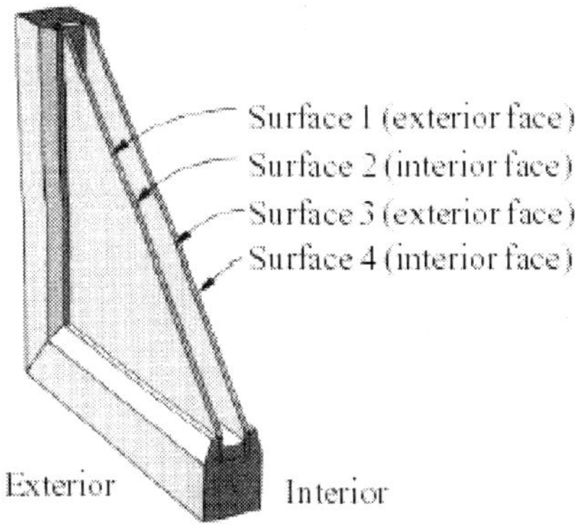

Fig 7.7 : Low-E coatings are placed on different surfaces to achieve different effects

Coating Materials

Two basic types of materials are used to make low-E coatings-sputtered and pyrolytic, referring to the process by which they are made. Ideally, each type of coatings are colorless and optically clear. Some coatings may have a slight hue or subtle reflective quality, particularly when viewed in certain lighting conditions or at oblique angles.

A sputtered coating has a multi layered structure (typically, three primary layers, with at least one layer of metal) and is deposited on glass or plastic film in a vacuum chamber. The gross thickness of a sputtered coating is only 1/10,000 of the thickness of a human hair. Sputtered coatings normally use a silver layer and must be protected from humidity and contact. For this reason they are sometimes called "soft coats." Since sputtering is a low-temperature process, these coatings can be deposited on flat sheets of glass or thin plastic films. Although, sputtered coatings are not durable in themselves, when placed into a sealed double- or triple-glazed assembly, they last as long as sealed glass unit. They are available commercially with emittance ranging from 0.20 to as low as 0.04. As explained earlier in this chapter, an emittance of 0.20 means that 80 percent of the long wavelength radiant energy received by the surface is reflected. For uncoated glass, emissivity is about 0.84, which means only 16 percent of the radiant energy received by the surface is reflected.

The second type of coatings, pyrolytic coatings are normally oxides of metals, most commonly tin-oxide and some additives deposited directly onto a glass surface in cold condition. After this deposition, glass is baked-on surface layer giving a quite hard and very durable coating. Due to this process, these are also called "hard coat". A pyrolytic coating is about 10 to 20 times thicker than a sputtered coating but is still extremely thin for all practical purposes. Pyrolytic coating can be exposed to air, cleaned with normal cleaning products, and subjected to general wear and tear without losing their low-E properties, unlike sputtered coatings. Because of their greater durability, pyrolytic coatings can also be applied on single pane glass and separate storm windows. These cannot be applied on plastics, since they require a high temperature process of baking. While there is a considerable variation in the specific properties of these coatings, they typically have emittance in the range of 0.40 to 0.15.

Spectrally selective coatings on plastic can also be applied to existing glass as a retrofit measure, thus reducing the SHGC of an existing clear glass considerably while maintaining a high visible light transmittance. Other conventional tinted and reflective films can also reduce the SHGC but at the cost of offering lower visible transmittance. Reflective films also reduce the U-factor as explained in previous section, since the surface facing the room has a lower emittance than uncoated glass.

7.2.2.4 Use of Multiple Panes

The insulating value of the window glass alone can be doubled (the U-factor is reduced by half) by adding a second pane. As expected, adding a third or fourth pane of glass further increases the insulating value of the window, but their effect is less pronounced as compared to the first case.

The common understanding of a double-glass glazing units is in the form of two glass layers fused around the perimeter to make a permanently sealed air space. Quite recently, specially developed spacers and polymer sealants have replaced glass-to-glass seals, and have proven sufficiently durable for almost all type of applications. In these windows, layers of glass are separated by and adhere to a spacer, and the sealant, which forms a barrier for diffusion of gas and moisture. Such spacer and sealant is applied around the entire perimeter. Normally, the spacer contains a desiccant material to absorb any residual moisture that may remain in the air space after manufacturing stage. Sealed insulating glass units are now a well proven technology. Designs utilizing high-quality sealants and manufactured with good quality control should normally last for decades without seal failure.

In addition to sealed insulating glass units, some manufacturers offer double-glazed units with non-sealed removable glazing panels. Such units offer flexibility of adding a blind or shade between the glazing, or addition or removal of the inner glazing in moderate climatic conditions. In these double-glazed designs, the inner glazing fits snugly to the sash, and the unsealed air space between the glass layers is normally vented to the exterior with a small tube to prevent condensation from forming in the air space. Three or more glazing layers provide even more insulating value as compared to double glazed composition, but their weight, and high cost cannot be justified for most situations.

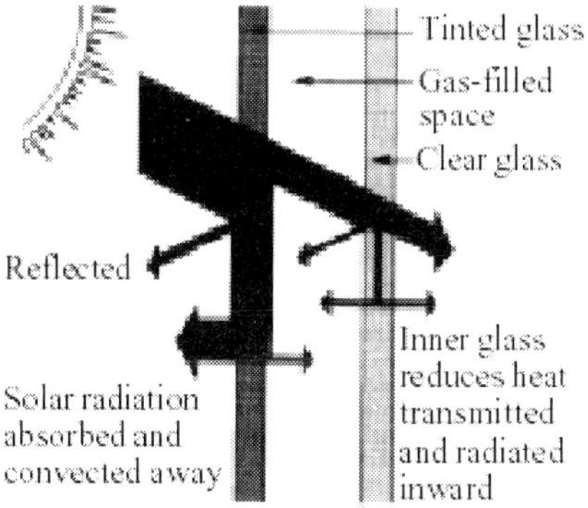

Fig 7.8:Using a tinted outer pane and a clear inner pane in a double-glazed window reduces heat gain. Most heat absorbed by the outer layer does not enter the building interior.

Double-pane units can be assembled using different glass types for the inner and outer layers as shown in Figure 7.8. Typically, the inner layer is standard clear glass, while the outer layer can be tinted, reflective, or both. The solar heat gain coefficient is reduced because the tinted glass and the clear glass, both reduce transmission of solar radiation. This combination further reduces the heat gain because of the inner clear glass, the gas fill, and low-E coatings.

The gap between the two glazing layers is responsible for minimizing the heat gain. It has been observed that the air space between layers of glass reaches its optimum insulating value at about 12 mm when filled with air or argon as shown in Figure 7.10. As the gap gets larger, convection through the air gap increases that increases heat transfer. Krypton gas has its optimum thickness at about 6 mm, so that if smaller air gaps are required, in a window whose overall exterior dimensions are limited, Krypton may be the best selection, although it is also more costly.

Triple and quadruple-glazed windows are commercially available in the Western and European countries but they are hardly available in Indian market. Their less popularity is due to a trade-off with their use. Addition of each layer of glass increases the insulating value of the assembly, but it simultaneously reduces the visible light transmission and the solar heat gain coefficient, thereby reducing the window's value for providing day-lighting or solar heating during winters. In addition, other issues that become important are increase in the weight of the unit, which makes mounting and handling more difficult. Due to the reasons mentioned above, the number of layers of glass gets limited to two in most cases.

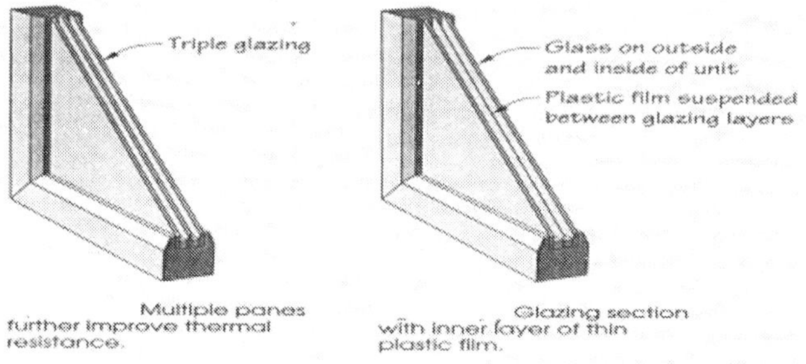

Figure 7.9: Multiple pane window sections

The concept of multiple pane units is not limited to multiple layers of glass only. One popular innovation is based on putting a plastic film in place of the middle layer of glass to develop configuration that is similar to triple glazed system. Weight of the plastic film is very less, and it is very thin. Therefore, it neither increases the weight nor the thickness of window unit. The glass layers protect the inner layer of plastic from scratching, mechanical abuse, corrosion, weathering, and visual distortions caused by external agencies. These plastic films are specially treated to resist UV degradation and they are heat shrunk for maintaining flat profile under all sets of conditions.

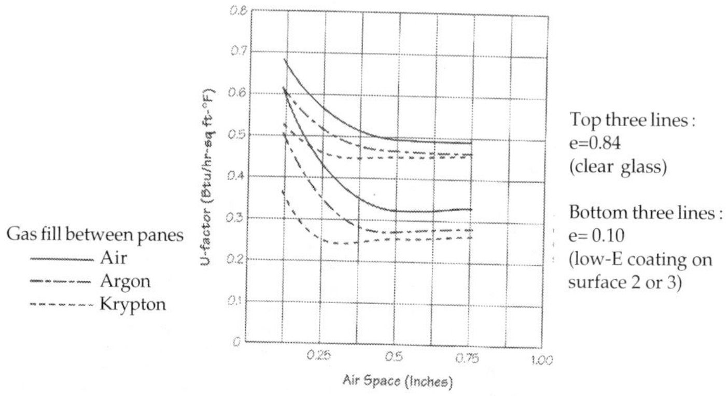

Fig 7.10:U-factor as a function of air-space thickness and emittance

The plastic inner layer decreases the U-factor of the window assembly by dividing the inner air space into multiple chambers. With use of plastic films, the restriction on width of air gap increases beyond half inch (nearly 12mm) to increase the insulation offered by air. Units are offered with one or two inner layers of plastic, depending upon the total gap between glass layers. Additionally, a low- E coating can be placed on the plastic film itself to further reduce the U-factor of the assembly. Further, the plastic film can also be provided with spectrally selective coatings to reduce solar gain in hot climates without significant loss of visible transmittance. The performance of multiple-pane window assemblies with low-emittance coatings and gas fills is described in the following sections.

7.2.2.5 Divided Windows

Manufacturers have been struggling with the problem of many building owners' preference for traditional, divided light windows, which have many small panes separated by thin bars called muntins. Thermal performance of a divided window gets improved as compared to window with a single glass. It is because of the reason that the wooden or PVC muntins have a higher insulating value than the glass. In case of metallic dividers, the effect is reversed. The insulating value of window gets increased due to enhanced heat transfer at increased edge-of-glass area. Typical example of such window is shown in Figure-7.11. Additional advantage of such windows is in terms of maintenance cost. On the event of breakage of glass, only small portion can be changed instead of changing the entire glass in case of undivided window.

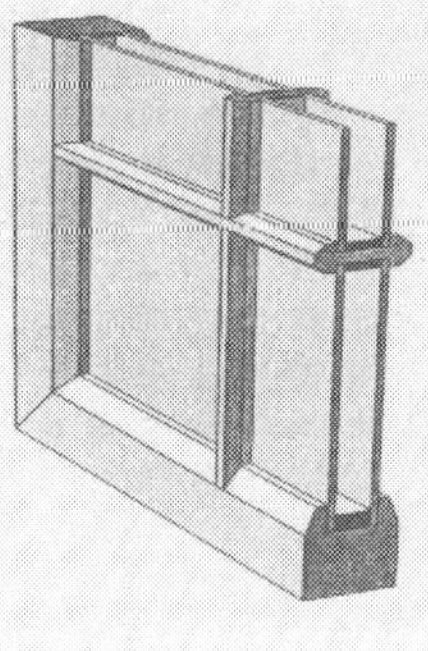

Fig 7.11: True divided light windows can be created with individual units of insulated glazing between muntins

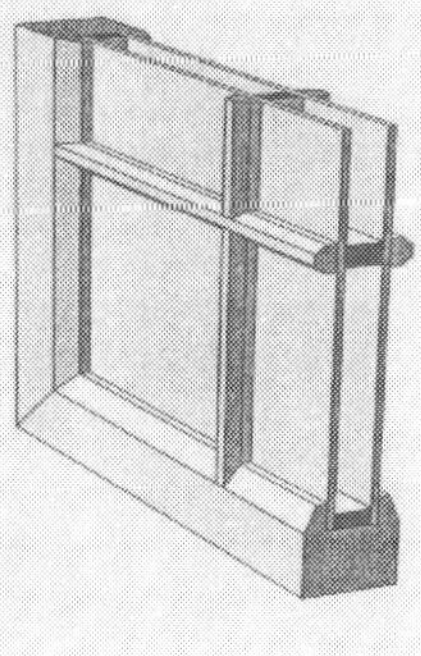

Fig 7.12: A realistic appearance of divided lights can be achieved by placing muntins over both sides of a single insulated glazing unit and a grid between the glazings. A lower cost alternative is to use the grid alone without the interior and exterior muntins

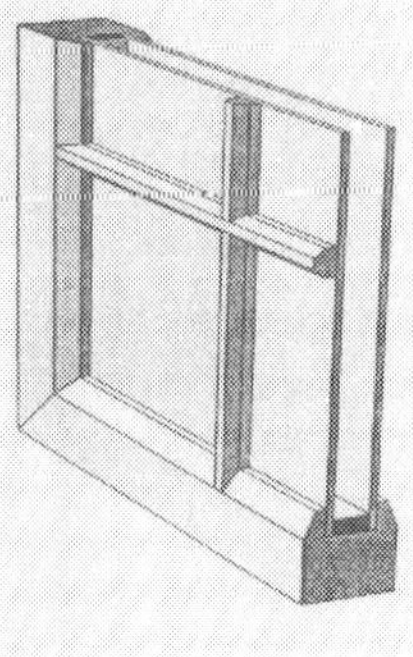

Fig 7.13: Divided lights are simulated in a simple way by placing muntins over the inside of a single insulated glazing unit.

Manufacturing of double glazed windows with dividers is more complicated than single glazed. An alternative to simplify manufacturing of such windows is by producing a single, large sealed glass unit with "muntins" glued to the inside and outside surfaces, while a grid is placed in the middle of one large insulated unit giving the visual effect of divided lights as shown in Figure 7.12. This reduces fabrication costs but does not reduce resistance to heat flow. The only increase is related to use of sealant that needs to cover larger edge length.

If the objective of divided window is just to provide divided light, a third option of building a large, double pane-insulated unit that has snap-on or glued-on grilles can be considered as shown in Figure 7.13. The energy performance of the simple snap-on grid will be similar to a unit without any mullions. Only in case of metallic frame the resistance to heat flow increases considerably with snap-on dividers because of reduction in the edge-effect heat transfer with the snap-on system.

7.2.3 Gas Fills Between Layers

Another improvement that can be made to the thermal performance of insulating glazing units is by reducing the conductance of the air space between the layers. Conventionally, the space is filled with air or flushed with dry nitrogen just prior to sealing. In a sealed glass insulating unit air currents between the two panes of glazing carry heat to the top of the unit and settle into cold pools at the bottom. By filling the space with a gas that is less conductive, more viscous, or slow-moving gas minimizes the convection currents within the space, conduction through the medium between layers can be reduced for controlling the overall transfer of heat.

Manufacturers have introduced the use of argon and krypton gas fills, with measurable improvement in thermal performance. Argon is an inexpensive, non-toxic, non-reactive, clear and odorless gas. The optimal spacing for an argon-filled unit is the same as for air, about 1/2 inch (12mm). Krypton has better thermal performance, but is more expensive as compared to argon. Krypton is particularly useful when the space between glazings must be thinner due to space restrictions. Optimal thickness of gap for this gas is 1/4 inch (6 mm). A mixture of krypton and argon gases can also be used as a compromise between thermal performances and cost. For filling the sealed unit completely with argon or krypton, a typical gas fill system adds the gas into the cavity with a pipe inserted through a hole at the edge of the unit. As the gas is pumped in, it gets mixed with the already existing air, making it difficult to achieve 100 percent purity. Upto 90 percent of purity can be practically achieved in such process. Through vacuum assisted process, purity of the order of 95 percent gas can be achieved. An uncoated double-pane unit filled with 90 percent argon gas and 10 percent air yields a slightly more than 5 percent improvement in the insulating value at the center of the glass compared to the same unit filled with air. However, when krypton fills are combined with low-E coatings and multi-pane glazing, more significant reductions of 15 to 20 percent can be achieved even with less purity of gas. These gases are inert, nontoxic, and occur naturally in the atmosphere, but maintaining their long-term thermal performance is an issue of research. Studies have shown that there is less than 0.5 percent leakage per year in a well-designed and well-fabricated unit, or a 10 percent loss in total gas over a period of twenty-years. Keeping the gas within the glazing unit depends largely upon the quality of the design, materials and, most important, assembly of the glazing unit seals. The effect of a 10 percent gas loss would only be a little change in U-factor on an overall product basis.

7.2.4 Thermally Improved Edge Spacers

The layers of glazing in a multi-pane window assembly are to be held apart at the appropriate distance by spacers. In addition to keeping the glass units at the proper dimension, the spacer system must provide a number of additional functions as mentioned below:

- Accommodate stress induced by thermal expansion and pressure differences;
- Provide a moisture barrier that prevents passage of water or water vapor that would fog the unit;
- Provide a gas-tight seal that prevents the loss of any special low-conductance gas in the air space;
- Create an insulating barrier that reduces the formation of interior condensation at the edge.

Traditional double-pane windows in colder countries used to have a wood spacer that was not able to provide hermetic seal. Therefore, the air cavity was usually vented to the outside for reducing fogging in the air gap. Modern versions of this system function well but, since they are not hermetically sealed, cannot be used with special gas fills or some types of low-E coatings. Ancient glass units were often fabricated with an integral welded glass-to-glass seal. These units used to be leak-proof but were difficult and costly to fabricate, and typically used to have a less-than-optimal narrow spacing. The standard solution for Insulating Glass Units (IGUs) came with use of metal spacers and sealants. These spacers, typically made of aluminium, also contain a desiccant that absorbs residual moisture in the air gap. The spacer is sealed to the two glass layers with the help of organic sealants that provide structural support as well as prevent entry of moisture. There are two approaches for making such IGUs: using a single-seal spacer and using a double-seal system. In the single-seal system as shown in Figure-7.14, an organic sealant, typically a butyl material is applied behind the spacer that holds the unit together and prevents moisture intrusion. These seals are normally not adequate to contain special low-conductance gases.

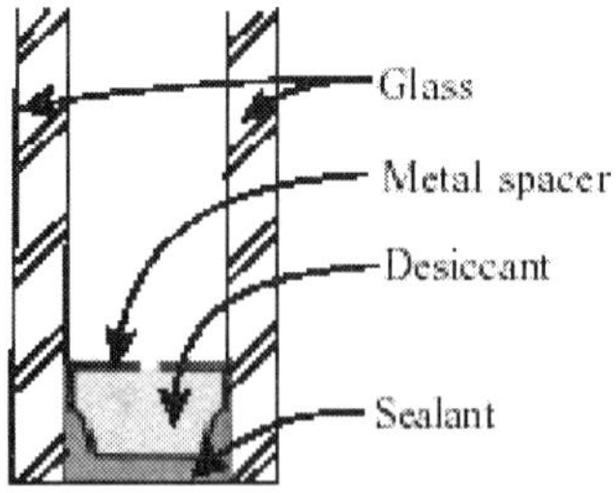

(a) Single-seal metal spacer

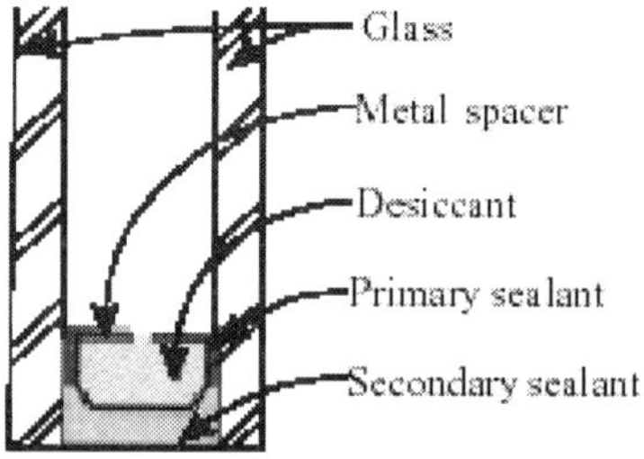

(b) Double-seal metal spacer

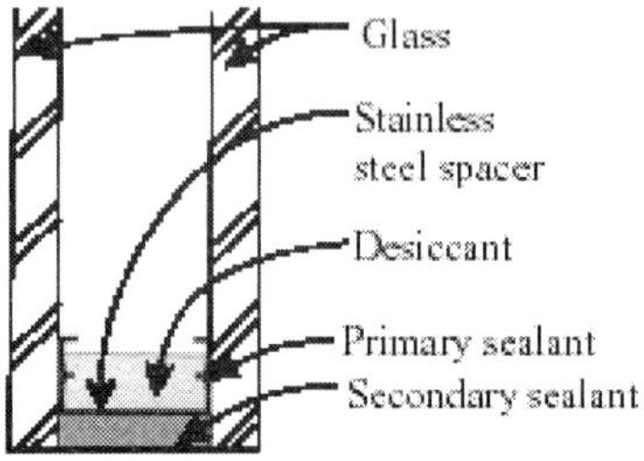

(c) Stainless steel spacer

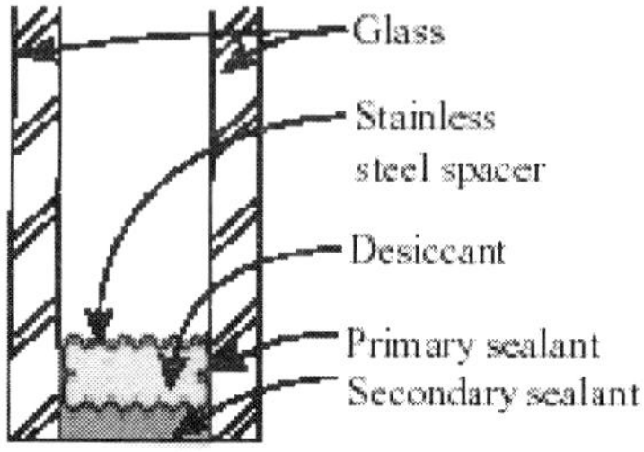

(d) Stainless steel spacer

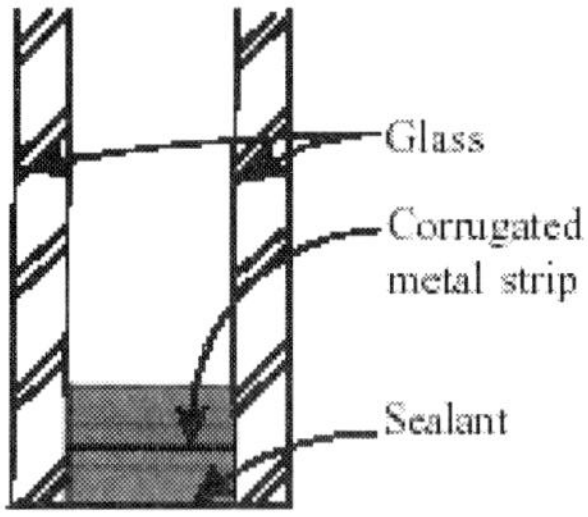

(e) Butyl tape spacer with metal

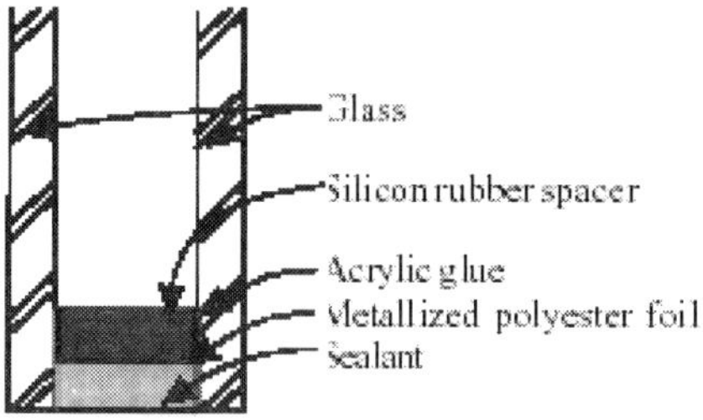

(f) Silicon foam spacer

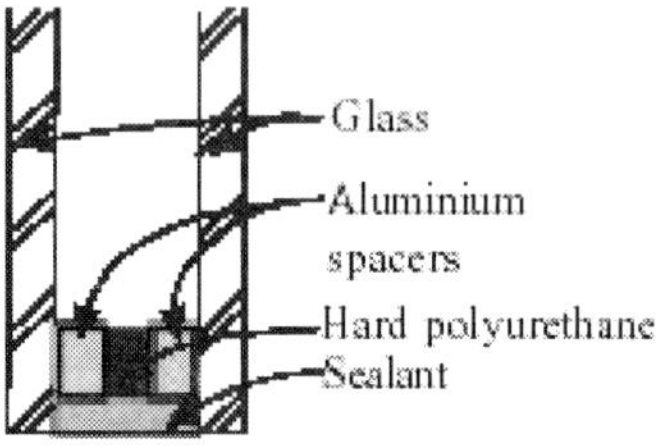

(g) Aluminium spacer with thermal break

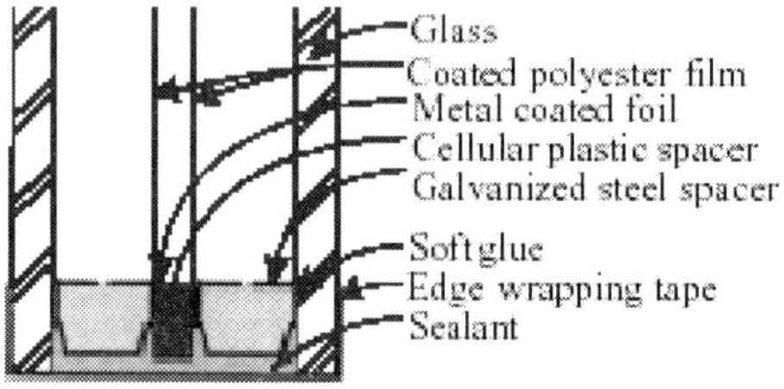

(h) Aluminium spacer with thermal break

Figure 7.14: Different types of spacers

In a double-seal system, shown in Figure 7.14, a primary sealant, typically butyl, seals the spacer to the glass to prevent moisture migration and gas loss, and a secondary backing sealant, silicone, provides structural strength. When sputtered low-E coatings are used with double-seal systems, the coating must be removed from the edge providing a better edge seal. Since aluminium is a very good conductor of heat, the aluminium spacer used in most standard edge spacer systems accounts for a significant thermal "short circuit" at the edge of the IGU. Such short circuit reduces the benefits of other improvements in glazing. The smaller the glass area, the larger is the effect of the edge on the overall product properties. In addition to the increased heat gain/loss, the colder edge is also more prone to condensation.

One approach for reducing heat gain/loss is by replacing the aluminium spacer with a metal that is less conductive material, e.g., stainless steel, and by changing the cross-sectional shape of the spacer as shown in Figure 7.14.

Another approach is by replacing the metal with better insulating materials. One such design alternative incorporates spacer, sealer, and desiccant in a single tape element. The tape includes a solid, extruded thermoplastic compound that contains a blend of desiccant materials and incorporates a thin, fluted metal shim of aluminium or stainless steel as displayed in Figure 7.14. In one more approach, an insulating silicone foam spacer that incorporates a desiccant and has a high-strength adhesive at its edges to provide good bonding to the glass. The foam is backed with a secondary sealant. Both extruded vinyl and pultruded fiberglass spacers are also used in place of metal designs.

There are several hybrid designs that incorporate thermal breaks in metal spacers or use one or more of the elements described above. Some of these are specifically designed to accommodate three and four-layer glazings or IGUs incorporating stretched plastic films. All such alternatives are designed to interrupt the path of heat transfer between two or more glazing layers at the glazing edge.

In order to achieve further enhanced performance from glazing, warm edge spacers have been developed. Warm edge spacer is state of the art three sided spacer bar replacing the traditional four sided aluminium spacer. In this spacer, a nickel plated steel is formed into a U-shape, eliminating the fourth side thereby increasing thermal resistance. During assembly, one fully automated, continuous spacer is bent on three corners and riveted in the fourth, decreasing the possibility of unit failure due to old style plastic corner keys with aluminium spacers.

For purposes of determining the overall window U-factor, the edge spacer has an effect that extends beyond the physical size of the spacer to a band about 2-1/2 inches (64 mm) wide. The contribution of this 2-1/2-inch-wide "glass edge" to the total window U-factor depends on the size of the window. Glass edge effects are much more important for smaller windows or windows with metallic dividers, that have a proportionately larger glass edge area. For a typical residential-size window (5 by 4 feet / 0.8 by 1.2 meters), changing from a standard aluminium edge to a good-quality warm edge will reduce the overall window U-factor by .05 to .06 W/sqm-°C. Another benefit is through the rise in interior surface temperature at the bottom edge of the window, which is most subject to condensation in cold climates. Here, a thermally improved, spacer results in temperature increase of 4-5°C at the window sight line-or 2-4°C at a point one inch in from the sight line, which is an important improvement.

7.2.5 Super windows

Advanced glazing products are generally available as an integrated product and the flexibility of selecting isolated features is not there. A window with a combination of all of the measures available to maximize its insulating value is termed as a "super window". Super windows are currently not available in Indian market due to their high cost as compared to other options. Most super windows available in Western and European countries consist of a triple or quadruple-layer design with two low-E coatings, krypton or argon gas fills, low-conductance spacers, and thermally improved frames. The center glazing layer(s) may be glass or plastic film.

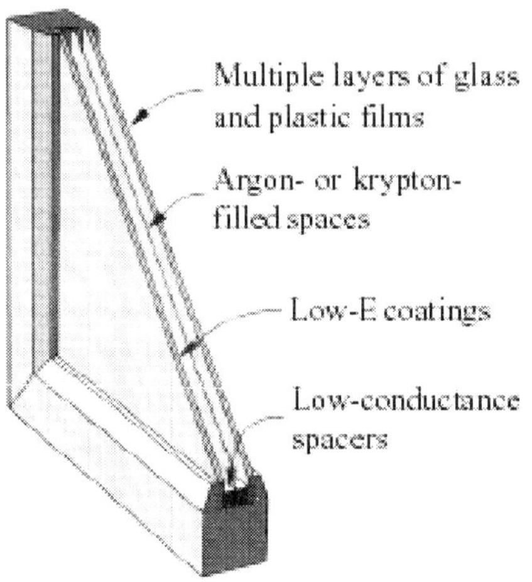

Superwindows improve thermal resistance with multiple layers of glass and suspended plastic films, argon and krypton gas fills, low-E coatings and low-conductance spacers.

Characteristics of superwindows

- Thermal resistance in north is increased with multiple layers of glass and suspended plastic films, argon and krypton gas fills, and low emittance coatings. This reduces winter heat loss and summer heat gain.
- Visible light transmittance is diminished slightly with each additional layer.

Application of superwindows

- Cold climates where reduction in heat loss is a priority.
- Where comfort is important particularly with large glazing areas.

Figure 7.15: Super window and its features

With the combination of features mentioned above, the resulting product is a highly transparent window with a center-of - glass U-factor below 0.90W/m^{2}K and an overall U-factor below 1.20W/m^{2}K. The overall SHGC of such product is about 0.40. With continuing improvements in frame and spacer design, overall window U-factors as low as 0.60 are also possible. The superwindow configuration presented above represents an improvement in U -factor but not in SHGC when compared to the double-glazed low-E case. As a result, the main impact is expected in the cold season, not the hot season. It can be noted that the double- glazed case with a selective coating (SHGC 0.26) has the best performance during the hot season demanding cooling. Such superwindows have a remarkable energy performance but they are cost-effective only at a very few places in India such as Leh. The loss of heat is so low that even heat gain from the diffused sunlight through a north-facing window on a cold, cloudy winter day is greater than the heat losses over remaining part of the day. At this threshold of performance, in very harsh conditions, a window can take on a new role in buildings as a net energy provider rather than a net energy looser. Such a superwindow has a lower heating loss than even a highly insulated wall in a cold climate. This development makes the direction of window less significant for the energy performance. South-facing windows have always had this property; however, highly efficient superwindow technologies mean that a window facing in any direction eventually acts as a passive solar heat collector.

7.2.6 Evacuated windows

It has been concluded that maximum thermal efficiency with gas fill would be in the case of a vacuum, no gas at all between the layers. If the vacuum is low enough, there would be no conductive or convective heat transfer between the panes of glass, thus lowering the U-value. A vacuum glazing must have a good low-E coating to reduce radiative heat transfer because the vacuum effect alone is not adequate. The same principle is used in the fabrication of thermos bottles, where the silver coating serves as the low-emittance surface. However, evacuated window assemblies present a number of engineering problems. One major issue is the structural requirement to resist normal air pressure and variable pressures caused by wind and vibrations. Additionally, in case of large panes, there can be large thermal stresses. The large, flat surfaces of a window tend to bow and flex with changing pressures. To maintain the separation between the panes, minute glass pillars or spheres have been developed. The pillars are very small but they are still visible, reducing the clarity of the window. Another important issue is the maintenance of an airtight seal around the edge of the unit. The seal must be maintained to eliminate gaseous conduction by keeping the air density within the unit to less than one millionth of normal atmospheric pressure. An air density of only ten times this amount is sufficient to re-establish conduction to its normal value. This vacuum seal must remain intact for the entire life of the window withstanding all the fluctuations in conditions.

7.2.7 Aerogel

Aerogel is a silica-based, open-cell, foam-like material that has about 4 percent silica and 96 percent air. Microscopic cells of the foam entrap gas, thereby preventing convection, while still allowing light to pass through. The particles that make up the thin cell walls slightly diffuse the light passing through, creating a bluish haze similar to that of the sky. Use of Aerogel for this purpose is generically referred to as "transparent insulation". It is technically possible to produce windows made of aerogel with a center-of-glass U-factor as low as 0.3W/m^{2}K. Aerogel is being produced in small quantities and small sizes, so that only tile-sized pieces of aerogel have been used as windows. Some manufacturers in western and European countries have produced double glazed windows filled with small beads of aerogel. Although the units have good insulating values, due to diffusion they do not provide a good view.

7.2.8 Smart Windows

"Smart windows" are able to dynamically change their solar- optical properties in response to changing performance requirements. The basic types of smart windows that directly respond to the environmental conditions such as light level, temperature, and active devices that can be directly controlled in response to occupant preferences or heating and cooling system requirements. The main passive devices used in smart windows are photochromics and thermochromics; active devices include liquid crystal, dispersed particle, and electrochromics.

Photochromics

Photochromic materials change their transparency in response to changes in the intensity of light. These materials have been used in sunglasses that change from transparent in the dim indoor light to dark in the bright outdoor conditions. Photochromics allowing just enough light to pass through for day-lighting purposes, while cutting out excess sunlight that creates glare and over-loads the cooling system.

Thermochromics

Thermochromics change transparency in response to changes in temperature. Such materials are gels sandwiched between glass and plastic that switch from a clear state when cold to a more diffuse, white, reflective state when hot. In their switched-on state, the view through the glazing gets lost due to diffusion. Such windows can, in effect, turn off the sunlight when the cooling loads become too high. Thermochromics can also be very useful for controlling the overheating for passive solar heating applications. The temperature of the glass, which is a function of solar intensity and outdoor and indoor temperature, would control the amount of sunlight reaching the thermal storage element. Thermochromics would be especially useful for use in skylights because their obscured state would not interfere with views as it would in a typical window.

Liquid Crystal Glazing

A variant of the liquid crystal display technology used in wristwatches can be used to serve as a privacy glazing for windows. A very thin layer of liquid crystals is sandwiched between two transparent electrical conductors on thin plastic films and the entire package is laminated between two layers of glass. When the power is off, the liquid crystals are in a random and unaligned state. The glass appears as a diffusing layer as they scatter light. Thus, the material transmits most of the incident sunlight in a diffuse manner; and its solar heat gain coefficient remains high. When power is applied, the electric field in the device aligns the liquid crystals and as a result the glazing becomes clear, permitting view in both directions. Limitation of this development is that the device has only two states, clear and diffusing, and the power must be continuously applied for the glazing to remain in the clear state.

Particle Dispersed Glazing

This electrically controlled concept utilizes a thin liquid-like layer in which numerous microscopic particles are suspended. In its state with no power supply, the particles are randomly oriented and thus partially block sunlight transmission and view. Transparent electrical conductors allow an electric field to be applied to the dispersed particle film, aligning the particles for increasing the transmittance. This glazing system can be partially transmitting between its clear and dark states.

Electrochromic Glazing

The most promising smart window technology are the devices using electrochromic coatings. Electrochromics can change transparency over a wide continuous range, from about 10 to 70 percent light transmittance in less than one minute, with a corresponding wide range of control over solar heat gain. The coating darkens as it switches and provides a view out under all switching conditions. Switching takes place at very low voltage (1-2 volts), therefore the cost of power supplies remains under control. On removal of the voltage, the electrochromic process is stopped without affecting the window's present state of transmittance. Reversing the voltage returns the window to its original state. The reversible process can continue over thousands of cycles with reasonably high frequency.

In contrast to thermochromic or photo chromic glazings, electrochromic windows offer more flexibility in control. Thermochromics and photochromics must have a preset threshold point at which they will change their state. Although a range of thresholds could be specified, the specified threshold becomes a permanent feature of that window. Electrochromics, in contrast, can be operated by computer, by occupant signal, or by simple thermostat or photocell controls. This offers the potential for occupant adjustments and calibration to changing local conditions.

7.3 WINDOW FRAME MATERIALS

The material that is used for making the window frame largely governs the physical characteristics of the window. Parameters such as frame thickness, width, weight, cross-section and durability are important to decide the thermal characteristics of the window. Hybrid or composite sash and frames have also been developed, in which multiple materials are selected and combined to best meet the overall required performance parameters. Thus, a simple inspection of the inner or outer surface of the frame is no longer an accurate indicator of the total material or its performance.

Table-7.2 shows the U-factors of various standard frame types. Since the actual U-factor depends on specific dimensions and design details, these values are only for explaining relative merits of various materials over each other. While it is useful to understand the role of frame type in window thermal performance, it is observed that manufacturers do not normally report the frame U-factor. Since the sash and frame represent from 10 to 50 percent of the total area of the window unit, the frame properties cannot be overlooked.

Table 7.2: Typical U factors for different frame materials

Frame material	*U (W/m²K)*
Aluminium (No Thermal Break)	10.8 – 12.5
Aluminium (With Thermal Break)	5.8
Aluminium-clad wood/Reinforced Vinyl	2.23 – 2.83
Wood and Vinyl	1.7 – 2.83

Wood, aluminium and vinyl frames are three most common types of frame materials. Their relative advantages and disadvantages have been described in the following sub-sections.

7.3.1 Wooden Frames

Wood is the most traditionally used frame material. The prime reason for its wide acceptability has been its availability and ease of milling into the complex shapes required for accommodating windows of almost any design. A decline in use of wooden frames has been observed over past decade because of emergence of other competing products that are either less expensive or more durable or perform better. Wood is not intrinsically the most durable material for window frame, because of its susceptibility to rot and threat from termite. However, well-built and well-maintained wooden windows can have a very long life.

Wooden frames have three positive and one negative characteristics: Good thermal performance, easy to mill into complex shapes suitable for windows, attractive interior appearance are positive points, whereas one negative point is requirement of exterior paint and maintenance unless clad with vinyl or aluminium.

Wood is easy to repair and maintain with simple tools and materials. A coat of paint protects the surface and allows an easy change in color schemes. Frames are generally made of dried timber to reduce shrinkage and bending that results in better operation and weather-tightness over their lifetime. Water-repellent and/or chemical treatments can be applied on wood to reduce swelling and warping, improve paint retention, and increase wood's resistance to decay and insect attack. Wooden windows are used in all configurations, from sliders to swinging windows. Wood is favored in many applications because of its appearance and traditional place in building design. A variation of the wooden window is by cladding the exterior face of the frame with vinyl or aluminium, thus creating a permanent weather-resistant surface. Clad frames offer lower maintenance requirements, while retaining the attractive wood finish on the interior.

Vinyl and enameled metal claddings offer much longer protection to wood frames. However, they are generally available in a limited number of colors, and refinishing these surfaces may be a difficult task. Dark-colored finishes absorb more of the solar radiation, and therefore, they tend to be more susceptible to aging from heat and ultraviolet damage. Many vinyl and plastic finishes and frame materials require special solvents and bonding agents for repair or refinishing.

From a thermal point of view, windows with wooden frame perform well. Amount of insulation is proportional to the thickness of wood. Metal cladding, metal hardware, or the metal reinforcing often used at corner joints tends to reduce the thermal performance of wooden frames. If the metal extends through the window from the cold side to the warm side of the frame, it creates a thermal short circuit, conducting heat more quickly through that remaining part of the frame.

7.3.2 Aluminium Frames

With increasing shortage and high prices of wood, towards the end of last century, aluminium has emerged out as a substitute of wood used in window frame. Aluminium is light, strong, durable, and it can be easily extruded into the complex shapes required for window parts. It can be fabricated to extremely close tolerances, to create special forms for the insertion of glazing, weatherstripping and thermal breaks. Aluminium frames are available in anodized and factory-baked enamel finishes that are extremely durable and require low-maintenance. Aluminium is widely used for industrial window units because of its lightweight and corrosion resistance.

The biggest disadvantage of aluminium as a window frame material is its high thermal conductance. It readily conducts heat that greatly raises the overall U-factor of a window unit. Due to its high thermal conductance, increase in frame thickness does not increase thermal resistance by significant amount. Focus therefore, should be kept on minimizing the width of frame that faces hot and cold sides of the building. Thus, an aluminium frame profile with a simple compact shape will perform much better than a profile with many fins and undulations. In cold climates, a simple aluminium frame can easily become cold enough to cause moisture condensation or frost on the inside surfaces of window frames. Even more than the problem of heat loss, the condensation problem spurred development of a more insulating aluminium frame.

The most common solution to the heat conduction problem of aluminium frames is providing a "thermal break" by splitting the frame components into interior and exterior pieces and using a less conductive material to join them as shown in Figure 7.16. There are many designs available for thermally broken aluminium frames. The most prevalent technique used in simple windows is called "pouring and de-bridging." The window frame part is first extruded as a single piece with a hollow trough in the middle. This is filled with a plastic that gets hardened to become a strong intermediate piece. The connecting piece of aluminium is then milled out, leaving only the plastic to join the two halves of aluminium. Functionally, the resulting piece is cut, mitered, and assembled like a simple aluminium extrusion. Thermally, presence of the plastic slows down the heat flow between the inside and outside. Use of thermal breaks reduces the U-value of aluminium frame from about 10-12W/m^{2}K to nearly half of this value.

It is easier to insert the thermal break in the bulkier main frame but it is problematic to include thermal breaks in thinner sash components that hold the glazing. In addition, as glazing systems with higher insulating values are developed, even the frame with a U-factor of 5-6W/m^{2}K are not considered to be consistent with the energy efficiency of the other window components.

Characteristics of aluminium frames can thus be summarized as: High thermal conductance resulting in poor U-factor, Necessity of thermal breaks, High strength-to-weight ratio, Lightweight compared to wood, and Durability with low maintenance requirement.

Aluminium frames are best suited for climates where high thermal resistance is not a priority. In more extreme climates, frames with thermal brakes are recommended to improve performance. Aluminium frames can be preferred in locations where lower maintenance and lower cost are important requirements.

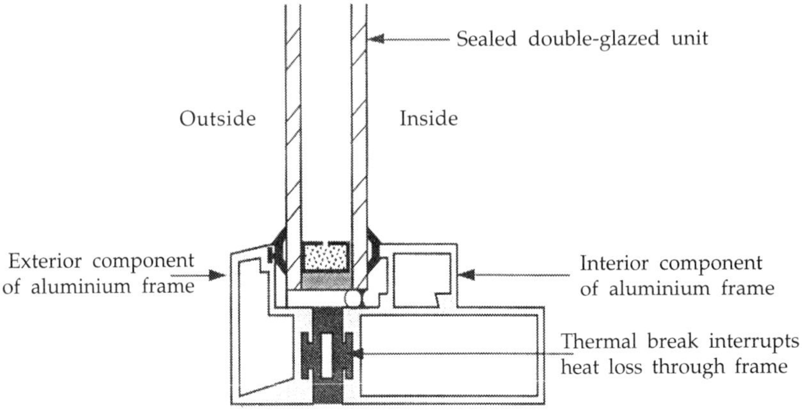

Figure 7.16: Thermal break in an aluminium frame

However, innovative new thermal break designs combined with changes in frame design have been used in Europe to achieve U-factors lower than 2.8 W/m^2K, but their costs are much higher than simple thermally broken frames. In hot climates, where controlling the direct solar gain is often more important than conductive heat transfer, investing money for a higher insulating value of the frame can be less important than using a higher-performance glazing system. However, in windows having higher proportion of frame area, specially multiple section or sliding windows, insulating frame is an important requirement.

7.3.3 PVC Frames

Poly-Vinyl Chloride (PVC) is relatively newcomer as window frame materials in India. Commonly known as 'Vinyl' or 'Plastic', Poly-Vinyl Chloride (PVC), is a very versatile plastic with good insulating properties, high resistance to impact, and excellent resistance to abrasion, corrosion, attack by air pollutants and termites. PVC frames do not require a finishing coat. This feature reduces maintenance requirement and reduce chances of deterioration over time. With recent advances in plastic technology, PVC frames now have much improved dimensional stability and resistance to degradation from the attack of sunlight and temperature extremes.

Similar to aluminium windows, vinyl windows are fabricated by cutting standard lineal extrusions to size and assembling the pieces into the form of complete sash and frame elements. This type of manufacturing process provides flexibility to readily fabricating the custom sizes needed.

Vinyl window frames require very little maintenance. In addition to good thermal resistance they have good moisture resistance. To provide the required structural performance, vinyl sections are usually larger than aluminium window sections, closer to the dimensions of wood frame sections. Very large PVC frames units may require metal stiffeners for increasing their strength.

Although vinyl as a material has a higher coefficient of expansion than either wood or aluminium, vinyl window frame profiles are designed and assembled in such a way that they eliminate dimensional change caused by thermal cycles. Vinyl frames with heat-welded joints are stiffer than mechanically joined vinyl frames, so they provide very good resistance to temperature and handling stresses, both at the job site and also during shipping. In some cases, a vinyl window assembly consists of both welded and mechanically fastened components. Interior webs can also be used to strengthen the frame that also enhances the thermal performance of window unit.

The thermal performances of good quality vinyl frames can be better than wooden frames. For simple PVC frames, the thermal resistance is usually of the same order as that of wood. Good frame designs including large hollow chambers within the frame can allow unwanted heat transfer through convection currents as shown in Figure-7.17. Creating smaller cells within the frame reduces this convection exchange, as does adding an insulating material. Most manufacturers are conducting research and development to improve the insulating value of their vinyl window assemblies.

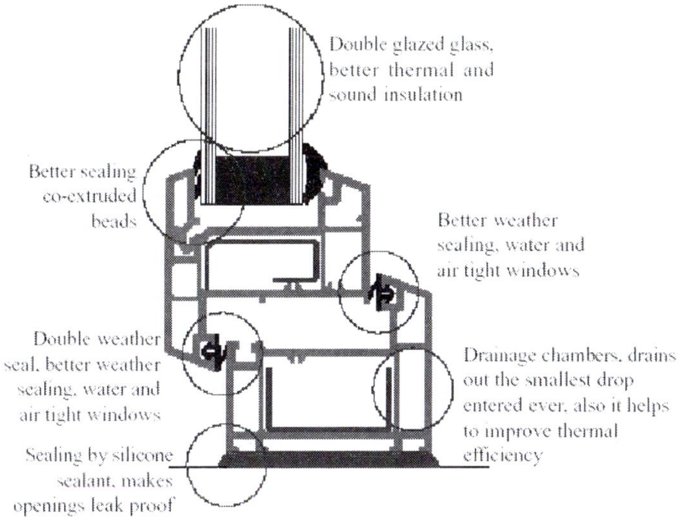

Figure 7.17: Cross section of hollow PVC frame for windows

Characteristics of Vinyl Frames can therefore, be summarized as: Very good thermal performance, flexibility for customized fabrication, and very low maintenance requirement. Windows with PVC frames can be used for almost all types of new buildings and also in cases of retrofitting.

7.3.4 Fiberglass and Engineered Thermoplastics

In addition to PVC frame, glass-fiber-reinforced polyester, or fiberglass can also be used for the same purpose. This material is extruded into lineal forms and then assembled into the final form. These frames are dimensionally stable and have good insulating value by incorporating air cavities (similar to vinyl). Since the material is stronger than vinyl, it can have smaller cross-sectional size and shape. Due to typical manufacturing process, fiberglass windows are likely to be more expensive than PVC windows. Another alternative to fiberglass is to use extruded engineered thermoplastics that comes from another family of plastics and is used extensively in automobiles and appliances. Similar to fiberglass, thermoplastics have some structural and other advantages over vinyl but they are also more expensive.

7.3.5 Wood Composites

Composite wood products, such as particle board and laminated strand lumber, in which wood particles and resins are compressed to form a strong composite material, are commonly used in building industry. The same material can be used by creating a new generation of wood/ polymer composites that are extruded into a series of lineal shapes for window frame and sash members. These composites are very stable, and have similar or even better structural and thermal properties than conventional wood. Additionally, they offer better moisture resistance and more decay resistance as compared to wood. They can be textured and stained or painted much like wood. This approach has the added environmental advantage of reusing a volume of sawdust and wood scrap that would otherwise be discarded.

7.3.6 Hybrid and Composite Frames

Hybrid frame designs use two or more of the frame materials described above to produce a complete window system. The wood industry uses vinyl and aluminium-clad windows to reduce exterior maintenance needs. Vinyl manufacturers and others offer interior wood veneers to produce the finish and appearance that many building-owners desire. Split -sash designs may have an interior wood element bonded to an exterior fiberglass element. We are likely to see an ever-increasing selection of such composite designs as manufacturers continue to try to provide better-performing products at lower cost. With increase in hybrid nature, it becomes increasingly difficult to estimate the thermal properties of such a frame from simple inspection, hence the end user should carefully interrogate manufacturer about thermal and other physical properties.

7.4 DESIGN CONSIDERATIONS AND IMPLICATIONS

The various technologies for energy efficient windows described in this book can have a major effect on comfort and on the annual energy performance of a building. Since the new glazing technologies provide highly effective insulating value and solar protection, there are important implications on the method of building design.

Designers are already aware of the window design guidelines and assumptions intended to reduce heating and cooling energy use. Most of these are based upon the relatively much poorer performance of windows. As a result, most of these assumptions frequently put limitations on design freedom or generate conflicts with other performance requirements, such as view. Traditional considerations include orientation, amount of glazing, and shading requirements for windows. With recent advancements in window technology, questions can be raised about the validity and need of revision in many of these restrictive suggestions.

Windows are one of the most multifaceted components in a building that address several purposes. They affect the aesthetics of the home, provide views, ventilation and daylight. They have a major impact on the indoor comfort and energy consumption of the building. The designer must determine the required amount and placement of glazing to provide natural ventilation in summer, solar heat gain in winter, or simply to allow egress from rooms as required. Decisions about window size and placement are also integral to the exterior appearance and the interior aesthetic qualities of the spaces. Additional design objectives include creating a sense of roominess or spaciousness and providing natural light or particular views. These architectural decisions are interwoven with site design and development since performance of window can be enhanced or diminished by landscape elements.

The first three of these - providing views, light, and fresh air-represent traditional window functions that do not change the window technology fundamentally with technological advancements. However, the next three objectives - decreasing summer heat gain, decreasing winter heat loss, and providing winter heat gain are influenced considerably by the quality and suitability of windows.

7.5 INDIAN CLIMATIC CONDITIONS AND WINDOW PERFORMANCE

Before selection of most appropriate window for any building, understanding of climatic conditions driving energy consumption in buildings is almost essential. Performance of windows is sensitive to local climatic conditions. Energy efficient window in one climate may turn out to be inefficient in other set of conditions.

7.5.1 Effect of climatic conditions on window performance

Due to different climatic conditions, especially the external heat transfer coefficient 'h_o', as well as internal heat transfer coefficient 'h_i', assume different values under standard conditions as per the international standards. Therefore, U-value, SHGC and VT values for all the six climatic zones have been calculated for the major types of window systems. The calculated values for Indian conditions are given in Table-7.3.

Table 7.3 reveals that the values of external and internal heat transfer coefficients found for Indian climatic conditions are quite different from those used in the USA or Europe. This difference is mainly due to presence of different combinations of wind velocity, ambient temperature and solar radiation. As a result of variation in external heat transfer coefficient, the overall U-value of the various window systems also varies from the values available in the international literature.

Table 7.3 : External (h_o) and Internal (h_i) heat transfer coefficients for the six climatic zones of India (for 3 mm single glazed clear window, at a sill height of 0.6 m)

S. No.	*Climate*	*External Heat Transfer Coefficient (h_o) W/m²K*	*Internal Heat Transfer Coefficient (h_i) W/m²K*
1.	Hot & Dry	15.36	4.49 [4.12]*
2.	Warm & Humid	14.66	4.65
3.	Composite Summer	14.44	4.49
4.	Composite Winter	11.48	4.11
5.	Moderate	8.76	3.01
6.	Cold & Cloudy	9.16	5.12
7.	Cold & Sunny	10.04	6.84 [8.04]*

The values in brackets shown in the last column of Table 7.3 are adopted from ASHRAE [2002] for summer & winter conditions.

Using the values of h_o and h_i given in Table 7.3 and the simulation software WINDOW 5.1, the values of thermo-optical parameters (U-value, SHGC and VT) obtained for different window systems in different climatic conditions in India are given in Figure 7.18. Summary of the results presented in the Figure 7.18 is:

1. The U value of all window assemblies is higher for hotter ambient conditions than the cooler ones.
2. The solar heat gain factor (SHGC) is marginally higher for cooler climatic conditions (in conformity with ASHRAE [1997] results).
3. The visual transmittance does not change with weather conditions, but the frame does have influence over this parameter.

Since the ambient conditions change all over the year, it is interesting to study the variation of U-value with possible temperature difference in different climatic conditions (incident solar radiation and wind velocity remaining constant). For single and double glazed windows (vinyl/ wood frames), the U value is minimum for a certain ambient temperature, but for higher insulating windows, U value increases almost linearly with increase in ambient temperature except for Low-

E with spectrally selective coating. The behavior of aluminium framed window units in different climatic zones for variation in ambient temperature is given in figure 7.18A to 7.18J.

Simulation studies carried out for variation in ambient temperature and its effect on the window U value show that for single glazed, double glazed with air in the cavity and double glazed with argon in the cavity, the general trend is that U value first decreases with increase in the ambient temperature, attains a minimum value and then starts increasing with increase in ambient temperature. For single glazed clear window U value is found to be minimum when the difference between the inside building temperature and the ambient temperature is minimum [Δt = 1°C (Cold & Sunny Climate) to 4°C (Hot & Dry Climate)]. For double glazed clear window with air filled cavity, the U value is found to be minimum for 10°C ambient temperature [Δt = 11°C (Cold & Sunny Climate) to14°C (Hot & Dry Climate)]. For double glazed argon filled windows, the U value is found to be minimum for 5°C ambient temperature [Δt = 16°C (Cold & Sunny Climate) to19°C (Hot & Dry Climate)]. For further improved glazing systems i.e., double-glazed spectrally selective (with air and argon as fill gas), triple-glazed clear (with air and argon as fill gas) and triple-glazed spectrally selective with argon filled window, the U value is minimum at lower ambient temperature and increases with increase in the ambient temperature.

The study also shows that the U value of window unit is higher for warmer climates as compared to the cold climates. The reason for this seems to be the temperature difference between inside and outside and the average temperature, which affects the air properties. The U value of double glazed bronze window increases with increase in the ambient temperature. Therefore, the advantage of low transmittance for solar radiation is therefore lost through increased heat transfer thereby inducing more load on the air-conditioning units. As expected, Triple glazed windows are outperforming the rest of the window units, but the simulation results show that triple glazed windows are performing better in cold climates. Moreover for Indian climatic conditions, the double-glazed window units with spectrally selective coating are performing in a similar fashion as triple-glazed windows. Therefore, it can very well be concluded that triple-glazed windows are not very useful in Indian climatic conditions.

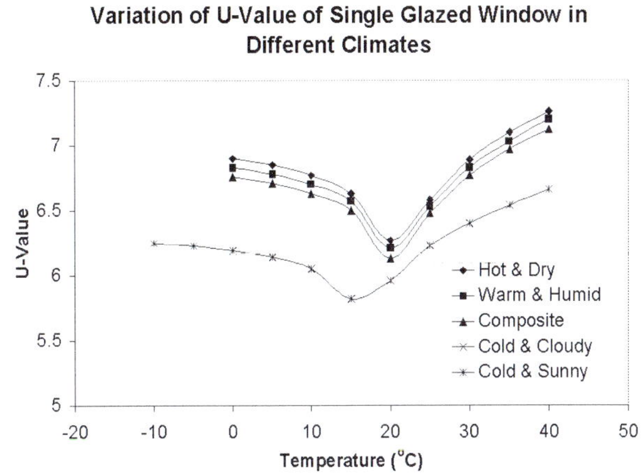

Figure 7.18A: Variation of U Value of Single Glazed Window in Different Climates

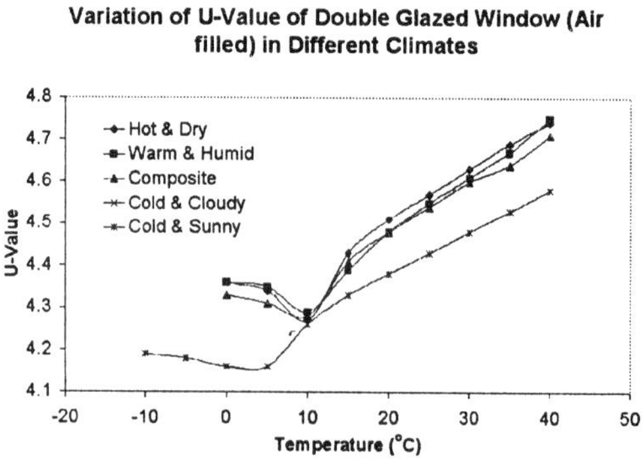

Figure 7.18B : Variation of U Value of Double Glazed Window (Air Filled) in Different Climates

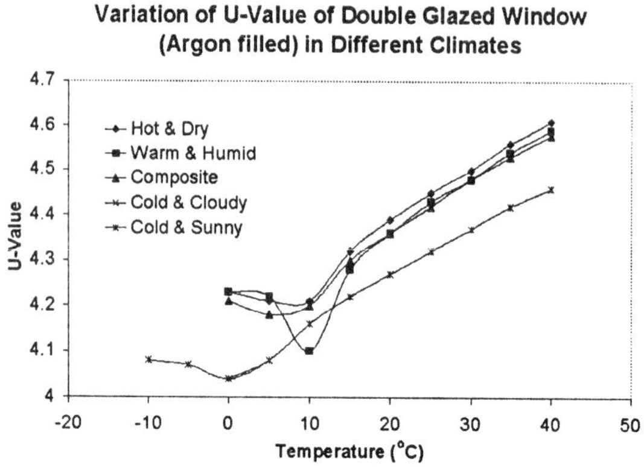

Figure 7.18C : Variation of U Value of Double Glazed Window (Argon Filled) in Different Climates

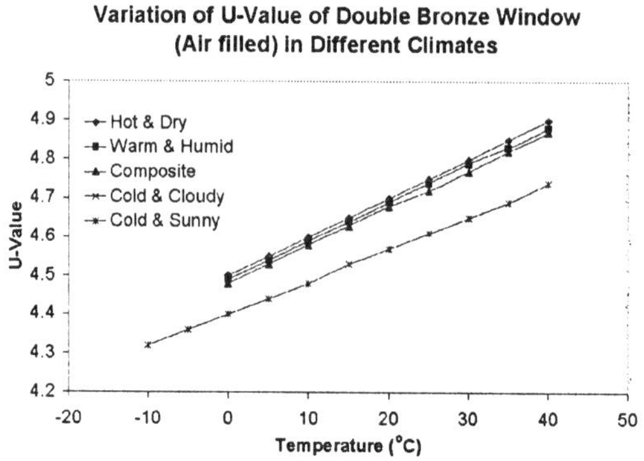

Figure 7.18D : Variation of U Value of Double Glazed Bronze Window (Air Filled) in Different Climates

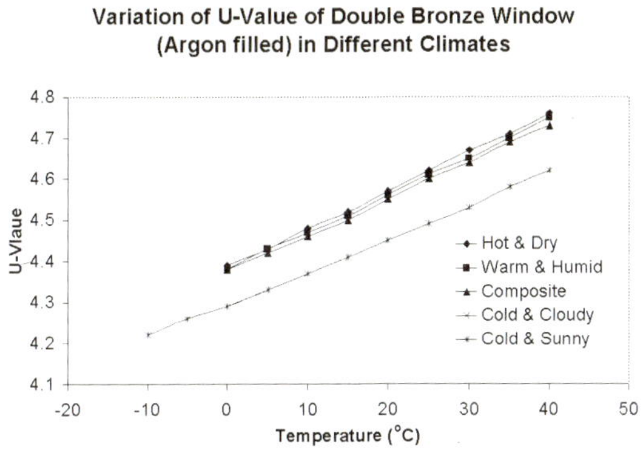

Figure 7.18E : Variation of U Value of Double Glazed Bronze Window (Argon Filled) in Different Climates

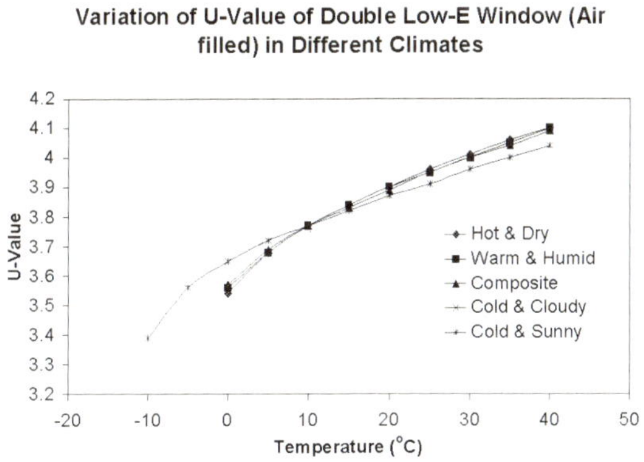

Figure 7.18F : Variation of U Value of Double Glazed Low-E Window (Air Filled) in Different Climates

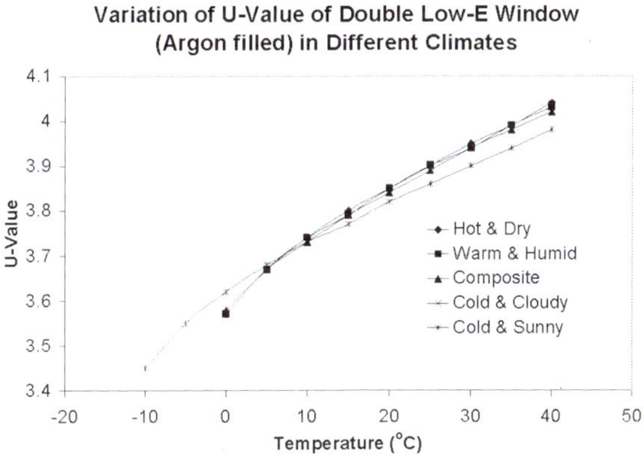

Figure 7.18G : Variation of U Value of Double Glazed Low-E Window (Argon Filled) in Different Climates

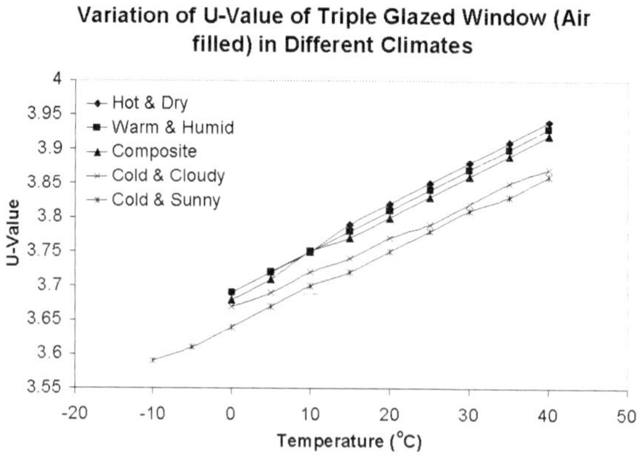

Figure 7.18H : Variation of U Value of Triple Glazed Window (Air Filled) in Different Climates

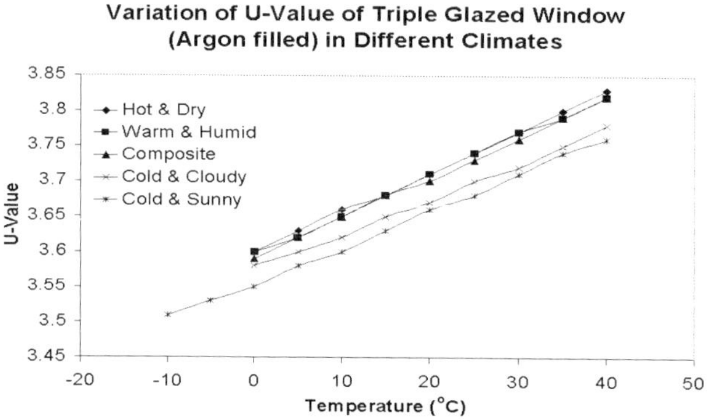

Figure 7.18I : Variation of U Value of Triple Glazed Window (Argon Filled) in Different Climates

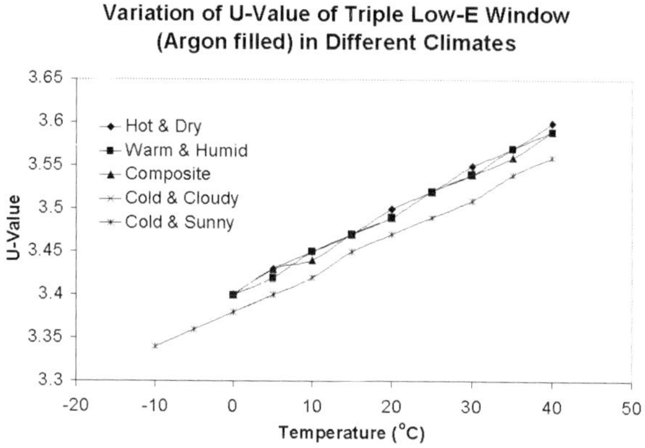

Figure 7.18J : Variation of U Value of Triple Glazed Low-E Window (Argon Filled) in Different Climates

Above mentioned details for the U-value can be used for fine-tuning the performance of windows to suit micro-climate. Codes and standards only cover the situation of commonly prevailing climatic conditions. Such exact calculation of the U-value becomes more important in air-conditioned buildings having large glazed area.

7.5.2 Energy saving potential in windows

A single room single story house with different types of window combination was analysed using the software DOE-2.1E by finding out the annual energy demand in different climates of India. The inside temperature was set at 24 °C for summer conditions and 21 °C for winter conditions. Tables 7.4 to 7.9 show the energy consumption in the building and change in energy consumption with change in the window type and window size.

Table 7.4: Specific Energy Demand and Peak Heating & Cooling Load (Hot & Dry Climate)

Window Type	*Window Area % to floor area*	*Frame Type*	*U-Value of the Building*	*Energy Demand per unit area (MWh)*	*Maximum Cooling Load per unit area (kW) (24°C)*	*Maximum Heating Load per unit area (kW) (21°C)*
Single Glazed Clear (3 mm)	5%	Aluminium	1.628	0.289	0.0933 (May)	0.0176 (Jan.)
Single Glazed Clear (3 mm)	10%	Aluminium	1.716	0.324	0.100 (May)	0.0191 (Jan.)
Single Glazed Clear (3 mm)	20%	Aluminium	1.892	0.400	0.123 (May)	0.024 (Jan.)
Double Glazed Clear (3 mm)	5%	Wood/ Vinyl	1.559	0.267	0.089 (May)	0.017 (Jan.)
Double Glazed Clear (3 mm)	10%	Wood/ Vinyl	1.579	0.307	0.098 (May)	0.019 (Jan.)
Double Glazed Clear (3 mm)	20%	Wood/ Vinyl	1.618	0.341	0.113 (May)	0.021 (Jan.)
Double Glazed Low-E with Argon filling (3 mm)	5%	Wood/ Vinyl	1.548	0.254	0.084 (May)	0.016 (Jan.)
Double Glazed Low-E with Argon filling (3 mm)	10%	Wood/ Vinyl	1.557	0.282	0.093 (May)	0.018 (Jan.)

Window Type	*Window Area % to floor area*	*Frame Type*	*U-Value of the Building*	*Energy Demand per unit area (MWh)*	*Maximum Cooling Load per unit area (kW) (24°C)*	*Maximum Heating Load per unit area (kW) (21°C)*
Double Glazed Low-E with Argon filling (3 mm)	20%	Wood/ Vinyl	1.574	0.298	0.112 (May)	0.021 (Jan.)
Triple Glazed Low-E with Argon filling (3 mm)	5%	Wood/ Vinyl	1.542	0.246	0.076 (May)	0.015 (Jan.)
Triple Glazed Low-E with Argon filling (3 mm)	10%	Wood/ Vinyl	1.544	0.267	0.083 (May)	0.014 (Jan.)
Triple Glazed Low-E with Argon filling (3 mm)	20%	Wood/ Vinyl	1.548	0.291	0.089 (May)	0.011 (Jan.)

Table 7.5: Specific Energy Demand and Peak Heating & Cooling Load (Warm & Humid Climate)

Window Type	*Window Area % to floor area*	*Frame Type*	*U-Value of the Building*	*Energy Demand per unit area (MWh)*	*Maximum Cooling Load per unit area (kW) (24°C)*	*Maximum Heating Load per unit area (kW) (21°C)*
Single Glazed Clear (3 mm)	5%	Aluminium	1.626	0.29	0.0776 (June)	0.0055 (Jan.)
Single Glazed Clear (3 mm)	10%	Aluminium	1.713	0.38	0.0821 (May)	–
Single Glazed Clear (3 mm)	20%	Aluminium	1.887	0.418	0.090 (May)	–
Double Glazed Clear (3 mm)	5%	Wood/ Vinyl	1.562	0.267	0.071 (May)	0.005 (Jan.)
Double Glazed Clear (3 mm)	10%	Wood/ Vinyl	1.584	0.350	0.076 (May)	–
Double Glazed Clear (3 mm)	20%	Wood/ Vinyl	1.628	0.385	0.083 (May)	–

Window Type	*Window Area % to floor area*	*Frame Type*	*U-Value of the Building*	*Energy Demand per unit area (MWh)*	*Maximum Cooling Load per unit area (kW) (24°C)*	*Maximum Heating Load per unit area (kW) (21°C)*
Double Glazed Low-E with Argon filling (3 mm)	5%	Wood/ Vinyl	1.548	0.257	0.069 (May)	0.005 (Jan.)
Double Glazed Low-E with Argon filling (3 mm)	10%	Wood/ Vinyl	1.557	0.336	0.073 (May)	–
Double Glazed Low-E with Argon filling (3 mm)	20%	Wood/ Vinyl	1.574	0.369	0.080 (May)	-
Triple Glazed Low-E with Argon filling (3 mm)	5%	Wood/ Vinyl	1.542	0.245	0.066 (May)	0.005 (Jan.)
Triple Glazed Low-E with Argon filling (3 mm)	10%	Wood/ Vinyl	1.544	0.322	0.070 (May)	–
Triple Glazed Low-E with Argon filling (3 mm)	20%	Wood/ Vinyl	1.548	0.354	0.076 (May)	–

Table 7.6: Specific Energy Demand and Peak Heating & Cooling Load (Composite Climate)

Window Type	*Window Area % to floor area*	*Frame Type*	*U-Value of the Building*	*Energy Demand per unit area (MWh)*	*Maximum Cooling Load per unit area (kW) (24°C)*	*Maximum Heating Load per unit area (kW) (21°C)*
Single Glazed Clear (3 mm)	5%	Aluminium	1.625	0.282	0.0927 (June)	0.0277 (Jan)
Single Glazed Clear (3 mm)	10%	Aluminium	1.711	0.339	0.111 (June)	0.033 (Jan)
Single Glazed Clear (3 mm)	20%	Aluminium	1.883	0.376	0.123 (June)	0.037 (Jan)

Window Type	*Window Area % to floor area*	*Frame Type*	*U-Value of the Building*	*Energy Demand per unit area (MWh)*	*Maximum Cooling Load per unit area (kW) (24°C)*	*Maximum Heating Load per unit area (kW) (21°C)*
Double Glazed Clear (3 mm)	5%	Wood/ Vinyl	1.559	0.254	0.083 (June)	0.025 (Jan)
Double Glazed Clear (3 mm)	10%	Wood/ Vinyl	1.578	0.299	0.092 (June)	0.027 (Jan)
Double Glazed Clear (3 mm)	20%	Wood/ Vinyl	1.616	0.334	0.101 (June)	0.030 (Jan)
Double Glazed Low-E with Argon filling (3 mm)	5%	Wood/ Vinyl	1.548	0.242	0.079 (June)	0.024 (Jan)
Double Glazed Low-E with Argon filling (3 mm)	10%	Wood/ Vinyl	1.557	0.286	0.087 (June)	0.026 (Jan)
Double Glazed Low-E with Argon filling (3 mm)	20%	Wood/ Vinyl	1.574	0.323	0.096 (June)	0.029 (Jan)
Triple Glazed Low-E with Argon filling (3 mm)	5%	Wood/ Vinyl	1.541	0.234	0.077 (June)	0.023 (Jan)
Triple Glazed Low-E with Argon filling (3 mm)	10%	Wood/ Vinyl	1.543	0.268	0.084 (June)	0.025 (Jan)
Triple Glazed Low-E with Argon filling (3 mm)	20%	Wood/ Vinyl	1.547	0.307	0.091 (June)	0.028 (Jan)

Table 7.7: Specific Energy Demand and Peak Heating & Cooling Load (Moderate Climate)

Window Type	*Window Area % to floor area*	*Frame Type*	*U-Value of the Building*	*Energy Demand per unit area (MWh)*	*Maximum Cooling Load per unit area (kW) (24°C)*	*Maximum Heating Load per unit area (kW) (21°C)*
Single Glazed Clear (3 mm)	5%	Aluminium	1.616	0.132	0.058 (March)	0.0142 (Dec.)
Single Glazed Clear (3 mm)	10%	Aluminium	1.693	0.148	0.064 (March)	0.015 (Dec.)
Single Glazed Clear (3 mm)	20%	Aluminium	1.847	0.163	0.071 (March)	0.017 (Dec.)
Double Glazed Clear (3 mm)	5%	Wood/ Vinyl	1.557	0.124	0.054 (March)	0.013 (Dec.)
Double Glazed Clear (3 mm)	10%	Wood/ Vinyl	1.574	0.139	0.059 (March)	0.014 (Dec.)
Double Glazed Clear (3 mm)	20%	Wood/ Vinyl	1.608	0.145	0.061 (April)	0.0124 (Dec.)
Double Glazed Low-E with Argon filling (3 mm)	5%	Wood/ Vinyl	1.546	0.116	0.0475 (April)	0.0117 (Dec.)
Double Glazed Low-E with Argon filling (3 mm)	10%	Wood/ Vinyl	1.552	0.134	0.050 (April)	0.012 (Dec.)
Double Glazed Low-E with Argon filling (3 mm)	20%	Wood/ Vinyl	1.564	0.137	0.055 (March/ April)	0.013 (Dec.)
Triple Glazed Low-E with Argon filling (3 mm)	5%	Wood/ Vinyl	1.540	0.109	0.046 (April)	0.0112 (Dec.)
Triple Glazed Low-E with Argon filling (3 mm)	10%	Wood/ Vinyl	1.541	0.124	0.048 (April)	0.0118 (Dec.)
Triple Glazed Low-E with Argon filling (3 mm)	20%	Wood/ Vinyl	1.542	0.129	0.053 (March / April)	0.0125 (Dec.)

Table 7.8: Specific Energy Demand and Peak Heating & Cooling Load (Cold & Cloudy Climate)

Window Type	*Window Area % to floor area*	*Frame Type*	*U-Value of the Building*	*Energy Demand per unit area (MWh)*	*Maximum Cooling Load per unit area (kW) (24°C)*	*Maximum Heating Load per unit area (kW) (21°C)*
Single Glazed Clear (3 mm)	5%	Aluminium	1.610	0.153	0.0415 (June)	0.0659 (Jan.)
Single Glazed Clear (3 mm)	10%	Aluminium	1.681	0.151	0.044 (June)	0.069 (Jan.)
Single Glazed Clear (3 mm)	20%	Aluminium	1.823	0.157	0.049 (June)	0.066 (Jan.)
Double Glazed Clear (3 mm)	5%	Wood/ Vinyl	1.553	0.147	0.040 (June)	0.063 (Jan.)
Double Glazed Clear (3 mm)	10%	Wood/ Vinyl	1.566	0.145	0.042 (June)	0.066 (Jan.)
Double Glazed Clear (3 mm)	20%	Wood/ Vinyl	1.593	0.150	0.047 (June)	0.064 (Jan.)
Double Glazed Low-E with Argon filling (3 mm)	5%	Wood/ Vinyl	1.544	0.144	0.039 (June)	0.062 (Jan.)
Double Glazed Low-E with Argon filling (3 mm)	10%	Wood/ Vinyl	1.549	0.142	0.0415 (June)	0.065 (Jan.)
Double Glazed Low-E with Argon filling (3 mm)	20%	Wood/ Vinyl	1.559	0.147	0.047 (June)	0.062 (Jan.)
Triple Glazed Low-E with Argon filling (3 mm)	5%	Wood/ Vinyl	1.539	0.133	0.036 (June)	0.057 (Jan.)
Triple Glazed Low-E with Argon filling (3 mm)	10%	Wood/ Vinyl	1.541	0.140	0.038 (June)	0.060 (Jan.)
Triple Glazed Low-E with Argon filling (3 mm)	20%	Wood/ Vinyl	1.544	0.145	0.043 (June)	0.057 (Jan.)

Table 7.9: Specific Energy Demand and Peak Heating & Cooling Load (Cold & Sunny Climate)

Window Type	*Window Area % to floor area*	*Frame Type*	*U-Value of the Building*	*Energy Demand per unit area (MWh)*	*Maximum Cooling Load per unit area (kW) (24°C)*	*Maximum Heating Load per unit area (kW) (21°C)*
Single Glazed Clear (3 mm)	5%	Aluminium	1.613	0.508	-	0.135 (Jan.)
Single Glazed Clear (3 mm)	10%	Aluminium	1.687	0.530	-	0.158 (Jan.)
Single Glazed Clear (3 mm)	20%	Aluminium	1.835	0.600	-	0.177 (Jan.)
Double Glazed Clear (3 mm)	5%	Wood/ Vinyl	1.551	0.453	-	0.107 (Dec.)
Double Glazed Clear (3 mm)	10%	Wood/ Vinyl	1.563	0.472	-	0.122 (Dec.)
Double Glazed Clear (3 mm)	20%	Wood/ Vinyl	1.586	0.514	-	0.132 (Dec.)
Double Glazed Low-E with Argon filling (3 mm)	5%	Wood/ Vinyl	1.540	0.412	-	0.100 (Dec.)
Double Glazed Low-E with Argon filling (3 mm)	10%	Wood/ Vinyl	1.540	0.428	-	0.114 (Dec.)
Double Glazed Low-E with Argon filling (3 mm)	20%	Wood/ Vinyl	1.540	0.446	-	0.127 (Dec.)
Triple Glazed Low-E with Argon filling (3 mm)	5%	Wood/ Vinyl	1.538	0.384	-	0.092 (Dec.)
Triple Glazed Low-E with Argon filling (3 mm)	10%	Wood/ Vinyl	1.541	0.401	-	0.098 (Dec.)
Triple Glazed Low-E with Argon filling (3 mm)	20%	Wood/ Vinyl	1.544	0.431	-	0.103 (Dec.)

Analysis of the results presented in tables above reveals the following inferences that may be helpful in making selection of widow type and size in different climatic conditions:

Hot & Dry Climate: In this climate cooling is the dominant requirement for most of the time in a year. It has been found that the use of triple glazed energy efficient low-E window gives maximum energy savings even if the window area of the building is increased up to 20% of the floor area or beyond. The percentage of the possible savings is as shown in Table-7.10.

Table 7.10: Energy Saving in Hot and Dry Climate

Type of Window	*Percentage Window Area to the Floor Area*	*Energy Consumption & Percentage Saving (As compared to Single Glazed Window with same opening area) kWh*
Single Glazed (Base Case)	5%	289
Single Glazed (Base Case)	10%	324
Single Glazed (Base Case)	20%	400
Double glazed window	5%	267 (7%)
Double glazed window	10%	307 (5%)
Double glazed window	20%	341 (14.7%)
Double glazed window with Low-E coating and Argon fill	5 %	254 (12%)
Double glazed window with Low-E coating and Argon fill	10%	282 (13%)
Double glazed window with Low-E coating and Argon fill	20%	298 (25.5%)
Triple Glazed Energy Efficient window	5%	246 (14.9%)
Triple Glazed Energy Efficient window	10%	267 (17.5%)
Triple Glazed Energy Efficient window	20%	291 (27%)

Warm & Humid Climate: In Warm & Humid climates also, cooling is the primary requirement. The air conditioning is basically required to remove the excessive moisture from the air for most of the time in a year. It has been found that all types of glazing behave in a similar fashion in warm & humid climate.

Composite Climate: Composite climate is also a cooling dominated climate because for most of the time in a year the temperature is more than the human comfort temperature and during the rainy season the presence of excessive moisture in the air keeps the air-conditioners busy thus air conditioning is basically required for approximately 8 - 9 months in the year. During brief winter period of December and January, heating is also needed. A triple glazed low-E window and a double-glazed low-E window with vinyl frame are good for such climatic conditions.

Moderate Climate: Moderate climate is the best climate for living because neither too much of heating nor excessive cooling is required. Most of the time, just providing enough ventilation outlets in the building can reduce the cooling load. However, for air-conditioned buildings triple-glazed low-E windows perform marginally better than the double-glazed low-E windows with vinyl frame.

Cold & Cloudy Climate: Cold & cloudy climate basically needs both cooling & heating only moderately. Most of the time in a year the temperature is more or less comfortable and just for 3-4 months in a year, heating is required and for 2 months in a year marginal cooling is needed but that is also marginal. It has been found that all types of glazing except single glazing behave in a different pattern during heating and cooling seasons. The most beneficial will be the provision of more window area to trap the solar energy to reduce the heating load.

Cold & Sunny Climate: Cold & sunny climate is a heating dominated climate and thus for most of the time in a year, heating is prime requirement. It has been found that the use of triple glazed energy efficient window gives the maximum energy savings even if the window area of the building is increased up to 20 % of the floor area or beyond.

Table 7.11: Energy Saving Potential of Multiple Glazed Windows Over Single Glazing

Window Type	*%age Area*	*Specific Energy Demand kWh/m²-a [Percentage saving as compared to the single glazing]*				
		Warm & Humid	*Composite*	*Moderate*	*Cold & Cloudy*	*Cold & Sunny*
Double Glazed	10%	350 [7.8]	299 [11.7]	139 [6.1]	145 [3.9]	472 [9.6]
	20%	385 [7.8]	334 [11.1]	145 [11]	150 [4.4]	514 [10.9]
Double Low-E with Argon	10%	336 [11.5]	286 [15.6]	134 [9.4]	142 [5.9]	428 [19.2]
	20%	369 [11.7]	323 [14.1]	137 [15.9]	147 [6.3]	446 [25.6]
Triple Glazed Energy Efficient Windows	10%	322 [15.3]	268 [20.9]	124 [16.2]	140 [7.8]	401 [24.3]
	20%	354 [15.3]	307 [18.3]	129 [20.8]	145 [7.6]	431 [28.1]

+ The %age area is window area (percent of floor area)

7.5.3 Optimization of Window Area

Based on detailed simulations, the optimized window area with respect to different window orientation is given in Table 7.12.

The lighting, heating, cooling and the total specific energy consumption in kWh/m^2 of the floor area are also given in Table-7.12.

Table 7.12: Optimum orientation and the corresponding specific energy consumption (kWh/m² /a)

Window Type	*Orientation*	*%age Window Area*	*Lighting Energy*	*Cooling Energy*	*Heating Energy*	*Total Energy*
						Hot & Dry Climate
Double Glazed	South	5	81.5	94.881	9.56	185.941
Double Glazed Low-E	South	5	82.9	88.391	9.42	180.711
Triple Glazed	South	7.5	82.4	77.647	8.97	169.017
						Warm & Humid Climate
Double Glazed	South	5	82.04	24.856	-	106.896
Double Glazed Low-E	North	7.5	83.57	22.396	-	105.966
Triple Glazed	North	12.5	84.12	18.653	-	102.773
						Composite Climate
Double Glazed	South	12.5	60.87	76.125	14.25	143.545
Double Glazed Low-E	South	15	60.71	62.249	11.25	134.209
Triple Glazed	South	15	61.34	52.267	10.51	124.117
						Moderate Climate
Double Glazed	North	25	36.92	23.688	3.563	64.171
Double Glazed Low-E	North	27.5	36.87	22.467	3.025	62.362
Triple Glazed	North	27.5	37.01	19.076	2.941	59.027
						Cold & Cloudy Climate
Double Glazed	South	17.5	55.08	9.813	94.75	159.643
Double Glazed Low-E	South	17.5	57.48	7.858	87.92	153.258
Triple Glazed	South	22.5	56.47	6.411	67.37	130.251
						Cold & Sunny Climate
Double Glazed	South	42.5	31.52	12.125	325.188	367.833
Double Glazed Low-E	South	42.5	33.18	10.954	297.143	341.277
Triple Glazed	South	42.5	34.56	8.995	247.27	290.825

7.6 ECBC REQUIREMENTS AND COMPLIANCE

As per the requirements under Energy Conservation Building Code of India, U-factors and SHGC shall be determined for the overall fenestration product (including the sash and frame) in accordance with ISO-15099, by an accredited independent laboratory, and labeled and certified by the manufacturer or other responsible party. U-factors for sloped glazing and skylights shall be determined at a slope of 20 degrees above the horizontal.

As exceptions Shading coefficient (SC) of the center glass alone multiplied by 0.86 is an acceptable alternate for compliance with the SHGC requirements for the overall fenestration area. Solar heat gain coefficient (SHGC) of the glass alone is an acceptable alternate for compliance with the SHGC requirements for the overall fenestration product.

Air leakage for glazed swinging entrance doors and revolving doors shall not exceed 5.0 l/s-m^2. Air leakage for other fenestration and doors shall not exceed 2.0 l/s-m^2.

Vertical fenestration shall comply with the maximum area weighted U-factor and maximum area weighted SHGC requirements of Table 7.13. Vertical fenestration area is limited to a maximum of 40% of the gross wall area for the prescriptive requirement.

Table 7.13: Vertical fenestration U-factor and SHGC requirements (U-factor in W/m^2 ^{0}C)

Climate	Maximum U-factor	Maximum SHGC (WWR* = 40%)	Maximum SHGC 40%< WWR* < = 60%
Composite	3.3	0.25	0.20
Hot and Dry	3.3	0.25	0.20
Warm and Humid	3.3	0.25	0.20
Moderate	6.9	0.40	0.30
Cold	3.3	0.51	0.51

* WWR = Window to Wall Ratio

Exception to vertical fenestration: Overhangs and/or side fins may be applied in determining the SHGC for the proposed design. An adjusted SHGC, accounting for overhangs and/or sidefins, is calculated by multiplying the SHGC of the unshaded fenestration product times a multiplication (M) factor. If this exception is applied, a separate M Factor shall be determined for each orientation and unique shading condition.

Table 7.14: SHGC "M" factor adjustments for overhangs and fins

		Overhang "M" Factors for 4 Projection Factors				Vertical Fin "M" Factors for 4 Projection Factors				Overhang+Fin "M" Factors for 4 Projection Factors			
Project Location	Orientation	0.25-0.49	-0.50 - 0.74	0.75 - 0.99	1.00 +	0.25 - 0.49	0.50 - 0.74	0.75 - 0.99	1.00 +	0.25 - 0.49	0.50 - 0.74	0.75 - 0.99	1.00 +
North latitude 15° or greater	N	.88	.80	.76	.73	.74	.67	.58	.52	.64	.51	.39	.31
	E/W	.79	.65	.56	.50	.80	.72	.65	.60	.60	.39	.24	.16
	S	.79	.64	.52	.43	.79	.69	.60	.56	.60	.33	.10	.02
Less than 15° North latitude	N	.83	.74	.69	.66	.73	.65	.57	.50	.59	.44	.32	.23
	E/W	.80	.67	.59	.53	.80	.72	.63	.58	.61	.41	.26	.16
	S	.78	.62	.55	.50	.74	.65	.57	.50	.53	.30	.12	.04

Exception to SHGC Requirements: Vertical Fenestration areas located more than 2.2 m (7 ft) above the level of the floor are exempt from the SHGC requirement in Table 7.14, if the following conditions are complied with:

- Total Effective Aperture: The total Effective Aperture for the elevation is less than 0.25, including all fenestration areas greater than 1.0 m (3 ft) above the floor level; and,
- An interior light shelf is provided at the bottom of this fenestration area, with an interior projection factor (PF) not less than:

  (i) 1.0 for E-W, SE, SW, NE, and NW orientations

  (ii) 0.5 for S orientation, and

  (iii) 0.35 for N orientation when latitude is < 23 degrees.

The "M" multiplication factor can also be calculated using equation given below. If the equation is used, a separate calculation shall be made for each orientation and unique shading condition.

$M = a.\ PF^2 + b.PF + 1$

PF here is projection factor. Projection factor for overhang is defined as the ratio of the horizontal depth of the external shading projection divided by the sum of the height of the fenestration and the distance from the top of the fenestration to the bottom of the farthest point of the external shading projection, in consistent units. Projection factor for fin is defined as the ratio of the horizontal depth of the external shading projection divided by the distance from the window jamb to the farthest point of the external shading projection, in consistent units.

Table 7.15: Coefficients for calculating M factor for overhangs and fins

Device	Coefficient	North	South	East/West
Overhangs	A	0.16	0.21	0.10
	B	-0.61	-0.83	-0.58
Side Fins	A	0.23	0.12	0.14
	B	-0.74	-0.59	-0.52

Minimum Visible Transmission (VT) of Glazing for Vertical Fenestration

To permit the use of available day lighting in place of electric lighting, glazing products used in offices, banks, libraries, classrooms with predominant daytime usage, must have the minimum visual transmittance (VT), defined as function of WWR, where Effective Aperture > 0.1, equal to or greater than the Minimum VT requirements of Table 7.16. The table also indicates recommended VT ranges for daylight applications in such spaces having different Window to Wall Ratio (WWR).

Table 7.16: Minimum Visible Transmittance requirements for fenestration

WWR	Minimum VT
0 - 0.3	0.27
0.31-0.4	0.20
0.41-0.5	0.16
0.51-0.6	0.13
0.61-0.7	0.11

Skylights

Skylights shall comply with the maximum U-factor and maximum SHGC requirements of Table-7.17 Skylight area is limited to a maximum of 5% of the gross roof area for the prescriptive requirement.

Table 7.17: Skylight U-factor and SHGC Requirements (U-factor in W/m2-°C)

	Maximum U-factor		Maximum SHGC	
Climate	With Curb	w/o Curb	0-2% SRR	2.1-5% SRR
Composite	11.24	7.717	0.40	0.25
Hot and Dry	11.24	7.717	0.40	0.25
Warm and Humid	11.24	7.717	0.40	0.25
Moderate	11.24	7.717	0.61	0.4
Cold	11.24	7.717	0.61	0.4

SRR = Skylight roof ratio which is the ratio of the total skylight area of the roof, measured to the outside of the frame, to the gross exterior roof.

Rated v/s Non-rated fenestration

All fenestration with U-factors, SHGC, or visible light transmittance determined, certified, and labeled in accordance ISO 15099 shall be assigned those values.

Unrated Vertical Fenestration. Unlabeled vertical fenestration, both operable and fixed, shall be assigned the U-factors, SHGCs, and visible light transmittance as shown in Table 7.19.

Unrated sloped glazing and skylights, both operable and fixed, shall be assigned the SHGCs and visible light transmittances in Table 7.17. To determine the default U-factor for unrated sloped glazing and skylights without a curb, multiply the values in Table 7.18 by 1.2. To determine the default U-factor for unrated skylights on a curb, multiply the values in Table 7.18 by 1.6.

Table 7.18: Defaults for unrated fenestration (overall assembly including sash and frame)

		Clear Glass			Tinted Glass		
Frame Type	Glazing Type	U-Factor (W/M^2–°C)	SHGC	VLT	U-Factor (W/M^2–°C)	SHGC	VLT
All frame types	Single Glazing	7.1	0.82	0.76	7.1	0.70	0.58
Wood, vinyl, or fiberglass frame	Double Glazing	3.3	0.59	0.64	3.4	0.42	0.39
Metal and other frame type	Double Glazing	5.1	0.68	0.66	5.1	0.50	0.40

Due to higher cost or availability, in case, it is difficult to comply with the requirements of ECBC for windows/fenestration, the option of 'trade-off' offers opportunity to still comply with the code by adopting measures in other areas that are even better than the code requirements. The code provided flexibility under the 'Building Envelope Trade-off Option' to pick and drop options as per their suitability provided high U-value etc. in one building component (e.g. roof having lower U-value than required) are enough to compensate for higher U-value for other component (say use of single glazed window in place of double glazed). This option has to be exercised through calculating the 'Energy Performance Factor' (EPR) for individual building components and the whole building. This method has been explained in ECBC 2007.

8

Lighting Techniques*

8.1 INTRODUCTION

In artificial lighting, the light source itself is under the designer's (user's) control. In daylighting, the source (sun and sky) is given. Thus if, control is necessary, it must be in transmission and distribution. Artificial lighting is practically independent of location and the climate. Daylighting, however, strongly depends on the externally given conditions and its control is only possible by a suitable building design.

The ultimate source of daylight is the sun, from which, we also receive a large amount of thermal radiation together with the light. During bright sunshine, the illumination is around 100 klux (100000 lux) and the intensity of thermal radiation is likely to be about 1 kW/m^2. In climates, where the heat balance is negative, i.e. overheating is not likely; thermal considerations will rarely restrict the amount of daylight to be admitted.

In the tropics, however, the situation is not quite as simple. Here the admission of an abundant quantity of daylight will be accompanied by radiant heat, which is probably excessive. Thus the 'filter' function of the envelope will be even more important. We must attempt to exclude radiant heat, whilst admitting daylight. In some impossible situations, thermal considerations will restrict the amount of light, which can be admitted. This means that there must be a fundamental difference in approach to daylighting design.

It is however, necessary to review some of the basic principles, before the methods of daylighting design are described.

8.2 THE LUMINOUS ENVIRONMENT: BASIC PRINCIPLES

The lighting inside a building is an extremely important issue. One can not design a building properly without lighting considerations such as daylight illumination, glare, visual contrast and comfort, privacy and view. The eye is stimulated by light reflected from objects, a prerequisite for being able to see (1 foot-candle= 10.764 lux).

8.2.1 The nature of light

What we perceive as light, is a narrow wavelength band of electromagnetic radiation from about 380 to 780 nm (1 nanometre = 10^{-9}m or 10^{-3} ìm) (Fig. 8.1). This energy radiation shows dual characteristics i.e.; it consists of energy particles-photons, but also shows transverse wave motion properties. The wavelength determines its colour (Fig. 8.2). Light containing all visible waves is

* Base document for this Chapter are Bansal N.K. and Minke G (1995), Climatic Zones and Rural Housing in India, Research Centre, Juelich, Germany and Watson D. (1993), The Energy Design Handbook, American Institute of Architects, Washington D.C.

perceived as white. The human eye's sensitivity varies with the wavelength and it is maximum at around 550 nm (yellow) as shown in Fig 8.2.

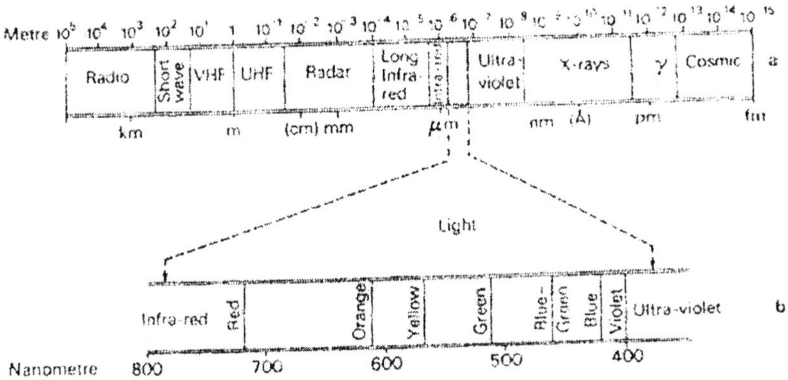

Fig. 8.1: Radiation spectrum

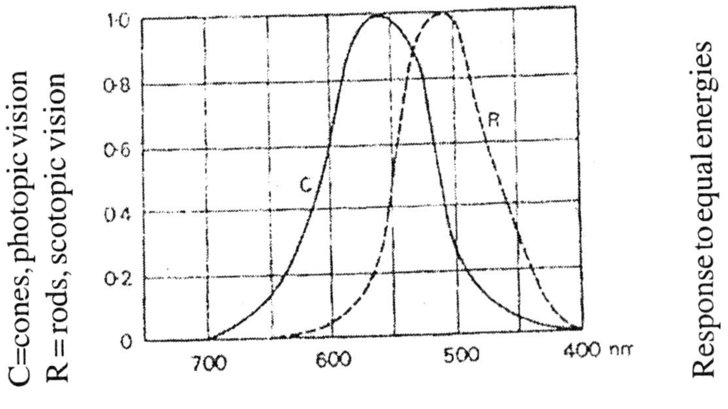

Fig. 8.2: Spectral sensitivity of the eye

In a homogenous medium, light travels along a straight path. Its velocity is about $3x10^8$m/s. More precisely, it has the following values in different mediums as:

vacuum	299792 $x10^3$ m/s
air	299724 $x10^3$ m/s
water	224915 $x10^3$ m/s
glass	198223 $x10^3$ m/s

8.2.2 Transmission

Some materials on exposure to light transmit a large part of it, so these are referred to as 'transparent' materials. Others, the opaque materials, block the passage of light. Behind an opaque object, there will be no light (no direct light), i.e. it will cast a shadow. The term 'translucent' is applied to such materials, which transmit a part of the incident light, but break its straight passage. These scatter light in all directions thus creating diffuse light. Light incident on an object can be distributed in three different ways i.e., reflected, absorbed and transmitted. Some important properties of the object and its material are described by the proportions of these three components i.e., reflectance (r) absorbance (a) and transmittance (t).

In all cases, $r+a+t = 1$ and, in case of opaque objects: $t = 0$, thus $r+a = 1$

8.2.3 Reflection

If, parallel rays of incident light remain parallel after reflection from a surface, the surface is a plane mirror. Thus we speak of specular reflection (Fig. 8.3 a). The rules of geometrical optics apply to such surfaces i.e.; the angle of reflection is the same as the angle of incidence. From a convex mirror, the reflected rays will be divergent and from a concave mirror, they will be convergent. Light reflected from a matt surface will be diffused (Fig. 8. 3 d).

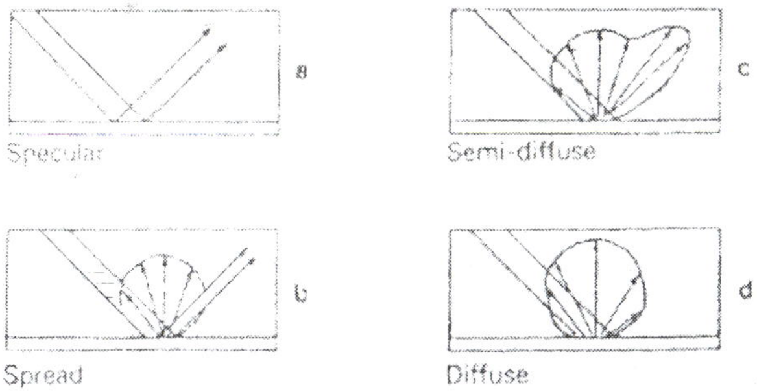

Fig. 8.3: Types of reflection

Most often, a mixture of the two kinds of reflections will occur, termed as 'semi-diffuse' or 'spread' reflection, depending on the relative magnitude of the two components (Figs. 8.3 b and 8.3 c). Some materials have practically the same reflectance for all wavelengths of light. These do not change the wavelength composition of light after reflection. Surfaces with such neutral reflection properties will be seen in white light as:

white	if r is above 0.75
grey	if r is between 0.05 and 0.75
black	if r is below 0.05.

Other materials are selective in their reflectance. They may absorb certain wave- lengths of the incident light; thus the remainder reflected will show a colour effect. Colour pigments are such selective absorbers, that they owe their colour to a subtractive process. In mixing coloured pigments, the absorptions are additive and the reflections will be subtractive, for example:

yellow paint	absorbs blue	reflects red, yellow, green
blue paint	absorbs red and yellow	reflects blue and green
a mixture of the two	absorbs blue, red and yellow	reflects only the green

A mixture of all kinds of pigments will be black, as it will absorb all the wavelengths. No mixture of pigments can give white, as there will always be some absorption in certain wavelengths.

8.3 PHOTOMETRIC QUANTITIES

The intensity of a light source (symbol: I) is measured in units of *candela* (cd). This is a basic assumed and agreed unit in the Systeme International (defined as the intensity of a 1/60 cm^2 uniformly emitting black body radiator at the melting point temperature of platinum, with all other units derived from this.

The flux (or flow) of light (symbol: F) is measured in lumens (lm). One lumen is the flow of light emitted by a unit intensity (1-cd) point source, within a unit solid angle. As the surface of a sphere subtends at its centre 4ð (= 12.56) units of solid angle, a 1 cd point source will emit a total of 12.56 lm in all directions.

Illumination (symbol, E) is measured as the amount of flux falling on unit area, i.e. lm/m^2 which is the lux- the unit of illumination in the Systeme International.

Luminance (symbol: *L)* is the measure of brightness of a surface. Units for its measurement can be derived in the following two ways:

(a) if, a light source of 1 cd intensity has a surface area of 1 m^2 (1 cd is distributed over 1 m^2), its luminance is 1 cd/m^2. This is the official SI unit.

(b) if, a completely reflecting and diffusing surface (r = 1.00) has an illumination of 1 lux, its luminance is 1 asb (apostilb)

The two units measure the same quantity and are directly convertible i.e.,

1 cd/m^2=3.14 asb.

8.3.1 Illumination

Illumination from a point source reduces with the square of the distance. A source of 1 candela emits a total flux of 4ðl lumens. At a distance (d), this flux will be distributed over a sphere of radius d, i.e. a surface of 4ðd^2. Thus the illumination at a distance d is.

E= 4ðl/4ðd^2= 1/d^2

This is known as the inverse square law and is applicable, when the illuminated plane is normal (perpendicular) to the direction of light, i.e., when the angle of incidence $\hat{a}=0^0$. However, when the plane is tilted, the same flux is distributed over a larger area. Thus the illumination is reduced. The reduction is proportionate to the cosine of the angle of incidence:

$E_{\hat{a}}=E_n \times \cos\hat{a}$

where E_n = illumination on a normal plane

$E_{\hat{a}}$ = illumination on a plane tilted by $\hat{a}$ degrees

$\hat{a}$ = angle of incidence

Illumination of a surface from several sources will be the simple sum of the component illuminations:

$E = E_1+E_2+E_3 ...$

Illumination from a linear source of infinite length reduces in direct proportion to the distance (and not the square of distance). Also, from an infinitely large luminous surface, (e.g. the sky), the illumination does not vary with the distance.

8.3.2 Scalar illumination

Lighting conditions are usually described, measured or specified in terms of illumination on a given plane. Most often, it is the horizontal working plane (taken desk or bench height), but possibly a vertical or inclined plane. In other words, we usually speak of planar illumination.

This however, does not describe all the luminous qualities of a space. Even if, the illumination on a horizontal plane is adequate, the vertical surfaces may remain dark. Further if, the visual task is other than two-dimensional, qualities other than the planar illumination must be considered.

Scalar illumination (or mean spherical illumination) is the average illumination received on the surface of a small sphere from all directions. It is denoted by E_s and measured in lux. It measures the total quantity of light present regardless of its direction.

The illumination vector is a composite quantity having both magnitude and direction. Its magnitude is the maximum difference in illumination between two diametrically opposed points on the surface of a small sphere (denoted $\ddot{A}E_{max}$ and measured in lux).

This direction is defined in terms of two angles, one horizontal (from a reference direction) and one vertical (from a horizontal up). The vector/scalar ratio is a measure of the directionality of light and a good indicator of its modeling qualities. When $\ddot{A}E_{max}/E_s= 4$, we have a completely mono-directional light. In practice, this value is always less than 4. A value of 0 would indicate a perfectly diffuse omni-directional lighting.

8.3.3 Visual efficiency

The purpose of lighting is two-fold:

1. practical-to facilitate the performance of a visual task and ensure visual comfort.

2. artistic (for lack of a better term)-to create certain emotional effects.

For practical purposes, we need to measure visual efficiency, as this strongly depends on lighting. It can be measured on its three facets:

1. **Visual acuity** or sharpness of vision, measured as the reciprocal of the visual angle ñ (expressed in minutes) subtended at the eye by the least perceptible detail. For example, if, the least perceptible detail subtends an angle of 2' the acuity will be: 1/ ñ=1/2=0.5
2. **Contrast Sensitivity (CS)**, measured as the ratio of the least perceptible luminance difference ($L_2 - L_1$) to the lower of the two luminances:

   CS= $(L_2 - L_1) \times 100\ (\%)/L_1$
3. **Visual performance**. i.e. the time required for seeing, expressed possibly as the number of characters perceived per second or on any comparative scale.

All the three facets, consequently visual efficiency itself depends on the level of illumination, as shown by the graphs in Fig. 8.4.

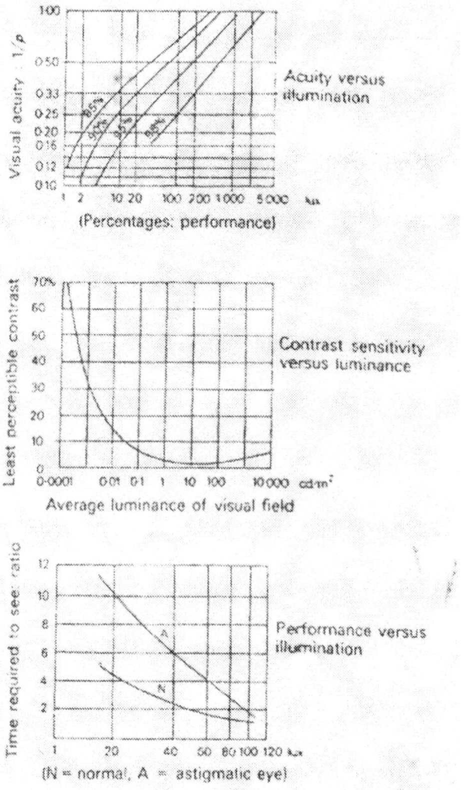

Fig. 8.4: Visual efficiency

8.3.4 Illumination quantity

The eye responds to a range of illumination levels extending over a million orders of magnitude:

from 0.1 lux (full moonlit night)

to 100000 lux (bright sunshine)

For practical situations and various activities (thus various visual tasks), detailed illumination requirements are given in various publications. The following values (in lux) can provide some general guidance:

casual seeing	100 lux
ordinary tasks, medium detail (e.g. wood machining, general office work)	400
severe, prolonged tasks (e.g. fine assembly, silk weaving)	900
exceptionally severe tasks (e.g. watch making)	2000-3000

8.3.5 The visual field

With stationary head and eyes, the visual field of an average person extends to 180^0 horizontally and 120° vertically. Within this, the central field is limited to 2° and the immediate background extends to about 40°. Visual comfort and efficiency can be ensured by the control of luminance distribution within the visual field,

The luminance ratios should be:

central field: background : environment

5: 2 : 1

but 10 : 3 : 1 should in no case be exceeded, as this may create glare.

The eye will adjust itself to the average luminance of the visual field (adaptation). With large contrasts, this may lead to loss of seeing the less luminous areas (under-exposure) and discomfort caused by the bright areas (over-exposure). Glare may also be caused by a saturation effect, even without any contrast, when the average luminance exceeds about 25000 cd/m^2 (80,000 asb). The magnitude of glare can be indicated by the terms discomfort glare (in a less severe case) and disability glare (in a severe situation).

8.3.6 Illumination quality

In a lighting design, the designer must ensure light, which is both adequate and suitable for the visual task. Suitability in this context would mean the following qualities:

a colour of light

b colour rendering

c light distribution (direct or diffuse; modeling)

d freedom from glare

e luminance distribution (consideration of surface qualities together with the lighting of these surfaces)

The first two depend on the light source subject to choice in electric lighting, but given in daylighting. Distribution in electric lighting depends on the fittings and their position. In daylighting, it depends on windows and reflective surfaces. In daylighting, the problem of glare is normally handled in qualitative terms only, but in electric lighting design, the glare index concept gives a quantitative evaluation method.

8.4 CLIMATE AND LIGHT

In high latitude moderate climates, where the sky is typically overcast, the whole of the sky hemisphere acts as a light source. Direct sunlight may occur, but can not be relied on. The sky itself has a luminance sufficiently high to provide lighting in normal rooms. On the basis of many observations, the Commission Internationale de l'Eclairage (CIE) has established the luminance distribution of a typical overcast sky, as varying according to the function:

$$L_{á} = L_{h} \times (1 + 2 \sin á)$$

where $L_{á}$ = luminance at á altitude angle ,

L_{h} = luminance at the horizon.

Thus the zenith luminance $(L_{z}) = 3L_{h}$.

Hot dry climates are characterized by strong direct sunlight from the cloudless skies. Direct sunlight is usually excluded from buildings for thermal reasons. The sky is typically of a deep blue colour and its luminance may be as low as 1700 cd/m^2-not enough to ensure adequate daylighting. This clear sky usually has the highest luminance near the horizon and the lowest luminance at right angles to the sun. The bare, dry, sunlit ground and light coloured walls of other buildings will reflect much light, which will be the main source of indoor daylighting. It may, however, also be the source of glare, when these strongly lit light surfaces are within the visual field. Light dust suspended in the air may create a haze and increase the apparent sky brightness up to 10000 cd/m^2, but the frequent heavy dust and sandstorms can reduce it to less than 850cd/m^2.

In warm humid climates, the sky is typically overcast with a luminance often exceeding 7000 cd/m^2. The proportion of diffused or skylight is predominant and the very bright sky viewed from a moderately lit room can cause discomfort glare. In composite climates, wide variations occur in natural lighting between the overcast and clear sky conditions.

8.4.1 Daylight in hot-dry climates

Direct sunlight must be excluded from the buildings partly for thermal reasons and partly, as it would unavoidably create glare. As windows in this climate tend to be small, not much sky would be visible from any point indoors. Thus, especially with low luminance blue skies, the sky component would be insufficient. On the other hand, luminance of the sky near the horizon is greater and it may be a source of glare if, not screened. Both the ground and the external surfaces of other buildings are usually light coloured: in the strong sunshine, these may also create glare (Fig. 8.5). Therefore, externally reflected light can only be used, provided sufficient care is taken to avoid glare.

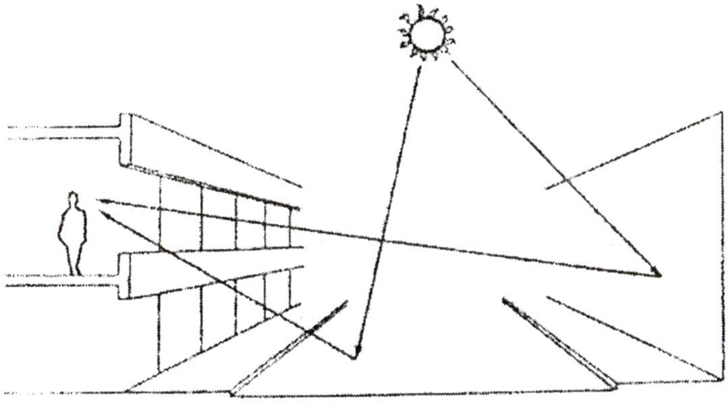

Fig. 8.5:Glare from sunlit surfaces

Internally reflected light would be the most convenient form of daylighting. One suitable arrangement is a high level window (with sill above eye-level), which would admit reflected light to the ceiling. If, the ceiling is white, this method would ensure adequate and well-diffused interior lighting through a comparatively small window (Fig. 8.6).

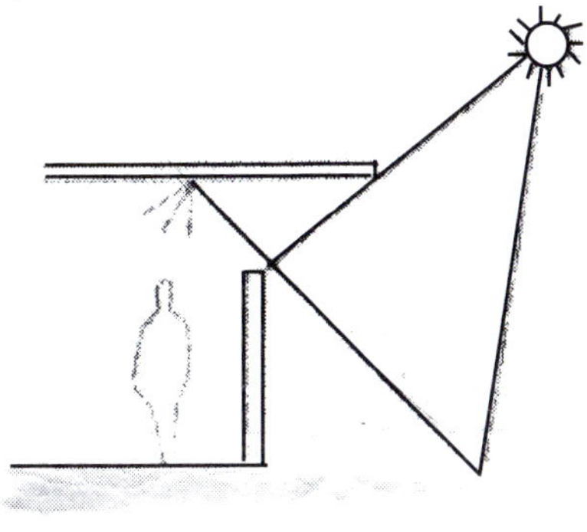

Fig. 8.6 : Well diffused interior lighting through a small window

8.4.2 Daylighting in the tropics

The above method ensures adequate daylight even with a very low level of outdoor lighting. Thus most of the time, the specified illumination levels will be exceeded. Physically-physiologically, this is advantageous (visual efficiency is improved) and in temperate climates, the psychological effect of such over-lighting is likely to be an increased sense of well being.

By contrast in warm climates, both the physical and the psychological effects would be disadvantageous. Due to the accompanying thermal radiation, over-lighting would mean overheating. This way, overheating would cause much greater discomfort than under lighting. Furthermore, a slightly under-lit room would be psychologically more acceptable, as light is mentally associated with warmth and reduced lighting with coolness. This, however, requires great skill in handling, partly to ensure an adequate illumination for the necessary visual efficiency and partly to avoid creating a gloomy effect. Visual gloominess is a subjective effect, created by an excessive contrast between the very bright outdoors and the dimly lit interior. It can be strengthened by factors affecting the other sense: dampness, stale air, smells and even by untidiness.

The tasks and problems of daylighting in tropical climates can be summarised as follows:

- to provide adequate daylight, even if, the windows are protected by louvers or grilles for thermal reasons.
- to exclude from the visual field excessively bright (light coloured, sunlit etc.) surfaces, which would cause glare.

If, shading devices are used, sunlit reflective surfaces of these devices can themselves become sources of glare. Hence, these surfaces should either be non-reflective, or positioned beyond being directly visible. Low level windows are acceptable if, they open onto a shaded and planted courtyard. When a sunlit view through a window is unavoidable, the strong luminance contrast between the view and the window surround can be reduced by:

- painting the adjacent wall by a light colour
- painting the inside of window frames white
- as the walls tend to be thick in this climate, the deep reveals should be splayed (and light coloured) to provide contrast grading
- other openings may be placed in opposite or flanking walls, to throw some light onto the wall surrounding the window

One solution for the avoidance of an excessively bright view is the use of a vertical strip-window at the corner of the room (Fig. 8.7). This would throw light onto the wall surface (as a wash) thus providing a larger apparent source of a lesser luminance.

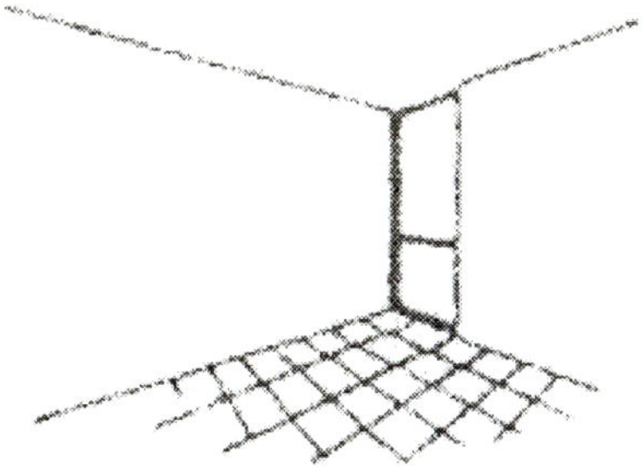

Fig. 8.7: A corner window

8.4.3 Daylight considerations in warm humid climates

Buildings in these climates are typically of lightweight construction, with large openings to ensure cross-ventilation and air movement and usually with wide over-hanging eaves or other shading devices. Direct sunlight is excluded for thermal reasons. The sky is bright, could provide sufficient light, but its high luminance would also cause glare. For this reason, view of the sky should be screened by shading devices or plants. As, however, the sky luminance is much less near the horizon than at higher altitude angles, a view of the sky up to about 15^0 from the horizon may be permissible.

The foregoing discussion establishes rather specific requirements for the design of shading devices. The criteria, far more stringent than just the exclusion of sunlight, can be summarised as follows:

- permit view of sky and ground near the horizon only, within about $\pm 15^0$ (up and down)
- exclude view of bright ground and sunlit blade or louver surfaces
- daylight is to be reflected from ground and blades up to the ceiling, which itself should be of a light colour

8.5 DAYLIGHT DESIGN

The daylight design depends upon a number of factors, which are discussed in various sections.

8.5.1 Site

Before beginning to design, the designer needs to examine the site for features that will help in using daylight. To ensure that the building is well integrated with the site and in that sense, responsive to its context, the designer should identify these features: Fig. 8.8 shows the ceiling reflected ground light.

- Vegetation that will filter sunlight, reduce glare or otherwise make sunlight usable for visual tasks in the building.

- Built features of the site or adjacent to the site that will increase or decrease the introduction of daylight into the building, unless they can be minimized.
- By manipulating trees, shrubs, vines and ground surfaces, a designer can control the quality and quantity of daylight entering a building and better integrate the building with its site. These elements of the site are probably some of the first things, a designer should think about, as he seeks a design solution.
- Vegetation filters daylight and thus eliminates glare and excessive thermal gain if, it is properly used.
- Ground surfaces can be used to reflect daylight into the building, once their approximate reflectivity has been calculated by following the accompanying chart.

High reflective surfaces near the site (such as buildings with reflective surfaces) can create unwanted glare.

Fig. 8.8: Ceiling reflected ground light

Table 8.1: Reflectance Values of Ground Surfaces

Ground Surfaces	%
Grass fields, lawns	6
Snow, tresh	74
Snow, old	64
Wild fields	25
Concrete	55
Macadam	18
Gravel	3
Bare earth	7

- Adjacent buildings on the east, west and north can be used to reflect sun and skylight into the building.
- Daylight reflected off the ground or other surfaces can be filtered by placing plants to block light, either before it strikes the reflecting surface or after it is reflected.

8.5.2 Building Form

If daylighting were the designers sole objective, it would be best to increase daylighting by extending the perimeter of the building. Often, however, a designer must also satisfy a competing need for reduced heat gain and heat loss through glazing. Figs. 8.9 a-e show various building forms.

In manipulating the building's overall form and geometry, the designer controls the aesthetic effect of daylight in the building. When the building's form has been chosen, the quantity of daylight entering can be roughly approximated. Precise calculations are made by manipulating controls at the building envelope once the overall form has been achieved.

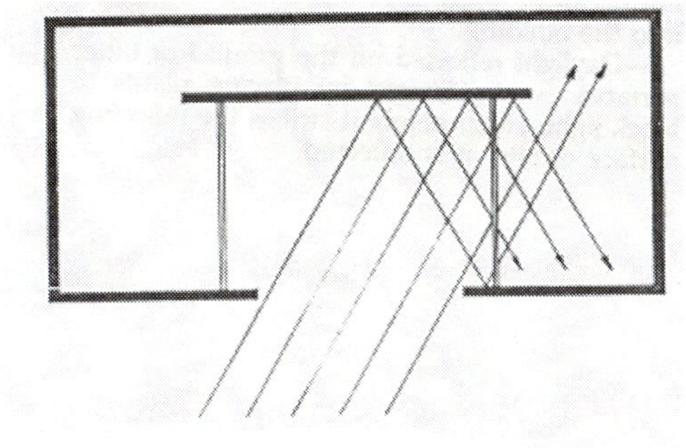

Figure 8.9(a): Plan with Exterior alcove for daylighting

- Clerestories, saw tooth roofs and light wells can be used to bring light in high and let it wash down the walls. Bringing daylight obliquely into a room in this way creates a soft ambience to the space.
- Ceiling height and window height can be raised in the room to bring in more daylight.
- Room depth can be reduced to get greater illumination towards the rear of a room.
- Daylight controls (light wells with shading, eggcrate diffusers, louvers, diffuser shades) can be used to get light from any orientation as soft and diffuse as north light.

Interior courtyards and open light wells can be used to bring light into the interior of buildings with deep plans; a designer can use these to enhance view and natural ventilation

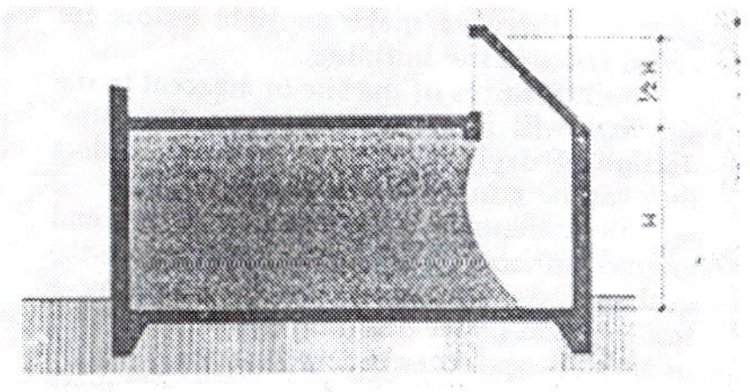

Figure 8.9(b): Effective proportions for clerestory wall wash using daylighting

- The perimeter of the building can be extended to gain increased exposure for daylighting.
- When overcast skies predominate during occupied periods, room depth should be limited to 2.5 times window height if, continuous or nearly continuous windows are used.

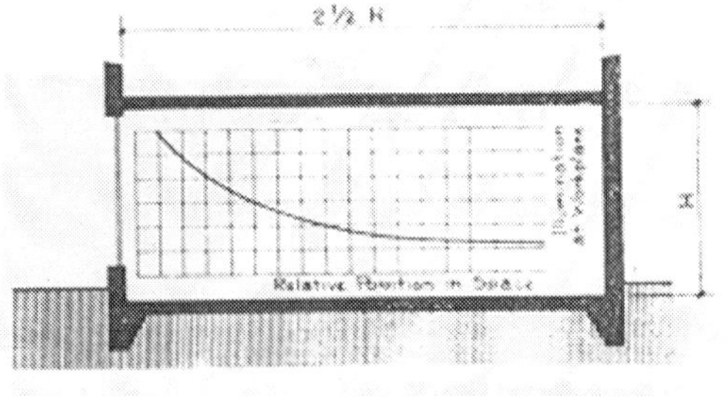

Figure 8.9(c): Relationship of room depth to window height for overcast sky conditions

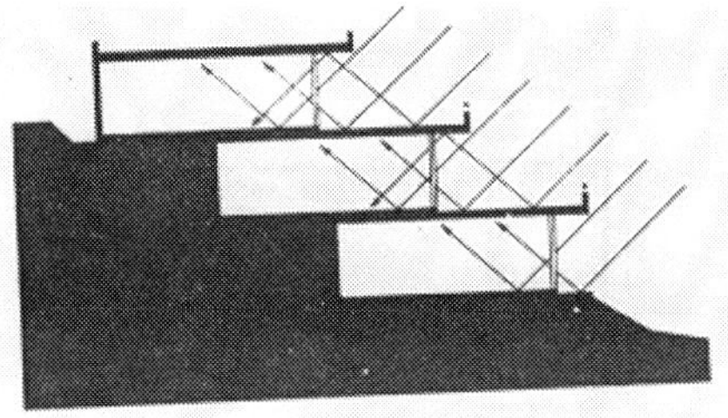

Figure 8.9(d): Stepped roof with reflective surfaces

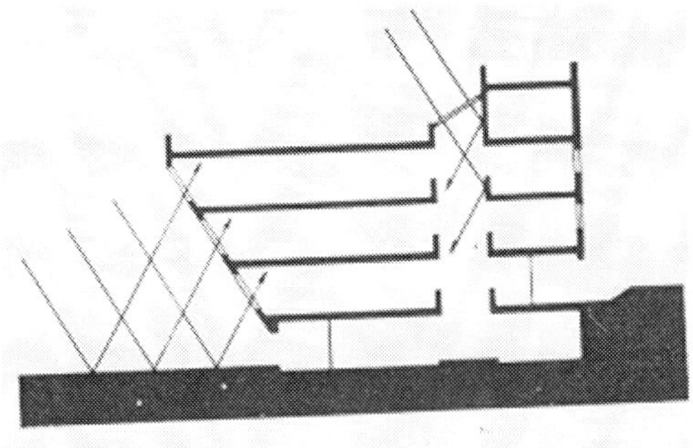

Figure 8.9(e): Stepped façade with reflective surfaces

- When clear skies predominate during occupied periods, depth should be limited to 3.5 times window height, if, continuous or nearly continuous windows are used.
- Enclosed atria can be used to bring in light to a protected central core, from which spaces within the building can gather light. Atria effectively increase the building perimeter.
- Windows can be located close to the ceiling or side walls to avoid strong brightness ratios.
- High reflectance ceilings and walls can help light penetrate deep into room.

8.5.3 Windows

Windows, clerestories and skylights transmit sunlight into the building, and it is here, at the building's envelope that the problems of overheating and glare are most easily solved by appropriate glazing and lighting controls.

- Ideally, glazing permits light to enter the building without significantly changing its colour, at the same time excluding weather and permitting a view outside. In practice, however, the glazing needed to control heat gain obscures the view. Float glass, sheet glass, wire glass, acrylic and polycarbonate plastic sheet and glass block-tinted, untinted or reflective-all have different transmittance values.
- Depending on the exposure or orientation, daylight passing through windows, clerestories or skylight all have different colours and modelling of shapes. Light from north is generally cool in colour and has a uniform, shadowless character. Light from south, east or west is tremendously varied in both colour and direction.
- Side lighting through windows is an excellent source of lighting, because its horizontal directionality provides good modelling shadows, minimal veiling reflections and excellent vertical surface illumination.
- Details of window can have significant effects on both the quantity and quality of light that enters a building; window details such as mullions, frames, heavy window supports and small glass lights can obstruct up to 20 % of the available light. Dirt accumulation and wired glass further obstruct light.
- If, windows are small relative to the wall surface, deep window wells, rounded jambs, or splayed window jambs can be used to soften brightness contrasts between interior and exterior surfaces.
- Louvers, Venetian blinds, curtains, overhangs or shading devices modify the introduction of sunlight into buildings, particularly east- or west-facing windows.

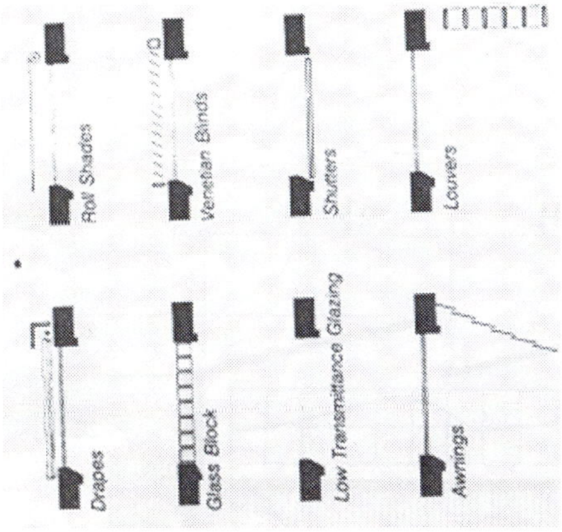

Figure 8.10: Sun control devices

- Too great a contrast between a window and a dark interior can be avoided by directing towards the ceiling or interior wall in rooms with excessive room-depth-to-window-height ratios (e.g., about 2 ½ to 1) continuous or nearly continuous windows are used.
- The light admitted to a space is proportional to the percentage of wall area occupied by windows.
- Windows on adjacent walls primarily light up these walls; windows on opposite side not only give good bilateral lighting, but illuminate adjacent walls as well.
- Tall, narrow windows generally give better penetration of skylights at points near the back of a room than long, low windows. When tall, narrow windows are widely separated, the distribution of daylight parallel to the window is uneven. Floor and wall area between the windows can appear rather dark.
- Windows on adjacent walls of square rooms give good penetration of daylight, unless they are comparatively narrow and placed close to the corners of the room. They also reduce glare by lighting the area of wall surrounding the opposite window.
- Bay windows can fully illuminate the area itself, but not the rest of the room, unless they are very high.
- Windows on opposite sides of a comparatively narrow room throw light onto the opposing walls and hence reduce the brightness contrast. However, in certain cases, e.g., a classroom with fixed seating and a chalkboard on one wall, bilateral lighting, unless properly controlled, could be distractingly bright for persons at the back of the room.
- Large windows extending the full width of a wall distribute daylight more uniformly than windows separated by substantial wall areas, but they also create glare under bright skies unless they are covered with suitable blinds, screens or overhangs.

8.5.4 Clerestories and Sawtooth roofs

Clerestories introduce light deep into a space without creating the excessive brightness that a direct view of the sky or sun produces

- Overhangs or horizontal louvers protect against the thermal effects of the sun, just as windows do
- Clerestories can be used on one side of a building for non-directional light and on two sides of a building for bi-directional lighting.

  Figs. 8.11 a-b demonstrate sawtooth roofs and clerestories.

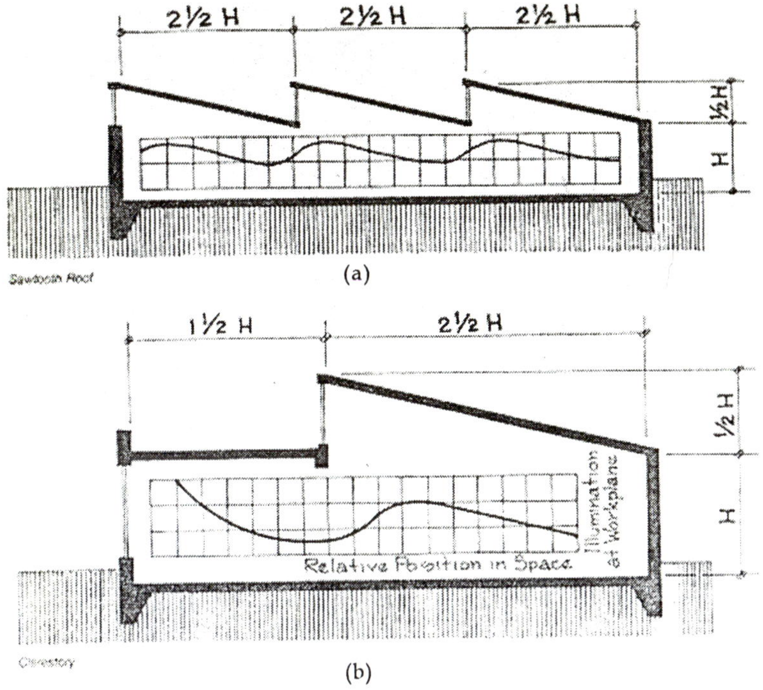

Figure 8.11: Effective proportions for sawtooth roofs and clerestories

8.5.5 Skylights

One of the most efficient means of introducing light deep into a building is through skylights, because the amount of light falling on the horizontal plane can be two times that on the vertical plane with overcast sky. Skylights must be used with caution, however, because they can also introduce direct sun into the building in summer and cause excessive heat loss in winter. This can be avoided through the careful use of shading and insulating controls or by limiting the skylight area to approximately 5% of the total roof area. Figures. 8.12 & 8.13 show both the large and small skylights along with the shading devices for skylights (Fig. 8.14).

- The most effective use of skylights is on top floor of a building. Light wells and other devices can bring light into the lower levels, but they are not always cost-effective.
- Clear glazing can be used in skylights, with an exterior screen to intercept unwanted direct sun; clear glazing permits a view of the changing sky.
- Skylights bring light deep into an interior space. They must be cleaned periodically to maintain their prime transmission qualities. Roof openings and skylights are useful in deep rooms with short windows where room-depth-to-window-height ratios exceed 2 to 1.

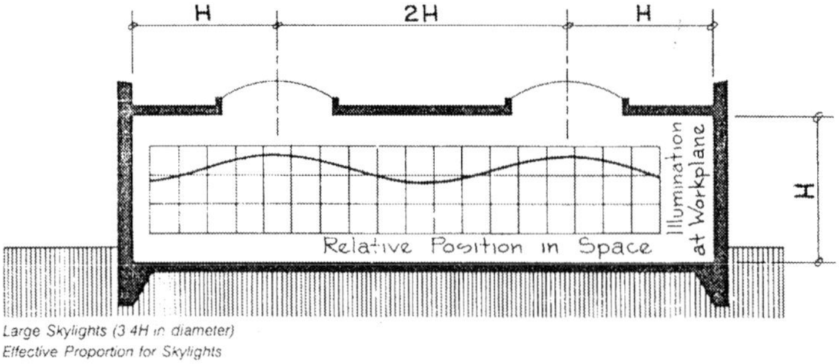

Figure 8.12: Effective proportions for large skylights

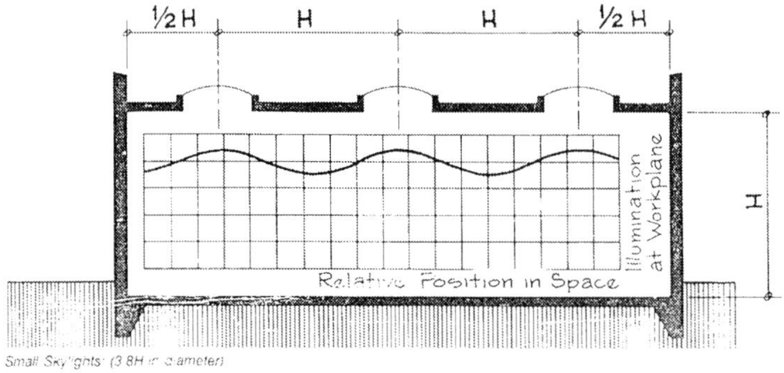

Figure 8.13: Effective proportions for small skylights

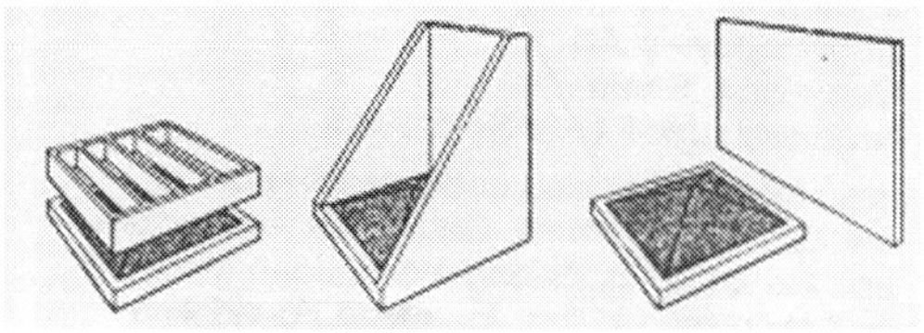

Figure 8.14: Shading devices for skylights

8.5.6 Light Shelves

Light Shelves, or horizontal projections at the building interior, bring light deep into a room by reflecting incoming light off the ceiling. If, these shelves are placed near the ceiling, a soft, diffuse light spreads out through the entire room as the light bounces off the ceiling. Figs.8.15 and 8.16 indicate different arrangements of light shelves.

- Through the use of cold mirrors, the infrared part of the spectrum can be separated from the visible. The infrared can then be used to generate heat, with the visible light directing various kinds of mirrors to produce diffuse or direct light.

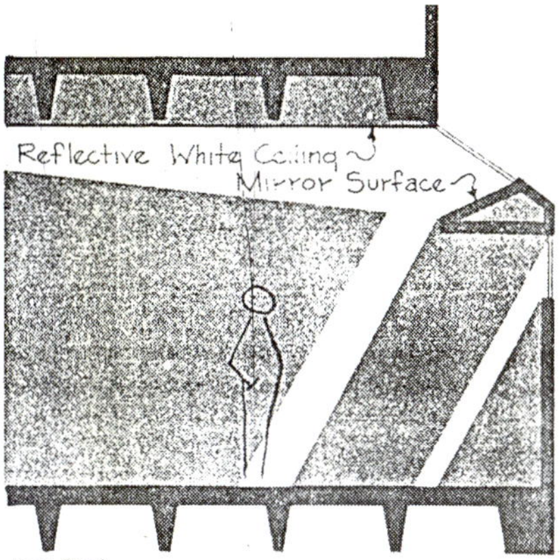

Light Shelf

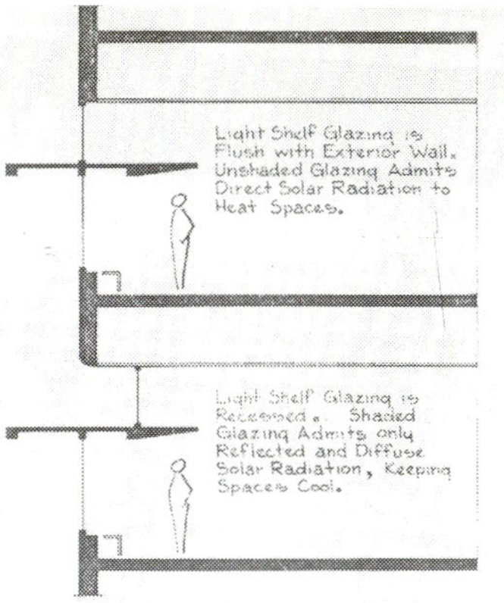

Location of Glazing in Light Shelves Affects Heat Gain

Figure 8.15: Location of glazing in light shelves affects heat gain

- Because daylight relies completely on fixed openings, the designer confronts two problems. First, as the sun moves across the sky, its most concentrated rays can be gathered only when they happen to be perpendicular to the fixed opening. Second, unless the building has only one storey, it can be difficult to get light deep into the building interior without a huge opening such as an atrium.

- Although still experimental, solar optics can be used to transmit concentrated quantities of sunlight deep into the interior of a building by using only a small amount of interior space. To do this, mechanical sun tracking instrument or heliostat, follows the sun and projects its rays through a small opening in the building envelope, guiding it down a narrow passageway such as stair tower or pipe chase with a system of lenses and mirrors. From these vertical shafts the sunlight can be brought into a room along the ceiling.

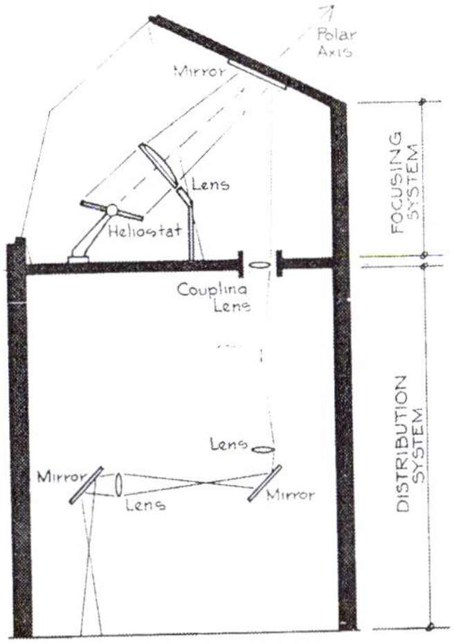

Heliostat Sun Tracking and Distribution Systems

Figure 8.16: Heliostat sun tracking and distribution system

8.6 INTERIOR SURFACES

Visual acuity is proportional to an object's physical size, perceived brightness and contrast. In general, the brighter the object, the easier it is to see. But our ability to see an object depends largely on its background. The greater the contrast between the object and its immediate surroundings, the easier it is to see. Figs. 8.17 indicates different forms of interior surfaces.

- Once daylight enters a building, it can be controlled to some extent by the interior surfaces. Rooms with dark coloured fabrics and wall surfaces have less daylight than rooms full of diffusively reflecting, light coloured surfaces. Highly reflective surfaces cause concentration of light which can be distracting if, in the field of view. They may also interfere with task performance if, excessive brightness on the task reduces contrast.
- Light coloured, diffusely reflecting surfaces facilitate the distribution of light.
- Reflectance of the ceiling should be 80% or higher.
- Reflectance of walls should be 50-60%.
- Light finishes on floors and interior furnishings add brightness and liveliness to interiors.
- Interior surface finishes have a significant effect on the amount of illumination reaching a task. The diagrams show the effect that painting various surfaces black has on the illumination at point X. In a room with all white surfaces, illumination at X is assumed to be 100%. The percentages given are the amount that illumination was reduced as a result of painting the room surfaces black. In the left hand diagrams, the window wall is in the foreground and is removed for the purposes of the illustration. In the diagrams, additional windows have been placed in the back of the room.

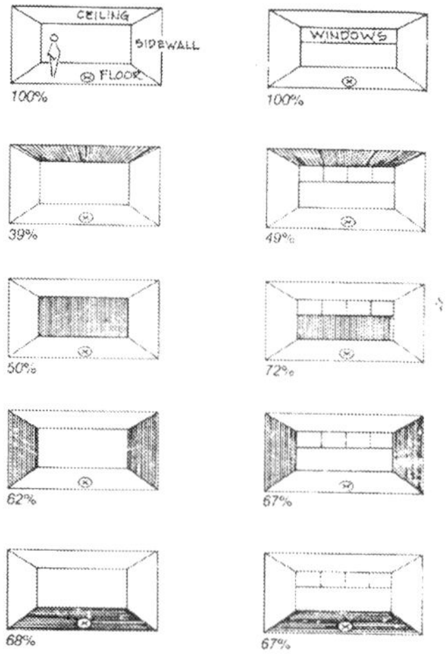

Fig. 8.17: Surface reflectance performance

Table 8.2 gives approximate reflection factors for various paints, while Table 8.3 mentions desirable reflection factors of interior surfaces.

Table 8.2: Reflecting factors of different colors

Colour	*Reflection factors (%)*
White	80-90
Pale yellow	80
Pale beige, lilac	70
Pale blue, green	70-75
Mustard yellow	35
Medium brown	25
Medium blue, green	20-30
Black	10

Table 8.3: Desirable reflecting factors of interior surfaces

Surface	*Reflection Factors (%)*
Ceilings	80
End walls	
in poorly lighted rooms	70
in well lighted rooms	25
Walls containing window (s)	80
Floors	25

8.7 ARTIFICIAL LIGHTING

When natural and artificial lighting are properly integrated, daylight minimizes the use and expense of artificial light, while artificial lighting compensates for inadequate daylight.

- In some daylighting designs, electric lighting is not needed at all, and is not even installed. Normally, however, daylighting does not save energy unless controls on the artificial lighting system- on off or dimming controls, manual or automatic-restrict electricity use, when daylight is sufficient.
- The following are some of the ways to enhance the natural effect of artificial lighting and make it compatible with the natural lighting.
- Use artificial lighting that is close in colour to the daylight.
- Avoid artificial lighting of different colours (e.g., a warm and cool wall of a single colour). If different colours of artificial light are played on a wall, the wall should be different

colours itself, with each colour compatible with its artificial light source; thus warm colour with a warm light and cool colour with a cool light.

- Place skylights and clerestories out of the line of vision to avoid glare and to better integrate daylight with artificial light.
- Use indirect electrical lighting to mimic the directional aspects of daylighting.

8.8 INTEGRATION OF NATURAL VENTILATION, SOLAR HEATING AND VIEW

Lighting, heating, cooling and ventilation and the esthetic satisfaction of a good view, can not always be accomplished through the same piece of glazing, especially if, we wish to maximize the benefits of these natural forces. Sometimes, these functions must be separated. In placing windows and other types of glazing, the designer can not afford to neglect one function entirely in satisfying another. Providing a view, for example, may preclude natural ventilation, because window placement is poor or causes glare.

The following are guidelines for integrating the various functions of lighting, heating, cooling and ventilation.

- Where possible, use different glazings to satisfy different building needs.
- Direct the light that accompanies solar heating away from task areas to avoid glare.
- In designing windows, take into account the acoustic problems they may create.

8.9 EVALUATION OF DAYLIGHTING

8.9.1 Physical Models

Procedures for evaluating daylighting designs should reflect the nature of information available at each phase of design. Thus, as the design proceeds and decisions become more refined, so should the means of evaluating these decisions.

- Scale models are useful in making the qualitative assessment that is the final arbiter of any good design. Light behaves in scale models exactly as it would in full sized buildings. Because accurate data on available daylight are not available in all locations, scale models are one of the better means of evaluating a design for daylighting. Models are of particular value in observing the effects of daylight in space, either with the naked eye or with a camera. An additional reason for using models is that there is no predictive technique that can evaluate the amount of illumination on a work surface when direct sun shines into a space.
- During the schematic phase of design, a rough scale model with openings cut for daylighting can provide a rough estimate of the amount of illumination (foot-candles) available on a work surface. Since these models can be constructed relatively quickly, several different concepts, as well as the same concept with the windows in different places can be compared.

- In the development phase of design, a more detailed scale model finalizes window sizes and locations. The model measures the amount of illumination on the work surface with an accuracy sufficient for this design stage.
- Finally, a full scale mock-up of key sections of the design can be made to finalize the daylighting decisions.

Model Geometry

- In any daylighting model, the size of openings should be accurate, as should window frames, mullions, sills, jambs and skylight wells. Louvers must be represented if they block or reflect light.
- Thickness of walls in the model is generally not important.
- Depth and reflectivity of window sill must be accurately represented.
- For blinds or louvers, the proportions of width to opening must be the same.
- In buildings with very large interior spaces uninterrupted by floor-to-ceiling walls, a typical bay or section can be simulated by enclosing the typical space with mirrored side walls.
- In comparing design changes in spaces with daylight openings on more than one wall, detect changes resulting from one opening by blacking out the other. The secondary opening can be covered with an opaque material painted black to simulate the light from inside that would be absorbed through the opening, when it is in operation, unless it has shades or Venetian blinds.

Materials

- Materials used in the model should have the same opacity, transparency, reflectance and texture as those to be used in the building. Paint can be used to simulate most wall surfaces.
- Colour has little significance, since the instruments measure only quantity of light reflected. Use grey paints on dark and light paper to simulate surfaces.
- Construct walls of plywood or cardboard and then paint appropriately. If, foam board is used, it must be painted or covered with opaque material.
- Glass can be simulated with real glass of float glass quality.
- For overcast skies, simulate plastic dome skylights with a flat covering of translucent or transparent material approximating the transmission properties of the dome material. Simulate sunny conditions with a plastic tent using the same angle of acceptance of the sun as the dome would have.
- To determine the normal transmission of transparent or translucent materials, place a

light cell in an opaque box opposite a small opening (about 2″ square) with some type of constant, relatively small, diffuse source light just outside the box (about 10 to 12 inches). With the light burning, the illumination on the light cells is recorded. Next, place the material to be tested over the opening in the box and record the illumination on the cell again. Calculate the material transmission by dividing the first measurement (box without material) with the second (material to be tested in place). Example: 144/180*100= 80% transmission.

Scale

- Models can be constructed at any convenience scale; however, they should be large enough to reproduce details accurately and to accommodate the illumination meter probe without causing excessive reflection.
- A scale of ¾ inches to 1 foot is convenient for daylighting studies of a room but ½ inch or 3/8 inch scale can be used, if care is exercised in construction and measurement.

Instrumentation

- Many kinds of photometers (light meters) and photocells are available for daylighting studies.
- Most suitable photometers use a photovoltaic power cell; however, battery operated photometers are also available.
- For measuring actual illumination levels, the photocell should be adapted with a colour corrector (a Viscor Filter) to screen out measurement of portions of the spectrum other than the visible.
- Because the photocells are not as sensitive to light striking them from a low angle (as opposed to direct or high angles), they must also be fitted with a cosine correction device.
- A photometer should provide a range in measurement of 1 to 12000 foot-candles.
- Caps can be made to adjust the percentage of light admitted to the photocell. For example, if the maximum range of the scale is 1000 foot-candles and one wishes to measure a lighting level of 2000 foot-candles, the cell can be covered with a cap allowing 50% of the light to penetrate; the indicated level is then multiplied by two. The cap is made by drilling holes equal to 50% of the total photocell area.
- Photometers with a photocell built into the display meter case are not suitable for model studies.

Model testing

- The outdoor location should approximate the sky and ground conditions for the proposed building.

- Ground conditions can make a large difference in interior illumination levels and distribution, because much of the light entering the building can be reflected from the ground.
- Exterior sky conditions must be measured at the beginning, during and at the end of a basis for test comparison and indicate changing sky conditions. They are especially important if design schemes are being compared.
- For the designer, two reference measurements E_v and Eh are important.

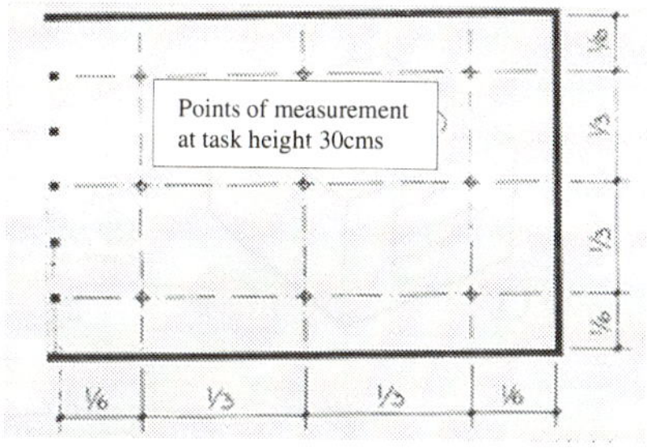

Figure 8.18: Suggested locations for measurement of daylight in models

E_v= illumination from the sky on the plane of the vertical fenestration or window wall and parallel to the wall (a few inches immediately outside the window but beyond any obstructing parts of the building, such as the overhangs and louvers. This measurement is made by placing the photocell on the center of the vertical window wall of the model, if, there are no protruding building parts to restrict the light reaching the cell. This measurement provides an indication of the total light from the sky, plus the light reflected from the ground and surrounding objects near window openings. If, the ground surface is to be altered in any way, only the light from the sky, by attaching a horizontal black shield to the light cell.

Eh= total hemispheric illumination on the unobstructed plane of the ground from both the sun and sky (any distance from the ground up to several hundred feet will suffice; usually the roof of the model is an appropriate place). This measurement is necessary when the model has horizontal openings. The measurement is made by placing the light cell on a flat surface, such as the model roof, where light from the sky will not be obstructed. This measurement provides an indication of the total light from the sky that is available to pass into a horizontal opening such as a skylight.

- Standard points for measurement in rectangular rooms are shown in the accompanying figure. If, the designer considers other points in the room particularly significant to the design, they can be used as reference points instead.

8.9.2 Lumen method

The Lumen method, which is the most widely used, was developed by J.W.Griffith for Libbey-Owens-Ford company. In this method, many different variables are taken into account, including sky conditions, position of sun, room size, glazing area and transmission characteristics such as overhangs, shades and blinds. The calculation technique is limited to a predicting amount of illumination on a centerline five feet from the window, five feet from the back wall and a point midway between, but can be modified by combining with area source comparative calculations to give reasonable values anywhere on a horizontal work plane. Fig. 8.19 shows the lumen method factors.

The Lumen method is as follows:

1. Determine solar altitude from the sun path diagram. (Please refer Annexure-2 at the end of this book)

2. Choose sky conditions. Determine illumination on a window (Ekw) and illumination on horizontal surfaces (Ekg) from figure 8.20.

3. Determine solar illumination value (Euw and Eug) from figure 8.21. Add to illumination on window (Ekw) and illumination on horizontal surfaces (Ekg)

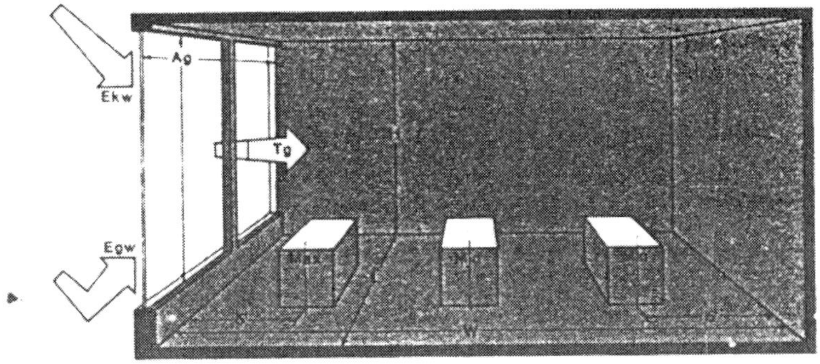

Figure 8.19: Lumen method factors

- Illumination on ground (Ekug)= illumination from sky on ground (Ekg) + illumination from sun on ground (Eug)

- Illumination on window (Ekuw)= illumination from sky on window (Ekw) + illumination from sun on window (Euw)

4. Multiply the illumination on the ground by the reflectance factor of ground (Rg) and the field proportion factor 0.5 to obtain the illumination on the window from the ground (Egw)

   - Illumination from ground on window (Egw)= illumination on ground (Ekug) x reflectance of ground surface (Rg) x 0.5

5. Determine the total transmitting area (Ag) of the window taking into account the metal frame. From manufacturers product data, find the transmittance factor of the glass itself (Tg) from Table 8.4.
6. Determine room dimensions and reflection of wall surfaces. Determine coefficients of utilization (C and K) from Table-8.5. For diffusing shades use ½ of total incident illumination from sun, sky and ground on window, or ½ x (Ekuw+ Egw)
7. Multiply the values of illumination on the window by the window factors and coefficients of utilization, separately for light from the ground and light from sky (Ekwp and Egwp)
   - Illumination from sky on work plane (Ekwp) = illumination on window (Ekuw) x window area of transmittance (Ag) x Transmittance of glass for average daylight (Tg) x coefficient of utilization (C) x coefficient of utilization (K)
8. Add the values found in step 7 in order to obtain the total illumination of the work plane in foot-candles.
   - total illumination on work plane= illumination from sky on work plane (Ekwp) + illumination from ground on work plane (Egwp)

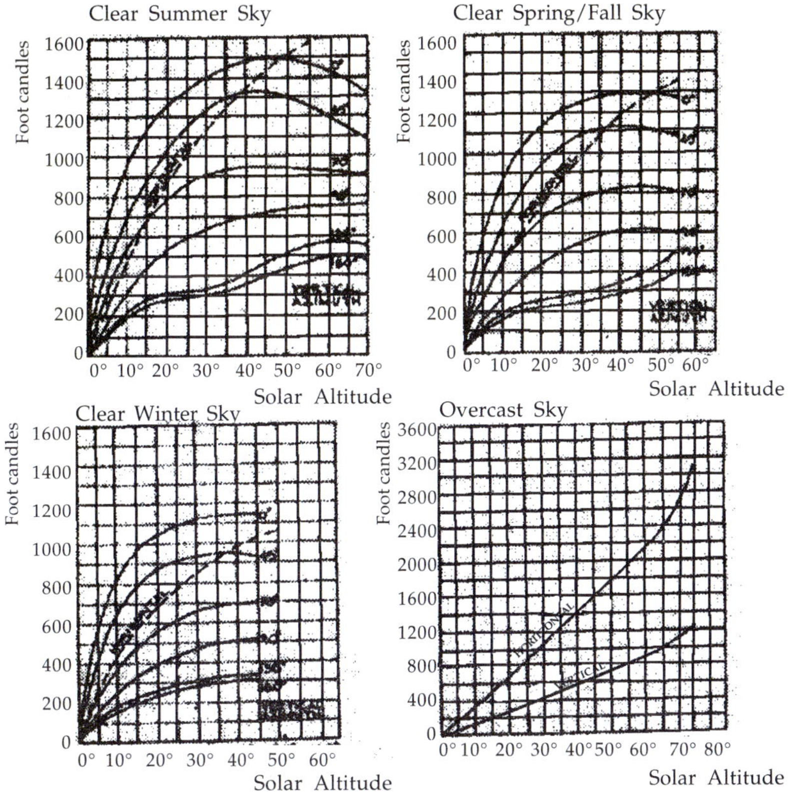

Source : Watson D. (1993), The Energy Design Handbook.

Figure 8.20: Illumination from sky on different planes

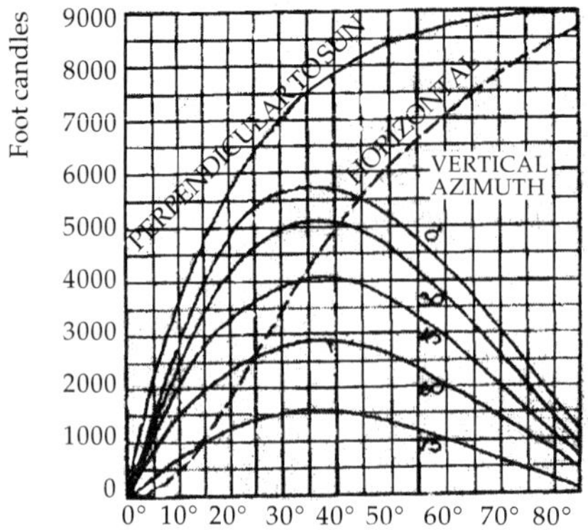

Source : Watson D. (1993) The Energy Design Handbook

Figure 8.21: Illumination variation with solar altitude

Table 8.4: Transmittance values of various kinds of glass

(a) Monolithic glass: clear and tinted

Glass	*Thickness*		*Transmittance*	
	Inch	*mm*	*Average Daylight %*	*Total Solar %*
Sheet	SS	2.5	90	85
	DS 3	3	89	80
	3/16	5	89	78
Clear	1/8	3	89	80
	3/16	5	88	78
	1/4	6	87	75
	5/6	8	86	70
Clear	3/8	10	84	67
Heavy duty	1/2	12	82	61
	5/8	15	80	56
	3/4	19	78	51
	7/8	22	75	48
Blue- green	1/8	3	83	63
	3/16	5	79	55
	1/4	6	75	47
Grey	1/8	3	61	63
	3/16	5	51	53
	1/4	6	44	46
	5/16	8	35	38
	3/8	10	28	31
	1/2	12	19	22
Bronze	1/8	3	68	65
	3/16	5	59	55
	1/4	6	52	49
	5/16	8	44	40
	3/8	10	38	34
	1/2	12	28	24

(b) Thermopane insulating glass

Glass	*Thickness*		*Transmittance*	
	Inch	*mm*	*Average Daylight* %	*Total Solar* %
Clear	1/8	3	80	69
	3/16	5	79	52
	1/4	6	77	59
Blue	1/8	3	75	52
	3/16	5	70	43
	1/4	6	66	36
Grey	1/8	3	55	52
	3/16	5	45	42
	1/4	6	39	35
Bronze	1/8	3	61	54
	3/16	5	53	43
	1/4	6	46	38

(c) Laminated safety glass with Vari-tan coating

Glass	Thickness		Vari-tan Coating		Transmittance	
	Inch	mm	Color	Number	Average Daylight %	Total Solar %
Clear	1/4	6	Silver	1-108	8 ±1.5	9
				1-114	14 ± 2.0	15
				1-120	20 ± 2.5	19
	1/4	6	Golden	1-208	8 ±1.5	8
				1-214	14 ± 2.0	13
				1-220	20± 2.5	20

Monolithic glass with Vari-tan coating

Glass	*Thickness*		*Vari-tan Coating*		*Transmittance*	
	Inch	*mm*	*Color*	*Number*	*Average Daylight %*	*Total Solar %*
Clear	1/4	6	Silver	1-108	8 ± 1.5	9
				1-114	14 ±2.0	16
				1-120	20 ± 2.5	20
	1/4	6	Golden	1-208	8 ± 1.5	9
				1-214	14 ± 2.0	14
				1-220	20 ± 2.5	21
B-green	1/4	6	Blue	2-350	50 ±5.0	35
Grey Tuf-Flex	1/4	6	Grey	3-108	8 ± 1.5	11
				3-114	14 ± 2.0	17
				3-120	20 = 2.5	24
Grey	1/4	6		3-134	34 ±4.0	36
Bronze Tuf Flex	1/4	6	Bronze	4-108	8 ± 1.5	9
				4-114	14 ±2.0	14
				4-120	20 ± 2.5	20
Bronze	1/4	6		4-134	34 ± 4.0	31

Thermopane glass with Vari-tan coating

Glass	*Thickness*		*Vari-tan Coating*		*Transmittance*	
	Inch	*mm*	*Color*	*Number*	*Average Daylight %*	*Total Solar %*
Clear	1	25	Silver	1-108	7 ±1.5	7
				1-114	13 ± 2.0	14
				1-120	18 ± 2.5	16
	1	25	Golden	1-208	7 ±1.5	7
				1-214	13 ± 2.0	12
				1-220	18 ± 2.5	17
Blue-green	1	25	Blue	2-350	45 ± 5.0	28
				2-350-2	38 ± 5.0	20
Grey Tuf-Flex	1	25	Grey	3-108	7 ± 1.5	9
				3-114	13 ± 2.0	14
				3-120	18 ± 2.5	20
Grey	1	25		3-134	30±4.0	29
Bronze Tuf Flex	1	25	Bronze	4-108	7 ± 1.5	7
				4-114	13 ± 2.0	11
				4-120	18 ± 2.5	15
Bronze	1	25		4-134	30±4.0	25

Table 8.5: Coefficient of utilization (C) for illuminance

(A)

Overcast Sky

Room length		20′		30′		40′	
Wall Reflectance		70%	30%	70%	30%	70%	30%
	Room Width						
Max	20′	0.0276	0.0251	0.0191	0.0173	0.0143	0.0137
	30′	0.0272	0.0248	0.0188	0.0172	0.0137	0.0131
	40′	0.0269	0.0246	0.0182	0.0171	0.0133	0.0130
Mid	20′	0.0159	0.0117	0.0101	0.0087	0.0081	0.0071
	30′	0.0058	0.0050	0.0054	0.0040	0.0034	0.0033
	40′	0.0039	0.0027	0.0030	0.0023	0.0022	0.0019
Min	20′	0.0087	0.0053	0.0063	0.0043	0.0052	0.0037
	30′	0.0032	0.0019	0.0029	0.0017	0.0020	0.0014
	40′	0.0019	0.0009	0.0016	0.0009	0.0012	0.0008

Coefficient of Utilization (C) : Clear Sky

Room length		20′		30′		40′	
Wall Reflectance		70%	30%	70%	30%	70%	30%
	Room Width						
Max	20′	0.0206	0.0173	0.0143	0.0123	0.0110	0.0098
	30′	0.0203	0.0173	0.0137	0.0120	0.0098	0.0092
	40′	0.0200	0.0168	0.0131	0.0119	0.0096	0.0091
Mid	20′	0.0153	0.0104	0.0100	0.0079	0.0083	0.0067
	30′	0.0082	0.0054	0.0062	0.0043	0.0046	0.0037
	40′	0.0052	0.0032	0.0040	0.0028	0.0029	0.0023
Min	20′	0.0106	0.0060	0.0079	0.0049	0.0067	0.0043
	30′	0.0054	0.0028	0.0047	0.0023	0.0032	0.0021
	40′	0.0031	0.0014	0.0027	0.0013	0.0021	0.0012

Coefficient of Utilization (C) : Ground

Room length		20′		30′		40′	
Wall Reflectance		70%	30%	70%	30%	70%	30%
	Room Width						
Max	20′	0.0147	0.0112	0.0102	0.0088	0.0081	0.0071
	30′	0.0141	0.0112	0.0098	0.0088	0.0077	0.0070
	40′	0.0137	0.0112	0.0093	0.0086	0.0072	0.0069
Mid	20′	0.0128	0.0090	0.0094	0.0071	0.0073	0.0060
	30′	0.0083	0.0057	0.0062	0.0048	0.0050	0.0041
	40′	0.0055	0.0037	0.0044	0.0033	0.0042	0.0026
Min	20′	0.0106	0.0071	0.0082	0.0054	0.0067	0.0044
	30′	0.0051	0.0026	0.0041	0.0023	0.0033	0.0021
	40′	0.0029	0.0018	0.0026	0.0012	0.0022	0.0011

(B)

Coefficient of Utilization (C) : Diffuse Shade

Sky

Room length	20′		30′		40′	
Wall Reflectance	70%	30%	70%	30%	70%	30%
Room Width						
20′	0.0247	0.0217	0.0174	0.0152	0.0128	0.0120
30′	0.0241	0.0214	0.0166	0.0151	0.0120	0.0116
40′	0.0237	0.0212	0.0161	0.0150	0.0118	0.0113
20′	0.0169	0.0122	0.0110	0.0092	0.0089	0.0077
30′	0.0078	0.0060	0.0067	0.0048	0.0044	0.0041
40′	0.0053	0.0033	0.0039	0.0028	0.0029	0.0024
20′	0.0108	0.0066	0.0080	0.0052	0.0063	0.0047
30′	0.0047	0.0026	0.0042	0.0023	0.0032	0.0020
40′	0.0027	0.0013	0.0022	0.0012	0.0018	0.0011

Ground

Room length	20′		30′		40′	
Wall Reflectance	70%	30%	70%	30%	70%	30%
Room Width						
20′	0.0147	0.0112	0.0102	0.0088	0.0081	0.0071
30′	0.0141	0.0112	0.0098	0.0088	0.0077	0.0070
40′	0.0137	0.0112	0.0093	0.0086	0.0072	0.0069
20′	0.0128	0.0090	0.0094	0.0071	0.0073	0.0060
30′	0.0083	0.0057	0.0062	0.0048	0.0050	0.0041
40′	0.0055	0.0037	0.0044	0.0033	0.0042	0.0026
20′	0.0106	0.0071	0.0082	0.0054	0.0067	0.0044
30′	0.0051	0.0026	0.0041	0.0023	0.0033	0.0021
40′	0.0029	0.0018	0.0026	0.0012	0.0022	0.0011

(C)
Coefficient of Utilization (C)
Horizontal Louvers

Sky

Room length	20′		30′		40′	
Wall Reflectance	70%	30%	70%	30%	70%	30%
Room Width						
20′	0.0556	0.0556	0.0392	0.0397	0.0298	0.0317
30′	0.0522	0.0533	0.0367	0.0389	0.0278	0.0311
40′	0.0506	0.0528	0.0359	0.0381	0.0270	0.0306
20′	0.0556	0.0556	0.0418	0.0411	0.0320	0.0364
30′	0.0372	0.0339	0.0278	0.0286	0.0220	0.0256
40′	0.0217	0.0211	0.0192	0.0186	0.0139	0.0164
20′	0.0556	0.0556	0.0422	0.0456	0.0320	0.0409
30′	0.0294	0.0233	0.0222	0.0203	0.0189	0.0194
40′	0.0139	0.0110	0.0133	0.0108	0.0120	0.0100

Ground

Room length	20′		30′		40′	
Wall Reflectance	70%	30%	70%	30%	70%	30%
Room Width						
20′	0.0556	0.0556	0.0392	0.0426	0.0303	0.0348
30′	0.0528	0.0539	0.0370	0.0433	0.0289	0.0337
40′	0.0506	0.0544	0.0359	0.0426	0.0278	0.0344
20′	0.0556	0.0556	0.0419	0.0459	0.0320	0.0381
30′	0.0367	0.0356	0.0274	0.0308	0.0217	0.027
40′	0.0239	0.0233	0.0192	0.0222	0.0153	0.0181
20′	0.0556	0.0556	0.0430	0.0486	0.0328	0.0398
30′	0.0261	0.0228	0.0217	0.0211	0.0170	0.0192
40′	0.0128	0.0108	0.0119	0.0107	0.0098	0.0097

(D)

Coefficient of Utilization (C)

Overcast Sky

Room length	8'		10'		12'		14'	
Wall Reflectance	70%	30%	70%	30%	70%	30%	70%	30%
Room Width								
20′	0.1250	0.1290	0.1210	0.1230	0.1110	0.1110	0.0991	0.0973
30′	0.1220	0.1310	0.1220	0.1210	0.1110	0.1110	0.0945	0.0973
40′	0.1450	0.1330	0.1310	0.1260	0.1110	0.1110	0.0973	0.0982
20′	0.0908	0.0982	0.1070	0.1150	0.1110	0.1110	0.1050	0.122
30′	0.1560	0.1020	0.0939	0.1130	0.1110	0.1110	0.1210	0.134
40′	0.1060	0.0948	0.1230	0.1070	0.1110	0.1110	0.1350	0.127
20′	0.0908	0.1020	0.0951	0.1140	0.1110	0.1110	0.1180	0.134
30′	0.0924	0.1190	0.1010	0.1140	0.1110	0.1110	0.1250	0.126
40′	0.1110	0.0926	0.1250	0.1090	0.1110	0.1110	0.1330	0.130

(E)

Coefficient of Utilization (C)

Clear Sky

Room length	8'		10'		12'		14'	
Wall Reflectance	70%	30%	70%	30%	70%	30%	70%	30%
Room Width								
20′	0.1450	0.1550	0.1290	0.1320	0.1110	0.1110	0.1010	0.0982
30′	0.1410	0.1490	0.1250	0.1300	0.1110	0.1110	0.0945	0.0101
40′	0.1570	0.1570	0.1350	0.1340	0.1110	0.1110	0.0964	0.0991
20′	0.1100	0.1280	0.1160	0.1260	0.1110	0.1110	0.1030	0.108
30′	0.1060	0.1250	0.1110	0.1290	0.1110	0.1110	0.1120	0.120
40′	0.1170	0.1180	0.1220	0.1180	0.1110	0.1110	0.1230	0.122
20′	0.1050	0.1290	0.1120	0.1300	0.1110	0.1110	0.1110	0.116
30′	0.0994	0.1440	0.1070	0.1260	0.1110	0.1110	0.1070	0.124
40′	0.1190	0.1160	0.1300	0.1180	0.1110	0.1110	0.1200	0.118

(F)
Coefficient of Utilization (C)
Ground

Ceiling Height	8'		10'		12'		14'	
Wall Reflectance	70%	30%	70%	30%	70%	30%	70%	30%
Room Width								
20′	0.1240	0.2060	0.1400	0.1350	0.1110	0.1110	0.0909	0.0859
30′	0.1820	0.1880	0.1400	0.1430	0.1110	0.1110	0.0918	0.0878
40′	0.1240	0.1820	0.1400	0.1420	0.1110	0.1110	0.0936	0.0879
20′	0.1230	0.1450	0.1220	0.1290	0.1110	0.1110	0.1000	0.0945
30′	0.0966	0.1040	0.1070	0.1120	0.1110	0.1110	0.1100	0.1050
40′	0.0790	0.0786	0.0999	0.1060	0.1110	0.1110	0.1180	0.1180
20′	0.0994	0.1080	0.1100	0.1140	0.1110	0.1110	0.1070	0.1040
30′	0.0816	0.0822	0.0984	0.1050	0.1110	0.1110	0.1210	0.1160
40′	0.0700	0.0656	0.0946	0.0986	0.1110	0.1110	0.1250	0.1320

(G)
Coefficient of Utilization (C)
Diffused Shade

Sky

Ceiling Height	8'		10'		12'		14'	
Wall Reflectance	70%	30%	70%	30%	70%	30%	70%	30%
Room Width								
20′	0.1450	0.1540	0.1230	0.1280	0.1110	0.1110	0.0991	0.0964
30′	0.1410	0.1510	0.1260	0.1280	0.1110	0.1110	0.0945	0.0964
40′	0.190	0.1570	0.1370	0.1270	0.1110	0.1110	0.0973	0.0964
20′	0.1010	0.1160	0.1150	0.1250	0.1110	0.1110	0.1010	0.1100
30′	0.0952	0.1130	0.1050	0.1220	0.1110	0.1110	0.1100	0.1220
40′	0.1110	0.1050	0.1240	0.1070	0.1110	0.1110	0.1300	0.1240
20′	0.0974	0.1110	0.1070	0.1210	0.1110	0.1110	0.1120	0.1190
30′	0.0956	0.1250	0.1030	0.1170	0.1110	0.1110	0.1150	0.1250
40′	0.1110	0.1050	0.1250	0.1110	0.1110	0.1110	0.1330	0.1240

Ground

Ceiling Height	8'		10'		12'		14'	
Wall Reflectance	70%	30%	70%	30%	70%	30%	70%	30%
Room Width								
20′	0.1240	0.2060	0.1400	0.1350	0.1110	0.1110	0.0909	0.0859
30′	0.1820	0.1880	0.1400	0.1430	0.1110	0.1110	0.0918	0.0878
40′	0.1240	0.1820	0.1400	0.1420	0.1110	0.1110	0.0936	0.0879
20′	0.1230	0.1450	0.1220	0.1290	0.1110	0.1110	0.1000	0.0945
30′	0.0966	0.1040	0.1070	0.1120	0.1110	0.1110	0.1100	0.1050
40′	0.0790	0.0786	0.0999	0.1060	0.1110	0.1110	0.1180	
20′	0.0994	0.1080	0.1100	0.1140	0.1110	0.1110	0.1070	0.1040
30′	0.0816	0.0822	0.0984	0.1050	0.1110	0.1110	0.1210	0.1160
40′	0.0700	0.0656	0.0946	0.0986	0.1110	0.1110	0.1250	0.1320

(H)
Coefficient of Utilization (C)
Horizontal Louvers

Sky

Ceiling Height	8'		10'		12'		14'	
Wall Reflectance	70%	30%	70%	30%	70%	30%	70%	30%
Room Width Max.	0.1540	0.1700	0.1290	0.1310	0.1070	0.1120	0.0910	0.0910
Mid 20′	0.1000	0.1060	0.1010	0.1060	0.0990	0.1020	0.0910	0.0910
Mid 30′	0.0740	0.0800	0.0860	0.0860	0.0910	0.0930	0.0910	0.0910
Mid 40′	0.0700	0.0740	0.0790	0.0790	0.0880	0.0910	0.0910	0.0910
Min 20′	0.0800	0.0800	0.0910	0.0910	0.0930	0.0930	0.0910	0.0910
Min 30′	0.0680	0.0680	0.0790	0.0790	0.0870	0.0870	0.0910	0.0910
Min 40′	0.0640	0.0640	0.0760	0.0760	0.0840	0.0840	0.0910	0.0910

Ground

Ceiling Height	8'		10'		12'		14'	
Wall Reflectance	70%	30%	70%	30%	70%	30%	70%	30%
Room Width Max.	0.1740	0.2000	0.1420	0.1570	0.1170	0.1230	0.0910	0.0910
Mid 20′	0.1040	0.1160	0.1100	0.1210	0.1060	0.1120	0.0910	0.0910
Mid 30′	0.0740	0.0820	0.0920	0.0990	0.0990	0.1060	0.0910	0.0910
Mid 40′	0.0580	0.0620	0.0790	0.0830	0.0920	0.0960	0.0910	0.0910
Min 20′	0.0780	0.0820	0.0930	0.0970	0.0990	0.1020	0.0910	0.0910
Min 30′	0.0580	0.0600	0.0740	0.0760	0.0900	0.0920	0.0910	0.0910
Min 40′	0.0520	0.0560	0.0700	0.0710	0.0860	0.0870	0.0910	0.0910

Example of calculation:

Location	Delhi (28.3^0 N) on July 30
Average Ground Reflectance:	6%
Floor Area	480 square feet
Height of window:	7 feet
Width of window:	24 feet
Room width:	20 feet
Room length:	24 feet
Ceiling height:	12 feet
Point of illumination:	Min (5 feet from back of wall)
Time of day:	12:00 p.m
1. Solar Altitude =	75^0
2. Ekw =	1200 fc from Fig. 8.20 for overcast sky
Ekg =	3100 fc from Fig. 8.20 for overcast sky
3. Euw =	0, overcast sky
Eug =	0, overcast sky
Ekug =	Ekg + Eug = 3100 + 0 = 3100 fc
Ekuw =	Ekw + Euw = 1200 + 0 = 1200 fc
4. Egw =	Ekug x 0.06 x 0.50 = 3100 x 0.06 x 0.50 = 93 fc
5. Ag =	24 feet x 7 feet =168 sq.ft
Tg =	0.50
6. Floor area =	480 sg.ft
Reflectance =	0.50

C = 0.0063 for overcast sky (by interpolation) from tables for C

C = 0.0081 for ground (by interpolation) from tables for C

K= 0.111 for overcast sky from tables for K

K = 0.111 for ground from tables for K

7. Ekwp = Ekuw x Ag x Tg x C x K

Ekwp = 1200 x168 x 0.50 x 0.0081 x 0.111

Ekwp = 71 fc.

Egwp = Egw x Aa x Tg x C x K

Egwp = 93 x 168 x 0.50 x 0.0081 x 0.111

Egwp = 7 fc.

8. Total illumination on work plane

   Ekwp + Egwp

   71 +   7

   78 fc.

8.10 DAYLIGHT FACTOR METHOD

The quantitative parameter that describes daylighting in a building is the daylight factor (DF) defined as :

DF= E_i x 100 %/E_o

Where

E_i= illumination indoors, at the point of observation (lux)

E_o= illumination outdoors from an unobstructed sky hemisphere (lux [1])

8.10.1 Sky conditions

The sky condition varies from place to place depending upon the cloud cover, as shown in the Fig. 8.22. Some of the sky conditions presented in literature are

- a uniform bright sky
- C.I.E. Standard overcast sky where the expression for brightness $B_{è}$ at an altitude è is given by

$B_{è}$= B_z x (1+ 2 sinè)/3

where B_z= Brightness at zenith

- clear sky expressed by Kittler (1965) is different from Indian sky described below
- for tropical (Indian) sky condition, the expression for brightness $B_{è}$ at an altitude angle of $_{è}$ is given by

$B_{è}$= B_z cosecè

when è lies between 15-90^0

The Indian code for daylighting in buildings (Indian Standard 240, 1976) has above equation for the outdoor sky condition within è= 15 ^{0}.

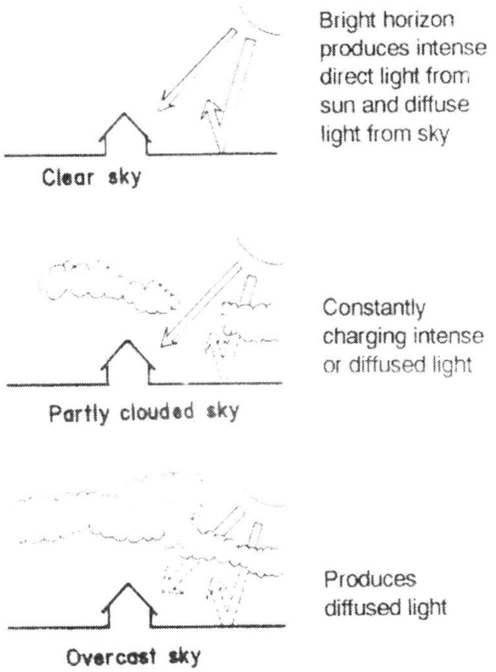

Fig. 8.22 : Various design skies

Some acceptable sky illumination for different locations are given in Table 8.9.

Table 8.9: Sky illumination levels at some locations

London	Lat 52^0	5000 Lux
Hobart	Lat 43^0	5500
Sydney	Lat 33^0	8000
Brisbane	Lat 27^0	10000
Darwin	Lat 10^0	15000
Nairobi	Lat 1^0	18000

For Indian conditions, normally, one takes a value of 8000 lux for sky illumination. Recommended values of daylight factors for domestic buildings are given in Table 8.10.

Table 8.10: Daylight factors for domestic buildings

Building/Function	*min DF*
Housing	
-kitchen, general	1.0
-kitchen, main workshops	1.5
-living room, general	0.5
-living room, desk for writing	1.5
-bedroom, general	0.25
-bedroom, dressing table	1.0
-circulation	0.2
Entrance halls and reception area	0.3
General offices	1.0
School assembly halls	0.2
School classrooms	1.0

8.10.2 Methodology

Based on the equations explained above a computer program has been developed which calculates the illumination at each grid node obtained by dividing the room into number of grids with the given grid spacing. The computer output has been validated through experimental results. From the calculated values ISO-daylight factor contours have been drawn. The grid spacing has been reduced near the window to improve the accuracy of the ISO-daylight factor contour. The area between the contours is measured and multiplied with the average daylight factor as the representative for that area and finally weighted average daylight factor is calculated. The weighted average is defined as

$$DF = +\int_0^A Df\,dA/A$$

and this is numerically computed as

$$DF = \sum^n Df_i\,A_i/\sum^n A_i$$

where

D= average daylight factor of a particular area

A= respective area

n= areas

The weighted average daylight factor variations have been plotted against various parameters given below:

(a) area of openings

(b) room height

(c) sill as compared to the height of working plane

(d) reflection coefficient of walls

(e) area of room

(f) aspect ratio of the opening

(g) location of window

Area of openings

Openings include both windows and ventilators, which differ themselves only in sill height and opening height. The area of openings is normally expressed as percentage of floor area. The area of openings was varied from 5%-30% in steps of 5%.

Room height

The illumination level varies with the room height even for fixed fenestration area, since the IRC changes as the surface area of the room changes with increased room height, according to split flux principle. The room height is varied from 2.8 m to 4.0 m in steps of 0.2 m, which is the normal range of room heights.

Sill height as compared to the height of working plane

The sill height of windows does not always coincide with the working plane height, to get the full utility of the opening. Hence to take account of the above, analysis have been carried out for the following conditions. Working plane height varying from–50% to + 100% that of window height, in steps of 25% such that the working plane height is below and above the sill height respectively for negative and positive increase.

Reflection coefficient of walls

Reflectances of walls normally range from 0.4 (grey or dark surface) to 0.85 (polished, white washed surface) which affects the daylighting inside the room especially in the IRC. For simplicity and by normal practice, the ceiling and the working plane reflectances are kept constant at 0.35 and 0.7 respectively, while wall reflectances are changed and analysed. But the program developed also has the flexibility of changing the ceiling and working plane reflectances.

Area of the room

Typically designers have been dealing with various room sizes in their practice. To cater to this and to get the effect of room size on daylighting for a given fenestration percentage, the effect of room area has been analysed. Rooms of 24 m^2, 48 m^2, 72 m^2 and 144 m^2 were taken for analysis. External obstructions have not been considered. The overhangs were assumed according to the room area from 0.6 to 0.9 m out from the windows and immediately above the top of window.

Aspect ratio of the opening

In general, it is known that high windows provide more penetration and correspondingly the spread is diffused. To quantify this, three cases of width to height ratio were used 1:1, 1:1.3 and 1: 1.6.

Location of window

For a particular fenestration percentage, many combinations of window locations and number of windows can be proposed. For example, windows may be in a larger wall or in shorter wall, centrally located or at the end, etc. To analyze these effects, about nine different locations have been considered and studied.

8.10.3 Results

The quantitative influence of various parameters have been clearly brought out in the graphs produced here.

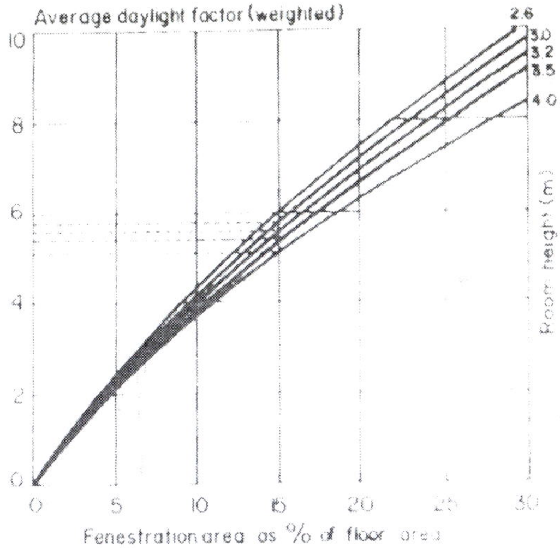

Fig. 8.23: Variation of daylight with fenestration area

- The average DF is directly proportional to the fenestration percentage (as expressed as % of the plot area as the area of sky seen is high).
- The average DF is inversely proportional to the room height, since the IRC decreases with increase in surface area for the same area of fenestration.

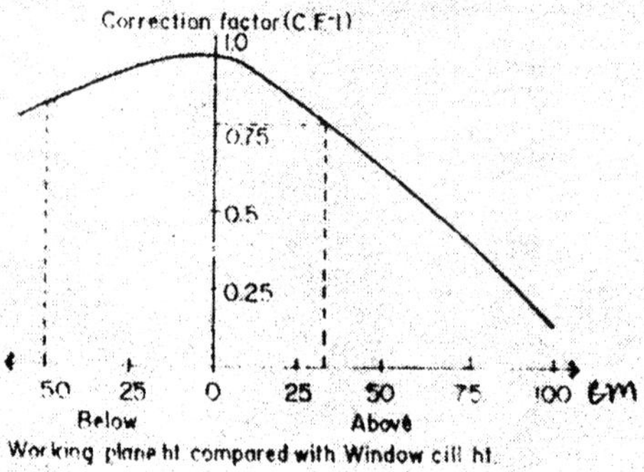

Fig. 8.24: Daylight level above and below sill height

- The average DF steeply decreases when the working plane is above the window sill since the area of window below the working plane is ineffective in illuminating the working plane.
- A correction factor CF1 is defined by taking the ratio between the average daylight factor obtained from a position off the working plane height with respect to the sill height compared to the average DF, when the working plane height coincides with the sill height.
- With the increase in reflection coefficient of surface there is an increase in average DF as the IRC increases. In Fig. 8.25 another correction factor CF2 is defined as the ratio between an average DF obtained with the given surface reflectance's and the average DF of a surface with reflectance 0.6

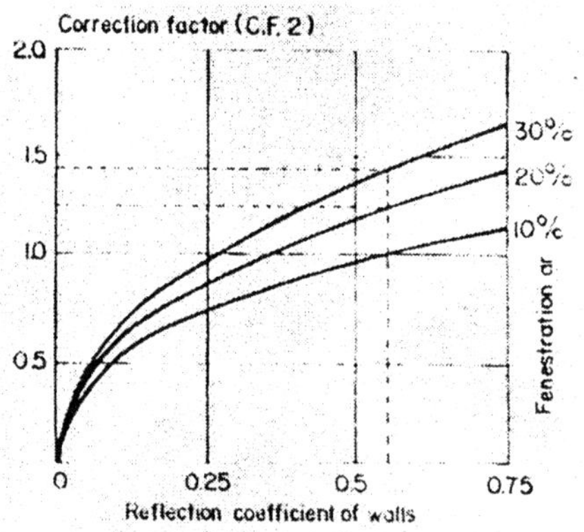

Fig. 8.25: Daylight variation with reflectance of walls

- An increase in DF is observed when the area of the room increases for the same percentage of fenestration. Correction factor CF3 is defined as the average daylight factor obtained in any room to the average daylight factor in 24 m^2 floor area.

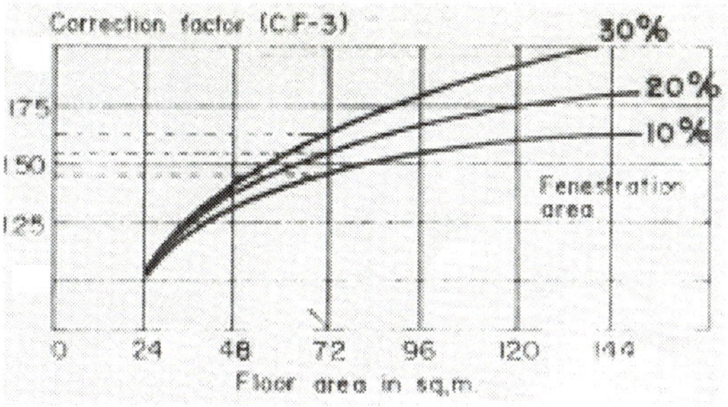

Fig. 8.26: Daylight variation with floor area

- Not much change is noticed when the width to height ratio is changed. However, the daylight distribution is even in case of less value of width/height, which can be seen in Fig.8.27.

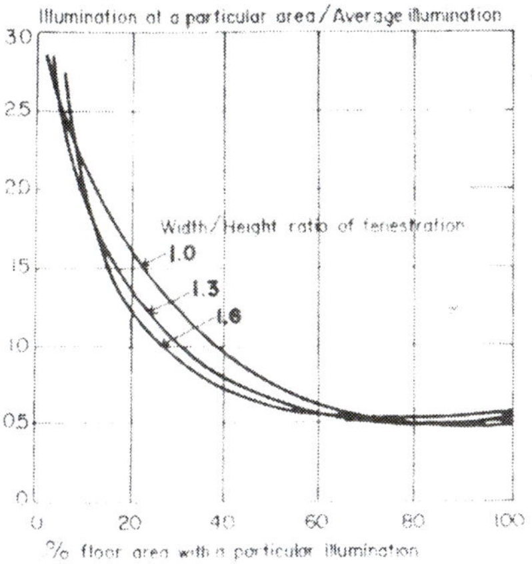

Fig. 8.27: Daylight variation with width to height ratio

- Finally from Figure 8.28, the idea of distribution can be obtained. The correction factor (CF4) is defined for various window locations, as the ratio between the average daylight factor obtained for that arrangement of windows and the average daylight factor obtained when the window is one in number and is at center of the longer wall. The average illumination decreases, when the window is in the shorter wall. It also decreases when the window is at the corner of the room since the area of sky seen from a point is less in these cases. If, the number of windows is increased, the spread of daylight is better while the penetration observed decreases.

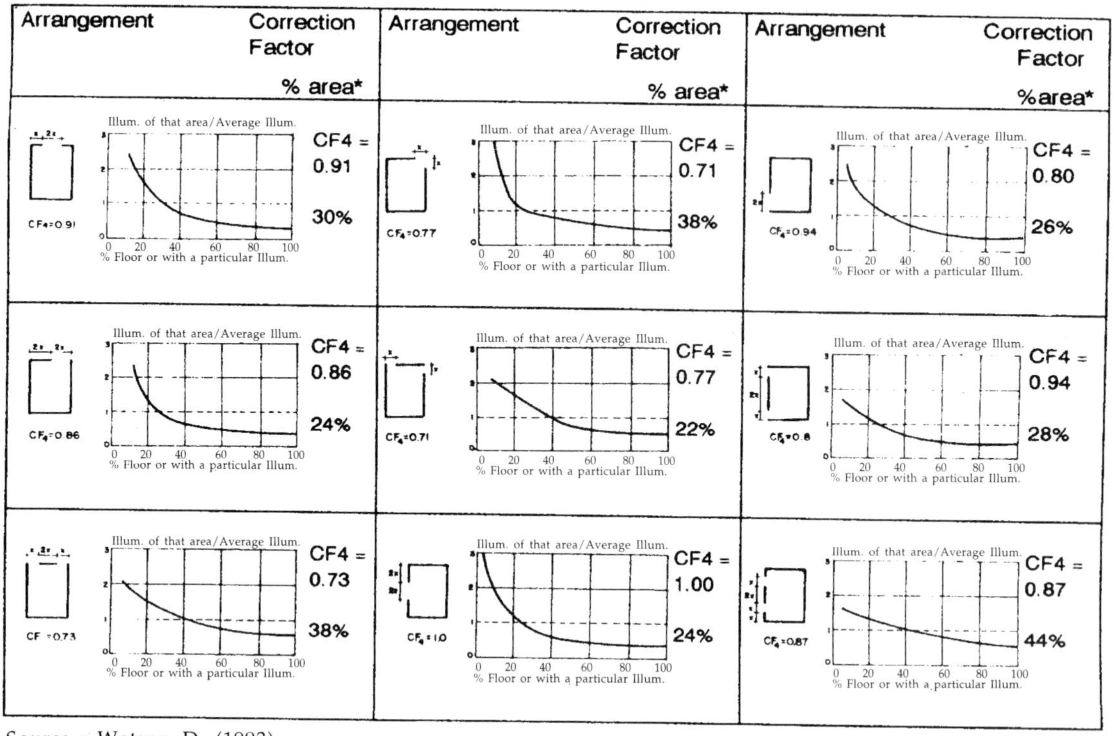

Source : Watson D. (1993)

Figure 8.28: Influence of window placement of daylight

As indicated in the goals of this study some simplified graphs for fenestration analysis pertaining to daylighting have been developed. The developed graphs can be used effectively by the designers in tropics for forward analysis stage of design, as follows:

To find the average illumination in a given room

(a) Required daylight factor is calculated by the ratio of required lux and the design sky (Fig. 8.23)

(b) The correction factor (CF1) for sill correction is divided by the above value from Fig. 8.24.

(c) The correction factor (CF2) is applied from Fig. 8.25 to incorporate the effect due to reflectance of walls

(d) Then the correction factor (CF3) for the area of the room from Fig. 8.26 is also divided by the above value of the daylight factor

(e) Finally, from table 8.27 (whichever case is to the given arrangement) correction factor (CF4) is selected and also applied

(f) Now by multiplying the final value with the design sky (say 8000 lux) the average illumination in the room can be obtained.

I= DF x 1/CF1 x 1/CF2 x 1/CF3 x 1/CF4 x design sky

where

I = average illumination

DF=average daylight factor

CF1 to CF4= various correction factors

8.11 USE OF DESIGN CURVES

The developed design curves for daylighting design can be effectively used as described below in the conceptual stage of the design of the building. To design the fenestration for a given lux level

Example

Room area	72 m^2
Required illumination	300 lux
Reflexion coefficient of walls Sill height= working plane height (0.75 m above the floor level)	0.6
Window to be at the center of the longer wall	
Length/width of room	1.5
Design sky	8000 lux

Calculation

Required daylight factor=

given lux/design sky= 300x100/8000=3.75

Applying necessary corrections

1. Sill height coinciding working plane height (Fig. 8.24), CF1= 1.
2. For 0.6 reflectance of wall (Fig. 8.25), CF2= 1.0
3. Area of the room 72 m^2 (Fig. 8.26), CF3= 1.4
4. For location of window at center of larger wall (Fig. 8.27), CF4= 1.0

Average daylight factor = 3.75/1 x 1/1 x 1/1.4 x 1/1.0 = 2.68

Required fenestration is about 7 m^2 from Fig. 8.23.

- The window area calculated this way should be uniformly distributed all over building facades to achieve uniformity of daylighting. Clerestories or skylights are usually much more effective in the distribution of daylight than the vertical windows.

- In any case, all buildings require artificial lighting to provide adequate lighting for occupants during the hours of no sunshine. Also in zones, where it is not possible or impracticable to provide daylight.
- Minimization of artificial lighting is desirable because of two reasons : One the lighting energy has to be paid for. Secondly, the lighting creates heat gain, which will increase the cooling load in an air-conditioned building, while in a non-conditioned building, it may create discomfort.
- Artificial lighting can vary a great deal in terms of energy requirements. A tungsten lamp in an inefficient luminaire can consume as much as 80 Watts/m^2 of electricity, whereas modern high efficiency discharge source with modern luminaire consumes only 12 Watts/m^2 for the same lighting levels.

A detailed discussion on artificial lighting is outside the scope of the present work, however, a brief description of artificial lighting concepts has been presented in the following section.

8.12 LIGHTING LEVEL WITH ARTIFICIAL LIGHTING

An artificial lighting (electric lighting in most cases) system is typically composed of lamps, circuitry, switches and controls and luminaries. Luminaries are fixtures into which lamps are placed; they usually include a reflecting surface to direct the light towards the space to be lighted. The characteristic of all the components must be included when considering the efficiency of a lighting system.

Lighting systems operate according to the relationship.

$$E = \frac{N\,(Lu)(Cu)(L_1)(L_2)}{A}$$

Where E = Illumination in lux

N = Required number of lamps

Lu = Lumen output per lamp

Cu = Coefficient of utilization for the luminaire and other reflecting surface

L_1 = Lamp depreciation factor

L_2 = Luminaire dirt depreciation factor

and A = Area to be lighted.

The lamp depreciation factor L_1 takes into account the deterioration of lamp output with time. It is usually specified by the manufacturer on the basis of testing programs. The luminaire dirt factor L_2, accounts for the effect of dirt accumulates on the luminaire.

The coefficient of utilization Cu, indicates how efficiently the luminaire illuminates the task plane. It is related to room geography and reflectance as well as the characteristics of the luminaire. The IES Lighting Hand Book contains Cu values for various types of luminaires and room characteristics. Manufacturer's literature may also contain Cu values.

A designer has several options for a light source. The light sources are classified as incandescent, fluorescent, high-intensity discharge lamps like mercury vapor, metal halide, high pressure/low pressure sodium etc.(Table 8.11).

Table 8.11: Light source characteristics

Characteristic	Incandescent Including Tungsten halogen	Fluorescent	High-intensity discharge lamps			
			Mercury Vapor (self-ballasted	Metal halide	High Pressure Sodium (improved color)	Low pressure sodium
Wattage (lamp only)	15-1500	15-219	40-1000	175-1000	70-1000	35-180
Life a(hr)	250-12000	7500-24000	10000-15000	1500-15000	24000-10000	18000
Efficacy (lumens/W) lamp only	15-25	55-100	50-60	80-100	75-140	Up to 180
Lumen Maintenance	Fair to Excellent	Fair to Excellent	Very good (good)	Good	Excellent	Excellent
Color rendition	Excellent	Good to excellent	Poor to excellent	Very good	Fair (very good)	Poor
Light direction Control	Very Good to excellent	Fair	Very Good	Very Good	Very Good	Fair
Source Size	Compact	Extended	Compact	Compact	Compact	Extended
Relight time	Immediate	Immediate	3-10 min	10-20 min	Less than 1 min	Immediate
Comparative fixture cost	Low: simple Fixture	Moderate	Higher than incandescent and fluorescent	Generally higher than mercury	High	High
Comparative operating cost	High: short life and low efficacy	Lower than incandescent	Lower than incandescent	Lower than mercury	High	High
Auxiliary equipment needed	Not needed	Needed: medium cost	Needed: high cost	Needed: high cost	Needed: high cost	Needed: high cost

Life and efficacy ratings subject to revision. Check manufacturer's data for latest information

8.13 TYPES OF LIGHTING

Incandescent lamps: An electric current flowing through a thin wire filament causes it to heat to the point of incandescence and to emit light. The required circuitry is very simple as shown in fig.1a. Incandescent lamps are the least efficient of all the commercially available light sources. This is shown in Table 8.11, where efficiency is given in lumens per watt.

A lumen is the amount of visible light fluxes which, falling normally on an area of 1 square foot, will produce an illuminance of 1 foot-candle. Illuminance E, is defined by

$$E = \frac{I}{d^2}$$

Where I is the luminous intensity of the light source and d is the distance from the source in feet. Illuminance has the units of foot-candles. Luminous intensity of various sources is standardized against platinum at 2033 K, which gives off 60 candles/cm^2. Luminous intensity is usually given in candlepower.

Incandescent lamps have shorter lives than light sources of other types. Their advantages are low initial cost and replacement costs, small physical size, and the fact that they can be dimmed to control the light output. Further more, no ballast is required in the circuit.

Fluorescent lamps: Light is produced by a discharge arc passing through a gas in the tube. Ultraviolet rays are converted into visible light by interacting with a phosphor coating on the inside of the tube. A ballast is required in the circuit to regulate current and starting voltage, as shown in Fig.8.29(b).

Fluorescent lamps are more efficient and have longer lives than incandescent lamps. Higher costs, larger size and the need for a ballast are their primary disadvantages.

High-intensity discharge Lamps: These are also discharge lamps and their operating characteristics are similar to those of fluorescent lamps. Figure 1c shows a circuit typical of a mercury vapor system.

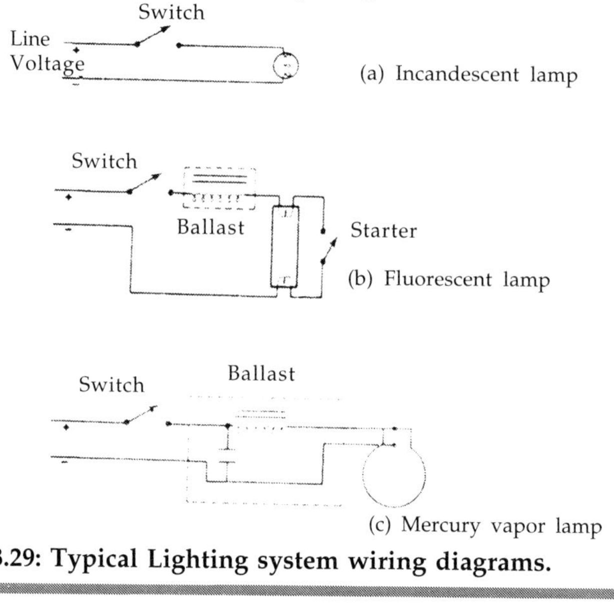

Figure 8.29: Typical Lighting system wiring diagrams.

High-pressure sodium lamps are the most efficient of the three types of HID lamps. All HID lamps take a few minutes to relight after they have been extinguished; thus an emergency auxiliary lighting system might be required.

Low-Pressure Sodium Lamps: These lamps are usually classified separately from fluorescent sources, although both are low-intensity discharge lamps. This is done because there is a difference in the color of the light produced, which may limit its suitability for certain applications. Low-pressure sodium lamps emit a monochromatic yellow light that is not pleasing to the eye. However, they are the most efficient lamps in current use and have relatively long lifetime. They have been extensively used in Europe.

LED Lighting

Light-emitting diodes (LEDs) are a relatively old technology (1970s) that has advanced from use in numeric displays and indicator lights to a range of new and potential applications, including exit signs, accent lights, task light, traffic lights, signage, cove lighting, wall sconces, outdoor lighting and downlighting.

LEDs offer benefits such as small size, long lamp life, low heat output, energy saving and durability. They also allow extraordinary design flexibility in color changing, dimming and distribution by combining these small units into desired shapes, colors, sizes and lumen packages. Currently, relatively low overall light output, poor color rendering and questions about advertised service life may indicate that LEDs, while very useful in many applications, are not yet ready for "prime time" in some architectural applications. Notably promising current applications include retail display, colored lighting, tight spaces, areas that require low light levels, exterior lighting and applications where the integration of light sources and architectural elements is critical.

LEDs currently dominate the exit sign market and many cities have adopted them as a replacement for incandescent lamps in traffic signals. In the architectural market, the development of a visible/white light LED has awakened lighting designers to new possibilities with this light source. White light LEDs, however, currently do not produce enough lumen output to make them competitive with many general light sources. This restricts their use in architectural projects to applications where small lumen packages are needed and where the characteristics of a lower CRI rating and high color temperature are acceptable.

Characteristics of LED

LEDs are solid state semi-conductor devices. LED illumination is achieved when a semiconductor crystal is excited so that it directly produces visible light in a desired wavelength range (color). LED units are small, typically 5mm (T 1-3/4)

Method of Operation of LED

When a LED unit is activated, a power supply converts AC voltage into sufficient DC voltage, which is applied across the diode semi-conductor crystal. This results in electrons (negative charge carries {N} in the diode's electron transport layer and holes (positive charge carriers [P]) in the diode's hole transport layer combining at the P-N junction and converting their excess energy into light. The LED is seated in clear or diffuse plastic lens that can provide a range of angular distributions of light.

Color with LED

The color composition of the light being emitted by the Led is based on the chemical composition of the material being excited. LEDs are available that can produce colors including white, deep blue, green, yellow, amber, orange, red, bright red and deep red.

Efficacy of LED lighting

LEDs are low-voltage, low-current devices and efficient light sources. For red, amber, yellow, green and blue LEDs, new materials have been developed that are more efficient than traditional materials, producing efficacies (lumen per watt) greater than incandescent lamps and rivaling fluorescent lamps. According to Phillips Lighting, "In 1993 an array of 200 LEDs was required whereas only 18 LEDs achieve the same performance today, with prediction of further reduction to only 10." Progress continues. Efficacies as high as 100 LPW have already been achieved in laboratory conditions. According to Steve Johnson, group leader of lighting research for the Lawrence Berkerly National Laboratory, "it is not unrealistic to expect the efficacy of solid-state sources to achieve 150-200 lumen per watt in the coming decades."

White Light LEDs

The utilization of indium gallium nitride (InGaN) as a semi-conductor material resulted in the brightest LEDs and enabled the development of the white light LED.

White light LEDs feature a phosphor added to a blue LED that converts some of the light emission into yellow, resulting in a bluish-white light. White light LEDs are therefore a cool light source with a spectrum of correlated color temperatures of 4,000-11,000K. Color rendering is considered poor. White light can also be achieved by color mixing the light produced by red, blue and green LEDs. The production of visible white light offers the promise that LEDs can be used in general lighting applications. As the light output and color rendering capabilities of LEDs improve, many more architectural applications will open up for this source.

Several manufactures currently offer a range of Led fixtures for replacing MR 16 lamps, display lighting, cove lighting, underwater lighting, architectural details and other applications. Some manufacturers are using colored LED array in these applications, combining red, blue and green LEDs to produce millions of colors, including white light. Designers should carefully consider requisite lumen package, source brightness, viewing angles and color rendering when considering use of this technology.

Advantages of LED Lighting

LEDs offer numerous benefits due to their mode of operation:

(a) Energy Efficiency

LEDs are highly efficient. In traffic signal lights, a strong market for LEDs, a red traffic signal head that contains 196 LEDs draws 10W versus its incandescent counterpart that draws 150W. Various estimates of potential energy savings range from 82% to 93%. With the red signal operating about 50% of the day, the complete traffic signal unit is estimated to save 35-40 %. It is estimated that replacing incandescent lamps in all of America's some 260,000 traffic signals (red, green, yellow) could reduce energy consumption by nearly 2.5 billion kWh. At the end of 1997, more than 150,000 signals were retrofitted, almost all of them red.

In architectural applications, the greatest penetration of LEDs has been in exit signs, both new signs and retrofits. Led retrofit products, which come in various forms including light bars, panels and screw in LED lamps, typically draw 2-5W per sign, resulting in significant savings versus incandescent lamps with the bonus benefit of much longer life, which in turn reduces maintenance requirements. Some of these products are designed specifically for either on-face or two face exit signs. Many new Led exit signs are also available, including edge-lit designs. LED products currently make up about 50% of the exit sign market. A study conducted by the Lighting Research Center in 1998 found that about 80% of the new signs being sold in the U.S utilize LEDs. Note that most retrofits are restricted to use in stencil-type signs versus panel-types signs.

(b) Long Life

Some LEDs are projected to produce a long life of about 100,000 hours. For this reason ideal for hard-to-reach/maintain fixtures such as exit sign lighting and, combined with its durability, pathway lighting. Their service life can be affected by the applications and environmental factors, including heat and if being overdriven by the power supply.

(c) No UV Emissions/Little Infrared

LEDs produce no UV radiation and little heat, making them ideal for illuminating objects, such as work of art, that are sensitive to UV light.

(d) Durable

LEDs are highly rugged. They feature no filament that can be damaged due to shock and vibrations. They are subject to heat, however, and being overdriven by the power supply.

(e) Small Size/design Flexibility

A single LED is very small and produces little light overall. However, this weakness is actually its strength. LEDs can be combined in any shape to produce desired lumen packages as the design goals and economic permit. In addition, LEDs can be considered miniature light fixtures; distribution of light can be controlled by the LEDs epoxy lens, simplifying the construction of architectural fixtures designed to utilize LEDs. A controller can be connected to a LED fixture to selectively dim individual LEDs, resulting in the dynamic control of distribution, light output and color. Finally, DC power enables the unit to be easily adaptable to different power supplies.

(f) Other Benefits

The other benefits of LEDs include:

- Light instantly
- Can be easily dimmed
- Silent Operation
- Low-voltage power supply (increased safety)

Disadvantages of LED Lighting

There are several major disadvantages of LEDs that restrict their application and slow their wider adoption in general lighting applications.

(a) Lack of Choice

There is currently a relative lack of availability of product choices for white LEDs. LEDs are undergoing continuous development, particularly in terms of lumen package per unit and lumens per watt. Progress is continuing rapidly. Philips Lighting and Hewlett-Packard, for example, recently launched LumiLEDs-a joint venture with a starting investment of $150 million, 1,000 employees and facilities in California, The Netherlands and Malaysia-with the goal of rapidly developing LED technology. Many other manufacturers are also exploring this emerging technology.

While some products are available now for the architectural market, it may take a while longer before fixture manufacturers begin to roll out a large selection of products that take advantage of this light source for general illumination.

(b) Color Quality

White LEDs currently offer poor color rendering and a high color temperature. As improvements are made to the technology in the lab, however, we can expect these problems to be corrected.

(c) Product Standardization

There is currently no standardization for this technology, raising questions about maintainability. Will the manufacturer offer matching spare parts when systems begin to fail or will entire systems need to be replaced?

8.14 REDUCTION OF LIGHTING POWER CONSUMPTION

Two choices can be made in changing lighting systems: modification of the existing system, or replacement of one system with another.

Modification of Existing System: several opportunities exist for power reduction in this category. One can:

- Remove lamps from fixtures. This is possible as a review of current accepted illuminance guidelines shows lower requirements than those for which the system was designed.

- Disconnect ballasts when lamps are removed. For systems other than incandescent ones, which have no ballast. The ballast dissipates energy even when the lamp has been removed.

- Replace lamps with lower-wattage lamps.

Table 1 shows comparison between incandescent lamps and various other types of lamps that could be substituted for them. It shows, for example, that one 100-watt incandescent lamp produces almost the same lumen as two 60- watt lamps although it has 16.7% less wattage.

The only discharge lamp that can be substituted for an incandescent lamp is the "self-ballasted" mercury vapor lamp. Standard mercury lamps are more efficient than self-ballasted mercury lamps, hence self ballasted lamps are not suitable for new installations. Self-ballasted lamps also have a high initial cost. Thus, even though they are easy to install in an existing incandescent fixture, economics might justify a complete replacement with standard mercury lamps.

Replacement of Existing System: An economic analysis might indicate that complete replacement of a lighting system is desirable. In that case, more options for a particular type of lamp exist.

The decision to replace is based on the following steps:

1. Select a light source that has the highest efficiency, compatible with other system requirements such as life, color rendition and other factors listed in Table 1.

2. Select the appropriate luminaire.

3. Estimate the required number of lamps per luminaire, and the number of luminaries.

4. Determine the initial and installation cost of the system and the energy savings compared to the old system.

5. Make an economic feasibility study.

The lighting designer is not constrained by existing equipment when designing a new installation, and can choose the most efficient available system that is compatible with a client's needs.

8.15 ELECTRICAL LIGHTING ANALYSIS

There are two fundamental approaches that are commonly used for calculating illuminance due to electrical lighting. The first approach (average illuminance determined by the lumen method) is derived from the lumen definition and the fact that one foot_candle is equal to one lumen incident on one square foot of area. The method is best suited to calculate the average illuminance over an area where luminaries are evenly spaced. The second approach (the point method) uses the candle power distribution curve in conjunction with the cosine effect and inverse square effect to calculate the illuminance at a single point due to one or two luminaries.

Average illuminance: Lumen Method

By definition we know that

$$\text{Illuminance} = \frac{\text{Luminous Flux}}{\text{Area}}$$

$$\text{Footcandles} = \frac{\text{Lumens}}{\text{Square feet}}$$

$$\text{Lux} = \frac{\text{Lumen}}{\text{per square meter}}$$

Coefficient of Utilization

In actual practice, only a portion of the lumen reaches the work place. This portion of lumen produced by a lamp depends upon selected luminaries as well as the environment around it. Coefficient of Utilization (CU) is the term used to describe the part of lumens reaching the task plane (express as percentage). It is a function of three factors:

- Room surface(ceiling, wall and floor) reflectors
- Room size and proportions
- Luminaires characteristics (efficiency and intensity distribution)

For example, if a particular luminaire/room combination had a CU of 0.75, the 75% of the lumen produced by the lamp would reach the work plane.

Room Surface Reflectance

All surfaces in the room (wall, ceilings, floors, furniture, machines, and people) absorb and reflect light. If these surfaces are highly reflective, less light is absorbed and more light is reflected back into space. Since some of the light will eventually reach the work plane, luminaries will perform more efficiently in rooms with high-reflectance surfaces.

Room size and proportions

Except in a totally indirect lighting system, light travels directly from the luminaire to the work plane while other light travels to the walls where some is absorbed and some reflected towards the workplane. In small rooms, a larger percentage of the total light produced by luminaries strikes the walls than in large rooms. As a result, the same luminaries will have a higher CU in large rooms. Similarly, luminaries will have a higher CU in rooms with a relatively low fixture mounting (or ceiling) height.

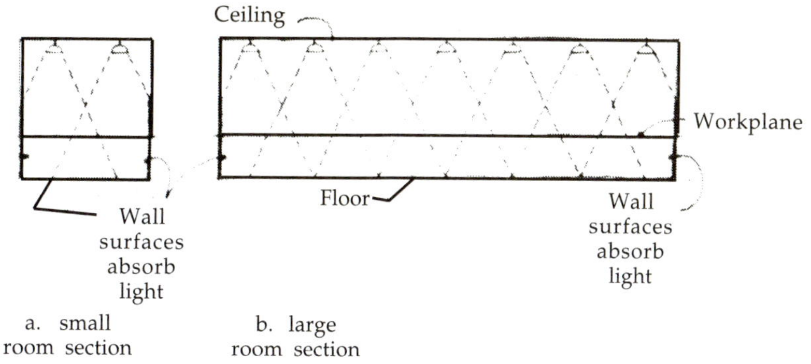

Figure 8.30: Room surface reflection

In small rooms, a larger percentage of the total light produced by the luminaries strikes the walls than in large rooms. It can be noted that in the small room a large part of the light from the luminaire strikes the walls, while in large room some of the light from the end luminaries hits the wall, but the luminaries in the center send all of their light directly to the workplane as shown in Figure 8.30. As a result, the same luminaries will have a higher CU in large rooms.

Type of luminaire

The design and light distribution characteristics and efficiency of the luminaire also affect the CU. Some luminaries (such as recessed deep-baffle down lights) have interior surfaces or cavities that tarp or absorb light; others have low or medium transmittance lenses or translucent closures that absorb light to varying degrees. Still others are designed to direct all of the light to the ceiling from which it is reflected back to the work plane. All of these types will typically be less efficient (and have a lower CU) than peon-bottom luminaries with high-reflectance interior surfaces that reflect and direct light $ñ_c$ to the work plane.

Initial Average Workplane Illuminance

The work plane is the height at which the task is performed; for office work, it is considered to be 75cm(30 inch) above the floor (normal desk/table height). The room cavity height is the distance from the luminaire to the workplane.

Consider an office 450cm (15 ft) long by 300cm (10 ft) wide by 255cm (8.5 ft) high, ceiling reflectance $ñ_c$ = 80 percent, wall reflectance $ñ_w$ = 50 percent, and floor reflectance $ñ_f$ = 20 percent, and a workplane height of 75cm (30 inch) Select 50 fc for this office environment from illuminance category E.

Calculate the room cavity ratio RCR:

$$RCR = \frac{5(\text{room cavity height})(\text{room length} + \text{room width})}{(\text{room length})(\text{room width})}$$

For the example room RCR = [5(6)(15+10)]/ [(15)(10)] = 5

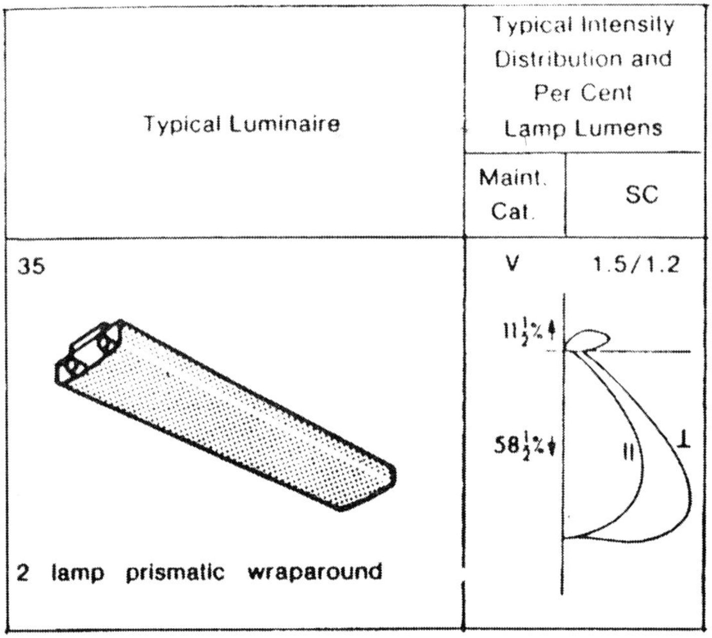

$\tilde{n}_{cc} \rightarrow$	80			70			50			30			10			0	WDRC
$\tilde{n}_{w} \rightarrow$	50	30	10	50	30	10	50	30	10	50	30	10	50	30	10	0	
RCR ↓	Coefficients of Utilization for 20 Per Cent Effective Floor Cavity Reflectance (ρ_{FC} = 20)																
0	0.81	0.81	0.81	0.78	0.78	0.78	0.72	0.72	0.72	0.66	0.66	0.66	0.61	0.61	0.61	0.59	
1	0.71	0.69	0.66	0.69	0.66	0.64	0.64	0.62	0.60	0.59	0.58	0.56	0.55	0.54	0.53	0.50	0.204
2	0.64	0.59	0.56	0.61	0.58	0.54	0.57	0.54	0.51	0.53	0.51	0.49	0.49	0.48	0.46	0.44	0.184
3	0.57	0.52	0.48	0.55	0.50	0.47	0.51	0.48	0.45	0.48	0.45	0.42	0.45	0.42	0.40	0.38	0.168
4	0.51	0.46	0.41	0.49	0.44	0.41	0.46	0.42	0.39	0.43	0.40	0.37	0.41	0.38	0.35	0.34	0.156
5	0.46	0.40	0.36	0.44	0.39	0.35	0.41	0.37	0.34	0.39	0.35	0.32	0.37	0.33	0.31	0.29	0.147
6	0.41	0.35	0.31	0.40	0.35	0.31	0.38	0.33	0.30	0.35	0.31	0.28	0.33	0.30	0.27	0.26	0.137
7	0.37	0.31	0.27	0.36	0.31	0.27	0.34	0.29	0.26	0.32	0.28	0.25	0.30	0.27	0.24	0.23	0.129
8	0.33	0.28	0.24	0.32	0.27	0.23	0.30	0.26	0.22	0.29	0.25	0.22	0.27	0.24	0.21	0.19	0.122
9	0.30	0.24	0.20	0.29	0.24	0.20	0.27	0.23	0.19	0.26	0.22	0.19	0.24	0.21	0.18	0.17	0.116
10	0.27	0.22	0.18	0.26	0.21	0.18	0.25	0.20	0.17	0.23	0.19	0.16	0.22	0.18	0.16	0.15	0.110

Figure 8.31: Typical coefficient of Utilization (CU) table for a fluorescent luminaire

Table 8.12: Data for Selected Lamps

Description	Watts	Base	Initial Lumens	Initial Lumens/ Watt	Lamp Lumen Depreciation, %	Rated Average Life (hours)
Incandescent A-19 frosted	100	Medium	1,740	17.4	90.5	750
Incandescent PS-30 frosted	200	Medium	3,700	18.5	85	750
Tungsten Halogen T-3 clear	500	RSC	10,500	20.8	96	1,500
Incandescent R-40 flood	300	Medium	3,600	12.0	90	2,000
Fluorescent 48" T-12 RS CW	41	Med.Bi.	3,150	76.8	84	20,000
Fluorescent 48" T-12 RS CWX	41	Med.Bi.	2,200	53.6	84	20,000
Fluorescent 96" T-12 RS CW	113	Rec Dc	9,150	76.8	82	12,000
Fluorescent 48" T-12 RS CWX	113	Rec Dc	6,533	53.6	82	12,000
Mercury HID H37KC-250/C	250	Mog.	18,850	75.4	89	24,000
Metal Halide HID M58PH-250	250	Mog.	20,500	82.0	78	10,000
HP Sodium HID S50VC-250	250	Mog.	26,000	104.0	90	24,000

Reading from the table in Fig.8.31 for RCR = 5, $ñ_c$ = 80 percent and $ñ_w$ = 50 percent, CU = 0.46. (In more typical cases, the values of the RCR will not be a simple integer and interpolation will be necessary.)

Modifying the formula:

Footcandles = lumens/Square feet

Footcandles =[(lumens per lamp)(no. lamps luminaire)(CU)]/ Floor area

From Table 8.12 (or the lamp manufacturer's literature). For a fluorescent 48" T-12 RS CWX lamp, the initial lumen output per lamp is 2.200lm. There are two lamps in this luminaire. Thus the average illuminance can be calculated:

Initial avarage illuminance per luminaire =

$$\frac{(200)(2)(0.46)}{150} = 13.5 \text{ fc}$$

LIGHT LOSS FACTORS

The initial illuminance must be reduced by the light loss factor, LLF, to determine the maintained illuminance. The LLF is the product of a number of sub factors (each of which is 1.0 or less):

Luminaire ambient temperature factor, LATF- if the ambient temperature of fluorescent lamps is significantly higher or lower than normal room temperature, then the lamp lumen output is reduced by the LATF (available from lamp manufacture's literature or see Fig.8.32(a). No adjustment is necessary for either incandescent or HID lamps because their output is not normally affected by temperature.

Voltage to luminance factor, VLF- if the service voltage will be predictably high or low, an adjustment factor should be applied [see Fig.8.32(b)]

Ballast factor, BF- typically use a 0.95 BF for fluorescent and HID lamps, and 1.0 for incandescent lamps.

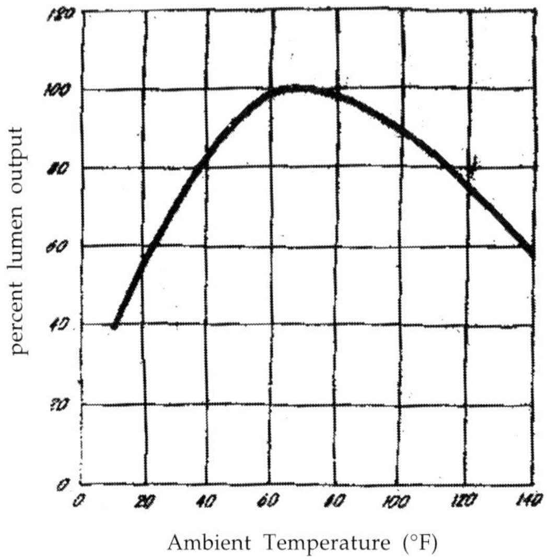

Figure 8.32(a): Luminaire ambient temperature factors, LATF, for F-40 fluorescent lamps

Luminaire surface depreciation factor, LSDF- Luminaire surfaces depreciate over time (due to corrosion of reflectors, lens discoloration, etc.). Unless specific data is available, assume 1.0.

Lamp burnout factor, LBF- in the past, it was common practice to allow a certain percentage of lamps to burn out before relamping. Presently, with higher energy costs, lamps are typically replaced immediately and this factor can be omitted (equal to 1.0).

Lamp Lumen depreciation factor, LLDF- lumen output gradually and predictably decreases throughout the life of the lamp. This factor depends on the construction of the Luminaire (varies with category of Luminaire, see manufacturer's literature), the dirt conditions within the space, and the frequency of luminaire washing (see Fig.8.33).

Room surface depreciation factor, RSDF-the accumulation of dirt on room surfaces reduces the amount of light reflected to the workplane (see Fig.8.34).

In the present example, these factors are:

Luminaire ambient temperature factor, LATF = 1.0 (operating at normal room temperature).

Voltage to Luminaire factor, VLF = 1.0 (operates at rated voltage).

Ballast factor, BF = 0.95 (ballast factor for fluorescent lamps).

Luminaire surface depreciation factor, LSDF = 1.0 (anticipate no deterioration due to age).

Lamp burnout factor, LBF = 1.0 (burnouts will be replaced immediately).

Lamp lumen depreciation factor, LLDF = 0.84 (from Table 8.12).

Luminaire dirt depreciation factor, LDDF = 0.86 (from Fig. 8.33: assumes "very clean" conditions for office environment: category V Luminaire maintenance)

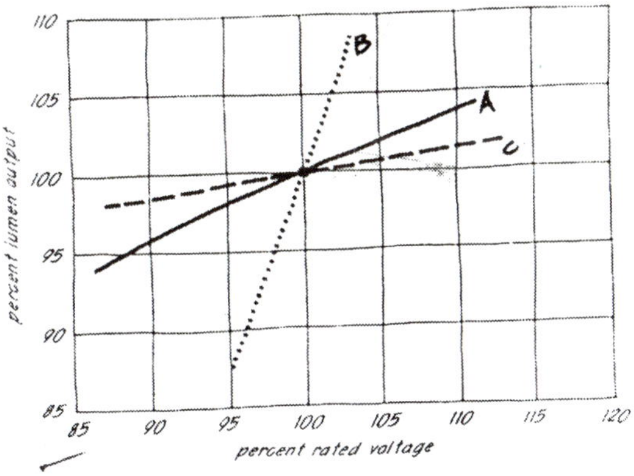

Figure 8.32(b): Voltage to Luminaire factor, VLF: (a) fluorescent, (b) incandescent and mercury with non-regulated ballast, and (c) mercury with constant-wattage ballast.

Classification from CU table in Fig.8.32(b) or manufacturer's literature; and 36 months Luminaire cleaning interval).

Room surface depreciation factor, RSDF =0.94 (see Fig.8.34: based on RCR = 5, 10 percent expected dirt depreciation with this "semidirect" Luminaire-some light is up, most is down).

Thus the light loss factor,

LLF = (LATF)(VLF)(BF)(LSDF)(LBF)(LLDF)(LDDF)(RSDF)

= (1.0)(1.0)(0.95)(1.0)(1.0)(0.84)(0.86)(0.94) = 0.69

MAINTAINED ILLUMINANCE PER LUMINAIRE

Average maintained illuminance per Luminaire

= (initial illuminance per Luminaire)(LLF)

= (13.5)(0.69) = 9.3 fc

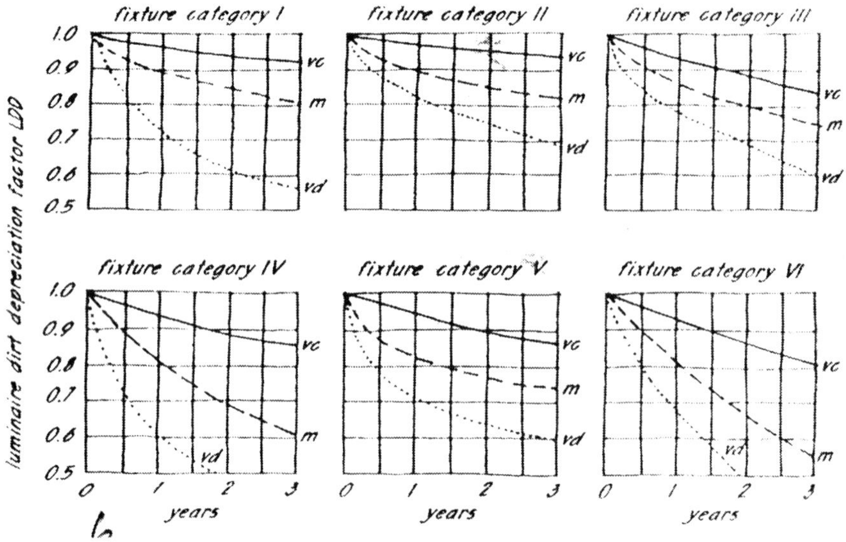

Figure 8.33: Luminaire dirt factor, LDDF

LDDF is a measure of the effect of air cleanliness and luminaire design on reducing lumen output over a period of time. The curves for very clean (solid line), average (dashed line), and very dirty (dotted line) for six maintenance categories of luminaires. See the coefficient of utilization table from manufacturer's literature to determine the maintenance category.

Table 8.13 : Room Surface Dirt Depreciation Factors

Per cent Expected Dirt Depre-ciation	Luminaire Distribution Type																			
	Direct				Semi-Direct				Direct-Indirect				Semi-Indirect				Indirect			
	10	20	30	40	10	20	30	40	10	20	30	40	10	20	30	40	10	20	30	40
Room Cavity Ratio																				
1	0.98	0.96	0.94	0.92	0.97	0.92	0.89	0.84	0.94	0.87	0.80	0.76	0.94	0.87	0.80	0.73	0.90	0.80	0.70	0.60
2	0.98	0.96	0.94	0.92	0.96	0.92	0.88	0.83	0.94	0.87	0.80	0.75	0.94	0.87	0.79	0.72	0.90	0.80	0.69	0.59
3	0.98	0.95	0.93	0.90	0.96	0.91	0.87	0.82	0.94	0.86	0.79	0.74	0.94	0.86	0.78	0.71	0.90	0.79	0.68	0.58
4	0.97	0.95	0.92	0.90	0.95	0.90	0.85	0.80	0.94	0.86	0.79	0.73	0.94	0.86	0.78	0.70	0.89	0.78	0.67	0.56
5	0.97	0.94	0.91	0.89	0.94	0.90	0.84	0.79	0.93	0.86	0.78	0.72	0.93	0.86	0.77	0.69	0.89	0.78	0.66	0.55
6	0.97	0.94	0.91	0.88	0.94	0.89	0.83	0.78	0.93	0.85	0.78	0.71	0.93	0.85	0.76	0.68	0.89	0.77	0.66	0.54
7	0.96	0.94	0.90	0.87	0.93	0.88	0.82	0.77	0.93	0.84	0.77	0.70	0.93	0.84	0.76	0.68	0.89	0.76	0.65	0.53
8	0.96	0.93	0.89	0.86	0.93	0.87	0.81	0.75	0.93	0.84	0.76	0.69	0.93	0.84	0.76	0.68	0.88	0.76	0.64	0.52
9	0.96	0.92	0.88	0.85	0.93	0.87	0.80	0.74	0.93	0.84	0.76	0.68	0.93	0.84	0.75	0.67	0.88	0.75	0.63	0.51
10	0.96	0.92	0.87	0.83	0.93	0.86	0.79	0.72	0.93	0.84	0.75	0.67	0.92	0.83	0.75	0.67	0.88	0.75	0.62	0.50

NUMBER OF LUMINARIES

Establish the design illuminance level for the room. In this example, the design illuminance level is established as 50 fc. Calculate the number of Luminaries required:

$$\text{Number of Luminaries} = \frac{\text{design illuminance level}}{\text{Net illuminance per luminaire}}$$

Thus, the number of Luminaries required = 5/9.3 = 5.4 or 6

LIMITATION OF METHOD

The lumen method as presented here is a simplification of the zonal cavity method. It assumes that Luminaries are surface-mounted; however, it may be applied where the luminaire-to-ceiling distance is comparatively small and wall reflectance above the luminaire plane equals the ceiling reflectance. For large ceiling cavities the more complex general zonal cavity procedure is recommended.

ILLIMINANCE AT A POINT- POINT METHOD

The lumen method discussed above calculates the illuminance in a work plane averaged over the entire floor area. However, the illuminance at any point may vary considerably at a specific location. For critical locations, it is desirable to calculate the illuminance at one specific point. This point method includes only the direct component of the illuminance from a luminaire; one of its principal disadvantages is that it does not include any indirect light reflected from ceilings or walls.

INVERSE-SQUARE EFFECT

The most widely used method of point illuminance calculation is based on the inverse-square effect which can be expressed:

$$E = \frac{I}{d^2}$$

where E = illuminance in footcandles

I = luminous intensity of the source in candelas

d = distance from the source in feet

In other words, if the source has a luminous intensity of one candela, then the illuminance on a surface at a distance of one foot the source is one lumen per square foot or one footcandle. When the area over which the same lumen is spread is proportionally doubled in width and doubled in height (or 4 ft^2) so that the illuminance is 02.5 fc (lumens per foot). Similarly, moving to three feet from the sources distributes the same one lumen over an area of 9 ft^2 resulting in an illuminance of 1/9 fc. In other words, there is an inverse relationship between illuminance and the square of the distance from the source.

COSINE EFFECT

While the above inverse-square formula gives the illuminance at a point on a plane normal (perpendicular) to the direction of light, in practice this perpendicular relationship is rarely encountered. In most instances, a correction must be applied that reduces the illuminance as the angle of incidence (tilt: the angle between light rays and the perpendicular of the plane) increases. This correction is equal to the cosine of the angle of incidence, and modifies the above formula to become:

$$E = \frac{I}{d^2} = \text{Cos } \beta$$

where β = angle of incidence (the angle between light rays and the perpendicular of the plane).

For more details about designing for day-lighting or artificial lighting, references listed in bibliography may be referred.

8.16 ECBC REQUIREMENTS AND COMPLIANCE

Skylights are very commonly used for improving day-lighting inside buildings. ECBC requirements for skylights have already been discussed in Chapter-7 along with discussing requirements for windows. This section primarily explains requirements for artificial lighting system.

Lighting systems and equipment shall comply with the mandatory provisions of this section and the prescriptive criteria. The lighting requirements in this section shall apply to:

(a) Interior spaces of buildings,

(b) Exterior building features, including facades, illuminated roofs, architectural features, entrances, exits, loading docks, and illuminated canopies, and,

(c) Exterior building grounds lighting that is provided through the building's electrical service.

Exceptions would be considered

(a) for emergency lighting that is automatically off during normal building operation and is powered by battery, generator, or other alternate power source; and,

(b) Lighting in dwelling units.

Mandatory Requirements

(a) Automatic Lighting Shutoff

Interior lighting systems in buildings larger than 500 m^2 (5,000 ft^2) shall be equipped with an automatic control device. Within these buildings, all office areas less than 30 m2 (300 ft2) enclosed by walls or ceiling-height partitions, all meeting and conference rooms, all school classrooms, and all storage spaces shall be equipped with occupancy sensors. For other spaces, this automatic control device shall function on either:

- A scheduled basis at specific programmed times. An independent program schedule shall be provided for areas of no more than 2,500 m2 (25,000 ft^2) and not more than one floor; or,
- Occupancy sensors that shall turn the lighting off within 30 minutes of an occupant leaving the space. Light fixtures controlled by occupancy sensors shall have a wallmounted, manual switch capable of turning off lights when the space is occupied.

Exception to this requirement is given to lighting systems designed for 24-hour use.

(b) Space control

Each space enclosed by ceiling-height partitions shall have at least one control device to independently control the general lighting within the space. Each control device shall be activated either manually by an occupant or automatically by sensing an occupant. Each control device shall :

- Control a maximum of 250 m^2 (2,500 ft^2) for a space less than or equal to 1,000 m^2 (10,000 ft^2), and a maximum of 1,000 m^2 (10,000 ft^2) for a space greater than 1,000 m^2 (10,000 ft^2).
- Be capable of overriding the shutoff control required in automatic lighting shotoff for no more than 2 hours, and
- Be readily accessible and located so the occupant can see the control.

The required control device may be remotely installed if required for reasons of safety or security. This would be treated as exception to the readily accessible requirement if considered. A remotely located device shall have a pilot light indicator as part of or next to the control device and shall be clearly labeled to identify the controlled lighting.

(c) *Control in day lighted areas*

Luminaries in daylighted areas greater than 25 m2 (250 ft2) shall be equipped with either a manual or automatic control device that:

- Is capable of reducing the light output of the luminaries in the daylighted areas by at least 50%, and
- Controls only the luminaries located entirely within the daylighted area.

(d) *Exterior lighting control*

Lighting for all exterior applications (unless exempted) shall be controlled by a photosensor or astronomical time switch that is capable of automatically turning off the exterior lighting when daylight is available or the lighting is not required.

(e) *Additional Control*

The following lighting applications shall be equipped with a control device to control such lighting independently of general lighting:

- Display/Accent Lighting. Display or accent lighting greater than 300 m^2 (3,000 ft^2) area shall have a separate control device.
- Case Lighting. Lighting in cases used for display purposes greater than 300 m^2 (3,000ft^2) area shall be equipped with a separate control device.
- Hotel and Motel Guest Room Lighting. Hotel and motel guest rooms and guest suites shall have a master control device at the main room entry that controls all permanently installed luminaries and switched receptacles.
- Task Lighting. Supplemental task lighting including permanently installed under shelf or under cabinet lighting shall have a control device integral to the Luminaries or be controlled by a wall-mounted control device provided the control device complies with space control conditions.
- Nonvisual Lighting. Lighting for nonvisual applications, such as plant growth and food-warming, shall be equipped with a separate control device.
- Demonstration Lighting. Lighting equipment that is for sale or for demonstrations in lighting education shall be equipped with a separate control device accessible only to authorized personnel.

(f) *Exit signs*

Internally-illuminated exit signs shall not exceed 5 W per face.

(g) *Exterior Building Ground Lighting*

Lighting for exterior building grounds luminaries which operate at greater than 100 W shall contain lamps having a minimum efficacy of 60 lm/W unless the luminaire is controlled by a motion sensor or exempt under the heading of automatic shutoff.

(h) *Interior Lighting*

The installed interior lighting power for a building or a separately metered or permitted portion of a building shall be calculated in accordance with installed interior lighting power norms and shall not exceed the interior lighting power allowance determined in accordance with either building area method or space function method. Tradeoffs of interior lighting power allowance among portions of the building for which a different method of calculation has been used are not permitted. The following lighting equipment and applications shall not be considered when determining the interior lighting power allowance, nor shall the wattage for such lighting be included in the installed interior lighting power. However, any such lighting shall not be exempt unless it is an addition to general lighting and is controlled by an independent control device:

- Display or accent lighting that is an essential element for the function performed in galleries, museums, and monuments,
- Lighting that is integral to equipment or instrumentation and is installed by its manufacturer,
- Lighting specifically designed for medical or dental procedures and lighting integral to medical equipment,
- Lighting integral to food warming and food preparation equipment,
- Lighting for plant growth or maintenance,
- Lighting in spaces specifically designed for use by the visually impaired,
- Lighting in retail display windows, provided the display area is enclosed by ceiling height partitions,
- Lighting in interior spaces that have been specifically designated as a registered interior historic landmark,
- Lighting that is an integral part of advertising or directional signage,
- Exit signs,
- Lighting that is for sale or lighting educational demonstration systems,
- Lighting for theatrical purposes, including performance, stage, and film or video production, and
- Athletic playing areas with permanent facilities for television broadcasting.

Internal lighting requirements can be complied with through three alternative routes:

Building Area method

Determination of interior lighting power allowance (watts) by the building area method shall be in accordance with the following:

- Determine the allowed lighting power density from Table 8.14 for each appropriate building area type.

- Calculate the gross lighted floor area for each building area type.
- The interior lighting power allowance is the sum of the products of the gross lighted floor area of each building area times the allowed lighting power density for that building area types.

Table 8.14 : Interior Lighting Power - Building Area Method

Building Area Type	LPD (W/m^2)	Building Area Type	LPD (W/m^2)
Automotive Facility	9.7	Multifamily	7.5
Convention Center	12.9	Museum	11.8
Court House	12.9	Office	10.8
Dining: Bar Lounge/Leisure	14.0	Parking Garage	3.2
Dining: Cafeteria/Fast Food	15.1	Penitentiary	10.8
Dining: Family	17.2	Performing Arts Theater	17.2
Dormitory	10.8	Police/Fire Station	10.8
Exercise Center	10.8	Post Office	11.8
Gymnasium	11.8	Religious Building	14.0
Healthcare-Clinic	10.8	Retail	16.1
Hospital/Health Care	12.9	School/University	12.9
Hotel	10.8	Sports Arena	11.8
Library	14.0	Town Hall	11.8
Manufacturing Facility	14.0	Transportation	10.8
Motel	10.8	Warehouse	8.6
Motion Picture Theater	12.9	Workshop	15.1

In cases where both a general building area type and a specific building area type are listed, the specific building area type shall apply.

Space Function Method

Determination of interior lighting power allowance (watts) by the space function method shall be in accordance with the following:

- Determine the appropriate building type from Table 8.15 and the allowed lighting power density.
- For each space enclosed by partitions 80% or greater than ceiling height, determine the gross interior floor area by measuring to the center of the partition wall. Include the floor

area of balconies or other projections. Retail spaces do not have to comply with the 80% partition height requirements.

- The interior lighting power allowance is the sum of the lighting power allowances for all spaces. The lighting power allowance for a space is the product of the gross lighted floor area of the space times the allowed lighting power density for that space.

Table 8.15: Interior Lighting Power – Space Function Method

Space Function	LPD (W/m^2)	Space Function	LPD (W/m^2)
Office-enclosed	11.8	Library	
Office-open plan	11.8	Card File & Cataloging	11.8
Conference/Meeting/Multipurpose	14.0	Stacks	18.3
Classroom/Lecture/Training	15.1	Reading Area	12.9
Lobby	14.0	Hospital	
For Hotel	11.8	Emergency	29.1
For Performing Arts Theater	35.5	Recovery	8.6
For Motion Picture Theater	11.8	Nurse Station	10.8
Audience/Seating Area	9.7	Exam Treatment	16.1
For Gymnasium	4.3	Pharmacy	12.9
For Exercise Center	3.2	Patient Room	7.5
For Convention Center	7.5	Operating Room	23.7
For Religious Buildings	18.3	Nursery	6.5
For Sports Arena	4.3	Medical Supply	15.1
For Performing Arts Theater	28.0	Physical Therapy	9.7
For Motion Picture Theater	12.9	Radiology	4.3
For Transportation	5.4	Laundry – Washing	6.5
Atrium-first three floors	6.5	Automotive – Service Repair	7.5
Atrium-each additional floor	2.2	Manufacturing	
Lounge/Recreation	12.9	Low Bay (<8m ceiling)	12.9
For Hospital	8.6	High Bay (>8m ceiling)	18.3
Dining Area	9.7	Detailed Manufacturing	22.6

For Hotel	14.0	Equipment Room	12.9
For Motel	12.9	Control Room	5.4
For Bar Lounge/Leisure Dining	15.1	Hotel/Motel Guest Rooms	11.8
For Family Dining	22.6	Dormitory – Living Quarters	11.8
Food Preparation	12.9	Museum	
Laboratory	15.1	General Exhibition	10.8
Restrooms	9.7	Restoration	18.3
Dressing/Locker/Fitting Room	6.5	Bank Office – Banking Activity Area	16.1
Corridor/Transition	5.4	Religious Buildings	
For Hospital	10.8	Worship-pulpit, choir	25.8
For Manufacturing Facility	5.4	Fellowship Hall	9.7
Stairs-active	6.5	Retail	
Active Storage	8.6	Sales Area	18.3
For Hospital	9.7	Mall Concourse	18.3
Inactive Storage	3.2	Sports Arena	
For Museum	8.6	Ring Sports Area	29.1
Electrical/Mechanical	16.1	Court Sports Area	24.8
Workshop	20.5	Indoor Field Area	15.1
Sleeping Quarters	3.2	Warehouse	
Convention Center – Exhibit Space	14.0	Fine Material Storage	15.1
		Medium/Bulky Material Storage	9.7
		Parking Garage – Garage Area	2.2
		Transportation	
		Airport – Concourse	6.5
		Air/Train/Bus – Baggage Area	10.8
		Terminal – Ticket Counter	16.1

Installed Interior Lighting Power

The installed interior lighting power calculated for compliance with shall include all power used by the luminaires, including lamps, ballasts, current regulators, and control devices except as specifically exempted. Exception is given if two or more independently operating lighting systems in a space are controlled to prevent simultaneous user operation, the installed interior lighting power shall be based solely on the lighting system with the highest power.

Luminaire Wattage with installed lighting power approach

Luminaire wattage incorporated into the installed interior lighting power shall be determined in accordance with the following:

- The wattage of incandescent luminaires with medium base sockets and not containing permanently installed ballasts shall be the maximum labeled wattage of the luminaires.
- The wattage of luminaires containing permanently installed ballasts shall be the operating input wattage of the specified lamp/ballast combination based on values from manufacturers' catalogs or values from independent testing laboratory reports.
- The wattage of all other miscellaneous luminaire types not described in (a) or (b) shall be the specified wattage of the luminaires.
- The wattage of lighting track, plug-in busway, and flexible-lighting systems that allow the addition and/or relocation of luminaires without altering the wiring of the system shall be the larger of the specified wattage of the luminaires included in the system or 135 W/m (45 W/ft). Systems with integral overload protection, such as fuses or circuit breakers, shall be rated at 100% of the maximum rated load of the limiting device.

(i) Exterior Lighting Power

For building exterior lighting applications specified in Table 8.16, the connected lighting power shall not exceed the specified lighting power limits specified for each of these applications. Trade-offs between applications are not permitted. Exterior lighting for all other applications (except those included in the concerned exceptions) shall comply with the requirements of exterior building ground lightings.

Table 8.16: Exterior Building Lighting Power

Exterior Lighting Applications	Power Limits
Building entrance (with canopy)	13 W/m^2 (1.3 W/ft^2) of canopied area
Building entrance (without canopy)	90 W/lin m (30 W/lin f) of door width
Building exit	60 W/lin m (20 W/lin f) of door width
Building facades	2 W/m^2 (0.2 W/ft^2) of vertical facade area

Exceptions to exterior lighting power requirements is given to lighting used for the following exterior applications is exempt when equipped with an independent control device:

- Specialized signal, directional, and marker lighting associated with transportation;
- Lighting used to highlight features of public monuments and registered historic landmark structures or buildings;
- Lighting that is integral to advertising signage; or
- Lighting that is specifically designated as required by a health or life safety statute, ordinance, or regulation.

9

Building Integrated Renewable Energy Technologies

9.1 INTRODUCTION

The potential threat of global climate change, the increasing energy demand and depletion of fossil fuels, has made sustainable energy supply a planetary issue. Today, buildings play a significant role in the total energy balance. The need for energy and environmentally conscious building design has become more and more pressing, as the ecological consequences of energy consumption become more and more important.

The building designer has already a number of energy saving technologies. This includes thermal insulation, insulated windows, advance heating, ventilation and air-conditioning equipment, passive solar design, climate conscious building orientation, daylighting, energy efficient lighting and applications etc. These measures, if suitably adopted can significantly reduce energy consumption in buildings.

Integration of renewable energy technologies especially solar thermal and solar photovoltaic providing ventilation water heating, cooking and also producing electricity become highly relevant to not only save energy but becoming energy producer. Systems can be installed on or near the host building and give a new dimension to energy conscious design.

9.2 SOLAR THERMAL OPTION

Solar thermal systems capture solar energy and convert it into heat to deliver either hot air or water at temperatures generally between 30 °C and 90 °C.

Systems using density gradients for transporting the working fluid are known as passive systems. Up to a certain capacity, such systems are used for supplying hot water in domestic buildings.

Active solar systems use mechanical means to transport heat from the collector system to locations where it is stored or used. Active systems are designed and applied to both residential and commercial buildings. A primary difference between the two applications is that a residential system, though requiring an auxiliary back up, tends to be designed as the building's primary system, while a commercial solar system is generally only an increment to the building's larger, more conventional mechanical system.

* Watson D. (1993) has been major reference for this Chapter.

Active solar systems can be applied to a variety of needs, including space heating, domestic or service (e.g., restaurant) hot water, space cooling, swimming pool heating and industrial process hot water. All involve solar collectors to absorb and retain solar energy (insulation). All involve a transport fluid, either air or a liquid (generally water or a water-antifreeze solution). The transport fluid requires a network of ducts and fans for air, or pining and pumps for liquid. If the heat is to be transferred from one fluid to another (e.g. from antifreeze solution to water or from water to air) heat exchangers will be required. These elements-collection, transport, heat exchange, distribution and storage-makeup what is normally considered a complete active solar system.

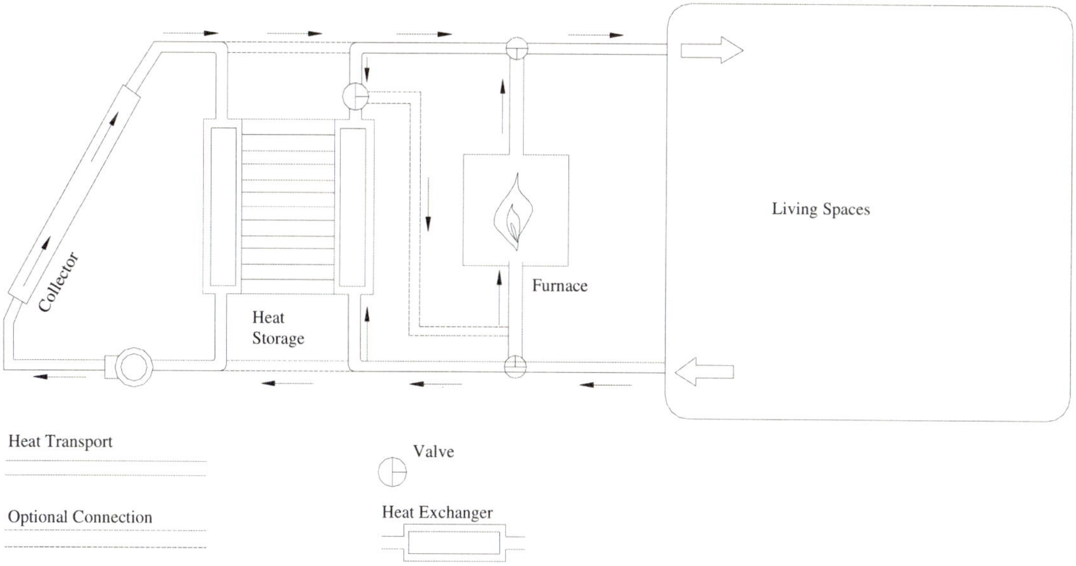

Figure 9.1: Basic solar thermal system

A major factor affecting solar systems is the delivery temperature required. Space heating can be accomplished at lower temperature than domestic water heating, for example, and space cooling usually at lower temperatures than industrial process water heating. This affects a wide range of design decisions (e.g., collector type, amounts of insulation, fluid flow rates, system pressure tolerance).

The symbols shown in Figure 9.2 are used to display various pieces of equipment and their location in the graphic illustrations are presented throughout this chapter.

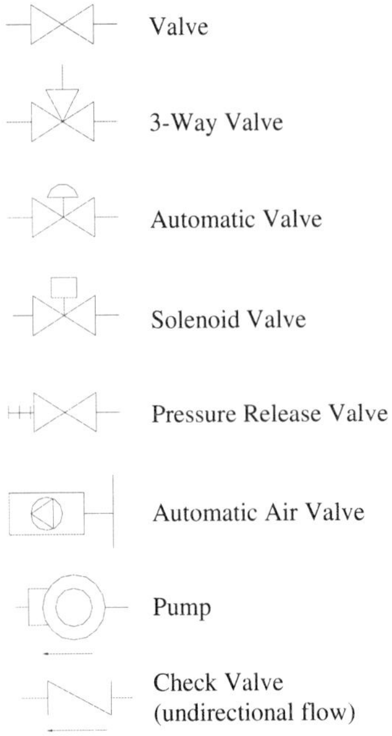

Figure 9.2: Symbols used in graphics

9.2.1 Feasibility Considerations

The feasibility of using an active solar system is best addressed with a focus on the problem to be solved and not a predetermined solution. For example, active solar systems are usually thought of as including collectors, transport systems, storage and perhaps, heat exchangers. Many solar applications, however, do not require all of these elements. Any application in which it is physically possible to collect and use solar energy is, theoretically, feasible. If it is also possible to reduce first costs without either increasing operating costs or decreasing efficiency, feasibility is improved.

An example illustrates the point. The owner of a building in Reno, Nevada, approached a design firm to investigate the possibility of adding a solar system. He was told that this building was well sited and structurally able to support roof-mounted collector arrays, but that a solar system would require an area of collectors four times the size of his roof and an addition to house heat storage. This design response is clearly based on a presumption that the solar system had to satisfy a certain percentage of the total load.

Without that assumption a different design might have been offered. Given the building's relatively constant daytime usage, it would have been possible to limit the number of collectors only to those needed to preheat incoming water for the existing boiler, with fluid transport accomplished by city water pressure. This solution would yield maximum possible collector efficiency and eliminate the first cost for heat exchange and storage.

Economic feasibility is defined here as lower life cycle cost, that is, over the life of a solar system the sum of all costs minus energy savings must be less than the sum of costs for a conventional system plus its energy costs.

Analysts at the National Bureau of Standards have identified five basic energy economic analysis approaches: net benefits or savings, savings-to-investment ratio, internal rate of return, discounted payback and life-cycle costs.

Life-Cycle Costs (LCCs), net benefits (B-C) and Savings-to-Investment ratio (SIR) analysis tools provide virtually the same savings result as would be arrived at by comparing LCC compilations. The SIR expresses not the savings amount, but the ratio of savings per unit of cost for the entire system.

The Internal-Rate-of-Return (IRR) on additional investment is expressed as a percentage. For IRR, only differences in savings and costs are considered. These four analysis tools are all comprehensive life-cycle cost methods that consider the time value of money over the life of a system.

The last method, discounted payback, again considers the time value of money, but only up to the point at which energy savings pay for all initial costs and replacement/maintenance cost incurred to that point.

The shorter the time frame in which specific clients operate, the more likely they are to prefer internal-rate-of-return and discounted-payback.

9.2.2 Site and Climate Analysis

A site and climate analysis for a solar system is performed to ensure that a sufficient quantity of solar radiation falls upon the given location and that it will not be shaded by existing or anticipated obstructions. More extensive information on this topic appears in the "Climate and Site" and "Shading and Sun Control" monographs in this handbook.

The two primary climatic factors to be considered are the geometric relationship at the site and the geometric relationship (angle of incident) between the sun rays and the absorbing collector surface. This amount of solar radiation varies depending on latitude and season, with higher values closer to the equator and the highest annual values around June 21 (*see* accompanying tables).

The incident angle determines percentages of radiation transmitted, reflected and absorbed by collector materials. The incident angle varies with altitude, which is the angle of sun above the horizon and with azimuth, which is the angle between the sun's position and true south. Collectors, other than motorized tracking collectors, are fixed in one plane. Thus the sun moves across the sky and its azimuth and altitude change, the angle of incident also changes. Less solar energy is reflected away from the collector absorber surface as the solar rays come closer to being perpendicular to the plane of the collector.

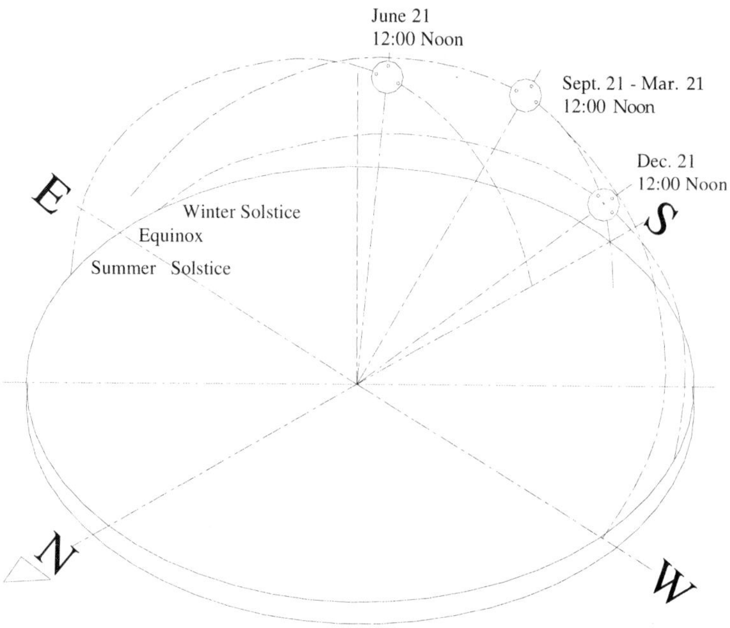

Figure 9.3: Seasonal variation in solar position

Any strategy that increases the amount of time that collectors are more nearly perpendicular to the sun's rays will increase system efficiency. Tracking collectors move continuously to follow the path of the sun. Flat-plate collectors can be mounted with adjustable tilt to be changed seasonally or even monthly. Fixed flat plate collectors are set at the tilt that optimizes the overall amount of heat collected. As a rule of thumb, fixed flat-plate collectors used year round should be mounted to true south and at a tilt equal to latitude plus 5 degrees. If the solar system is designed for use in the heating season only, a higher tilt, of latitude plus 15 degrees, will be more nearly perpendicular to the winter sun.

Site shading patterns and local climatic patterns will determine whether the collectors will see an asymmetrical solar day. If there is a persistent pattern of morning cloudiness or morning shading, for example, then the designer can consider orienting the collectors west of south to maximize collection of afternoon sun.

Existing shading conditions can be subject to changes caused by subsequent growth of trees or construction on adjacent land.

9.2.3 System Types

In active systems, either air or a liquid can be used to collect solar heat. The heat can subsequently be transferred to another fluid using heat exchangers, allowing the manner of supplying heat to the load to be independent of the nature of the heat collection medium.

A solar collector of the liquid or air-heating type, in combination with an insulated storage reservoir with associated pumps (or blowers), piping (or ducting) and a control system are the components necessary for solar heating a space or heating domestic or service hot water.

The collectors can be of the flat plate, evacuated tube, or concentrating type, depending on the temperatures required by the load. Storage can be by a hot-water tank, a rock bed (for air system) or phase-change material.

In residential applications a control system consisting of thermostats and relays controls the solar collection system, the heat distribution system, and their interaction with the auxiliary heating or cooling system. In commercial applications of the solar system itself is more likely to be an auxiliary system, controlled by the controls for the larger HVAC system.

Several additional subsystem components common to most conventional heating, ventilating and air-conditioning systems, but designed specially for the requirements of solar systems, are heat exchangers, pumps and expansion tanks.

In the simplest analysis, there are two system types, air and liquid (primarily water). The major differences in these two approaches are that liquids transport and store heat more efficiently than air and that water freezes.

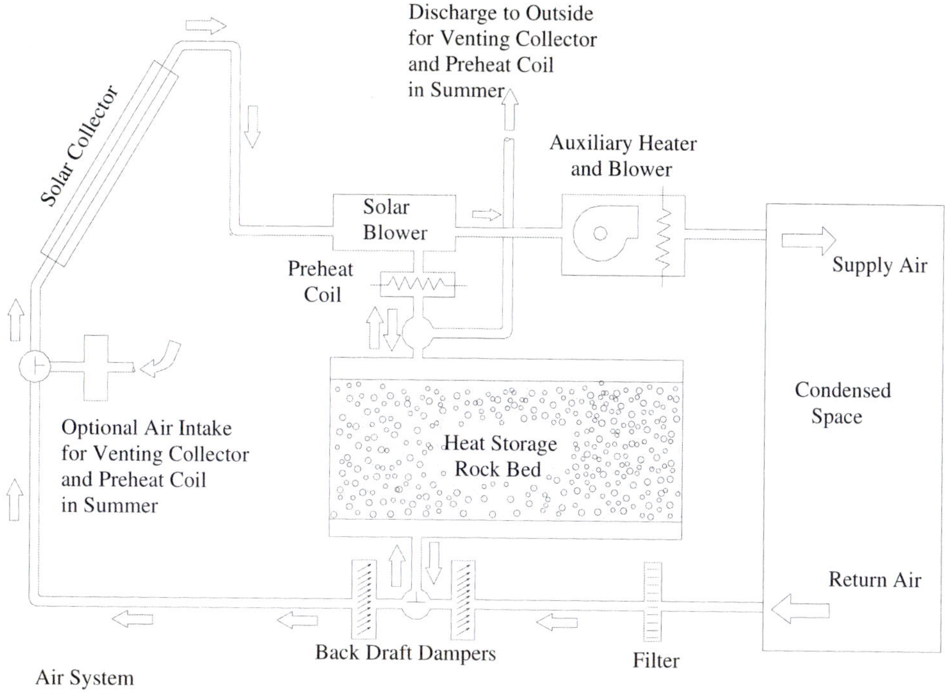

Figure 9.4: Solar air heating system

Using air as the transport medium avoids the freezing problem associated with water collectors, but creates a substantial penalty in additional space requirements. Forced convection of air transfers 30-300 w/m²°C while the same value for water is 300-600 w/m²°C. Air systems also generally use rock storage, which has a similar space penalty. Rocks are 50% more dense than water but will hold only 20% as much heat per pound; three times as much space is required.

There are freezing problems associated with water systems. Most of the conventional means of providing freeze protection diminish system efficiency and increase power requirements.

One common solution to the freezing problem is to circulate an antifreeze solution, rather than water, through the collectors. The antifreeze is less efficient than water as a heat transfer fluid and requires the use of a heat exchanger (double-jacked for domestic hot water systems to preserve purity) and the use of two pumps rather than one. Hydrocarbon and silicon fluids also can be used but are less efficient. These systems are referred to as indirect (double loop) systems.

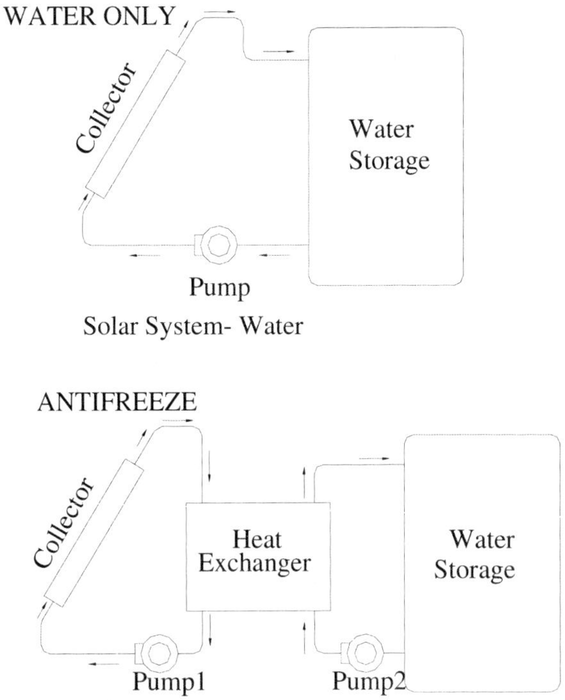

Figure 9.5: Different versions of solar water heating system (Contd.)

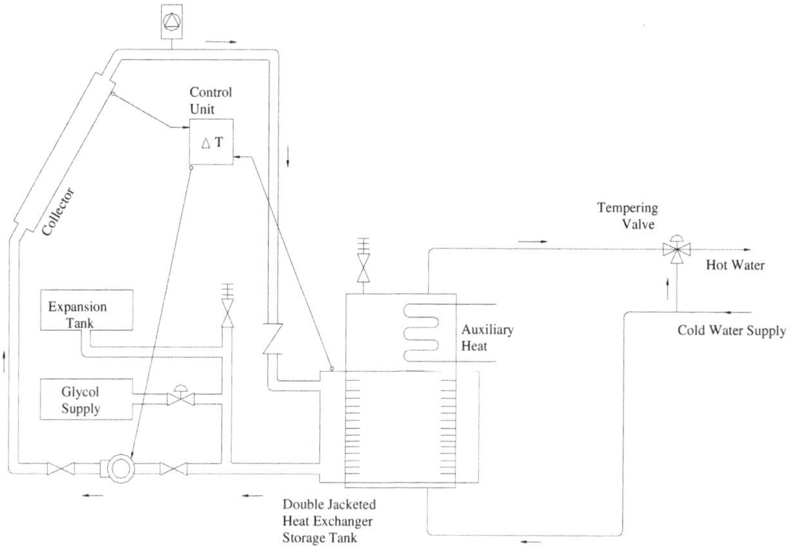

Indirect, Single Tank Liquid System

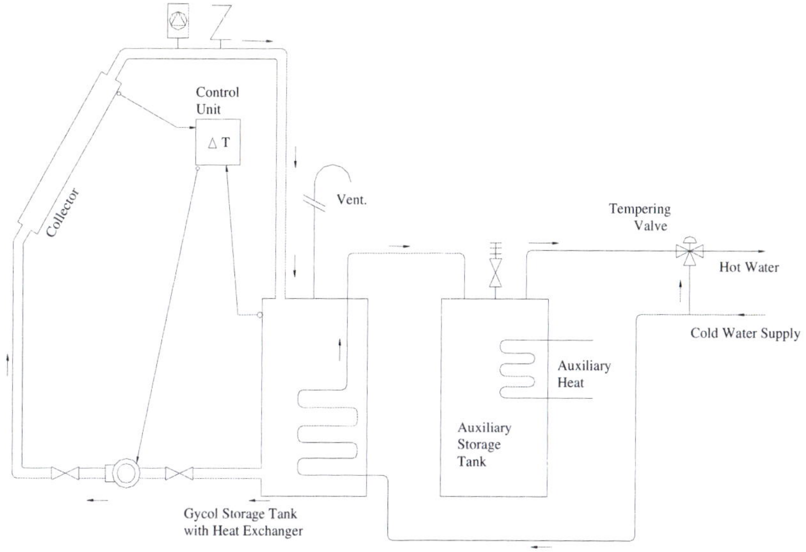

Indirect, Double Tank Liquid System

Figure 9.5: Different versions of solar water heating system (Contd.)

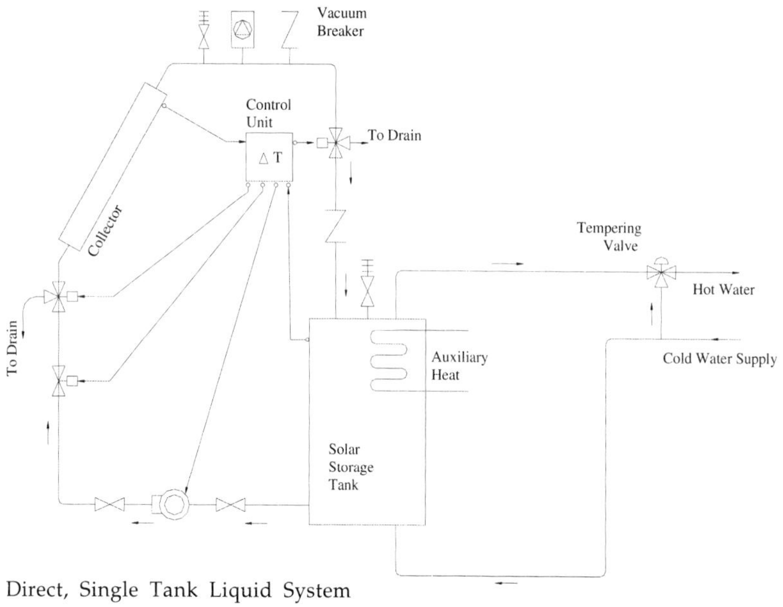

Direct, Single Tank Liquid System

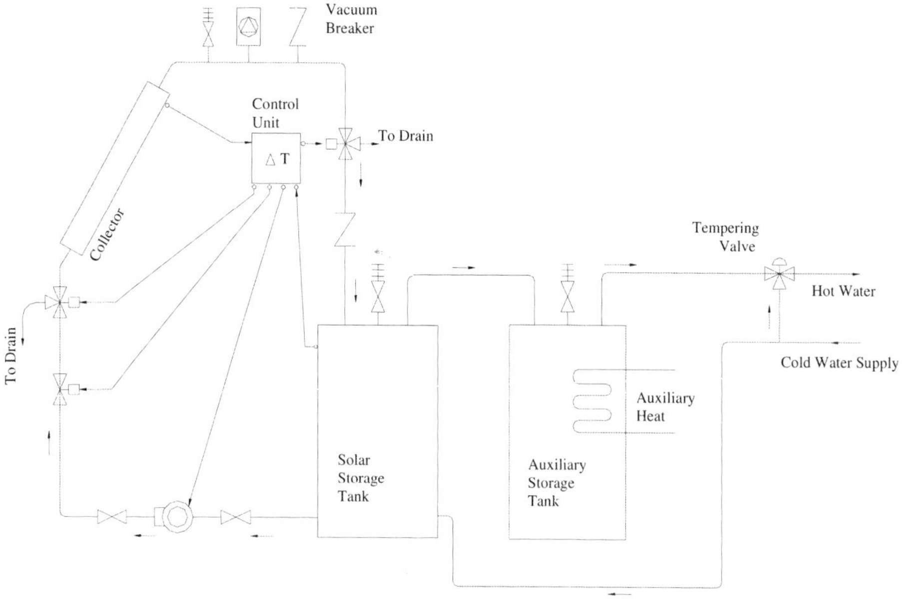

Direct, Single Tank Liquid System

Figure 9.5: Different versions of solar water heating system

Direct systems (single loop) generally circulate water through the collectors only during the heating periods. Provision of draining the collector during freezing weather has to be provided. This generally introduces air into the system each time it is drained, requiring vacuum breakers, air vents, additional sensors and valves. Another method is to re-circulate warm water to heat the collectors above freezing, which obviously cause energy losses.

There are a few variations in the air system and because of considerable space requirement, it is used mainly for the residential market. In commercial buildings, however, considerable amount of heat is available due to internal loads. The air systems can thus be effectively used when combined with forced air duct system.

In commercial and industrial applications, systems tend to be large, the compactness of water systems can therefore be an advantage.

In summary, air and liquid systems offer the following advantages and disadvantages:

Liquid	*Air*
Collector generally more efficient.	Collectors generally operate at slightly lower efficiency.
Can be combined with domestic hot water system and air-cooling systems possible in the future.	Simpler; space heat can be supplied directly. Can preheat domestic hot water. Does not adapt easily to air cooling.
Freeze protection can require antifreeze and heat exchangers; costlier and less efficient.	No freeze protection required.
Precautions must be taken against corrosion, leakage and boiling.	Low maintenance requirements. Leak easily repaired with duct tape; however, they may be difficult to find.
Insulated pipes take up nominal space. Usually higher installation costs for collectors and storage components.	Ductwork and rock storage bed are bulky. Lower equipment costs.
	More energy required to drive fans than pumps. Noisier in operation.

9.2.4 Collectors

The three major types of active solar collectors used in building applications are flat plates, evacuated tubes and various linear concentrator types. Flat plates are by far the most common type used for heating and hot water. Evacuated and concentrating collectors are more often used for applications requiring higher temperatures.

Flat-Plate Collectors :

A flat-plate solar collector consists of the following components.

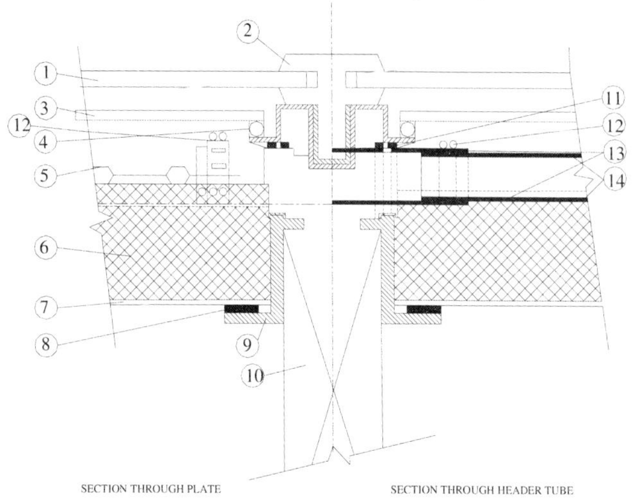

1. OUTER GLASS
2. MEOPRENE GLAZING GASKET
3. INNER GLASS
4. HEAT RESISTANCE GLAZING TAPE
5. FLUID CIRCULATING PLATE
6. RIGID FIBREGLASS INSULATION
7. VAPOR BARRIER BACKING
8. SEALING BED
9. ALUMINIUM EXTRUDED FRAME
10. SUBSTRUCTURE
11. GROMMET AND DESICCANT
12. NOSE CLAMP
13. FLEXIBLE HOSE
14. HEADER TUBE

Figure 9.6: Details of solar collector for water/liquid heating

Absorber plate- metal (usually copper, steel or aluminium) or plastic surface covered with flat black paint or a special selective coating to maximize absorption and minimize re-radiation.

Flow passage- liquid flow is usually through tubes attached to or integral with the absorber plate; air flow occurs above and/or below the plate; the heat-transfer surface area is maximized by means of fins, slots or metal screening.

Cover plate(s)- transparent cover (one, two or three) of tempered glass or various plastic materials are used to reduce convective and radiative heat losses to the outside air.

Insulation- reduces conductive heat losses at the back and side of the collector.

Enclosure—a box to protect collectors components from the weather.

Fluid flow tubes in a flat-plate collector are spaced several inches apart, with the absorber surfaces between acting as fins that absorb heat and conduct it to the tubes. Tube spacing is an efficiency-versus-cost tradeoff. Copper tubes can be welded or soldered to copper plates or clamped to aluminium plates. The thermal conductance of the bond is critical and can vary by a factor of 200. A better technique is to extrude or otherwise form a tube pattern into the plate during manufacture. Tubes can be in parallel from inlet to outlet header or in a single serpentine. The later technique eliminates the possibility of header leaks and ensures uniform flow but also increases pressure drop. When water is used as the heat-transport fluid, drain down freeze protection requires that flow passages be easy to drain.

Unlike liquid collectors, air-collector absorber plates do not require high thermal conductivity because air comes in contact with the entire surface. Routing the air flow beneath the absorber plate reduces thermal loss through the glazing. Heat transfer is enhanced by both increasing surface area and creating turbulent flow, but with a penalty of increased fan power requirements. Air collectors eliminate both freezing and boiling problems. Leaks are also not damaging, though they can degrade performance significantly.

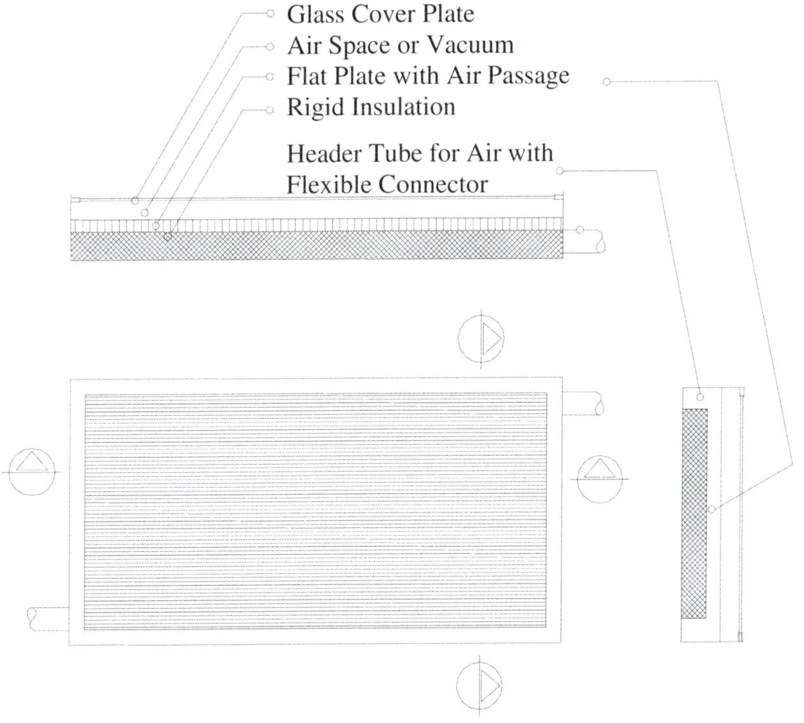

Figure 9.7: Solar collector details for air heating

Table 9.1: Characteristics of Absorptive Coatings

Property or Material	*Absorptance a*	*Emittance ε*	*a/ε*	*Breakdown Temperature F(°C)*	*Comments*
Black Chrome	87-93	.1	-9		
Alkyd Enamel	9	9	1		Durability limited at high temperatures
Black Acrylic Paint	.92-.97	.84-.90	-1		
Black Inorganic Paint	.89-.96	.86-.93	-1		
Black Silicone Paint	.86-.94	.83-.89	1		Silicone binder
Pbs/Silicone paint	.94	.4	2.5	662 (350)	Has a high emittance for thickness>10μm
Flat Black Paint	.95-.98	.89-.97	-1		
Ceramic Enamel	.9	.5	1.8		Stable at high temperature
Black Zinc	.9	.1	9		
Copper Oxide over Aluminium	.93	.11	8.5	392 (200)	
Black Copper over Copper	.85-.90	.08-.12	7-11	842 (450)	Patinates with moisture
Black chrome over Nickel	.92-.94	.07-1.2	8-13	842 (450)	Stable at high temperature
Ni-Zn-S over Nickel	.96	.97	14	536 (280)	May be influenced by moisture at elevated temperatures
Black Iron over Steel	.90	.10	9		

The coating on the absorber plate determines in large part the plate's absorptance and emittance. Absorptance is the measure of how much energy is absorbed rather than reflected or transmitted. Emittance is the measure of how much is reradiated rather than contained. One would like to maximize the first and minimize the latter, or increase the ratio (á/å) between the two. Flat black paint is inexpensive and has a high absorptance (.95-.98), yielding an á/å ratio of 1. Selective surface is the term given to coatings with both high absorptance and low emittance. Black Chrome, one of the more widely used selective surface, has an á/å ratio of 9 (á, 0.9 and å, 0.1). selective surfaces improve collector performance, but increase the cost; their long-term durability has not yet been determined.

Table 9.2: Characteristics of cover plate materials

Test	*Poly-vinyl Fluo-ride*	*Poly-ethylene Tereph-thalate or Polyester*	*Polycar-bonate*	*Fiber-glass Rein-forced Plastics*	*Methyl Meth-acrylate*	*Fluorinated Ethylene Propylene*	*Ordinary Clear Lime Glass (Float) (0.10-0.13% Iron)*	*Sheet Lime Glass ().05-0.06% Iron)*	*Water White Glass (0.01% Iron)*
Solar Trans-mission (%)	92-94	85	82-89	77-90	89	97	85	87	85-91
Maximum Operating Temp. (°C)	227	220	250-270	200 pro-duces 10% transm-ission loss	180-190	248	400	400	400
Tensile Strength (psi)	13000	24000	9500	15000-17000	10500	2700-3100	1600 annealed 6400 temp-ered	1600 annealed 6400 temp-ered	1600 anneal ed 6400 temp-ered
Thermal Expansion Coefficient (in/in/F° x10^{-6})	24	15	37.5	18-22	41.0	8.3-10.5	4.8	5.0	4.7-8.6
Elastic Modulus (psi x 10^{-6})	0.26	0.55	0.345	1.1	0.45	0.5	10.5	10.5	10.5
Thickness (in)	0.004	0.001	0.125	0.040	0.125	0.002	0.125	0.125	0.125
Weight (lb/ sq. ft.) for above thickness	0.028	0.007	0.77	0.30	0.75	0.002	1.63	1.63	1.63
Greatest Load Area (psf; sq. ft.)	-	-	-	-	-	-	-	-	30:30 anne-aled 100:28 temp-ered
Length of Life (yr.)	In 5 years retains 96% of total trans-mission	4	-	7-20	-	-	-	-	-

Table 9.3: Characteristics of insulating materials

Material	*Density (Lb/Cu.ft.)*	*Thermal Conductivity at 200 (°F) (BTU/Hr.Sq.Ft.°F/In.)*	*Temperature Limits (°F)*
Fiberglass with organic Binder	0.6	0.41	350
	1.0	0.35	350
	1.5	0.31	350
	3.0	0.30	350
Fiberglass with Low Binder	1.5	0.31	850
Ceramic Fiber Blanket	3.0	0.4 at 400 °F	2300
Mineral Fiber Blanket	10.0	0.31	1200
Calcium Silicate	13.0	0.38	1200
Urea-Formaldehyde Foam	0.7	0.20 at 75 °F	
Urethane Foam	2-4	0.20	250-400

Characteristics of Insulation Materials

Cover plates are normally of glass or one of several plastics. The two primary considerations are transmittance and durability. Window glass tempered to withstand high temperatures is most commonly used. Transmittance (T) of solar radiation is affected primarily by iron content. Transmittance can be .85 for an iron content of 0.12% and 0.92 for water white glass with an iron content of 0.01%. Glass is practically opaque to longwave, thermal radiation, which helps to trap the heat collected by the absorber plate. Plastics used as cover glazing are cheaper and lighter than glass. Since they are thinner, often have higher transmittance as well. Disadvantages of plastics are that they generally do not trap heat as well and degrade under both high temperature and ultraviolet radiation.

The number of cover plates depends on the type of application and involves a tradeoff between cost and performance. As a rule of thumb, the higher the differential between ambient and absorber temperatures the more cover plates are required, except that a single-glazed collector with a selective surface will often out perform a double-glazed one with a nonselective surface.

Various types of insulation are used in collectors to minimize heat losses from the back and sides. It is important that the insulation not outgas under stagnation conditions (that is, when heat builds up because the heat transport fluid is not flowing). Such gases can coat the inside of the glazing and greatly reduce transmittance. For this reason, fiberglass insulation is preferred over Styrofoam and urthanes.

Collector enclosures are ordinarily made of steel, aluminium or fiberglass. The enclosure should allow for differential expansion while remaining air and watertight. External pipe connections are particularly vulnerable; sealing compounds and gaskets must be able to withstand both stagnation temperatures and thermal cycling.

The performance of flat-plate collectors can be increased by an antireflective coating plate on cover plates, honey combs between absorber and cover to reduce connective heat loss, and exterior planer reflectors to increase incident radiation.

Flat-plate collector will not be economical for space cooling until both collector performance is improved and absorption units are produced that operate at 160 to 180 degree (F).

For the present, however, advanced collectors design must be used for higher temperature applications.

Evacuated tube collectors

Evacuated tubes provide higher temperatures than flat-plate collectors because the vacuum surrounding the fluid-transport tube restricts connective heat loss. Evacuated tubes can collect both direct and diffuse radiation.

Several types of evacuated tubes are in the market. Basis options are either two or three cylindrical glass tubes with the evacuated space between the outer and second tube. A selective surface is applied to the outside of the second cylinder. The three tube version delivers fluid between the second and third tube and remove it within the third tube.

Various configurations of reflectors can be used behind evacuated tubes to provide a small degree of concentration. Extremely high stagnation temperatures over 600 degree (F.)- can cause thermal shock with cold water as well as boiling water.

Parabolic troughs

Another way to cut down on heat loses and achieve higher temperatures is to concentrate the solar energy into a smaller absorber surface. The most commonly used concentrator is a parabolic reflector trough with an absorber pipe located along the focal line. The concentrators require continuous tracking but only about a single axis. A parabolic dish will achieve higher concentration but only through the significant increase in mechanical complexity and most required to track simultaneously in two planes (altitude and azimuth).

Parabolic concentrators can collect only direct sunlight, not diffuse. As a result, they receive less of the available sunlight than flat plates, which in particularly cloudy climates can completely offset the gain in efficiency.

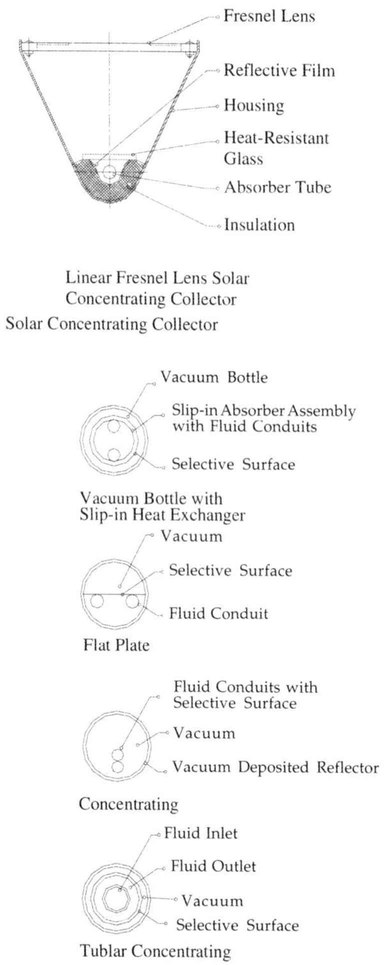

Figure 9.8: Different types of concentrating collectors

Fresnel lens collectors also concentrate sunlight, but they do so by refracting (bending) the light instead of reflecting it as do parabolic concentrators.

Fresnel lens applications are generally more expensive, but have the same advantages and disadvantages of parabolic troughs. One problem is the dust accumulation on specular and lens surfaces.

The compound parabolic collector is a promising design still in the development stage. This collector essentially "funnels" the light down to the absorber surface rather than reflecting it. It requires only seasonal adjustment, accepts both direct beam and diffuse radiation over a wide angle and does not require highly polished reflector surfaces, thereby tolerating dust and degradation better. The cost disadvantage is that a large amount of reflector surface is required.

9.2.5 Collector Efficiency

Collector efficiency is a measure of the percentage of available solar energy that the collector will transmit to the heat transport fluid. Two generic methods of measuring collector efficiency are the calorimetric and instantaneous methods.

The calorimetric method uses a closed system consisting of collector and small storage tank and provides a good method for determining the day-long efficiency of a collector. It requires measurement of the quantity of incident solar radiation, the time period of measurement and the temperature change of the system.

The instantaneous method uses an open system, an isolated collector and it performs at solar noon under steady-state conditions. The method requires measurement of the mass of the transport fluid, fluid temperature change as it flows through the collector (air or liquid) and amount of solar radiation.

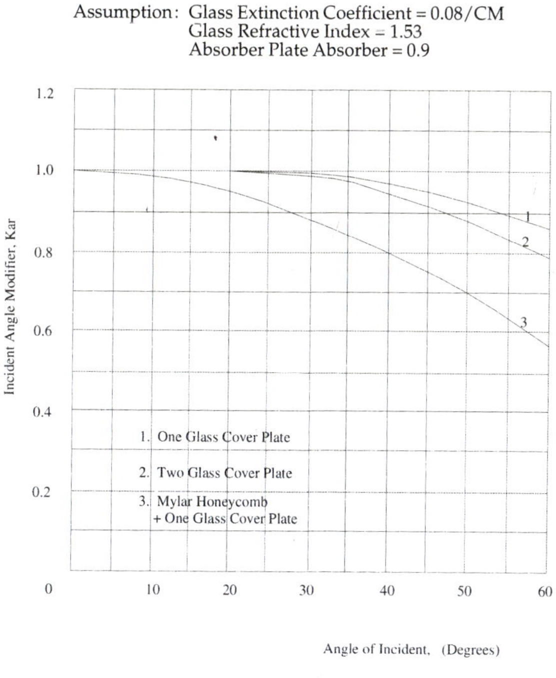

Figure 9.9: Incidence angle modifier

The American Society of Heating, Refrigerating and Air-conditioning Engineers, using a test method developed by the National Bureau of Standards (NBS), has adopted standard 1993-97, Methods of Testing to Determine the Thermal Performance of Solar Collectors. This standard uses the instantaneous method for determining collector efficiency based on gross collector area. Two procedures are used to determine the following:

- collector time constant
- instantaneous efficiency.

The collector time constant is a measure of the thermal inertia of the collector, which is determined by its mass. The smaller the time constant, the more rapidly a collector will respond to short periods of insulation.

The efficiency test is as described earlier. An incident angle modifier (see accompanying figure) adjusts for the decrease in collector efficiency that occurs as more of the incident solar radiation is reflected away from the absorber. This varies for different collectors, but as a rule of thumb, the day-long modifiers for single and double glass can be given as 0.93 and 0.91 respectively.

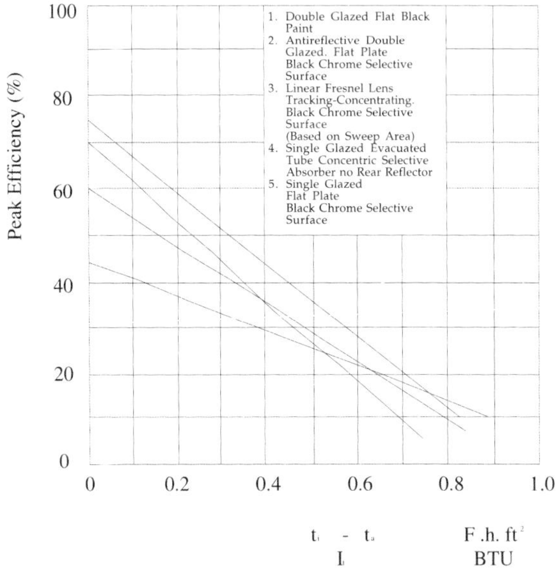

Figure 9.10: Collector efficiency curves

The U.S. Department of Housing and Urban Development (HUD) requires that efficiency test of collectors be performed both before and after a 30-days stagnation test. This test is described both in HUD's Intermediate medium Property Standards for Solar Heating and Domestic Hot Water Systems and NBS's Interim Performance Criteria for Solar Heating and Cooling.

The accompanying figures indicate the effects of a variety of flat-plate and liquid collectors.

Moving from left to right on the horizontal axis of these graphs, the temperature differential between the fluid temperature entering the collector (t_i) and outside air (t_a) increases. The curve show that for constant insolation striking the absorber plate (I_t), efficiency is inversely proportional to this temperature differential. As shown, the evacuated tube is less affected than the other collector types.

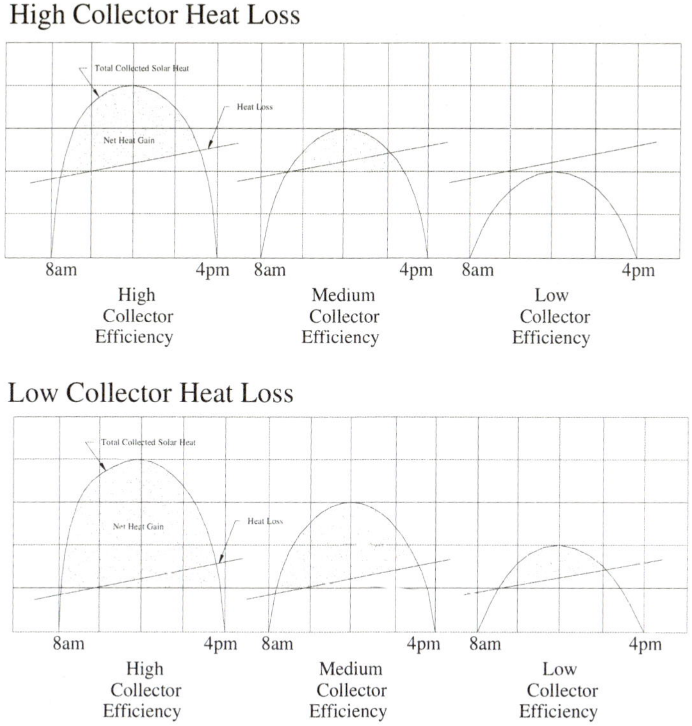

Figure 9.11: Heat losses from collectors

Designers who have reached the stage of selecting collectors will know the weather patterns (the ambient temperature) and will also have made assumptions about the range of storage temperatures. Comparison of the efficiencies of different collectors within the limits dictated by these two temperatures enables designers to make tradeoffs among cost, efficiency, etc.

9.2.6 Thermal Storage

Most effective solar applications benefit from some form of thermal storage. Thermal storage enables the solar system to collect more heat than is immediately required and store it for later use. The size of the storage system depends on how long heat must be stored, which varies for different applications. Residential space heating storage may be sized for a period of two or three cloudy days. Commercial applications are often sized in relation to the diurnal (24-hours) cycle, though they can be designed for much longer periods.

The design tradeoffs involved in incorporating storage into energy delivery systems can be complex.

- storage temperature versus container and heat exchanger size.

- power requirements versus heat exchanger size.
- efficiency versus duration of storage.
- efficiency versus storage and heat exchanger size.
- energy density versus materials corrosion.
- energy density versus container cost.

Thermal storage consists of a storage medium, a container and input-output devices. Containers must both retain the storage medium and prevent the loss of thermal energy. Stratification of the medium within the container causes vertical "layers" of different temperatures, which can be used by the designer to determine placement of inlets and outlets. Outlets high in the container will deliver the medium to the end use at a higher temperature. Return outlets to collector placed low in the tank will return cooler medium, allowing the collectors to operate at higher efficiency.

Table 9.4(a): Properties of heat storage materials

Sensible-Heat Storage	*Sp. Ht. BTU/Lb, °F*	*True Density, Lb./ft³*	*Heat Capacity, BTU/Ft.³°F*	
Water	1.00	62	62	63
Scrap Iron	0.12	490	59	41
Magnetite	0.18	320	57	40
Scrap Aluminium	0.23	170	39	27
Concrete	0.27	140±	38	26
Stone	0.21	170±	36	25
Brick	0.20	140	28	20
Sodium (to 208 °F)	0.23	59	14	-

Heat Storage Materials

The capacity of thermal storage is proportional to the differences between storage input and output temperatures times the heat storage capacity of the particular medium used.

If water is the storage medium, the storage capacity will be the product of the volume, the specific heat of water and the operating temperature range. The specific heat of water, taken from the accompanying table, is 1 BTU/lb./degree (F).

Highest temperature obtained	=	150 degree (F).
Lowest useful temperature	=	85 degree (F.)
Operating range	=	65 degree (F.)

One cubic foot of water, again from the table, would give a storage capacity of 1x62x65 = 4030 BTU. If the daily heat requirement of a house is 40 kWh (1 kWh = 3413 BTU) and two days' heat (273,040 BTU) is to be stored, the volume will be:

$$\frac{40 \times 2 \times 3413}{4030} = 68 \text{ cubic feet}$$

One gallon of water weighs approximately 8.3 pounds, which yields 7 ½ gallons per cubic foot of water (62/8.3 = 7.5). Thus the storage requirement, 68 cubic feet of water is 508 gallons.

Often the recommended storage volume is related to the collector area. Rules of thumb are in the range of 10 to 20 pounds (1-3 gallons) of water for each square foot of collector.

If the storage medium is crushed rock or gravel, the heat storage capacity can be established as the product of the volume of container, the solidity ratio, the density and the specific heat of the stone, and the operating temperature range. The solidity ratio may be typically around 0.7 (meaning there is 30 percent void between the solids). The density of stones, from the table, is then 110 lbs./cu./ft. Thus the 68 cubic feet of storage in the above example, if filled with crushed stone instead of water, would give a storage capacity of 68 cu.ft. x 110 pounds/cu.ft. = 102,102 BTU, which is approximately 37 percent of the storage capacity of the water.

To date, the majority of active solar storage systems have used water and rock beds. Water storage predominates in domestic hot water applications and rock-bed storage predominates in space heating applications.

Insulated leak-proof tanks are the major cost component of water-based storage systems. Tanks can be steel, fiberglass or reinforced plastics, concrete or woolen. Characteristics, advantages, disadvantages and costs of such tanks are presented in the accompanying table.

The cost ranges listed are approximate and are in 1979 dollars. Such costs depends on tank size, location, installation requirements, temperature ranges and insulation needs. The cost for much larger tanks for longer duration storages can be substantially lower.

Rock beds are much simpler to construct than water tanks. Common materials can be used, and excessive insulation is not required because rock has rather low thermal conductivity. In addition, corrosion problems are eliminated and small leaks cause little problem.

Thermal stratification of storage will improve system performance significantly, from 5 to 10 percent. For water storage a temperature difference of up to 10 degrees (F) can be maintained in a carefully designed system. Stratification can be facilitated by the use of vertical tanks and baffles or anti-bending headers at the top and bottom of storage tanks.

Ensuring stratification is much easier in rock beds than in water tanks because the rocks are immovable. Rock beds need an adequate plenum over the top to ensure that stratification is not upset by causing the hot injected air to move from top to bottom of the storage before spreading over the entire top surface of all the rocks.

Table 9.4(b) : Water storage tank characteristics

Type	*Advantages*	*Disadvantages*	*Temperature Limitations*	*Cost range (S1 gal.)*
Steel	Can be pressurized. Much field experience.Easy plumbing connections.	Complete tanks difficult to install indoors.Subject to rust and corrosion.	None	0.70-0.96
Fiber glass	Factory insulated tanks available.Much field experience.No corrosion.	Maximum temperature is limited. Cannot be pressurized. Complete tanks difficult to install indoors	<150-200°F	1.29-2.42
Concrete	Can be pre-cast or cast in place.	Possibility of cracks and leaks.Cannot be pressurized. Difficult to make leak-tight plumbing connections.	<210°F	0.69-0.92
Wooden	Indoor installation	Maximum temperature limited.Cannot be pressurized. Not suitable for underground installation.	<160°F	0.62-1.78

Storage efficiency, the ability to retard heat losses, can be increased by insulation- at a cost. The sheet metal and Air Conditioning Contractors National Association recommends a maximum loss of 2% in 12 hours. The U.S. Department of Housing and Urban Development Immediate Minimum Property Standards suggest a maximum loss of 10% in 24 hours. When the thermal losses supplement the building's heating load and overheating can be easily vented in summer, lower storage efficiencies are acceptable.

Insulation is also a consideration for ducting and piping, which can lose thermal energy coming from collectors to the load or to storage and from storage to the load.

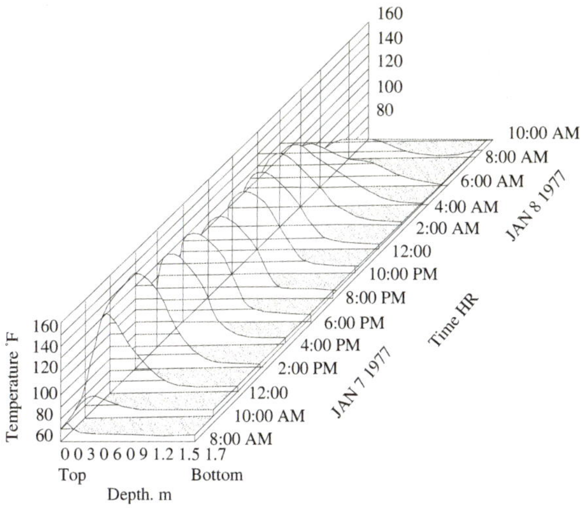

Figure 9.12(a): Temperature profiles in pebble bed during peak heating

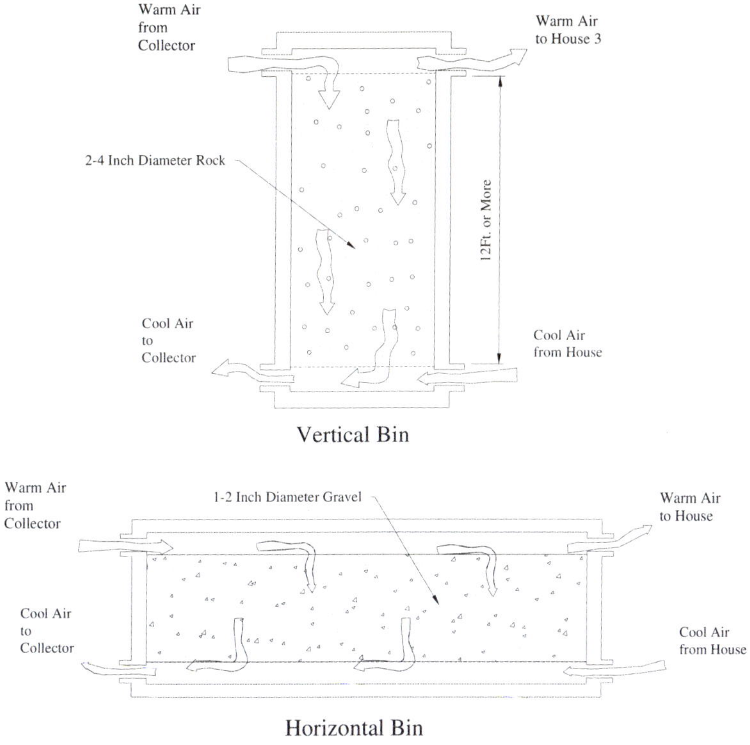

Figure 9.12(b): Rock bed heat storage

The accompanying figure lists the variety of possible strategies for strong low-temperature thermal energy, a number of which are in the research and development stage.

Table 9.5: Storage Locations in residence

Stratification	*Advantages*	*Disadvantages*
Room or basement	• Minimal insulation requirement. • Insulation protected from weather.· • Thermal losses contribute to building heat in winter. • Leaks easily detected. • Easy access for repairs.	• Reduced living space. • Thermal losses increase summer air conditioning load. • Leaks possibly damaging interior. • Difficult to install steel or FRP tanks in an existing building.
Garage	• Insulation protected from weather. • Leaks easily detected. • Easy access for repair.· • Easy installation of steel or fiber reinforced plastic tanks in an existing garage.	• Reduced garage space. • Extra insulation required. • Freeze protection most often required.· • Possible damage to garage from leaks. • Thermal losses not recovered.
Crawl space	• Insulation protected from weather. • Thermal losses may contribute to building heat in winter.	• Thermal loses may add to summer air-conditioning load. • Difficult access to retrofit or repairs. • Usual shaped tank may require extra insulation.
Outdoors, above grade.	• Easy access. • No increased airconditioning load from thermal loss. • No reduction in living space.	• Extra insulation required. • Weather protection required. • No recovery of thermal losses. • Freeze protection usually required • Possibility of vermin attacking insulation.
Outdoors, below grade	• No increased airconditioning load from thermal losses. • No living space reduction.	• Access for repair difficult. • Several problems can be caused by contact with ground water.· • Thermal losses not recovered. • Possibility of vermin attacking insulation· • Careful design required to ensure sufficient net positive suction head for the pump • Cost for excavation.

Annual cycle storage have a number of advantages. Solar energy collected on long, hot summer days can be used in the winter, reducing collector area, reducing summer stagnation problem, and greatly reducing if not eliminating backup energy needs. Sizing does become more critical, however.

Solar ponds function as both energy collector and storage, which allows simplicity of design and can result in lower cost. Solar energy is trapped in the pond because the behavior of salt water at the bottom counteracts the natural tendency to lose energy by convective currents. Salt-gradient solar ponds can be economically attractive in areas where land is readily available and little snow falls.

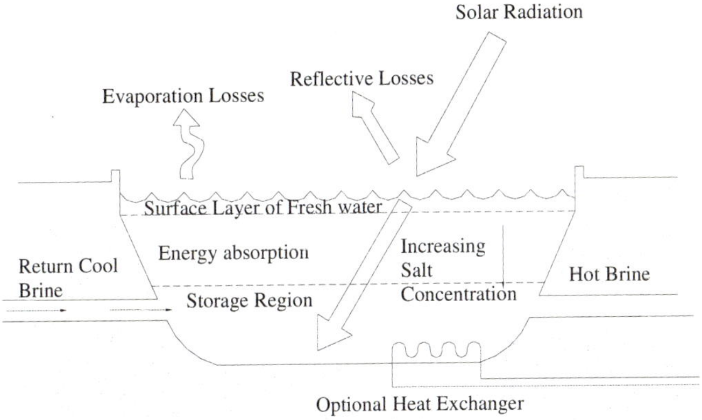

Figure 9.13: Solar pond

Larger sensible heat or phase-change storage generally have unit heat losses. Community systems offer the potential for use of only one backup system, statistical averaging of shared loads and other economies of scale' although there will be increased distribution losses due to long distance runs. Annual storage may prove to be economical only in multifamily dwelling and large commercial applications.

Table 9.6: Salt hydrates for solar heat storage

Phase changing salts	*Melting point, ^0F*	*Heat fusion BTU per pound*	*Density lb/ft*
Calcium chloride hexahydrate	84-102	75	102
Sodium carbonate dehydrate	90-97	106	90
Disodium phosphate dehydrate	97	114	95
Calcium nitrate tetrahydrate	102-108	60	114
Sodium sulphate decahydrate (Gluber's salt)	88-90	108	97
Sodium thisulphate pentahydrate	118-120	90	104

Table 9.7(a): Relative volume of water and phase changing Glauber's salts required to store equal amounts of heat as the usable temperature range varies

Solution	*Water: 1ft³ 62 lbs. Salt: 0.11ft³ 10 lbs*	*Water: 1ft³ 62 lbs. Salt: 0.35ft³ 32 lbs*	*Water: 1ft³ 62 lbs. Salt: 0.50ft³ 45 lbs*
BTU stored	1240	4960	9300
Temperature range (°F)	80-100	50-130	50-200
Temperature difference (°F)	20	80	150

Latent heat-of-fusion storage for air systems is represented by eutectic salts. The heat storage principle of salts is that a material stores significant amounts of heat as it changes phase from solid to liquid (melts) and gives that heat up again as it solidifies. The advantage of these salts is that they change state at very convenient temperatures and require small volumes of space. After 30 years of investigation, the primary disadvantage continues to be that after a number of cycles the anhydrous salts tend to separate from the water, which shows down the reverse phase change, and makes the storage much less effective.

9.2.7 Heat Transport Fluids

Selection of the heat transport fluid dictates much of the remaining design. The primary advantages and disadvantages of air and water as heat transport fluids are discussed earlier in the section on system types.

The larger the building, the more likely the use of liquid systems since distribution piping consumes relatively small amounts of space. For air to be as efficient as liquid, large ducts and/or rapid air velocities must be used in contribution with large fans required to provide higher initial and operating costs. Higher air speeds also require higher air temperatures so that people will feel warm drafts rather than cool ones. One way to use air-type collectors effectively is to feed the air directly to ventilation equipment as preheated intake air, reflected to as air tempering.

Table 9.7(b): Collector fluid options

Collector Fluid Options	*Heat Storage Options*	*Space Conditioning Options*
Air	Rocks Small containers of water Small containers of phase-changing salts.	Forced warm or cool air.Air-warmed (or cooled) radiant panels.
Water or other fluid such as oil or a water-anti-freeze solution.	Large containers (usually tanks) of water. Large containers of water encircled by pebbles.	Forced hot or cold water, for example base-board or fan coil units. Hot or cold water radiant panels. Forced warm or cool air (this requires a heat exchanger to remove the heat or coldness from storage and transfer it to the air.)

Collector Fluid Options:

Building designs that limit the location of solar collectors to the roof (rather than to the south-facing walls) are more likely to require the use of liquid systems because of the extra distance involved in transporting fluid to and from heat storage, which is usually located close to the ground because of its weight.

The primary advantages of air as transport fluid are avoidance of the freeze problem and absence of damage from leakage. Leakage can, however, cause serious degradation of performance. Duct insulation (at least 1 inch) is recommended, even in heated space.

Fan sizing will depend on the desired air flow rates and the cumulative pressure losses through collectors, ducts and rock bed storage. Factory- assembled air-handling units complete automatic dampers and connections for auxiliary heat input are often effective solutions.

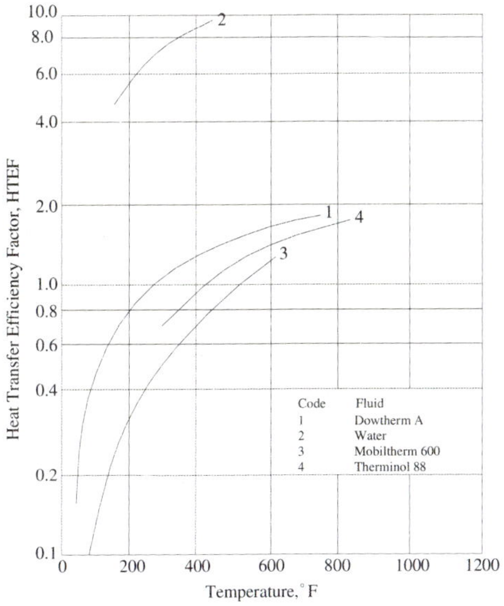

Figure 9.14: Heat transfer efficiency factors

Table 9.7(c): Collector Fluid Characteristics

Characteristics	*Water*	*50% Ethylene glycol/water*	*50% Propylene glycol/water*	*Silicone fluid*	*Synthetic hydro-carbon*
Freezing point (°F)	32	-33	-24	-120	-70
Boiling point	212°F	230°F	225°F	400°F	550°Z
Fluid stability	Requires pH or inhibitor monitoring	Requires pH or inhibitor monitoring	Requires pH or inhibitor monitoring	Good	Good
Corrosion	Corrosive to iron and aluminium	Corrosive to iron and aluminium	Corrosive to iron and aluminium	Non-corrosive	Non-corrosive
Specific Heat (BTU/Lb.°F@ 100°F)	1.0	83	.87	.30	.51
Viscosity (Lb./Ft-Hr.@ 100°F)	1.66	2.5	3.0	17	11
Potability	Potable	Very toxic	Non-toxic, non potable	Non-toxic non-potable	Non-potable

The ideal heat transport liquid has good heat transfer capabilities, requires slow pumping power, remains in a liquid state at the range of possible temperatures and pressures, does not promote corrosion, is safe to use, and is inexpensive. Water can meet all these criteria with one exception- it freezes.

One common solution to water's freezing is to mix glycol antifreeze (either ethylene or propylene) with water in a 50% solution. This degrades water's beneficial physical properties; the glycol-water solution has greater density, lower specific heat, and greater viscosity, all of which require increased pumping power. Several organic fluids can also be utilized as transport fluids.

Table 9.8: Toxicities of Heat Transfer Fluids

Fluid	LD_{50}
Water	-
100% Ethylene Glycol (No inhibitors)	8.0
100% Propylene Glycol (no inhibitors)	34.6
100% Diethylene Glycol (no inhibitors)	30
100% Triethylene Glycol (no inhibitors)	30
100% Downtherm SR-1	4
Mobitherm Light	20
SF-96(50) (Silicon)	50
Q2-1132 (Silicon)	50
Downtherm J	1.1
Therminol 44	13.5
Therminol 55	15.8
Therminol 60	13.0
Sun-Temperature	No test information available.

Toxicities of Heat Transfer Fluids:

Toxicity is a significant problem in all situations in which heat transfer fluids can contaminate potable water. LD-50 values from the accompanying table refer to the quantity of substance (g/kg) that kills 50% of dosed test animals in 14 days.

For domestic hot water applications, the U.S. Department of Housing and Urban Development (HUD), National Bureau of Standards and many local codes require a double walled heat exchanger whenever a toxic collector fluid is used. Fill locations should be carefully marked, designating the proper coolant used.

The various parameters involved in corrosion are well described in HUD's Intermediate Minimum Property Standards for Solar Heating and Domestic Heat Water Systems.

Corrosion is a more significant problem with aqueous solution and tends to increase with high oxygen and chloride content, higher temperatures and improper pH. Corrosion problems can take several forms: Galvanic corrosion is caused by the junction of two dissimilar materials in an electrolytic solution. Insulating couplings used between dissimilar metals can sometimes eliminate this problem; however, in many cases metal can still enter the fluid and travel to the site of another metal. Pitting corrosion involves rapid local metal loss. Aluminium and steel are susceptible to the presence of chloride ions. Crevice corrosion is similar to pitting corrosion but occurs at crevice in the system, such as those at spot-welded joints.

9.2.8 Heat Transport Equipment

A heat exchanger is a device for transferring thermal energy from one fluid to another. Heat exchangers in active solar systems are used primarily to isolate collector piping loops containing toxic antifreeze solutions from storage and space heating or domestic hot water loops. They are also used to avoid use of the more expensive antifreeze solutions for storage.

Heat exchangers can be used to reduce hydrostatic head on storage tanks when collectors are mounted at a considerable height above the water storage tank.

Heat exchanger effectiveness is defined as the actual heat transfer rate divided by the theoretical maximum heat transfer rate.

Effectiveness for typical liquid exchangers is 0.5 to 0.8. Sizing is usually done using manufacturers' literature. Most manufacturers will provide technical assistance in the selection process. Required information is:

- fluid inlet and outlet temperature.
- heat transfer rate (in BTUs per hour) or fluid flow rate (in gallons per minute).

A number of heat exchanger types are available. Remote heat exchangers are separate from the tank and require two pumps to circulate the fluids. More power is consumed, but forced convection on both sides of the exchanger results in higher heat transfer. Tube-in-shell heat exchangers are widely used in solar hot water systems. They contain tightly packed tube bundles inside an outer jacket. The collector fluid is circulated across the tubes, while the storage fluid flows through tubes.

The shell and double-tube heat exchanger is similar to the shell and tube except that a secondary chamber containing an intermediate fluid is located within the shell to surround the water tube in which potable water circulates. The heated toxic liquid circulates in the outer shell, transferring heat to the intermediate fluid, which in turn transfers heat to the tube carrying potable water. The exchanger should be equipped with a sight glass to detect leaks by a change in color-toxic liquid can contain dye or by a change in the liquid level in the intermediate chamber, which would indicate a failure in either the outer shell or the intermediate tube lining.

Double separation can be provided by using two separate heat exchangers between the collector and storage. The two heat exchangers may be of the same or different types and are generally of the shell and tube type.

Jacket type of heat exchangers are either tubing or plate coils wrapped around and bonded to the outside of the metal storage tank.

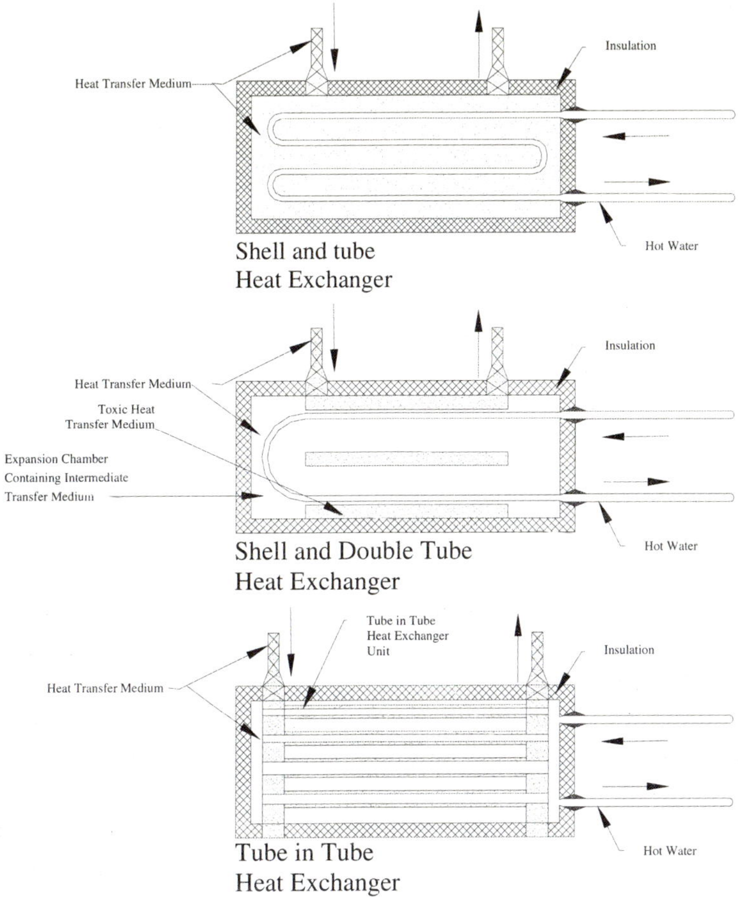

Figure 9.15: Heat transport equipment

There is forced convection in the outer loop and natural convection between the wall of the tank and the storage liquid. They provide both excellent stratification in the storage tank and double separation.

Immersion heat exchangers are either a coiled-tube or a tank-within-a-tank. They have forced convection through the internal tubing or tank and natural convection in to the storage liquid. The tube bundles come with or without fins and single-or-double-sleeve construction. Tank-within-a-tank exchangers arc metal tanks fitted with standard piping with the fluid circulating through them. Variations include finned tubes or discs on the piping.

Double separation is possible with a continuous piping loop. Special provisions may be necessary on the storage tank so that it can accommodate these types of heat exchangers.

The air-to-liquid heat exchanger (hydronic fin coil) is a standard theme of HVAC equipment. It is used in a large portion of commercial buildings. In active solar systems it is used primarily for hot water preheat or delivery of heat from storage to load.

Pumps

The efficiency of a pump is basically the work output divided by energy (electrical) input. The work is defined as flow rate time fluid head. Head is the combination of pressure or resistance to flow within the piping loop and any height to which the fluid must be raised, expressed as a vertical column (in feet) of the given fluid. No more than the equivalent of 1 to 3.5 percent of the energy collected by the solar energy system should be consumed by the pump(s) used to circulate the fluids. This factor can be much higher (7 to 8 percent), degrading system efficiency.

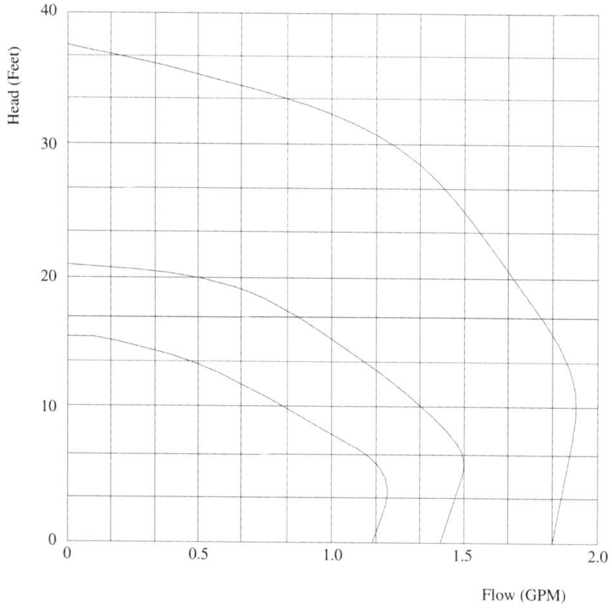

Figure 9.16: Typical pump curves

The flow rate is number of gallons of fluid or cubic feet of air per minute of heat transfer fluid that should flow through the collectors. The collector manufacturer will specify the most efficient flow rate.

Flow/head requirements are critical to pump selection and can be highly significant for overall system design.

Closed-loop systems are characterized by a continuous fluid loop with the pump installed in the fluid circuit. Since the fluid loop is continuous, the pump discharge pressure (or head pressure developed by the pump) must be sufficient to provide the proper flow characteristics to overcome the pressure loss of the entire loop, including exchangers. If the system is full and closed, there is no vertical head requirement due to the balance effect of fluid in the return line. This lack of a vertical head requirement means that pump power requirements are reduced and pumps with low discharge pressure can be used. Start-up head requirement must be available, however.

Open-loop systems include a wide variety of configurations including drain-down and drain-back as well as loops that vent to the atmosphere. Certain collector loops create vertical pump-heat requirements to lift fluid to the highest point in the collector system.

Pump Connections

Strainers are advisable on the inlets of all pumps. Periodic maintenance is required to clean out impurities.

Check valves should be located in pumping loops to prevent reverse thermo-siphoning.

Provisions for pump servicing should be made. Some methods are unions, bolted flanges, or flexible connections.

Expansion tanks are designed into fluid loops to maintain required system pressures. For solar energy systems they require special consideration because of the volumes of liquid and wide temperature ranges involved.

Piping design also involved sizing, configuration, fittings and insulation.

Many engineering handbooks have pertinent tables. Standard pipe friction tables should be used. Pipe friction will vary with heat transfer fluid, flow rate and plumbing material.

Drain-down and drain-back system require substantially more pump pressure, to recharge the system (i.e. create a new siphon effect). This can require either multiple-or-two stage pump and control arrangements.

Centrifugal pumps are generally preferred over the piston-type, positive-displacement pumps. They provide the safety feature of only creating pressures slightly above those rated if the fluid loop becomes blocked or a valve is inadvertently left closed.

Pump materials that will come into contact with circulating fluid must be compatible with a fluid to ensure extended pump life. A bronze or stainless steel pump should be used when the pump is to be exposed to air. With antifreeze liquids (but not with glycols), a cast iron pump can be used. Some antifreeze liquids or inhibitors can be harmful to pump seals and gaskets. Magnetic-drive pumps have no seals to wear and leak and can be used with any transfer fluid. Polyethylene and polypropylene seals interact with petroleum-based transfer fluids; pumps without seals or ones with special seals of elastomeric materials should be used.

Pumps should be durable as they must run long periods of time at high temperatures and pressures. A pump failure will cause collector stagnation and can damage the entire system.

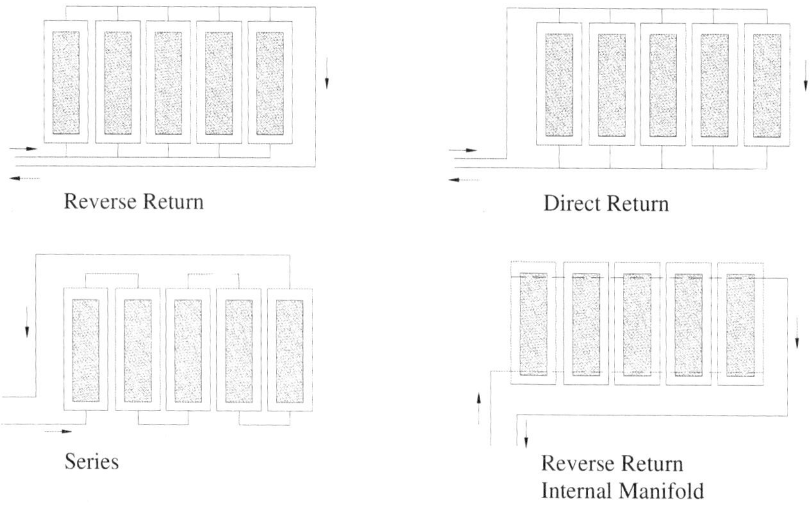

Figure 9.17(a): Collector piping configuration

Collector piping and manifolding design should minimize installed cost, leakage, maintenance problems and heat losses. It should provide uniform flow to all collectors to maximize collector efficiency, minimize pump power requirements and provide for air purging. Internal manifolds using piping within the collector have great potential for reducing piping and insulation costs but require careful design to maintain proper flow to all collectors.

Reverse-return arrangements are generally preferred because they provide equal flow to all collectors when low, uniform resistance is maintained in the manifolds- but generally require more piping and additional cost.

Expansion

All pipes should be hung or anchored loosely enough to allow expansion and contraction with temperature changes. A 100 feet length of copper pipe will expand approximately 1 inch with a 100 degree (F.) temperature rise. This expansion can be compensated with silicon bulbs, bellows, braided wire, pipe elbows, or swings. Silicon hoses are often used as expansion joints in arrays where there is little room for pipe expansion. Standard corrugated expansion joints made of copper alloy can also be used. Elbows also allow for some expansion, usually a sufficient amount for a small system.

A primary source of parasitic losses in solar energy systems is the energy transport system (i.e. piping, fitting, and pipe insulation). Significant thermal losses can occur if piping is incorrectly circulated or insufficiently insulated.

9.2.9 Controls

The controls of active solar system-sensors, valves, dampers, differential thermostats, etc.- are the physical manifestation of the system's design logic. The controls should accomplish the following tasks:

- fluids-flow management to maximize collection of solar energy
- system protection from temperature extremes (e.g., freezing, overheating, malfunction)
- heat delivery; storage/auxiliary interconnections.

A control system has three major components: sensors, actuated devices and the "controller" or decision-making device.

Typically, sensors and visual monitors in an active solar energy system sense temperature, pressure and flow rate. Common problems associated with sensors are improper or inadequate selection (mismatch of sensor and task), improper location and inaccessibility.

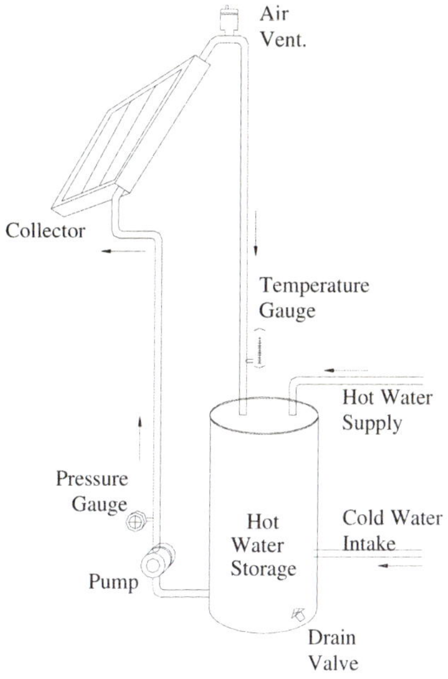

Figure 9.17(b): Monitoring devices, drains and vents

Collector temperature sensors are critical to determining when solar energy is available. More accurate control is achieved when sensors are located directly on the absorber or on the outlet rather than in the return pipe above the collector. If located on the return pipe, no flow is allowed to pass the sensor prior to start-up and it therefore relies on conduction and convection of heat from the collector and can give only an indirect measurement of the collector temperature. This can result in unnecessary delays in system start-up.

A loosely mounted sensor or one that is not well-connected to the collector can cause cooling of storage at the end of the day by retaining enough heat after the solar input drops off to indicate falsely that solar heat is still available.

Storage tank sensors are generally placed as close to the outlet to collectors as possible. Attention should be paid to the effects of tank stratification; if sensors are placed in the hot portion of a storage tank they can erroneously indicate that collectors are not substantially warmer than storage- both delaying system start-up and causing premature shut-down.

An actuated device is any component that executes the command of the control logic selectors. Pumps, fans, mixing valves, motorized dampers, flow switches and auxiliary water heater elements are examples. These devices control the fluid flow in the system and provide scale protection and auxiliary water heating. In drain-down or drain-back systems, their reliable operation is critical to providing freeze protection to the entire system.

Valves control fluid flow, water pressure and air in the system. All of the valves necessary in a liquid solar system are common plumbing fixtures (see accompanying chart).

Table 9.9: Valves and Vents

Type	*Purpose*	*Location*	*Comment*
Blackflow Preventor	Prevents mixing of potable water with non-potable fluid	On city water supply	Required in some code jurisdictions, don't install near electrical component
Check Valve	Permits liquid flow in only one-direction	Closed loop systems; between storage & collector to prevent reverse thermo-siphoning	Ensure arrow on valve points in direction of flow
Pressure Relief Valve	Allows fluid to escape closed loop if working pressure is exceeded	Collector loop at return to storage	
Temperature and Pressure Relief	Same as above (with temperature sensor attached)	Top of storage tank and/or DHW tank	Connect to container or waste drain required in most areas; don't use threaded fittings
Tempering and Mixing Valve	Mixes cold water to water from storage tank when it exceeds set point	12" elbow HW outlet with CW entering from bottom	Remove temperature sensing element before soldering and replace afterwards; check position of fittings
Pressure regulator	Reduces incoming water pressure to prevent damage to components	Drain-down	Proceed by strainer, isolate with shut-offs for cleaning

Type	*Purpose*	*Location*	*Comment*
Air Vent	Eliminates air bubbles from system	High points of system (above collector manifold)	Mount vent vertically; make sure cap is loose.
Air Eliminator	Removes air from heat transfer fluid	Above expansion tank	
Balancing Valve	Controls flow of fluids through system piping	System without reverse return piping; between manifold & each collector	Can be square head cock, ball or globe valve; do not use a gate valve
Vacuum Relief Valve	Permits system to drain by gravity	Drain-down; above collector at high point; above CW inlet of storage to prevent vacuum conditions to prevent collapse of tank	
Solenoid Valve	Starts, stops or diverts flow of heat transfer fluid	Drawn-down system	Often 2 valves used; one for collector circulation; one for drain
Isolation (shut-off) Valves	Permits components to be serviced without heaving to drain system	Either side of pump and strainer; either side of external Hx; either side of pressure reg.	Don't use globe valves; they restrict flow & reduce efficiency; don't isolate collector from relief valves
Fill Valve	Manual fill-up with transfer fluid	High point of system (low point if transfer pump is used)	Gate valve with open end facing up or quick connect valves
Drain Valve	Draining & periodic cleaning	Bottom of storage tank; one on collector loop for draining system	Removing valve handles prevents tempering (store in a safe place)

Early active solar systems experienced significant problems with leaking three-way valves. Problems can also arise from the substitution of check valves for approved back-flow preventors.

As a rule, all valves in a pipeline should be the same size as the lines in which they are installed to permit a rapid drain-down, especially when using the drain-down freeze-protection method. Stop cocks should be the same size as their line.

The container uses sensors to determine whether the difference between the solar collector and storage temperatures is sufficient to justify pump operation. An adequate temperature dead band should be incorporated into the control design to prevent harmful cycling of the pump in the morning and evening and intermittently during cloudy periods. As a rule of thumb, pumps should be activated when a temperature difference of 8 to 10°F is detected between collectors and storage. Shut-off should occur when this differential drops 3 to 5°F.

If the collector is drained when not in use, the control should allcw slight collector overheating before start-up and some thermal response lag in the collector sensor to avoid premature shutdown when the first cool water from the piping enters the collector.

The control subsystem should ensure that temperatures and/or pressures developed in the solar energy system because of a power or system component failure do not damage any of the system components or the building. For example; high-temperature limiting devices should be installed to protect the system from damage resulting from rapture, etc., and a low temperature limiting device should be installed to protect the system against the free-up damage. Applications of dampers is critical. Control dampers can be either proportional (regulating or balancing) or open/close (shut-off). Back draft dampers control the direction of flow, like the check valves in liquid systems.

Damper material must be appropriate for prolonged exposure to dry, high-temperature air. Air leakage past dampers degrades system performance significantly. High quality dampers designed for minimum air leakage and air tight inspection ports to facilitate maintenance and frequent inspection are required.

An active solar system's controller receives output signals from the sensors, selects the desired control strategy and transmits the appropriate order to the actuated devices, whether directly or via relays.

The central computerized Energy Management and Control System (EMCS) installed in many large buildings can incorporate solar control, but this requires careful integration of the solar and conventional systems. For simpler systems a central control panel can be provided to consolidate the circuits, fuses and relays that provide the control functions.

The model codes for solar energy systems proposed by the U.S. Department of Energy calls for controls to prevent the following:

- The addition of energy to the storage medium when the temperature of the storage medium has reached its maximum design operating temperature.
- Thermo-siphoning that will cause damage by freezing.
- Heat transfer fluids rising above the maximum design operating temperature of liquid system; damage from thermal shock.

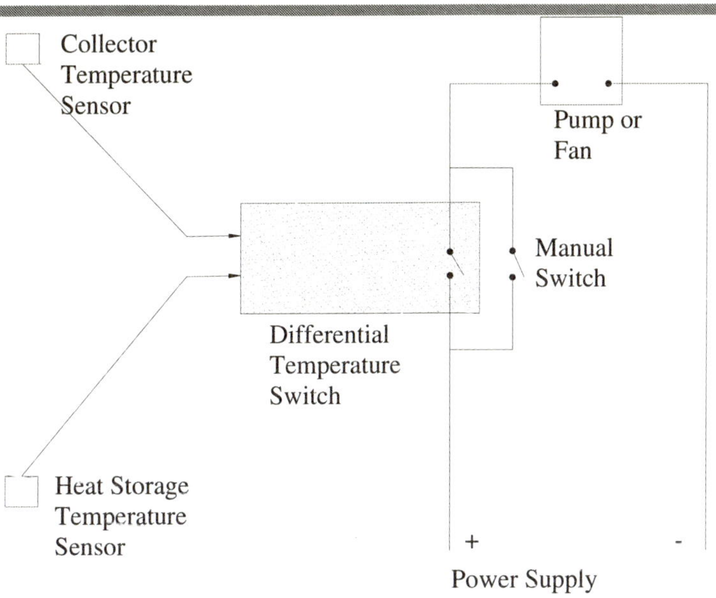

Figure 9.18: Basic solar differential control system

9.2.10 HVAC Integration

Residential air systems have three basic thermal operating modes: collector-to-storage, storage-to-load and collector-to-load. For liquid systems (especially commercial), operating modes are less straightforward, varying more with specific applications. A critical factor in every case is the manner in which auxiliary energy is integrated into the solar system, or *vice versa.* This can be done in many ways; no effort is made here to discuss them all, only to indicate relevant issues.

The simplest active solar system would be one without storage that operated only when solar energy was available and the load demanded energy. The next level of complexity, as the accompanying diagrams for an air system illustrate, includes storage but keeps auxiliary heat entirely separate. Note diagram 3; this is not entirely satisfactory because in the intermediate seasons and on mild winter days it is possible that solar collection will suffice to meet the entire diurnal load.

Systems increase in complexity as an attempt is made to integrate all of the components. For example, in large installations it is generally undesirable to have two separate heat delivery systems, one for the solar and the other for the backup. Integrating these two in one ducting system (for forced air systems, for example) causes dampering and other control complications but can reduce the initial cost of heat delivery system. Several of the liquid systems in early federal active solar demonstration programs were found to be heating storage inadvertently with auxiliary energy. This is generally a question of whether the auxiliary is piped in series or in parallel. If designed in series the possibility exists that the return water temperature will exceed the storage temperature. If allowed to continue this connection will degrade collector efficiency.

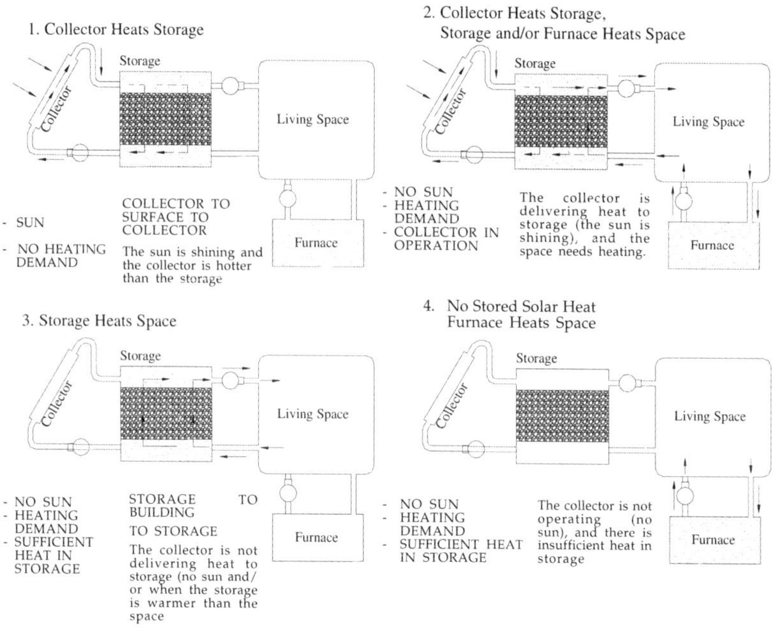

Figure 9.19 : Collector-Storage relationships

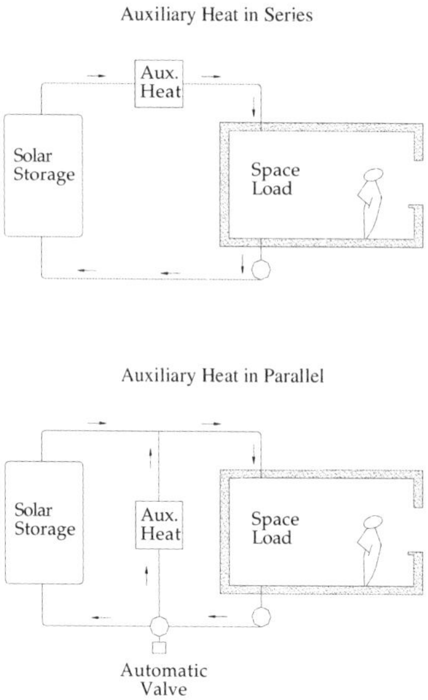

Figure 9.20: Auxiliary heat interfacing with solar storage

Auxiliary fuel use is minimized if the auxiliary is in parallel with the load, using solar heated water exclusively whenever the storage temperature exceeds the required heating coil temperature. When the storage temperature coil is too low, circulation of solar-heated water is discontinued and auxiliary heat is used exclusively. Piping and valving in such a system must be arranged so that the water bypasses the storage tank when auxiliary heat is in use; an automatic valve and single pump provide heat from the appropriate source. In severely cold weather, it can sometimes be better to leave comparatively warm water in storage unused for a time while the auxiliary supply is meeting the high demand in the building. The storage water would not be useful until the load is less severe or the storage temperature has been increased by addition of solar heat. This suggests the desirability of higher system operating temperatures at the same time that collector efficiency argues for lowering them.

With air-delivery systems it is possible to solve this problem by using two separate hydronic coils in the air-stream- a lower-temperature one from solar-heat water and a higher-temperature one from auxiliary.

A similar design problem is encountered with flat plate collectors used to activate absorption chillers. Promising research is under way attempting to lower the required temperatures, but at present the Coefficient-of-Performance (COP) of these units' falls off rapidly as regeneration water temperatures drop below 170 degree (F.).

The system schematic and mode description for the Santa Clara Community Center, a case study presented later in this section, illustrates one design solution to the problem above. This system has three thermal operating modes.

Mode 1- Auxiliary or Storage to load. This mode is used when there is little or no solar energy available. Heating is supplied either from the stored hot water or from the boiler. Cooling is supplied from the cool storage which is maintained by the boiler/absorption chiller combination.

Mode 2 – Collector to Storage Load. This mode is used when the solar flux is sufficient to provide efficient building heating and hot water storage but is insufficient to drive the absorption chillers. The system operates in this mode during the early morning and late afternoon hours. Cooling is supplied as described for Mode-1.

Mode 3 – Collector to chillers. This mode is used when the isolation is adequate to provide efficient firing of one or both absorption chillers. The active period for this mode center on solar noon in summer. Chilled water is drawn from the bottom of the cold storage tank where it is coldest and deposited on the top of the tank on its return from the cold tank fan coils. If the temperature at the top of the cold reservoir rise above 55 degree (F.), the boiler comes to fire the absorption chillers.

Because solar collector efficiency improves as collection temperatures are reduced, and conventional air-to-air heat pump system performance rises as heat-source temperature increases, a heat pump could be used advantageously to draw heat from storage, thus lowering the temperature of storage fluid fed to the collectors. Present indications are that such an operating mode can offer energy savings.

Table 9.10: Recommended Solar System Design Parameters

S. No.	*Parameter*	*Recommended*
1.	Collector area	Determined by life-cycle cost analysis
2.	Collector tilt	Lat +5° (water heating only) or Lat +15° (space and water heating)
3.	Collector orientation	Due south
4.	Storage mass	15 Lb.Water/Sq.Ft = 1.8 Gal/Sq.Ft. (air system)
5.	Heat exchanger heat transfer coefficient	10 BTU/Hr, °FSq.Ft (5-15 F approach)
6.	Collector heat transfer	10 BTU/Hr, °FSq.Ft. or 4 BTU/Hr, °FSq.Ft (air system)
7.	Number of glazings	1
8.	Collector surface absorption	≥ 0.9 with selective surface.
9.	Collector coolant flow rate	10 Lb./Hr, °FSq.Ft = 0.02 gpm water/Sq.Ft. (Liquid system) or 2 CFM/Sq.Ft (air system)
10.	Collector back insulation	U = 0.1d BTU/Hr, °FSq.Ft.
11.	Distribution pipe insulation	U = 0.15 BTU/Hr, °FSq.Ft of pipe

The integration of solar and conventional HVAC system is in several ways simpler for commercial than for residential buildings. A solar system in a commercial building is generally only a relatively small increment in an already complex mechanical system. More highly trained operating personnel are generally available, reducing maintenance problems. Solar applications are also generally consistent with current design and economic analysis efforts to diminish commercial peak loads by spreading them over larger time cycles, both diurnal and seasonal. On the other hand, cooling tends to be much larger portion of the mechanical system load, and the solar cooling technology is not as advanced or cost-effective as solar heating.

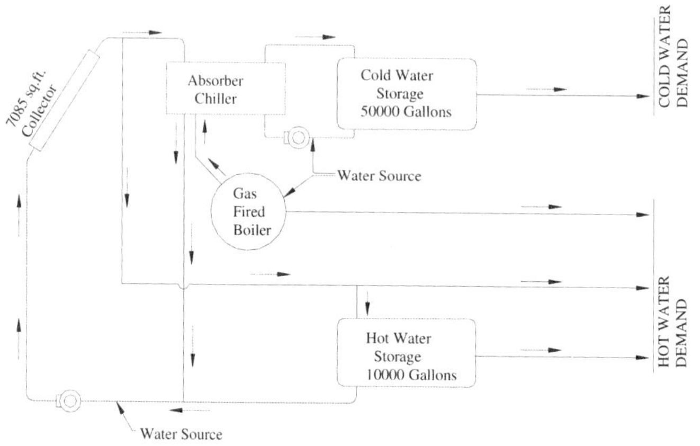

Figure 9.21: Solar water heating system at Santa Clara Community Centre

9.2.11 System Simulation

A variety of methods have been developed for the analysis and design of active solar heating, cooling, building service hot water, and industrial process heat systems. These includes manual methods, hand-held calculator (programmable) methods and detailed computer simulations.

There are three primary purposes to be served by these analyses and design methods. Foremost is the determination of an appropriate size for the collector array. Secondarily the components, (e.g., storage, heat exchangers etc.) must be selected and sized, and the system configuration and control strategy selected.

The third purpose, which is circular and interactive with the two above, is the determination of economic feasibility. This involves assessing the costs of the solar system and the value of the fuel saved.

Solar system performance and collector sizing requirements differ from conventional systems in three significant respects. First, collection of solar energy and demand for its use do not always occur at the same time. Peak demand is generally at night or during cloudy weather. Sizing of solar system components is therefore based on overall system performance rather than on peak load calculations. Only auxiliary energy supply systems are sized for peak loads.

Second, both energy demand and thermal storage mass influence the operating temperature of solar collectors. This affects the amount of efficient solar energy a given collect array can collect. The consequence is that seasonal building load variations strongly influence the annual performance of a solar energy system and must be considered.

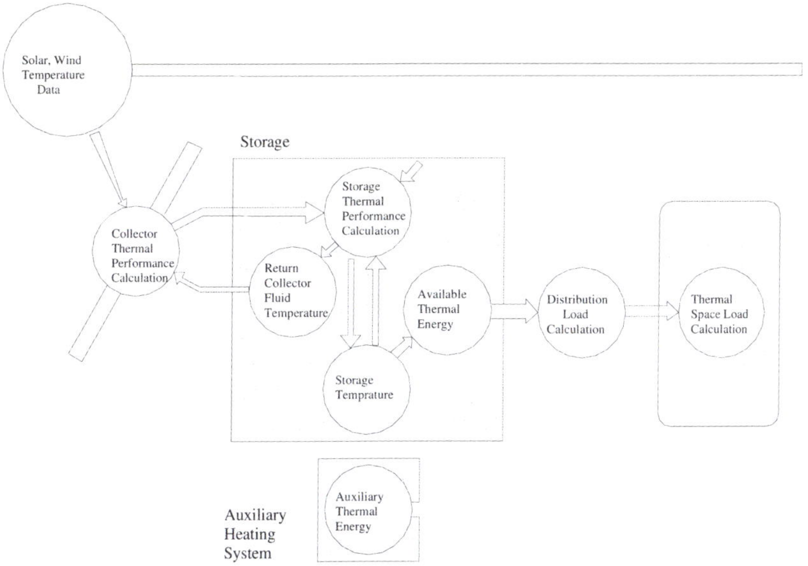

Figure 9.22: Typical simulation model

Third, solar energy is typically collected and delivered over a wide range of temperatures, which influences the performance of heating coils and absorption chillers. Conventional "Peak Load" design methods are, therefore, not appropriate for solar systems.

The performance of any solar heating or cooling system depends on the solar radiation available to the collector, the outside ambient air temperature and wind condition, the collector design, the inlet fluid temperature from storage, and the thermal load on the system. General understanding of how the above factors affect system performance in various locations requires a system simulation.

Building loads vary somewhat but not the extend or frequency of variations in both weather and solar incidence. Long-term system performance can only be accurately predicted with computer programs that perform hour-by-hour simulations (8,760 per year). Most of the simpler design and analysis methods are derived from statistical collections of the results of these annual simulations. Many of the methods (from simple to complex) have been tested against actual installed solar systems. This is done by comparing predicted to monitored system performance.

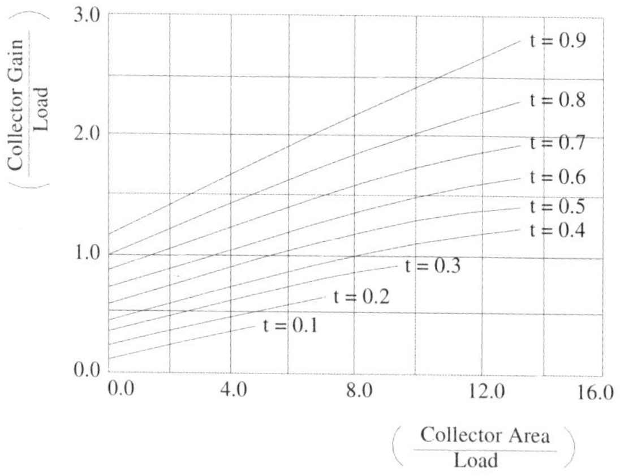

Figure 9.23a: f-chart for liquid system

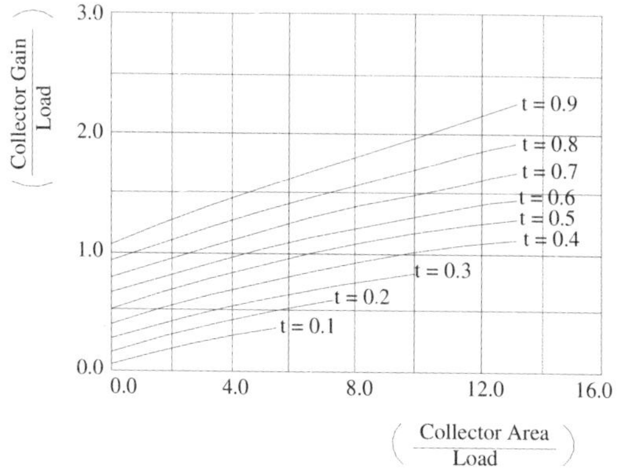

Figure 9.23b: f-chart for air system

The advantages of the simplified manual methods are simplicity of use, low cost, computational speed, rapid turnaround and accessibility to persons with little technical experience. The simplified methods are generally more appropriate for use in design of hot water system for residential or small commercial buildings dominated by external loads.

The most comprehensive and widely used simplified methods is the f-chart method. It was developed using the TRASYS program to simulate representative types of solar heating (air and water, space and hot water) systems in several different geographical locations. It is available on magnetic cards for programmable calculators, for microcomputers and on time sharing basis on large main frame computers. A manual f-chart user must calculate solar fractions for each month of the year for use in determining an annual solar fraction of the energy provided by the solar system.

In the pursuit of even greater time saving several manual methods have been developed that yield an optimum collector area and an annual solar fraction directly. The Relative Areas program, developed at Colorado State University and the GFL method are both such annual methods. Each was developed from correlations of f-chart results.

The Solar Load Ratio (SLR) method for liquid systems was developed from the detailed hour-by-hour simulation results from a computer program developed at the Los Alamos Scientific Laboratory. It is a very simple design and sizing procedure originally developed for residential use but now extended to small externally dominated commercial buildings as well.

The SLR results are presented in terms of the ratio of building load to collector area for liquid systems in the accompanying tables. These tables present the ratio in terms of the solar heating percentage of the total space heating requirement. The Load Collector Ratio (LCR) is defined as:

$$\text{LCR} = \frac{\text{Building Load (BTU/Degree day)}}{\text{Collector Area (Ft}^2\text{)}}$$

To use the Load Collector Ratio (LCR) for determining the size of the collector for one of the cities listed (or an equivalent location), one must (1) determine the building's thermal load and (2) decide what percentage of solar heating the system is to provide.

For example, a 2,000-square-foot building Boise, Idaho, with a load of 6 BTU/Degree Day/ S.F. for which 50% solar fractions desired will have a load collector ratio of 39. Using the above formula:

$$\text{LCR} = \frac{\text{Building Load}}{\text{Collector Area}}$$

$$39 = \frac{2000 \times 6}{\text{Collector Area}}$$

Collector Area = 308 square feet.

One problem with both the SLR and f-chart methods is that their accuracy is limited to the reference solar systems originally modeled in the hour-by-hour simulations.

The TRNSYS simulation program developed at the University of Wisconsin and the DOE-2/CBS (Component-Based-Simulator-based on TRNSYS) are much more sophisticated than what has been discussed so far. Use of these simulation programs requires both engineering and computer training. Aside from the refined results made possible by the hourly integration of all variables, the significant advantage of these programs is that they allow users to build complete systems for simulation, mixing equipment and design strategies as desired.

9.3 PHOTOVOLTAIC SYSTEMS

Photovoltaic systems convert sunlight into direct electric current. Given the recent and projected growth of PVs, they are already becoming rival to solar thermal systems in market penetration. The primary applications of PVs will likely be:

- roof mounted residential systems with capacities of 2-8 kilowatts
- commercial, industrial and institutional building systems with capacities of about 500 kilowatts
- control station systems integrated into utility and possibility near major load centers with capacities of 10-100 megawatts.

Photovoltaic systems used in most buildings are expected to connect with grid. These systems will typically consist of the following two elements:

- an array which converts sunlight into electricity without any moving part.
- A power conditioner, which converts for D/C electricity from array into A/C electricity, then supplies this power to building loads and to grid.
- In this section, we describe major components of a PV system and provide background information on design concerns.

9.3.1 System Definition

Since most of the building integrated systems are grid connected, we concentrate on the description of such systems. There are four major subsystems of such a grid connected photovoltaic system:

- A photovoltaic array
- Power conditioning and control system
- Protection / safety subsystem
- Optional storage system

The array subsystem is a mechanically and electrically integrated assembly of photovoltaic modules designed to provide a specified amount of dc electrical power under specified operating conditions. Typical components of an Array Subsystem include the following:

- photovoltaic modules
- module mounting hardware
- positive and negative bus bars or cables
- module electrical interconnects
- manual disconnect switches.

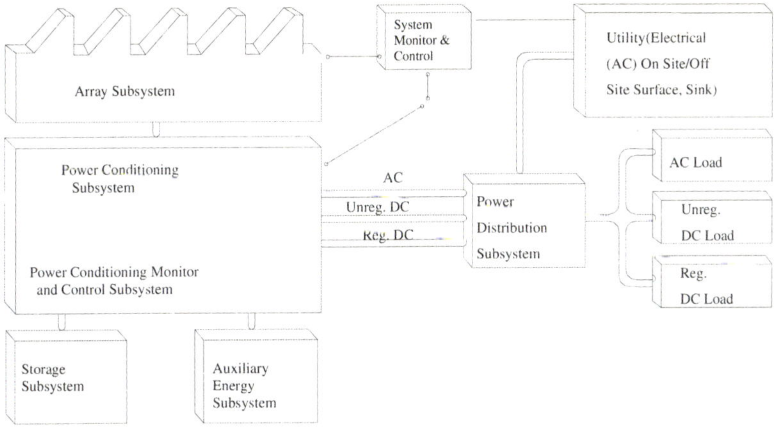

Figure 9.24: Generalized photovoltaic power system

- The Power Conditioning and Control Subsystem (PCS) operates as a current source, inverting the dc array output to ac, and acts in parallel with the utility to supply power to building loads. Typical components of the Power Conditioning and Control Subsystem include the following:
  - dc/ac inverter
  - control protection sensors and feedback circuits
  - ripple filter
  - isolation transformer
  - surge arrestors
  - manual disconnect switches and circuit breakers.

- The Protection Subsystem protects people, system components and the utility's line from damage in case of abnormal system operation. Typical components of the Protection Subsystem include the following:
  - frame and system grounding
  - ground fault detectors
  - surge arresters, voltage regulators and blocking diodes
  - manual disconnect switches and circuit breakers
  - isolation transformers
- If a storage Subsystem is included in a grid-connected PV system, its use is generally limited to a few hours of capacity for peak saving or leveling loads. The duty cycle for batteries operating in grid-connected systems is characterized by relatively high maximum charge and discharge rates. In addition, frequent cycling occurs, on a daily basis, although all cycles may not involve a complete discharge or a complete charge. The batteries may also experience rapid shifts between charge and discharge, such as might occur as the result of an abrupt change in load demand.
- A typical residential utility-connected PV system with a roof mounted photovoltaic array is shown. The PV array converts solar radiation to dc electricity for input to the power conditioner. The array writing is shown running through a conduit to a fused outdoor electrical disconnect. Although over-current conditions are not likely to occur from the PV array, fusing may become a code requirement in order to protect the power-conditioning unit from extreme currents in array writing; e.g., those induced by a close lightning flash.

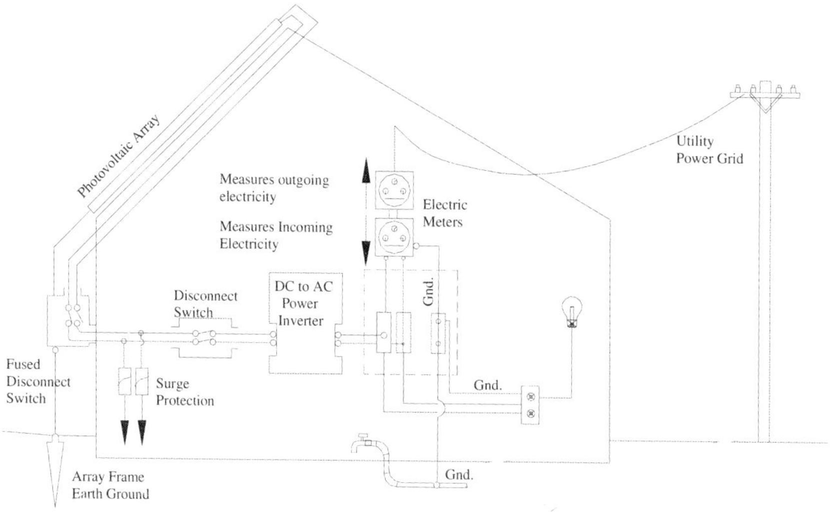

Figure 9.25(a): Typical utility-interactive PV system

- Also shown in this example is an earth ground wire coming from a metallic frame for the array. This ground wire eliminates the shock hazard potential in static charge build up or in an electric fault from a solar cell to the frame. The array wiring is protected from lightning included high voltage by surge arresters located in the array circuit panel board inside the residence. A second manual disconnect is provided to insure isolation from the PV array when required during power inverter maintenance or repair.

- The power conditioner converts the array dc to residence-compatible ac and also contains the system controls. The inverter executes the following functions: automatic start-up (morning), automatic shut-down (evening), and array voltage control. When electrical loads are not satisfied by the PV system, auxiliary power is drawn from the utility grid. When PV system output exceeds electrical loads, that excess power is fed back to the utility. In addition to these normal operations, the control must provide for automatic disconnection from the utility lines in the event of utility power loss- a safety feature to protect those working on downed lines.

- Since the generic system allows two-way power flow to the local utility, ratcheted kilowatts-hour meters are provided to record the flow of energy to and from the utility.

9.3.2 The Photovoltaic Array

The two types of array subsystems are concentrating arrays and flat-plate arrays. Flat-plate array subsystems use no special optics and are usually installed in a fixed position, tilted from the horizontal at an angle calculated to optimize the amount of sunlight received throughout the day. Concentrating arrays generally must track the sun and are further distinguished by their ability to track on one or two axes.

- To further understand the operation of array subsystems it is necessary to view both the mechanical and electrical characteristics of their components. Comparisons are shown for both flat-plate and concentrating systems.

- Concentrating arrays operate according to a fundamental characteristic of photovoltaic cells whereby the current density (in amperes per square meter) produced by a single cell is proportional to the amount of sunlight (insulation) it receives. There are two types of optical concentrating technologies: point focus concentrators and linear focus concentrators.

- As their names imply, point focus concentrators, utilize Fresnel lenses to concentrate light into a single PV cell. Linear focusing systems use parabolic trough mirror to focus light along PV cells, mounted upon a linear receiver located within the focal point of the trough. These systems reduce the cell area necessary to produce the equivalent amount of power with a flat-plate array.

- The basic elements of all PV systems is the photovoltaic cell, a semi-conductor device that converts sunlight into dc electricity. Although all cells produce about the same amount of voltage (approximately 0.5v), their efficiencies (power output divided by power input) vary considerably, depending on a variety of factors. The most commonly used semiconductor material- practically to the exclusion of all others at this time- is crystalline silicon. Encapsulated silicon cells have a typical electrical conversion efficiency of 11.5 percent to 100 mW/cm² insolation, 25°C (77 degrees F.), and 1.0m/sec wind speed. The photovoltaic module is a portion of array packaged in a unit that can be shipped, installed and replaced easily. The module provides a means of packaging the PV cell circuit so that it is environmentally sealed.

Table 9.11: Comparison of flat plate and tracking collector

Category	Flat Plate	Tracking Concentrator
Diffuse radiation Collection	Yes	No
Type of cooling	Passive	Active-liquid coolant (some passive)
Power Requirements for Operations	None	a) 1 hp for tracking b) ½ hp to 2hp water pump
Total Radiation Collection	Depending on tilt	One axis- Depending on tilt
Moving parts	None	a) Collector structure b) Pumps c) Motors d) Cooling Fluid
Lb/Ft² Aperture Area	3 to 8	4 to 6
Collector Efficiency	8% to 13%	One-Axis 15% to 18% Two-Axis 15% to 20%
Heat Available for Other Uses	Insufficient for Economical Collection	30,000 to 50,000 kWh/Yr/ft² Collector Area
O&M Requirements	Infrequent electrical checking, Module cover cleaning	Machinery checks, Electrical Checking, Reflector cleaning
Control Devices Required	None	Tracking Controller (Pre-programmed, Sun following, or combination)
Manufacturers (1980)	15-20 companies currently in production	One Axes- Several companies in production Two Axes- Several companies in testing

Collector Comparisons

- A concentrating module consists of a number of optical units with mounted PV cells connected in series mechanically and electrically integrated to form a single unit. A flat plate module is composed of a number of cells connected in series and parallel to obtain the desired voltage and current characteristics. The ratio of cells surface to module surface determines the aerial efficiency or packing density of the module. As shown in the accompanying figures, circular cells are not an efficient use of module surface area. This has encouraged development of high-density modules that rely on rectangular or square cells.

- Within a typical flat-plate module, the cells are interconnected not only to derive the desired voltage and current, but also to isolate defective cells. Protection from soiling is provided usually by a cover sheet of glass. Rigidity and back support is provided by a layer of Crane glass or a similar material. The cell circuit is encapsulated in a reliable sealant, such as Ethylene Vinyl Acetate (EVA), to protect it from moisture. The current trend in flat-plate technology has been to eliminate module frames, allowing the mounting hardware to provide edge support.

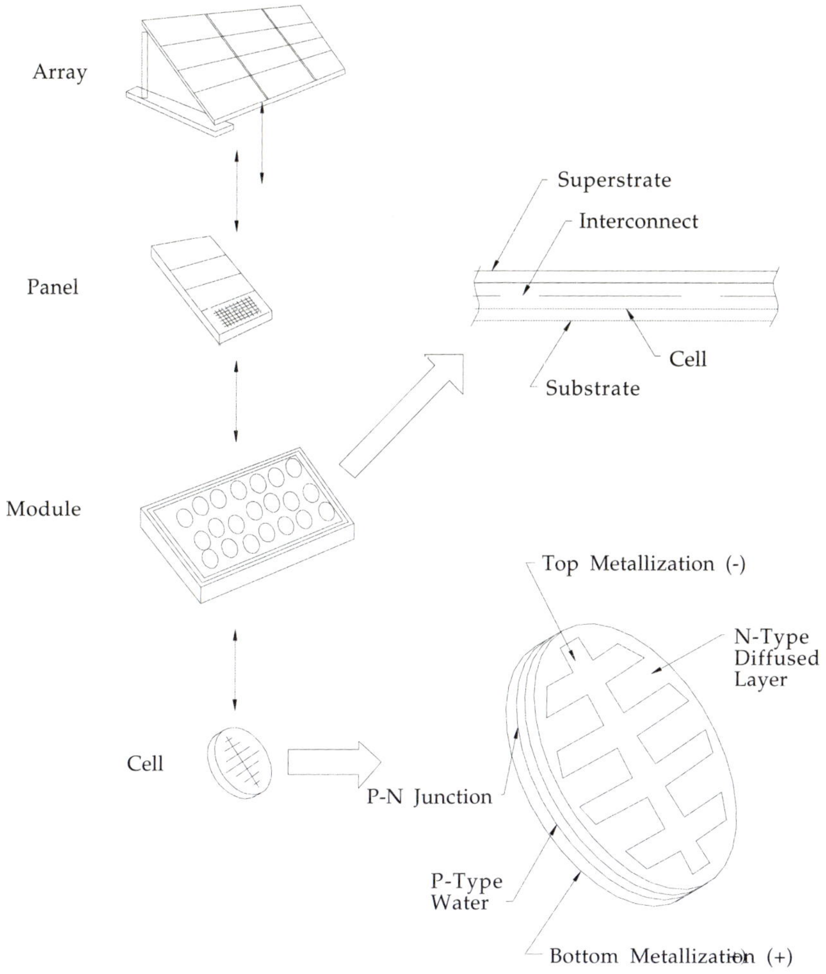

Figure 9.25(b): Flat plate array components

- Panels are a mechanical assembly of modules. In concentrator subsystems, panels are usually a single free-standing unit, motorized to provide tracking. The array then consists of a mechanical assembly of PV panels electrically interconnected to produce a specified quantity of dc power.
- Just as the array subsystem has a mechanical modality of modules and panels there is also an electrical modularity of modules and source circuits. Module voltage is the sum of the series-connected cell voltages. Module current is the current produced by the parallel strings of series-connected cells. Characteristics of dc to ac conversion exhibited by modern inverters require the series connection of modules in a source circuit to achieve sufficient operating voltage that minimizes power losses. Source circuit voltage is the sum of the series-wired module voltages, while source circuit current is produced by all modules. Several source circuits are connected in parallel to achieve total power output of the array subsystem. Array subsystem voltage is the voltage produced by all source circuit.
- The accompanying graphs illustrate the current-voltage (IV) relationships for photovoltaic devices. Single-cell output characteristics are shown in the upper graph. The power output of the cell is equal to the product of the current (I) and voltage (V): watts = I x V. The short circuit current, isc. and open circuit voltage, Voc, are also shown. The maximum power point is identified as P_M . Note that power decreased sharply after voltage exceeds about .45 volts.
- The middle graph shows the variation of output current and voltage for various Nominal Operating Cell Temperatures (NOCT). This graph shows that an increase in temperature produces a slight increase in cell current (constant voltage) and a significant decrease in voltage (at constant current).
- The general principles for combining the voltage and current of photovoltaic devices are shown. These principles apply to the cell circuit in each module as well as a source circuit in an array. For example, if the three IV curves in the upper left represent three modules in a short circuit IV curve is shown in upper right. If this source circuit is combined with another one having the same characteristics, the resulting array IV curve is shown in the lower right.

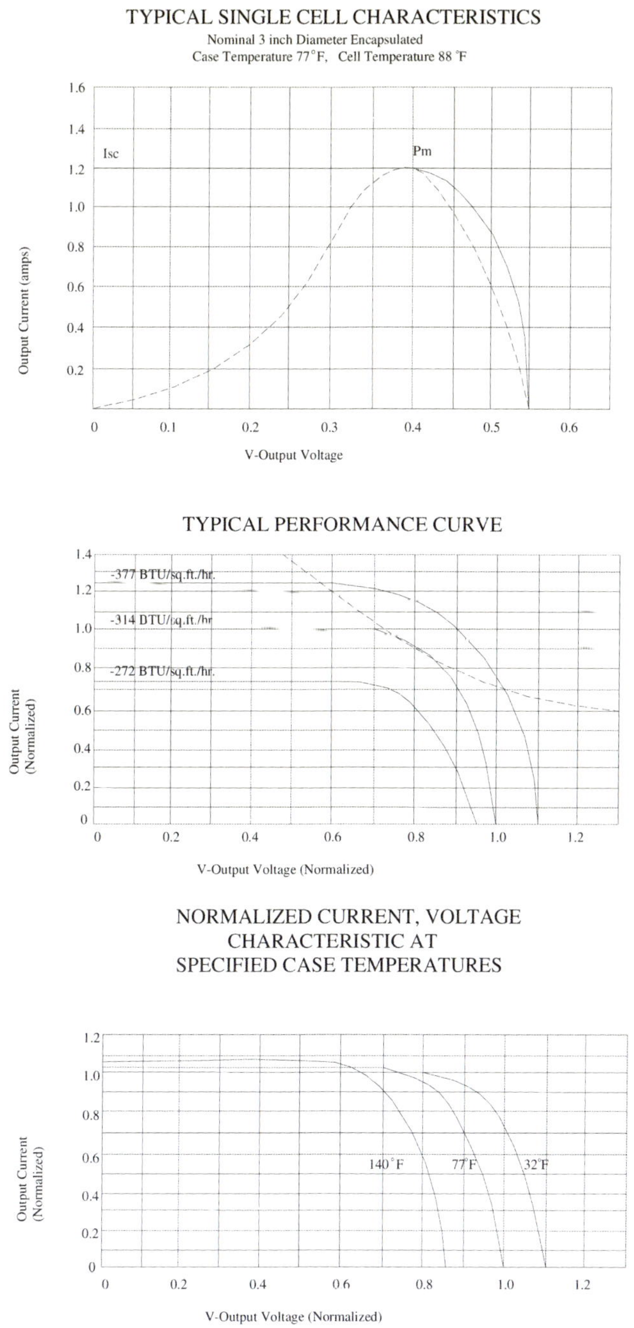

Figure 9.26: Relationship between voltage and current for typical PV cell

9.3.3 Power conditioning and Control Subsystem

The Power Conditioning and Control Subsystem (PCS) includes all the PV system electrical equipment (power and control) except the solar array, dc wiring from the array, ac wiring to the residence electric service panel and associated components. In addition to its primary function of converting dc energy from the array to ac energy of suitable quality for use in utility interconnected systems, the PCS is responsible for overall PV operation, control and protection. The PCS discussed in this section is intended for indoor installation and operation.

- Power Conditioning for the PV system is used to produce utility-compatible ac power from a dc solar array source. It uses in inverter plus ac and dc interface hardware and all necessary control logic and protection. Two types of inverters, line-commutated and self commutated, are available to convert array dc input into ac output. The line commutated inverters use the utility's signal to transform or commute, array dc input into ac output. The self commutated inverters commute array dc input using an internally driven rotating mechanism. Trade-offs exist in the selection of an inverter type. The dc interface is composed of elements that effectively join the dc from the array to the dc/ac inverter section of the PCs. The ac interface is composed of elements that provide electrical isolation and buffering impedance between the inverter and the ac utility system. This interface includes control and protective devices that make it compatible with both the PV system's and the utility system's operational capabilities and constraints.
- Power Conditioning and Control Subsystems used in residential 240 V ac, single phase applications are normally rated for an input voltage of about 200 V dc. They are capable of operating in a voltage window from 160 Vdc to 240 vdc to interface with as many array types and configurations as practical. Normally rated input voltages for nonresidential 180 Vac, three phase applications is about 400 Vdc operating in a voltage window from 320 to 480 Vdc. Since there is only one maximum power point product of array voltage and current, maximum power tracking by the PCS manipulates current and voltage so that the array operates as close to this point as possible, this maximum power tracking manipulation is as frequently specified in system designs as fixed voltage operation. Either fixed voltage operation or automatic tracking of the array maximum power point voltage can be used. However, the selection of a constant voltage level is important since available array energy loss can be predicted as a function of PCs input voltage.
- The available array output current varies with insolation and weather conditions. When the array output current increases beyond the operating capability of the PCS (e.g., very cold, sunny day), the unit will either limit the array current by increasing the dc voltage at the array terminals or otherwise protect itself. At low levels of array output current the PCs will shut down. Direct current input power to the PCS is equal to the ac output power divided by the PCS internal or through efficiency.
- A measure of how efficiently the PCS converts available array energy is its Energy Conversion Performance Factor (ECPF). The ECPF accounts for array energy utilization capability, weighted average conversion efficiency and miscellaneous losses. Although a

ripple current is generated by the PCS, this current is usually limited to 5 percent of the nominal or rated dc input current from the array. A conversion ECPF value is typically at least 86 percent. Factors used to determine the ECPF include the following:

- part-load and full-load efficiencies
- standby hours
- operating hours
- no-load losses
- average array output
- rated array output

Table 9.12: Inverter Characteristics

Inverter Type	*Characteristics*
Line Commutated	- Currently more efficient - Less expensive - Utility may require extra equipment to reduce current harmonics - Power factor not as good - Cannot operate when utility is down
Self Commutated	- Less efficient - More expensive - More operation and maintenance may be required due to moving parts, extra equipment etc. - Power factor better - Current harmonics - Can operate when utility is down

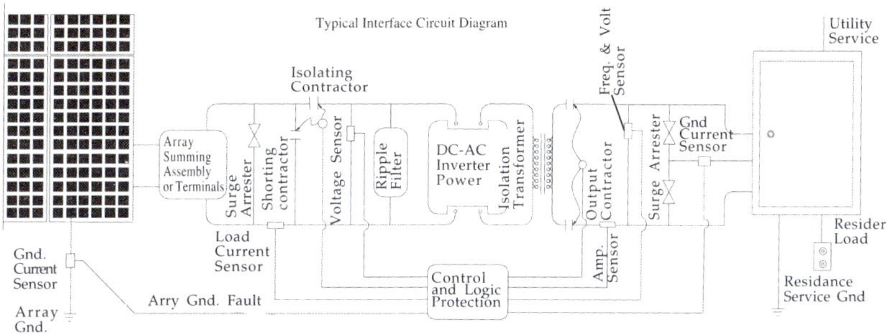

Figure 9.27: Circuit diagram of power-conditioning subsystem interface

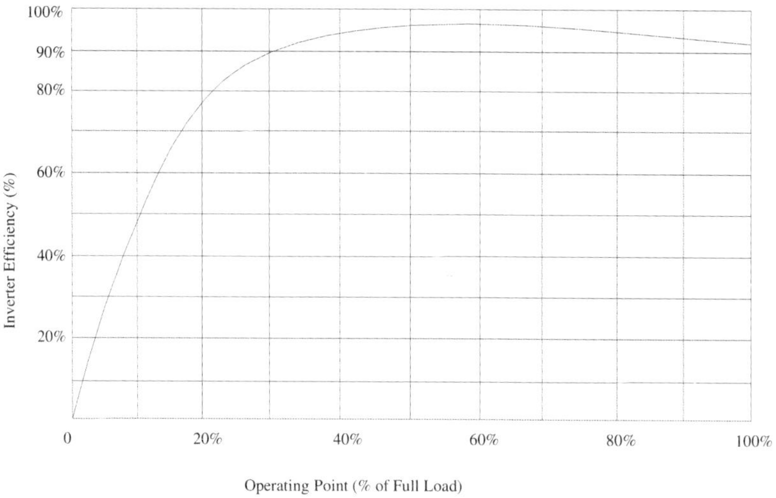

Figure 9.28: Efficiency of solid-state inverter as function of load

Rated PCS power is delivered at or above the minimum specified efficiency during steady state utility voltage swings within the typical range of 86.7 percent to 105.8 percent Vac of utility voltage. The PCS power rating is based on its ac output power capability at the nominal input (dc) voltage rating at the low end of the required ac voltage operating range (e.g., 86.7 percent of a nominal 240 Vac rated utility service).

- Normal (automatic) operation of the PCS consists of the following actions. When the solar radiation incident of the PV array is intense enough to generate an array output power that exceeds the no-load losses of the PCS, the PCs will automatically start, synchronize and connect to the utility line to deliver real power based on power available from the array. The PCS will simultaneously control Volt-Ampere-Reactive (VAR) flow. When array power falls below the level required to support a positive power output, the PCS will automatically stop converting energy, disconnect from the utility and shutdown within one to five minutes.
- Advanced PCS design will generally incorporate the features described below:
  - Start-up. The PCS starts automatically for array input voltage within a pre-set range and array input power above the no-load loss for a pre-set duration.
  - Line-Tie. The PCS incorporates a "walk in" feature whereby, after synchronization with the utility, the output level is gradually increased over several seconds to the full power available at the time of line-tie.
  - Cycling. Excessive cycling is prevented during periods of low solar insolation (e.g., late afternoon and during heavy clouds).

- PCS operating and storage conditions typically assume any combination of the following external environmental conditions without mechanical or electrical damage or degradation of operating characteristics:

  - Ambient temperature.

  Operating   -18°C to +45°C*

  * Maximum operating temperature for installation elevations above 1 km is 40°C.

  - Relative humidity. 0 to 100 percent**

  ** 95 percent is acceptable if the unit does not require internal air flow for cooling.

- The total acoustical noise generated by the PCS, under any condition of operation should be reduced by 75 db measured at a distance of 2m from any point on the surface of the PCS cabinet. To accommodate the temperature, humidity and acoustical noise conditions the PCS is usually located in an unconditioned, isolated space.

- A number of general utility-interconnection parameters affect the selection and specifications of PCS. The objectives are to ensure compatibility of the signal produced by the PV system with that from the utility. The primary parameters are listed below. The local utility must be contacted to verify all site-specific requirements.

  - Reactive Current. The power factor may be limited to 0.95 leading to 0.95 leading at the output terminals of the PCS while powering from 1/8 to full rated load.

  - Harmonic Distoration. Total Harmonic Distoration (THD) in the current waveform may be limited to 5 percent Root-Mean-Squared (RMS) at full rated current. The maximum single harmonic current may not exceed 3 percent rms. Total voltage harmonic voltage may not exceed 1 percent rms.

  - Frequency. The PCS may be required to operate over a frequency range of 58 to 62 Hz, synchronous with the utility.

  - Electrical Isolation. A dry type isolation transformer may be required at the PCS ac interface and to automatically disconnect when the PCS is in a standby mode.

- Electro Magnetic Interference (EMI) must be minimized in the PCS to prevent the adverse interaction between the PCS and equipment operating at 2 meters or greater distance away, such as telephones, radio and television.

- Since the dc wiring and array can act as an antenna for interference generated within the PCS, EMI radiated from the array must be suppressed. Typically EMI must meet the FCC "Incidental Radiator" classification.

- Final acceptance of the PCS can be given after installation and upon successful completion of specified site tests, to be conducted by the system installer. Required field tests and corresponding factory tests are listed.

- The PCS protects the PV system against damage as the result of abnormal conditions detected at its dc and ac interface. Typical protection equipment includes transient overvoltage suppressors, ac and dc undervoltage and overvoltage trip devices, overload current and short circuit protection and ground fault detection. Examples of abnormal conditions for which protection is required are listed below:
  - over or under frequency at ac output terminals (e.g., utility frequency out-of-tolerance for > 2 sec.)
  - alternating current fault, overvoltage or undervoltage
  - direct current fault or overvoltage
  - abnormal current flow and grounding conductor (green wire) (e.g. current in ac ground exceeding 5 milliamps root mean square (ma rms) (ac or dc)
  - PCS component malfunction (e.g. internal failure in PCS (no automatic start-up)
  - Loss and return of utility line voltage (e.g. utility voltage below 87 percent nominal for 2 sec. or above 106 percent nominal for 1 sec.)
  - Array output overcurrent.

Table 9.13: Tests and checks for PV systems

Name of Test	*Factory Tests*		*Field Tests*
	Type	*Routine*	
Interconnection Cable Check	X	X	X
Load Test	X	X	X
Operational Mode Tests (Start-up,	X	X	X
Synchronize, Shutdown			
Utility Disconnect Tests	X	X	X
Devices Properly Functioning			X
Ground Connection	X	X	X

- Under several of these conditions the PCS will disconnect from the utility within 0.5 seconds and shut down. Upon return to normal conditions, the PCS will typically start-up automatically and line-tie within one to five minutes. At no time may the PCS inject DC into the utility line under either normal or abnormal conditions including internal component failure. Protection purposes and devices are summarized in the Table 9.14.
- Table 9.15 indicates the differences among controls built into power-conditioning units, automatic switching using electromechanical controls, and microprocessors. The choice among these depends on several factors:
  - how critical the array output is to application
  - distance from array to application

- availability of monitoring room and personnel to monitor array
- size of the array field and complexity of wiring
- degree of load management required
- availability of maintenance personnel and frequency of maintenance.

Table 9.14: Typical Protection Devices for Power Conditioning

Purpose	*Device*
System & Worker Protection may be integral part of PCU	- Circuit Breakers - Ground Fault Protection - Surge Arrestor
Utility Protection may be required by Utility	- Harmonic Distortion Monitor - Power Factor Monitor - Isolation Transformer - Alarm & Annunciator
System Protecting for self commutated inverters only	- Intertrip & Auto-synchronizing for low or loss of utility voltage
System Protecting for commercial and industrial applications. May be in existing electrical system	- Phase Over-Current Relays - Over/Under Frequency Relays - Zero Sequence Voltage - Grand Fault Relays (High Voltage)

Table 9.15: Control Systems

Category	*Inverter Self-Contained*	*Automatic Switching*	*Microprocessor*
Cost	Included as part of inverter cost	\$ 1000 or \$ 5000 (~20 kW or less)	\$10000 to \$50,000 for24 channels
Complexity	No extra equipment required	Electromechanical Switches	Extra wiring, switches, electrical interfaces required (in addition to microprocessor)
Applications Recommended	Residential and small commercial	Medium to large commercial	Medium to large commercial and all industrial
Disadvantages	No control available for partial system failure or planned shutdown (whole system must be shutdown)	Cannot easily change control sequence once installed	Major cost
Advantages	Simple, no monitoring required	Can control many aspects of system in a limited way. Control may go to main control center if special control panel is provided	Available to monitor & control any aspects of system; control sequence can be programmed. Control can go to main control centre

9.3.4 The Storage Subsystem

Unlike the power-conditioning and PV array subsystems, an electrical storage subsystem is entirely an option for a utility-connected photovoltaic power system. Its principal uses include:

- reduction of peak electrical demand or usage during periods of higher electricity cost.
- service as a backup energy supply during utility outages
- increased displacement of on-site loads by PV output.

- Since the first two uses of storage are independent of the use of photovoltaic power systems, they may be considered independent advantages in deciding whether storage would be cost effective alternative to sellback. From the standpoint of designing utility connected PV systems, the overriding factor in choosing a storage system is economics.
- The desirable characteristics of a battery storage system for PV applications include:
    - accepts deep discharge number of charge-
    - accept a large number of charge-discharge cycle without a failure
    - requires little or no maintenance
    - does not generate significant quantities of dangerous gases
    - is cost effective
- if batteries are included in grid-connected PV systems, they are generally limited to a few hours of capacity for peak saving or leveling loads. The duty cycle for batteries operating in these types of systems is characterized by relatively high maximum charge and discharge rates. In addition, although all cycles may not involve a complete discharge or a complete charge. The batteries may also shift rapidly between charge and discharge, as the result of a transient cloud on an otherwise sunny day or an abrupt change in load demand.
- Two types of batteries suitable for PV systems are currently commercially available; Lead Acid (PbH_2SO_4) and Nickel-Cadmium (NiCd). A comparison is shown for these batteries types in terms of their important characteristics. The comparison also indicates other possible by-product hazards.
- The use of a battery storage system generally also requires additional power conditioning equipment to regulate voltages during charging and discharging cycles. A typical arrangement is shown for interfacing batteries with the PV system. The voltage regulator controls battery charge and discharge voltage levels and rates in response to the state of charge.

Table 9.16: Factors Determining Desirability of Storage

Factors favoring A Storage Subsystem	*Factors Reducing Desirability Of Storage*
Low cost/ kWh	High cost / kWh
Utility sell-back rate is a small percentage of normal rate	Utility sell-back rate is a large percentage of normal rate
Utility requires extensive PC equipment to remove harmonics and improve power factor	Utility requires only an isolation transformer
Utility charges by peak load in addition to net kWh (commercial & industrial)	Utility charges by net kWh only (residential)
Some dc loads exist or may be introduced (water heater coil, etc.)	All loads are ac
There is adequate area or existing architecture in which to put the batteries	A new building or wing will have to built to house batteries
Use	Approximate Storage Size
Reduce sell-back to utility	Difference between: array typical day output and typical day fraction of array output which goes directly to the load
Peak saving	Amount of energy used above the typical peak kW level for which the application is charged
Dc Loads	Typical day dc load energy requirements
Nighttime ac loads	Storage is not a good application for grid-connected systems for nighttime ac loads

- Several factors in addition to basic design decisions may affect battery sizing, such as the amount of storage capacity required with respect to the load magnitude and the desired safety factor. These factors include the amount of capacity necessary to accommodate self-discharge and parasitic energy losses for ventilation and other auxiliary equipment.
- Another important consideration in battery sizing is the fact that many types of batteries do not fail catastrophically, but experience a gradual decline in available capacity as they approach the end of their useful life. For example, it is common practice among lead-acid battery manufacturers to specify end of life as the point at which available capacity falls below 80 percent of rated capacity. In such a case it would be necessary to specify an initial capacity equal to 125 percent of the capacity desired, in order for available capacity to adequate throughout the battery life, in addition, battery degradation strongly depends on cycling frequency and depth of discharge. Thus, an economic trade-off exists between selection of the design point depth of discharge, the cost of installing sufficient rated capacity to meet the system requirements, and the cost of battery replacement over the life of the system.

Factors Determining Desirability of Storage

- Care should be taken to distinguish between battery energy capacity and the manufacturer's rated battery capacity. The energy capacity is of primary interest to the designer and is defined as the total energy (kWh) that can be withdrawn from a fully charged battery. The energy capacity of a given battery varies with temperature, rate of discharge, age of the battery and the allowable depth of discharge (usually determined by some minimum cut off voltage). The manufacturer's rated capacity is generally specified as the total number of ampere-hours (current multiply by hours) that can be withdrawn from a new battery at a specified discharge rate, temperature and recommended cutoff voltage. The specified discharge rate is often stated in terms of the number hours over which full discharge occurs (e.g., 10 amp-hours at the 10 hour discharge rate).

Battery Characteristics and Design Considerations

- Battery terminal voltage can be affected by many parameters, including details of cell construction, charge or discharge rate, state of charge, battery age, operating temperature, and for lead acid batteries, specific gravity of the electrolyte. Fluctuations in battery terminal voltage during operation can affect the performance of the photovoltaic power system, particularly with regard to array efficiency if DC voltage regulators or other types of power conditioning equipment are used. Therefore, it is important that all parameters affecting terminal voltage be identified for the type of cell being considered and that these factors be accounted for in the system design.
- Proper charging conditions are very important to ensure efficient battery operations as well as maximum battery life. In most non-solar battery applications, however, energy dispatching requirements and variations in insulation may result in significantly less control over charging conditions. Battery efficiency decreases at higher charge/discharge rates.
- The ambient conditions under which a battery operates can affect its performance characteristics and life. For example, available capacity and voltage of lead acid cells are a function of operating temperature. Drastic reductions of available capacity occur at very low temperatures and permanent damage can result if the electrolyte freezes. Also, operation at elevated temperatures will reduce battery life.
- Other battery characteristics such as operating voltage range (which can affect conditioner designs), efficiency and self-discharge rate are also temperature-dependent. In addition, humidity, wind, rain, snow, ice, air-borne pollutants and other ambient conditions may affect the performance of batteries and auxiliary equipment.

Table 9.17: Battery Characteristics and Design Considerations

Battery Characteristics	*Design Considerations*
Equalization	Lack of equalization may result in reduced lifetimes, particularly for extended discharge periods
High charge/Discharge Rate	High charge/discharge rate can increase temperature, decrease efficiency and shorten battery life.
Self-Discharge Rate	Self-discharge causes battery energy losses
Parasitic Power Needs	Auxiliary equipment may require continuous power sources (e.g. ventilation)
Extended Operation at Partial State-of-Charge	Partial state-of-charge can decrease charge acceptance (e.g., via sulfation in lead-acid) and reduce capacity.
Corrosion	Chemical degradation may limit battery lifetimes independent of the number of discharge cycles.
Rated Cycle Life	Cycle life divided by cycle frequency is an upper bound on battery life.
Duty Cycle	Cyclic operation, partial charge operation and periods of deep discharge can adversely affect battery life.
Current-Voltage Characteristics	I-V characteristics affects system operation, voltage levels, battery charge/discharge.
Auxiliary Systems	Ventilation and/or air-lift stratification systems may be required. Flowing electrolytes batteries (REDOX, zinc-chlorine) require pumps, valves, control systems.
Capacity Degradation Over Time	Capacity will degrade over time, especially for deep discharge duty cycles.
Maintenance Requirements	Maintenance is a key tradeoff of battery performance, lifetime and life-cycle costs.
Ambient Conditions	Battery characteristic are strongly affected by ambient conditions, especially temperature; low temperature reduce available capacity, high temperatures reduce lifetime (lead acid)
Safety Requirement	Controlled access, over-current protection, circuit isolation, fire protection, procedures to avoid shorting battery terminals, ventilation, and other safety features may be required.

- Many types of batteries contain or produce potentially hazardous or corrosive materials at some point in the charge / discharge cycle. These may include flammable and/or toxic gases, liquids, and solids. Also, auxiliary systems may contain moving or high temperature parts from which personnel must be protected.
- Overcurrent protection, circuit insulation, and other electrical safety features may be required. The need to protect personnel from electrical shocks hazards must also be considered. Care in design and operational procedures should be taken to preclude short-circuiting of battery terminals with tools. Showers or eyewash stations may be required if personnel are exposed to the risk of contact with acid from lead-acid batteries.

Table 9.18 : Battery specifications

Category	*Lead-Acid (Deep Cycle)*	*Nickel-Cadmium*
Weight/Capacity	100 to 145 Lb/kWh	66 to 100 Lb/kWh
Life in Cycles	1500 to 2000	2000 to 3000
Hazards	Hydrogen gas evolution acid electrolyte spills/leaks	
Self Discharge	Possible problem after a few weeks	A problem only after long time intervals (month or greater)
Overcharging Tolerance	Will be damaged by overcharging	Will accept 5% to 10% capacity overcharge for extended periods
Failure Mechanisms	- A battery rated 75 °(F.) will lose half its lifetime if it operates at 110 °(F.) - Freezing problem: at near or full discharge, freezes at 32°(F.) - Water Loss	- Can operate up to 115°(F.) with no loss of capacity or lifetime - Can operate down to -40°(F.) without failure, although operation at this extreme should be avoided due to efficiency loss - Internal short circuits towards end of life - Water loss towards end of life.
Required Maintenance	Water replacement	- Water replacement (none for sealed)
Recommended Temperature Range (Typical)	75° ± 10°(F.)	75° ± 40°(F.)
Typical Energy Efficiency	70 to 80%	80 to 85%
Battery Voltage	Varies with state of charge	Fairly constant with state of change

- Design features necessary to ameliorate safety and environmental concerns will depend on the specific nature of the battery, as well as the type and location of the installation. For example, an application to which the general public could have access may require more stringent safety provisions than one in which physical assess to components is restricted to skilled workers. In addition, all applications will be required to conform to local or national safety codes and specifications.

- Depending on the types of battery used and the specific nature of the application, various auxiliary devices and equipment may be required for proper operation. For example, lead-acid, battery installations may require ventilating systems to maintain hydrogen concentrations below dangerous levels. Airlift system to prevent stratification of the electrolyte may also be required in some instances. Similarly, the flowing electrolyte battery designs (for example, zinc-chlorine) require pumps, valves, and associated control systems, while the advanced high temperature batteries require auxiliary heating and cooling equipment.

- The photovoltaic system designer may also be responsible for supplying racks or other support structures in addition to intercell bus connectors, cabling, disconnect switches, fuses, or circuit breakers. Protective housing or special rooms may be required to protect or isolate the battery.

- Certain physical or operating characteristics of the battery may impose special requirements on the design of the battery enclosure and support systems.

- For example, lead-acid batteries may rest directly on the floor or may be placed in tiered racks and stacked three or four layers high. This latter arrangement creates a significant concentrated floor loading condition and can affect building design requirements. Similarly, flowing electrolyte batteries may require special damping measures to ameliorate vibration induced by electrolyte pumping systems, while the high temperature batteries may present thermal stress problems.

- If the batteries contain acid or alkaline solutions, corrosion-resistant coatings may be required on the walls, floor and other structures in the batteries room. Corrosion-resistant floor drains and plumbing should also be provided. The floor drain sump must be of adequate size to contain the total volume of any potential spill, including water used for cell washing, or by fire extinguishing systems.

- Many types of battery systems require periodic maintenance to ensure safe and efficient operations as well as to provide maximum life time. Maintenance may include periodic visual inspection, checking of electrical connections and replacement of air filters or other service to auxiliary equipment. Aqueous batteries, such as the lead-acid type, may also require periodic measurement of electrolyte specific gravity and addition of water.

- In many applications, selection of the optimum battery type can be significantly affected by both first and life-cycle costs. For example, if maintenance or replacement costs are likely to be high, it may be advantageous to select a battery with low maintenance requirements and long life, even though this may result in high first cost. Economic evaluation should therefore be a life-cycle dollars per kilowatt-hour basis, rather than simply first cost dollars per kilowatt or kilowatt-hour. The actual cost of the battery energy storage subsystem over the life of the photovoltaic power system is determined by:

- first cost (dependent on battery type)
- impact on design requirements of other system components, such as the required voltage range of the power-conditioning equipment (dependent on battery type, ambient conditions and system configuration)
- maintenance costs (dependent on battery type duty cycle, ambient conditions, system location and economic factors such as inflation)
- salvage value (dependent on battery type and system location)
- energy efficiency (dependent on battery type, duty cycle and ambient conditions)
- auxiliary equipment requirements (dependent on battery type).

Table 9.19: Lead-Acid Battery Types

Type	*General characteristics*	*Typical Applications*
Automotive (SLI) and Diesel Starting	High discharge rate, relatively low cost, poor cycle life	Automotive starting, lighting and ignition; tractors, snowmobiles and other small engine starting; large diesel engine starting
Motive Power (Traction)	Moderate discharge rate, good cycle life	Fork lifts, mine vehicles; golf carts, submarines; other electric vehicles
Stationery (Float)	Medium discharge rate, good life (years), some type have low self-discharge rates, poor cycle life	Telephone power supplies; uninterrupted power supplies (UPS); other standby and emergency power supply applications
Sealed	No maintenance, moderate rate, poor cycle life	Lanterns, portable tools, portable electronic equipment, also sealed SLI
Low Rate Photovoltaic	Low maintenance, low self-discharge, special designs for high and low ambient temperatures, poor deep cycle life	Remote, daily shallow discharge, large reserve (stand-alone) photovoltaic power systems
Medium rate Photovoltaic	Moderate discharge rate, good cycle life, low maintenance	Photovoltaic power systems with on-site backup or utility interface, requiring frequent deep cycle operation

9.3.5 System Design Concerns and Comparison

Several design concerns result from detailed design issues subsystem interfaces within the PV system. Issues discussed in this section address array sizing, roof constraints, array mounting, array wiring, module interconnection, power conversion operation, battery location and fire safety. These concerns are currently the focus of detailed field studies.

- There is concern about roof-mounted array sizing when too many site-specific variables exist to provide any natural limits other than available roof area or source circuit size. Usually the system is expected to deliver energy to the building load at the minimum life cycle cost, including the cost of back-up utility are at least 50% of those charged to customers, the largest possible array size produces the lest life-cycle cost. Otherwise the array subsystem is limited by site specific series and parallel circuit layout, module mounting details, roof weather protection, and esthetic integration.
- The choice of array mounting technique has significant effects on overall system costs. However, it is not apparent from the distinct array roof mounting approaches- integral, direct or stand-off- which is the most cost effective. Each approach has offsetting advantages and disadvantages. Module layout, array operating voltage, wiring methods, weather seals and replacement or maintenance access are affected by mounting technique selection.

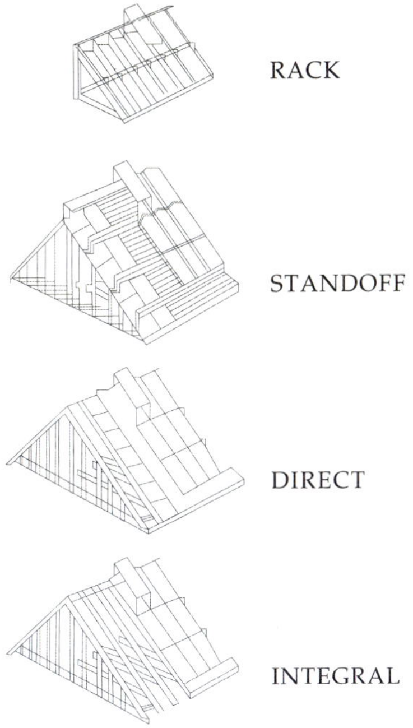

Figure 9.29: Array mounting types

Comparison of Features and Liabilities of Mounting Types

- Temperature and humidity cycling stresses can cause cell and interconnection failures as well as the de-lamination of a module's incapsulant system. Other potential degradation agents include ultraviolet irradiation and corrosion. Candidate modules should be carefully selected on the basis of material characteristics to withstand anticipated environmental and mechanical stress conditions.

Table 9.20: Comparison of Features and Liabilities of Mounting Types

Mounting Types	*Features*	*Liabilities*
Rack	- More options in array placement (ground or roof) - More tilt angle control - Maintenance and installation access - Good for flat roofs	- Structural, material and labor costs - Roof availability - Land availability - Zoning - Vandalism protection (Ground mounts) - Esthetics - Wind uplift
Stand-off	- Back venting of array - Retrofit applicability - Need not be waterproofed - Lower-profile, more esthetic	- Access more difficult - Roof penetration waterproofing required
Direct	- Structural materials minimized - Array acts as waterproofed membrane - Roofing materials minimized	- Must withstand same loading as code requires for roof - Minimal array cooling, thus higher operating temperatures - Must access electrical connections from top - Access for maintenance difficult - Achieving watertight seal
Integral	- Minimizes roofing materials - Minimizes structural materials - Provides back access through attic for maintenance	- Water tightness critical - Special truss system may be required - Not especially suited to retrofit work - Must withstand same loading as code requires for roof.

- The primary structural requirement for each module is to limit breakage of cover material cells and interconnects due to wind, snow, hail and seismic loads. Selection of load combinations should reflect a balance between values that have a low probability of being exceeded and values that do not result in a costly overdesign of the module mounting.

- The choice of array wiring methods and system layout has an important effect on overall system costs. While dry location wiring appears least costly, it is not apparent which distinct layout approach is the most cost effective. For example, many roof mounted designs locate the negative bus along the eave, with the positive bus along the ridge. A wired connection to the earth ground for the negative bus may be provided as an additional safety precaution in case of accidental contact. This connection requires an isolation transformer in the power conversion subsystem. However, the transformer adds economic penalties to initial cost and reduces net power output over the life of the system. If the array bus ground can be safely eliminated, then a lower overall cost results.

- Modules with accessible conductive parts are limited by safety standards to produce no more than 30 Vdc at 0°C, to provide protection from electric shock hazard. Trade-offs between low voltage (<30 Vdc) and advanced module designs that allow higher voltages by elimination of exposed conductive parts should be examined for circuit or layout flexibility. Since PV modules cannot be switched off easily during hours of sunlight and the current limiting character of PV cells makes the use of circuit breakers and fuses infeasible, careful consideration of installation and maintenance procedures must be made.
- An array subsystem incorporates a variety of features to ensure safety from the low voltage (<30 Vdc) end of a branch circuit to its high voltage (~200 Vdc) end. Appropriate safety features can include the following.
  - System, enclosure and equipment grounding, accompanied if necessary by ground fault sensors to short the array or open the array circuit to ground connector.
  - Adequate conductor ampacity for the highest expected (i.e. short-circuit) current and operating temperature at that location in the circuit
  - Adequate insulation for the highest expected (i.e. short-circuit) voltage at that location in the circuit
  - Redundant safety measures for fail-safe operations.
  - Minimizing potential effects of voltage arcs between an open-circuit cell and adjacent components.
  - Surge protection for circuit elements.
- Module interconnection methods must satisfy the National Electrical Code. The key design concern is whether the application can be classified as a wet or dry location. Since, low cost wet location methods do not presently exist, wiring weather protection critical. In addition, the location and method of splice connections must be carefully considered from a standpoint of both code compliance and cost savings. The number of slice connections as well as length of wiring runs depend on such things as module layout, series and parallel circuit layout, module mounting details and outdoor disconnect location.
- Two primary design concerns exist in the area of power conversion. These concerns affect the relationship between power conversion design and operation.
- Power-conditioner sizing attempts to achieve sometimes two conflicting objectives. Optimal sizing may require a compromise between the following approaches,:
  - PCS sized to handle expected peak array output

- PCS sized to maximize periods during which it operates at higher efficiencies.

  Present solutions to this problem have first considered the effects of location and temperature on peak array power. The most economical system has been found to be one in which the array subsystem is slightly oversized in relation to the input PCS rating.

- Another set of tradeoffs result in the use of maximum power tracking or constant voltage power conversion. From a design standpoint, there is perhaps a 5% life-cycle cost difference.

- Field experience has indicated problems in startup and maximum power tracking. The designer must be aware of the high open circuit voltage that can exist during start-up conditions when there is a low total power output. The specifications of the unit must accommodate these initial conditions.

- It is easy to specify a Power Conversion Subsystem operation with ranges within a few percent of the maximum power point; however, test data on maximum power tracking options has indicated difficulty in achieving these specifications. Though not yet perfected, alternative schemes are under development, including the use of a pilot cell. This approach is an open loop control method and although relatively simple, may not represent the true array operating point over the lifetime of the system as module performance is degraded due to dirt, electrical problems or shadowing.

- Location of batteries within a building presents several concerns. Tradeoffs between an interior location for the batteries usually result in an interior location based primarily on the requirements for maintaining environmental control and access for maintenance. This location assumes battery placement in an equipment room with the equipment for power conversion, control and monitoring.

- Design of the room should consider the following requirements: sufficient ventilation to remove any hydrogen buildup; incorporation of a wet area; accommodation for spillage of active battery ingredients; tool and equipment storage; and minimization of unauthorized access to the equipment. A guaranteed amount of ventilation at all times is required to dissipate the small amount of hydrogen and chemicals emitted under normal operating conditions to prevent hydrogen buildup within the room. A positive 30 to 60 cfm ventilation is suggested to remove hydrogen during equalization of battery charge. These ventilation requirements may produce a slightly greater infiltration loss. To accommodate any possible spillage, a 5 cm drop in the slab can be designed around the battery racks. The batteries can be located in a metal enclosure to minimize general access. If used the cabinet should have heavy louvers and a locked door. As electrochemical storage systems become more widespread, standard components may be developed to resolve these concerns.

Table 9.21: Comparison of PV system types

Description	*Advantages*	*Disadvantages*	*Conclusions*
ALL-ELECTRIC SYSTEM/BATTERY STORAGE This system involves all-electric loads with space heating and cooling provided by a heat pump. The PV system includes batteries connected directly across the solar array bus, with the solar array operating point established by the voltage of the battery. Battery change accomplished by limiting the battery charge voltage to a prescribed level. Control is exerted by partial shunting of discrete section of the solar array current to limit battery charge voltage.	No max power tracker Does not require feed back to utility	Initial cost and maintenance of batteries Energy dissipated through shunt when PV system output exceeds what load and battery will accept. Energy losses through battery heat dissipation Digital shunt and battery charge control devices required. Somewhat lower annual energy displacement than with no-battery system Battery generated hydrogen gas explosive hazard. Cost of safety features to meet local codes.	This PV only system is less economical and displaces less energy than a system without battery storage utilizing a maximum power tracker and utility feedback. Major factors contributing to disadvantage of this system include cost of battery storage and the losses associated with the charge/discharge cycles.
2. ALL-ELECTRIC/ FEEDBACK This system involves all-electric loads, with space heating and cooling provided by a heat pump. The PV system includes a maximum power tracking inverter and permits feedback of excess PV energy to the utility grid connected in parallel with the photovoltaic system.	Simplest system Utility essentially acts as electrical storage medium for all access energy generated by PV array.	Acceptance of feedback by utility Low buyback rate makes system less attractive	This system is the least complex to implement, assuming utility acceptance of access PV array output. Large scale sellback of power to the utility from many residences can pose a serious problem to the utility.Of the PV-only investigated, the feedback system provided the highest energy displacement for an all-electric residence.

- Fire safety is an important design concern that must be specifically addressed for each application. One concern is the likely classification of the roof-mounted installation by local building code officials. Another concern is the installation's fire rating classification. Local fire companies may need to be alerted and instructed regarding the potential danger of the energy producing roof. The location of the dc power line adjacent to the normal utility line and the exterior disconnect switch should alert fire personnel that the building has an additional power supply. However, fire personnel must be informed that a disconnect at the switch still permits the array to operate as an active generator in the daylight and only interrupts power supply to the building.

9.3.6 System Feasibility

Preliminary estimates of cost effectiveness and requirements are an important first step in deciding whether or not to utilize a photovoltaic power system, this section provides simple nomographs which give quick, rough estimates of PV system economics and PV collector area.

- Solar energy is an inherently diffuse power source and large areas are required to collect it. A flat-plate PV system, for example, requires about 10m^2 (100 square feet) of collector area to generate a peak output of 1 kW at noon on sunny days assuming 10% overall system efficiency). The array size is a key parameter in PV system design because it determines the peak output of the system and also many of the requirements for other PV subsystems. The purpose of this section is to provide a preliminary estimate of PV collector area.
- Collector sizing for utility-connected systems is essentially an economic tradeoff analysis. An array size too small will produce too little energy relative to the initial fixed cost of installing the system (many of these initial costs are independent of the array size). On the other hand, an array size too large will provide a large amount of energy, but much of the output will be in access of the on-site loads, and hence would be less valuable. Because the utility is always present to provide backup power, the availability of PV power at all times is not a factor. Thus, it is not cost-effective to size the array so large (with storage) as to meet all of the electric demands, including cloudy days, because then the array energy is not being fully used (significant excess would occur on sunny days). The proper size is a balance which depends on the type of collector, the location, the electric loads, PV system costs, utility electricity costs and many other design variables.
- PV systems are likely to be cost effective for arrangement of array sizes. This is important because it means that there is some flexibility in the design and that the array area itself need not be critically dependent on particular assumptions about future electricity costs, sell back rates, inflation, etc. (Economic feasibility remain very sensitive to these factors, however). In the future standard package systems may be developed for specific building types or application. For now, however, the designer should not be too concerned with using the exact "optimum" array area.
- To a large extent the array size may be dictated by the available area, especially for roof-mounted systems. In estimating the available area for horizontal mounting surfaces, the designer must also account for the spacing between PV modules to prevent shading. Typical cover ratios (ratio of array area to total ground or roof area required) are given for estimating purposes. These cover ratios minimize shading effects to a few percent and may be increased if area is limited. The designer should also consider aesthetic aspects such as visual interest or structural appearance in estimating area availability.

Economic Feasibility

- Economic analysis for PV system involves the following steps:
  1. Estimate PV System Performance.
     - Estimate Average Daily Insolation (kWh/m^{2}d). The adjoining map can be used to estimate daily mean direct normal solar radiation for a particular location.
     - Estimate Average System Efficiency. The PV system efficiency is usually taken to be about 10%, based on nominal estimates for typical equipment.
     - Determine System Output (kWh/m^{2}d).
     - Estimate Utilization factor. The utilization factor depends on the match between load and PV output, but can be estimated as 0.8 assuming "good" design.
  2. Estimate PV System Cost
     - Estimate Alternate Electricity Cost (Rs./kWh). An electric energy cost should be estimated based on average daytime Rs./kWh energy charges, but not fixed on demand charge which the PV system does not offset.
     - Determine Annual Fuel Savings (Rs./m^2).
     - Estimate Installed System Costs (Rs./m^2). The installed PV system cost should be adjusted for available tax credits. For example tax credit alone can be as much as 40% of installed cost for homeowners and 25 % for businesses. Depreciation should also be included.
  3. Estimate Rate of Return on Investment.
     - Determine Simple Payback (years).
     - Estimate Rate of Return on Investment.
     - Determine Simple Payback (years).
     - Estimate Time Horizon (years). The useful life of the PV System is usually 20 to 30 years.
     - Estimate Energy Escalation Rate (%/y). It is important to estimate an annual electricity escalation rate, since electricity costs will probably increase over time.
     - Determine Rate of Return on Investment.

9.4 ECBC REQUIREMENTS FOR SOLAR WATER HEATING

The Energy Conservation Building Code, as a mandatory requirement requires that Residential facilities, hotels and hospitals with a centralized system shall have solar water heating for at least 1/5 of the design capacity.

Exception to this requirement is given to systems that use heat recovery for at least 1/5 of the design capacity.

The application for approval shall furnish detailed calculation showing the design to ensure that at least 20% of the heating requirement shall be met from solar heat/heat recovery and not more than 80% of the heat shall be met from electrical heating. Wherever gas is available, not more than 20% of the heat shall be met from electrical heating.

10

Energy Audit in Buildings*

The energy audit in a building is a feasibility study to identify energy use among the various services, to identify opportunities for energy conservation, and to act as the first step in establishing an energy management program. The audit will produce the data on which such a program is based. The study should reveal the options available for reducing energy waste, the costs involved, and the benefits achievable from implementing those Energy-Conserving Opportunities (ECOs). The energy management program is a systematic on-going strategy for controlling a building's energy consumption pattern. It is adopted to reduce waste of energy and money to the minimum level as permitted by the climate, functions of the building, its occupancy schedules, and other factors. It establishes and maintains an efficient balance between a building's annual functional energy requirements and its annual actual energy consumption.

10.1 PRE-AUDIT STAGE

10.1.1 Preparing For The Audit

Before undertaking an energy audit, the following preparations should be made to ensure that the audit goes smoothly and that all required information is available in a timely manner:

1. Establish contact with the senior individual with responsibility for the audit in the facility/building to be audited. All communications concerning the audit and recommendations from the audit should go through this individual.
2. Give the facility at least one week prior notice of an audit visit in order to allow sufficient time for the facility managers to obtain the required documentation and inform the staff of the audit. Identify in writing the documented information that you require, such as electrical bills and plans/drawings.
3. Request that a facility staff member who is familiar with the facility and able to explain your presence to staff to accompany you on your audit rounds.
4. Before entering any area of a facility, always announce your presence and ask permission. Respect facility rules, which may delay or prevent entry into some areas. When these situations occur, try to obtain information about energy using equipment in these areas by talking with staff. Obtain and use any required personal protective equipment required by facilities to allow entry to certain areas.

* Base document for this chapter is Kumar P. and Tyagi A.K. (2002), "Managing Energy Efficiency in Hotels and commercial building" and Tyagi A.K. (2003), " Hand Book on energy audits and management"

10.1.2 Common Sense Based ECOs

Even before formal energy audit, some major checks and solutions can be adopted in a building. These opportunities do not involve much technicalities but they are more common sense based practices. The identification of such opportunities to reduce energy consumption requires on-site inspection. These opportunities fall in two categories:

1. Changing operating practices so as to reduce energy consumption.
2. Retrofitting the building so as to make the building itself more energy efficient.

Changing Operating Practices

Opportunities to reduce energy consumption that fall into this category have to do with changing people's behavior in the workplace. The following measures should be implemented and adhered to since they can result in immediate and significant energy savings at no cost:

1. All lights, computers and other electrical equipment should be turned off when not in use. At the end of the work day a staff person should be designated to ensure that all lights, computers and other electrical equipments in the workplace are switched off.
2. Windows and doors in an air conditioned room should never be left open. If a natural breeze is desired, switch off the air conditioning.
3. The use of equipment bearing a certification of energy efficiency.

Making A Building More Energy Efficient

A wide range of measures may be taken to make a building more energy efficient. Determining which measures to implement often requires detailed calculation of use within the building and heat gain/loss from the building, and the costing of retrofit options to determine which are cost effective; professional assistance will often be necessary to perform these analyses. The least cost approach is to ensure that energy efficiency is designed into buildings in the first instance. The following retrofit measures, however, will typically result in significantly reduced energy usage and significant energy cost savings:

1. Sealing air-conditioned spaces so that cooled air stays within the space and warmer outside air does not enter the space.
2. In hotels, installing mechanisms in guest rooms that require the insertion of the guest's key while the guest is in the room to activate the electrical system of the room, and which results in all electrical systems shutting off when the key is withdrawn when the guest leaves the room.
3. Installation of insulation in the ceiling/roof of all air-conditioned spaces.
4. Options may also be available for introducing more energy efficient equipment into a building to improve overall energy efficiency.

10.2 PHASES OF ENERGY AUDIT

The energy audit contains several phases. These phases include a simple walk-through survey, followed by monitoring of energy use in the building services, and then model analysis using computer simulation of building operation. The complexity of the audit is therefore directly related to the stages or degree of sophistication of the energy management programme and the cost of the audit exercise. The first stage is to reduce energy use in areas where energy is wasted and reductions will not cause disruptions to the various functions. The level of service must not be compromised by the reduction in energy consumed. It begins with a detailed, step-by-step analysis of the building's energy use factors and costs, such as insulation values, occupancy schedules, chiller efficiencies, lighting levels, and records of utility and fuel expenditures. It includes the identification of specific ECOs, along with the cost-effective benefits of each one. The completed study would provide the building owner with a thorough and detailed basis for deciding which ECOs to implement, the magnitude of savings to be expected, and the energy conservation goals to be established and achieved in the energy management programme. However, the ECOs may yield modest gains. The second stage is to improve efficiency of energy conversion equipment and to reduce energy use by proper operations and maintenance. For this reason, it is necessary to reduce the number of operating machines and operating hours according to the demands of the load, and fully optimize equipment operations. Hence the ECOs would include the following:

- Building equipment operation,
- Building envelope,
- Air-conditioning and mechanical ventilation equipment and systems,
- Lighting systems,
- Power systems, and
- Miscellaneous services.

The first two stages can be implemented without remodeling buildings and existing facilities. The third stage would require changes to the underlying functions of buildings by remodeling, rebuilding, or introducing further control upgrades to the building. This requires some investment.

The last stage is to carry out large-scale energy reducing measures when existing facilities have past their useful life, or require extensive repairs or replacement because of obsolescence. In this case higher energy savings may be achieved. For these last two stages, the audit may be more extensive in order to identify more ECOs for evaluation, but at an increased need for heavier capital expenditure to realize these opportunities.

10.2.1 Surveying the Building

A walk-through survey of a building may reveal several ECOs to the experienced eye of the auditor. The survey could be divided into three parts.

Preliminary survey

Prior to the walk-through survey, the auditor may need to know the building and the way it is used. The information can be obtained from:

- architectural blueprints,
- air-conditioning blueprints,
- electrical lighting and power blueprints,
- utility bills and operation logs for the year preceding the audit,
- air-conditioning manuals and system data, and
- building and plant operation schedules.

Walk-through

Thus having familiarized with the building, the walk-through process could be relatively straightforward if the blueprints and other preliminary information available describes the building and its operation accurately. The process could begin with a walk around the building to study the building envelope. Building features such as building wall color, external sun-shading devices, window screens and tint, and so on are noted as possible ECOs. If a model analysis is included in the study, the building must be divided into zones of analysis. The survey inside the building would include confirmation that the air-conditioning system is as indicated on plans. Additions and alterations would be noted. The type and condition of the windows, effectiveness of window seals, typical lighting and power requirements, occupancy and space usage are noted. This information could be compared against the recommendations in the relevant Codes of Practices. System and plant data could be obtained by a visit to the mechanical rooms and plant room. Nameplate data could be compared against those in the building's documents, and spot readings of the current indicating panels for pumps and chillers recorded for estimating the load on the system.

Operator's input

The auditor may discuss with the building maintenance staff further on the operating schedules and seek clarification on any unusual pattern in the trend of the utility bills. Unusual patterns such as sudden increase or decrease in utility bills could be caused by changes in occupancy in the building, or change in use by existing tenants. It is not uncommon for tenants to expand their computing operations that may increase the energy use significantly.

Report

At this stage, ECOs could be found in measures such as:

- Reduce system operating hours,
- Adjust space temperature and humidity,

- Reduce building envelope gain,
- Adjust space ventilation rates and building exfiltration,
- Review system air and water distribution,
- Adjust chiller water temperatures, and
- Review chiller operations.

The benefit from adopting each ECO should be compared against cost of implementation. Caution should be exercised in the cost-benefit analysis given the wider range of certainty of the projections made. However, a survey at this level may be sufficient for small buildings.

10.2.2 Measurements

The capability of the energy auditor and the scope of an audit could be extended by the use of in-place instrumentation and temporary monitoring equipment. In-place instrumentation refers to existing utility metering, air-conditioning control instrumentation and Energy Management Systems (EMS). The use of in-place utility metering and temporary monitoring equipment in energy auditing can yield valuable information about the building systems such as:

- Energy signature and end-use consumption analysis,
- Discovery and identification of ECOs,
- Quantification of energy use and misuse,
- Establishing bounds for potential energy reduction, and
- Data acquisition for further calculation and analysis.

Existing information

Existing instrumentation such as utility meter readings, and energy billings could be used to establish energy consumption patterns for the building. The regularity of consumption pattern is an indicator that no significant change in consumption occurred prior to the audit. This can also be used to check the validity of projections based on extrapolated short-term monitored data. Utility data could be used to establish useful indices such as kWh/m^2/year to compare relative energy performance of buildings. Air-conditioning control instrumentation such as chilled water temperature probes, water flow meters could be used to estimate cooling load demand and plant operation. For example, chilled water temperature outside the designed range may indicate that cooling coils may be operating under off-design conditions.

Short term monitoring

The building may not be equipped for monitoring energy consumption and it may be necessary to install temporary measurement devices such as instantaneous recorders (strip chart, data loggers, etc.) and totalizing recorders (kWh meters) to obtain data over the period of a week for the study. Monitored data is also useful for completing the energy model of a building for use in some building energy simulation software. For example the total building energy consumption would include energy used in the vertical transportation system and potable water pumps which are not modeled in the software. An estimate for annual consumption is extrapolated from the typical week consumption profile. Regularity of the weekly consumption profile means that the annual consumption could be estimated with confidence and the value used to cross check with the annual energy bills.

10.2.3 Model Analysis

Building energy consumption in simplest terms is just the product of rate of consumption of a system and the period of operation. In lighting systems, its energy consumption could be determined manually with precision as it does not interact with other consumption variables. Energy consumption of cooling systems, however, is many times more complicated as it is affected by the internal heat gain within a building as well as weather variables, which varies in a complex manner over time. Building model analysis using computers offers several improvements over manual calculations. These include:

- Precise schedule of building parameters,
- Precise determination of weather impact,
- Specification of part load performance of plant and equipment, and
- Consideration of parameter interactions such as lighting load on air-conditioning consumption.

Software

Some software such as Visual DOE, eQUEST, Energy Plus, TRNSYS, EcoTect, permit hour-by-hour calculations of building consumption for the entire 8760 hours of the year, but require thorough knowledge of the software to carry out accurate and meaningful analysis. Few simplified software based on consumption analysis on characteristic days in a year may also be considered. However, the improvements in computational power of the desktop PC has introduced several powerful features and user-friendly graphical interface possible in more recent versions of such software making it more accessible to the practicing engineer.

Analysis

The general procedure for an analysis would be to establish a model giving an annual consumption within 10% of the measured data. This establishes the base model. The impact of ECOs on energy consumption would be compared against the base model. ECOs could be considered singly or in combinations to determine interactions between them. The results of the energy savings in each analysis should not be taken as absolute but rather taken to be relative to the base run so as to give an indication of the order of magnitude of savings. Thus those ECOs which show significant gains would be implemented.

10.2.4 Use of Data Collection Sheets

Energy audits should be performed using the following worksheets:

Energy Audit Checklist: These worksheets provide the basic data-gathering tool for performing an energy audit. As appropriate to the facility to be audited, the following sections of the Energy Audit Checklist should be completed:

- General
- Architectural Components
- Mechanical Systems, having regard for blowers and fans, boilers and steam systems, chillers and refrigeration systems, cooling towers, compressors and compressed air systems, heating/ventilation/air conditioning (HVAC) systems, drying systems, fire protection systems, heat exchangers, pumping systems, vacuum systems, energy recovery systems and water and sewer systems
- Electrical Systems, having regard for lighting, motors and drives
- General Electrical Information
- Motor Data
- Room Lighting Assessment

A typical energy audit checklist is given below:

Energy Audit Checklist

Lighting:

- Is your facility using the most energy efficient lighting options (fluorescent, mercury vapor, etc.)?
- Are there areas that have excessive or unneeded lighting?
- Are you making effective use of available lighting, such as natural sunlight?
- Have you installed lighting management equipment such as dimmers, timers and sensors?

Building Envelope:

- Is the building well insulated?
- Does weather stripping around doors and windows need to be replaced?
- Are cracks around doors, windows and foundations properly sealed?
- Are there open doors around loading docks or other frequently accessed areas?

Heating and Cooling:

- Are furnaces, boilers and air conditioning systems operating efficiently?
- Is there a regular maintenance and update schedule for these systems?
- Are filters replaced regularly?
- Is the building properly ventilated?

Motors and Equipments:

- Is your equipment maintained so that it is operating at maximum efficiency?
- Is equipment load compatible with manufacturer specifications?
- Are machines shut down when not in use?
- Are fan belts at the proper tension and in good condition?

Energy Behavior:

- Are lights, fans and equipment (computer, printers, etc.) turned off when not in use?
- Are building temperatures set back when not in use?
- Are thermostats set to higher or lower than necessary in summer and winter?

The following steps should be taken to complete the energy audit, as appropriate to the facility being audited, and data should be entered onto the relevant worksheets:

1. Obtain and review electricity and fuel use records for the facility; records for the previous 14 months are preferred.
2. Obtain and review any facility drawings showing details of electrical and mechanical systems as well as building construction details. Use drawings to determine the extent of systems and level of building envelope insulating value.
3. Use information gathered as well as interviews with facility maintenance staff to determine age and general condition of the facility and its systems. Determine, from interviews, if any major system or facility upgrades are planned or have been recently completed.
4. Physically inspect and record information on all small portable electrical appliances used in the facility. This should include, for example, computers, printers, photocopiers, printers, refrigerators, small kitchen appliances and televisions. Try to determine the approximate number of operating hours per week.
5. Physically inspect and record information on electric motors in the facility. If the motors are integrated into equipment such as air conditioners or refrigerators, just obtain information on the equipment, not the individual motors. For motors that are not included with equipment, record motor information on the audit data sheet. For each motor, record

sufficient information about motor size, duty, and location to uniquely identify it. Also record information about how the motor is controlled such as simple on/off control or automatic control. If motor is running, obtain running amperage at motor starter using a clip on ammeter if one is available.

6. Inspect and record all light fixtures in the facility. In each room or area that can be uniquely identified, measure and record the light level at working surfaces. In each area, determine the number and type of fixtures as well as fixture age, number of lamps , and fixture control. Also inspect and record information on any emergency fixtures in the area.
7. Inspect and record information on all individual unitary and mini split air conditioners in the facility. Determine electrical load information or unit capacity or both. For mini split systems, remember to obtain information from both the internal evaporator section and the external condenser/ compressor section. Also record information about unit location and if it is blocked by furniture or other equipment. Also record information about how each unit is controlled and the location of the controller.
8. Inspect and record information on central air conditioning systems in the facility. Record location, area served, unit type and capacity, condenser location, ductwork size and extent, unit controller type and location, and condition of equipment, filters, ductwork and controls. Ask building occupants served by each system to describe the level of comfort provided by each system. Determine weekly operating hours of each system. Check level and condition of ductwork insulation and vapor seal.
9. Inspect and record information on fuel using appliances in the facility such as boilers, domestic hot water heaters, emergency generators, and kitchen appliances (if applicable). Determine appliance capacity, age, condition, and fuel consumption. Also inspect fuel storage tanks, piping systems, pumps etc. Look for signs of leakage or system restrictions or blockages that can reduce efficiency.
10. Inspect and record information about other electrical equipment such as elevators, water pumps, exhaust fans, domestic hot water heaters and transformers. Record information on equipment age, condition, capacity, and weekly operating hours. Also determine and record how the equipment is controlled.
11. Review the energy audit checklist for buildings once the initial audit review is completed. Review each item and ensure it has been addressed (if applicable) or if sufficient information has been gathered to allow it to be addressed. If not, repeat audit steps necessary to address the item.

10.2.5 Using Energy Audit Data

An energy audit generates the data on which to develop options and recommendations for improved energy efficiency. Using the data from the audit, options can be developed and costing can be done to determine how energy use within a building can be made more efficient. A recommendation on a specific course of action can then be developed based on the technical options available, the cost of those options and the significance of the opportunity. Typically, options for enhanced energy efficiency are evaluated in financial terms, using the concept of simple payback. Simple payback is calculated by dividing the cost of an energy conservation enhancement by the annual savings that are projected from the investment; the figure resulting from this calculation gives the number of years that are required for the savings in energy use to pay for the investment. For example:

If an option is identified that will incur a cost of Rs.10,000 to implement and will result in saving Rs.4,000 per year in energy costs, then:

Rs. 10,000 = Saving in 2.5 years @4,000/year

In this example, the investment would pay for itself in 2.5 years. Most energy efficiency initiatives are capital intensive and the calculation of simple payback does not therefore address labor and other non-capital costs of an initiative; these costs can be factored into the analysis as appropriate. Generally, investment options with a simple payback of about 3 years or less are considered worthwhile in financial terms as well as energy conservation terms; options with a 3-5 years simple payback are also frequently acted upon, particularly in a climate of rising energy prices since increasing energy costs will decrease the simple payback period. Options with a simple payback of greater than 5 years may not be considered financially justifiable; in this instance, although significant energy efficiency enhancements may still be achieved, the cost of these enhancements may not be considered to warrant action. As noted above, some of the simplest energy efficiency actions can also be the most effective. Turning off lights in an office building, use of roof insulation and ensuring that air conditioned rooms are sealed are simple initiatives that can generate significant energy savings.

The focus must be on cost effective measures that bring immediate savings and reduce pay-back time. The cost should be low relative to savings, and the methods easily applied and as simple as possible. Product-oriented solutions that replace an older, obsolete component one-for-one with a newer, more efficient product result in a short pay-back.

As lighting is a major consumer of electricity in commercial buildings, this is an area to target for substantial savings. Opportunities for improving lighting efficiency are:

Replace or retrofit old fixtures for greater efficiency and performance.

Replace incandescent lamps with more efficient lighting sources.

Install controls such as occupancy sensors to shut off unnecessary lighting.

Increase use of natural light through a daylighting design.

Replace old ballasts with electronic ballasts. Note that this also removes a potential contaminant—PCBs are frequently used in older ballasts. Savings of 40 - 50% on lighting may even be expected with the installation of a custom Metal Optics aluminum film reflector, customized louver, T8 lamps, and an electronic ballast. The new lighting systems may even bring a more contemporary and pleasing look to tenants, as well as creating a more productive work environment.

Design-oriented solutions buildings may involve the heating, ventilation and air conditioning systems. HVAC must respond to the building envelope, lighting, and internal loads and accounts for about half of all energy consumed in buildings.

Opportunities for improving HVAC efficiency are:

- Improve efficiency of equipment when central plant equipment is replaced.
- Improve control and management of systems using direct digital controls.
- Use "free" cooling with outdoor air, which reduces mechanical cooling and improves indoor air quality.
- Add variable frequency drives that manage air and fluid flows to match actual building needs.
- Use high efficiency motors. A control center may allow the building engineer to monitor and change parameters of the HVAC and lighting system. This interaction should result in reduced operating hours and a high efficiency operation.

10.2.6 Prepare realistic estimates of cost

The study needs to be specific to the building, and result in measures that can be implemented. Some solutions sound good conceptually, but for practical reasons they cannot be used. For example, two of the air handlers in a building that were originally chosen for modification could not be changed to variable air handling systems because of their physical configuration and cost.

Care should be taken to involve stake-holders e.g. owners & occupants, in the process for finding solutions. The owners and managers need to feel excited about changes and eager to execute those changes. Energy calculations may be wonderful on paper, but they must work on a practical level. The study needs to be transformed into reality. Communicating with tenants is very important and can make a retrofit go more smoothly. In this case, tenants were consulted daily during the construction phase in order to coordinate installation of replacement fixtures and lighting.

Develop a cost effective construction package

Exact steps should be defined. The construction package will list points to be controlled, how they are controlled now, and what has to change. Building owners and engineers must work together to insure satisfaction with vendors, products and method of installation.

Reassess cost vs. budget and savings vs. action.

Costs need to be re-evaluated for periodic reality checks. For example, some building owners may decide to replace glazing on windows (for various reasons this was not an option for Standard's buildings). The cost estimate may be Rs. 800 per square foot ($20), with a pay-back of twelve years. In the design phase, however, it may be discovered that the window frames holding the heavier, glazed windows are inadequate for current seismic standards and must be replaced. Suddenly, costs soar to Rs. 1200 per square foot ($30), with a pay-back of twenty years. Implementing this idea would not be practical for most building owners.

10.2.7 Select a competent implementation team

Contractors should have a proven track record. Methods used should be reliable and guaranteed. Standard used a mix—for the HVAC air handling systems they used proven methods and known contractors, and in lighting and control systems they incorporated new technology. Some cost effective measures may involve calculated risk taking, and in Standard's case, the choices they made were well worth it in terms of reduced project cost and increased effectiveness. After selecting a competent construction firm, the owners, engineers and construction team must work together to make sure renovation measures are properly implemented and that expected results are achieved. Feedback from all parties involved (including tenants) is necessary to identify and correct any potential problems. The careful preparation and follow through provided by the steps above will lead to a successful renovation. By bringing together computer modeling and energy conservation analysis with new technology in HVAC and lighting, these renovations were possible. Teamwork and communication from the initial energy model to the implementation of all the steps made this renovation successful on all levels.

10.3 ENERGY AUDIT INSTRUMENTS

Details of few basic energy audit instruments are given below. These instruments are often required for conducting energy audits. Table 10.1 below shows major energy audit instruments and their description of their features.

Table 10.1: Energy audit instruments

 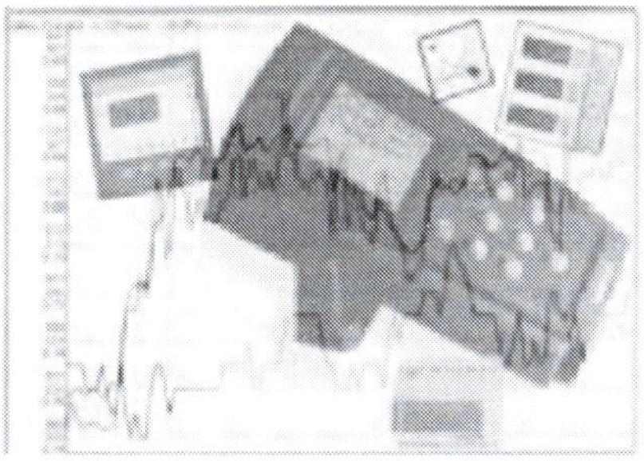	**Electrical Measuring Instruments:** These are instruments for measuring major electrical parameters such as kVA, kW, PF, Hertz, kVAr, Amps and Volts. In addition some of these instruments also measure harmonics. These instruments are applied on-line i.e on running motors without any need to stop the motor. Instant measurements can be taken with hand-held meters, while more advanced ones facilitates cumulative readings with print outs at specified intervals.

	**Combustion analyzer:** This instrument has in-built chemical cells which measure various gases such as O_2, CO, NO_X and SO_X.
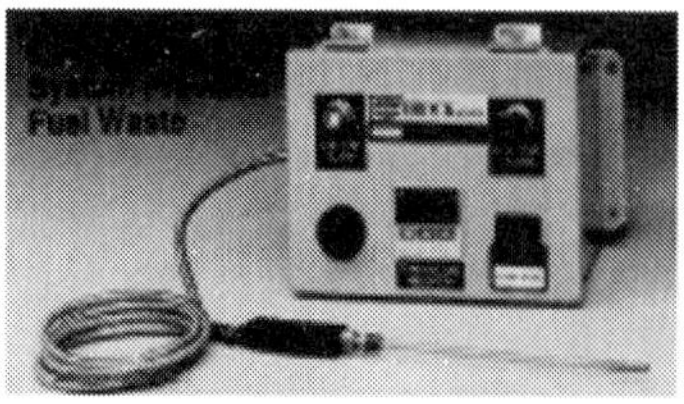	**Fuel Efficiency Monitor:** This measures oxygen and temperature of the flue gas. Calorific values of common fuels are fed into the microprocessor which calculates the combustion efficiency.
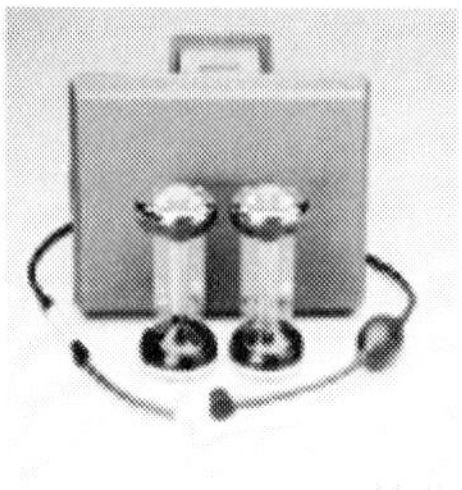	**Fyrite :** A hand bellow pump draws the fuel gas sample into the solution inside the fyrite. A chemical reaction changes the liquid volume revealing the amount of gas. A separate fyrite can be used for O_2 and CO_2 measurement.
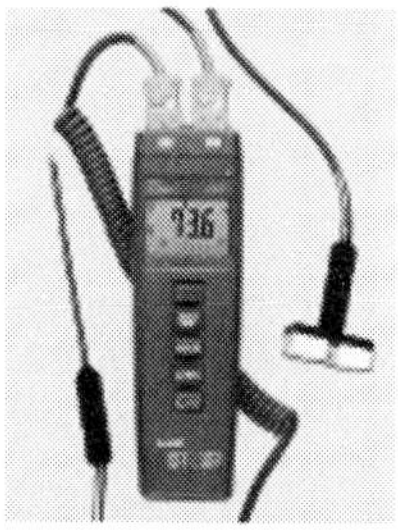	**Contact thermometer:** These are thermocouples which measures for example fuel gas, hot air, hot water temperatures by insertion of probe into the stream. For surface temperature, a leaf type probe is used with the same instrument.
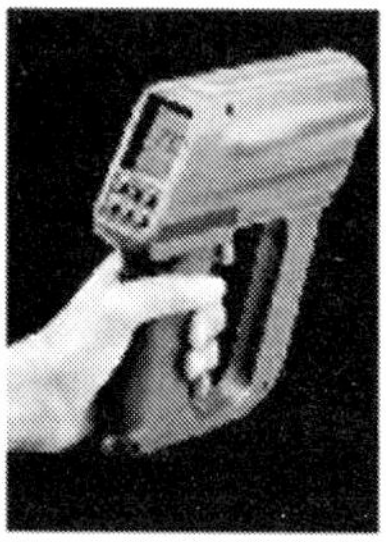	**Infrared Thermometer:** This is a non-contact type measurement which when directed at a heat source directly gives the temperature read out. This instrument is useful for measuring hot spots in furnaces, surface temperatures etc.

	**Pitot Tube and manometer:** Air velocity in ducts can be measured using a pitot tube and inclined manometer for further calculation of flows.
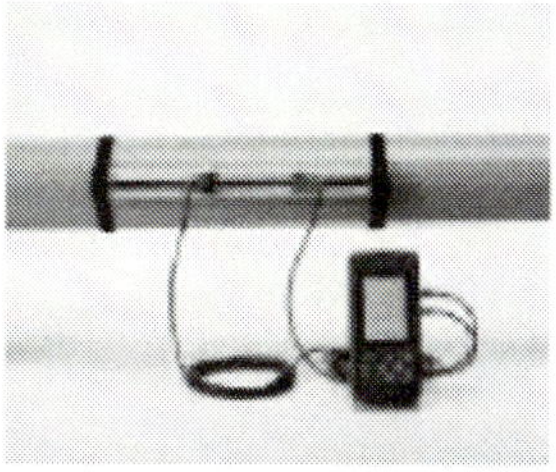	**Water flow meter:** This non-contact flow measuring device using Doppler effect / Ultra sonic principle. There is a transmitter and receiver which are positioned on opposite sides of the pipe. The meter directly gives the flow. Water and other fluid flows can be easily measured with this meter.
 Tachometer  Stroboscope	**Speed Measurements:** In any audit exercise speed measurements are critical as thay may change with frequency, belt slip and loading. A simple tachometer is a contact type instrument which can be used where direct access is possible. More sophisticated and safer ones are non contact instruments such as stroboscopes.
	**Leak Detectors:** Ultrasonic instruments are available which can be used to detect leaks of compressed air and other gases which are normally not possible to detect with human abilities.
	**Lux meters:** Illumination levels are measured with a lux meter. It consists of a photo cell which senses the light output, converts to electrical impulses which are calibrated as lux.

10.4 PERFORMANCE EVALUATION AND MAJOR AREAS OF EFFICIENCY IMPROVEMENT

(a) Air conditioning unit

The parameters needed to be looked for evaluating performance of air conditioning unit are:

- Indoor and outdoor design conditions
- Measured flows and capacities of all equipment used in the system
- Comparison of the measured and design capacities
- Comparison of energy consumption with the design value

An air conditioner is efficient when all of its components i.e. compressor, condenser, evaporator and condenser cooling (heat rejection) system are working in matched conditions. This means that under peak operating conditions, they must perform to their optimum output. To evaluate the performance following approach is followed:

Compressor:

From the operating suction and discharge pressure, the capacity may be evaluated from the rating charts. The operating kilowatt input can give the value of input power. This can be compared with the rated input power.

Condenser:

Water or air-flow rate and temperature rise across the condenser gives the heat rejection rate. The flow rates and temperature rise can be compared with the design parameters and any variation must be analysed. Following equation can be used for water-cooled condenser:

Heat rejected (kW) = 4.182 × water flow rate in liter per second × temperature rise in ^{0}C

Equation for air cooled condensers is:

Heat rejected (kW) = 1.20 × air flow rate in liter per second × temperature rise in ^{0}C

Heat rejected must be compared with the rated heat rejection rate as per the rating chart.

Cooling coil:

Air flow rate and enthalpy drop across the cooling coil will give the cooling load. The flow rates and enthalpy drop should be compared with the design parameters. The equation for cooling coil is:

Cooling produced (in kW) = 1.2 × air flow rate in liter per second × enthalpy drop.

Enthalpy difference between the return air and supply air are measured in kilo joules per kilogram in SI units.

Cooling tower:

Heat rejected at the condenser must match the heat rejected at the cooling tower. The equation for cooling tower is same as the equation for water cooled condenser. Additionally, for cooling tower, efficiency of cooling tower can be calculated as:

$$\text{Efficiency} = \frac{\text{Entering water temperature} - \text{leaving water temperature}}{\text{Entering water temperature} - \text{ambient wet bulb temperature}}$$

The efficiency thus obtained must be compared with the rated efficiency.

Following are major energy conservation opportunities in air conditioning systems:

Installation of variable speed drives:

Variable speed drives typically use electronic circuitry to vary the output frequency, which, in turn, varies the speed of motor. Since the power required by the fan or pump is proportional to cube of its speed, large reduction in power consumption can be obtained by this method. Since the air handling units are designed for peak load conditions, if the VSDs are installed at different air handling units of the HVAC system, the daily and seasonal variation in the required CFM can be translated into energy savings.

Design of cooling towers is also done to meet the worst combination of peak load and wet bulb temperature. However the condition of water entering the tower varies with time and season changing the operating conditions for the tower. In order to utilize the tower efficiently, the fan output must be optimally adopted to the cooling requirement governed by the climatic conditions and load.

Low leakage dampers:

If the dampers are not closed properly, unwanted outdoor air can enter the building and increase the load on cooling system. Use of low leakage dampers restrict air leakage to less than 1% as compared to common dampers allowing 5-30% air leakage even in closed position.

Reduced minimum outdoor air:

Use of outdoor must be minimized to its minimum as per the ventilation standards. Any extra outdoor air usually increases load on heating or cooling system/ this can be done by adjusting the damper linkage to minimum position.

Unoccupied ventilation reduction:

Outdoor air is to be supplied to meet the ventilation requirement as mentioned above. In unoccupied spaces, such use of outdoor air should be eliminated to reduce the load. By the addition of the time clock or the automation system, provisions must be made to shut the outdoor air during unoccupied period and during the night hours.

Enthalpy control/dry bulb economizer

Using outside air to cool a building can result in lower mechanical refrigeration costs wherever the outdoor air has a lower total heat content (enthalpy) than the return air. This can be accomplished by an 'integrated economizer' or enthalpy control.

The dry-bulb economizer or the integrated economizer can be made automatic by providing dampers capable of providing 100% outdoor air with local controls that sequence the chilled water or DX coil dampers. During economizer operation when space temperature rises, the outdoor air damper opens first, then on a further rise, the cooling coil is switched on. Economizer operation is activated by outside air temperature say 23°C. If the outside air temperature is below 23°C, the above described economizer operation takes place. Above 23°C, outside air-cooling is not economical, and the outdoor air damper opening reduces to its minimum position as per ventilation requirement only.

If an economizer is equipped with an enthalpy control, savings will get accrued due to a more accurate change-over point. The load on a cooling coil of air handling system is a function of the total heat (enthalpy) of air entering the coil. The total heat is a combined function of dry bulb temperature and relative humidity. In a typical enthalpy control system both the conditions DBT and RH are measured in the return air path and outdoor. The system calculates best route for cooling of air to keep lowest load on itself.

Exhaust air control

Energy can also be saved by controlling operation of exhaust fans in such a way that it operates only when there is requirement. In normal situations, exhaust fans operate for much more duration than their requirement for removal of odor/fumes and to remove heat built-up. The operation of removal of fumes/odor can be scheduled automatically in such a way that they operate only when objectionable air contaminants are getting generated. Exhaust fans of laboratory hoods, kitchen vents and toilets for example can be coupled with facility usage. The other family of exhaust fans that is used to avoid heat built-up, can be automated by thermostatic control.

Retrofit of central fans for variable air volume usage

Conversion of constant speed fans or constant volume air distribution system to a Variable Air Volume (VAV) system can be helpful in saving energy. Such retrofitting also results into considerable reduction in fan horsepower. Fans with air foil or backward curved impellers without vortex vanes require additional vanes or some means to control flow volume, such as eddy current clutch or variable speed drive, for realizing the advantages of VAV system. With a fan with forward curved impeller mounted on roof-top, the supply fan does not need any retrofitting. The fan may just require the addition of a damper in the return duct system if building statics become objectionable. This damper can be controlled by space static sensor referenced to outdoor condition.

Fans with vortex vanes require a different approach. In this scheme, the supply fan static control maintains the minimum supply duct static required for delivering the minimum CFM. The return fan static control senses change in space pressure relative to outdoors and maintains the space at slightly positive pressure to prevent infiltration of outdoor air. A VAV system delivers air in quantities based on the actual instantaneous load requirements. Amount of energy saved by VAV system is proportional to variation in building loading, typically in offices the savings of the order of 30% can be achieved. This system is much efficient than the dual duct system in which air from hot and cold ducts are mixed to achieve desired temperature.

Advanced heat exchangers

The availability of air-to-air heat exchangers namely, air-to-air heat plate exchangers, heat pipes, heat wheels offer energy savings in the field of air conditioning. The air-to-air plate heat exchanger has a series of plates to provide large area to facilitate heat transfer over low temperature differences. These systems are very energy efficient in low-humidity conditions.

Heat pipes are devices that usually consist of sealed finned tube with a wick lining on the inner side. The tube contains a working fluid, which evaporates from the hot end of the tube and condenses at the cold end, thus transferring heat. The working fluid is returned to the hot end by capillary action of the wick. The heat conductivity of heat pipes is about 1000 times of copper and the system offers ability to operate at very low temperatures even.

Heat wheels are rotary heat exchangers packed with aluminum honeycomb fill. One half of the wheel is in contact with warm air and the other half with cold air. The sensible heat of the incoming warm air is given to the aluminum and the wheel rotates slowly releasing the heat to the exhaust cold air during the second half of the revolution. Desiccant coated heat wheels are also available where, in addition to sensible heat transfer, latent heat transfer also takes place as the desiccant absorbs moisture in one half of the revolution and releases it in the second half of the revolution.

Operation and maintenance practices to be ensured:

- The system should be reset and rebalanced at regular intervals. Often the initial balancing gets disturbed with passage of time.
- Provisions should be made for shutting down equipment when not needed.
- Set back temperatures should be assigned when space is not occupied.
- Shut down should start shortly before the occupants leave and it should start as late as possible before the occupants arrive.
- Cool night air should be utilized for pre-cooling of space through ventilation.
- Solar shading devices must be working properly.
- Air filters must be checked and replaced if chocked.
- Coils and tubes of all heat transfer surfaces must be clean.

- Water treatment plant should work properly to avoid scale formation in tubes.
- Air-vents should be working properly.
- In case of multiple equipment, sequential starting should be adopted.
- Lubrication, belt tension should be checked periodically.
- Room thermostat and humidistat should be at tamper proof locations but remain clean.

(b) Lighting system

Lighting is a very important area for energy auditors. It involves several issues such as use of daylight, choice and proper installation of luminaries, operation and control of lighting devices. Due to special importance of this field, in this handbook, a separate chapter has been given to this topic. However, to maintain comprehensiveness of this chapter, salient points related to lighting are being covered again from the point of view of energy audit.

For evaluating efficiency of lighting system, the total installed load should be divided by the floor area of the building to determine the loading in watts per square meter. This value can be compared with typical values of good lighting practices recommended in various lighting codes. A lighting scheme loading in the range of 7-11W/m^2 is considered an efficient scheme. However, besides comparing lighting load a comparison with power consumption for lighting per unit floor area is another important criteria for lighting evaluation. This energy consumption can be derived from the multiple of lighting load and usage duration. The chapter on building energy code contains a table that presents recommended lighting energy consumption per unit floor area for different types of building usages. The efficient lighting scheme should however ensure right lighting levels at the work plane or working area. For example office table, conference rooms, shops require 300lux level, whereas, corridors etc. require only 70lux. Drafting tables, operation tables etc. require illumination level of 750-1500lux and efficient lighting scheme should not compromise on this level.

Over the time, luminaries and room surfaces get dirty and the light output of the lamp decreases. Simple cleaning of lamps and luminaries can substantially improve the lighting of space and help reduce energy wastage.

Following are potential energy saving actions related to lighting:

- remove unnecessary lamps
- turn-off lights near windows
- turn-off lights when an area is unoccupied
- keep lamps and fixtures clean
- eliminate unnecessary outside lighting
- install high efficiency fluorescent lamps to replace standard ones

- replace conventional ballast with conventional one
- install dimmer switches
- install timers for external lighting
- install task lighting replacing general lighting

(c) Pumps and motors

Efficiency of a pump is defined as ratio of useful power output to the power input to the pump shaft. The input power can be estimated by measurement of current drawn and supplied voltage. The power output of a pump is basically the energy delivered to the fluid:

$P_{out} = \rho QH$

Where ρ is density of fluid (N/m^3), Q is volumetric flow rate (m^3/s) and H is total dynamic head (m) which is the sum of total static head, entrance head-loss, frictional head-loss, head-loss due to fittings and valves, velocity head in discharge pipe.

It has been observed that large safety margins are kept on the head of the pump that results in a condition in which the pump does not operate at specified most energy efficient duty point. Large differences are found in the efficiency of pumps manufactured by organized sector and small-scale manufacturers. Selection should not be only based upon the initial cost alone, efficiency and running costs should also be given due weight. In case where the operating condition is unclear or is likely to be variable, effective method of efficient modulation like variable speed drives should be used.

The case of motors is quite similar to pumps. Motor efficiency, avoiding partial loading condition, are similar measures for ensuring energy efficiency.

10.5 ECBC REQUIREMENTS FOR ELECTRICAL POWER

Electric equipment and systems shall comply with the mandatory requirements.

10.5.1 Mandatory Requirements

10.5.1.1 Transformers

Maximum Allowable Power Transformer Losses

Power transformers of the proper ratings and design must be selected to satisfy the minimum acceptable efficiency at their full load rating. In addition, the transformer must be selected such that it minimizes the total of its initial cost in addition to the present value of the cost of its total lost energy while serving its estimated loads during its respective life span. Transformers used in buildings shall be constructed with high quality grain oriented low loss silicon steel and virgin electrolytic grade copper and the manufacturer's certificate to this effect shall be obtained.

Table 10.2: Maximum Allowable Losses of 11,22 kV Transformers

Transformer Capacity, kVa	Maximum Allowable Losses at Full Load in % of Rating	
	11 kV Transformer	22 kV Transformer
100	2.5	2.7
160	2.3	2.2
250	2.1	1.8
400	1.5	1.5
630	1.4	1.5
800	1.4	1.5
1000	1.2	1.2

Reference conditions: 100% of nameplate load at temperature of 75° C

Measurement and Reporting of Transformer Losses

All measurement of losses shall be carried out by using calibrated digital meters of class 0.5 or better accuracy and certified by the manufacturer. All transformers of capacity of 500 kVA and above would be equipped with additional metering class current transformers (CTs) and potential transformers (PTs) additional to requirements of Utilities so that periodic loss monitoring study may be carried out.

10.5.1.2 Energy Efficient Motors

Motors shall comply with the following:

(a) All permanently wired polyphase motors of 0.375 kW or more serving the building and expected to operate more than 1,500 hours per year and all permanently wired polyphase motors of 50kW or more serving the building and expected to operate more than 500 hours per year shall have a minimum acceptable nominal full load motor efficiency not less than shown in Table 8.2.2 or the BIS for energy efficient motors.

(b) Motors of horsepower differing from those listed in the table shall have efficiency greater than that of the next listed kW motor.

(c) Motor horsepower ratings shall not exceed 200% of the calculated maximum load being served.

(d) Motor nameplates shall list the nominal full-load motor efficiencies and the full-load power factor.

(e) Motor users should insist on proper rewinding practices for any rewound motors. If the proper rewinding practices cannot be assured, the damaged motor should be replaced with a new, efficient one rather than suffer the significant efficiency penalty associated with typical rewind practices.

(f) Certificates shall be obtained and kept on record indicating the motor efficiency. Whenever a motor is rewound, appropriate measures shall be taken so that the core characteristics of the motor is not lost due to thermal and mechanical stress during removal of damaged parts. After rewinding, a new efficiency test shall be performed and a similar record shall be maintained.

Table 10.3: Minimum Acceptable Motor Efficiencies

Motor Size (kW)	Efficiency (%) 2 Pole	Efficiency (%) 4 Pole
1.1 (1.5 hp)	82.2	83.8
1.5 (2 hp)	84.1	85.0
2.2 (3 hp)	85.6	86.4
3.0 (4 hp)	86.7	87.4
4.0 (5.5 hp)	87.6	88.3
5.5 (7.5 hp)	88.5	89.2
7.5 (10 hp)	89.5	90.1
11.0 (15 hp)	90.6	91.0
15.0 (20 hp)	91.3	91.8
18.5 (25 hp)	91.8	92.2
22.0 (30 hp)	92.2	92.6
30.0 (40 hp)	92.9	93.2
37.0 (50 hp)	93.3	93.6
45.0 (60 hp)	93.7	93.9
55.0 (75 hp)	94.0	94.2
75.0 (100 hp)	94.6	94.7

10.5.1.3 Power Factor Correction

All electricity supplies exceeding 100 A, 3 phase shall maintain their power factor between 0.98 lag and unity at the point of connection.

10.5.1.4 Check-Metering and Monitoring

(a) Buildings whose maximum demand is greater than 250 kVA shall have the electrical distribution system with their energy consumption being check-metered.

(b) Services exceeding 1000 kVA shall have permanently installed electrical metering to record demand (kVA), energy (kWh), and total power factor. The metering shall also display current (in each phase and the neutral), voltage (between phases and between each phase and neutral), and total harmonic distortion (THD) as a percentage of total current.

(c) Services not exceeding 1000 kVA but over 65 kVA shall have permanently installed electric metering to record demand (kW), energy (kWh), and total power factor (or kVARh).

(d) Services not exceeding 65 kVA shall have permanently installed electrical metering to record energy (kWh).

10.5.1.5 Power Distribution Systems

Thermal Monitoring of Main Distribution System

All the power junction boxes and main power distribution board and cable termination points shall be provided with temperature monitoring mechanism comprising of sensors in the enclosed chambers and properly visible temperature indicators outside. Record of temperature during commissioning and subsequently on a daily basis shall be maintained.

Power Distribution System Losses

The power cabling shall be adequately sized as to maintain the distribution losses not to exceed 1% of the total power usage. Record of design calculation for the losses shall be maintained.

Annexure 10.1 : Case study of Rail Bhawan, New Delhi
(Courtesy: Bureau of Energy Efficiency)

EXECUTIVE SUMMARY OF SAVINGS IN RAIL BHAWAN

A consortium of Energy auditors conducted the study during Nov. 2002-Jan. 2003. Following are the major energy saving potential, identified during the study.

1.0 Lighting system

The present energy consumption in the lighting system at Rail Bhawan is 4,56,000 kWh/Year which translates to Rs. 29.05 lakhs per annum. The anticipated energy saving due to the recommended measures are 1,50,484 kWh/year (replacement with electronic ballast & high lumen tubes and de-lamping), which translates to a saving of Rs. 9.59 lakhs per annum. About 33 % saving are envisaged in the annual cost of the energy used for lighting systems.

2.0 Canteen

Presently about 360 LPG cylinders (14 kg capacity each) are used only for water heating and 27,216 kWh of electrical energy for water heating requirement in the canteen/Annum. It is proposed to replace this LPG and electrical heater with solar water heating system, of capacity 4,500 LPD. This will lead to a savings of 2.97 lakhs per year [1.23 lakhs from LPG Heating and 1.74 Lakhs from electrical heating]. The investment on the solar water heating system will be around Rs. 8.0 lakhs and the pay back period is 2.7 years.

3.0 Pumping system

The present energy consumption for the pumping system at Rail Bhawan is 24,000 kWh/Year which translates to Rs. 1.53 lakhs per annum. The anticipated energy saving due to the recommended measure is 5,093 kWh/year (replacement with a new monoblock pump set, having a system efficiency of 60 %), which translates to a saving of Rs 0.32 lakhs per annum.

4.0 HVAC system

The present energy consumption HVAC system at Rail Bhawan is 9,36,000 kWh/Year which translates to Rs. 59.62 lakhs per annum. The anticipated energy saving due to the recommended measures are 4,16,000 kWh/year (introduction of central AC system & room heating, through hot water generated from LDO), which translates to a saving of Rs. 26.5 lakhs per annum. About 44% saving are envisaged in the annual cost of the energy used for HVAC systems.

The summary of overall saving is given as a Table below.

Summary of Energy Saving

Sl. No	*Area*	*Saving potential /Year*			*Capital investment, Rs. Lakhs*	*Simple pay back period, Years*
		kWh	*Rs. Lakhs*	*%*		
1	Lighting	1,50,484	9.59	33	24.85	2.59
2	Pumping system	5,093	0.32	19	0.30	0.92
3	Canteen LPG heating	5,040 kg of LPG	1.23	25	8.0	2.70
4	Canteen electrical heating	27,261	1.74	57		
5	HVAC system	4,16,000	26.50 [a]	44	130.0	4.91
6	**Total**	**5,98,838 & 5,040 kg of LPG**	**39.38**	**25**	**163.15**	**4.14**

[a]: Annual running cost for LDO (16,998 kg/year) & electricity are deducted.

Note: Energy cost Rs. 6.37/kWh & LPG cost Rs. 24.5/kg.

By optimizing the loading pattern & operational time of various loads, about 10-12 % yearly energy consumption can be reduced/controlled.

1.0 Introduction

Rail Bhawan is the office building of Ministry of Railways where planning, decisions regarding operation and control of entire Railway network in the country are carried out. The built-up area of the building is 2,910 square metres and there are about 4,850 employees. The regular office timing is 9.00 hours to 17.00 hours and five a week operation.

It is highly appreciable that the officials of Rail Bhawan have introduced 515 nos. of 11W CFLs for corridor lighting and also modified the passenger lift system with microprocessor-based system as an energy conservation measures.

2.0 Energy Source and Distribution

The Energy demand for the facility is met from Electricity, LPG and diesel. Major source of energy is electricity and LPG is used for cooking in canteen. Diesel is used to run the emergency Generator set. The total connected load in the facility is 2,187 kW and the load distribution is shown below. The sanctioned load is 1,210 kW.

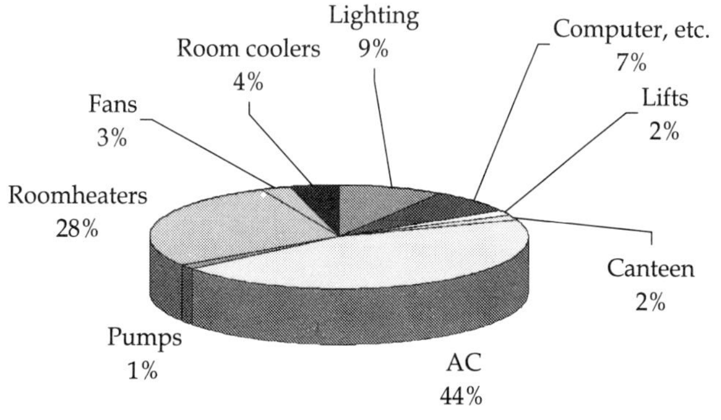

Distribution of connected load

The load distribution during summer and winter seasons were analysed and given below.

Load distribution during summer

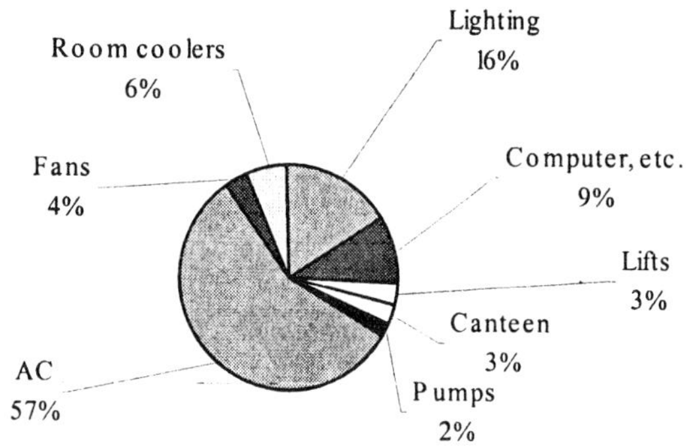

Total load is 1053 kW

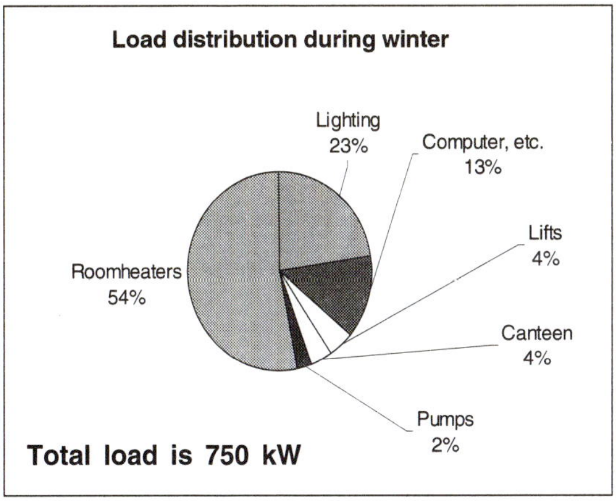

Based on the operating power & duration of running of various loads, the annual energy consumption for various loads were established and depicted below. It is seen that AC accounts for 32%.

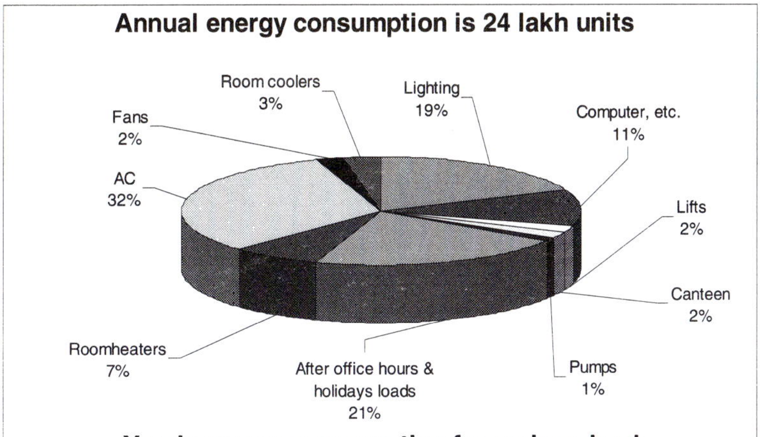

Yearly energy consumption for various loads

The Facility is getting electrical power supply from New Delhi Municipal Council (NDMC) at 11 kV and also having two Diesel generator set of 500KVA & 166KVA capacity as a back up supply. The power is distributed through three step down (11,000/415 V) transformers of 750 kVA each. Presently two transformers are working and one is standby. There are five interconnected LT bus for distribution of power, out of which three are for power and two for emergency loads like lighting and lifts. Normally all five LT bus are energized from NDMC power supply and in case of failure of power supply, the DG sets are started and only the two emergency panel are energized. (Annexure #1 - Single line diagram)

The monthly energy consumption details for the last two years are provided in Annexure II.

The daily energy consumption pattern for the last two years is shown below (Graph # 1). It is evident from the above graph that energy consumption is almost double during the summer period May–September because of cooling need (Air conditioners, fans and air coolers). The usage pattern is almost similar with slight upward variation of 3% for the last two years except for the dip in the month of June 2002 which is due to increased usage of emergency power from Diesel generating sets due to power cuts.

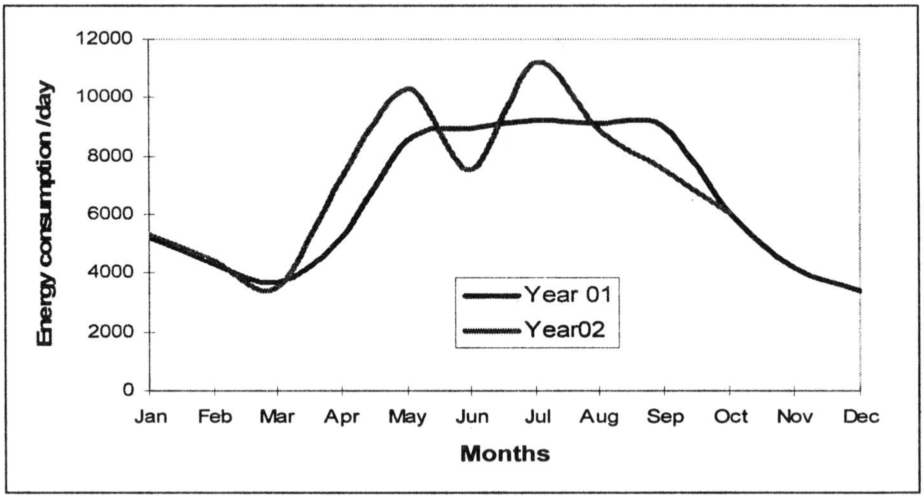

Study has been conducted during winter season hence there was no AC load. During the study period, the electrical power was measured over a period of 24 hours and it was found that the peak demand of the facility in winter is around 550 KW and the minimum demand is 63 KW (during night time).

Power consumption and power factor variation plot for 24 hours (graph # 2)

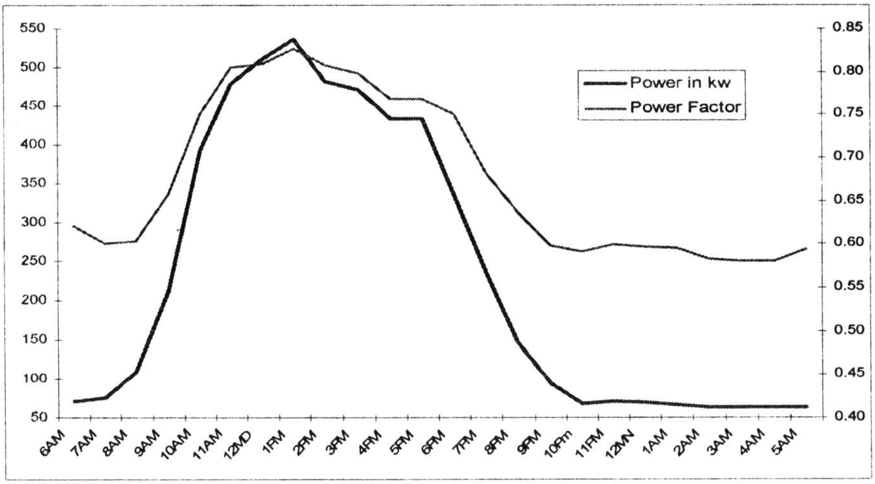

It is very evident from the graph#2 that average load during working time (10AM to 6PM) is around 430 kW and peak demand of 550 kW occurs during lunch time (12.30PM–1.30PM) this is because of heavy usage of lift by the staff and heating food articles in the canteen.

Graph #2 also shows the variation in power factor from low loads to peak loads and it is very low at light loads. The average power factor during the night time from 7PM to 7AM is 0.6 and during the working time (i.e. 10AM to 6PM) it is 0.79.

3.0 Study Results

The study results are presented in the following sections.

3.1 DG set

The plant has two DG sets (166 kVA x 1 no. & 500 kVA x 1 no.) which are run only during NDMC power failure. During the course of the study, it was observed that the loading of the two DG sets were less than 50% and the 500 kVA DG set is sufficient to cater to the load requirement during winter season (loading pattern during summer has to be observed). Trials were taken and the plant authority has taken the decision to run only one DG set hence optimized the DG loading.

The NDMC power supply is quite reliable and the DG sets are operated occasionally for smaller duration hence further study on DG was not required.

3.2 Lighting system

Adequate and proper lighting contributes both directly and indirectly towards productivity and safety, and towards providing an improved work atmosphere. In fact, all these are inter-related and complimentary to each other. There are several factors which contribute towards proper lighting and it would be very difficult to deal with all of them when providing general illumination to a large area. However, all efforts were made to study and include these factors.

To study, analyze and identify energy conservation options in lighting, a study of the plant lighting load was conducted. The purpose of the study was to determine the lighting load and its distribution in various sections of the Building, determine the quality of illumination provided, and recommend measures to improve illumination and reduce electricity consumption.

A high quality and accurate digital lux meter was used to measure the illumination level at various sections of the building during working hours. Other performance indicators such as type of lamps used, type of luminaries, mounting height, physical condition of lamps and luminaries, use of day lighting, etc. were also noted down.

3.2.1 Lighting inventory and lux level

To determine the total lighting load, a physical count of the number of light fixtures provided in different floors of the Building was carried out. It was found during the survey that mainly twin 40-W fluorescent tube light have been used in the building.

The illumination level was also measured primarily at working planes at various rooms of the building. Care was taken to reduce the effect of day lighting while taking the measurements.

The recorded inventory and measured illumination levels in the facility are provided in Annexure III along with the list of numbers of light fittings installed.

Based on the measured lux levels, it was found that about 65% of the measurement points showed lux level of less than 100 and the lighting level distribution is depicted below.

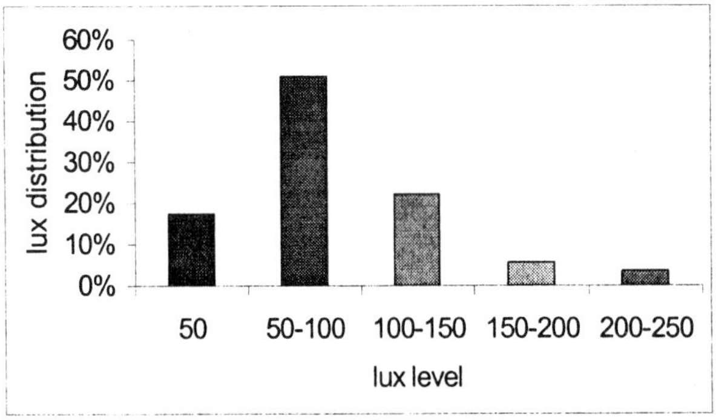

It is clear from the above Figure that about 50% of the measured illumination level falls in the range between 50 to 100 lux. It is evident that more than 65% of lighting points have lux level less than 100 and 35% more than 100 lux level. Therefore improvement in lux levels would be one of the major thrust areas of improvement in the illumination system.

It could be seen from Table A of Annexure III that the second floor accounts for the highest numbers of installed fitting as well as highest lighting lux level in the building.

Major reasons for poor illumination levels are as follows :

- Poor reflectors / no reflector installed for the tube lights
- Large height of installed fittings from the working plane
- Reduction in lumen due to ageing
- Improper design of furniture and seating arrangement

3.2.2 Setting baseline in lighting system

Metering and monitoring are the major activities of any energy audit and the results of energy audit are based on the quality of data collected and measurements carried out. For realizable energy savings care should be taken during audit period so that after implementation of energy saving measures saving should be measurable.

In Rail Bhavan, the electrical distribution (Annexure –I) of Lighting load is in emergency bus along with the lift loads. From emergency bus bar, it goes to each floor and each wing then further distributed from Distribution board. Total lighting load measurement at single point and floor wise was envisaged but due to lifts load and some wings of ground floor and second floors are getting supply from 1st floor lighting circuit, the circuit could not be segregated from lift loads. It was also informed by the Rail Bhavan authority that possibility of small mixed loads like computer, AC may also be there in the circuit.

The power distribution in each floor was measured and given in Annexure IV. To arrive at per tube light power consumption, measurements at following different points were carried out.

1. Floor wise (ground,1st and second floor metering at different wings at different DB's)
2. Incoming feeder of emergency bus
3. Lighting DB of conference hall
4. Single tube light

Particulars	Power in KW	No. of tube light	Per tube consumption in watts	Remarks
Ground &1st floor	55	1126	48.8	Mostly lighting loads
Emergency panel	209 -280*	3438	61 - 81	Lift loads included
Conference hall	4.45	96	46.4	Only lighting load
Single tube light	0.080	2	40	Only lighting load

*Variation is due to lift loads.

It is clear from the above table that variation in the consumption is from 40 watts to 49 Watts (excluding the jerk from lifts) from the emergency panel. It was informed by Rail Bhavan authority that apart from lift load, small load of AC, computer and fax machine are also connected. Hence, ***if these loads can be segregated from the emergency lighting panel, the total building load can be measured at the incoming feeder of emergency panel.*** Variation in per tube consumption from 40 watt to 46.4 watt in pure lighting circuit is because of poor power factor of 0.6 and number of tube-lights.

Based on measurements in pure lighting load circuit, power consumption per tube light of 46.4 watt can be considered as base line and savings can be measurable by slightly changing the present circuit for metering. Based on 46.4 watt, the total lighting load (40 W FTL) for 3,550 tube lights is around 164.7 kW.

3.2.3 Options for improvements in lighting system

The conventional fluorescent tube lights (FTLs) form a major portion of office lighting. There are almost 3,606 FTLs and 515 CFLs. Lighting system accounts for 36,000 kWh per month of energy consumption. Based on the measurements and observations made during energy audit, the following options have been evolved for reducing energy consumption as well as improvement in lux levels in lighting system.

(a) The tube lights energized at the outer windows in each room may be put off when sufficient day light is available. The savings are difficult to quantify.

(b) In a few of the rooms (Room no. MSR 245, 243, 247, 249, 251 A & 252), tube light is energized (total 19 nos.) on the top of twin tube fittings to illuminate the ceiling. It is suggested to remove such fittings. It is also suggested to replace each 40 W tube light (standard FTL) with high lumen tube light (36 W) with electronic ballast. This will improve the lux level substantially, which in turn may improve the working efficiency of the employees because of better working condition. In order to improve the lux level further and to avoid stroboscopic effect (as tube is above the fan), it is suggested that fittings which are ceiling mounted should be transformed to suspended one. This care should be taken during the implementation of the above.

The capital cost required for the modification is Rs. 24.85 Lakhs and energy saving envisaged is 1,50,484 kWh/year and the pay back period is 2.59 years.

3.3 Water pumping system

At Rail Bhavan, major portion of water is received from NDMC at pump house where three pumps (1 x 10 HP submersible: 3-4 years old & 2 x 7.5 HP centrifugal which are more than 30 years old) are installed to pump water to overhead tanks from where it is distributed to various end use points. In addition to the above, two tube well pumps (one at exit gate & other at Nursery) are installed to supplement the water supply.

Initially, there was another 7. 5 HP centrifugal pump (in pump house) which was later replaced by this submersible pump with casing being there and other piping circuit remaining same. We brought to the notice of the Rail Bhavan officials that the casing is stagnating the flow & affecting the performance of the pump considerably.

The electrical power consumption of various motor-pump units are measured and given in Annexure V. The performance of the submersible pump at pump house is evaluated and presented below.

Sl. No.	*Particular*	*Value*	*Unit*	*Remark*
1	Rating of Pump	7.5	kW	
2	Electrical consumption	8.85	kW	Measured
3	Flow rate	490.4	LPM	Measured
4	Delivery head	28	m	After Pr. Gauge
5	Delivery head	1.5	m	Before Pr. Gauge
6	Total head	29.5	m	Calculated
7	Motor-pump efficiency	26.7	%	Calculated

It is seen from the Table that the overall efficiency is low. Hence, it is suggested to replace the pump with a new mono-block pump set which will have an overall efficiency of 60 %. The annual saving expected is 5,093 kWh. The investment is Rs. 30,000- and the pay back period is 0.92 years.

Since the other pumps are run for 1-4 hours/day, further energy saving potential is negligible.

3.4 Canteen

At Rail Bhavan, canteen facility (located at third floor) is provided for employees. On an average 8,000 visitors (no. of visits of each employee) avail the facility, out of which 1,000 visitors take lunch daily. Majority of the items in canteen are being cooked using LPG. Electrical heaters are also being used for heating water which in turn is used for various applications like tea/coffee warmer, for making tea/coffee, plate washing, etc.. The details of loads at canteen is given below.

Since the requirement for heating is quite high, it is suggested to introduce **solar hot water system** on the terrace of the building. **It is established that each 100 litres capacity solar hot water system can save either 1500 kWh of electricity per year or 195 kg of LPG per year** (Source: MNES, 1998). The capital cost for 4,500 litres capacity system is Rs. 8.0 lakhs, and the saving envisaged is 5,040 kg of LPG and 27,216 kWh of electricity per year. The pay back period is 2.70 years.

Use of electricity for heating application is not an efficient route. Hence, hot water from solar system may be used to the maximum extent in place of electrical heating. Even for heating of milk, etc. LPG, is a better option than electricity.

Sl. No.	*Location*	*Application*	*Power Consumption (kW)*	*Operating Hrs per day*	*Working days per week*
1	Third Floor Canteen	Tea warmer	2	7	5
2	Third Floor Canteen	Coffee maker (3 no.)	2 each	7	5
3	Third Floor Canteen	Geyser for plate washing (2 no.)	2 each	12	5
4	Second Floor - Pantry	Coffee maker	2	12	5
5	Second Floor - Pantry	Boiler - milk heating	2	8 to 10	5
6	Second Floor - Pantry	Boiler - Water heating	2	8	5
7	Second Floor - Pantry	Boiler - Water heating	2x2 No.	8	5
8	Second Floor - VIP canteen	Water Heater	2x2 No.	12	5

3.5 HVAC system

AC and room heaters are the heating, ventilation and air conditioning (HVAC) provided in the facility.

3.5.1 Air conditioning system

The plant has installed 410 no. of 1.5 TR window air conditioners (AC) of various makes/ models at different locations. There are also 1.5 TR x 9 no.; 4.3 TR x 10 no. and 7.5 TR x 4 no. of split package units to cater to the cooling need. On an average, these AC units are used 6 months in an year.

Sample measurement was taken on a few of the ACs and the results are given in Annexure VI. Since there are lot of AC units in 1st to 5th floor of the building and air cooled AC systems consume more specific power, it is suggested to go for **centralized AC system** with chilled water as secondary refrigerant. The plant can be either installed on the terrace of the building or on the terrace of the 'F' wing. The chilled water line can pass through the existing ducting in the verandah of each floor. Fan Coil Units (FCUs) with modulating motorized valves can be installed to replace the existing units. In Ministers' rooms, the existing AC units may be retained so that the units may be run when the central plant is not working, if required. 2x 200 TR screw chiller, which has better energy efficiency both at full load & part load (0.46-0.66 kW/TR) is recommended. The feasibility of the proposed system is to be considered from the civil angle also.

3.5.2 Room heaters

Rail Bhavan has 435 nos. of room heaters of combination of 2 & 0.7 kW capacity to use during winter season. On an average, these heaters are used for 2 months in a year.

Use of electricity for heating application is not an efficient route. Hence, it is suggested to install a Light Diesel Oil (LDO) fired **hot water generator** on the terrace of the building. The hot water can be circulated through the same water circuit (of centralized AC system) so that individual rooms are kept warm. The capital cost of the system is Rs. 5.0 lakhs and the annual net cost saving is Rs. 5.0 lakhs.

3.6 Energy usage pattern

The energy consumption for different days in various months were collected; plotted and depicted below. It is seen that there is 10-12 % variation in daily energy consumption. This variation can be minimized/controlled by optimizing the running of loads like lifts (operating minimum no. of lifts by increasing the load factor), exhaust fan in toilets (through timer), etc.

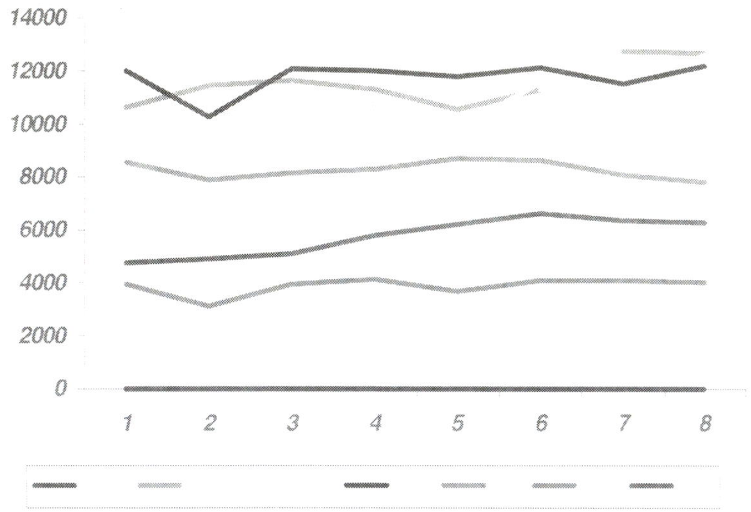

USAGE PATTERN:10-12% VARIATION IN CONSUMPTION

The saving calculation for various systems are presented in Annexure VII. The proposed measurement & verification (M&V) protocol are provided in Annexure VIII.

4.0 Conclusions

Presently, the average annual energy consumption is 24 lakh units. The possible saving by implementing the proposed measures are 5.98 lakh units of electricity & 5,040 kg of LPG used in canteen which comes to about 25 % reduction of annual energy bill, at a capital investment of Rs. 163.15 Lakhs.

Data Sheets prepared under the energy audit

Sl. No.	*Month*	*From*	*To*	*kWh Consumption*	*Amount, Rs.*	*Rs/kWH*	*MWh/ month*
1	Nov. 2000	27-10-00	27-11-00	120763	712622	5.90	120.763
2	Dec. 2000	27-11-00	27-12-00	113400	669166	5.90	113.4
3	Jan. 2001	27-12-00	30-01-01	177300	1046247	5.90	177.3
4	Feb. 2001	30-01-01	26-02-01	116280	686153	5.90	116.28
5	March 2001	26-02-01	27-03-01	106560	628822	5.90	106.56
6	April 2001	27-03-01	27-04-01	161400	952279	5.90	161.4
7	May 2001	27-04-01	31-05-01	290190	1711909	5.90	290.19
8	June 2001	31-05-01	28-06-01	250890	1480109	5.90	250.89
9	July 2001	28-06-01	27-07-01	267360	1577253	5.90	267.36
10	Aug. 2001	27-07-01	21-08-01	227580	1342622	5.90	227.58

Sl. No.	*Month*	*From*	*To*	*kWh Consumption*	*Amount, Rs.*	*Rs/kWH*	*MWh/ month*
11	Sept. 2001	22-08-01	27-09-01	323250	2059413	6.37	323.25
12	Oct. 2001	27-09-01	30-10-01	199470	1270934	6.37	199.47
13	Nov. 2001	30-10-01	27-11-01	116640	743307	6.37	116.64
14	Dec. 2001	27-11-01	28-12-01	105527	672629	6.37	105.527
15	Jan. 2002	28-12-01	28-01-02	164622	1049301	6.37	164.622
16	Feb. 2002	28-01-02	26-02-02	127470	812494	6.37	127.47
17	March 2002	26-02—02	27-03-02	102210	651588	6.37	102.21
18	April 2002	27-03-02	26-04-02	216840	1381781	6.37	216.84
19	May 02	26-04-02	26-05-02	308310	1964551	6.37	308.31
20	June 2002	26-05-02	28-06-02	247740	1578599	6.37	247.74
21	July 2002	28-06-02	29-07-02	347880	2216506	6.37	347.88
22	Aug. 2002	29-07-02	29-08-02	275010	1752323	6.37	275.01
23	Sept. 2002	29-08-02	30-09-02	240240	1530839	6.37	240.24
24	Oct. 2002	30-09-02	30-10-02	181650	1157621	6.37	181.65

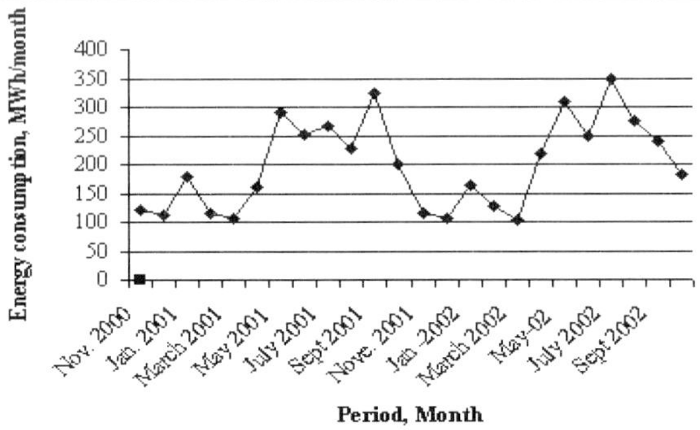

Figure : Variation of monthly energy consumption with time.

Single line electrical power distribution diagram.

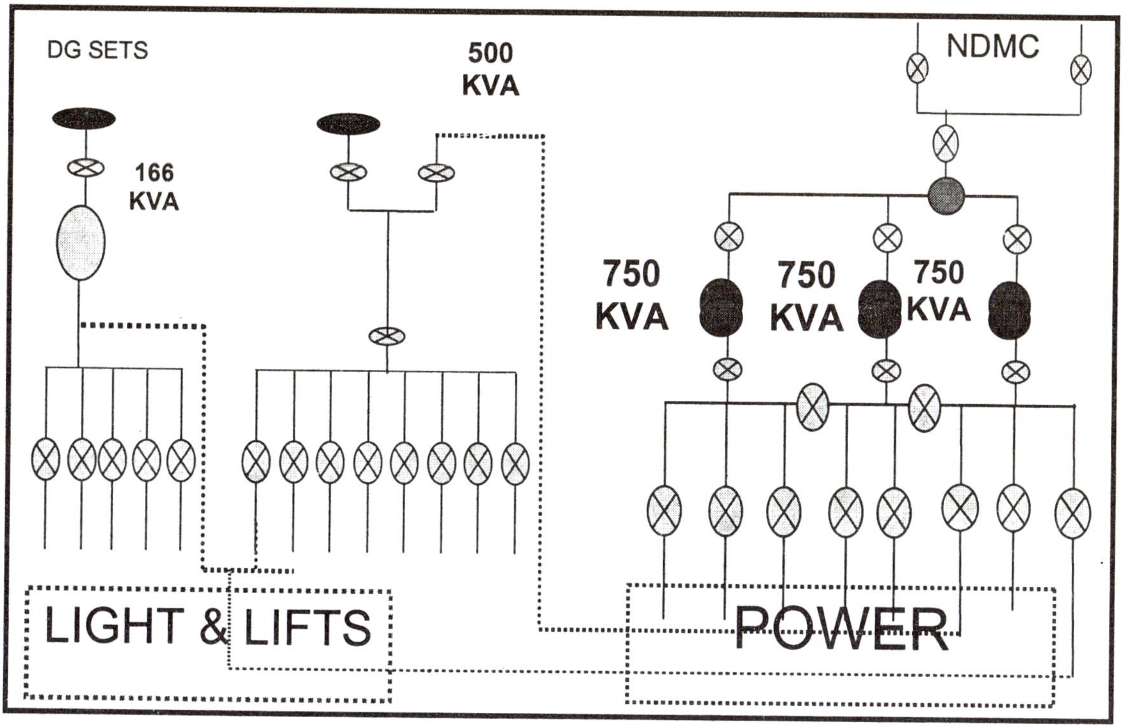

Measured electrical parameters at various DB's for Lighting

Sl. No.	*Floor*	*Wing*	*Voltage, V*	*Current, A*	*Power factor*	*Power, kW*
1	Ground Floor	D	232 235 234	22.7 2.29 5.92	0.88 0.61 0.59	4.7 0.32 0.8
2	First Floor	D	232 232 232	0.38 25.5 28.9	0.98 0.72 0.7	0.086 4.3 4.7
3	Ground & First Floor	C & D	231 235 235	26.3 0.19 15.1	0.66 0.67 0.68	4 0.03 2.4
4	Ground Floor	C	231 234 235	0.08 0.36 0.11	0.17 0.97 0.75	0.003 0.081 0.018
5	First Floor	C	233 233 234	20.4 27.2 23.2	0.64 0.74 0.72	3 4.7 3.9
6	Ground & First Floor	A	231 233 233	22 39 43.1	0.66 0.65 0.72	3.4 5.9 7.3
7	Second Floor	Conference Hall	233 234 233	9.27 8.65 15.2	0.51 0.51 0.52	1.1 1.03 1.96

Electrical power consumption of various motor-pump units

Sl. No.	*Location*	*Pump*	*Rating, KW*	*Voltage, V*	*Current, A*	*P.F.*	*Power, kW*
1	Pump House	Submersible	7.5	237 237 237	19.7 20 19.8	0.64 0.63 0.6	2.95 2.99 2.9
2	Pump House	Pump No. 1	5.5	235 234 237	6.51 6.51 6.68	0.72 0.75 0.76	1.09 1.15 1.12
3	Pump House	Pump No. 4	5.5	236 236 238	8.72 9.45 8.8	0.9 0.85 0.76	1.85 1.89 1.59
4	Exit Gate Pump (Bore Well)	Submersible	2.98	236 235 232	5.7 5.47 5.76	0.6 0.64 0.66	0.812 0.823 0.88
5	Nursery (Bore Well)	Submersible	5.5	234 236 236	13.2 12.8 13.1	0.48 0.44 0.42	1.47 1.34 1.29

Results of performance evaluation of Air conditioners

Sl. No.	*Location*		*Room 223*	*Tel. Excha.*	-	*Room 236*	-
1	Identi. No.		LT 308	LT 295	LT 358	LT 471	LT 131
2	Make		Carrier	Accaire	Accaire	Carrier	Usha
3	Capacity, TR		1.5	1.5	1.5	1.5	1
4	Incoming Air	Temp., C	10.6	16.5	12.4	13.4	13.4
		RH, %	70.4	53	75.4	67.3	73.3
5	Outgoing Air	Temp., C	5.9	5.2	3.8	5	6.5
		RH, %	81	89	84.6	90	88
6	Ave. velocity	m/s	1.74	1.74	2.19	2.33	1.88
7	Suction area, cmxcm	Length	33	50	49.5	36	16
		Breadth	45	23	24.5	41	29
8	TR delivered		0.65	1.03	1.43	1.51	1
9	Power consumed, kW		1.83	1.63	1.26	1.37	0.9
10	SPC, kW/TR		2.82	1.58	0.88	0.91	0.90
					Average KW /TR		1.42

SPC - Specific power consumption; Ambient (condensing) condition: 15 deg. C & 67.3 %

Saving calculation for various systems

Saving Calculation for Lighting				
Sl No.	**Parameter**	**Value**	**Unit**	**Remark**
(A)	**Present status**			
1	Present rate of electricity	6.37	Rs.	
2	Consumption for existing tubelight	46.4	W	
3	Total no. of 40 Watts tube lights in rooms	3516	No.	
4	Operating hours/year	2500	hour	
5	40 Watts tubelight in staircase	34	No.	
6	Operating hours/year	8760	hour	
(B)	**Proposed Modification :**			
1	Replacing each FTL with high lumen TL & Electronic ballast	30	W	
2	Delamping the single FTL which illuminates the ceiling	19	No.	
(C)	**Saving :**			
1	Saving on account of replacing FTL in rooms	148279.93	kWh/year	
2	Saving due to delamping	2204.2821	kWh/year	
3	Total energy saved due to lighting modification	150484.21	kWh/year	
4	Total amount saved due to lighting modification	9.59	Rs Lakhs	
(D)	**Investment :**			
1	Cost per high lumen TL with electronic ballast	700	Rs.	
2	Total Investment	24.85	Rs lakhs	
(E)	**Payback**	2.59	Years	

Saving Calculation for pump

Sl No.	Parameter	Value	Unit	Remark
(A)	**Present status**			
1	Present rate of electricity	6.37	Rs.	
2	Rating of pump	7.5	kW	
3	Power consumption pump	8.85	kW	
4	Present efficiency of motor-pump unit	26.7	%	
5	Running hours of pump during working day	6	hours	
6	Running hours of pump during holiday	2	hours	
7	No. of working days/month	21	days	
8	No. of holidays/month	9	days	
9	Pump running months/year	12	months	
10	Annual energy consumption	15292.8	kWh	
(B)	**Proposed Modification :**			
1	Replace the motor-pump with a monoblock pump set	7.5	kW	
2	Motor-pump efficiency of new pump	60	%	
(C)	**Saving :**			
1	Annual energy saving due to replacement	5092.5	kWh/year	
5	Total amount saved due to replacement	32439.24	Rs	
(D)	**Investment :**			
1	Capital investment for the monoblock pump	30000	Rs.	
(E)	**Payback**	0.92	Years	

Saving calculation for canteen

Sl No.	*Parameter*	*Value*	*Unit*	*Remark*
(A)	**Present Status :**			
	LPG			
1	Average consumption of LPG cylinders per month.	120	No.	
2	Cylinders used only for heating water.	30	No.	
3	Capacity of each LPG cylinder	14	kg	
4	Total LPG consumption for heating water	420	kg	
5	Cost of LPG per kg	24.5	Rs.	
	Electricity			
6	Power consumption of geyser used for plate washing (hot water)	4	kW	2kW*2No.
7	Power consumption of boiler in pantry	6	kW	2 kW*1No. & 2kW*2No.
8	Power consumption of boiler in VIP pantry	4	kW	2kW*2No.
9	Running hours of geyser and boiler in VIP pantry per day	12	Hrs	
10	Running hours of boiler in pantry per day	8	Hrs	
11	No of actual working days per month	21	Days	
12	Total kWh consumption for 9 months per year	27216	kWh	Calculated
13	Cost of electricity per kWh	6.37	Rs.	
(B)	**Established facts :**			
1	100 litres of solar hot water system can save electricity per year	1500	kWh	
2	100 litres of solar hot water system can save LPG per year	195	kg	
(C)	**Modification :**			
1	No. of 100 litres capacity system required to replace the 360 cylinders/year	25.85	No.	30*12=360cylinders
2	No. of 100 litres capacity system required to replace the 27126 kWh/year	18.144	No.	
3	Total No. of collectors required	43.99	No.	
4	Nearest standard system capacity available	45	No.	
(D)	**Saving :**			
1	Saving due to LPG replacement	1.23	Rs. Lakhs	
2	Saving due to electricity replacement	1.73	Rs. Lakhs	
3	Total saving	2.97	Rs. Lakhs	
(E)	**Investment :**			
1	Cost of 4500 LPD system	8	Rs Lakhs	
(F)	**Payback period**	2.70	years	

Saving calculation for HVAC systems

Cooling	Average SPC of existing air conditioners	1.42	kW/TR
	Present condensing temp. (winter season)	15	deg. C
	Average condensing temp. during summer	35	deg. C
	Increase in SPC of compressor due to higher condensing temp. (Taking that for every 1 deg. C rise in condensing temp., there is 2.0 % increase in SPC of compressor)	40	%
	Expected SPC of air conditioners during summer	1.99	kW/TR
	Presently installed capacity of AC with a diversity of 25%	400	TR
	Capacity of central AC system required	400	TR
	Installed window AC	358	Nos
	Installed AC load	751.8	kW
	Present AC running load from Energy bill	600	KW
	Presently delivered TR	301.81	TR
	Loading with central AC plant with 75%	300	TR
	Power required by central plant/TR	1.10	kW
	KW consumption of central AC plant with 75% loading	330	KW
	Power Saving	270	kW
	Working Hrs /day	10	
	Working days /year	125	
	Working Hrs /Yr	1250	
	Energy cost	6.37	Rs.
	Energy saving kWh /year	337500	kWh
	Energy saving Rs. /year	21.4988	Rs Lakhs
Heating	Room heating load for two months/year	400	kW
	Energy consumed for room heating /Year	168000	kWh
	Energy cost/yr	10.70	Rs Lakhs
	Equivalent kcal (capacity of hot water generator)	**3.44**	**Lakh kcal**
	Hot water flow required to carry the above heat (35/40 deg. C)	72	M3/Hr
	Calorific value of LDO	10000	kcal/kg
	Thermal efficiency of hot water generator	85%	%
	Annual LDO requirment	16998	kg
	Cost of LDO/Kg	20	Rs.
	Running energy cost for pump&FCUs/year	2.30	Rs. Lakhs
	LDO cost/year	3.40	Rs. Lakhs
	Annual savings	**5.00**	Rs. Lakhs
Total system	Total saving	**26.50**	Rs. Lakhs
	Investment		
	Central AC plant	125	Rs. Lakhs
	Hot Water generator	5	Rs. Lakhs
	Total	130	Rs. Lakhs
	Payback period	**4.91**	Years

It may be noted that the existing window AC may be sold out to reduce the net capital investment.

M&V protocol for various systems

Saving calculation protocol for Lighting

Sl No.	Item	Formula	Unit	Remark
1	No of running hours per day	H	Hrs	As per baseline
2	No of actual working days per month	D	Days	From actual month calendar
3	Average consumption per existing tubelight	W1	Watts	As per baseline
4	Total no. of 40 W fittings	Ns	No.	3550 no. as counted
5	Total no of single fittings for ceiling illumination	Nd	No.	19 no as counted
6	Rate of electricity	R	Rs/kWh	Rs 6.37 per kWh (During the study)
7	Average consumption per tubelight after modification	W2	Watts	From actual measurement after modification
8	Monthly saving due to delamping of tubelights which are for ceiling illumination	Sd = Nd*W1* H*D/1000	kWh	Calculated
9	Monthly saving due to modification of single fitting	Ss = Ns*(W1-W2)*H*D/1000	kWh	Calculated
10	Total monthly saving	S = Sd+Ss	kWh	Calculated
11	Total monthly amount saved due to lighting modification	A = S*R	Rs.	Calculated

Saving calculation protocol for pump

Sl No.	Item	Formula	Unit	Remark
1	No of running hours per month	H	Hrs	As per baseline
2	Present power consump. Of pump	P1	kW	measured
3	Present water flow rate	F1	M3/sec.	measured
4	Present head developed	Hd1	Metre	measured
5	Present pump efficiency	E1=9.81*Hd1*F1*100/P1	%	Calculated
6	Rate of electricity	R	Rs/kWh	Rs 6.37 per kWh (During the study)
7	Power consump. of new pump	P2	kW	From actual measurement after modification
8	Water flow rate from new pump	F2	M3/sec.	measured
9	Head developed by new pump	Hd2	Metre	measured
10	New pump efficiency	E2=9.81*Hd2*F2*100/P2	%	Calculated
11	Energy saving/month	Se=(H*P1*(E1-E2)/100	kWh	Calculated
12	Total monthly amount saved due to the modification	A = Se*R	Rs.	Calculated

Saving calculation protocol for canteen

Sl No.	Parameter	Formula	Unit	Remark
1	Total LPG Consumption for heating water	Ncyl	No.	As per base line
2	Total energy consumption for heating water	Et	kWh	As per base line
3	LPG Consumption to achieve the desired temperature if required	N(cylfut)	No.	From current month
4	Rate of electricity	R0	Rs./kWh	As per base line
5	Rate of LPG cylinder	R1	Rs./cylinder	As per base line
4	Saving due to redundancy of boiler and geyser	Se=Et*R0	Rs.	Calculation
5	Saving due to Reduced usage of LPG	Slpg=(Ncyl - N(cylfut))*R1	Rs.	Calculation
6	Total Savings	S=Se+Slpg	Rs.	Calculation

Saving calculation protocol for HVAC system

Sl. No.	Item		Formula	Unit	Remark
(A)	**AC system**				
1	No of running hours per day	:	H	Hrs	As per baseline
2	No of actual working days per month	:	D	Days	From actual month calendar
3	Total no of window a/c units	:	Nwac	Nos.	As per baseline
4	Specific power consumption for Window a/c unit	:	SPCwac	kW/TR	As per baseline
5	Energy consumption for New Screw Chiller	:	Psc	kWh	From actual metering
6	Total TR developed by New Chiller.	:	Ttr	Ton-hour	From actual metering
7	Minimum Ton-hour developed by new chiller (based on the current running pattern & 75 % loading)/month	:	Trmin.=63000	Ton-hour	As per baseline
8	Ton-hour considered for calculation	:	Tcal = Max. of (Ttr or Trmin.)	Ton-hour	As per baseline
9	Energy consumption by auxiliaries like Ch. W pump, Cond W Pump, CT and FCU's.	:	Paux	kWh	From actual measurement after modification
10	Total energy consumption by new Chiller System	:	Ptotal = Psc + Paux	kWh	Calculated
11	Specific power consumption of New Chiller	:	SPCsc = Ptotal / Ttr	kW/TR	Calculated
12	Estimated consumption for existing system for future running hours.	:	Pexis = SPCwac * Tcal	kWh	Calculated

13	Monthly saving due to modification of A.C. System	:	S = Pexis - Ptotal	kWh	Calculated
14	Rate of electricity	:	R	Rs/kWh	From current bill
15	Total monthly amount saved due to A.C modification	:	A = S*R	Rs.	Calculated
(B)	**Room heating system**	:			
1	Total no of heaters	:	Nh	Nos.	As per baseline
2	Rating of each heater	:	Rh = 2	kW	As per baseline
3	Running hours per month	:	H = 170	Hrs	As per baseline
4	Energy consumption per month	:	Ph = Nh * Rh * H	kWh	Calculated
5	Fuel consumption for hot water generator	:	F	Lit	From actual metering
6	Future rate of fuel	:	Rf	Rs/lit	Market rate
7	Energy consumption for pump and FCU's	:	Pp	kWh	From actual metering
8	Monthly energy cost for heating system	:	C = (F * Rf) + (Pp * R)	Rs/month	Calculated
9	Total monthly amount saved due to Heating System modification	:	A = (Ph * R) - C	Rs/month	Calculated

11

Building Automation and Controls

11.1 FUNDAMENTALS OF CONTROL SYSTEMS

Control systems are everywhere around us, they regulate temperature in homes, stabilize aircraft and spacecraft, affect production of food by regulating the quality and purity of produce, are used in refineries, and so on. Automatic control has played a vital role in the advances of engineering and science. In addition to its extreme importance in space-vehicle systems, missile-guidance systems, robotic systems and the like, automatic control has become an important and integral part of modern manufacturing and industrial processes. From a simple on-off control of thermostat for temperature control in buildings, the building automation and control area has advanced to self learning and adaptive controls using PID, fuzzy logic and other advanced control strategies.

A system is generally made up of components which could be mechanical, electrical, hydraulic, and/or pneumatic. The function of the control system is to regulate the output of the system in accordance with some input signal. The controlled output may be position, velocity, acceleration, temperature, etc. The output is required to track and follow the input signal as closely as possible. The output is measured by using transducers and, fed back to the controller in order to correct deviations from the input signal. This is referred to as feedback and is an essential element of closed-loop control systems. When feedback is not used, we have an open-loop control system.

In closed-loop control systems, feedback is used for calculating the error which is the difference between the input and output signals. The error signal is then filtered, amplified and applied to a power element within the system such as an electrical motor, hydraulic valve/ram that acts upon the quantity to be controlled.

Modern control is increasingly based on having an electrical signal as input and having transducers that produce electrical signals as a measure of the output. These are then fed into the controller which acts upon the system being controlled. Computers are increasingly used in control applications.

11.2 DEFINITIONS AND TERMINOLOGY

Controlled Variable and Manipulated Variable:

The controlled variable is the quantity or condition that is measured and controlled. The manipulated variable is the quantity or condition that is varied by the controller so as to affect the value of the controlled variable. Normally, the controlled variable is the output of the system.

Control:

Control means measuring the value of the controlled variable of the system and applying the manipulated variable to the system to correct or limit deviation of the measured value from a desired value.

Plants:

A plant may be a piece of equipment, perhaps just a set of machine parts functioning together, the purpose of which is to perform a particular operation. In this book, we shall call any physical object to be controlled (such as a mechanical device, a heating furnace, a chemical reactor, or a spacecraft) a plant.

Processes:

Defined as natural, progressively continuing operation or development marked by a series of gradual changes that succeed one another in a relatively fixed way and lead toward a particular result or end; or an artificial or voluntary, progressively continuing operation that consists of a series of controlled actions or movements systematically directed towards a particular result or end. In this book we shall call any operation to be controlled a process. Examples are chemical, economic, and biological processes.

Systems:

A system is a combination of components that act together and perform a certain objective. A system is not limited to physical ones. The concept of the system can be applied to abstract, dynamic phenomena such as those encountered in economics. The word system should, therefore, be interpreted to imply physical, biological, economic, and the like, systems.

Disturbances:

A disturbance is a signal that tends to adversely affect the value of the output of a system. If a disturbance is generated within the system, it is called internal, while an external disturbance is generated outside the system and is an input.

11.3 TYPES OF CONTROL SYSTEMS

11.3.1 Feedback Control systems:

A system that maintains a prescribed relationship between the output and the reference input by comparing them and using the difference as a means of control is called a feedback control system. An example would be a room-temperature control system. By measuring the actual room temperature and comparing it with the reference temperature (desired temperature), the thermostat turns the heating or cooling equipment on or off in such a way as to ensure that the room temperature remains at a comfortable level regardless of outside conditions.

Example

An example of a closed-loop system is a temperature-control system in a room. For this system we wish to maintain, automatically, the temperature of the room at a desired value. To control any physical variable, which we usually call a signal, we must know the value of this variable, that is, we must measure this variable. We call the system for the measurement of a variable a sensor. In this system, the sensor is a thermistor. Thermistor is a device which has a resistance that varies with temperature. By measuring this resistance, we obtain a measure of the temperature.

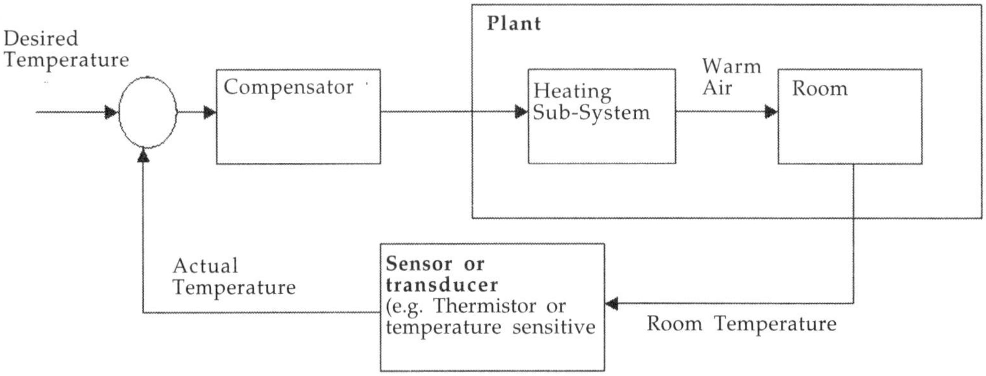

Figure 11.1: Schematic diagram of a typical building control system

We defined the plant of a control system as that part of the system to be controlled. It is assumed in this example that the temperature is increased by activating a gas furnace or a heating sub-system. Hence the plant input is the electrical signal that activates the furnace, and the plant output signal is the actual temperature of the living area. The plant is represented as shown in the above figure. In this example, the output of each of the systems is connected to the input of the other, to form the closed loop. In most closed-loop control systems, it is necessary to connect a third system into the loop to obtain satisfactory characteristics for the total system. This additional system is called a compensator or a controller.

The usual form of a single loop closed-loop control system is as follows:

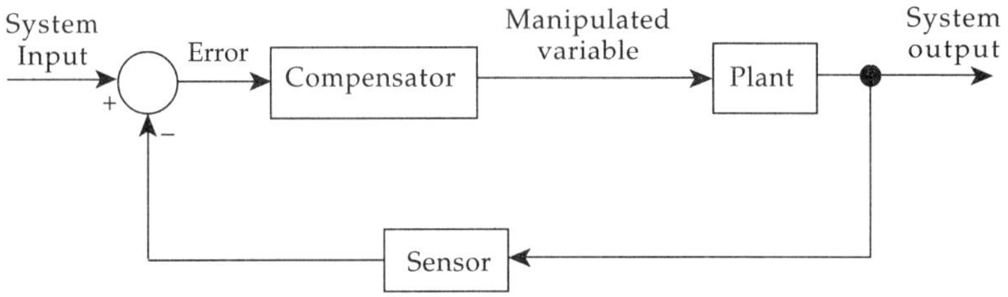

Figure 11.2: Single loop closed loop control system

The system input is a reference signal; usually we want the system output to be equal to this input. In the temperature-control system, this input is the setting of the Desired Temperature. If we want to change the temperature, we change the system input. The system output is measured by the sensor, and this measured value is compared with (subtracted from) the input. This difference signal is called the error signal, or simply the error. If the output is equal to the input, this difference is zero, and no signal reaches the plant. Hence the plant output remains at its current value. If the error is not zero, in a properly designed system the error signal causes a response in the plant such that the magnitude of the error is reduced. The compensator is a filter for the error signal, since usually satisfactory operation does not occur if the error signal is applied directly to the plant.

11.3.2 Closed-Loop and Open-Loop Control Systems

Open-loop control systems

Those systems in which the output has no effect on the control action are called open-loop control systems. In other words, in an open-loop control system the output is neither measured nor fed back for comparison with the input. One practical example is a washing machine. Soaking, washing and rinsing in the washer operate on a time basis. The machine does not measure the output signal, that is, the cleanliness of the clothes.

In any open-loop control system the output is not compared with the reference input. Thus, to each reference input there corresponds a fixed operating condition; as a result, the accuracy of the system depends on calibration. In the presence of disturbances, an open-loop control system will not perform the desired task. Open-loop control can be used, in practice, only if the relationship between the input and output is known and if there are neither internal nor external disturbances. Clearly, such systems are not feedback control systems. Note that any control system that operates on a time basis is open loop. For instance, traffic control by means of signals operated on a time basis is another example of open-loop control.

Closed-loop control systems

Feedback control systems are often referred to as closed-loop control systems. In practice, the terms feedback control and closed-loop control are used interchangeably. In a closed-loop control system the actuating error signal, which is the difference between the input signal and the feedback signal (which may be the output signal itself or a function of the output signal and its derivatives and/or integrals), is fed to the controller so as to reduce the error and bring the output of the system to a desired value. The term closed-loop control always implies the use of feedback control action in order to reduce system error.

Closed-loop versus open-loop control systems

An advantage of the closedloop control system is the fact that the use of feedback makes the system response relatively insensitive to external disturbances and internal variations in system parameters. It is thus possible to use relatively inaccurate and inexpensive components to obtain the accurate control of a given plant, whereas doing so is impossible in the open-loop case. From the point of view of stability, the open-loop control system is easier to build because system stability is not a major problem. On the other hand, stability is a major problem in the closed-loop control system, which may tend to overcorrect errors that can cause oscillations of constant or changing amplitude.

11.3.3 Types of Closed loop control

Most control systems utilize feedback in some manner. Here's a look at several fundamental feedback mechanisms. Many real-time embedded systems make control decisions. These decisions are usually made by software and based on feedback from the hardware under its control (termed the plant). Such feedback commonly takes the form of an analog sensor that can be read via an A/D converter. A sample from the sensor may represent position, voltage, temperature, or any other appropriate parameter. Each sample provides the software with additional information upon which to base its control decisions.

Systems that utilize feedback are called closed-loop control systems. The feedback is used to make decisions about changes to the control signal that drives the plant. An open-loop control system doesn't have or doesn't use feedback.

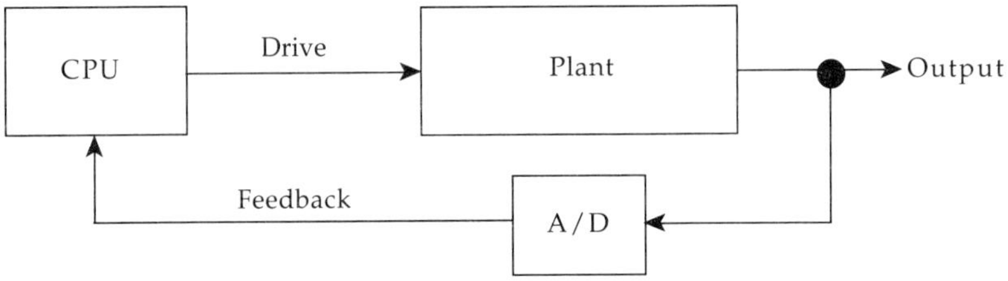

Figure 11.3: A closed-loop control system

A basic closed-loop control system is shown in Figure 11.3. This figure can describe a variety of control systems, including those driving elevators, thermostats, and cruise control.

Closed-loop control systems typically operate at a fixed frequency. The frequency of changes to the drive signal is usually the same as the sampling rate, and certainly not any faster. After reading each new sample from the sensor, the software reacts to the plant's changed state by recalculating and adjusting the drive signal. The plant responds to this change, another sample is taken, and the cycle repeats. Eventually, the plant should reach the desired state and the software will cease making changes.

If feedback indicates that the temperature at home is below the desired setpoint, the thermostat will turn the heater on until the room is at least that temperature.

On/Off (Bang Bang)

How much should the software increase or decrease the drive signal? One option is to just set the drive signal to its minimum value when you want the plant to decrease its activity and to its maximum value when you want the plant to increase its activity. This strategy is called on-off control, and it is how many thermostats work. On-off control doesn't work well in all systems. If the thermostat waits until the desired temperature is achieved to turn off the heater, the temperature may overshoot. See Figure 11.4. The same amount of overshoot and ripple probably isn't acceptable in an elevator.

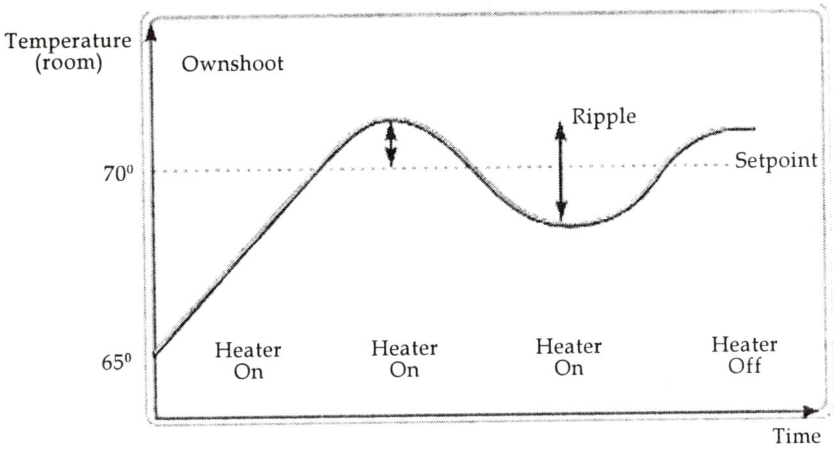

Figure 11.4: Control example

Proportional control

Proportional control is the primary alternative to on-off control. If the difference between the current plant output and its desired value (the current error) is large, the software should probably change the drive signal a lot. If the error is small, it should change it only a little. In other words, we always want a change like:

P * (desired — current)

where P is a constant proportional gain set by the system's designer.

For example, if the drive signal uses PWM, it can take any value between 0% and 100% duty cycle. If the signal on the drive is 20% duty cycle and the error remaining at the output is small, we may just need to tweak it to 18% or 19% to achieve the desired output at the plant.

If the proportional gain is well chosen, the time the plant takes to reach a new setpoint will be as short as possible, with overshoot (or undershoot) and oscillation minimized.

Unfortunately, proportional control alone is not sufficient in all control applications. One or more of the requirements for response time, overshoot, and oscillation may be impossible to fulfill at any proportional gain setting.

Differentiation

The biggest problem with proportional control alone is that you want to reach new desired outputs quickly and avoid overshoot and minimize ripple once you get there. Responding quickly suggests a high proportional gain; minimizing overshoot and oscillation suggests a small proportional gain. Achieving both at the same time may not be possible in all systems.

Fortunately, we do generally have (or can derive) information about the rate of change of the plant's output. If the output is changing rapidly, overshoot or undershoot may lie ahead. In that case, we can reduce the size of the change suggested by the proportional controller.

The rate of change of a signal is also known as its derivative. The derivative at the current time is simply the change in value from the previous sample to the current one. This implies that we should subtract a change of:

D * (current — previous)

where D is a constant derivative gain. The only other thing we need to do is to save the previous sample in memory.

In practice, proportional-derivative (PD) controllers work well. The net effect is a slower response time with far less overshoot and ripple than a proportional controller alone.

Integration

A remaining problem is that PD control alone will not always settle exactly to the desired output. In fact, depending on the proportional gain, it's altogether possible that a PD controller will ultimately settle to an output value that is far from that desired.

The problem occurs if each individual error remains below the threshold for action by the proportional term. (Say the error is 3, P = 1/8, and integer math is used.) The derivative term won't help anything unless the output is changing. Something else needs to drive the plant toward the setpoint. That something is an integral term.

An integral is a sum over time, in this case the sum of all past errors in the plant output:

$$I * \sum_{t} (\text{desired current})$$

Even though the integral gain factor, I, is typically small, a persistent error will eventually cause the sum to grow large and the integral term to force a change in the drive signal.

In summary, on-off and proportional control are the two basic techniques of closed-loop control. However, derivative and/or integral terms are sometimes added to porportional controllers to improve qualitative properties of a particular plant's response. When all three terms are used together, the acronym used to describe the controller is PID.

11.4 SENSORS AND TRANSDUCERS

Sensor is the eye of the system. It senses the measured variable and produces an output signal that represents the status of the controlled variable. Examples in a process control system may include a thermistor to measure temperature or a humidity detector to measure moisture. Examples in a motion control system may be an optical device to measure position or a tachometer to measure rotational speed. In the water reservoir system, the float is the measurement device. Other terms used are detector, transducer, and measurement device.

11.5 ACTUATORS

Actuator. The actuator is the "muscle" of the system. It is a device that physically alters some type of energy or fuel supply, causing the controlled variable to match the desired set point. Examples of energy or fuel are the flow of steam, water, air, gas, or electrical current. A practical application is a commercial bakery where the objective is to keep the temperature in an oven at 375 degrees. The temperature is the controlled variable. The temperature is determined by how much gas is fed to the oven burner. A valve in the gas line controls the flow by the amount it opens or closes. The valve is the actuator in the system. In the reservoir system, the actuator is the flow control valve, connected to the inlet pipe. Other terms used are the final control element, or final correcting device. Common types of actuators are louvers, hydraulic cylinders, pumps, and motors.

11.6 AUTOMATION SYSTEMS FOR BUILDING AUTOMATION

11.6.1 Building Automation

Building Automation is the process of integrating systems such as environmental control, access control, closed circuit TV, elevator control, parking lot supervision, fire alarm monitoring and other building systems into one network. It enables facilities to be driven and managed by sophisticated electronics. In a broad sense, these "smart buildings" are designed so that the HVAC (heating, ventilating, and air conditioning) environment, lighting, and security systems perform at the highest efficiency possible. From an HVAC perspective, the automated systems that produce smart buildings are often referred to as Facility Management Systems (FMS) or Building Automation Systems (BAS). Building Automation Systems (BAS) optimize the start-up and performance of HVAC equipment and alarm systems. BAS greatly increases the interaction of mechanical subsystems within a building, improve occupant comfort, lower energy use and allow off-site building control.

11.6.2 Constituents of a Building Automation System

A building automation system is comprised of electronic equipment that automatically performs specific facility functions. The commonly accepted definition of a BAS includes the comprehensive automatic control of one or more major building system functions required in a facility, such HVAC systems. In many cases a BAS includes lighting, security, fire safety, industrial processes, and more. Automated systems include a collection of sensors that determine the condition or status of parameters to be controlled, such as temperature, relative humidity, and pressure. Similarly, output devices impart electronic signals or physical action to the control devices. Examples include electric relays or damper and valve actuators. The sensors and output devices are connected either to a unitary controller or to a distributed processor. Unitary controllers are limited to the needs of an intended function and have limited capabilities, such as memory size. Distributed processors can accommodate the needs of several unitary controllers as well as connect directly to input and output devices.

Common applications include

- Equipment scheduling (turning equipment off and on as required).
- Optimum start/stop (turning heating and cooling equipment on in advance to ensure the building is at the required temperature during occupancy).
- Operator adjustment (accessing operator set-points that tune system to changing conditions).
- Monitoring (logging of temperature, energy use, equipment start times, operator logon, etc).
- Alarm reporting (notifying the operator of failed equipment, out of limit temperature/pressure conditions or need for maintenance).

11.6.3 Functions of building automation

- Building Automation systems provide operators a central location to receive building alarms and operating conditions. By utilizing local area networks or wide area networks multiple workstations can be incorporated.
- Remote alarming is available through networks and phone modems.
- An automation system can provide scheduling and tracking of after hours building use to ensure tenant comfort and allow operating costs to be assessed to the appropriate cost center.
- Abnormal operating conditions can often be detected and corrected before tenant comfort or safety is compromised.
- Mechanical systems can be monitored and preventative maintenance scheduled on run time or other user defined variables.
- Digital control systems provide precise control of environmental conditions as well as operating schedules for mechanical equipment. This equates to dollar savings through reduced energy consumption.

11.6.4 Features and benefits

DDC Controls - Using low cost, reliable Direct Digital Controls (DDC) increases overall system reliability, reduces wiring costs, and provides for system expansion without performance degradation. Existing outdated controls can be replaced with new controllers which are more reliable, require less maintenance, provide more sophisticated control, and are less expensive to purchase and operate.

Outside Air Optimization - Proper control of outside air provides necessary inside air changes for occupant comfort and health, minimizes energy costs by space pre-conditioning, allows for enthalpy based free cooling, and reduces the use of outside air when it is not needed.

Coordinating Equipment - Orchestrating the operation of building systems, so that equipment works together, saves energy and improves comfort. Individual control systems that are not centrally monitored and coordinated can fight each other or malfunction, causing comfort problems and wasting considerable energy. We can interface to existing or planned systems so that the building will run smoothly and at peak efficiency without expensive duplication of controls or unnecessary complexity.

Graphical Operation - Simplifying facility operation and integrating data from various systems in a "seamless" manner is best accomplished with a graphical user interface. This eliminates the need to memorize commands or point numbers, and allows the operator to take a walking tour of the facility from the console. Existing systems can be easily upgraded to add this powerful operational tool. Point and shoot graphics empowers management by letting everyone see what's going on and taking the mystery out of proper operations.

Tighter Scheduling - Conventional controls, such as timeclocks, are inaccurate and are typically setup to run equipment longer than the actual need. By automating this function with computerized controls, the computer can predict the optimum time to start/stop equipment and eliminate waste caused by excessive runtime.

Smarter Control - HVAC equipment is typically sized to handle the building load under worst case conditions. Most conventional controls are set up to meet these design criteria at all times. With the automation system, control setpoints and strategies can be adjusted to meet only the actual load, eliminating unnecessary waste.

11.6.5 The impact of automation

It makes quantum improvements possible.

There is a connection between operating cost, environmental quality, and profitability. Computer technology is the key to managing facilities and costs effectively. Without better tools, the existing personnel can't keep up with increasing demands. Either quality suffers or costs increase in other areas (like contracted services, utility charges, or personnel).

It manages direct and hidden costs –

Recognizing the real costs (both direct and hidden) and how they are controlled affects an organization's ability to compete. The following costs can be significantly reduced using facility automation technology:

Personnel - Operating personnel need the tools that technology provides to leverage their expertise and time. Without better systems, quality will degrade and overall costs will rise.

Utilities - Energy costs are a large part of the controllable facility budget. Integrated facility automation makes controlling utility costs possible.

Equipment Repair and Replacement - Repair and replacement of aging building equipment is a fact of life. Newer technology equipment is generally less expensive to purchase, install, operate and service. Every significant equipment repair or replacement should be evaluated against the cost of upgrading to the newest technology.

Lost Opportunity - There is a direct correlation between comfort and the productivity, receptiveness and efficiency of conducting business. Even small percentage losses due to equipment breakdowns or comfort problems represent huge costs and can easily justify providing a proper building environment.

11.7 APPLICATION AND COMPONENTS OF BUILDING AUTOMATION SYSTEMS

Following are key areas that can be improved by using building automation systems:

- Heating, Ventilation and Air Conditioning, and Indoor Air Quality
- Lighting
- Voice and Data Communications
- Energy Efficiency/Energy Management
- Security
- Elevators and Escalators
- Life Safety Systems
- Building Condition Monitoring

11.7.1 Heating, Ventilation and Air Conditioning, and Indoor Air Quality

HVAC systems are generally controlled by building automation systems that can:

- permit individual occupants to adjust workspace temperatures (within prescribed limits);
- monitor temperatures, and adjust according to a usage profile;
- adjust indoor air quality based on room occupancy and building standards;
- adjust humidity, temperature and air flow speeds; and
- use either variable air volume or constant volume air distribution designs. The former allows greater individual control.

11.7.2 Lighting

Technologies for lighting include many lighting types and functions. Lighting needs vary with each building. The functional goal is to furnish occupants of the building with the lighting required to complete specific visual tasks effectively and productively. Current lighting systems can:

- automatically turn on and off lights by photocell or computer schedule;
- modify lighting levels through the use of photochromatic windows;
- allow individuals to adjust their lighting through computer or telephone interfaces;
- link the lighting controller to a graphic user interface with icons, for centralized control;
- turn circuits on and off through computer control; and
- manage energy consumption by monitoring room occupancy and adjusting lighting to suit.

11.7.3 Voice and Data Communications

Voice and data communication capabilities are integral to the effective operation of a building and its occupants. In an integrated automated building, data communication is vital to the integration of all other automated building systems, e.g., lighting, energy management and HVAC. Generally "data" in the context of "voice and data", refers only to end-user data, such as email, Internet and database access. Voice and data in-building communications include:

- voice services, e.g., telephones, voicemail and intercoms;
- building systems, e.g., paging, elevator music and kiosks;
- video and audio conferencing;
- local and wide area networks, e-mail, internet access, database access;
- ability to access building services remotely, e.g., when working from home; and
- television systems.

11.7.4 Energy Efficiency/Energy Management

The objective of energy management is to ensure maximum efficiency and lowest operating cost. Opportunities for reducing heat gain in the summer and reducing heat loss in the winter will lower energy costs. Energy deregulation brings opportunities to select the most effective source of heat, be it steam, oil, natural gas or electricity. In some buildings, multiple fuels are used together, whereas in other situations, each source of heat generates warmth in a distinct manner. For example, baseboard electrical heaters may supplement circulating warm air. Furnaces capable of burning either natural gas or oil exist, and electric heater systems compete with the ability to purchase steam from external sources. Management of these energy sources depends on the infrastructure that exists within the building, as well as the "spot costs" of each of these energy sources. Intelligent building technologies permit each of the following energy sources to be managed based on criteria that can include the fluctuating pricing of:

- traditional electrical generating and distribution sources;
- new electrical generating agencies;
- oil;
- gas;
- co-generation; and
- future opportunities that may involve photovoltaic sources and wind.

11.7.5 Security

Security systems are generally divided into three sub-components:

- access control;
- intrusion; and
- surveillance.

Effective security systems integrate these three areas, allowing the building mode, function and operation to be pre-scheduled or controlled by individual access requests. A typical system will involve:

- access card;
- elevator interface;
- door interface;
- intrusion detection;
- sensor detection, such as temperature, moisture, glass breakage, etc.;
- guard tours; and
- parking controls.

Many of the functions of an access control system are subordinate to the life safety system, which may deactivate parts of the access control system in an emergency.

11.7.6 Elevators and Escalators

Building automation systems can provide occupants with improved elevator service. Elevator control can be quite complex, particularly with multiple elevator groupings and incorporating traffic patterns into the system. Some elevators may be shut down for part of the day to conserve energy. Current designs frequently include communications within the elevators to permit the use of access control cards, and closed circuit surveillance is becoming widespread. An effective access control system can permit dynamic changes to user privileges so that, for example, certain floors may not be accessible even with an approved access control card, unless there are already people occupying that floor.

Escalators can save energy by slowing down or stopping when detectors indicate no traffic. This approach to energy savings also benefits the mechanical components that need not run continuously.

11.7.7 Life Safety Systems

Life safety systems, often called "fire systems", are typically driven by code considerations. Security systems are required to release doors per code constraints under emergency conditions. HVAC systems are also driven by life safety needs, e.g., smoke extraction, stairwell pressurization and elevator recall. The advent of intelligent building technologies facilitates additional functionality. For example, in a fire, lighting can be turned on throughout the building, and networks can enhance information provided to individuals, e.g., the state of the fire system, emergency broadcast messages, etc. Paging systems, normally restricted to being part of the fire system, can be used in intelligent buildings to broadcast pre-recorded status messages, which can be far more informative than messages spoken by nervous staff.

11.7.8 Building Condition Monitoring

Building automation technologies facilitate monitoring of a building's condition. Since transducers or sensors can measure most building-related parameters, needs will drive their specific use. Under appropriate conditions, any or all of these may be appropriate:

- areas with heavy snowfalls may monitor the loads imposed by such snow on their roofs;
- monitoring the strain in key structural members may be important with regards to wind loads, suspension of exhibits, loud speakers, and crowd loading in stadiums;
- moisture detectors laid beneath membranes in a building can prevent significant damage;
- monitoring the temperature in fuse panels, electrical switchgear and transformers can warn of impending failure;
- monitoring current flow in conductors can identify trouble in lamps or other electrical devices;
- monitoring vibration on mechanical systems can identify bearings needing maintenance; and
- monitoring conductivity of lubricating oil can identify metal buildup due to wear.

All of these examples may be built into a building condition monitoring system via the security system.

11.8 INTEGRATED COMMUNICATION FOR BUILDING AUTOMATION

The full benefits of building automation technologies are only fully realized through integration, such as:

- building condition monitoring depends on many parameters;
- occupancy monitoring can provide input for lighting, HVAC and elevators; and
- voice and data can be integrated for those who use telephones and computers.

The communications infrastructure must be designed and developed to support all possible applications in the building. These include voice and data systems, data processing needs, security systems, building automation systems, lighting systems and other systems that combine to create an intelligent building. Under current practice, many subsystems in a construction project, e.g., elevator monitoring and control systems, voice systems, and security systems, are covered by separate construction contracts. Each specialty in a construction project is a division within the overall contract. As a result, each sub-contractor installs its own communication system, with dedicated conduits, separate communication terminal locations and different staff pulling similar cables.

11.8.1 Radio Frequency Technologies

Many wireless devices and protocols are currently being promoted. Burglar alarm systems for residential applications, patient wandering systems for hospitals and other applications of voice systems, such as Bluetooth™ or IEEE 802.11b, communicate without a hard wired infrastructure.

Wireless communications are particularly attractive where offices and partitions are frequently reconfigured, and applications change frequently. The wireless solution competes favourably with wired alternatives. HVAC requirements can be economically and efficiently met using wireless controls.

Evolving wireless technologies enable one antenna to serve a wide range of frequencies, so that a single antenna and wireless infrastructure can serve telephones, pagers, local area networks and signalling for building automation systems. The active components of these wireless systems should be installed in the centralized communications rooms alongside their wired system equivalents.

11.8.2 Communication Issues

The ability of a standard digital data transmission protocol, e.g., TCP/IP (Transmission Control Protocol/Internet Protocol) to transmit many forms of data enables a single infrastructure to transport multiple, independent data elements. Both analogue and digital data can be handled, serving, for example, security, voice and traditional data processing information. Bandwidth needs for voice and security applications are small compared to data processing, so network performance would not be prejudiced.

Security and redundancy needs must be well addressed, within the network design. Appropriate protection is essential, to ensure security and to protect against viruses, hackers and other intruders. A very large number of individual IP addresses can be used to uniquely identify each device attached to the network while also respecting naming conventions.

11.8.3 Standards and Protocols

Standards and protocols are an area of contention in the intelligent building technologies industry. The industry would benefit from universal or widespread acceptance of a small suite of standards and protocols. There are, at present, a number of different standards available, but no general consensus apparent. Adoption of a universal or widely accepted standard industry wide would be very helpful.

Standards define the arrangements under which devices and systems interact and communicate with each other. The terminology is complicated by the frequent interchange of the terms "standard" and "standard compliant". Some vendors will certify that their products comply with other vendors' implementations. Sometimes, vendors will publish their standards, allowing competitors to use a subset. Switch manufacturers typically employ a range of protocols, some of which adhere to published standards and some of which are only available through their own proprietary products. The following arrangements generally apply.

- a standard is normally written through a national organization. Organizations such as the American National Standards Institute (ANSI) and the American Society of Heating, Refrigeration, and Air-conditioning Engineers (ASHRAE) are among those writing standards. Such standards are developed in a public forum that generally includes representatives from a number of corporate organizations and manufacturers who participate in a carefully structured vote to ensure that the document represents all interests. Canada, sometimes through the Canadian Standards Association (CSA), writes some of its own standards and often participates in the U.S. process so that standards will be compatible between the two countries and may be issued simultaneously in both countries;
- an open standard may be owned by a company or a consortium of companies and disclosed to the public. In some cases, open standards require payment of a licence fee.

11.9 EXAMPLE OF LIGHTING AUTOMATION

How do you decide what detector to use for your light sensing application?

The choices can seem overwhelming: photodiodes, phototransistors, photodarlingtons, photomultiplier tubes, photo resistors, integrated circuits, various hybrids and even thermopiles. This application note provides insights on selecting the best approach for your ultraviolet, visible and near-infrared light sensing applications. Specific application needs considered include:

- image size
- signal-to-noise ratio
- frequency bandwidth
- cost

Available Light Sensing Options

Light sensing applications vary widely from specialized scientific instrumentation that needs to detect individual light particles (photons) to systems that control high speed welding and cutting lasers that produce kilowatts of optical power. Fortunately, there are sensors for almost any application imaginable: from a photomultiplier tube which gives a large voltage pulse for every photon it detects, to cooled thermopiles that absorb kilowatts of power providing a thermocouple voltage proportional to the optical power absorbed. The following describes the most popular light sensing technologies. Their characteristics are summarized.

Table 1 – Comparison of Light Sensor Characteristics

Electrical Characteristics	Photo-Multiplier Tubes	Photo-diodes	Photo-transistors	CdS Photocells	Other Photo-conductors	Integrated circuits	Hybrids	Sensor Electronic Assembly
Available Wave lengths (m)	0.2-0.9	0.2-2.0	0.4-1.1	0.4-0.7	2-15	0.2-1.1	0.2-15.0	0.2-15.0
Performance-to-cost-ratio	Fair	Good	Excellent	Excellent	Fair	Fair	Fair	Good
Sensitivity	Excellent	Very Good	Very Good	Very Good	Very Good	Very Good	Very Good	Very Good
Linearity	Good	Excellent	Good	Good	Good	Good	Good	Good
Ambient Noise Performance	Fair	Very Good	Very Good	Very Good	Very Good	Excellent	Excellent	Excellent
Dynamic Range	Very Good	Excellent	Very Good	Good	Good	Very Good	Very Good	Very Good
Stability	Very Good	Very Good	Good	Poor	Fair	Very Good	Very Good	Very Good
Other Characteristics								
Reproducibility	Fair	Excellent	Fair	Poor	Fair	Very Good	Very Good	Very Good
Cost	High	Low	Very Low	Very Low	High	Medium	High	Medium
Ruggedness	Poor	Excellent	Excellent	Excellent	Good	Excellent	Very Good	Excellent
Physical Size	Large	Small	Small	Small	Small	Small	Medium	Medium
Ease of Customization	Poor	Easy	Fair	Fair	Poor	Poor	Poor	Fair
Cost of Customization	Very High	Low	Medium	Low	High	Very High	High	Medium
Lead time for Customization (weeks)	40	12	14	12	20	40	30	16

Photomultiplier Tubes: Photomultiplier tubes are special vacuum tubes that have a light sensing surface (the photocathode) that absorbs incoming light photons and emits secondary electrons. These secondary electrons are accelerated and multiplied within the photomultiplier tube by dynode plates. Each time an electron strikes a dynode, it has gained enough momentum to create a larger number of secondary electrons. This multiplication process continues for each dynode within the tube. Tubes with ten to twelve dynodes can easily generate multiplications of more than a million, resulting in sufficient current to develop hundreds of millivolts across an output 50 ohm load resistor for a single incident photon. Photomultiplier tubes provide the ultimate in detection sensitivity. They can sense the smallest amount of optical energy there is an individual photon. When cooled, it can be essentially noise free, with at most one false photon pulse in a one second time period. However, there are many tradeoffs for this light sensor:

- It's mechanically fragile.
- It needs an extremely stable high voltage power supply.
- It's expensive.
- Shapes and sizes are very limited.
- It's susceptible to external magnetic fields.
- The available photo cathodes are limited to sensing ultra-violet to near infrared wavelengths (190 to 900 nm, with special's to 1100 nm) Photomultiplier tubes are generally used to detect the lowest light levels where the application demands their superior sensitivity.

Photodiodes: Photodiodes are light sensitive semiconductor devices that are manufactured in essentially the same way as semiconductor diodes used in conventional electronic circuits. The primary differences are that photodiode chips are larger and they are packaged to allow light onto the sensitive area of the diode. Photodiodes offer many conveniences and advantages that make them very practical for a wide range of applications:

- They can easily measure from Pico watts to mill watts of optical power.
- They come in standard packages or the package can be tooled to fit your application exactly.
- Depending on the semiconductor material used, they can detect wavelengths from 190 to > 2,000 nm.
- They are small and light weight.
- Almost any photosensitive shape can be fabricated for as little as $3,000 tooling.
- They have very reproducible sensitivity.
- They are inexpensive, with million piece pricing for small area detectors less than $0.25.
- Very large areas can be fabricated (> 10cm2, but with cost increasing with area).
- They can be very responsive, with risetimes as fast as 10 picoseconds.

If noise presents a problem when measuring a few Pico watts of light with a standard photodiode, consider the advantages of an avalanche photodiode which offers a current gain internal to the photodiode structure of up to about 100. Photodiodes generally require a pre-amplifier to give signal gain for applications to detect picowatts of light power. But for high optical power (<10 microwatt) levels, a simple load resistor configuration can give adequate performance and TTL compatible voltage swings. Silicon based photodiodes cover the wide range of wavelengths from 190 to 1100 nm (the lower limit is set by absorption of ultraviolet light in air). Germanium (Ge) photodiodes overlap the silicon response spectrum and are usable to about 1600 nm. Semiconductors that are compounds of gallium, arsenide, indium, antimonide and phosphorous can be specially fabricated to cover small sections of the 190 to 2000 nm spectral range. For instance, the fiber optics industry uses indium-gallium-arsenide (InGaAs) detectors for the 800 to 1800 nm range. More exotic and expensive photodiodes can sense energy much further out in the IR spectrum. Photodiodes are widely used in our high-tech society, in applications ranging from sensors for door openings, assembly line controls, load levelers in luxury cars, to personal blood sugar meters for diabetics, sun-tan exposure meters, smoke detectors, x-ray baggage inspection systems and even cranial pressure sensors for head injury patients.

Phototransistors and Photodarlingtons: Phototransistors are transistors designed to capture light and are assembled in a transparent package. They are often more convenient than photodiodes because they have built in gain: the absorbed light creates a current in the base region of the phototransistor, resulting in current gains from 100 to several thousands. Photodarlingtons have two stages of gain, with net gains that can be greater than 100,000. The built in gain allows the phototransistor to be coupled with a load resistor to accommodate TTL level voltages for a wide range of light levels. Because of their ease of use, low cost and TTL compatible signal levels, phototransistors have become popular for applications where there is more than a few hundred nanowatts of available optical power. These devices however, do have some drawbacks compared to photodiodes. The frequency bandwidth and linearity are relatively limited and spectral response is restricted to between 350 and 1100 nm. In addition, there are very large variations in sensitivity between individual devices and few standard package options.

Photoconductive Sensors: A photoconductive sensor is a thick film semiconductor material whose electrical resistance decreases with increasing incident light. These rugged assemblies that can withstand hundreds of volts are typically smaller than 0.25 inch diameter. Photoconductive sensors based on cadmium sulfide (CdS) have sensitivity curves that closely match the sensitivity of the human eye. Accordingly, they are useful in applications involving human light perception such as headlight dimmers and intensity adjustments on information displays. These sensors can be designed for measuring microwatts to milliwatts of optical power and are very inexpensive at high volume (less than $0.10 each). These characteristics make CdS photoconductors the sensor of choice in applications such as street light control and in the toy industry where economy is a major consideration. There are, however, considerations that limit the use of CdS photoconductors in more sophisticated applications requiring sensitivities over a wide spectral range, small variations between individual parts, or no history-dependent response. The resistance of these sensors depends on the thick-film microstructure, so the resistance specification has a wide tolerance – a max/min ratio of 3 is not uncommon. The resistance also has long term memory which depends, at any given time, on the amount of light actually incident on the sensor plus the sensor light history for the past several days.

Photoconductors made from materials other than CdS such as lead telluride and mercury cadmium telluride are also available. These materials have spectral sensitivities that cover the range that photodiodes cannot: above 2 ìm out to 15 ìm. This longer wavelength sensitivity is very important for infrared imaging cameras and for long wave instrumentation such as is used to monitor carbon dioxide laser emission and atmospheric physics. Hence sensors tend to be more expensive than both silicon photodiodes and CdS photoconductors.

Integrated Circuits: Incorporating additional electronics directly onto a semiconductor sensor chip makes it possible to add additional functions to the sensor. An optical IC is an integrated circuit comprising photodiode and electronic-signal-processing-circuits. Such additional functions as current-to-voltage conversion and reference-level sensing (a Schmitt trigger, for example) can be incorporated. Other optical ICs can provide signals highly immune to noise, such as a current-to-frequency conversion. The principal advantages of an optical IC are ease of use, small size and immunity to electronic noise compared to a photodiode with separate electronics. Typically these devices are much more expensive and offer a very limited active light-sensing area. Custom tooling for specific applications is also expensive.

Hybrids: The electronic functions of an optical IC can also be provided by a hybrid circuit that has unpackaged IC components (die) attached to a substrate that also contains a photodiode. This type of sensor combines the ease of use and immunity to electrical noise of an optical IC with increased design flexibility and lower tooling costs. In addition, the sensitivity can easily be increased with a larger photodiode active area without the added cost of a separate detector. The primary disadvantages of a hybrid sensor are its cost and reliability. Cost can be several times higher than the electronic-assembly option discussed below and reliability testing is difficult to amortize, so either limited reliability screening is implemented, or the piece cost becomes high.

Sensor Electronic Assemblies: Combining any of the sensors listed above with printed-circuit-based electronic signal processing creates sensor assemblies or black boxes. The user defines specifications for light input and the desired output response; the vendor builds and tests the systems to ensure that the specifications are met. An assembly can also include optical components such as lenses and special wavelength filters. The user just bolts the assembly in place and connects it to the high-level electronics; there are no concerns about mismatch between the purchased sensor and front-end amplifiers or diagnostic electronics. The system is relatively immune from noise and is highly reliable because of the mature manufacturing technologies used. Sensor electronic assemblies are easy to implement. Experienced vendors can often deliver better reliability and lower cost products compared to an OEMs in-house manufacturing. Less flexibility in making changes on the fly is the main disadvantage, but this is not an issue for a responsive vendor or mature designs.

Other Sensors: There are many other types of sensors. These include avalanche photodiodes, bolometers, self-scanned arrays and photon drag detectors. A sensor vendor can provide information about these devices and can discuss the physics and advantages of each detector technology.

Selecting a Sensor: Reviewing a few key design aspects generally provides enough information for making an optimum choice of detector for a given application (see Figure)

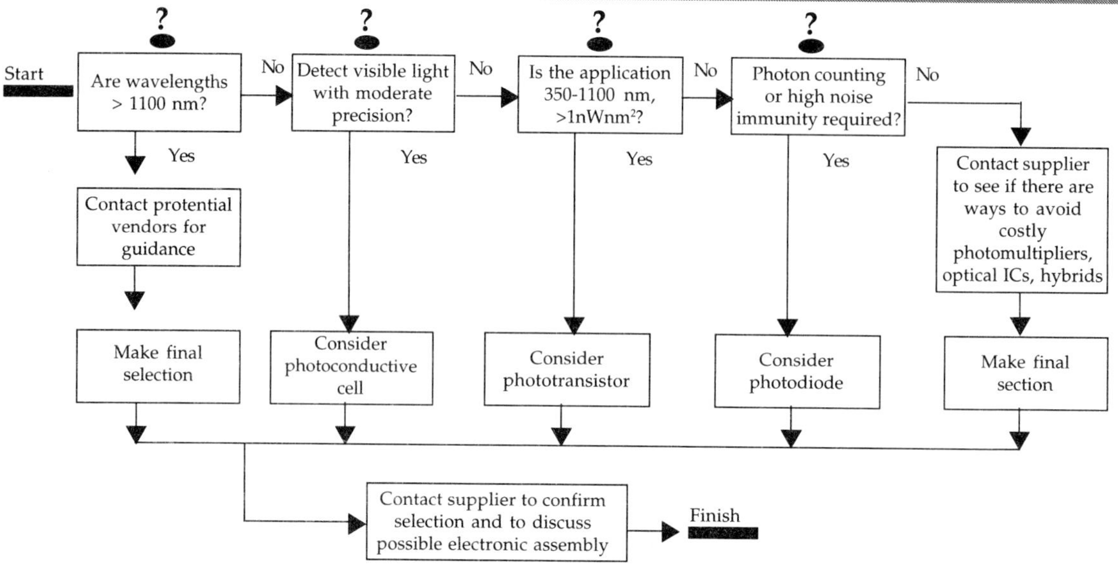

Is my light in the infrared?

For sensing of wavelengths below 1100 nm, photoconductive cells or a silicon-based detector should be appropriate. At wavelengths above 1100 nm, the costs and technology options are not straightforward, and a detector vendor consulted at the beginning of a design program will provide the most effective guidance.

Do I have plenty of light in the visible region?

Applications at visible wavelengths with at least microwatts of optical power, in which the sensor is simply required to detect if light is present, can use one of the least expensive and most rugged detectors available - the photoconductive cell. There are many standard devices available as well as custom-design options including complete electronic assemblies.

Do I have nanowatts of power?

Silicon phototransistors and photodarlingtons; the second-lowest-cost sensors, are also convenient and should be considered next. At least nanowatts of optical power within a 5 mm diameter spot are required at wavelengths between 350 and 1100nm. The application must also tolerate some unit-to-unit sensitivity variation.

Should I consider a higher performance photodiode?

For UV to near IR wavelengths, photodiodes offer the best overall performance. They are only slightly more expensive than phototransistors, but their spectral range is broader and they have lower noise, more uniform sensitivity and reproducibility, a larger dynamic range, better linearity and more package options. Also, photodiodes can routinely detect picowatts of optical power. Thus, if phototransistors or photoconductive cells are not appropriate for an application, more often than not a photodiode will afford the best alternative.

Other Options

At least 90% of detector applications should be satisfied by one of the sensors discussed above. However, when light levels are extremely low, or ambient electronic noise levels are high, or space requirements are particularly limited, other alternatives, such as optical ICs, hybrids or photomultipliers should be seriously investigated.

What's next?

After selection, develop a partnership with your opto sensor manufacturer. The manufacturer is the sensor expert, and working together usually results in a successful project design. Most important, supply the vendor with specific application information about technical specifications, ambient light levels, operating lifetime, operation and storage environment, project schedules, anticipated production volumes and cost targets for tooling and unit price objectives. And remember to discuss the electronic assembly operation – you could reduce costs and improve performance! With this information the sensor vendor can help a system designer make informed decisions after considering trade-offs between reliability, technical performance and cost.

Annexure 1

SI Units and Conversion Factors

Introduction

The "Systeme International d'Unites" – The International System of Units abbreviated as SI was formally recognised by the General Conference on Weights and Measures in 1960. Most of the countries in the world have subsequently decided to adopt SI units.

The salient features of the SI units are:

1. **Comprehensive** Only 7 base units and 2 supplementary units to cover the entire spectrum of science and engineering as listed in Table A.7-1
2. **Coherent** Product or quotient of the units of two or more quantities comprises the unit of the resultant quantity. Coherence of the derived units is observed in Table A. 7-2 whereas that for the physical quantities in Table A. 7-3
3. **Rational** It absorbs the rationalised MKS system and also the multiples and submultiples concept as given in Table A. 7-4
4. **Brief** The symbol and punctuation in writing the abbreviation of the units are standardised for the sake of complete uniformity and consistency of brevity.

Table 1: SI base units

Base Units	*Unit Symbol*	*Dimensions*	*Physical Quantity*
kilogram	kg	M	mass
metre	m	L	length
second	s	T	time
degree kelvin	K	t	temperature
ampere	A	I	current
candela	cd		luminous intensity
mole	mol		amount of substance
Supplementary Units			
radian	rad	-	plane angle
steradian	sr	-	solid angle

Definitions of the base and the supplementary units

kilogram (kg)	The kilogram is the unit of mass equal to the mass of the international prototype of the cylinder at Sevres.
metre (m)	The metre is the length equal to 1 650 763.73 wavelengths in vacuum of the radiation corresponding to the transition between the levels $2p_{10}$ and $5d_5$ of the krypton-86 atom.
second (s)	The second is the duration of 9 192 631 770 periods of the radiation corresponding to the transition between the two hyperfine levels of the ground state of the caesium-133 atom.
kelvin	The kelvin, unit of thermodynamic temperature, is the fraction 1/273.16 of the thermodynamic temperature of the triple point of water.
ampere (A)	The ampere is that constant current which, if maintained in two straight parallel conductors of infinite length, of negligible circular cross-section, and placed 1 metre apart in vacuum, would produce between these conductors a force equal to $2x10^{-7}$ newton per metre length.
candela (cd)	The candela is the luminous intensity, in the perpendicular direction, of a surface of 1/600 000 square metre of a black body at the temperature of freezing platinum under a pressure of 101 325 newton per square metre.
mole (mol)	The mole is the amount of substance of a system which contains as many elementary entities as there are atoms in 0.012 kilogram of carbon 12.
radian (rad)	The radian is the plane angle between two radii of a circle which cut off on the circumference an arc equal in length to the radius.
steradian (sr)	The steradian is the solid angle which, having its vertex in the centre of a sphere cuts off an area of the surface of the sphere equal to that of a square having sides of length equal to the radius of the sphere.

Table 2 : SI derived units with new names

Derived Unit	*Unit Symbol*	*Physical Quantity*
newton	J = NM = kgm^2/s^2	force
joule	J = Nm = kg m^2 / s^2	energy, work, heat
watt	W = J / s = Nm / s = kg m^2 / s^3	power
pascal	Pa = N/m^2 = kg/ms^2	pressure, stress
hertz	Hz = S^{-1}	frequency

volt	V = W/A	potential
ohm	Ω = V/A=W/A^2	resistance
coulomb	C = As	charge
farad	F = As/V = A^2s/W	capacitance
weber	Wb = As/V = A^2s/W	magnetic flux
henry	H = Vs/A = Ws/A^2	inductance
siemen	S = V/A = W/A^2	conductance
tesla	T = Wb/ m^2 = Vs/ m^2 = Ws/ Am^2	magnetic induction
lumen	Im = cdsr	luminous flux
lux	Im/m^2 = cd sr / m^2	illuminance

Definitions

newton N(=kgm/s^2) — The newton is that force which, when applied to a mass of 1 kilogram gives it an acceleration of 1 metre per second squared.

joule J (=Nm) — The joule is the work done when the point of application of a force of 1 newton is displaced through a distance of 1 metre in the direction of the force.

watt W (=J/s) — The watt is the power which in 1 second gives rise to energy of 1 joule.

hertz Hz(= s^{-1}) — The hertz is the number of repetitions of a regular occurrence in 1 second.

pascal Pa(=N/m^2) — The pascal is the pressure produced by a force of 1 newton applied, uniformly distributed, over an area of 1 square metre.

poise P (=g/cms) — The poise is a non-SI unit of viscosity. The coherent SI unit is Pas=kg/ms=Ns/m^2 which is 10 times larger than the poise.

stoke St (=cm^2/s) — The stoke is a non-SI unit of kinematic viscosity. The coherent SI unit is m^2/s which is 10^4 times larger than the stoke.

Notes:

A. Note that kilogram is written as kg, not kgm, not kgf etc. Similarly second as s, not sec or sec. etc. *No fullstops, No plurals, No dots, No dashes.* For example, torque is in Nm, not N.m, not N-m etc.

B. The unit of force is newton with symbol N and there is no such thing as kilogram force in SI units. Just N and its multiples and submultiples. Whether the energy is in electrical, mechanical, optical or any other form, the unit is joule,

symbol J=Nm

similarly power is referred to as watt, symbol W irrespective of form.

No horsepower. No metric horsepower. Just watt,

W = J/s = Nm/s

and its multiples and submultiples.

C. Always leave a space between the number and the unit symbol, e.g., 23.2 cm and 2500 N.

D. For numbers less than unity, zero must be put on the left of the decimal and for larger numbers exceeding five figures one space after every three digits counting from the right end must be left blank without any commas, e.g., 0.23 cm and 15 232 756 are the correct ways of writing these numbers.

E. SI Units are the easiest for numerical and practical purposes, when used all by themselves. However, confusions arise because of mixing of MKS and SI units. Reference to the Conversion Table 5 will be found useful.

Table 3 : SI Units of Common Physical Quantities

Physical Quantity	*Unit*	*Unit Symbol*	*Dimensions*
Acceleration	metre/second^2	m/s^2	LT^{-2}
Angular acceleration	radian/second^2	rad/s^2	T^2
Angular displacement	radian	rad	–
Angular momentum	kilogram metre^2/second	kgm^2/s	ML^2T^{-1}
Angular velocity	radian/second	rad/s	T^{-1}
Area	square metre	m^2	L^2
Calorific value	joule/metre^3	J/m^3	$ML^{-1}T^2$
Capacitance	farad	F(= As/V)	$I^2T^1M^{-1}L^{-2}$
Charge	coulomb	C(≡As)	IT
Circulation	metre^2/second	m^2/s	L^2T^{-1}
Concentration	kilogram/metre^2	kg/m^3	ML^{-3}
Conductance (electrical)	siemen (mho)	S(≡A/V)	$I^2T^3M^{-1}L^{-2}$
Conductance (thermal)	watt/metre^2 kelvin	W/m^{2}K	$MT^{-3}t^{-1}$
Conductivity	mho/metre	S/m	$I^2T^3M^{-1}L^{-3}$

Physical Quantity	*Unit*	*Unit Symbol*	*Dimensions*
Conductivity /thermal)	watt/metre kelvin	W/mK	$MLT^{-3}t^{-1}$
Current	ampere	A	I
Density	kilogram/metre^3	kg/m^3	ML^{-3}
Discharge	metre^3/second	m^3/s	L^3T^{-1}
Displacement	metre	m	L
Electrical dipole mom.	coulomb metre	p(≡Cm)	ITL
Electrical field strength	volts/metre	V/m	$MLT^{-3}I^{-1}$
Electrical flux density	coulomb/metre^2	C/m^2	ITL^{-2}
Electrical polarisation	coulomb/metre^2	C/m^2	ITL^{-2}
Energy Enthalpy	joule	J(≡Nm)	NK^3T^{-2}
Entropy	joule/kilogram kelvin	J/kgK	L^2T^{-2}t-1
Force	newton	N(≡kg m/s^2)	MLT^2
Frequency	per second	Hz (≡/s)	T^{-1}
Heat	joule	J(≡Nm)	ML^2T^{-2}
Illuminance	lux	IX (≡Im/m^2)	
Inductance	henry	H(≡ Vs/A)	$ML^2T^{-2}I^{-1}$
Length	metre	m	L
Luminance	candela/metre^2	cd/m^2	
Luminous flux	lumen	Im(≡ cd sr)	
Luminous intensity	candela	cd	
Magnetic field strength	ampere turns /metre	A/m	IL^{-1}
Magnetic flux	weber	WB (≡VS)	$ML^2T^{-2}I^{-1}$
Magnetic flux density	weber/metre^2	WB/m^2	MT-$^2I^{-1}$
Magnetic induction	tesla	T(≡Wb/m^2)	MT^2I-^{1}
Magnetic moment	weber metre	Wbm	$ML^3T^{-2}I^{-1}$
Magnetisation intensity	weber/metre^2	Wb/m^2	$MT^{-2}I^{-1}$
Mass	kilogram	kg	M
Moduli of elasticity	newton/metre^2	Pa(≡N/m^2)	$ML^{-1}T^{-2}$
Moment	newton metre	Nm	ML^2T^{-2}
Momentum	kilogram metre/second	kgm/s	MLT^{-1}
Moment of inertia	kilogram metre^2	kgm^2	ML^2
Permeability	henry/metre	H/m	$MLT^{-2}I^{-2}$
Permittivity	farad/metre	F/m	$I^2T^4M^{-1}L^{-3}$

Physical Quantity	*Unit*	*Unit Symbol*	*Dimensions*
Plane angle	radian	rad	
Potential	volt	V(≡W/A)	$ML^3T^{-3}I^{-1}$
Power, Radiation flux	watt	W(≡Nm/s)	ML^2T^{-3}
Pressure, Stress	newton/metre^2	Pa(≡ N/m^2)	$ML^{-1}T^{-2}$
Resistance	ohm	Ω (≡V/A)	$ML^2T^{-3}I^{-2}$
Resistivity	ohm-metre	Ω m	$ML^3T^{-3}I^{-2}$
Solid angle	steradian	sr	
Specific energy and Specific enthalpy	joule/kilogram	J/Kg	L^2T^{-2}
Specific volume	kilogram/metre^3	kg/m^3	ML^{-3}
Specific heat	joule/kilogram K	J/kgK	$L^2T^{-2}t^{-1}$
Speed	metre/second	m/s	LT^{-1}
Stream function	metre^2/second	m^2/s	L^2T^{-1}
Surface tension	newton/metre	N/m	MT^{-2}
Temperature	kelvin	K	t
Time	second	s	T
Thermal capacity	joule/kilogram K	J/kgK	$L^2T^{-2}t^{-1}$
Torque	newton metre	Nm	ML^2T^{-2}
Velocity	metre/second	m/s	LT^{-1}
Velocity potential	metre^z/second	m^2/s	L^2T^{-1}
Viscosity (dynamic)	newton second/metre^2 or kilogram/metre second	Ns/m^2 (≡Pas) kg/ms	$ML^{-1}T^{-1}$
Viscosity (kinematic)	metre^2/second	m^2/s	L^2T^{-1}
Volume	metre^3	m^3	L^3
Weight	newton	N(≡kg m/s^2)	MLT^{-2}
Work	joule	J (≡Nm)	ML^2T^{-2}

Table 4 : Multiples and Submultiples

tera	T	10^{12}	milli	m	10^{-3}
giga	G	10^9	micro	μ	10^{-6}
mega	M	10^6	nano	n	10^{-9}
kilo	k	10^3	pico	P	10^{-12}
deci	d	10^{-1}	femto	f	10^{-15}
centi	c	10^{-2}	atto	a	10^{-18}

Table 5 : Conversion Tables

To Convert the following	*Into SI*	*Multiply by*	*Conversely, multiply by*
LENGTH (m, km, cm, mm, nautical miles acceptable in SI)			
feet	m	0.3048	3.2808
inches	cm	2.5400	0.3937
miles	km	1.6093	0.6214
miles, nautical	km	1.852	0.540
yards	m	0.9144	1.0936
mils	m	$25.4 x 10^{-6}$	$39.37 x 10^{3}$
micron	m	10^{-6}	10^{6}
angstrom	m	10^{-10}	10^{10}
links (surveyor's)	m	0.2012	4.972
chains	m	10.12	$4.972 x 10^{-2}$
AREA			
$feet^2$	m^2	0.0929	10.764
$inch^2$	cm^2	6.542	0.1550
acres	m^2	$4.047 x 10^{3}$	$2.471 X 10^{-4}$
$yards^2$	m^2	0.8361	1.196
circular mils	mm^2	$0.5067 x 10^{-3}$	$1.973 x 10^{3}$
are(a)	m^2	100	0.01
hectare (ha)	m^2	10^{4}	10^{-4}
VOLUME			
$feet^3$	m^3	0.0283	35.3147
$inch^3$	cm^3	16.387	0.0610
$yard^3$	m^3	0.7646	1.308
bushels	m^3	0.0363	27.50
gallons	m^3	$4.546 x 10^{-3}$	$0.2199 x 10^{3}$
gallons (US)	m^3	$3.785 x 10^{-3}$	$0.2642 x 10^{3}$
litres (I)	m^3	10^{-0}	10^{3}
hectolitres	m^3	0.1	10
mililitres (ml)	m^3	10^{-6}	10^{6}
pints	m^3	0.000 568	1760
quarts	m^3	$1.136 x 10^{-3}$	879.9
barrels (US)	m^3	0.1590	6.2893

To Convert the following	*Into SI*	*Multiply by*	*Conversely, multiply by*
acre feet	m^3	1233.5	$0.811x10^3$
fluid ounces	cm^3	28.41	0.0352
ANGLE (rad.sr and degrees to be used as appropriate)			
degrees	rad	0.017 453	57.2958
minutes	rad	0.000 291	$3.436x10^3$
seconds	rad	0.000 004 8	$0.2083x10^6$
MASS (kg, Mg, g, mg, t and carat acceptable			
grams	kg	10^{-3}	10^3
quintals	kg	100	0.01
pounds	kg	0.4536	2.2046
tons	kg	1016.0	$9.842X10^{-6}$
tonnes (t)	kg	10^3	10^{-3}
slug	kg	14.59	0.0685
slug (metric)	kg	9.807	0.1020
grain	g	0.0648	15.432
carat	g	0.2	5.0
ounce (oz)	g	23.8	0.035
stone	kg	6.35	
hundredweight (cwt)	kg	50.8	
long ton	ton	0.98	1.016
short ton	ton	1.1	0.907
VELOCITY AND ACCELERATION (m/s, km/h, knots, Hz, rad/s, m/s^2 and rad/s^2 acceptable in SI)			
feet/second	m/s	0.3048	3.281
miles/hour	m/s	0.447	2.237
miles/hour	km/h	1.609	0.6213
knots	m/s	0.5144	1.943
r.p.m.	rad/s	0.1047	9.550
r.p.m.p.s.	rad/s^2	0.1047	9.550
c. p. s. (cycles/ second	Hz	1	1
DENSITY AND SPECIFIC VOLUME (kg/m^2, g/cm^2, m^3/kg acceptable			
$grams/cm^3$	kg/m^3	10^3	10^{-3}
$pounds/foot^3$	kg/m^3	16.03	0.0624

To Convert the following	*Into SI*	*Multiply by*	*Conversely, multiply by*
pounds/inch^3	kg/cm^3	27.679x10^{-3}	0.0361
feet^3/pound	m^3/kg	0.0624	16.02
gallons/pound	cm^3/kg	0.010	100
DISCHARGE (m^3/s, I/s, kg/s acceptable in SI			
cusecs (feet^3/ seconds)	m^3/s	0.02832	35.33
cumecs (metre^3/sec.)	m^3/s	1	1
gpm (gallons/ minute)	cm^3/s	0.0758x10^{-3}	13.20x10^7
litres/second (l/s)	m^3/s	10^{-3}	10^3
pounds/sec.	kg/s	0.4536	2.204
tons/hour	kg/s	0.282	3.546
FORCE AND WEIGHT (N, kN, MN, μN and mN acceptable in SI			
dynes	N	10^{-5}	10^5
kgf	N	9.807	0.1020
lb_f	N	4.448	0.2248
poundals	N	0.1383	7.233
tonf	kN	9.964	0.1003
PRESSURE, STRESS AND ELASTIC MODULI (Pa, kPa, MPa, GPa, bar, mPa and μPa acceptable in SI)			
kgf/metre^2	Pa (≡N/m^2)	9.807	0.1020
kg_f/cm^2	kPa(= kN/m^2	98.07	0.0102
bar	kPa	100	0.01
atm (atmospheres)	kPa	101.325	9.869x10^{-3}
at (technical atmospheres)	kPa	98.07	0.0102
psi (Ibf/inch^2)	kPa	6.895	0.145
psf (Ibf/foot^2)	Pa	47.88	0.0209
dynes/cm^2	Pa	0.1	10
tonf/inch^2	MPa	15.44	0.0647
feet of water	kPa	2.989	0.3345
inches of water	kPa	0.249	4.016
torr (mm of mercury)	kPa	0.1333	7.501
inches of mercury	kPa	3.386	0.2953
ENERGY, WORK AND HEAT (J, kJ, MJ, mJ and kWh acceptable in SI)			
kg, metres	J (≡Nm)	9.807	0.1020

To Convert the following	*Into SI*	*Multiply by*	*Conversely, multiply by*
ergs	J	10^{-7}	10^{7}
foot pounds	J	1.356	0.7376
kilowatt hours	M J	3.6	0.2778
therms	M J	105.51	0.0094
calories	J	4.187	0.2388
horse power hours	M J	2.685	0.3724
Btu	kJ	1.055	0.9478
Chu	kJ	1.900	0.526
POWER (W, kW, MW, GW, mW and μW acceptable in SI)			
ergs/second	W(≡Nm/ s≡ J/s)	10^{-7}	10^{7}
foot Ib/second	W	1.356	0.7376
horse power	kW	0.7457	1.341
horse power (metric)	kW	0.7355	1.360
kilocalories/ minute	W	69.77	0.0143
TORQUE AND MOMENT (Nm, kNm, MNm and μNm acceptable in SI)			
kgf metres	Nm	9.807	0.1020
Ibf feet	Nm	1.356	0.7374
Ibf inches	Nm	0.1130	8.850
tonf inches	Nm	3.0370	0.3622
MOMENTUM AND ANGULAR MOMENTUM (kgm/s and kgm²/s respectively acceptable in SI)			
Ib foot/second	kgm/s	0.1383	7.230
Ib foot²/second	kgm²/s	0.0421	23.75
MOMENT OF INERTIA (kgm² acceptable in SI)			
Ib foot²	kgm²	0.0421	23.75
Ib inch²	kgm²	0.2926×10^{3}	3.417×10^{3}
slug foot²	kgm²	1.3558	0.7375
CONCENTRATION (kg/m³ and g/m³ acceptable in SI)			
grams/litre	kg/m³	1	1
Ib/foot³	kg/m³	6.236	0.1603
grains/gallon	g/m³	14.254	0.0701
VISCOSITY, Dynamic and Kinematic (Ns/m² = kg/ms = Pas, p, cP and cST recommend			
poise (gram/ cm Second) (P)	kg/ms (≡Ns/m²)		0.1 10

To Convert the following	*Into SI*	*Multiply by*	*Conversely, multiply by*
centipoise (cP)	Ns/m^2	0.001	1000
kgf sec/metre^2	Ns/m^2	9.807	0.1020
slug/foot sec.	kg/ms (≡Pas)	47.88	0.0209
Ibf sec/foot^2	Ns/m^2	47.88	2.089x10^{-2}
Ibf sec/inch^2	Ns/m^2	6895	1.45X10^{-4}
stokes (centimetre^2/sec) (St)	m^2/s	10^{-4}	10^4
centistokes (cSt)	m^2/s	10^{-6}	10^6
foot^2/second	m^2/s	0.0929	10.76
Inch^2/second	m^2/s	6.45x10^{-4}	1550
THERMAL QUANTITIES Thermal Conductivity: (W/m°C recommended)			
Btu/ft^2 hour (°F/inch)	W/m°C	0.1442	6.940
Btu/ft^2 hour (°F/ft)	W/m°C	1.7307	0.5778
kcal/m^2 hour°C	W/m°C	1.163	0.8600
HEAT -TRANSFER COEFFICIENT, CONDUCTANCE: (W/m^2 °C recommended)			
Btu/ft^2 hour °F	W/m^2 °C	5.678	0.1760
kcal/m^2 hour °C	W/m^2 °C	1.163	0.8600
Temperature (°C and K used in SI)			
°C	K	ADD 273.15	Subtract 273.15
°F	°C	5(F-32)/9	9/5x°C+32
°F	K	5(F-32)/9+ 273.15	9(K-273.15)/ 5+32
°R	K	5(R-491.) / 9+273.15	9(K-273.15) / 5+491.67
TEMPERATURE INTERVALS IN °C AND K ARE USED INTER CHANGEABLY			
ton of refrigeration	kW	3.517	0.2848
ENTROPY, SPECIFIC HEAT, LATENT HEAT: (kJ/kg and kJ(kgK recommended)			
Btu/lb °R	kJ/kg K	4.187	0.2388
Btu/lb	kJ/kg	2.326	0.4299
kcalorie/kg	kJ/kg	4.187	0.2388
kcalorie/kg°C	kJ/kg K	4.187	0.2388
THERMAL CAPACITY, CALORIFIC VALUE: (kJ/kg°C, kJ7m^3 °C and kJ/m^3 recommended)			
kcal/kg °C	kJ/kg °C	4.187	0.2388
kcal/m^2 °C	kJ/m^2 °C	4.187	0.2388

To Convert the following		*Into SI*	*Multiply by*	*Conversely, multiply by*
$kcal/m^3$		kJ/m^3	4.187	0.2388
ELECTRICAL QUANTITIES				
oersted, field strength		A/m	$1000/4\pi$	$4\pi X10^{-3}$
maxwell, flux		Wb	10^{-8}	10^{8}
gauss, flux density		T	10^{-4}	10^{4}
kilovolt/inch, stress		kV/m	39.37	0.0254
emu	current		10	0.1
esu	current	A	0.1c	10/c
emu	potential		10^{-8}	10^{8}
esu	potential	V	$10^{-6}c$	$10^{6}/c$
emu	charge		10	0.1
esu	charge	C	0.1c	10/c
emu	power			
esu	power	W	10^{-7}	10^{7}
emu	resistance		10^{-9}	10^{9}
esu	resistance	Ω	$10^{-5}c^2$	$10^{5}/c^2$
emu	conductance		10^{9}	10^{-9}
esu	conductance	S	$10^{5}/c^2$	$10^{-5}/c^2$
emu	inductance		10^{-9}	10^{9}
esu	inductance	H	$10^{-5}/c^2$	$10^{5}/c^2$
emu	capacitance		10^{9}	10^{-9}
esu	capacitance	F	$10^{5}/c^2$	$10^{-5}c^2$
emu	flux density		10^{5}	10^{-5}
esu	flux density	C/m^2	$10^{3}/c$	$10^{-3}c$
esu	permittivity	F/m	$10^{7}/4\pi\ c^2$	$4\pi c^2 x10^{-7}$
esu	permeability	H/m	$4\pi x10^{-7}$	$10^{7}/4\pi$

To Convert the following	*Into SI*	*Multiply by*	*Conversely, multiply by*
emu magnetisation esu	A/m	10^3 $10/c$	10^{-3} 0.1c
emu displacement esu	C/m^2	$10^5/4\pi$	$4\pi x10^{-5}$ $4\pi x10^{-3}$
OPTICAL QUANTITIES			
lumens / sq. feet	Ix (≡lm/m^2)	10.764	0.0929
foot candles	Ix	10.764	0.0929
candles / sq. foot	cd/m^2	10.764	0.0929
candles / sq. inch	cd/m^2	1550	0.6451x10^3
foot lamberts	cd/m^2	3.426	0.2918
MISCELLANEOUS QUANTITIES			
million electron volts	kWh	4.44x10^{-20}	2.252x10^{-19}
electron volts	J	16022x10^{-19}	6.241x10^{-18}
atomic mass units	kg	16605x10^{-27}	6.022x10^{-26}
pH valu (= $-\log_{10}$ CH_{30})	pH	1	1
astronomical units	m	0.1496x10^{12}	6.6844x10^{-12}
light years	m	1.4605x10^{15}	0.1057x10^{-15}
angstrom	m	10^{-10}	10^{10}
barns	m^2	10^{-28}	10^{28}
curies	s^{-1}	3.7x10^{10}	0.2703x10^{-10}
rads	J/kg	0.01	100
rontgens	C/kg	2.58x10^{-4}	3875
gals	m/s^2	0.01	100
lusecs	μNm/s	133.32	7.502x10^{-3}
torre/second	Nm/s	0.1333	7.5018
frigorie	kJ	4.1855	0.239
sthene	N	1000	10^{-3}

Table 6 : Physical Constants

Constant quality	*Symbol*	*Value*	*SI Units*
(a) Atomic and Nuclear			
Electron rest mass	m_e	$9.1085 x 10^{-31}$	kg
Electron rest energy	$m_e c^2$	$8.1873 x 10^{-14}$	J
Specific charge on an electron	e/m_e	$1.7588 x 10^{-11}$	C/kg
Compton electron wavelength	λ_e	$2.4263 x 10^{-12}$	m
Classical electron radius	γ_e	$2.8180 x 10^{-15}$	m
Charge on an electron	e	$1.6022 x 10^{-12}$	C
Proton / electron mass ratio	$m_o m_e$	1836	-
Proton rest mass	m_o	$1.6724 x 10^{-27}$	kg
Proton rest energy	$m_o c^2$	$1.5033 x 10^{-10}$	J
Specific charge on a proton	e/m_o	$9.5790 x 13^{-15}$	C/kg
Compton proton wavelength	λ_{en}	$1.3214 x 10^{-15}$	m
Gyromagnetic ratio	γ	$2.6752 x 10^{-8}$	/ST
Neutron rest mass	m_o	$1.6748 x 10^{-27}$	kg
Neutron rest energy	$m_o c^2$	$1.5053 x 10^{-10}$	J
Bohr magneton	μ	$9.2741 x 10^{-21}$	J/T
Bohr radius	a_o	$5.2917 x 10^{-11}$	m
Rydberg constant	R_ε	$1.0974 x 10^{-7}$	/m
Zeeman splitting constant	μ/h_c	46.686	/Tm
Magnetic moment of electron	μ_e	$9.284 x 10^{-24}$	J/T
Magnetic moment of proton	μ_o	$1.4106 x 10^{-25}$	J/T
Atomic mass unit	a	$1.6605 x 10^{-27}$	kg
(b) General			
Speed of light in vacuo	c	$2.997\ 925 x 10^{31}$	m/s
Planck's constant	h	$6.6253 x 10^{-34}$	Js
Gravitational constant	G	$6.670 x 10^{-14}$	Nm^2/kg2
Fine structure constant	α	$7.2974 x 10^{-3}$	-
Permittivity constant (free space)	ε	$8.8542 x 10^{-12}$	F/m
Permeability constant (free space)	μ_o	$4\pi x 10^{-7}$	H/m
Impedance constant (free space)	Z_o	$3.7673 x 10-^{2}$	Ω

Faraday's constant	F	9.650×10^{-5}	C/mol
Boltzmann constant	k	1.3806×10^{-23}	J/K
Avagadro's number	N	6.0248×10^{-6}	/kg mol
Stephan's constant	ρ	5.6695×10^{-8}	W/m^2K^4
Universal gas constant	R_o	8.314	J/K mol
Zero celsius (centigrade)	O°c	273.15	K
Triple point of water	tx	273.16	K
(c) Atmospheric and Geophysical			
Characteristic gas constant for air	R_a	287	J/kgK
Mean molecular weight of air	M_a	28.966	-
Mean ICAO air viscosity	μa	1.79×10^{3}	Ns/m^2
Standard atmosphere (pressure)	atm	101.325	kN/m^2
Standard atmosphere (temperature)	T_s	288.15	K
Lapse rate for standard atmosphere	L	6.5	K/km
Mass of atmosphere		5.27×10^{18}	kg
Voltage gradient, fine weather; average		100	V/m
Solar constant for earth	Sc	1400	J/m^2s
Sonic speed in air at S.T.P.	a	340.3	m/s
Gravitational parameter	GM	3.986×10^{-14}	m^3/s^2
Mass of earth	M	5.976×10^{-24}	kg
Standard gravitational acceleration	g_c	9.806 65	m/s^2
Mean radius of the earth	r_m	6371	km
Mean density of the earth	ρ_e	55.17	kg/m^3
Escape velocity at the surface	V_e	11.2	km/s
Rotational velocity at the equator		465	km/s
Mean velocity in the orbit about the sun		29.78	km/s
Approximate age of the earth		4.5×10^{9}	years
Area of land surface		148.9×10^{12}	m^2
Area of water surface		361.2×10^{12}	m^2
Height of Mount Everest		8847.7	m
Depth of Marianas Trench		11.033	km
Seismic wave velocity compressive		8	km/s
Shear		4.5	km/s
Acceleration $g = 9.80616 - 0.025928 \cos 2\lambda + 0.000069 \cos^2 2\lambda - 0.000003\,h$ m/s^2 at a place with latitude and a height h metres above the sea level for the earth.			

TEMPERATURE CONVERSION FACTORS

Temperature

Difference of temperature
1 degree on the Centigrade or Celsius scale (degC)
= 1.8 degrees on the Fahrenheit scale (degF)

Temperature reading on thermometer
0°C = 32°F (water freezing point)
100°C = 212°F (water boiling point)

Calculation of temperature difference
1 degC = 9/5 degF
1 degF = 5/9 degC

Calculation of temperature level
°C = 5/9 x (°F - 32)
°F = 9/5 x °C + 32

Angles and slopes

These are mainly required for sloping roofs, which are generally expressed in degrees, but which are difficult for the worker to measure out on the site. Therefore, roof slopes are best expressed in simple relations between height and span, preferably using round numbers. Since they are difficult to visualize, the approximate relations between some common slopes (given in ratios and percentages) and angles (in degrees) are shown in the following table:

Ratio of slope	*Percentage of slope*	*Angle*
1 : 50	2%	≈ 1°
1 : 25	4%	≈ 2°
1 : 20	5%	≈ 3°
1 : 10	10%	≈ 5.5°
1 : 5	20%	≈ 11.5″
1 : 4	25%	≈ 14°
1 : 3	33.3%	≈ 18.5°
1 : 2	50%	≈ 26.5°
2 : 3	66.7%	≈ 33.5°
3 : 4	75%	≈ 37°
4 : 5	80%	≈ 38.5°
1 : 1	100%	≈ 45°
5 : 4	125%	≈ 51.5°
4 : 3	133.3%	≈ 53°
3 : 2	150%	≈ 56.5°
2 : 1	200%	≈ 63.5°
3 : 1	300%	≈ 71.5°
4 : 1	400%	≈ 76°
5 : 1	500%	≈ 78.5°
10 : 1	1000%	≈ 84.5°

Calorific value of various energy resources

Extra light heating oil	11.9 kWh/l
Natural gas	6.9 - 9.2 kWh/m^3
Liquified petroleum gas (propane, butane)	12.8 kWh/kg
Electricity	1 KWh
Hard coal, charcoal	8.1 kWh/kg
Lignite bricquetts	5.6 kWh/kg
Timber (deciduous tree, 15% ML and 500 kg/m^3	4.1 kWh/kg
Pine wood (15% moisture content, 360 kg/m^3)	4.4 kWh/kg
Wood pieces (30% moisture, 250 kg/m^3)	3.3 kWh/kg
Latent heat: 1 m^3 water on cooling by 1 K	1.16 kWh

Saturation-point humidities

°c	*Moisture Content g/kg*	*Density of Dry Air kg/m³*	*Moisture Content g/m³*
-20	0.63	1.396	0.879
-15	1.01	1.368	1.381
-10	1.60	1.342	2.147
- 5	2.47	1.317	3.253
0	3.78	1.293	4.887
5	5.40	1.270	6.858
10	7.63	1.248	9.522
15	10.6	1.226	12.995
16	11.4	1.222	13.930
17	12.1	1.217	14.727
18	12.9	1.213	15.648
19	13.8	1.209	16.684
20	14.7	1.205	17.713
21	15.6	1.201	18.736
22	16.6	1.197	19.870
23	17.7	1.193	21.116
24	18.8	1.189	22.353
25	20.0	1.185	23.700
26	21.4	1.181	25.273
27	22.6	1.177	26.600
28	24.0	1.173	28.152
29	25.6	1.169	29.962
30	27.2	1.165	31.688
35	36.6	1.146	41.943
40	48.8	1.128	55.046

Annexure-2

Sun Path Diagrams

LATITUDE 15" NORTH

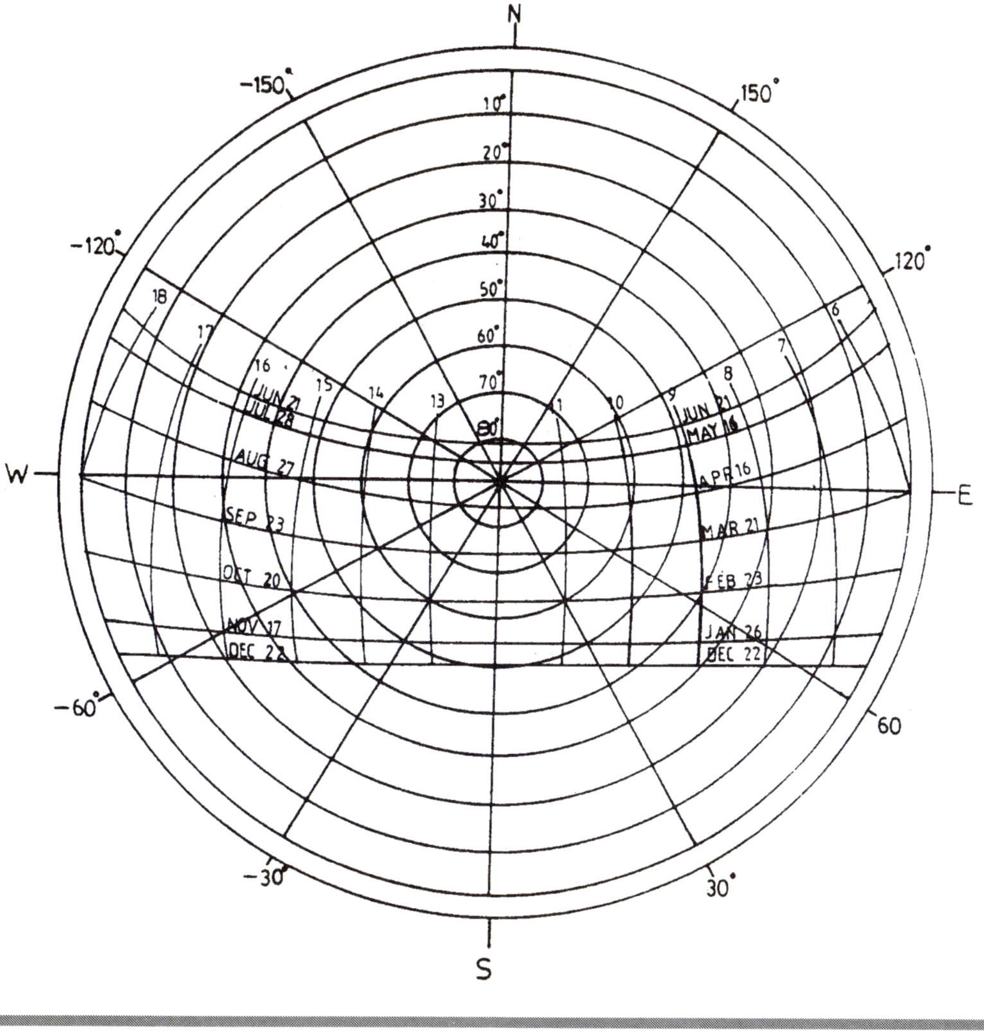

LATITUDE 17" NORTH

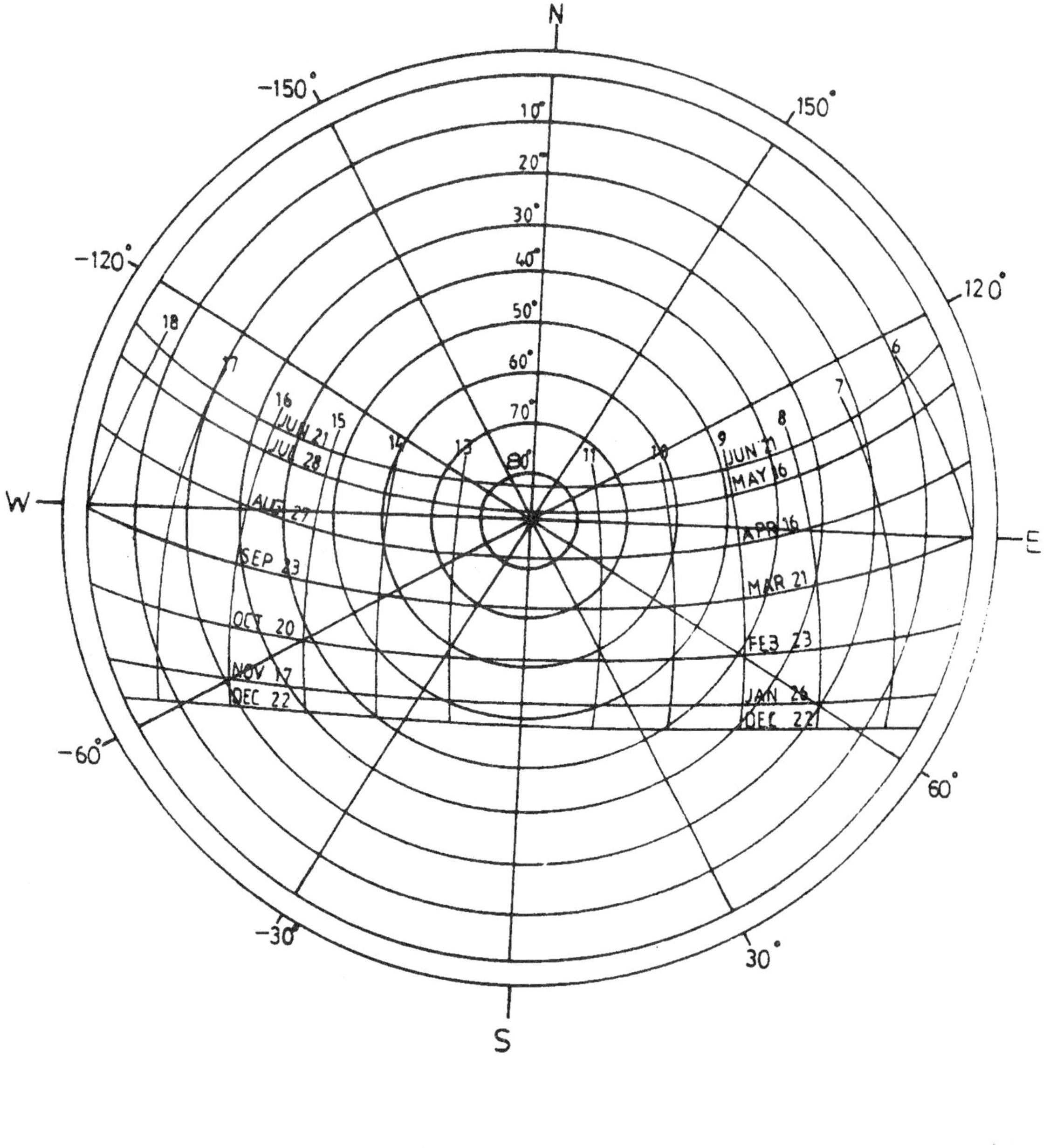

LATITUDE 19" NORTH

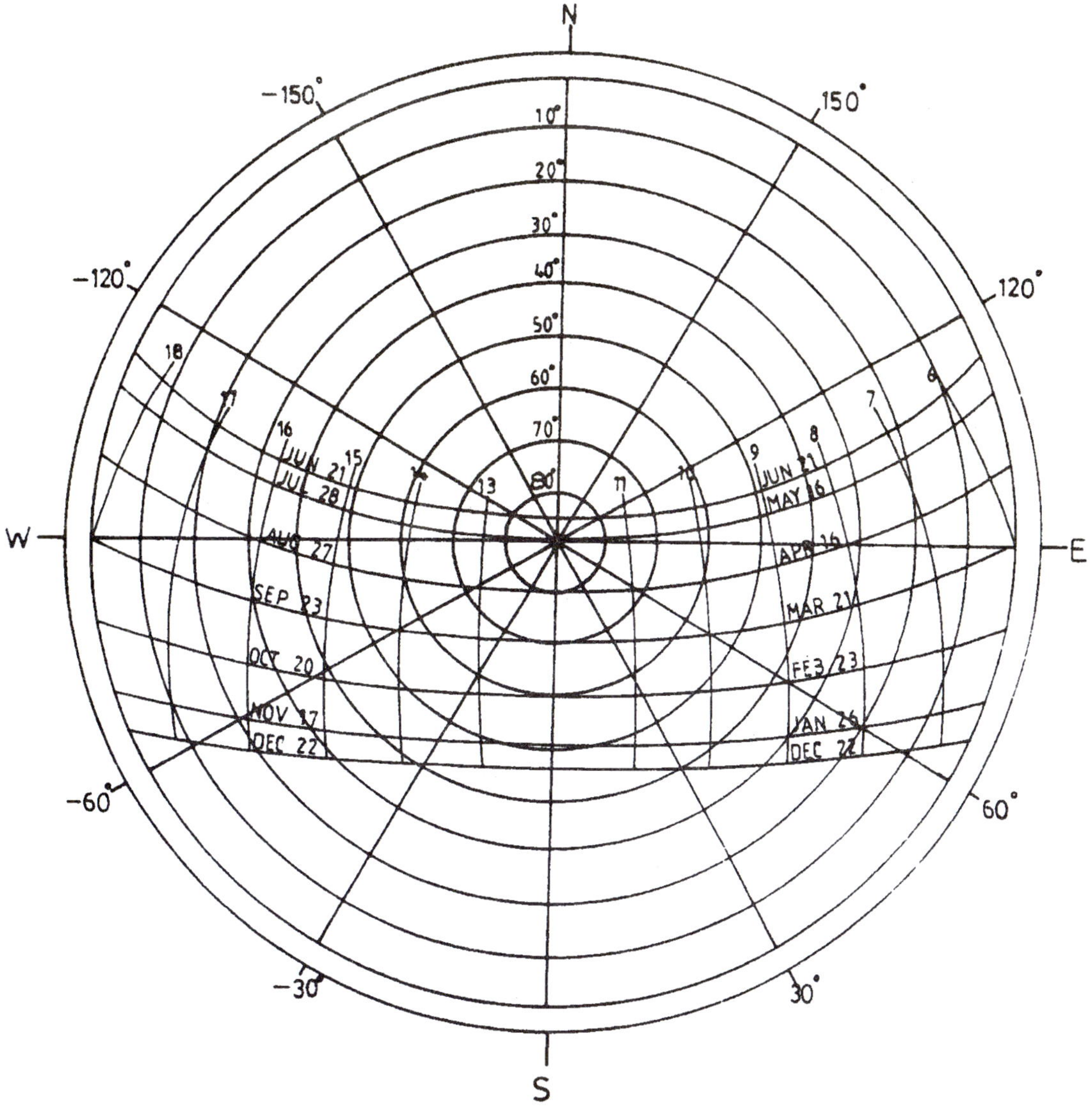

LATITUDE 21" NORTH

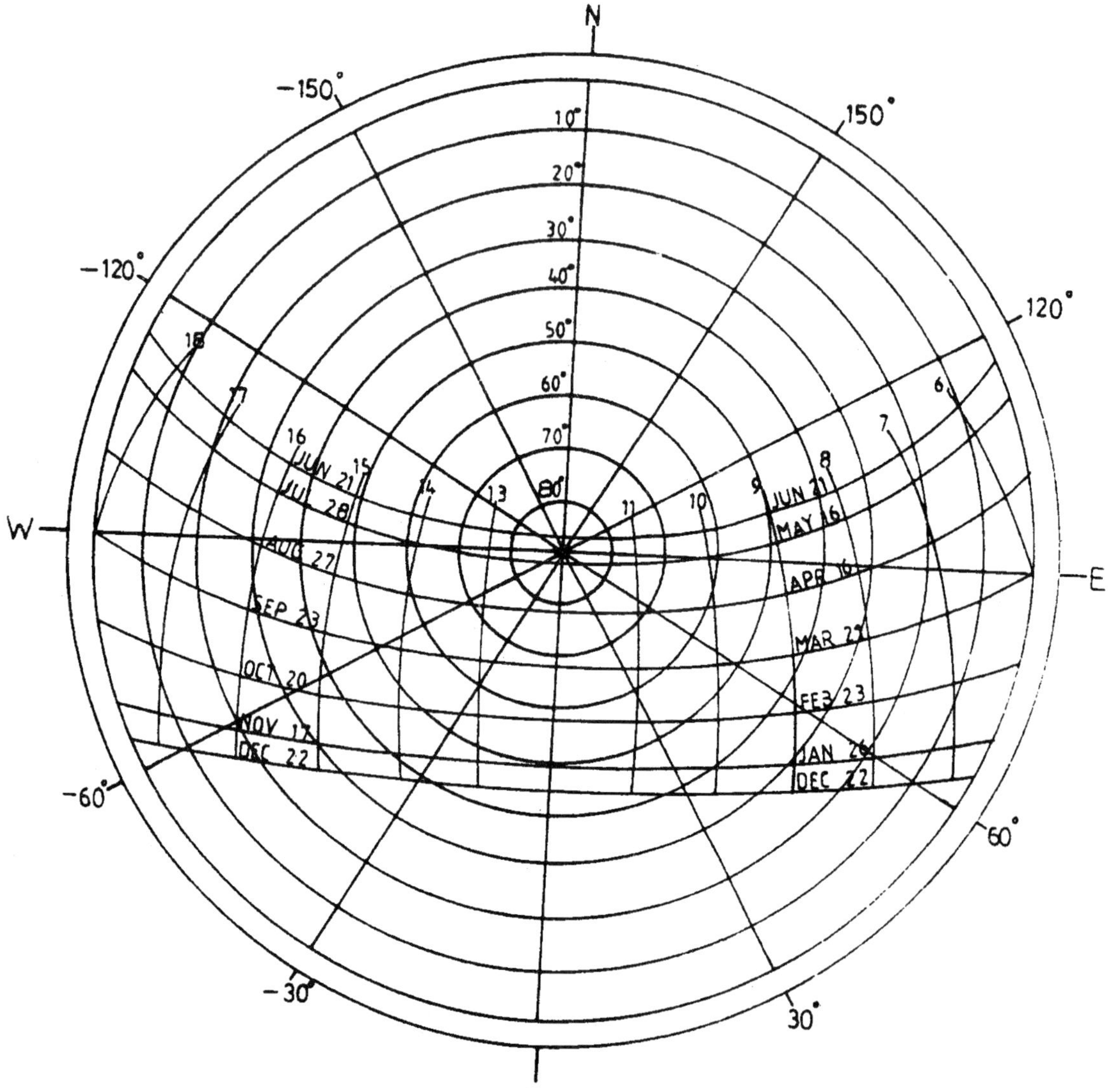

LATITUDE 23" NORTH

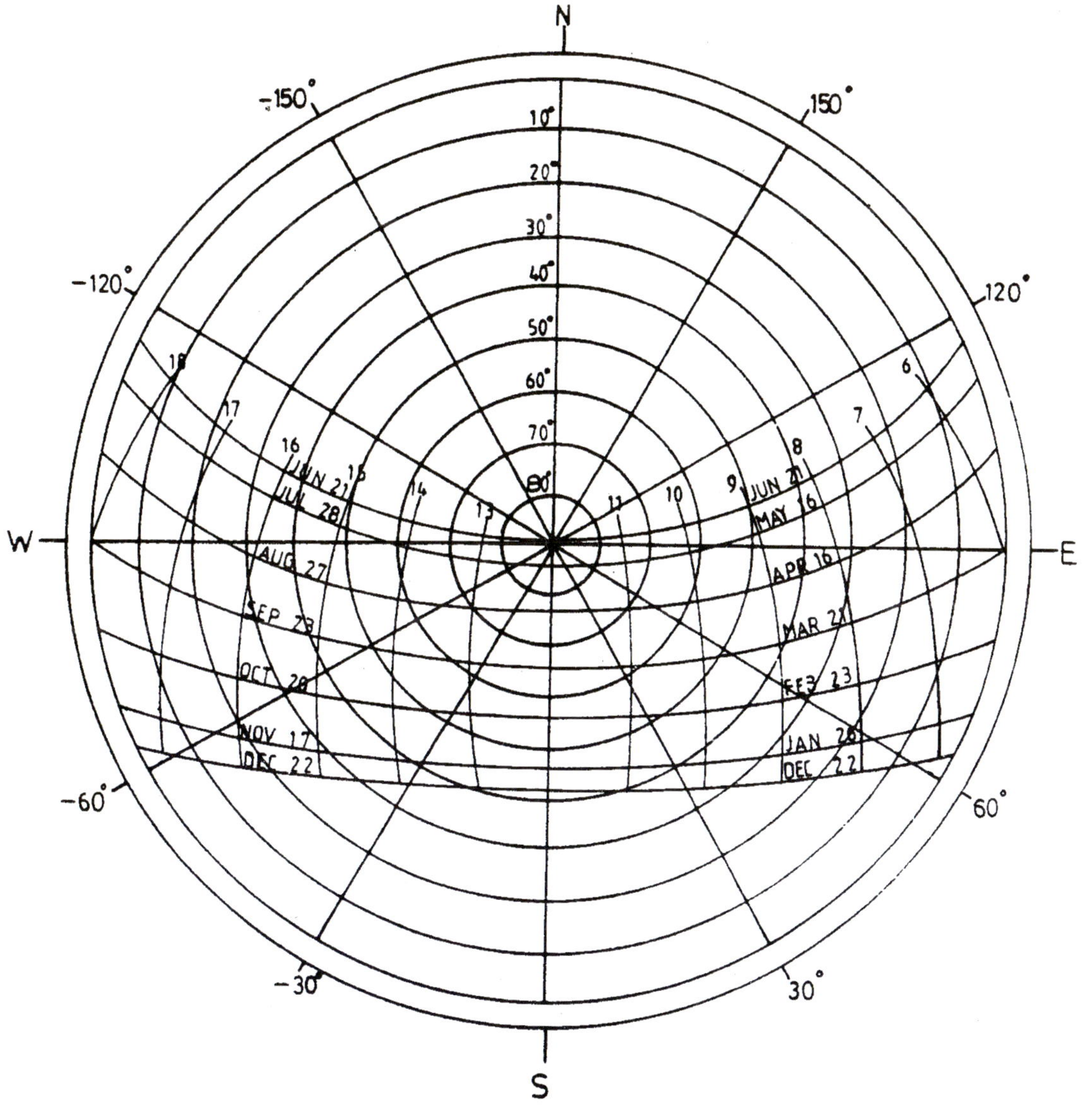

LATITUDE 25" NORTH

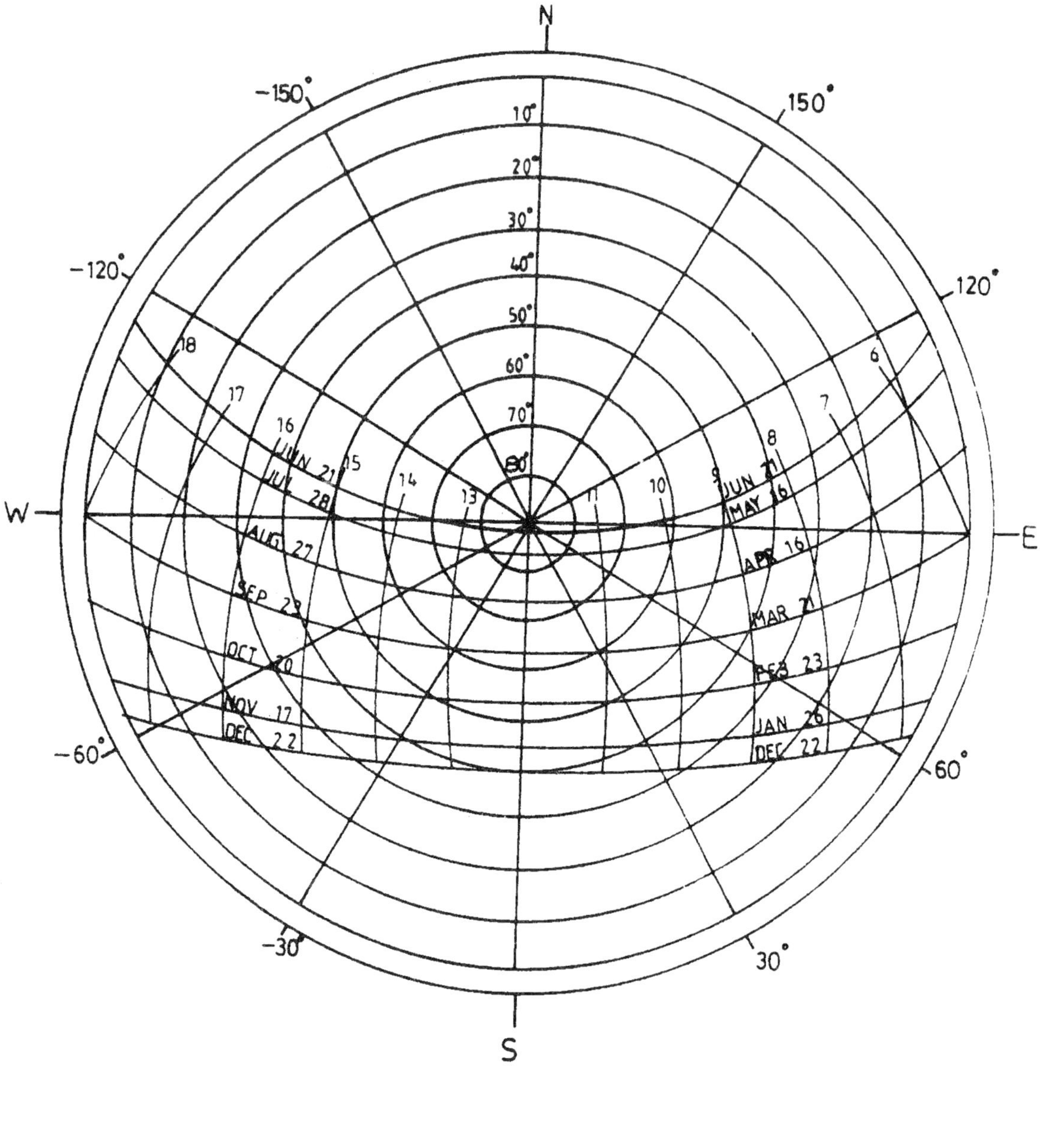

LATITUDE 27" NORTH

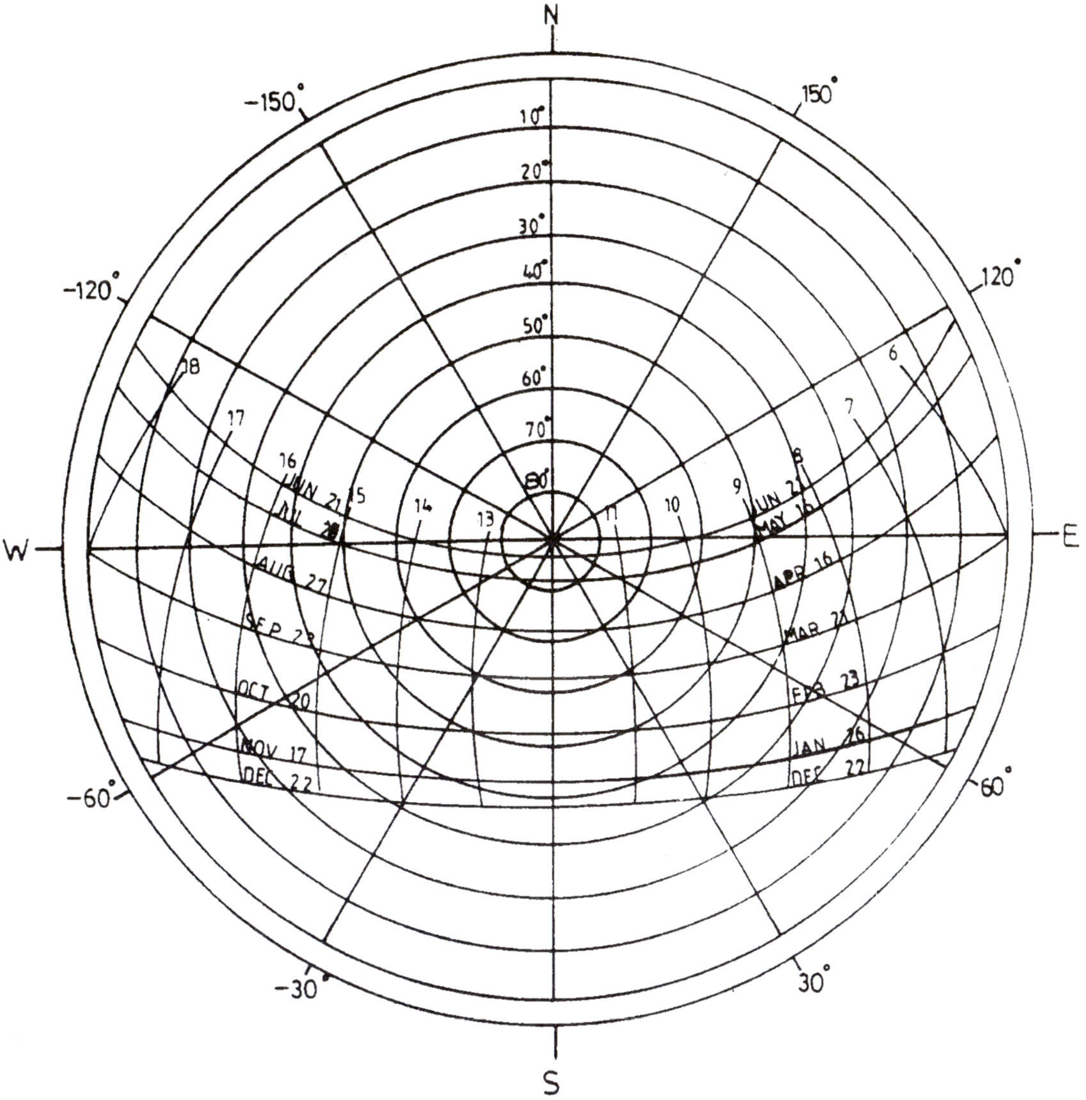

LATITUDE 29" NORTH

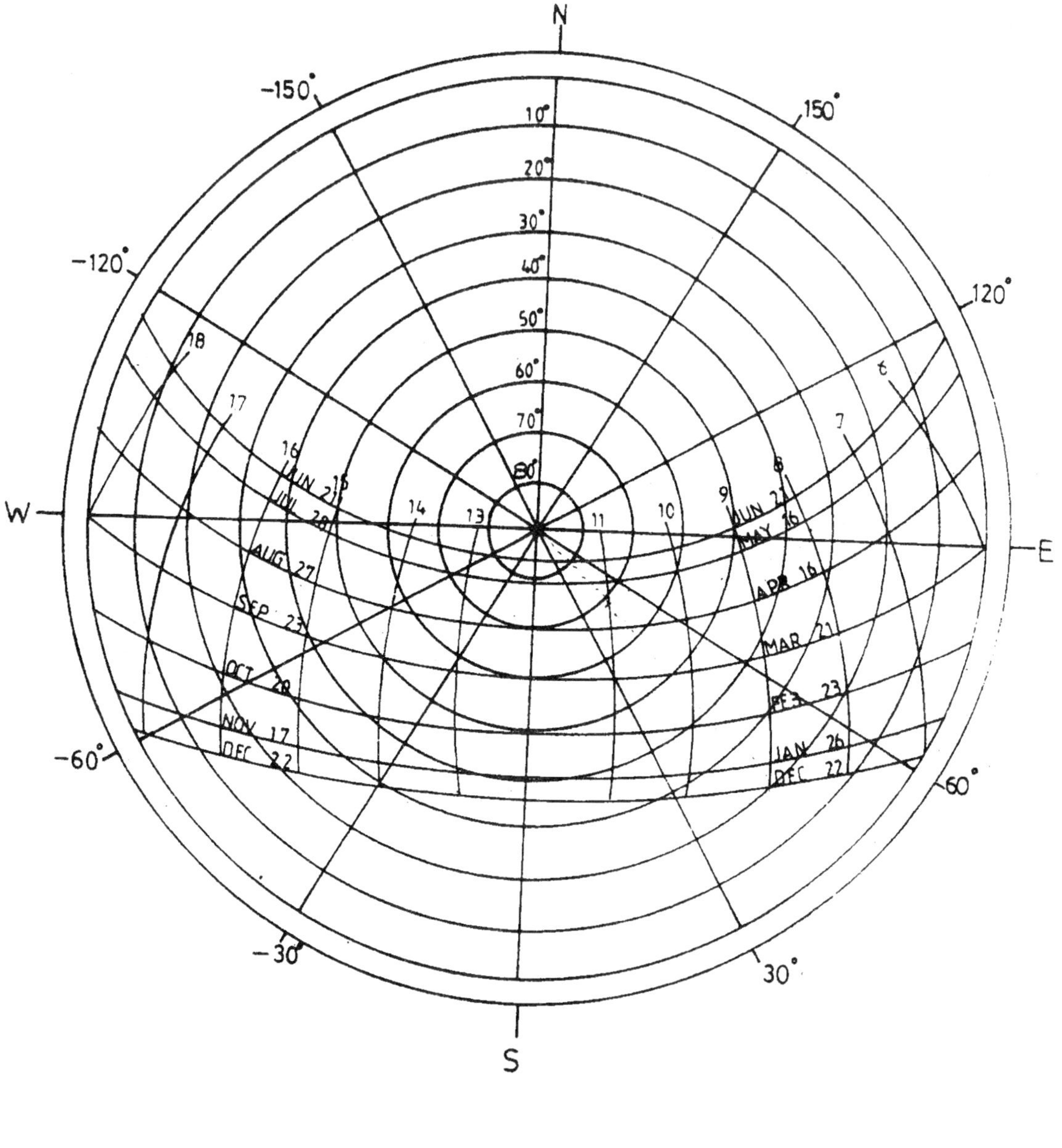

LATITUDE 31" NORTH

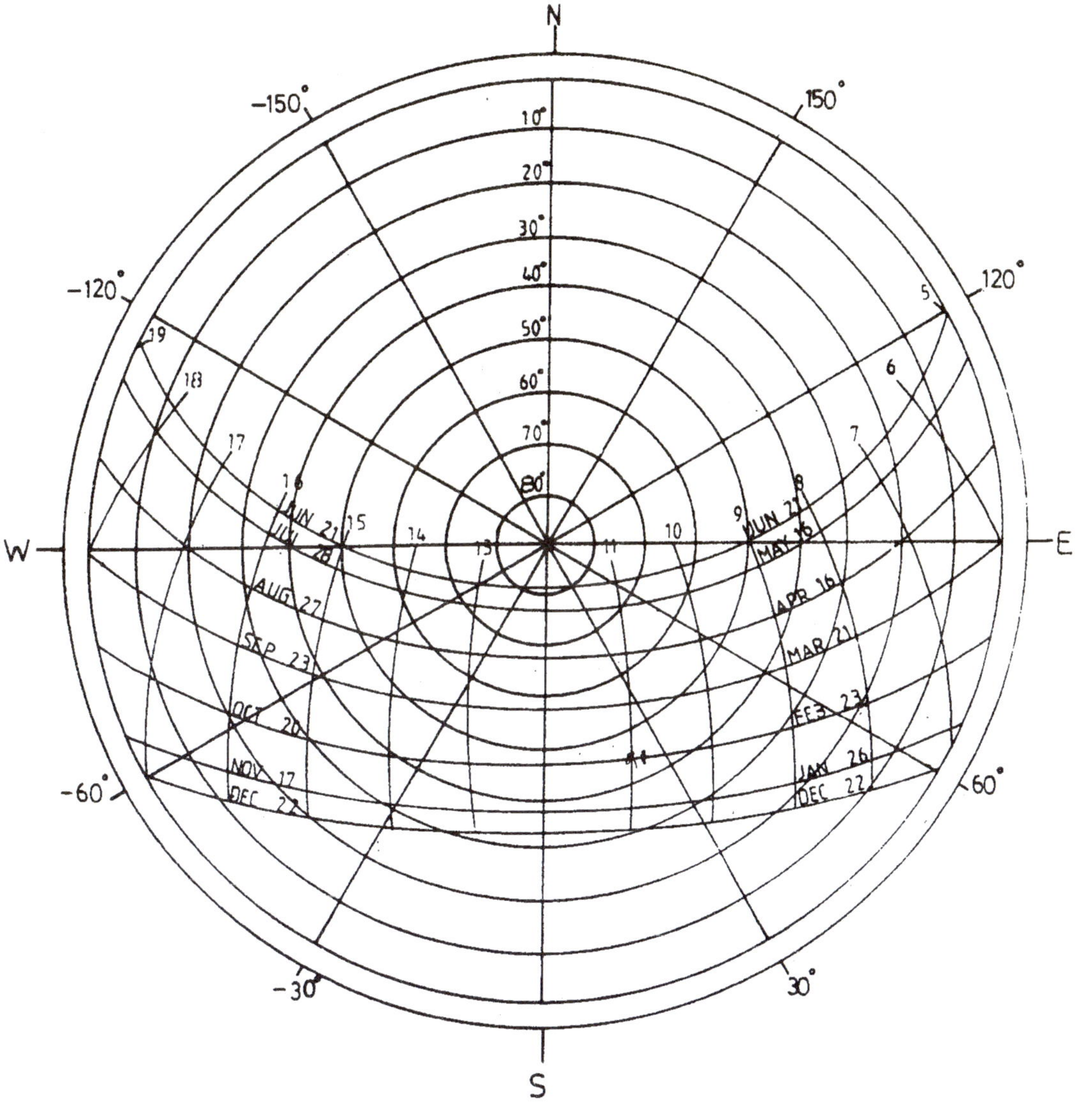

LATITUDE 33" NORTH

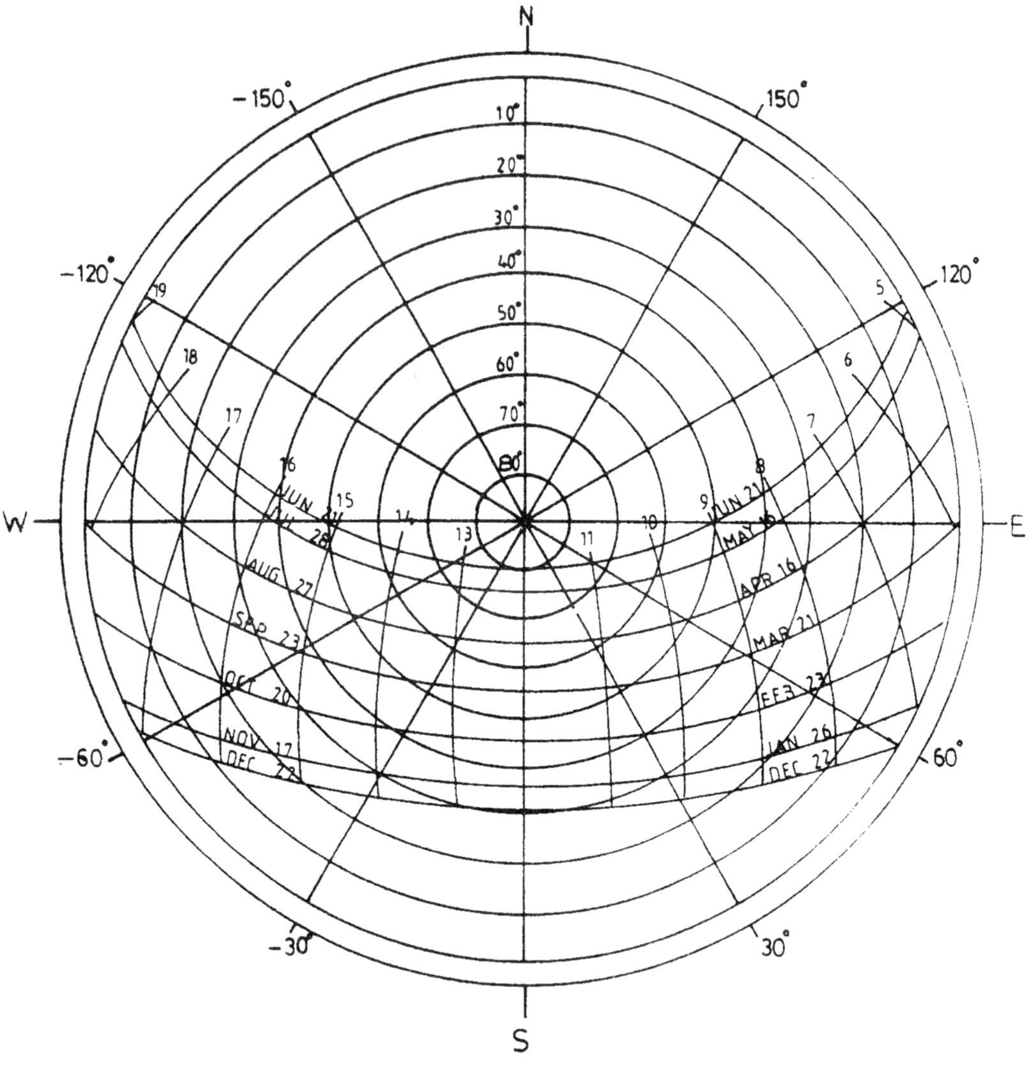

LATITUDE 35" NORTH

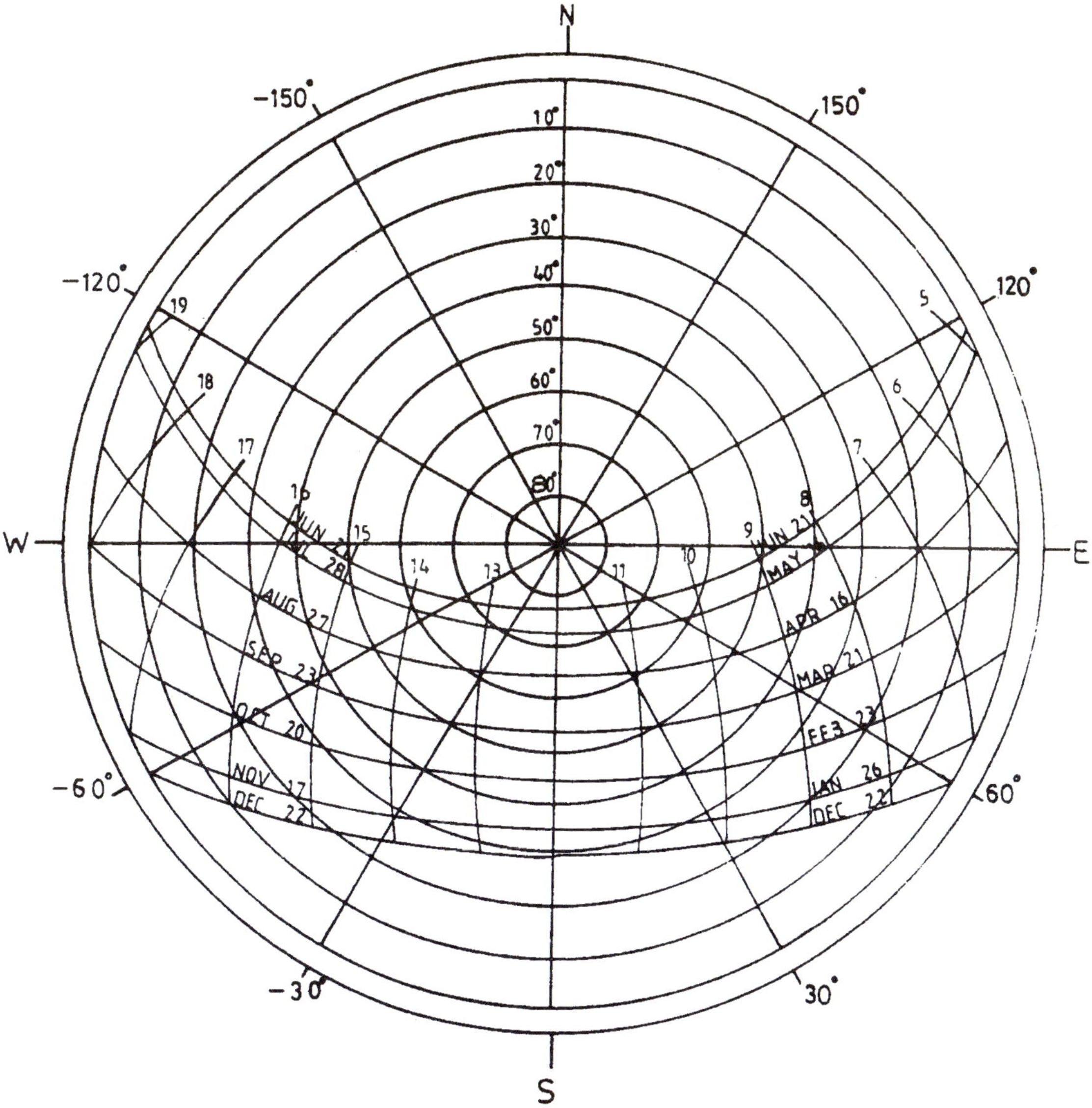

Bibliography

1. Tyagi Amit Kumar (2003), " Hand Book on energy audits and management", published by TERI. ISBN-81-8541971-X
2. ASHRAE HAND BOOK (2005), " Fundamentals", ISBN 978-1-931862-71-4
3. ASHRAE HANDBOOK (1996), "Heating, Ventilation and Air-conditioning systems and Equipment, ISBN-1-883413-35-4
4. Bansal N.K. and Minke G (1995), Climatic Zones and Rural Housing in India, Research Centre, Juelich, Germany.
5. Bansal N.K., Mathur J. (2006), Energy Efficient Windows, Anamaya Publishers, India, ISBN-81-88342-73-4.
6. Clarke J.A (2001), "Energy Simulation in Building Design", Butter worth HEINEMANN Melborne ISBN-0-7506-5082-6
7. CMIE (2004), Energy Report, Center for Monitoring the Indian Economy, New Delhi, India.
8. Dean Heerwagen(2004) "Passive and active Environment Controls" Mc Graw Hill ISBN 0-07-250173-1
9. ECBC 2007 : Energy Conservation Building Code, Bureau of Energy Efficiency, Ministry of Power, Govt. of India.
10. Illuminating Engineering Society Handbook.
11. ISO 6946, Building Components and Elements — Thermal Resistance and Thermal Transmittance — Calculation Method.
12. ISO 7345, Thermal Insulation Physical Quantities and Definitions
13. ISO 8301, Thermal Insulation - Determination of Steady — State Thermal Rresistance and Related Properties — Heat Flow Meter Apparatus.
14. ISO 8302, Thermal Insulation — Determination of Steady — State Thermal Resistance and Related Properties — Guarded hot Plate Apparatus
15. ISO 9050, Glass in building - Determination of Light Transmittance, Solar Direct Transmittance, total Solar Energy Transmittance, Ultraviolet Transmittance and Related Glazing Factors.
16. ISO 10211- 1: Thermal Bridges in Building Construction - Heat Flow and Surface Temperatures, Part 1. General Calculation Methods.
17. Kreider Jan F., Curtiss Peter S., ARI Rabi (2002)," Heating and Cooling of Buildings, Design for Efficiency", by McGraw Hill Higher Education, ISBN-0-7-237341-5

18. Cook Jeffery (1989), " Passive Cooling", The MIT Press, Cambridge Massachusetts London, England. ISBN 0-262-03147-7

19. Kaufman M (1984), Daylight Design & Analysis: IES Lighting Handbook, Reference Volume, New York, Illuminating Engineering Society of North America, NY.

20. Daniels Klaus (2003), "Advanced Building Systems, A technical Guide for Architects and Engineers. Birkhuser publishers for Architecture.

21. Koenigsberger, Ingersoll, Mayhew, Szokalay (1975), "Manual of Tropical Housing and Buildings", Orient Longmann, New Delhi.

22. Krieder J.F., Curtiss P.S., Rabi A., "Heating and Cooling of Buildings: Design for efficiency", Mc Graw Hill, 2002, ISBN- 0-07-237341-5.

23. Kreith Frank and West Ronals. E (1997), "CRC Hand Book of Energy Efficiency", CRC Press Inc. ISBN-0-8493-2514-5

24. M. Santamouris and D. Asimakopoulous (2001) "Passive Cooling of Building" James & James (Science Publishers) Ltd. UK ISBN 1873936478

25. Sodha M.S, Bansal N.K, Kumar A., Bansal P.K, Malik M.A.S (1986), "Solar Passive Building, Science and Design", Pergamnon Books Ltd. ISBN 0-08-030550-4

26. Majumdar Mili "Energy Efficient Buildings in India (2002) Tata Energy Research Institute, New Delhi ISBN 81-85419-82-5

27. Bansal Naredra. K., Hauser Gerd, Minke Gernot (1994), "Passive Building Design, A Handbook of Natural Climatic Control", by ELSEVIER SCIENCE B.V. ISBN -0-444-81745-X

28. Olgyay and Olgyay (1973), Design with Climate, Princeton University Press.

29. Paul W.O' Callaghan (1993), "Energy Management", by Mc Graw-Hill Book Company Europe. ISBN-0-07-707678-8

30. Kumar Pradeep, Tyagi Amit Kumar (2002), "Managing Energy Efficiency in Hotels and commercial building", by TERI. ISBN 81-85419-98-1

31. Prakash Sanjay (1991) Solar Architecture and Earth Construction in the North west Himalaya Har Anand Publication, New Delhi ISBN 0-7069-4933-1

32. Kornher Steve and Zaugg Andy "Solar air heating systems" Rodale press Emmaus.PA. ISBN 087857-442-5

33. TERI Energy Data Directory and Year Book 2004-05

34. The Gazette of India (2001), Registered No. DL-33004; Energy Conservation Act 2001.

35. Watson D. (1993), The Energy Design Handbook, American Institute of Architects, Washington DC, ISBN 1-55835-094-2.